STUDY GUIDE: TOOLS FOR SUCCESS

Principles of Economics

Second Edition

Fred M. Gottheil
Professor of Economics
University of Illinois

Prepared by
David M. Wishart
Wittenberg University

With the Assistance of
Margaret Landman
Bridgewater State College

South-Western College Publishing
an International Thomson Publishing company I(T)P®

Cincinnati • Albany • Boston • Detroit • Johannesburg • London • Madrid • Melbourne • Mexico City
New York • Pacific Grove • San Francisco • Scottsdale • Singapore • Tokyo • Toronto

Team Director / Publisher: Jack W. Calhoun
Acquisitions Editor: Keri Witman
Developmental Editors: Kurt Gerdenich and Thomas S. Sigel
Production Editor: Peggy K. Buskey
Marketing Manager: Lisa L. Lysne

Copyright © 1999
by South-Western College Publishing
Cincinnati, Ohio

All Rights Reserved
The text of this publication, or any part thereof, may not be reproduced or transmitted in any form or by any means, electronic or mechanical, including photocopying, recording, storage in an information retrieval system, or otherwise, without prior written permission from the publisher.

Study Guide: Tools for Success to accompany Principles of Economics, 2nd edition ISBN: 0-538-86822-8
Study Guide: Tools for Success to accompany Principles of Microeconomics, 2nd edition ISBN: 0-538-86826-0
Study Guide: Tools for Success to accompany Principles of Macroeconomics, 2nd edition ISBN: 0-538-86827-9

3 4 5 6 7 8 PN 5 4 3 2 1 0 9

Printed in the United States of America

I(T)P®
International Thomson Publishing
South-Western College Publishing is an ITP Company.
The ITP trademark is used under license.

TABLE OF CONTENTS

Preface   v

Part 1   The Basics of Economic Analysis

1. Introduction   1
2. Production Possibilities and Opportunity Costs   17
3. Demand and Supply   33
   Part 1 — Comprehensive Sample Test   50

Part 2   Introduction to Microeconomics

4. Elasticity   60
5. Marginal Utility and Consumer Choice   75
6. Price Ceilings and Price Floors   109
7. Business Ownership and Organization   126
   Part 2 — Comprehensive Sample Test   138

Part 3   The Microeconomics of Product Markets

8. Costs of Production   149
9. Maximizing Profit   167
10. Identifying Markets and Market Structures   182
11. Price and Output in Monopoly, Monopolistic Competition, and Perfect Competition   194
12. Price and Output Determination Under Oligopoly   212
13. Antitrust and Regulation   230
14. Externalities, Market Failure, and Public Choice   242
    Part 3 — Comprehensive Sample Test   257

Part 4   The Microeconomics of Factor Markets

15. Wage Rates in Competitive Labor Markets   267
16. Wages and Employment: Monopsony and Labor Unions   287
17. Interest, Rent, and Profit   301
18. Income Distribution and Poverty   314
    Part 4 — Comprehensive Sample Test   330

Part 5   Employment, Inflation, and Fiscal Policy

19. Aggregate Demand and Aggregate Supply   338
20. Gross Domestic Product Accounting   354
21. Consumption and Investment   367
22. Equilibrium National Income   382
23. Fiscal Policy: Coping with Inflation and Unemployment   401
24. Economic Growth, Business Cycles, and Countercyclical Policy   417
    Part 5 — Comprehensive Sample Test   431

Part 6 — Money, Banking, and Monetary Policy

25. Money	441
26. Money Creation and the Banking System	455
27. The Federal Reserve System and Monetary Policy	467
Part 6 — Comprehensive Sample Test	479

Part 7 — Government and the Macroeconomy

28. Can Government Really Stabilize the Economy?	488
29. Government Spending	503
30. Financing Government: Taxes and Debt	514
Part 7 — Comprehensive Sample Test	526

Part 8 — The World Economy

31. International Trade	534
32. Exchange Rates, Balance of Payments, and International Debt	551
33. Economic Problems of Less-Developed Countries	567
Part 8 — Comprehensive Sample Test	580

Preface

My first contact with Fred Gottheil came some 30 years ago when my Dad enlisted my aid typing a long, long book review as part of Professor Gottheil's graduate level History of Economic Thought course that he was taking at the University of Illinois. Typing was one of the more useful things I learned in junior high school, and my Dad, no slouch of an economist, knew how to exploit cheap labor. Fifty cents per page was the going rate. Either that or mow the yard. Never in my wildest 13-year-old imagination did I dream that I'd go on to major in economics after having taken Fred's Principles course in economics at Illinois (mainly to defend myself in arguments with my Dad), become good friends with Fred, write a Ph.D. thesis under his supervision, and be involved in this textbook/study guide project through two editions. Working with Fred has been one of the joys of my life. I owe him a debt of gratitude for teaching me about economics and much more. That Fred is a wonderful soul comes through in his text.

Writing this study guide has been fun and rewarding. I haven't done it alone. Hundreds of my students at Wittenberg University have been subjected to dozens of questions and problems, variants of which appear in this book. My students have been quick to point out flaws in the questions, doing a first round of editing for me. Especially helpful in this regard for the first edition were Deborah Goldstein, Ed Hasecke, Chris Murray, Kristen Neubaurer, Ryan Terry, Steve Valenti, and Bethany Young. Mojca Fink read the entire first edition and pointed to many corrections that were necessary. Mojca's eye for detail was a great help.

For this edition, Chris Taendler and Javier Herrera helped with editing and locating Web sites for the Economics Online segments in each chapter. Thanks guys. Javier read the entire manuscript, some of it twice, and checked answers carefully. He was a tireless worker, always willing to challenge me. Professor Gottheil offered feedback on many of the chapters. There was no shortage of red ink from Fred's pen, all of it constructive. Margaret Landman edited the entire manuscript and helped write some of the Chapter in a Nutshell and Graphing Tutorial/Pitfalls segments. Her help sharpening the questions and the prose throughout has been invaluable. Thanks also go to the editorial staff at South-Western — Jack Calhoun, Dennis Hanseman, and Rebecca Robey on the first edition. Thomas Sigel's editorial help on this edition has been terrific. Tom deserves credit for many of the new features in the second edition. The second edition is vastly improved as a result of Tom's many helpful suggestions. Peggy Buskey gave me quick feedback on the format of the book and kept the final copy editing rolling at a fast clip. Errors that remain are my responsibility. Any questions about the study guide can be addressed to me by e-mail — (*dwishart@wittenberg.edu*).

Finally, my wife Jo Wilson gets special thanks for her patient support over many months of writing. My sons Tony and Jacob have put up with a distracted parent for too long. We're overdue for a fishing trip.

David M. Wishart
Wittenberg University
June 1998

CHAPTER 1

INTRODUCTION

Chapter in a Nutshell

Economics is an important branch of the social sciences where study is focused on three critical areas of human behavior. First, economists study the problems that arise because **resources are scarce and people's wants are insatiable**. If resources are scarce and human wants are unlimited, then it makes sense that **choices have to be made**. It's the making of these choices that forms the other two areas of human behavior that economists study. Choices have to be made about **allocating scarce resources to produce goods and services to satisfy insatiable wants**. The third area of human behavior that economists study is **distribution**. Once goods and services are produced, they have to be distributed to people. The way goods and services are distributed is crucial to understanding how an economy performs. In our society, **consumer sovereignty** drives the production of most goods and services, meaning that consumers are free to decide what they want to purchase in the marketplace. Consumers form households that supply renewable and nonrenewable resources to firms that produce goods and services.

Production and distribution are complicated social processes. Economists use **models to help simplify the study of real-world economic relationships**. These models help economists to understand cause-and-effect relationships in the economy. Economists use models to study microeconomic and macroeconomic relationships. **Microeconomics** focuses on **individual economic relationships**. **Macroeconomics** studies the **behavior of the economy as a whole**. Economists use **positive analysis — the study of the economic relationships that exist** in the economy and **normative analysis — the study of what ought to be** in the economy. Economists have made substantial progress toward a better understanding of the economy due to the collection of better economic data over the last 50 years and the use of new statistical methods to test the accuracy of economic models. **Econometrics** is the branch of economics that deals with the **use of statistical methods to analyze economic data**. Even though economists' predictions aren't perfect, they are improving as economic knowledge advances.

After you study this chapter, you should be able to:

- Describe the finite character of the earth's **resources**.
- Distinguish between **renewable and nonrenewable resources**.
- Discuss people's **insatiable wants**.
- Tell how **scarcity** and choice are related to each other.
- Explain why **economic models** are used.
- Define and contrast **microeconomics** and **macroeconomics**.
- Compare **positive** and **normative economics**.

Concept Check — See how you do on these multiple-choice questions.

1. The **finite character of resource supplies** combined with **insatiable wants** results in
    a. normative economics
    b. *ceteris paribus*
    c. the problem of scarcity
    d. the circular flow model
    e. consumer sovereignty

All of our resource supplies are finite. And, for practical purposes, human wants can be described as insatiable. Do you see a problem here?

2. Economists who study **microeconomic questions** focus on
    a. national saving and investment
    b. unemployment and inflation
    c. the economy as a whole
    d. individual economic behavior
    e. circular flows

Economic analysis can be carried on at the level of households and firms, or it can be done at the level of the economy as a whole.

3. Which of the following statements makes a **positive economics** statement?
    a. Greenhouse gas emissions should be cut by 10 percent from 1990 levels
    b. Carbon dioxide emissions contribute to global warming
    c. A tax should be placed on gasoline to decrease carbon dioxide emissions
    d. Developing countries ought to limit their greenhouse gas emissions
    e. Slowing down global warming should be a top priority for the United States

Positive economics describes what exists in the economy.

4. A major advantage of using **economic models** is that they
    a. allow us to focus on only the most important variables
    b. are expressed algebraically and not in words
    c. are able to capture all the elements in economic relationships
    d. force us to use econometric methods
    e. emphasize the role played by scarcity and insatiable wants

Economic models are used to simplify real-world economic relationships in order to understand them better.

5. The primary reason for using the *ceteris paribus* **assumption** is that it allows us to
    a. examine a relationship where all variables change together
    b. predict economic changes with nearly perfect accuracy
    c. examine the impact of changes in variables one at a time
    d. distinguish between microeconomics and macroeconomics
    e. hold stocks of nonrenewable resources constant

Can cause-and-effect economic relationships be identified if all variables change simultaneously?

THE BASICS

Am I on the Right Track?

Your answers to the questions above should be **c, d, b, a,** and **c.** It's very important that by now you appreciate that scarcity forces people in a society to make choices about what is produced and how the output is distributed. Scarcity and choice are at the heart of economic analysis. You should also have an appreciation for the ways that economic analysis is conducted. For example, the distinction between microeconomics and macroeconomics should be clear. Positive economic analysis and normative economic analysis are also easily distinguishable. Try using the *ceteris paribus* assumption in a conversation with one of your friends. If you can explain it to them after they give you a strange look, then you are probably on the right track.

Key Terms Quiz — Match the terms on the left with the definitions in the column on the right.

1. natural resources
2. macroeconomics
3. insatiable wants
4. positive economics
5. scarcity
6. normative economics
7. economics
8. econometrics
9. consumer sovereignty
10. social sciences
11. economic model
12. ceteris paribus
13. circular flow model
14. household
15. firm
16. microeconomics

___7___ a. social science that studies scarcity and choice
___8___ b. statistical methods for testing economic models
___6___ c. what ought to be
___9___ d. free choice in the market on what to buy
___11___ e. simplification of real-world economic relationships
___3___ f. unlimited desires for goods
___16___ g. the study of individual economic behavior
___10___ h. the study of human behavior generally
___12___ i. other things being equal
___13___ j. exchange relationships between households and firms.
___4___ k. what is
___14___ l. people living under one roof with a source of income
___15___ m. an enterprise that produces goods and/or services for market
___1___ n. renewable and nonrenewable gifts of nature
___2___ o. the study of the economy as a whole
___5___ p. finiteness of resources relative to unlimited wants

True-False Questions — If a statement is false, explain why.

1. Economists regard natural resources as gifts of nature. (T/F) T

2. Scarcity is created only through the advertisements in the marketplace. (T/F) F

3. If resources are limited and people's wants are insatiable, then scarcity exists. (T/F) T

4. Economics is the study of how people make money in the stock market. (T/F) F

5. Economists use graphs and models to simplify complex economic problems. (T/F) T

6. An economic model is an exact representation of an economy. (T/F) F

7. The circular flow model would better represent the real world if flows of money, resources, goods, and services to and from government were included. (T/F) T

8. The *ceteris paribus* assumption is often used to simplify economic analysis. (T/F) T

9. Economics is considered to be a social science because it examines individual and social behavior. (T/F) T

10. Microeconomics is more useful than macroeconomics because it gives a more detailed picture of the economy. (T/F) F

11. Macroeconomic analysis focuses on economic activity at the level of the whole economy rather than at the level of the individual. (T/F) T

12. Positive economics is involved in policy formation, stating positively what ought to be. (T/F) F

13. Normative economics involves value judgments. (T/F) T

14. An economist hired to plan economic policies for a presidential candidate would never engage in positive economic analysis. (T/F) F

15. Because social scientists work with models that are 100 percent precise, they can develop policies that will solve any social problems we face. (T/F) F

Multiple-Choice Questions

1. The difference between a renewable resource and a nonrenewable resource is that
    a. a renewable resource can never be depleted while a nonrenewable resource is depleted as it is used
    b. a nonrenewable resource can never be depleted while a renewable resource is depleted as it is used
    c. the stock of a renewable resource can be maintained forever
    d. conservation efforts cannot save renewable resources
    e. renewable resources are liquids and nonrenewable resources are solids

2. Economics is a social science that explores the problem of
    a. how society transforms scarce resources into goods and services
    b. persuading people to reduce their insatiable wants
    c. scarcity in poor countries but not rich countries
    d. what ought to be done to make the world a better place
    e. circular flows within the family unit

3. Economists use the *ceteris paribus* assumption in their analysis because it
    a. converts positive economic statements to normative ones
    b. converts normative economic statements to positive ones
    c. is the only way to move from theoretical model building to the real world
    d. allows us to develop one-to-one, cause-and-effect relationships
    e. broadens the scope of analysis, creating a social science approach to the subject

THE BASICS

4. Positive economics deals with _____ while normative economics considers _____.
   a. what ought to be; what is
   b. what is; what ought to be
   c. good policies; policies for normal times
   d. improvements in living standards; how to keep the economy steady over time
   e. a positive approach to economic problems; a normal approach to problems

5. Microeconomics is the branch of economics that analyzes _____ while macroeconomics is the branch of economics that analyzes _____.
   a. the behavior of individual economic units; how national economies work
   b. how national economies work; the behavior of individual economic units
   c. positive questions; normative questions
   d. historical issues on a micro scale; contemporary issues on a large scale
   e. economic details; broader aspects of economic issues

6. In the circular flow model, households furnish labor, capital, land, and entrepreneurship to businesses for which they are paid _____, _____, _____, and _____, respectively.
   a. profit, interest, rent, wages
   b. wages, interest, rent, profit
   c. wages, interest, profit, rent
   d. wages, profit, interest, rent
   e. wages, rent, interest, profit

7. If we accept the assumption that people have insatiable wants and that the resources available to satisfy these wants are finite, then
   a. misery is guaranteed for all
   b. the economy is easy to model
   c. because of scarcity, people are forced to make choices
   d. consumer sovereignty can be invoked to eliminate scarcity
   e. firms and households will cooperate to decrease wants and increase resource supplies

8. An economist who is attempting to accurately estimate the unemployment rate for a national economy is practicing
   a. microeconomics
   b. normative economics
   c. positive economics
   d. consumer sovereignty
   e. sociology

9. The branch of economics that deals with individual economic behavior is
   a. microeconomics
   b. macroeconomics
   c. normative economics
   d. positive economics
   e. econometrics

10. Models that economists use are
    a. perfect representations of the real world
    b. typically useless oversimplifications of the real world
    c. abstractions of an economic reality
    d. exempt from *ceteris paribus*
    e. applicable only to macroeconomics

11. Money flows in resource markets represent payments to _____ whereas, money flows in product markets represent payments to _____.
    a. business firms; workers
    b. natural resource owners; banks
    c. the government; private businesses
    d. property owners; only the most productive individuals
    e. households; firms producing goods and services

12. Scarcity is a term used by economists to describe the fact that
    a. people's wants are limited
    b. natural resources are available to us in fixed amounts
    c. there will always be poverty in the world
    d. abundance and affluence are never permanent
    e. people's wants are insatiable relative to the availability of resources

13. Which of the following statements is **not** a normative statement?
    a. Low-income individuals ought to be exempt from income taxes
    b. Unemployment and inflation should be minimized
    c. The unemployment rate is 10 percent
    d. The government should cut funding for the arts
    e. The money supply should grow at a constant rate

14. Which of the following statements is **not** a positive statement?
    a. Prices of essential goods and services should be set by the government
    b. The economy is extremely complex
    c. People's wants are insatiable
    d. Payments for resources are made in factor markets
    e. Unemployment last year was 7.3 percent of the labor force

15. Economists use abstractions in their analysis of the economy because
    a. information is insufficient to allow for detailed consideration of any economic problem
    b. abstractions are useful when economic model building is inappropriate
    c. they want to reduce the complexity of the world to more manageable dimensions
    d. abstractions are used by all social scientists
    e. the real world they want to understand is itself an abstraction

16. All of the following are examples of nonrenewable resources **except**
    a. forests
    b. iron ore
    c. coal
    d. oil
    e. natural gas

THE BASICS

17. All of the following are examples of renewable resources **except**
    a. the sea
    b. fish in the sea
    c. gold used to make earrings ✓
    d. labor used to grow corn
    e. corn used to feed hogs

18. Although scarcity exists today, it is not nearly as severe as it was in ancient times. Looking to the future, economists believe that societies will better cope with scarcity
    a. by developing new technologies that create greater supply to satisfy human wants ✓
    b. by producing enough to completely satisfy human wants
    c. by doing better positive economic analysis
    d. by doing better normative economic analysis
    e. with more accurate economic models

19. Using the *ceteris paribus* assumption to study the effect of an increase in the price of mustard on the amount of ketchup that is purchased requires that
    a. the price of mustard be held constant
    b. both the price of mustard and the amount of ketchup purchased be held constant
    c. everything except the price of mustard and the amount of ketchup purchased be held constant ✓
    d. nothing should be held constant
    e. econometrics be used

20. The circular flow model presented in the text includes which participants?
    a. firms and the government
    b. households, banks, and firms
    c. households and the government
    d. firms, households, and the government
    e. firms and households ✓

Fill in the Blanks

1. Resources that are _renewable_ can be maintained forever with properly managed conservation.

2. Examples of disciplines that are part of the social sciences include _economics_, _sociolgy_, _anthropology_, _political science_, and _psychology_.

3. In order for an economist to make the statement that as its price increases, the quantity demanded for filet mignon will decrease, the _ceteris paribus_ assumption will have to be introduced.

4. Households _supply_ land, labor, capital, and entrepreneurship to firms in return for _payments_ that they use to _purchase_ goods and services produced by firms.

5. Economists who make normative statements concerning economic issues apply their own personal and social _values_ to make these statements.

Discussion Questions

1. What do economists study? Identify the main branches of economics and the types of analysis that are used.

2. How do social values and responsibilities influence economic behavior?

3. Can you imagine scarcity becoming a thing of the past? Think about what was available to your grandparents compared to what you have at your disposal. What does it tell you?

4. Why aren't economists' predictions perfect?

THE BASICS 9

5. Suppose that you were to make the circular flow model more detailed by including banks and the government. How would the addition of these groups change the model?

Everyday Applications

1. Go to the business pages of a newspaper and survey the content of the articles there. How many of the articles are about microeconomic topics? How many are about macroeconomics? Can you pick out any predictions that economists or business analysts are making in these articles? What sort of economic models seem to be the basis for their predictions?

2. Watch the Jim Lehrer News Hour on PBS some evening and analyze the discussions between interviewers and guests for positive and normative content. How do the people being interviewed use positive analysis to support their normative arguments? Can you see how the two types of analysis can work together?

Economics Online

For a peek into the wild and wonderful world of econometrics, visit the SHAZAM homepage (*http://shazam.econ.ubc.ca/*). SHAZAM is an econometrics computer program. You probably won't understand many of the technical terms on this homepage, but if you continue with your study of economics, you'll come to appreciate how useful econometrics can be. Better yet, it can be fun, especially with the computer technologies now available.

Answers to Questions

Key Terms Quiz

a. 7   f. 3   k. 4   p. 5
b. 8   g. 16   l. 14
c. 6   h. 10   m. 15
d. 9   i. 12   n. 1
e. 11   j. 13   o. 2

True-False Questions

1. True
2. False. People don't need to be convinced to want more than they have. That is why economists say wants are insatiable.
3. True

4. False. Economics is the study of how we work together to transform scarce resources into goods and services to satisfy the most pressing of our infinite needs, and how we distribute those goods and services among ourselves.
5. True
6. False. An economic model is an abstraction of our economic reality, focusing on just a few principal features of the way an economy operates.
7. True
8. True
9. True
10. False. Whether micro or macroeconomics is more useful depends on what problems are under consideration.
11. True
12. False. Positive economics examines the economic relationships that exist in an economy.
13. True
14. False. The economist would certainly want to understand how the economy works to draw cause-and-effect conclusions.
15. False. The social sciences use models that are not perfect representations of the world.

Multiple-Choice Questions

1. c
2. a
3. d
4. b
5. a
6. b
7. c
8. c
9. a
10. c
11. e
12. e
13. c
14. a
15. c
16. a
17. c
18. a
19. c
20. e

Fill in the Blanks

1. renewable
2. economics, sociology, anthropology, political science, psychology
3. *ceteris paribus*
4. supply, payments, purchase
5. values

Discussion Questions

1. Economists study how societies cope with the problem of scarcity. For example, economists study the allocation of scarce resources for production of goods and services. Distribution of these goods and services is also a focus of analysis. Economists develop theoretical models to help them sort out the core issues in economic questions. It is possible to test these theoretical models against real-world data. The main branches of economics are microeconomics and macroeconomics, while econometrics is also an important field. Economists pursue both positive and normative analysis in their work.

2. Even though consumer sovereignty guides what we buy and, therefore, what we produce for the market, our economic choices are nonetheless constrained by social values and responsibilities. For example, most cultures find extremely excessive and wasteful behavior to be inappropriate. Certain types of drugs are illegal in most cultures, though this varies from society to society. We feel a responsibility to pay taxes even though we would prefer not to. So, even though the consumer is mostly sovereign, limits are placed on economic behavior by our shared cultural values and responsibilities.

THE BASICS

3. We will always have scarcity because of unlimited wants. However, the advances of the industrial revolution in recent history have helped to diminish the severity of scarcity. Pick up a 1950s Sears catalog and look at the mix of goods that was available to American consumers then. Or read the opening pages of Dickens's *A Tale of Two Cities*. Imagine yourself using these goods to satisfy your wants. Would you trade places with these earlier consumers?

4. Economists' predictions aren't perfect because it is impossible to control for changes in the myriad variables that may affect the variable being predicted. Sometimes the data used by economists turn out to be flawed.

5. Households contribute savings to banks, which, in turn make loans to firms and to households. Households also furnish resources to banks, as they do to other firms, and banks make payments to households for supplying resources. Households pay taxes to the government and, in return, receive payments such as Social Security from the government. Moreover, government makes payments to business firms for products that they supply to government. Also, households supply resources to government and the government makes payments for these resources in return.

APPENDIX

ON READING GRAPHS

Appendix in a Nutshell

The appendix acquaints you with some of the techniques that economists use in translating economic concepts to mathematical and graphical forms. Remember, anything that is expressed mathematically or graphically can also be expressed in words. The reason we use math and graphs in economics is because they simplify discussions. The intention is not to make life more difficult for those trying to do economics but, rather, to make concepts that would be difficult to express in prose more easily understandable. Graphs in economics are a classic case of pictures being worth a thousand words. None of the mathematics and graphs in this text are terribly difficult. So, relax, graphing can be fun.

After you study this appendix, you should be able to:

- Find the **origin** of a graph.
- Measure distances on graphs.
- Graph relationships between **independent and dependent variables**.
- Connect points representing data from a table to form a graph.
- Explain what is meant by the **slope of a curve**.
- Describe various shaped curves by their slopes.
- Measure the **slope at a point on a curve**.

Concept Check — See how you do on these multiple-choice questions.

1. The **origin** of a graph is
   a. the end of the line that describes the independent variable
   b. the slope of the curve
   c. the graph's point of reference
   d. the sum of the horizontal and vertical distances on the graph
   e. where one starts to connect points to form a curve

What are the x and y coordinates that we associate with the origin?

2. The **independent variable** and the **dependent variable** in a relationship reflect a linkage between them such that
   a. changes in the dependent variable depend on changes in the value of the independent variable
   b. the dependent variable always has a larger value than the independent variable
   c. the dependent variable is always some multiple of the independent variable
   d. as the independent variable increases, so does the dependent variable
   e. as the independent variable increases, the dependent variable decreases

Typically, economists work with **relationships that express dependence**. For example, the amount of a good that people are willing to buy depends on its price.

3. The **slope** of a curve measures the
   a. ratio of the change in the variable on the horizontal axis to the change in the variable on the vertical axis
   b. ratio of the change in the variable on the vertical axis to the change in the variable on the horizontal axis
   c. rate of decrease in the dependent variable
   d. rate of increase in the independent variable
   e. percentage change in the dependent variable divided by the percentage change in the independent variable

Slopes can be either positive or negative, and they can be either constant or changing.

4. Curves that are **U-shaped** have slopes that are first _____ and then turn _____, while curves that are **hill-shaped** have slopes that are first _____ and then turn _____.
   a. decreasing; increasing; increasing; decreasing
   b. negative; positive; positive; negative
   c. positive; negative; negative; positive
   d. rising; falling; falling; rising
   e. zero; infinite; infinite; zero

Sketch a U-shaped curve and a hill-shaped curve and use the definition of slope to determine the correct answer.

5. In order to measure the **slope at a point on a curve**, one should
   a. find the x and y values of the point
   b. divide the x value of the point by the y value
   c. draw a line from the origin to the point and find the slope of the line
   d. divide the y value of the point by the x value
   e. draw a tangent through the point and find the slope of the tangent

Measuring the slope at a point on a curve is necessary if the slope is not constant. If the slope of a curve is

THE BASICS

constant, then it is a straight line.

Am I on the Right Track?

Your answers to the questions above should be **c, a, b, b,** and **e**. Some of the terms used in the concept check show up in the key terms quiz below. Make sure you clearly understand their meanings.

Key Terms Quiz — Match the terms on the left with the definitions in the column on the right.

1. origin
2. independent variable
3. dependent variable
4. slope of a curve
5. tangent
6. slope of a tangent

_2_ a. a variable whose value influences the value of another variable
_5_ b. a straight line that touches a curve at only one point
_6_ c. the slope of a curve at its point of tangency
_1_ d. a graph's point of reference
_3_ e. a variable whose value depends on the value of another variable
_4_ f. the slope of the tangent to the curve at a point

Graphing Tutorial

The best way to learn to read graphs is to construct a few of them and begin to interpret them. This tutorial is far from exhaustive. However, it will show you how to construct a graph from values that are listed in a table. The graph will be interpreted. Then, the problems below will help you apply different concepts relevant to reading graphs.

Suppose you are operating a lemonade stand during the hottest part of the summer and you vary the price of lemonade from day to day to see how changes in the price affect the amount of lemonade purchases. The data from your experiment on changing the price are shown in the table below.

Price per Cup ($)	Quantity Demanded
2.50	0
2.00	3
1.50	5
1.00	8
0.50	12

Each of these pairs of price and quantity demanded values can be translated into a point on a graph. Then the points can be connected to form a curve. In this case, the curve that is formed is called a demand curve because it reflects the quantity demanded of lemonade at different prices. You will learn more about demand curves in Chapter 3. The curve constructed from the table is shown on the next page, with the price measured along the vertical axis and the quantity demanded measured along the horizontal axis.

14   CHAPTER 1   INTRODUCTION

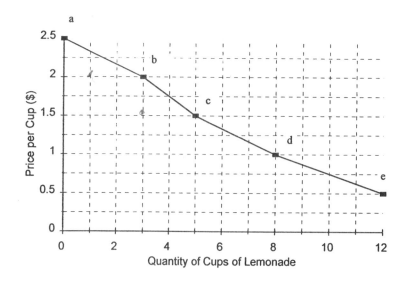

Each of the points shown in the table is labeled with a letter in the graph. Point a in the graph corresponds to a price of $2.50 and 0 cups of lemonade purchased. Points b, c, d, and e correspond to the other pairs of values listed in the table. What can be said about the slope of this curve? Clearly, the slope is negative because the curve is downward sloping. That is, as price decreases, the quantity demanded increases. For every decrease in value of the variable measured on the vertical axis, there is an increase in the value of the variable measured along the horizontal axis. Furthermore, the slope of this curve is not constant. Look at what happens as we decrease the price by $.50 from point to point along the curve. The quantity demanded increases by 3 cups, then 2 cups, then 3 cups, then 4 cups.

The problems below will delve somewhat deeper into interpreting graphs.

Problems

1. Using the example in the graphing tutorial, compute the slope of the curve between the following prices:

   a. From a price equal to $2 to a price equal to $1.50

   b. From $1.50 to $1.00

   c. From $1.00 to $.50

THE BASICS

d. What happens to the value of the slope over this range of prices? How does this influence the shape of the curve?

2. Consider the graph shown below and explain how the slope changes along the graph by drawing tangent lines at various points along the curve.

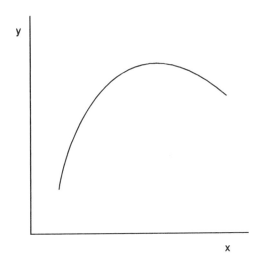

3. Explain the changes that occur in the slope along this curve from the origin to point A, then from point A to point B.

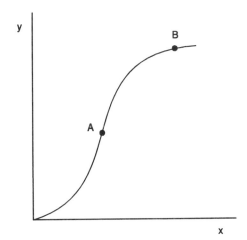

Answers to Questions for the Appendix

Key Terms Quiz

a. 2
b. 5
c. 6
d. 1
e. 3
f. 4

Problems

1. a. The slope between prices of $2 and $1.50 is $(2 - 1.50)/(3 - 5) = -.5/2 = -.25$

    b. The slope between prices of $1.50 and $1 is $(1.5 - 1)/(5 - 8) = -.5/3 = -.167$

    c. The slope between prices of $1 and $.5 is $(1 - .5)/(8 - 12) = -.5/4 = -.125$

    d. The value of the slope is negative but increasing over this range, meaning that the slope becomes less negative and the curve is becoming flatter.

2. Starting at the point on the curve closest to the origin, the slope is positive but decreasing until it becomes zero at the peak of the curve beyond which the slope becomes increasingly negative.

3. From the origin to point A, the slope is positive and increases as the curve gets steeper. From point A to point B, the slope is positive and decreases as the curve becomes flatter.

CHAPTER 2

PRODUCTION POSSIBILITIES AND OPPORTUNITY COSTS

Chapter in a Nutshell

This chapter considers how **productive resources** — labor, capital, land, and entrepreneurship — are combined to produce goods. A model is developed to represent an economy's **production possibilities**. Our model of production possibilities highlights the need for societies to make choices in the face of scarcity — a concept that was stressed in the first chapter. There is an **opportunity cost** associated with any choice that is made. For example, in order for an economy to produce more of one good, it will be forced to sacrifice units of production of other goods. Moreover, we will find that shifting resources from the production of one good to another involves increasing sacrifices of the first good in order to generate equal increases in the second good. This phenomenon is called **the law of increasing costs**.

   Economic growth occurs in an economy where the supplies of productive resources increase over time. Economic growth is an expansion of an economy's production possibilities. Another source of economic growth is ideas that take the form of **new applied technology**, or **innovations**. Innovation allows a given quantity of resources to produce a larger output. **Division of labor and specialization** is yet another way that an economy can experience economic growth. As people specialize in specific tasks, they are able to produce more than if they spread their talents and energies over many unspecialized tasks. **Division of labor and specialization** occur at the international level. We will learn that economies specialize at the international level in activities for which they have an **absolute advantage** — that is, the country can produce a good with fewer resources than can other countries. Specialization also occurs according to **comparative advantage**. A country has a comparative advantage if it can produce a good at a lower opportunity cost than can other countries.

After studying this chapter, you should be able to:

- Name the **factors of production**.
- Describe an economy's **production possibilities**.
- Distinguish between **capital goods** and **consumption goods**.
- Define **opportunity cost**.
- Explain the **law of increasing costs**.
- Show how new **technology** and **innovation** lead to **economic growth**.
- Explain how **specialization and division of labor** increases productivity.
- Account for international specialization according to **absolute and comparative advantage**.

Concept Check — See how you do on these multiple-choice questions.

1. An economy that experiences **the law of increasing costs** and shifts resources from automobile production to computer production in order to increase computer output by fixed increments is
   a. inefficient
   b. suffering from a declining industry
   c. growing
   d. operating beyond its production possibilities curve in the impossibilities region
   e. giving up increasing amounts of automobiles

As resources are shifted from automobile production to computer production, what happens to the opportunity cost of producing more computers?

2. An **innovation** is a change in the way that a good is produced such that
   a. economic growth decreases
   b. the amount of labor used increases
   c. the same amount of resources can produce a larger output
   d. computers are used in production
   e. scarcity is abolished

Recall that an innovation is the introduction of a new applied technology to production that reduces the severity of scarcity.

3. All of the following except _____ will result in **economic growth**.
   a. growth in the labor force
   b. growth in the capital stock
   c. improvements in technology
   d. an increase in entrepreneurship
   e. an increase in the unemployment rate

Economic growth is a shift to the right in the production possibilities curve. Which of the above possible answers would not result in a shift in the production possibilities curve?

4. **Capital accumulation** is limited in poor countries because
   a. their citizens don't want to work
   b. most of their resources must be devoted to production for subsistence
   c. of the law of increasing costs
   d. people in these countries are quite satisfied to be poor
   e. wars in these countries have wiped out the advanced technology that used to exist

A poor economy must necessarily devote most of its resources to the production of consumption goods just to provide for subsistence. If few resources are devoted to capital goods production, how can a poor country begin to grow?

5. The **opportunity cost** of going to see a movie is equal to
   a. the cost of the ticket
   b. the time lost while watching the show
   c. the value of the next best possible action
   d. five points that you missed on the economics quiz you could have studied for
   e. the pleasure you could have enjoyed watching TV instead

What is given up in going to see the movie?

Am I on the Right Track?

If your answers to these questions were **e, c, e, b,** and **c**, then you are on the right track. Perhaps the best study hint for mastering this chapter (and one that applies to all subsequent chapters) is to learn the jargon used by economists. Economists use language that appears rather ordinary, but the meanings they attach to these words are often quite different from the ordinary meanings usually associated with them. So, learn the concepts of opportunity cost, law of increasing cost, technological change, innovation, labor specialization, among others. Progress will be much easier if we all agree on definitions to specific terms. The key terms quiz

THE BASICS

below should help.

Key Terms Quiz — Match the term on the left with the definition in the column on the right.

1. factors of production
2. labor
3. capital
4. human capital
5. land
6. entrepreneur
7. production possibilities
8. opportunity cost
9. law of increasing costs
10. innovation
11. underemployed resources
12. economic efficiency
13. labor specialization
14. absolute advantage
15. comparative advantage

_13_ a. division of labor into specialized activities
_3_ b. manufactured goods used to make other goods and services
_7_ c. combinations of goods and services that can be produced
_9_ d. the opportunity cost of producing a good increases as its output rises
_10_ e. an idea that becomes an applied technology
_14_ f. producing a good with fewer resources than another producer
_11_ g. resources that are less than fully utilized
_15_ h. producing a good at a lower opportunity cost than another producer
_2_ i. physical and intellectual effort by people in the production process
_8_ j. the quantity of goods that must be given up to obtain a good
_1_ k. land, labor, capital, and entrepreneurship
_4_ l. the knowledge and skills acquired by labor
_12_ m. the maximum possible output with resources fully employed
_5_ n. a natural-state resource such as real estate
_6_ o. a person willing to assume the risks of a business

Graphing Tutorial

From a graphing perspective, this chapter is fairly straightforward. There is really only one type of graph presented in the chapter — the production possibilities curve (or frontier). The production possibilities curve is drawn bowed-out from the origin. The bowed-out shape of the curve reflects the law of increasing costs. However, once you draw a production possibilities curve, many economic principles can be illustrated with it beyond the law of increasing costs. The example presented below will help you appreciate the variety of applications that the production possibilities model affords.

Suppose an economy can produce pizzas or ovens in the combinations shown in the table below.

Pizzas	Ovens
0	10
5	9
10	7
15	4
20	0

This information is presented as a graph on the following page.

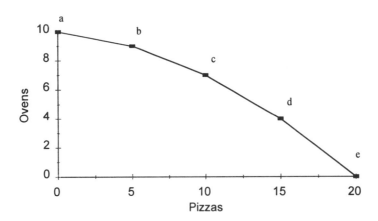

Production Possibilities Frontier for Pizza and Ovens

Note how the production possibilities frontier is bowed-out from the origin. Clearly, the law of increasing costs is at work in this case. Looking at the graph, let's start with 10 ovens and no pizza, at point a. To produce the first 5 pizzas, resources are shifted from oven making to pizza making. One oven is sacrificed. We move from the vertical intercept at 0 pizzas and 10 ovens toward the right on the curve to point b at 5 pizzas and 9 ovens. But look at what happens as we increase pizza production again. Resources must be shifted out of oven production, and we give up more ovens for each additional batch of 5 pizzas. Increasing costs show up as consecutive sacrifices of 2, 3, then 4 ovens as we increase pizza output from 5 to 20, finally ending up at point e.

The production possibilities table and curve assume full employment. Suppose this economy was producing only 10 pizzas and 4 ovens. Find this point on the graph. It lies inside the production possibilities frontier, indicating that resources are either unemployed or underemployed. Find the point represented by 15 pizzas and 8 ovens. This point lies outside the curve in what is termed the impossibilities region of the economy. Over time, with increases in the supplies of resources, new innovations, and greater labor specialization, we can expect the production possibilities for this economy to expand. The values shown in the table for pizza and oven output will increase, and the curve will shift to the right. This shift represents economic growth.

The questions and problems that follow will provide you with ample opportunity to develop your skills interpreting and drawing production possibilities frontiers.

True-False Questions — If a statement is false, explain why.

1. Factors of production include consumption goods. (T/F)

2. Slave labor is an important factor of production in some countries. (T/F)

3. When my hired housekeeper vacuums my home, he is performing labor. (T/F)

4. Capital is a good used to produce or market other goods. (T/F)

THE BASICS   21

5. Personal computers are considered capital goods because they are so expensive. (T/F) F

6. Entrepreneurs share the risks and uncertainties of business ventures with the labor they hire. (T/F) F

7. The opportunity cost of a bushel of wheat is the money that must be sacrificed in order to produce it. (T/F) F

8. An economy that operates on its production possibilities curve is efficient. (T/F) T

9. The production possibilities for an economy expand as the supplies of factors of production increase. (T/F) T

10. All economies' production possibilities curves always shift to the right. (T/F) F

11. A pair of countries where one has an absolute advantage over the other in all areas of production will find it impossible to benefit from trade. (T/F) F

12. The richer the economy, the more easily it can grow because the opportunity cost of shifting resources to capital goods becomes less painful. (T/F) T

13. An economy that has underemployed resources can still operate on its production possibilities curve. (T/F) F

14. If Japan can produce more automobiles and more computers than the United States using the same amount of resources, then Japan has an absolute advantage in both activities. (T/F) T

15. If the opportunity cost of producing one car in Japan is 10 computers and the opportunity cost of producing one car in the United States is 5 computers, then the United States has a comparative advantage in computer production. (T/F) F

Multiple-Choice Questions

1. Lumber, used in the construction of a farmer's barn, is considered
    a. a consumption good because the farmer will use the barn
    b. entrepreneurship if the farmer is an independent operator
    c. capital because it is a good used to make other goods
    d. human capital because it contains labor that made the lumber from the tree
    e. neither a consumption good nor a factor of production because it is raw material

2. Points A and B on the production possibilities curve shown below represent combinations of consumption goods and capital goods produced in country A and country B, respectively. These positions suggest that in the future
    a. country A will grow faster than country B
    b. country B will grow faster than country A
    c. they will grow at the same rate because they are on the same curve
    d. neither will grow because both are producing fewer capital goods than consumption goods
    e. both countries will have unemployed resources

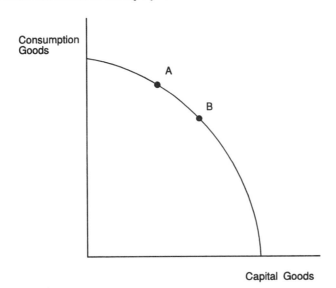

3. The production possibilities model applies
    a. only to economies that produce simple goods like the Crusoe economy described in the text
    b. to economies without labor specialization
    c. to economies without division of labor
    d. to economies whose factors of production are fully employed
    e. universally to all economies regardless of their differences

4. If an economy experiences unemployment, it would show up as a point
    a. on the production possibilities curve but on one of the axes
    b. outside the production possibilities curve
    c. inside the production possibilities curve
    d. on the production possibilities curve
    e. on a production possibilities curve that is shifting to the right

5. The opportunity cost of producing a good is
    a. the dollar amount paid to produce the good
    b. the quantity of other goods that must be sacrificed in order to produce the good
    c. the labor hours required to produce the good
    d. the amount of capital used to produce the good
    e. higher than most people realize because scarce resources are expensive

THE BASICS

6. The law of increasing costs suggests all of the following **except** that
   a. resources, such as labor and land, are not of equal quality or fertility
   b. resources, such as labor and land, are of equal quality and fertility
   c. switching from producing one good to another involves increasing sacrifices of the first good
   d. the opportunity cost of producing a good is not constant along a bowed-out production possibilities curve
   e. the opportunity cost of producing more of a good increases as resources are shifted away from producing other goods

7. To economists, the term "capital" refers exclusively to
   a. goods used to produce other goods and services
   b. money used to purchase capital in the form of stocks and bonds
   c. savings accumulated by households to purchase capital
   d. money used by an entrepreneur to purchase capital
   e. real estate, forests, metals, and minerals

8. An entrepreneur, as distinct from other factors of production, is a person who
   a. earns an income higher than those earned by workers
   b. is a hired manager
   c. assumes all the risks and rewards associated with a business venture
   d. buys and sells stocks and bonds
   e. hires and fires workers

9. All of the following statements about technological change are true **except** that
   a. an idea that eventually takes the form of newly applied technology is described as innovation
   b. technological change can shift the production possibilities curve to the right
   c. new technology reduces the severity of scarcity
   d. our grandchildren will no doubt regard our technology as rather primitive
   e. new technology, although productive, must create unemployment in the long run

10. Capital accumulation (addition to capital) occurs in an economy when
    a. more inputs are used in production
    b. resources are shifted from the production of consumption goods to the production of capital goods
    c. new technologies are adopted
    d. workers work longer hours
    e. the economy operates at full employment

11. One of the reasons that poor economies tend to stay poor is that
    a. workers in these economies are not sufficiently motivated because their consumption goods are insufficient to satisfy their needs
    b. their governments tend to shift resources from capital goods to consumption goods
    c. most of their resources are devoted to consumption goods production so little capital accumulation occurs
    d. they are exploited by the industrially advanced economies
    e. they do not have a production possibilities curve

12. If an economy is operating along its production possibilities curve, then it is clear that
    a. all factors of production are fully employed
    b. poverty is eliminated
    c. technological change is assured
    d. some resources may still be underemployed
    e. economic growth must slow down

13. The most likely explanation for the shift in the production possibilities curve shown below is
    a. a decrease in the supplies of some inputs
    b. a decrease in the supplies of all inputs
    c. the adoption by the government of a full employment policy
    d. a shift from capital goods to consumer goods production
    e. technological change which occurs in the production of both capital and consumption goods

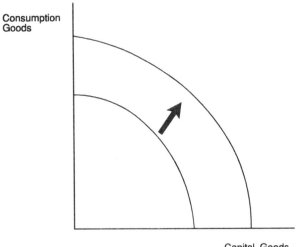

14. An entrepreneur _____ manager of a firm, and/but assumes _____ for the success or failure of the firm.
    a. is the sole; no responsibility
    b. may or may not be the sole; full responsibility
    c. cannot be the sole; full responsibility
    d. desires to be; full responsibility
    e. is the sole; partial responsibility

15. Specialization and division of labor take place at the international level according to the
    a. law of increasing costs
    b. principle of comparative advantage
    c. principle of economic efficiency
    d. rate of new innovation
    e. universality of the production possibilities model

16. Which of the following is a clear example of underemployment?
    a. a young man works as a carpenter
    b. a middle-aged man works as a bank manager
    c. a retired woman works as a hospital volunteer
    d. an African American man is not hired as a police officer because he lacks a high school diploma
    e. a young woman is denied a promotion only because she is a woman

THE BASICS 25

17. Although countries may experience devastating losses of human life and physical capital during a war, their postwar economies typically recover quickly because
   a. citizens are motivated by patriotism to rebuild quickly
   b. the ideas on which production technologies are based are indestructible
   c. other countries will typically come to the devastated country's aid
   d. entrepreneurs usually find great investment opportunities right after a war
   e. political leaders use great care in planning for recovery

18. Given the following production possibilities frontier, the opportunity cost of increasing capital goods production from one to two is
   a. five consumption goods
   b. four consumption goods
   c. three consumption goods
   d. two consumption goods
   e. one consumption good

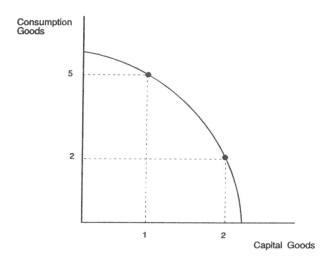

Questions 19 and 20 are based on the data in the following table. In one day, Mexico can use all of its resources to produce either 100 bushels of corn or 200 pounds of avocados. Similarly, the United States can use all of its resources to produce either 80 bushels of corn or 80 pounds of avocados in one day.

Quantities of Corn and Avocados Produced in Mexico and the United States in One Day

	Corn (bushels)	Avocados (pounds)
Mexico	100	200
United States	80	80

19. Which country has an absolute advantage in what?
   a. Mexico in avocados; the United States in corn
   b. Mexico in corn; the United States in avocados
   c. Mexico in avocados
   d. the United States in avocados
   e. the United States in corn

20. In the United States, the opportunity cost of one bushel of corn is _____ pound(s) of avocados while in Mexico the opportunity cost of one bushel of corn is _____ pound(s) of avocados so the United States has a comparative advantage in _____ production.
    a. one; two; corn
    b. one; two; avocado
    c. 80; 200; corn
    d. 80; 200; avocado
    e. 100; 200; corn

Fill in the Blanks

1. The _opportunity cost_ of producing more capital goods is the amount of _consumption goods_ sacrificed.

2. As resources are shifted from producing one good to producing another, the opportunity cost of the second good _increases_, which illustrates the _law of increasing costs_.

3. Because a poor society must devote so many resources to the production of _consumption_ goods, it is very difficult for it to produce _capital_ goods in order to encourage faster economic growth.

4. If an economy operates inside its production possibilities frontier, it is an indication of _underemployed_ or _unemployed_ resources.

5. To say that the United States produces computer software at lower opportunity cost than does Great Britain suggests that the United States has a _comparative advantage_ in software production.

Discussion Questions

1. Does my son, who weeds the backyard because I insist, constitute labor? Does your answer change if my son and I agree that he will be paid $0.25 per bucket of weeds pulled? Explain.

2. What is the opportunity cost of your college education? How does the opportunity cost change if you had been offered a job paying $75,000 a year in a field you love at the beginning of this academic year? Would you still be in college this year?

THE BASICS

3. Why do entrepreneurs hire specialists, sometimes at very high wage rates?

4. Carefully distinguish between the terms absolute advantage and comparative advantage.

5. How does specialization according to comparative advantage affect labor productivity?

Problems

1. The figures in the table below represent the production possibilities for a country that produces capital goods and consumer goods.

Capital Goods	Consumer Goods
1,000	0
800	400
600	750
400	1,000
200	1,150
0	1,200

a. Sketch a graph with capital goods on the horizontal axis and consumer goods on the vertical axis and draw the production possibilities curve that corresponds to these data.

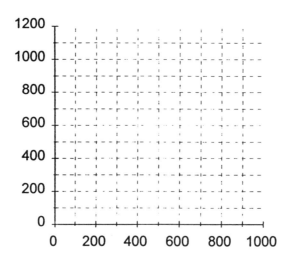

b. Does the graph you have drawn exhibit the law of increasing costs? How do you know? Use the concept of opportunity cost and the data provided to explain the law of increasing cost.

2. The following table shows the amounts of apples or cheese that can be produced in Washington and Wisconsin in one day.

	Apples(bushels)	Cheese(pounds)
Washington	400	100
Wisconsin	400	200

If these two states specialize, what should each one produce? Why? Explain carefully using the concepts absolute and comparative advantage.

THE BASICS

3. Return to the graphing tutorial presented on pages 19-20 above. Suppose that the resources available in the economy were to double, that is, twice as much labor, capital, land, and entrepreneurship. How would the economy's production possibilities change? Construct a table to show the new production possibilities and draw a graph to show how the production possibilities curve changes.

4. The following table shows the **labor time in hours** required to produce skis and chocolate in Switzerland and the United States.

	United States	Switzerland
One pair of skis	10	8
One pound of chocolates	2	1

a. Given this information, which country has an absolute advantage in skis? In chocolate? Explain.
   (Hint: Be careful because the units in this table are in hours of time required to produce each good, not in physical units.)

b. Which country has a comparative advantage in chocolate? In skis? Explain.

Everyday Applications

1. What was the opportunity cost of your working through these study guide exercises? Was it worth it? How will you know? Knowing the concept of opportunity cost won't necessarily make you a better decision maker, but it should change the way you evaluate the decisions you make.

2. North Korea is a desperately poor country right now. Will North Korea stay poor because it currently is poor? What would happen if North Korea were to allocate more of its resources to the production of capital goods rather than consumption goods?

Economics Online

The Internet is likely to change the way we do business in ways that we cannot even imagine today. One of the pressing issues facing firms that want to expand their Internet sales is how to safeguard transactions that are done over the Internet. Check out the site (*http://policyworks.gov/org/main/mg/intergov/oisnews.htm*) for information about how the Internet will facilitate commerce. What will happen to production possibilities curves as we learn to better use this new technology?

Answers to Questions

Key Terms Quiz

a. 13   f. 14   k. 1
b. 3   g. 11   l. 4
c. 7   h. 15   m. 12
d. 9   i. 2   n. 5
e. 10   j. 8   o. 6

True-False Questions

1. False. Consumer goods are some of the final goods and services produced by factors of production.
2. False. The absence of coercion is necessary for the economists' definition of labor.
3. True
4. True
5. False. Expense does not tell you whether a good is capital or not.
6. False. An entrepreneur is solely responsible for the business's success or failure.
7. False. The opportunity cost is the quantity of other goods that must be given up to produce the bushel of wheat.
8. True
9. True
10. False. Growth doesn't always occur in an economy.
11. False. Trade can benefit both countries if comparative advantages exist.
12. True
13. False. Full employment of all resources in the economy is a requirement for its being on the curve.
14. True

THE BASICS 31

15. False. The United States would have the comparative advantage in car production because the opportunity cost of producing cars in the United States is less than in Japan (5 computers compared to 10 computers).

Multiple-Choice Questions

1. c	6. b	11. c	16. e
2. b	7. a	12. a	17. b
3. e	8. c	13. e	18. c
4. c	9. e	14. b	19. c
5. b	10. b	15. b	20. a

Fill in the Blanks

1. opportunity cost; consumption goods
2. increases; law of increasing costs
3. consumption; capital
4. underemployed or unemployed
5. comparative advantage

Discussion Questions

1. My son will tell you that the only way he will weed the backyard without pay is if I coerce him. This is not labor. However, if we agree on a wage, then the work is labor.

2. The opportunity cost of going to college is the money you give up not working during the time you are in college. If the described job offer is better than your next best alternative now, then your opportunity cost has risen, and you are less likely to go to college this year.

3. Entrepreneurs hire specialists because these people are very productive. That is, a specialist can produce more in a given period of time than a nonspecialized worker. Because specialists produce more, they are paid a higher wage.

4. An absolute advantage exists if one country can produce more of a good than another country with the same resources. A country has a comparative advantage in the production of a good if it can produce the good at a lower opportunity cost than can another country. That is, the country with the comparative advantage gives up less to produce the good than does the other country.

5. Specialization according to comparative advantage will increase labor productivity because countries and their labor forces will be specializing in activities that they perform at relatively lower opportunity costs. For example, a country that begins to specialize according to its comparative advantage shifts its productive resources into producing goods that have a lower opportunity cost to produce. If the country gives up less to produce these goods, it necessarily ends up with more output from its workers. Hence, labor productivity is higher.

Problems

1. a. Your graph should look like the one shown below.

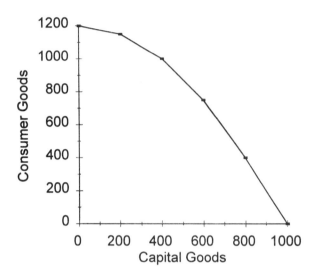

b. This graph does exhibit the law of increasing costs because it is bowed-out from the origin. Furthermore, for each 200-unit increase in capital goods production, the sacrifice in consumer goods rises. These sacrifices, or opportunity costs, are 50, 150, 250, 350, and 400 for each additional 200 units of capital goods produced.

2. Washington will specialize in apple production because the opportunity cost of one bushel of apples is one-fourth pound of cheese. Wisconsin will specialize in cheese production because the opportunity cost of producing a pound of cheese is two bushels of apples whereas the opportunity cost of producing a pound of cheese in Washington is four bushels of apples. Wisconsin has an absolute advantage in cheese production while Washington has a comparative advantage in apple production.

3. All the numbers in the table would double and the production possibilities curve would shift out to the right so that all the values along the curve double too.

4. a. Switzerland has an absolute advantage in both activities because it does both in less time than does the United States.

   b. The opportunity cost of one pound of chocolates in the United States is one-fifth pair of skis. In the two hours it takes to produce one pound of chocolate in the United States, one-fifth pair of skis is given up. By similar reasoning, the opportunity cost of one pound of chocolates in Switzerland is one-eighth pair of skis. It takes one hour to produce a pound of chocolate in Switzerland and eight hours to produce a pair of skis. Therefore, Switzerland has a comparative advantage in chocolate production because the opportunity cost of producing chocolate is lower there.

CHAPTER 3

DEMAND AND SUPPLY

Chapter in a Nutshell

How are prices determined? This is the basic question we explore in this chapter. Let's conclude before we start our analysis of price determination: Price depends on **demand and supply**. That's it. But what's **demand and what's supply**? **Demand** represents people's **willingness to buy goods and services at different prices**. Price is a reflection of how willing people are to buy goods and services. Supply can be interpreted similarly. **Supply** represents the **willingness of producers to supply goods and services at different prices**. However, supply depends on the time frame being considered to a greater extent than does demand. Producers can better adjust to changes in the market given more time. We'll develop three time frames in which to consider supply — **the market day, the short run, and the long run**.

With an understanding of demand and supply, it is possible to describe how **equilibrium prices** are determined in markets for goods and services. The equilibrium price equates the **quantity demanded** and the **quantity supplied** in a market. **Changes in demand** and **changes in supply** cause changes in equilibrium prices and quantities demanded and supplied in markets. Prices effectively **ration goods and services** in our economy. Price increases ration the available supply of a good to those who can still afford it. A price decrease makes a good available to a wider segment of the market.

After you study this chapter, you should be able to:

- Discuss how **consumer demand** is measured.
- Describe the **inverse relationship** between price and quantity demanded.
- Discuss how **supply** is measured.
- Distinguish between **market-day supply, short-run supply, and long-run supply**.
- Explain how **equilibrium prices** are determined.
- Define **normal goods, substitute goods, and complementary goods**.
- Show how **changes in demand** and **changes in supply** cause changes in equilibrium prices.
- Give examples of **price as a rationing mechanism**.

Concept Check — See how you do on these multiple-choice questions.

1. A decrease in price causes an increase in the **quantity demanded** because
   a. consumers cannot afford to buy as much
   b. consumers are willing to buy more at a lower price
   c. consumers' tastes change as the price decreases
   d. consumers' incomes increase as the price decreases
   e. the number of consumers increases as the price decreases.

Be careful to keep separate in your mind the difference between a change in quantity demanded and a change in demand.

2. One characteristic of the **market-day supply** is that
   a. the time period is too short to allow changes in the quantity supplied
   b. it applies in the short run
   c. it applies in the long run
   d. it depends on the demand
   e. it depends on the quantity demanded

Think about the shape of the market-day supply curve.

3. A **change in demand** can be caused by all of the following except a
   a. change in income
   b. change in the prices of other goods
   c. change in tastes
   d. change in population
   e. change in the price of the good being considered

Again, think about what is meant by a **change in demand** versus a **change in quantity demanded**.

4. An improvement in the **technology** for producing a good will cause
   a. an increase in the demand for the good
   b. a shift to the left in the short-run supply curve
   c. a shift to the left in the long-run supply curve
   d. an increase in the supply of the good
   e. an increase in the incomes of consumers

Improvements in technology permit a larger quantity of a good to be produced with the same amount of resources.

5. To say that **price serves as a rationing mechanism** means that
   a. only those with the willingness to pay for goods in a market get them
   b. demand is limitless
   c. supplies keep dwindling
   d. wants are insatiable
   e. resources are scarce

If wants are insatiable and resources are scarce, then a mechanism must exist for allocating products among the consumers who desire them.

Am I on the Right Track?

Your answers to the questions above should be **b, a, e, d,** and **a**. Understanding demand and supply is key to your understanding all that follows in this text. If the answers to the questions above weren't readily apparent to you, then you may want to return to the text and re-read some or all of the chapter. Be sure that you understand the difference between changes in demand and quantity demanded, the different time frames in which to consider supply, and the role that prices play in rationing goods and services in markets. Then come back and work carefully through the exercises that follow. This is an extremely important chapter!

THE BASICS

Key Terms Quiz — Match the terms on the left with the definitions in the column on the right.

1. change in quantity demanded
2. law of demand
3. demand schedule
4. demand curve
5. market demand
6. supply schedule
7. market-day supply
8. supply curve
9. excess supply
10. excess demand
11. equilibrium price
12. short run
13. long run
14. change in demand
15. normal good
16. substitute goods
17. complementary goods
18. change in supply

___4___ a. a curve that relates price and quantity demanded
___5___ b. the sum of all individual demands in a market
___9___ c. quantity supplied greater than quantity demanded at a price
___11___ d. the price that equates quantity demanded to quantity supplied
___13___ e. supplier can change all resources used in production
___14___ f. a shift in the entire demand curve
___16___ g. goods that can replace each other
___18___ h. a shift in the entire supply curve
___1___ i. a change in the amount purchased due to a price change
___2___ j. inverse relationship between price and quantity demanded
___7___ k. quantity supplied is fixed, regardless of price
___3___ l. a schedule of quantities of goods purchased at different prices
___6___ m. a schedule of quantities of goods supplied at different prices
___17___ n. goods that are used together
___10___ o. quantity demanded greater than quantity supplied at a price
___8___ p. a curve that relates price and quantity supplied
___12___ q. supplier can change some resources used in production
___15___ r. a good whose demand increases when income increases

Graphing Tutorial

Drawing and interpreting demand and supply diagrams is easy. Consider the data presented below for the market for brooms during a month-long period. The first column shows the price per broom in dollars, the second column shows the quantity demanded at each price, and the third column shows the quantity supplied at each price. The table combines information for the demand schedule and the supply schedule.

Price ($ per broom)	Quantity Demanded (per month)	Quantity Supplied (per month)
6	10	70
5	20	60
4	30	50
3	40	40
2	50	30
1	60	20

Note that the information contained in the table corresponds to the market for brooms. Therefore, the demand schedule represents the sum of all the buyers' individual demand schedules. Likewise, the supply schedule represents the total number of brooms put on the market by suppliers at different prices during a month. It is a simple matter to plot these data on a graph with quantities measured horizontally and prices measured vertically. The graph is shown below.

The demand curve is drawn as a downward-sloping line starting at the point 10 brooms per month and $6 per broom. At a price of $6, 10 brooms per month are demanded by consumers. The demand curve shows that for each $1 decrease in the price of a broom, the quantity demanded increases by 10 brooms per month. The supply curve is an upward-sloping line starting at the point 20 brooms per month and $1 per broom. For each $1 increase in the price of a broom, the quantity of brooms supplied increases by 10 per month.

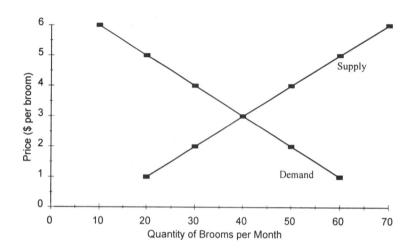

Consider the point where the demand curve and the supply curve intersect. This point is 40 brooms per month at a price of $3 per broom. At a price of $3 per broom, the quantity of brooms demanded is equal to the quantity of brooms supplied. In other words, all the brooms that are offered for sale are purchased at this price. In this example, $3 is the equilibrium price.

Suppose the price were $2 per broom. At $2 per broom, the quantity of brooms demanded is 50 while the quantity of brooms supplied is 30. There is an excess demand for brooms, represented on the graph as the horizontal distance between the points on the demand curve and the supply curve at a price of $2, which is 20 brooms. Would the price stay at $2 per broom? Of course not. The excess demand for brooms will generate competition between buyers that will push the price of brooms higher, causing the quantity demanded to decrease and the quantity supplied to increase until equilibrium is reached at a price of $3 per broom.

Consider a price above equilibrium at, say, $4 per broom. At $4 per broom, the quantity of brooms supplied is 50 while the quantity of brooms demanded is 30. At this price, an excess supply of brooms exists, represented by the horizontal distance between the points on the supply curve and the demand curve at a price of $4 per broom, which is 20 brooms. Suppliers are trying to sell 20 brooms more than consumers are willing to buy at $4 per broom. In this case, the price will begin to decrease as suppliers lower price, causing the quantity demanded to increase and the quantity supplied to decrease until the equilibrium is reached at a price of $3 per broom.

What sort of supply curve have we drawn in this example? We know that it cannot be a market-day supply curve because it isn't drawn vertically at a specific quantity level. This supply curve could either be a short-run supply curve or a long-run supply curve, depending on how easily suppliers can adjust the quantities of resources used to produce brooms.

A variety of factors influence the position of the demand and supply curves we have drawn. These are discussed at length in the text. Make sure you understand how demand and supply curves shift due to changes

THE BASICS   37

in these factors. Any time there is a shift in one or the other or both curves, the equilibrium price will change, as will the quantity demanded and supplied. The exercises below will give you the opportunity to practice drawing and interpreting demand and supply diagrams.

Graphing Pitfalls

Consider the graph shown below. What is wrong with it? In a purely technical sense, nothing at all. The only difference between this graph and the one shown above is that price is measured along the horizontal axis and quantity is measured on the vertical axis in the graph below. The information conveyed by the graph is exactly the same. So, does this mean it doesn't matter which axis we label price and which we label quantity? No! By convention, economists measure price on the vertical axis and quantity on the horizontal axis. You'll decrease the level of confusion if you stick to this convention in drawing your graphs!

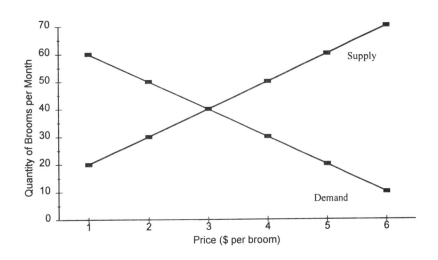

The axes are switched on this graph! Measure quantity on the horizontal axis and price on the vertical axis!

True-False Questions — If a statement is false, explain why.

1. The law of demand states that as price decreases, quantity demanded decreases. (T/F)

2. A demand schedule shows people's willingness to buy specific quantities of a good at different prices. (T/F)

3. The market demand for a good is the sum of individual demands for the good. (T/F)

4. In the time period known as the market day, producers can sell more goods as their prices rise. (T/F)

5. A supply schedule depends upon the willingness of demanders to buy the quantities supplied at various prices. (T/F)

6. The short run is a period in which producers can devote larger quantities of some resources to production as prices increase. (T/F)

7. An excess demand exists when the price is below its equilibrium level. (T/F)

8. The equilibrium price equates the quantity demanded to the quantity supplied. (T/F)

9. An increase in supply causes an excess demand at the original price, and competition between sellers leads to a lower equilibrium price. (T/F)

10. An increase in demand causes an excess demand at the original price, and competition between demanders leads to a higher equilibrium price. (T/F)

11. An excess supply exists when the price is below the equilibrium price. (T/F)

12. If the price of one good increases and the demand for another good increases as a result, then the goods must be substitutes. (T/F)

13. Two goods that can replace each other in consumption are called complements. (T/F)

14. The long run is a time period sufficient to allow suppliers to make some, but not all, of the changes necessary to adjust the quantity supplied to price changes. (T/F)

15. A change in demand refers to a movement along a demand curve due to a price change, but a change in quantity demanded refers to a shift in the entire demand curve. (T/F)

Multiple-Choice Questions

1. If a market is in equilibrium, then
   a. demand curves and supply curves are the same
   b. at the equilibrium price, quantity supplied is equal to quantity demanded
   c. the short-run quantities of supply and demand equal the long-run quantities of supply and demand
   d. the short-run equilibrium price equals the long-run equilibrium price
   e. all demanders receive the goods they want, and all suppliers sell the goods they want

THE BASICS

2. If excess demand exists in a market, then
   a. excess supply will emerge to absorb the excess demand
   b. the quantity supplied is less than the quantity demanded
   c. the quantity demanded is less than the quantity supplied
   d. the equilibrium price will fall
   e. the price will fall

3. The market demand for fish represents the
   a. sum of all individual demands for fish
   b. specific quantities consumers will buy, given the market-day supply
   c. relationship between price and quantity of fish demanded by a consumer on the fish market
   d. maximum quantity consumers will buy, given the limitations of their income
   e. changing tastes of consumers

4. An increase in demand causes
   a. an increase in supply as new firms enter the market
   b. an increase in price and an increase in supply
   c. an increase in price and an increase in the quantity supplied
   d. a decrease in demand in the future
   e. a decrease in price and an increase in the quantity supplied

5. If supply increases and demand does not change, then price
   a. as well as quantities demanded and supplied will increase
   b. will decrease, and quantity demanded and supplied will increase
   c. will decrease, and quantity demanded and supplied will decrease
   d. and quantity demanded remain unchanged
   e. remains unchanged, but both quantities demanded and supplied will decrease

6. If, at a specific price, quantity demanded is greater than the quantity supplied, then price will
   a. increase until the excess supply is eliminated
   b. decrease until the excess supply is eliminated
   c. increase until the excess demand is eliminated
   d. remain unchanged, and quantity demanded will decrease
   e. decrease, and quantity supplied will increase

7. Suppose there is a widespread rumor that Japanese car manufacturers plan to increase the price of their cars by 50 percent next month. You would expect that in the United States, the demand curve for Japanese cars would
   a. shift to the left next month
   b. shift to the right next month
   c. shift to the right before next month
   d. shift to the left before next month
   e. remain unchanged, but the price of U.S. cars would decrease next month

8. In the graph below, an increase in the price from 3 to 5 causes
   a. a market-day supply curve to shift to the right
   b. a short-run supply curve to shift
   c. suppliers to increase their use of all resources to produce 10 units
   d. the quantity supplied to increase from 5 to 10
   e. the supply to increase from 5 to 10

9. The basic difference between the short run and the long run is that in the
   a. short run, suppliers cannot adjust output to changes in demand
   b. long run, suppliers can make any necessary adjustments to output
   c. short run, a new business can enter an industry
   d. short run, suppliers can devote more resources of all kinds to production
   e. long run, demanders can adjust their demands to their incomes

10. When economists refer to price as a rationing mechanism, they mean that
    a. the government can establish a rationing program by setting prices
    b. price weeds from the market those who want the good, but can't afford it
    c. most markets have chronic problems with excess demand so rationing is necessary
    d. suppliers ration goods by setting a price demanders can afford
    e. demanders ration their incomes by choosing only low-priced goods

11. Which of the following will not cause a change in demand for a particular good?
    a. a change in the price of a related good
    b. a change in income
    c. a change in tastes
    d. a change in expectations about future prices
    e. a change in the price of the good

THE BASICS

12. When price is higher than its equilibrium level, we can expect that
    a. as the equilibrium price rises, the quantity supplied will increase
    b. as the equilibrium price rises, the quantity demanded will decrease
    c. the quantity supplied and demanded will both fall as the equilibrium price adjusts
    d. the quantity supplied and demanded will both rise as the equilibrium price adjusts
    e. as the price falls to its equilibrium level, the quantity demanded will increase

13. The market-day supply is drawn as a vertical line at a particular level of production because
    a. output can easily be adjusted
    b. chronic excess supply is permanent
    c. output can completely adjust to price changes
    d. output can partially adjust to price changes
    e. output cannot be changed on the market day

14. The demand and supply curves shown in the diagram below represent which of the following changes?
    a. an increase in demand and an increase in the equilibrium price
    b. a decrease in demand and a decrease in the equilibrium price
    c. a decrease in demand and a decrease in the quantity supplied
    d. an increase in the quantity demanded and an increase in supply
    e. an increase in the supply and an increase in the equilibrium price

15. If consumers are presented with hard scientific evidence that a diet including moderate red wine consumption leads to lower rates of heart disease, which of the following changes is likely to occur?
    a. an increase in red wine prices
    b. an increase in white wine prices
    c. a decrease in brie cheese prices
    d. a decrease in grape prices
    e. an increase in beer prices

16. In general, as the time period considered moves from the short run to the long run, supply curves
    a. become steeper
    b. are perfectly vertical
    c. become flatter
    d. shift toward the left
    e. intersect with demand at a higher price

17. Which of the following will not cause a change in the supply of pencils?
    a. a change in pencil-making technology
    b. a change in resource prices associated with pencil making
    c. a change in the price of pens and other substitute goods
    d. a change in the price of pencils
    e. a change in the number of pencil suppliers

18. Suppose the demand and supply for strawberries decrease, but the decrease in demand is major while the decrease in supply is minor. Under these conditions
    a. price increases, and quantities demanded and supplied decrease
    b. price decreases, and quantities demanded and supplied increase
    c. price decreases, and quantities demanded and supplied decrease
    d. price increases, and quantities demanded and supplied increase
    e. price remains unchanged, but quantities demanded and supplied increase

19. Stan the news man on Channel 6 reports that the automobile prices were unchanged over the last year, yet automobile sales increased by 5 percent. In the same year, incomes rose by 2.5 percent. Based on this information, you could reasonably conclude that automobiles are
    a. substitute goods
    b. complementary goods
    c. normal goods
    d. priced below their equilibrium level
    e. priced above their equilibrium level

20. A change in quantity demanded of a good always results from a change in
    a. tastes
    b. the price of that good
    c. income
    d. the price of substitutes
    e. the price of complements

Fill in the Blanks

1. From the shortest to the longest, the time periods in which we consider supply are __The market day__, __short run__, and __long run__.

2. Pairs of goods for which a price increase in one causes an increase in the demand for the other are called __substitutes__.

3. When the __quantity demanded__ is equal to the __quantity supplied__, the price is an __equilibrium__ price.

4. Price serves as a __rationing__ mechanism by removing from the market those who are __less willing__ to purchase the good.

5. The market demand for a good is calculated by __summing__ all of the __individual__

THE BASICS

demand curves of consumers in the market.

Discussion Questions

1. Richard III was willing to exchange his kingdom for a horse. What was the opportunity cost of his having a horse?

2. What is the difference between a change in quantity demanded and a change in demand?

3. Contrast market-day supply, short-run supply, and long-run supply. Why does the nature of supply depend so much on the length of the time period being considered?

4. Would the following events cause a change in demand or a change in quantity demanded in the market for automobiles? Explain.

    a. A limit is placed on the number of cars that can be imported from Japan.

    b. Malaysia becomes a major new exporter of cars to the United States.

    c. Congress passes a big income tax increase in an attempt to deal with the deficit.

d. A report is issued suggesting that air travel has become much less safe in recent years.

e. The legal driving age is lowered to 15.

Problems

1. The following table shows the demand and supply schedules for an initial release of the first compact disc by the new female pop group from England, the Nice Girls.

Price ($/CD)	Quantity Demanded (1,000s)	Quantity Supplied (1,000s)
24	0	100
22	20	100
20	40	100
18	60	100
16	80	100
14	100	100
12	120	100
10	140	100

a. Sketch a demand and supply diagram to represent the data from the table in the space below.

b. What time frame is represented by the supply curve you have drawn? How do you know?

THE BASICS

c. What is the equilibrium price, quantity demanded, and quantity supplied?

d. At each price listed in the table, note whether an excess demand or supply exists and its magnitude.

e. Suppose that record executives had initially issued 120,000 compact discs for the Nice Girls's first album? How would your answers to parts c and d change?

2. Draw the market-day, the short-run, and the long-run supply curves. Why do the slopes of these supply curves differ?

3. The graph below shows the market for British beef after the announcement that consumption of beef posed the risk of Mad Cow Disease. The demand curve shifts to the left, from D to D'. Explain in detail how the market adjusts from a price of $6 per pound to $4 per pound as a result of the shift in demand.

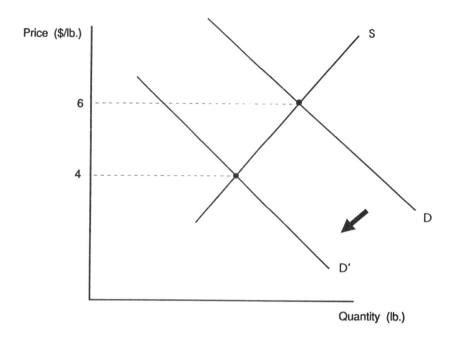

Everyday Applications

A fairly painless way to become better acquainted with the business world is to watch Nightly Business Report a few nights a week on your local PBS station. It's usually on in the early evening. Check your local listings. As you watch the show, keep in mind that a separate market exists for every stock and bond discussed. We'll present more detail on stocks and bonds in Chapter 7. For now, it's enough to know that the prices that you hear quoted on the show are set by the interaction of demand and supply, just as has been discussed in this chapter. Listen to the discussion of the "most active" stocks — those whose prices have changed most dramatically. Typically, something has happened in these markets to make the stock more or less attractive. Think about how various factors shift the demand and supply curves for stocks and bonds to change their prices.

Economics Online

Business researchers are constantly searching for new products that consumers are willing to pay for. One of the commodities that consumers seem increasingly willing to pay for is information. The Internet is a convenient way to provide cheap information. Increasingly, consumers are willing to pay for information about utility energy services. Technology will make a wide range of utility energy services available to consumers, like time-of-day pricing, but they need to have information about the services before they order them. Visit the address (*http://www.aesp.org/htdocs/strategies/str-cons.htm*) to find out more about consumer

THE BASICS

willingness to pay for utility energy services. How would the market for these information services be affected by an increase in energy prices that might be part of the policy to cope with global warming?

Answers to Questions

Key Terms Quiz

a. 4	f. 14	k. 7	p. 8
b. 5	g. 16	l. 3	q. 12
c. 9	h. 18	m. 6	r. 15
d. 11	i. 1	n. 17	
e. 13	j. 2	o. 10	

True-False Questions

1. False. The law of demand states that as price decreases, quantity demanded increases.
2. True
3. True
4. False. In the market-day period, quantity supplied is fixed no matter what happens to the price.
5. False. The supply schedule shows the quantities that producers are willing to supply at different prices.
6. True
7. True
8. True
9. False. An increase in supply will cause an excess supply at the original price, then competition between sellers leads to a lower equilibrium price.
10. True
11. False. When price is below the equilibrium, an excess demand will exist.
12. True
13. False. Two goods that can replace each other in consumption are called substitutes.
14. False. The long run is a time period long enough to allow producers to make any changes necessary to adjust the quantity supplied to price changes.
15. False. A change in demand is a shift in the entire demand curve due to a change in income, tastes, prices of other goods, expectations of price changes, and/or a change in the number of consumers. A change in quantity demanded is a movement along a demand curve due to a change in price.

Multiple-Choice Questions

1. b	6. c	11. e	16. c
2. b	7. c	12. e	17. d
3. a	8. d	13. e	18. c
4. c	9. b	14. a	19. c
5. b	10. b	15. a	20. b

Fill in the Blanks

1. the market day; the short run; the long run
2. substitutes
3. quantity demanded; quantity supplied; equilibrium
4. rationing; less willing

5. summing; individual

Discussion Questions

1. If Richard III was willing to give up his kingdom for a horse, then the opportunity cost of his having a horse was his kingdom. Remember that opportunity cost represents what we are willing to sacrifice in order to have something or do something. Prices and opportunity costs are linked in this way. The price that Richard III was willing to pay for a horse was his kingdom.

2. A change in quantity demanded is always the result of a change in the price of the good. When the price changes, there is a movement along a specific demand curve between the two prices. On the other hand, when demand changes, it is due to a change in income, tastes, prices of other goods, expectations about future prices, and/or the number of consumers in the market. A change in demand results in a shift in the demand curve.

3. The market-day supply corresponds to the shortest time period a supplier faces. In fact, it is so short that production cannot be adjusted at all in response to price changes. The short-run supply allows the supplier to change the quantities of some (but not all) resources used in production. The long-run supply is a time period long enough to allow for changes in the quantities of all resources used in production. The market-day supply curve is drawn as a vertical line at the quantity that is put on the market and can't be changed. The short-run and the long-run supply curves are drawn as upward sloping so that as price increases, the quantity supplied increases. However, the long-run supply curve is flatter than the short-run supply curve because in the long run a producer can make greater adjustments to the resources used in production; hence, for any price change, the change in output will be greater in the long run than in the short run.

4. a. A limit on the number of cars imported from Japan will cause the supply curve for automobiles to shift to the left; therefore, the quantity demanded of cars will decrease.

   b. If Malaysia becomes a major new exporter of cars to the United States, then the supply of cars will increase, and the quantity demanded of cars will increase as the price falls.

   c. A big tax increase will decrease consumers' after-tax incomes; therefore, the demand for cars will decrease.

   d. If air travel is reported to have become much less safe, then tastes for automobiles will change and the demand for cars will increase.

   e. If the legal driving age is lowered to 15, then the number of consumers of cars will increase and the demand for cars will increase.

Problems

1. a. See the diagram shown on the following page. Note that the units on the quantity axis are 1,000s of CDs.

THE BASICS 49

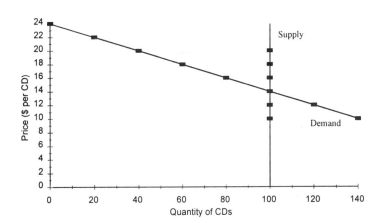

b. The supply curve shown above is a market-day supply because it is drawn vertically at the level of output equal to 100,000 compact discs. This output cannot be changed on the market day no matter what happens to price.

c. At a price equal to $14 per CD, the quantity demanded equals the quantity supplied at 100,000 compact discs.

d. When the price is $24 per disc, the excess supply is 100,000.
When the price is $22 per disc, the excess supply is 80,000.
When the price is $20 per disc, the excess supply is 60,000.
When the price is $18 per disc, the excess supply is 40,000.
When the price is $16 per disc, the excess supply is 20,000.
When the price is $12 per disc, the excess demand is 20,000.
When the price is $10 per disc, the excess demand is 40,000.

e. If 120,000 compact discs had been issued initially, the market-day supply would shift to the right by 20,000. The new equilibrium price would be equal to $12 per disc. Excess supply at each price would increase by 20,000 until a price of $10 per disc was reached where the excess demand would be 20,000 discs.

2. The market-day supply curve is drawn as a vertical line at the output level that is given. The short-run supply curve has a positive slope, as does the long-run supply curve, but the short-run supply curve is steeper. The slopes of these curves differ because they reflect the different abilities of producers to alter resources devoted to production in response to price changes in different time periods. In the market day, the amount of resources devoted to production cannot be changed, no matter what the price change is. In the short run, some resources devoted to production can be changed, but not all of them. In the long run, the producer can change the level of all the resources devoted to production in response to price changes.

3. The announcement that consumption of British beef might lead to a risk of contracting Mad Cow Disease caused a decrease in demand for British beef due to a change in tastes. The demand curve shifted to the left, and, at the original price of $6 per pound, an excess supply of beef existed. Beef producers competed with one another to lower the price in order to eliminate the excess supply. As price fell, quantity demanded increased along D' and quantity supplied decreased along the supply curve until the new equilibrium price of $4 was reached. At $4 per pound, the quantity of beef demanded along D' equals the quantity of beef supplied.

PART I — THE BASICS OF ECONOMIC ANALYSIS

COMPREHENSIVE SAMPLE TEST

Give yourself 50 minutes to complete this exam and see how you do. The answers follow. Don't look until you are finished!

True-False Questions — If a statement is false, explain why. Each question is worth 2 points.

1. Normative economic analysis addresses questions about what ought to be. (T/F)

2. When the *ceteris paribus* assumption is introduced, many variables are assumed to be changing at the same time. (T/F)

3. A forest is an example of a renewable resource that can be depleted if timber is cut faster than trees can mature. (T/F)

4. A capital good is a good used only to produce more capital goods. (T/F)

5. An innovation is an applied technology that permits a larger output to be produced with a given amount of resources. (T/F)

6. If a country has a comparative advantage over another country in the production of shirts, then it can produce shirts in less time than the other country. (T/F)

7. The market-day supply curve is vertical because the market day is a period of time too short for a producer to alter production levels in response to price changes. (T/F)

8. Given a short-run supply curve, an increase in demand will cause an increase in the equilibrium price and a decrease in the quantity demanded and supplied. (T/F)

9. The circular flow model excludes the fact that households supply resources to business enterprises. (T/F)

10. A production possibilities curve that is bowed-out from the origin exhibits the law of demand. (T/F)

THE BASICS 51

Multiple-Choice Questions — Each question is worth 2 points.

1. The circular flow model depicts the flows of resources, goods and services, and money in an economy in order to
   a. perfectly represent the economy
   b. shift attention away from the roles of banks and government in the economy
   c. allow us to focus on the main elements of an economy
   d. give some attention to all the elements in an economy
   e. accurately measure the importance of imports and exports to an economy

2. _____ analysis is used to study the behavior of individual economic units like households and firms while _____ analysis is used to understand the behavior of the economy as a whole.
   a. Microeconomic; macroeconomic
   b. Macroeconomic; microeconomic
   c. Positive; normative
   d. Normative; positive
   e. Econometric; modeling

3. The goal of positive economic analysis is to answer questions concerning
   a. specific relationships that exist in the economy
   b. what ought to be
   c. issues that can be cast in a positive light
   d. positive policy options
   e. statistical methods used to test the accuracy of economic models

4. Given an economy with the choice to produce either capital goods or consumption goods, a shift of resources from the production of consumption goods to the production of capital goods could cause all of the following **except**
   a. an immediate decline in living standards
   b. an increase in living standards in the long run
   c. a slowdown in economic growth
   d. an increase in the production of consumption goods in the long run
   e. an increase in the production of capital goods

5. An economy whose resources are fully employed will produce combinations of goods that correspond to points
   a. inside the production possibilities curve
   b. outside the production possibilities curve
   c. on the market-day supply curve
   d. on the long-run supply curve
   e. on the production possibilities curve

6. A change in any of the following will cause a change in demand for a good **except**
   a. the price of that good
   b. income
   c. tastes
   d. population
   e. the prices of related goods

7. Most of the income earned by an entrepreneur comes from
   a. loans
   b. wages
   c. salaries
   d. interest
   e. profit

8. The opportunity cost of putting an unemployed worker back on the job is
   a. $54,000
   b. the value of her unemployment insurance
   c. zero
   d. greater than her income
   e. equal to the wages she earns at the new job

9. We analyze supply in the context of three time periods — the market day, the short run, and the long run — in order to show that
   a. supply is always changing
   b. producers are able to respond more flexibly to changes in the market given more time
   c. producers are unwilling to change their output in the short run
   d. producers use econometrics to arrive at their equilibrium output levels
   e. markets adjust slowly to supply changes

10. A producer who is able to make partial adjustments in output in response to price changes by hiring or laying off workers is
    a. operating in the short run
    b. operating in the long run
    c. still in the market-day period
    d. anticipating a price increase
    e. anticipating a price decrease

11. If the price in a market starts out above the equilibrium price, then it is clear that
    a. the excess demand will cause the price to rise higher
    b. the demand curve will shift to the right in order to adjust to an equilibrium
    c. the excess supply will result in a decrease in price and an adjustment to equilibrium
    d. the economy is operating inside its production possibilities curve
    e. consumers are trying to purchase more goods than are available

12. When economists argue that prices set in markets serve as a rationing mechanism for goods and services, they mean that
    a. goods and services are provided to those people who have the strongest taste for them and can afford them
    b. markets are always in equilibrium
    c. the market will never provide a large enough supply to satisfy all those with the ability to pay
    d. everyone with a willingness to pay gets some of the product
    e. rationing by other means is ineffective

THE BASICS

13. An increase in the price of Pepsi will likely lead to an increase in the demand for Coke because the two goods
    a. are complements because they are consumed together
    b. are normal goods
    c. are substitutes because they can replace each other in consumption
    d. people's tastes for the two drinks change as a result of a price change in one of them
    e. the incomes for Coke drinkers will increase

14. To say that Brazil has a comparative advantage in sugar production relative to Florida means that
    a. Brazil can produce a given amount of sugar in less time than can Florida
    b. Brazil can produce more sugar in a given amount of time than can Florida
    c. sugar is cheaper in Brazil
    d. the opportunity cost of producing sugar is lower in Brazil
    e. Brazil has an advantage over Florida because it is a nation and Florida is a state

15. Demand for a good will always rise when
    a. the price of a complementary good falls
    b. the price of a substitute good falls
    c. tastes change
    d. income decreases
    e. the price of the good falls

16. The recent weather patterns caused by El Niño wreaked havoc on South American countries, especially Ecuador, destroying much of the country's infrastructure (roads, telephone systems, homes, and factories). An economist using the production possibilities model to describe the effect of El Niño on Ecuador would show
    a. an inward shift in the country's production possibilities curve
    b. an outward shift in the country's production possibilities curve
    c. a movement along the production possibilities curve from consumption goods to capital goods
    d. a movement along the production possibilities curve from capital goods to consumption goods
    e. a movement from a point on the curve to a point inside the curve

17. Suppose the Ecuadoran government announces a program to rebuild the country's infrastructure financed by higher taxes on the Ecuadoran people. The immediate effect noted in the production possibilities model is
    a. an inward shift in the country's production possibilities curve
    b. an outward shift in the country's production possibilities curve
    c. a movement along the production possibilities curve from consumption goods to capital goods
    d. a movement along the production possibilities curve from capital goods to consumption goods
    e. a movement to a point beyond the curve in the impossibilities region

18. At $2 per gallon, John buys 50 gallons of gasoline per week, Mary buys 20 gallons per week, and Tom buys 30 gallons per week. Which of the following is a point on their combined market demand curve for gasoline?
    a. Q = 120 gallons per week, P = $2
    b. Q = 100 gallons per week, P = $3
    c. Q = 100 gallons per week, P = $2
    d. Q = 120 gallons per week, P = $6
    e. Q = 70 gallons per week, P = $2

19. In Adam Smith's famous pin factory example, one man draws out the wire, another straightens it, and a third cuts it. Other people are employed, some pointing the pins, others whitening them, and still others packaging pins. The total output from this factory is much higher than if each person employed performed all the operations necessary for making a pin individually. Smith's example illustrates
    a. comparative advantage
    b. absolute advantage
    c. the law of increasing costs
    d. economic efficiency
    e. labor specialization

20. Economists classify resources as factors of production. The four factors of production are
    a. rent, wages, interest, and profits
    b. land, labor, capital, and entrepreneurship
    c. plant and equipment, labor, management, inventories
    d. human capital, physical capital, money, rent
    e. entrepreneurship, technology, innovation, land

Discussion Questions/Problems — Each question is worth 10 points.

1. In the space provided below, draw a production possibilities curve to show an economy that can produce either consumption goods or capital goods or both. On the curve, label two points A and B to show positions that emphasize consumption goods production and capital goods production, respectively. Why is a move from point A to point B much harder for a poor country to make than for a rich country?

2. The table below shows the world demand for U.S. corn and the quantities U.S. farmers will supply at different prices.

Price ($/bushel)	Quantity Demanded (millions of bushels per year)	Quantity Supplied (millions of bushels per year)
5	1	5
4	2	4
3	3	3
2	4	2
1	5	1

THE BASICS

a. On the axes provided below, draw the demand and supply curves that correspond to the data shown in the table. Carefully label your graph.

b. What is the equilibrium price and what is the quantity demanded and supplied at that price?

c. Suppose that because of a financial crisis in Asia, the world demand for U.S. corn is cut in half; that is, at each price, only 50 percent of the previous quantity is now demanded. What are the new quantities demanded at each price shown in the table above? Plot these values in the graph you drew above and label the new demand curve D'.

d. What is the new equilibrium price and what is the quantity demanded and supplied at that price?

e. Explain in detail how the market adjusts from the original equilibrium price to the new one.

3. The following table shows the amounts of sugar or oranges that can be produced in one month in Florida and Brazil.

	Sugar (tons)	Oranges (tons)
Florida	300	300
Brazil	400	300

a. Which producer has an absolute advantage in sugar production? Orange production? Explain.

b. Which producer has a comparative advantage in sugar production? Orange production? Explain.

c. Could Florida and Brazil benefit from specialization? Explain.

4. Use a production possibilities curve diagram to show the impact of losing a war on a country's economy. How does one explain John Stuart Mill's observation that countries recover remarkably quickly after wars are lost?

Answers to the Sample Test on Part I

True-False Questions

1. True
2. False. The *ceteris paribus* assumption holds all but one variable constant so that one-on-one cause-and-effect relationships can be identified.
3. True
4. False. A capital good is a good used to produce other goods. The other goods may be either capital or consumption goods.

THE BASICS   57

  5. True
  6. False. If the country has a comparative advantage in shirt production, then it can produce shirts at a lower opportunity cost.
  7. True
  8. False. An increase in demand will cause an increase in the equilibrium price and an increase in the quantity demanded and supplied in the short run.
  9. False. The circular flow model shows households supplying resources to business enterprises.
  10. False. A production possibilities curve that is bowed-out from the origin exhibits the law of increasing costs.

Multiple-Choice Questions

1. c	6. a	11. c	16. a
2. a	7. e	12. a	17. c
3. a	8. c	13. c	18. c
4. c	9. b	14. d	19. e
5. e	10. a	15. a	20. b

Discussion Questions/Problems

1. The graph below shows the production possibilities curve for this problem.

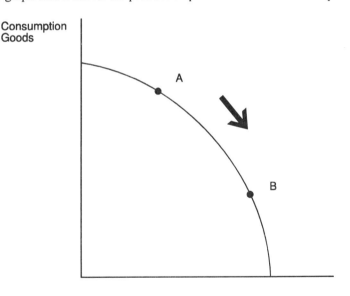

   Point A shows that mostly consumption goods are being produced while point B shows that resources have been shifted to the production of more capital goods. The move from point A to point B is harder for a poor country because a large portion of a poor country's resources must be devoted to consumption goods production just to provide for subsistence. Moreover, as a poor country shifts resources from producing consumption goods to producing capital goods, it will give up larger and larger amounts of consumption goods just to increase capital goods production by equal amounts because of the law of increasing costs.

2. a. The graph that corresponds to the answers to part a and part c is shown on the next page.

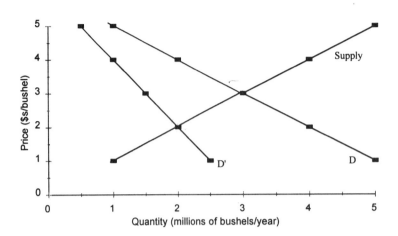

b. The equilibrium price is $3, and the quantity demanded equals the quantity supplied at 3 million bushels per year.

c. At each price, the quantity demanded is half what it was on the original demand curve. D' shows these points.

d. The new equilibrium price is $2, and quantity demanded now equals quantity supplied at 2 million bushels per year.

e. Once demand decreases to D', there is an excess supply at the original price of $3. In this case, the excess supply is 1.5 million bushels of corn. Producers compete with one another to lower price. As the price decreases, quantity demanded increases along D', and quantity supplied decreases along the supply curve until the new equilibrium is reached at a price of $2 per bushel.

3. a. Brazil has an absolute advantage in sugar production because it can produce more sugar in one month than Florida— 400 tons versus 300 tons. Neither Brazil nor Florida has an absolute advantage in orange production — they both produce 300 tons.

   b. Brazil has a comparative advantage in sugar production. The opportunity cost of one ton of sugar in Florida is one ton of oranges. The opportunity cost of one ton of sugar in Brazil is 3/4 ton of oranges. Brazil gives up fewer oranges to produce sugar than does Florida. Florida has a comparative advantage in orange production. The opportunity cost of one ton of orange in Florida is one ton of sugar, while the opportunity cost of one ton of oranges in Brazil is 4/3 tons of sugar.

   c. Florida should specialize in oranges and Brazil should specialize in sugar. At the end of a month, there would be 300 tons of oranges and 400 tons of sugar between them. This is more than could be had if each producer split resources evenly between the production of the two goods.

4. If we suppose that the country's output is split between consumption goods and capital goods, the impact of losing a war is shown graphically below. The curve shifts inward toward the origin. The bigger the losses, the bigger the shift. Countries are able to recover faster than one might expect after losing a war because, in spite of the losses of human resources and physical resources (capital destroyed and land unsuitable to cultivation or habitation), the ideas on which production had been based cannot be destroyed. The

THE BASICS

knowledge that guided the applied technology in the country prior to the war still exists after the war. Once the technology is applied again, perhaps even in improved form, the production possibilities curve will shift back to its original position or beyond.

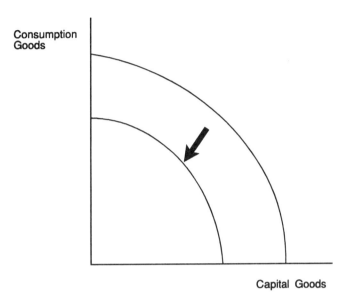

CHAPTER 4

ELASTICITY

Chapter in a Nutshell

When economists use the word **elasticity**, they mean **sensitivity**. **Price elasticity of demand** is a measure of buyers' **sensitivity to price changes**. The elasticity of demand to price changes varies among different categories of goods. The reasons for this variation in elasticity are explored in the chapter. The **price elasticity of demand** can be calculated as the **ratio of percentage change in quantity demanded to the percentage change in price**. **Cross elasticity of demand** is the percentage change in quantity demanded for one good divided by the percentage change in price of another good. **Price elasticity of supply** can also be measured. Supply becomes more sensitive to price changes given a longer time frame. The **market-day supply** is totally **insensitive, or inelastic**, to price changes while **long-run supply** is fairly **elastic** for most goods. Elasticity is an extremely useful concept for politicians as well as economists. Elasticity can be used to design more effective policies to generate **tax revenues**.

After you study this chapter, you should be able to:

- Explain how **elasticity** means **sensitivity**.
- List the determinants of **price elasticity of demand**.
- Distinguish between the **elastic, inelastic,** and **unit elastic** ranges on a straight-line demand curve.
- Contrast the **cross elasticity of demand** for **substitutes** and **complements**.
- Categorize goods as **normal** or **inferior** using the **income elasticity of demand**.
- Calculate **price elasticity of supply** for short-run and long-run supply curves.
- Use elasticity concepts to evaluate **tax policies**.

Concept Check — See how you do on these multiple-choice questions.

1. The **price elasticity of demand** is a measure of **demand sensitivity** to
    a. supply changes
    b. price changes
    c. income changes
    d. changes in tastes
    e. changes in the prices of other goods

What kind of elasticity are you trying to describe?

2. Which of the following *is not* a **determinant of the demand sensitivity to price changes**?
    a. income level
    b. whether the good is a basic item
    c. time to adjust
    d. the availability of substitute goods
    e. the number of producers in the market

Focus on factors that apply to the demand side of the market.

INTRO TO MICROECONOMICS 61

3. Goods can be classified as **substitutes** and **complements** using the concept of _____, while goods can be classified as **normal** or **inferior** using the concept of _____.
   a. income elasticity; cross elasticity
   b. cross elasticity; income elasticity
   c. price elasticity; income elasticity
   d. income elasticity; price elasticity
   e. price elasticity; cross elasticity

Know the various types of elasticity measures that we can use.

4. As producers are given more time to respond to price changes, the **elasticity of supply**
   a. increases
   b. decreases
   c. approaches infinity
   d. approaches zero
   e. become equal to the demand elasticity

Time has an important role to play in the elasticity of supply too.

5. Colbert, Louis XIV's finance minister in France during the seventeenth century, thought **air would be the perfect good to tax** because
   a. the demand for air is elastic
   b. the demand for air is inelastic
   c. the tax would be a small burden for the peasantry
   d. air was one of the few things the king could tax
   e. the tax would be easy to calculate using a demand-supply diagram

What types of commodities generate the most revenue when they are taxed?

Am I on the Right Track?

Your answers to the questions above should be **b**, **e**, **b**, **a**, and **b**. Elasticity is a concept used routinely by economists. It has many applications in the analysis of demand and supply. There is a formula to learn for calculating elasticities. With some practice, it is easy to use. Elasticities are always ratios of percentage changes in two variables. We use the elasticity value to understand the size of the impact that a change in one variable has on another. An example of the price elasticity of demand is as follows. If the price of strawberries increases by 10 percent and people buy 5 percent fewer strawberries, then the price elasticity of demand for strawberries is 5 percent divided by 10 percent or .5. Note that we adopt the convention of dropping the minus sign. An elasticity of .5 means that a 1 percent increase in the price of strawberries leads to a .5 percent decrease in the quantity demanded. Because the value for elasticity is less than one, we say that the demand for strawberries is insensitive to price changes or price inelastic.

Key Terms Quiz — Match the terms on the left with the definitions in the column on the right.

1. elasticity
2. price elasticity of demand
3. total revenue
4. unit elastic
5. price elastic
6. price inelastic
7. cross elasticity of demand
8. income elasticity
9. income elastic
10. income inelastic
11. Engel's law
12. inferior goods
13. price elasticity of supply

_____ a. price elasticity coefficient less than one
_____ b. the sensitivity of demand to income changes
_____ c. price elasticity coefficient greater than one
_____ d. low income elasticities for basic foods
_____ e. price times the quantity purchased
_____ f. as income decreases, the quantity demanded increases
_____ g. the sensitivity of supply to price changes
_____ h. price elasticity equal to one
_____ i. sensitivity of demand for one good to price changes in another good
_____ j. the sensitivity of one variable to changes in another
_____ k. income elasticity greater than one
_____ l. income elasticity less than one
_____ m. the sensitivity of demand to price changes

Graphing Tutorial

An important concept developed in this chapter is that of price elasticity of demand. Suppose that during the summer, you sell ice cream cones on the Boardwalk at Coney Island. You find that the data in the table below represent the demand schedule for ice cream cones:

Price ($)	Quantity Demanded (hundreds)
4	0
3	1
2	2
1	3
0	4

By plotting and connecting these points as shown below, you can draw the demand curve and see that it is linear. The slope is a constant, equal to -1, meaning that every $1 decrease in price causes an increase of 1 (hundred) in quantity demanded.

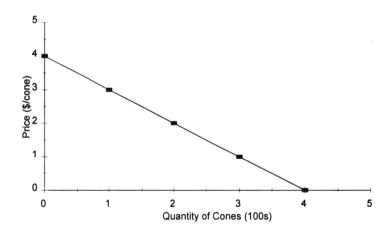

INTRO TO MICROECONOMICS 63

Even though the demand curve is a straight line, this is not a case of constant or unit elasticity. In fact, the price elasticity of demand changes as you change the price of an ice cream cone and move along the demand curve. For example, when you lower the price from $4 to $3, quantity demanded increases from 0 to 1, yielding a price elasticity of demand equal to 7. When you lower the price further from $3 to $2, quantity demanded increases from 1 to 2, so that the price elasticity of demand is now 1.66. The numerical value of the price elasticity changes at each point, becoming smaller as the price is lowered and quantity demanded increases.

The concept of price elasticity can help answer the question of whether you could increase total revenue by raising or lowering the price of an ice cream cone. If you are currently charging $3, then our calculation above shows that the price elasticity is 1.66 there. By lowering the price to $2, the theory indicates that total revenue should increase because you are operating in the elastic portion of the demand curve. Let's check the numbers. If the price is $3, total revenue will be $3 times 100, or $300. When the price is reduced to $2, total revenue will become $2 times 200, or $400. Thus, total revenue will increase by $100 if you lower the price of an ice cream cone to $2.

For almost all demand curves, the price elasticity varies at different points along the curve. A business owner can use information about the price elasticity of demand to help determine whether price should be raised or lowered from its current level. Similarly, the government can use information about price elasticity to predict how consumers will respond to the change in the price of a good that occurs when a higher tax is imposed.

True-False Questions — If a statement is false, explain why.

1. The price elasticity of demand measures the sensitivity of demand to price changes. (T/F)

2. If a good has no close substitutes and is regarded as a necessity by many consumers, then demand for the good will be quite elastic. (T/F)

3. Cross elasticity of demand is the ratio of the percentage change in quantity demanded for a good to the percentage change in price for another. (T/F)

4. A 50 percent increase in price that results in a 90 percent decrease in the quantity demanded indicates that demand is elastic in this price range. (T/F)

5. Price elasticity of demand is constant along a straight-line demand curve. (T/F)

6. If two goods are substitutes, then an increase in the price of one good will lead to an increase in the quantity demanded for the other good. (T/F)

7. If two goods are complements, then a decrease in the price of one good will result in a decrease in the quantity demanded of the other good. (T/F)

8. The price elasticity of demand is the same as the slope of the demand curve. (T/F)

9. A used car purchased by a consumer because his or her income increased by 10 percent is an inferior good. (T/F)

10. Engel's law expresses the fact that people spend large percentages of any increase in income on food. (T/F)

11. Demand for low-priced goods like salt tends to be price inelastic because they usually comprise a small percentage of a consumer's budget. (T/F)

12. The passage of time leads to a more price inelastic demand because consumers' habits become more fixed. (T/F)

13. A long-run supply curve is relatively more price elastic than a short-run supply curve. (T/F)

14. If demand is unit elastic, then for any percentage change in price, the percentage change in quantity demanded will be one. (T/F)

15. Total revenue increases if price decreases when demand is inelastic. (T/F)

Multiple-Choice Questions

1. If the price elasticity of demand is 2.5, then a 1 percent increase in price will lead to a
   a. 2.5 percent increase in the quantity demanded
   b. decrease in demand but we cannot tell how big
   c. 2.5 percent decrease in demand
   d. 2.5 percent decrease in the quantity demanded
   e. 2.5 percent increase in demand

2. Suppose that Freddy's quantity demanded for plums increases from two pounds to four pounds per week when price decreases from $1.25 per pound to $.75. Freddy's demand is
   a. inelastic since the elasticity is .75
   b. elastic since the elasticity is 1.33
   c. unresponsive to price changes since the elasticity is so small
   d. elastic because he buys more as price decreases
   e. inelastic since he buys only twice as much

INTRO TO MICROECONOMICS

3. In 1857 a Prussian statistician calculated the income elasticity of demand for basic foods. His discovery that the income elasticity is _____ is known as _____.
   a. less than one; the cross elasticity of food
   b. greater than one; the cross elasticity of food
   c. less than one; the law of income elasticity of basic goods
   d. greater than one; Engel's law
   e. less than one; Engel's law

4. The concept of _____ compares the percentage change in quantity demand of one good to the percentage change in price of another, while _____ is the concept used to examine the percentage change in quantity demanded that results from a percentage change in income.
   a. cross elasticity of demand; price elasticity of demand
   b. price elasticity of demand; cross elasticity of demand
   c. cross elasticity of demand; income elasticity of demand
   d. income elasticity of demand; price elasticity of demand
   e. price elasticity of demand; income elasticity of demand

5. If the price of asparagus rises by 25 percent and the quantity demanded of artichokes increases by 75 percent then artichokes and asparagus are
   a. complementary goods with a cross elasticity of 1/3
   b. inferior goods with an income elasticity of 1/3
   c. substitute goods with a cross elasticity of 3
   d. price elastic goods with elasticity equal to 3
   e. price inelastic goods with elasticity equal to 1/3

6. Given an income elasticity of demand of .5, we would expect that
   a. for a .5 percent increase in income, quantity demanded will increase by 1 percent
   b. for a 1 percent increase in income, quantity demanded will increase by .5 percent
   c. the good is an inferior good
   d. the good is definitely a luxury good
   e. the good may not have close substitutes

7. If the price elasticity of demand is 2 and the quantity demanded increased by 25 percent, then price must have
   a. increased by 50 percent
   b. increased by 12.5 percent
   c. decreased by 50 percent
   d. decreased by 12.5 percent
   e. decreased by 25 percent

8. In the inelastic region along a straight-line demand curve, a price decrease leads to a total revenue decrease since
   a. price decreases proportionately more than quantity demanded increases
   b. price decreases proportionately less than demand
   c. price decreases but demand does not increase
   d. price decreases proportionately more than quantity demanded decreases
   e. the elasticity is greater than one

9. Given the low price elasticities of demand for agricultural goods, we would expect that in years when harvests are near record
   a. total revenue for farmers increases since so much is sold
   b. total revenue for farmers stays the same since harvests don't vary in size much from good years to bad years
   c. total revenue decreases since price falls by a larger percentage than the quantity demanded increases
   d. total revenue decreases since price falls by a smaller percentage than quantity demanded increases
   e. farmers have the opportunity to purchase new equipment

10. The tax revenue is greater if the demand for the good is relatively inelastic because
    a. the supply curve will shift vertically by a greater amount if demand is inelastic
    b. the quantity demanded decreases more as price increases along an inelastic demand curve
    c. the quantity demanded increases more as price decreases along an inelastic demand curve
    d. the supply curve will become steeper as the good is taxed
    e. the quantity demanded decreases very little as price increases along an inelastic demand curve

11. Along a linear demand curve, from top to bottom (higher price levels to lower price levels), elasticity varies from
    a. elastic, to unit elastic, to inelastic
    b. inelastic, to unit elastic, to elastic
    c. unit elastic, to elastic, to inelastic
    d. elastic, to inelastic, to unit elastic
    e. unit elastic, to inelastic, to elastic

12. If a seller finds it possible to increase total revenue by cutting price, then the demand for the good must be
    a. price inelastic
    b. unit elastic
    c. increasing
    d. related to the income elasticity
    e. elastic

13. An increase in the price of aspirin is likely to be paired with a(n) _____ in the quantity demanded of Tylenol because the two goods are _____.
    a. increase; complements
    b. decrease; complements
    c. increase; substitutes
    d. decrease; substitutes
    e. increase; elastic

14. Over time, both price elasticities of demand and elasticities of supply tend to increase because consumers and producers
    a. are always less responsive given enough time
    b. are noted for taking a long time to make decisions
    c. are able to make adjustments to price changes given sufficient time
    d. prefer higher prices in the long run
    e. cannot be expected to make important decisions too rapidly

INTRO TO MICROECONOMICS

15. If two goods are close substitutes for one another, then we would expect the cross elasticity of demand between them to be
    a. large and positive
    b. large and negative
    c. small and positive
    d. small and negative
    e. indeterminate unless we are given specific numbers for the calculation

16. One would expect the cross elasticity of demand between apple pie and ice cream to be _____ and the cross elasticity of demand between ice cream and frozen yogurt to be _____.
    a. negative; positive
    b. positive; negative
    c. one; greater than one
    d. one; less than one
    e. less than one; greater than one

17. Suppose that a video rental shop opens in a small town with one movie theater. *Ceteris paribus*, one would expect that the demand for movie tickets will become
    a. less elastic as a result
    b. much greater since most videos are of mediocre quality
    c. much smaller because videos are cheaper
    d. more elastic as a result
    e. more negatively cross elastic since videos and movies are substitutes

18. Suppose you are given data showing that a 50 percent increase in airline ticket sales is associated with a 10 percent increase in the incomes of frequent flyers. It would be correct to assert that
    a. a 5 percent increase in income leads to a 1 percent increase in ticket sales
    b. a 1 percent increase in income leads to a 5 percent increase in airline ticket sales so the demand for airline tickets is income elastic
    c. a price decrease for airline tickets would lead to a total revenue increase
    d. the demand for airline tickets is sensitive to price changes
    e. people view air travel as an inferior good

19. As incomes increase, the demand for food tends to increase less than proportionately, suggesting that
    a. the demand for food is sluggish
    b. the supermarket business is likely to go sour in the long run
    c. food is an inferior good
    d. the demand for food is income elastic
    e. the demand for food is income inelastic

20. Calculations of income elasticities of demand for food show them to be higher for poorer countries than for rich countries because
    a. food is not an inferior good in poorer countries
    b. the demand for food does not obey Engel's law in poorer countries
    c. the demand for food is so price inelastic in rich countries
    d. a larger percentage of any given change in income will be spent on food in poor countries
    e. such income elasticities are often negative in rich countries

Fill in the Blanks

1. The price elasticity of demand is calculated as the _____ divided by the _____.

2. An inferior good has an income elasticity of demand that is _____ while a normal good has an income elasticity that is _____.

3. If the intent of government policy is to raise revenue through taxation, then goods with _____ demands should be taxed.

4. When demand is elastic, a(n) _____ in price leads to an increase in total revenue.

5. The price elasticity of demand increases in the long run because consumers have time to _____, while the price elasticity of supply increases in the long run because producers have time to _____.

Discussion Questions

1. Explain why a firm would never price in the inelastic region of its demand curve if it could avoid doing so.

2. Why are income elasticities for basic foods relatively low?

3. Would you expect the cross elasticity of demand for Budweiser with respect to changes in the price of Coors to be positive or negative? Why? Would the cross elasticity of demand for Budweiser with respect to the price of pretzels be positive or negative? Explain.

INTRO TO MICROECONOMICS

4. Explain the logic behind Colbert's desire to tax air.

Problems

1. Why are numerical values for price elasticity large, indicating an elastic demand, at high prices along linear demand curves and smaller, indicating an inelastic demand, at low prices? (Hint: Consider the formula we use for calculating elasticity coefficients and the nature of percentage changes for small numbers and large numbers.)

2. The following table shows Spike's demand for New York Knicks' basketball tickets:

Price ($/ticket)	Quantity Demanded (number of tickets purchased)
$10	20
20	15
30	10
40	5
50	0

a. Calculate the price elasticity of demand between the prices of $10 and $20.

b. Calculate the price elasticity of demand between the prices of $20 and $40.

c. Calculate the price elasticity of demand between the prices of $40 and $50.

d. Identify each of the elasticities you calculated above as elastic or inelastic and calculate the changes in total revenue between each pair of prices.

3. The graph below shows the market for cigarettes.

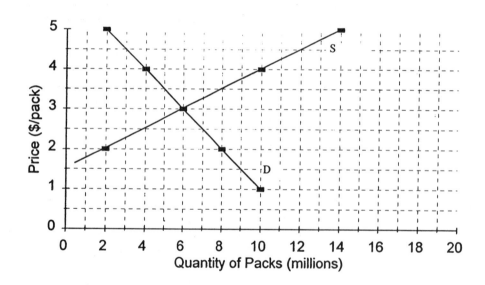

a. Identify the equilibrium price and the quantity demanded and supplied at that price.

b. Suppose a tax equal to $1 per pack is placed on cigarettes. Draw the new supply curve. Explain how you drew the new supply curve.

c. What is the new equilibrium price, and what are the quantity demanded and supplied at this price?

d. How much revenue does the government receive from this tax? How would the revenue generated from the tax change if the demand for cigarettes became more elastic? Explain.

Everyday Applications

1. This morning's paper had an ad in it for Click Camera, which was running a film sale — buy two rolls and get the third one free. Does this marketing strategy embody assumptions about the price elasticity of demand for film? Explain.

2. Why do we often see two-liter bottles of Pepsi and Coke both priced at $.99 sitting next to each other on grocery shelves? Does the cross elasticity of demand have anything to do with this observation?

Economics Online

Is the lack of available substitute products in stores causing your price elasticities to be too low? Can you feel producers taking advantage of your inelastic demand by raising prices and their revenues? If so, then this might be the Web site for you. Formula Freedom Software lets you make your own household products from scratch. The claim is made that the products are either cheaper or safer than the store-bought variety. If this kind of do-it-yourself information becomes widely available and is utilized by many people via the Internet, what will be the impact on price elasticities of demand? Visit the site (*http://www.autonomy.com/freedom7.htm*). If you try some of these recipes and they work, drop me an e-mail (*dwishart@wittenberg.edu*).

Answers to Questions

Key Terms Quiz

a. 6
b. 8
c. 5
d. 11
e. 3
f. 12
g. 13
h. 4
i. 7
j. 1
k. 9
l. 10
m. 2

True-False Questions

1. True
2. False. If a good has no close substitutes and is a necessity, then demand will be relatively inelastic.
3. True
4. True
5. False. The elasticity ranges from elastic at the top of a linear demand curve to inelastic at the bottom.
6. True
7. False. For complements, a decrease in the price of one good will lead to an increase in the amount purchased of the other good.
8. False. The price elasticity of demand is equal to the percentage change in quantity demanded divided by the percentage change in price, whereas the slope of the curve is the change in price divided by the change in quantity.
9. False. Income has increased and the quantity of used cars purchased increased as a result so the used car is a normal good.
10. False. Engel's law suggests that the demand for food is income inelastic so that a 1 percent increase in income leads to a less than 1 percent increase in the quantity of food demanded.
11. True
12. False. Given more time, the price elasticity of demand increases because consumers have more time to search out substitute goods.
13. True
14. False. Unit elastic means that for a 1 percent increase in price, the quantity demanded decreases by 1 percent and vice versa.
15. False. Total revenue increases if price decreases when demand is elastic.

Multiple-Choice Questions

1. d
2. b
3. e
4. c
5. c
6. b
7. d
8. a
9. c
10. e
11. a
12. e
13. c
14. c
15. a
16. a
17. d
18. b
19. e
20. d

Fill in the Blanks

1. percentage change in quantity demanded; percentage change in price
2. negative; positive
3. inelastic
4. decrease
5. search for substitutes; adjust production levels

INTRO TO MICROECONOMICS

Discussion Questions

1. If demand is price inelastic, an increase in price results in an increase in total revenue. This is because a 1 percent increase in price leads to a less than 1 percent decrease in quantity demanded. Therefore, the decrease in quantity demanded is more than offset by the increase in price. If the firm is able to raise price when the demand is inelastic, it will do so in order to raise total revenue.

2. The fact that the demands for basic foods are income inelastic was discovered by the Prussian statistician Engel and is called Engel's law. It makes sense that these demands would be income inelastic. As our incomes rise, we will purchase somewhat larger amounts of food and, perhaps, better selections of food too. However, one can eat only so much. Thus, the demand for food isn't terribly sensitive to income changes, translating into a low income elasticity.

3. Budweiser and Coors are substitute goods. Therefore, an increase in the price of Coors will lead to an increase in the quantity demanded of Budweiser. It makes sense that most of these close substitutes have very similar prices based on the fact that they are close substitutes, so the cross elasticities will be positive. Budweiser and pretzels are complements. Therefore, an increase in the price of pretzels will lead to a decrease in the quantity demanded of Budweiser. These two goods are consumed together, so the cross elasticity will be negative.

4. From the perspective of a finance minister like Colbert, the problem with a tax on a particular good is that a consumer can avoid the tax by not consuming the good. For example, the simple way to avoid an increase in the tax on cigarettes is to stop smoking! But that might not be so simple since cigarettes are addictive, causing their demands to be quite inelastic. The trick for a finance minister is to find a good for which the demand is so inelastic that the consumer cannot cut back the amount purchased as it becomes more expensive. Air is such a good. A tax on air would be completely unavoidable for consumers. And the king owned the air in France at the time! So, it was his to tax.

Problems

1. In the elastic region, at the top of the linear demand curve, a change in quantity demanded is a large percentage change since the quantity values are small numbers, e.g., from 1 to 2 or from 2 to 3. The changes in price are small percentage changes since the price figures are relatively large. Therefore, the quotient of percentage change in quantity demanded and percentage change in price is a large number, so the demand is elastic. By similar reasoning, at the bottom of the linear demand curve, a change in quantity demanded is a small percentage change since the quantity values are bigger numbers. The changes in price are big percentage changes since the price values are low. Thus, the elasticity value we get is small, so the demand is inelastic there.

2. a. .43; For a 1 percent increase in price, there is a .43 percent decrease in the quantity demanded.

   b. 1.5; For a 1 percent increase in price, there is a 1.5 percent decrease in the quantity demanded.

   c. 9; For a 1 percent increase in price, there is a 9 percent decrease in the quantity demanded.

   d. At P = $10, total revenue = $200; at P = $20, total revenue = $300; at P= $30, total revenue = $300; at P = $40, total revenue = $200; at P= $50, total revenue = $0. As price increases when demand is inelastic, total revenue increases. As price increases when demand is elastic, total revenue decreases.

3. a. The original equilibrium price is $3 per pack, and the quantity demanded is equal to the quantity supplied

at 6 million packs.

b. The new supply curve is shown in the diagram on the next page as S'. If you look closely, S' is shifted up vertically from the original supply curve by the amount of the tax, $1. The original supply curve and S' are parallel with the vertical distance between them equal to $1. This reflects the fact that the producer must pay $1 to the government for every pack of cigarettes that is sold. Therefore, to supply any quantity, the price must be $1 higher.

c. Reading from the graph below, the new equilibrium price is approximately $3.60 per pack, and the new quantity demanded equals quantity supplied at about 4.8 million packs.

d. The revenue is shown in the diagram below as the area of the rectangle marked by heavy lines. This area can be computed as $1 times 4.8 million packs or $4.8 million dollars. If the demand for cigarettes becomes more elastic, tax revenues would decrease. Fewer than 4.8 million packs would be sold as the price rose with the tax.

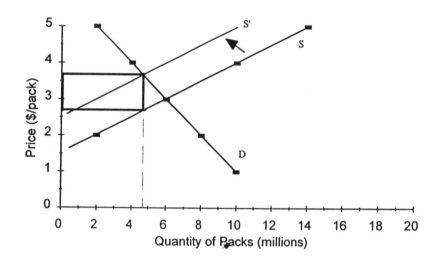

CHAPTER 5

MARGINAL UTILITY AND CONSUMER CHOICE

Chapter in a Nutshell

In Chapter 3, we studied the law of demand, noting that when price falls, quantity demanded increases. But why? It seemed obvious, didn't it? In this chapter, we explore the obvious to explain the law of demand. We'll find that the explanation for the law of demand lies in the concepts **marginal utility**, **total utility**, and the **marginal-utility-to-price ratios** for different goods. Some other new concepts that are presented in this chapter to help us understand consumer choice include the **law of diminishing marginal utility**, **consumer surplus**, and **interpersonal comparisons of utility**. This chapter gets to the bottom of why people buy what they do.

After working through this chapter, you should be able to:

- Explain what is meant by the term **marginal utility**.
- Relate the concepts **total utility** and **marginal utility** to each other.
- Describe the meaning of the **law of diminishing marginal utility** with an example.
- Present an explanation for the **water-diamond paradox**.
- Account for the law of demand using **marginal-utility-to-price ratios**.
- Explain the logic behind the **marginal-utility-to-price ratio equalization rule**.
- Give an example of **consumer surplus**.
- Discuss how **interpersonal comparisons of utility** can be useful to policymakers.

Concept Check — See how you do on these multiple-choice questions.

1. The **law of diminishing marginal utility** holds that
   a. as people consume more of a good, total utility increases, then decreases
   b. both water and diamonds have a low marginal utility in the desert
   c. marginal utility diminishes when too much is consumed
   d. increasing consumption leads to smaller additions to total utility
   e. total utility actually decreases for some consumers if they consume too much

Think about the definition of marginal utility as you consider the possible answers to this question. Marginal utility is the addition to total utility from consuming one more unit. What must happen to the marginal utility for most goods as more and more units are consumed?

2. The paradox in the **water-diamond paradox** is that
   a. water is very useful but has a low value and diamonds are less useful but have a high value
   b. diamonds are expensive and water is cheap
   c. diamonds have a high total utility but a low marginal utility
   d. the price of water is high but its marginal utility is low, while the opposite is true for diamonds
   e. water is a very abundant but priceless resource, while diamonds are scarce but easy to price

A paradox is a seemingly contradictory statement. What is paradoxical about the value of water and diamonds?

3. The **marginal-utility-to-price ratio** is a representation of the
   a. law of demand
   b. total satisfaction a consumer gets from a good
   c. additional satisfaction a consumer gets from a good
   d. satisfaction per dollar spent that a consumer gets from a good
   e. true market value of a good determined by supply and demand

Marginal utility is the satisfaction generated by the last unit consumed. Price is the dollar amount spent for the last unit. What's the right answer?

4. To say that some people enjoy **consumer surplus** means that they
   a. pay less than they would have been willing to pay for a good
   b. are accomplished shoppers who only purchase products that are good values
   c. pay exactly what a good is worth to them
   d. only purchase items that are on sale since the sale increases the marginal utility-to-price ratio
   e. pay a price that is higher than they expected to pay for an item

Do the prices you pay for goods match what you are willing and able to pay for them? Consider items that you buy in bundles of units like a six-pack of soda. How much are you willing to pay for the first can of soda versus the second, the third, and so on? Is the price different for each can? Consumer surplus relates to the fact that although the price is the same for each can (the price of the six-pack divided by six), your willingness to pay is probably greater for the first can than it is for the sixth can.

5. We are unable to make **interpersonal comparisons of utilities** of money because
   a. the law of diminishing marginal utility does not apply to money
   b. it is impossible to compare the satisfaction different people get from money
   c. the measurement of utility in hypothetical units makes comparisons impossible
   d. money has a high total utility but a low marginal utility
   e. money has a low total utility but a high marginal utility

Utility is the satisfaction that *a person* enjoys from consuming a good. Are tastes the same for all people? How can we compare the satisfaction that different people enjoy from consuming the same good? How can we compare the satisfaction different people experience from their last dollars of income?

Am I on the Right Track?

Your answers to the questions above should be **d, a, d, a,** and **b**. Utility may sound like a strange concept for economists to use, but it is really quite simple. Utility is the satisfaction one derives from consuming a good. Though it is difficult to measure in a precise way, we all know that we do experience satisfaction from consumption. Marginal utility and total utility are related. Marginal utility is the extra satisfaction a person enjoys from consuming one more unit of a good. Total utility is the satisfaction experienced from consuming a certain amount of a good. Marginal utility can be divided by the price of a good to get the extra satisfaction per dollar spent. These marginal-utility-to-price ratios can then be used to show that demand curves slope downward. That is to say, as the price of a good decreases, the marginal-utility-to-price ratio increases, so a person will consume more of a good. Other concepts related to utility and consumer choice are consumer surplus and the problems inherent in making interpersonal comparisons of utility. Work through the exercises that follow to make sure that you thoroughly understand these concepts.

INTRO TO MICROECONOMICS

Key Terms Quiz — Match the terms on the left with the definitions in the column on the right.

1. utils
2. marginal utility per dollar
3. utility
4. MU/P equalization principle
5. marginal utility
6. consumer surplus
7. total utility
8. interpersonal comparisons of utility
9. law of diminishing marginal utility

_____ a. comparison of marginal utilities between people
_____ b. the total satisfaction from consumption
_____ c. smaller additions to total utility from consumption
_____ d. the feeling of satisfaction from consumption
_____ e. hypothetical units for measuring utility
_____ f. satisfaction per dollar spent for a unit of a good
_____ g. principle by which consumers arrange consumption
_____ h. addition to satisfaction from consuming one more unit
_____ i. utility that a consumer enjoys by paying less than he or she is willing and able to pay for a good

Graphing Tutorial

If we agree to measure utility in utils, then graphing total utility and marginal utility functions is uncomplicated. Suppose that the information in the following table represents Jo's total utility and marginal utility measured in utils from drinking cups of herbal tea. A larger number of utils means that Jo is more satisfied from drinking tea.

Jo's Total and Marginal Utility from Cups of Herbal Tea Consumed per Day (measured in utils)

Cups per Day	Total Utility	Marginal Utility
0	0	
1	20	20
2	38	18
3	52	14
4	60	8
5	64	4

Note how marginal utility can be calculated from total utility. Marginal utility is defined as the change in total utility divided by the change in the quantity consumed. Written mathematically, we have $MU = \Delta TU/\Delta Q$. Each value in the marginal utility column is the difference in total utilities between the pair of consumption levels. For example, as consumption increases from zero to one cup, total utility increases by 20 utils, so the marginal utility of the first cup is 20 utils. Marginal utility and total utility are the same for the first cup. But for the second cup, total utility increases by only 18 units, from 20 to 38. Hence, the marginal utility of the second cup is 18.

The graph on the following page shows Jo's total utility function for consuming herbal tea. This total utility function illustrates the law of diminishing marginal utility because it becomes less steep as more tea is consumed. Drinking more cups per day increases total utility, but at a decreasing rate so the total utility function becomes flatter as consumption increases. For example, moving from point a at the origin to point b, we see that total utility increases to 20 from drinking the first cup. However, drinking the second cup moves Jo to point c where total utility is 38, an increase of only 18 utils compared to 20 for the first cup. Trace out the smaller and smaller increases in total utility that Jo derives from drinking the third, fourth, and fifth cups by moving along the total utility function through points d, e, and f. All total utility functions that exhibit the law of diminishing marginal utility become flatter as consumption increases.

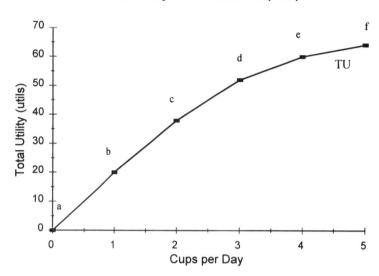

Total Utility from Herbal Tea (utils)

The figures for marginal utility from the table are represented graphically below. Note how the law of diminishing marginal utility shows up as a negative slope for the marginal utility function. Points a through e on the graph show the marginal utility Jo derives from the first through the fifth cups of tea. Even though total utility is rising, each cup of tea consumed adds less to total utility than the cup consumed previously. Makes sense doesn't it? If the total utility function increases at a decreasing rate, then the marginal utility function must have a negative slope.

Marginal Utility from Cups of Tea

INTRO TO MICROECONOMICS

Ultimately, the shapes of total utility and marginal utility functions depend on an individual's tastes. You can create examples of different individual utility functions for a variety of goods and practice graphing them.

Graphing Pitfalls

Consider the total utility function drawn below. This total utility function has a positive slope, and the slope gets steeper as consumption increases. Does this make sense given what you know about the law of diminishing marginal utility? If the total utility function has an increasingly steep slope, then marginal utility must be increasing, not diminishing. While this might be true for some individuals consuming some goods, such as a person who is completing a stamp collection, it isn't the shape we usually expect when considering utility functions. So, if you happen to draw a total utility function with an increasingly steep slope, go back and carefully check the numbers on which you based your graph. Either you are describing some unusual tastes, or you've made a mistake drawing the graph.

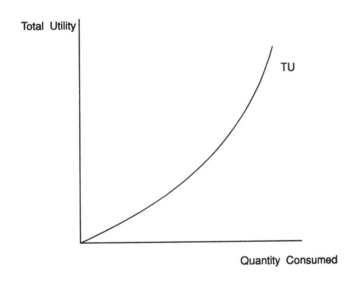

You won't find too many total utility functions that look like this!

True-False Questions — If a statement is false, explain why.

1. Utility is the satisfaction or enjoyment that a person obtains from consuming a good that can be measured precisely by psychological tests. (T/F)

2. Utils are the units in which psychologists' testing devices are calibrated to determine the utility people obtain from consumption. (T/F)

3. The total amount of satisfaction someone enjoys from consuming a specific quantity of goods is called total utility. (T/F)

4. Two people who consume precisely the same quantity of a particular good will enjoy the same total utility levels. (T/F)

5. Marginal utility is always a very small quantity. (T/F)

6. The law of diminishing marginal utility suggests that as the quantity consumed increases, the addition to total utility from an additional unit consumed will decrease. (T/F)

7. The marginal-utility-to-price ratios of goods can be compared to determine the order in which a person will purchase them. (T/F)

8. If the marginal-utility-to-price ratio is the same for all but a few goods, then a consumer has maximized total utility. (T/F)

9. If Ruth's consumer surplus is zero, then she must be paying exactly the highest amount that she was willing to pay for a good. (T/F)

10. Marginal utility analysis can be used to explain government policies regarding taxation and the redistribution of income from the rich to the poor given the "reasonableness" of diminishing marginal utility of income. (T/F)

11. A lower marginal-utility-to-price ratio for a particular good compared to others means that more of it should be consumed. (T/F)

12. In choosing to purchase a combination of goods, consumers must consider prices and not just utilities because goods are not free. (T/F)

13. A total utility curve should become steeper as more is consumed if the law of diminishing marginal utility applies. (T/F)

14. Consumer surplus is the difference between what a consumer is willing to pay for a good and what the consumer actually pays. (T/F)

15. If water is extremely scarce, then the marginal utility of an additional unit is high and the water-diamond paradox is less apparent. (T/F)

INTRO TO MICROECONOMICS

Multiple-Choice Questions

1. The law of demand tells us that
   a. the quantity demanded increases as price falls
   b. demand increases because price falls
   c. people respond to price changes
   d. demand creates its own supply, meaning that if there's a demand, supply will be created to satisfy it
   e. demand depends on people having income to satisfy it

2. The law of diminishing marginal utility
   a. is another way of expressing the law of demand
   b. states that people's inclination to consume basic goods falls as incomes increase
   c. shows that goods lose their individual values as the total utility of all goods decreases
   d. is the utility equivalent to the law of increasing costs
   e. states that total utility rises at a decreasing rate as consumption increases

3. The water-diamond paradox can be explained by showing that
   a. water's total utility may be lower than diamonds', but its marginal utility is higher
   b. water's total utility may be lower than diamonds', and its marginal utility is lower as well
   c. water's total utility is less than its marginal, but diamonds' total utility is higher than their marginal
   d. water's total utility may be higher than diamonds', but its marginal utility is lower
   e. total utility for both water and diamonds decreases as their marginal utilities increase

4. Given the marginal-utility-to-price ratio equalization principle, if $MU_1/P_1 > MU_2/P_2$,
   a. the consumer should consume more of good 1 and less of good 2
   b. the consumer should consume more of good 2 and less of good 1
   c. total utility of good 1 is greater than total utility of good 2
   d. total utility of good 2 is greater than total utility of good 1
   e. the price of good 1 must fall

5. The law of diminishing marginal utility suggests that
   a. total utility will begin to diminish
   b. additional units of consumption will add less to total utility
   c. consumers' wants are insatiable
   d. most consumers will limit their consumption even when they earn high incomes
   e. marginal utility diminishes faster than total utility as more goods are consumed

6. The marginal-utility-to-price ratio tells us that if the price of a good falls, then, *ceteris paribus*
   a. its marginal-utility-to-price ratio falls
   b. its marginal-utility-to-price ratio rises
   c. its marginal utility falls
   d. its marginal utility rises
   e. consumers buy less of the good

7. The value of a good to a consumer depends on
   a. its total utility
   b. the marginal utility of the first unit consumed
   c. the average utility of the units consumed
   d. the marginal utility of the last unit consumed
   e. the ratio of its marginal utility to total utility

8. Consumer surplus
   a. is the value you place on the sum of the marginal utilities of a good
   b. is the difference between what you pay for a good and what you would have been willing to pay
   c. corresponds to the area below the market price in a graph of the demand curve
   d. is the utility that is left over after a consumer pays for a good
   e. emerges when the consumer pays the equivalent of the good's marginal utility

9. You would be inclined to bid on a good at an auction if
   a. its MU/P was higher than those for other goods you consume
   b. its MU/P was lower than those for other goods you consume
   c. the consumer surplus was less than its price
   d. the consumer surplus was greater than the marginal utility from consuming the good
   e. the marginal utility was higher than its price

10. All of the following are true for interpersonal comparisons of utility **except** that
    a. they are used to justify higher tax rates for rich people than poor people
    b. it is possible to justify not taxing the rich at higher rates than the poor
    c. confidence in measuring utilities increases if it is strictly personal
    d. it is impossible to compare with perfect confidence utilities among different people
    e. it is possible to compare with perfect confidence utilities among different people

11. Suppose that Ron paid a scalper (a seller in the black market for tickets) $100 for a ticket to see the Rolling Stones and his true willingness to pay was $250. We can be sure that
    a. the ticket scalper extracted all the possible consumer surplus from Ron
    b. Ron's consumer surplus was low because he paid more than face value for the ticket
    c. Ron's consumer surplus was the $60 face value of the ticket
    d. Ron's marginal-utility-to-price ratio for the concert was extremely high compared to that for other goods
    e. Ron enjoyed $150 of consumer surplus from the purchase

12. Suppose that development of oil fields around the Caspian Sea leads to an increase in the world supply of gasoline. This change in the market for gasoline would lead to
    a. an increase in the equilibrium price and lower consumer surplus
    b. a decrease in the equilibrium price and greater consumer surplus
    c. an increase in the equilibrium price and greater consumer surplus
    d. a decrease in the equilibrium price and lower consumer surplus
    e. no change in consumer surplus

13. In the economist's abridged version of *Beauty and the Beast* that is presented in the text, Beauty decides to return to the Beast because
    a. she knows that he'll soon be transformed into a handsome prince, giving her enormous utility
    b. the utility she gains from being with the Beast offsets the utility lost from being apart from her father
    c. she gains consumer surplus from being with the Beast
    d. being around her two jealous sisters creates more negative utility for her than does the Beast's ugliness
    e. the utility she gains from enjoying the Beast's roses more than offsets the negative utility of his ugliness

INTRO TO MICROECONOMICS 83

14. As the price of a good falls, people buy more of it because
    a. the demand for the good increases
    b. they have more income to spend on the good
    c. the marginal utility from additional units of consumption of the good increases
    d. the marginal-utility-to-price ratio for the good increases
    e. consumer surplus from consumption of the good increases

15. An increase in the price of a good causes people to buy less of it because
    a. the demand for the good decreases
    b. they have less income to spend on the good
    c. the marginal utility from additional units of consumption of the good decreases
    d. the marginal-utility-to-price ratio for the good decreases
    e. consumer surplus from consumption of the good decreases

16. If there is diminishing marginal utility of income, then it may increase social welfare (assuming that it is reasonable to compare utility levels among people) to increase taxes on
    a. the incomes of the rich and give the funds to the poor
    b. the incomes of the poor to provide funds for job training
    c. cigarettes
    d. the incomes of the poor and give it to the richer classes
    e. consumption goods

17. According to the law of diminishing marginal utility, consumers will
    a. arrange their purchases of goods so that the marginal-utility-to-price ratios are the same
    b. always receive positive utility from consuming more
    c. beyond some point, experience smaller increases in total utility from more consumption
    d. become satiated in all their wants
    e. experience negative utility from overeating

18. One might argue that French chefs understand the law of diminishing marginal utility better than American chefs because
    a. French chefs are able to price their meals higher than American chefs
    b. the French serve many courses of small portions, keeping the marginal utility of each one high
    c. the French focus on large portions and unlimited trips to the salad bar, keeping total utility high
    d. the only way to get people to eat American cuisine is to keep prices very low, suggesting a low marginal utility
    e. the waiters in French restaurants are instructed to help customers to equate the MU/P among different menu items by carefully explaining the various choices

19. Suppose that your roommate comes back to the dormitory exclaiming about what a great deal she got on a new shirt that she would have purchased at the regular price for $35, but she bought on sale for $6. An appropriate response would be to
    a. make an interpersonal comparison of utility and remark that the shirt is ugly and not worth even $6 to you
    b. suggest that your roommate is now enjoying $29 of consumer surplus
    c. suggest that the shirt was on sale because it has a low marginal utility
    d. suggest that your roommate's total utility from the shirt is 35 utils
    e. suggest that your roommate's total utility from the shirt is at least $29

20. A consumer who has spent all of her income on clothes and food and finds that her marginal-utility-to-price ratio is higher for clothes than for food should, in the future, rearrange purchases to maximize total utility by
    a. purchasing more food and less clothes
    b. purchasing more of both commodities
    c. purchasing more clothes and less food
    d. purchasing less of both commodities
    e. paying closer attention to the law of diminishing marginal utility for both commodities

Fill in the Blanks

1. Utility is the _____ or _____ a person obtains from consuming a good.

2. The law of diminishing marginal utility suggests that as more is _____ the _____ a person derives from each additional unit _____.

3. A person's utility is _____ when the ratios of _____ for each of the goods consumed are _____.

4. The difference between the _____ amount a person would be willing to pay for a good or service and the amount actually paid is called _____.

5. We are unable to make precise _____ of the marginal utilities of money, which has sobering implications for tax policies that impose higher _____ on the wealthy.

Discussion Questions

1. Why do economists find utility theory useful?

2. What is the law of diminishing marginal utility? Do all people consuming all goods exhibit this law? Give some examples of possible exceptions to the law of diminishing marginal utility.

3. How can the water-diamond paradox be resolved by using the concept of marginal utility?

4. Explain the logic behind the marginal-utility-to-price ratio equalization principle.

5. Why are demand curves for most goods downward sloping?

6. Typically, people pay less for goods and services than they are willing and able to pay. What is the concept that economists have developed to explain this phenomenon?

7. Economists try to avoid making interpersonal comparisons of utility. However, such comparisons may seem reasonable and useful to make, especially from the standpoint of social policies like taxation and programs to aid the poor. Explain.

Problems

1. a. The following table portrays Tony's total utility from consumption of Spiderman comic books — he is an avid collector. The column for marginal utility has been left blank. Calculate the values for marginal utility and fill in the blanks in the marginal utility column.

Number of Comics	Total Utility	Marginal Utility
0	0	
1	100	
2	190	
3	270	
4	330	
5	380	

b. Does Tony experience the law of diminishing marginal utility from consuming Spiderman comics? How do you know?

c. In the space below, sketch graphs for the total utility function and the marginal utility function.

2. Jacob is a lego maniac, but he also likes Super Soaker squirt guns. The following table shows Jacob's total utility and marginal utility from legos and squirt guns measured in utils.

Quantity of Legos	TU	MU	MU/P	Quantity of Sq.Guns	TU	MU	MU/P
0	0			0	0		
1	20	20		1	50	50	
2	37	17		2	25	25	
3	50	13		3	15	15	
4	60	10		4	10	10	
5	65	5		5	2	2	

a. Suppose the price of legos is $5 per set and the price of a squirt gun is $8 per gun. Compute the marginal-utility-to-price ratios for legos and squirt guns and enter these values in the table.

b. How many sets of legos and how many squirt guns will Jacob purchase if he has $26 to spend? Carefully explain how you arrived at your answer.

c. Now suppose the price of legos falls to $2.50 per set while the price of squirt guns stays the same. How many sets of legos and how many squirt guns will he purchase? Show how you arrived at your answer.

d. Draw Jacob's demand curve for legos between the prices $5 per set and $2.50 per set. Why does it have a negative slope?

3. Pat has $30 to spend on sugar and spice. Pat's marginal utilities from sugar and spice are shown in the following table.

Quantity of Sugar	MU	MU/P	Quantity of Spice	MU	MU/P
1	20		1	40	
2	12		2	20	
3	9		3	9	
4	5		4	7	
5	3		5	5	
6	1		6	3	

a. Suppose that a unit of sugar is priced at $5 and the price of a unit of spice is $10. Compute the marginal-utility-to-price ratios for sugar and spice and enter these values in the table.

b. Given Pat's $30 budget, how many units of sugar and spice will be purchased? Explain how you arrived at this answer.

c. Suppose the price of spice stays constant at $10 and the price of sugar falls to $3. How many units of sugar will be demanded at this price? Carefully explain your reasoning.

d. How many units of sugar will Pat purchase if the price falls to $2, holding the price of spice constant at $10 per unit?

e. Draw Pat's demand curve for sugar. Does it conform to the law of demand? Why?

4. The following table shows Chloe's demand schedule for Beanie Baby Dolls.

Price per Doll ($)	Quantity Demanded
20	0
16	1
12	2
8	3
4	4
0	5

a. Use the information in this table to sketch a graph of Chloe's demand curve for Beanie Baby Dolls.

b. Suppose that the price of Beanie Baby Dolls is $8. How much consumer surplus does Chloe enjoy? How did you arrive at this answer?

c. How does Chloe's consumer surplus change if the price of dolls falls to $4? What is her consumer surplus if Beanie Baby Dolls are free? Justify your answers.

INTRO TO MICROECONOMICS

Everyday Applications

1. The next time you go shopping for groceries, think about the implications of the marginal-utility-to-price equalization rule. Does this rule make sense in the context of your everyday experience? Why or why not? Do people who haven't studied principles of economics really behave according to this principle?

2. As part of the same shopping trip, do a rough calculation of your consumer surplus. What you are doing in computing your consumer surplus is estimating your demand curve for different goods. How do price elasticities of demand for various goods that you purchase compare to one another? Did you pass by goods in the store because they were too expensive? What price would have induced you purchase these goods? Did you go for any "buy one at the regular price and get the second at half price" deals? Do store owners seem to intuitively understand the role that marginal-utility-to-price ratios play in consumer choices?

Economics Online

Using your favorite Web search engine, type in "virtual mall" and embark on an extraordinary shopping trip. Using Yahoo, I found 457 shopping centers online the last time I typed "virtual mall." Consider the implications for the creation of consumer surplus from shopping online. On the one hand, the potential for consumers to compare prices is much greater as a result of online shopping. Travel time between stores has been dramatically reduced. But consider the individual who likes to shop in person. Will this sort of individual — one who likes to touch the merchandise, discuss options with a salesperson, etc. — find it advantageous to shop online? Suppose a person derives substantial utility from the shopping experience. Will shopping online ever compare to the real thing for these people?

Answers to Questions

Key Terms Quiz

a. 8
b. 7
c. 9
d. 3
e. 1
f. 2
g. 4
h. 5
i. 6

True-False Questions

1. False. We measure utility in hypothetical units called utils because utility cannot be measured precisely.
2. False. Utils are hypothetical units. There are no machines calibrated in utils to measure utility.
3. True.
4. False. Each person has a unique utility function for the good. Therefore, their total utility levels are probably different. Remember, it is impossible to make precise interpersonal comparisons of utility.
5. False. Marginal utility is the addition to total utility from consuming one more unit of a good. Marginal utility may be large or small. For example, the marginal utility of the first gulp of water you take after a long run on a hot day is quite high.
6. True.
7. True.
8. False. In order to maximize utility, a consumer must equate the ratio of marginal utility to price for all goods.

9. True.
10. True.
11. False. A lower marginal-utility-to-price ratio for one good compared to other goods means that less of it should be consumed with expenditures diverted to other goods, thus equating the marginal-utility-to-price ratios for all goods.
12. True.
13. False. The law of diminishing marginal utility causes total utility curves to become flatter as more is consumed.
14. True.
15. True.

Multiple-Choice Questions

1. a	6. b	11. e	16. a
2. e	7. d	12. b	17. c
3. d	8. b	13. b	18. b
4. a	9. a	14. d	19. b
5. b	10. e	15. d	20. c

Fill in the Blanks

1. satisfaction; enjoyment
2. consumed; extra utility; diminishes
3. maximized; marginal utility to price; equal
4. maximum; consumer surplus
5. comparisons between people; taxes

Discussion Questions

1. Economists developed utility theory in order to explain consumer choice and the principles underlying demand. For example, why does quantity demanded increase as price decreases? Consumers purchase more of a good as its price falls because the marginal-utility-to-price ratio for that good has risen relative to the marginal-utility-to-price ratio for other goods. It is perfectly clear that people gain satisfaction, or utility, from consumption. Consumers compare the additional satisfaction (marginal utility) per dollar spent between different goods in making their choices.

2. The law of diminishing marginal utility states that as consumption increases, the addition to total utility from more consumption will eventually decrease. Thinking about exceptions to this law only seems to reinforce its universality. Perhaps certain kinds of addictions like alcoholism and drug addictions could be considered exceptions. But even in these cases, individuals eventually experience diminishing marginal utility (if not negative utility) as their lives unravel around them.

3. The water-diamond paradox is easy to explain with utility theory. Since diamonds are scarce, most people have very few of them, and the marginal utility of the last one consumed is very high. Therefore, even though the total utility of diamonds is low relative to the total utility of water, the marginal utility of diamonds is very high compared to the marginal utility of water, which is abundant in most parts of the world. Therefore, people value the last unit of scarce diamonds they consume at a much higher rate than the last unit of abundant water they consume.

4. Consumers maximize utility from consumption when the ratios of marginal utility to price are the same for all goods consumed. This is logical because the sensible consumer will always rearrange purchases from

INTRO TO MICROECONOMICS

goods whose MU/Ps are lower to ones whose MU/Ps are higher. After all, consumers are always trying to get the most possible satisfaction per dollar spent. By consuming more of the goods with the high MU/P and less of the goods with low MU/P, these ratios are brought into equality. The marginal utility of the next units consumed of the high MU/P goods is a little bit lower because of the law of diminishing marginal utility. Similarly, the marginal utility of the low MU/P goods increases a little bit as fewer of these goods are consumed. Therefore, the rearrangement of goods consumed drives the MU/Ps into equality.

5. The law of demand tells us that demand curves will be downward sloping. That is, as the price decreases, quantity demanded increases. Marginal utility analysis tells us why. When the price of a good decreases, its MU/P increases relative to the MU/P for other goods. Therefore, consumers will rearrange their purchases to buy more of the good whose price has fallen. After all, this good has a higher satisfaction per dollar spent than other goods, given the drop in its price.

6. Consumers are seldom charged their exact willingness to pay for each unit of a good that they consume. That is, they aren't charged prices directly from their demand curves for all the units of various goods they purchase. Therefore, consumers are able to enjoy utility expressed as the difference between the dollar amount that they were willing to pay and the price they actually paid. This difference between what people pay for a good and what they would have been willing to pay is called consumer surplus.

7. Interpersonal comparisons of utility can never be exact. It is natural that people's tastes differ from one another, and this is as true for money as it is for any other good. Some people have a stronger taste for money than do others. And, while it may be possible, in some cases, that the marginal utility of the last dollar earned by a rich person exceeds the marginal utility of the last dollar earned by a poor person, it seems reasonable in most cases that the reverse is true. That is to say, in most instances, the marginal utility of the last dollar to the poor person (who may be purchasing necessities with it) is higher than the marginal utility of the last dollar to the rich person (who may be enjoying luxury goods with the last dollar). Therefore, given the reasonableness of such interpersonal comparisons of the marginal utility of money, it follows that total utility in the economy rises when the rich are taxed at a higher rate than the poor and some of these tax revenues are used to support programs that aid the poor. Hence, interpersonal comparisons of the marginal utility of money do have a role to play in the creation of social policies.

Problems

1. a. The table with the marginal utility column completed is shown below.

Number of Comics	Total Utility	Marginal Utility
0	0	
1	100	100
2	190	90
3	270	80
4	330	60
5	380	50

b. Tony does experience the law of diminishing marginal utility in his consumption of Spiderman comic books. The figures in the marginal utility column of the table decrease from 100 to 50 from the first comic book through the fifth.

c. Tony's total and marginal utility functions are shown below.

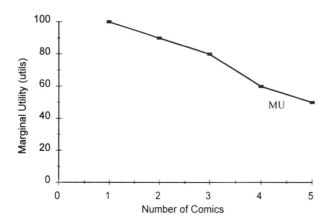

2. a. The completed table with the marginal-utility-to-price ratio computations is shown below.

Quantity of Legos	TU	MU	MU/P	Quantity of Sq.Guns	TU	MU	MU/P
0	0			0	0		
1	20	20	4	1	50	50	6.25
2	37	17	3.4	2	25	25	3.125
3	50	13	2.6	3	15	15	1.875
4	60	10	2	4	10	10	1.25
5	65	5	1	5	2	2	.25

b. With $26 to spend, Jacob will purchase 2 legos sets and 2 squirt guns. He begins by purchasing a squirt gun with its MU/P equal to 6.25. Then he purchases 2 legos sets, which leaves him with $8 that he spends on a second squirt gun. Each purchase corresponds to the highest possible MU/P that is available to him.

INTRO TO MICROECONOMICS

c. A decrease in the price of legos sets to $2.50 changes the values in the MU/P column for legos. Each of these numbers doubles since the price falls in half from $5 to $2.50. So, we have values in the column equal to 8, 6.8, 5.2, 4, and 2 for the first through fifth legos sets, respectively. If Jacob still has $26 to spend, he will purchase items in the following order — 2 legos sets, a squirt gun, 2 more legos sets, and a squirt gun. He will end up with 4 legos sets and 2 squirt guns.

d. Jacob's demand curve for legos sets between the prices $5 and $2.50 per set is shown below. The demand curve has a negative slope because a decrease in the price of legos relative to other goods (squirt guns in this case) raises the MU/P for legos. As the price of legos decreases, Jacob's quantity demanded increases because his satisfaction per dollar spent on legos increases.

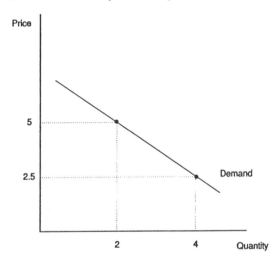

3. a. The completed table is presented below.

Quantity of Sugar	MU	MU/P	Quantity of Spice	MU	MU/P
1	20	4	1	40	4
2	12	2.4	2	20	2
3	9	1.8	3	9	.9
4	5	1	4	7	.7
5	3	.6	5	5	.5
6	1	.2	6	3	.3

b. Pat will purchase 2 units of sugar and 2 units of spice. She purchases these items in the following order — sugar, spice, sugar, spice. Each purchase corresponds to the next highest MU/P ratio, which are, in order, 4, 4, 2.4, 2.

c. A fall in the price of sugar to $3 changes the MU/P column to 6.67, 4, 3, 1.67, 1, and .33. Pat will purchase these items in the order sugar, spice, sugar, sugar, and spice. Pat spends $29 of her budget this way. If she had an additional $2, her next purchase would be sugar. So, at $3 per unit, Pat buys 3 units of sugar.

d. A fall in the price of sugar to $2 changes the MU/P column to 10, 6, 4.5, 2.5, 1.5, and .5. Pat will purchase items in the order sugar, sugar, sugar, spice, sugar, sugar, and spice to completely exhaust her budget. She will have purchased 5 units of sugar at $2 per unit.

e. The graph is shown below.

4. a. Chloe's demand for Beanie Baby Dolls is shown below.

b. If the price of dolls is $8, then Chloe enjoys $8 of consumer surplus on the first doll, $4 on the second doll, and $0 on the third doll for a total of $12. Consumer surplus is the sum of the difference between the price she was willing to pay (read from the demand curve) and the price she actually paid ($8).

c. If the price falls to $4, then Chloe's consumer surplus rises to $12 on the first doll, $8 on the second doll, $4 on the third doll, and $0 on the fourth doll for a total of $24. These values are the differences between the price she was willing to pay and the $4 price she actually paid. If the dolls are free, Chloe enjoys $40 of consumer surplus — $16 + $12 + $8 + $4.

INTRO TO MICROECONOMICS

APPENDIX

THE INDIFFERENCE CURVE APPROACH TO DEMAND CURVES

Appendix in a Nutshell

Utility analysis suffers from the defect that the unit of measure — utility — cannot itself be measured. No one has yet invented a utilometer! However, it is possible to derive demand curves without using the concept utility in the sense of counting utils. The **indifference curve** approach only relies on our knowledge of the consumer's preferences between sets of goods and the consumer's **budget constraint**. The only assumption necessary in this analysis is that consumers can rank their preferences. That is, the utilities of goods are not really measured with the indifference curve approach. Rather, consumers only need to be able to rate the utilities of sets of goods as greater, less than, or equal to the utilities of other sets of goods. If two sets of goods have equal utilities, then a consumer is said to be indifferent between them.

Indifference curves are defined by combinations of goods that yield identical utility to a consumer. Therefore, all the combinations of goods represented by indifference curves are rated as equally preferred by the consumer. The slope of the indifference curve reflects a **declining marginal rate of substitution**. As a consumer gives up units of one good along an indifference curve, increasing amounts of the other good are required in order to maintain the consumer's level of satisfaction constant. Sets of indifference curves can be drawn as an ascending series with the curve farthest from the origin representing the combinations of goods that yield the highest utility. These sets of indifference curves are called **indifference maps**.

The amount of each good that a consumer will purchase depends on the prices of the two goods and the consumer's income. This information defines the **budget constraint** — the sum of the price times the quantity of each good that is consumed must be equal to the consumer's income. Algebraically, we can write the budget constraint as

$$I = P_1 Q_1 + P_2 Q_2$$

where P_1 and P_2 stand for the prices of the two goods, Q_1 and Q_2 stand for the quantities, and I is income. A consumer's choice of a combination of goods 1 and 2 that maximizes utility given prices and income is the point where the budget constraint (or line) lies tangent to an indifference curve. As the price of one of the goods is allowed to change — suppose it increases — then the budget line rotates toward the origin along the axis of the good whose price is rising. The increase in price will map out tangent points on indifference curves that yield smaller quantities consumed of the good whose price increases. Thus, as the price of a good increases, the quantity demanded decreases, and we can draw the familiar downward-sloping demand curve.

After you study the material in this appendix, you should be able to:

- Explain why economists use the **indifference curve approach** to study consumer choice.
- Construct **equally preferred sets of goods** to form an **indifference curve**.
- Show that the **marginal rate of substitution** declines as one good is substituted for another.
- Rank the levels of utility for indifference curves that form an **indifference map**.
- Shift a **budget constraint** by changing the prices of goods and/or a consumer's income.
- Derive a demand curve by changing the price of a good to shift a budget constraint across a consumer's indifference map and locating **tangent points** between the budget constraints and indifference curves.

98 CHAPTER 5 MARGINAL UTILITY AND CONSUMER CHOICE

Concept Check — See how you do on these multiple-choice questions.

1. The **indifference curve approach** to demand curves requires that
    a. a consumer be able to put precise utility values on different sets of goods
    b. utils be counted very carefully
    c. we make interpersonal comparisons of utility
    d. a consumer have a sufficiently large budget to buy many different items
    e. a consumer be able to rank utilities of different goods

Remember that we are using the indifference curve approach because counting utils seems farfetched.

2. An **indifference curve** is formed by constructing combinations of goods that
    a. are rated with higher utilities than other goods
    b. are within the consumer's budget constraint
    c. are not subject to the law of diminishing marginal utility
    d. yield identical levels of utility for a consumer
    e. are substituted for one another at a constant marginal rate

Think about what the term *indifference* means. If someone is indifferent between two combinations of goods, then that person is equally satisfied with either one.

3. The **marginal rate of substitution** is the rate at which a consumer
    a. measures utils for additional units of consumption
    b. will give up units of one good for units of another good while holding utility constant
    c. runs up against the monthly budget constraint
    d. finds substitute goods for goods whose prices are increasing
    e. compares the utility rankings of sets of goods that might be substitutable

Utility is constant along an indifference curve. To keep utility constant, a consumer must substitute increasing amounts of one good in order to accept equal cuts in the amount consumed of the other good.

4. A consumer's **budget constraint** is formed by
    a. subtracting the cost of various budget items from the consumer's income
    b. setting the consumer's income equal to the sum of the price times the quantity for all goods consumed
    c. adding up the prices of all the items in the household budget
    d. comparing the marginal-utility-to-price ratios of the most preferred goods the consumer buys
    e. dividing income by the price of the most expensive good consumed

A budget constraint simply shows the various combinations of goods that a consumer can purchase given the prices of the goods and the consumer's income.

Am I on the Right Track?

Your answers to the questions above should be **e, d, b,** and **b**. Probably the best way to learn the indifference curve approach to demand curves is to work through some numerical examples that allow you to see indifference curves being constructed and their relationship to budget constraints in determining a consumer's choices of combinations of goods to purchase. The graphing tutorial and the questions that follow give you a chance to do this.

INTRO TO MICROECONOMICS

Graphing Tutorial

Graphing indifference curves and budget constraints in order to derive demand curves is a fairly sophisticated procedure. However, if you keep in mind the definitions for the concepts that lie behind the graphs, it isn't that difficult to do. Remember, our goal here is to derive a downward-sloping demand curve, just as this was our goal in the main part of the chapter.

An indifference curve consists of a set of combinations of goods that yield identical utility to a particular person. The table below shows combinations of bananas and boxes of cereal that provide identical utility to Jerry.

Combination	Bananas	Boxes of Cereal
a	1	15
b	3	9
c	5	6
d	7	4
e	9	3

These equally preferred combinations of bananas and boxes of cereal are plotted below as an indifference curve.

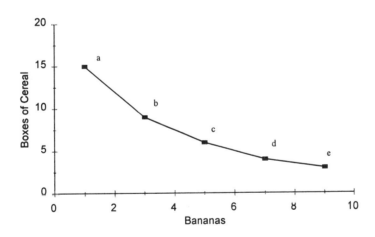

Note that Jerry's indifference curve exhibits the principle of declining marginal rate of substitution. Starting at point a and moving to point b, Jerry is willing to give up 6 boxes of cereal for 2 more bananas, giving us a marginal rate of substitution equal to -3. From point b to point c, Jerry is willing to give up only 3 boxes of cereal for 2 more bananas — a marginal rate of substitution equal to $-3/2$. From point c to point d, the marginal rate of substitution is -1 and from point d to point e, the marginal rate of substitution is $-1/2$. Jerry trades fewer and fewer boxes of cereal for 2 more bananas while keeping his utility constant because he experiences diminishing marginal utility from more bananas. He isn't a chimp after all! Because of the declining marginal rate of substitution, the indifference curve is downward sloping and convex with respect to the origin.

We can create another indifference curve for Jerry showing a set of combinations of bananas and cereal that have equal but higher utility than the set of combinations we just considered. Such a set of combinations would lie above and to the right of the indifference curve we just drew. Suppose we simply add 5 boxes of cereal to every level of banana consumption shown in the graph above. This would do the trick wouldn't it? A plot of the two indifference curves is shown below.

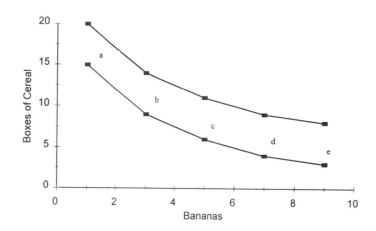

Now let's put prices on bananas and boxes of cereal and give Jerry some income and see how much of each good he will purchase. Suppose that bananas are selling for $2 each, cereal costs $1.67 per box, and Jerry has $20 of income. If he spends all of his income on bananas, he can purchase 10. This point, 10 bananas and 0 boxes of cereal, is an endpoint on Jerry's budget constraint (or line) that is shown below in the graph. The other endpoint is at 11.97 boxes of cereal and 0 bananas, corresponding to Jerry spending all his income on cereal — $20 divided by $1.67 per box. Given these prices and his income, Jerry purchases 5 bananas and 6 boxes of cereal. This choice is the tangent point between Jerry's budget line and the indifference curve.

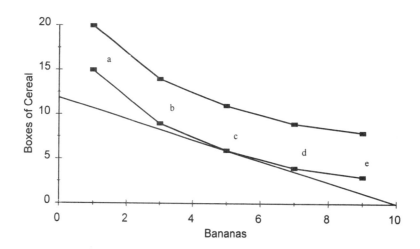

INTRO TO MICROECONOMICS

Suppose that we let the price of cereal drop to $1 per box and see what Jerry chooses to buy. The price of bananas and Jerry's income are held constant — $2 per banana and $20. At a price of $1 per box, Jerry could spend all of his income on cereal and buy 20 boxes. Therefore, the budget line rotates up the cereal axis to intersect at the point 20 boxes of cereal and 0 bananas. This rotation of the budget line is shown in the graph below.

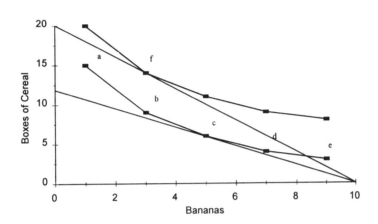

Now that the price of cereal has fallen, Jerry chooses to purchase 14 boxes (he's stocking up for Kramer) and only 3 bananas. This is the point labeled f. We have generated enough information to draw Jerry's demand curve for cereal between the prices $1.67 per box and $1 per box. At $1.67 Jerry buys 6 boxes, and at $1 per box Jerry buys 14 boxes. As an exercise, sketch this demand curve.

True-False Questions — If a statement is false, explain why.

1. A consumer's indifference curve reflects combinations of goods that yield identical utility levels. (T/F)

2. Ian's utility increases as he moves down along his indifference curve. (T/F)

3. Brian has maximized utility if he consumes at the tangent point between his indifference curve and his budget constraint. (T/F)

4. As the price of a good falls, the intercept for that good on a budget constraint shifts away from the origin. (T/F)

5. The marginal rate of substitution is the rate at which one good can be substituted for another, which is constant along an indifference curve. (T/F)

6. An indifference map consists of many indifference curves drawn in ascending order of utility level as one moves away from the origin. (T/F)

7. If the price of a good doubles, then one intercept for that good on a budget constraint will shift halfway toward the origin. (T/F)

8. If income increases, a budget constraint will shift outward from the origin so that the new constraint is parallel to the old one. (T/F)

9. Deriving the demand curve for a good using the indifference curve approach requires that both goods' prices be changed simultaneously. (T/F)

10. The indifference curve approach leads to more frequent violations of the law of demand than does the marginal-utility-to-price ratio approach to constructing demand curves. (T/F)

Multiple Choice Questions

1. Which of the following is true about combinations of goods represented by an indifference curve?
    a. the marginal utilities of the combinations decrease, descending along the curve
    b. combinations are equally preferred to one another
    c. the marginal utilities of the combinations increase, descending along the curve
    d. each combination matches its price
    e. they lie on a straight line

2. A budget line
    a. represents the total value of all combinations on an indifference curve
    b. is determined by a set of prices, indicating combinations of goods a consumer can buy with given income
    c. is derived by consumers to fix the combinations of goods they can buy and how much they can save
    d. is an equation representing what a consumer would buy if income matched prices
    e. curves inward (is concave) to the origin.

3. The indifference curve approach to demand derivation is based on
    a. precise comparisons of measurements of utility levels from the consumption of sets of goods
    b. a recent invention called the utilometer
    c. interpersonal comparisons of utility
    d. the fact that the marginal utility of money is diminishing
    e. consumer preferences between sets of goods

4. Indifference curves that are downward sloping and convex to the origin reflect
    a. the abandonment of utility theory with the indifference curve approach
    b. the increasing marginal utility of certain goods
    c. the increasing ease of substituting one good for another
    d. the declining marginal rate of substitution
    e. the rising marginal rate of substitution

5. Suppose a consumer, with an income of $100, faces a $1 price for soda and a $2 price for hot dogs. The consumer's budget line will intersect the hot dog and soda axes at
   a. 100 hot dogs and 50 sodas
   b. 50 hot dogs and 100 sodas
   c. 100 hot dogs and 200 sodas
   d. 75 hot dogs and 150 sodas
   e. points that cannot be determined without an indifference map

6. Given the information in question 6, suppose that the price of hot dogs increases to $4 each. This price increase would result in all of the following **except** a
   a. change in the soda intercept
   b. decrease in the maximum number of hot dogs that can be purchased
   c. shift to an indifference curve corresponding to a lower utility level for the consumer
   d. possible decrease in soda consumption since hot dogs and sodas are complementary goods
   e. nonparallel shift in the budget constraint toward the origin

7. Suppose the consumer's income in questions 5 and 6 increases to $200. If the prices of sodas and hot dogs are $1 and $2, respectively, the increase in income would result in all of the following **except**
   a. a doubling of each intercept to the axes for sodas and hot dogs
   b. a change in the shape of the consumer's indifference curves
   c. a shift to an indifference curve corresponding to a higher utility level for the consumer
   d. a parallel shift in the budget constraint
   e. an increase in either or both soda and hot dog consumption

8. One problem with the marginal-utility-to-price ratio approach to understanding the law of demand is that
   a. it forces us to make interpersonal comparisons of utility
   b. the measurement of utility seems so unrealistic
   c. people find it impossible to rank their preferences
   d. many times, the law of diminishing marginal utility is violated
   e. the theory is useless for the development of tax policies

9. The distinction between an indifference curve and an indifference map is that
   a. an indifference curve allows utility levels to fluctuate while utility is constant on an indifference map
   b. indifference curves are convex toward the origin while indifference maps are concave
   c. an indifference map is comprised of many indifference curves
   d. an indifference map has a rising marginal rate of substitution
   e. the law of diminishing marginal utility is less evident in an indifference map than on an indifference curve

10. A demand curve that is derived using the indifference curve approach will
    a. be more sensitive to income changes than one derived using the marginal-utility-to-price ratio approach
    b. have the same characteristics as one derived using the marginal-utility-to-price ratio approach
    c. allow for interpersonal comparisons of utility to be made with precision
    d. show a declining marginal rate of substitution
    e. be more likely to have a positive slope than one derived using the marginal-utility-to-price ratio approach

Discussion Questions

1. What motivated economists to develop the indifference curve approach to the derivation of demand curves? What is required of consumers in order for this approach to be feasible?

2. Why do indifference curves show a declining marginal rate of substitution?

3. Why are total utility levels for indifference curves that lie farther from the origin higher than total utility levels for indifference curves close to the origin?

4. Explain how it is possible to derive a demand curve given a consumer's indifference curves and budget lines that reflect changes in the price of one good, holding income constant.

INTRO TO MICROECONOMICS

Problems

1. Bill is a big Phish fan. He follows Phish from show to show and tapes each concert. Bill is indifferent between the following combinations of tickets to Phish shows and cases of blank recording cassettes.

Tickets	Cases of Tapes
4	15
6	8
8	4
10	3

   a. Sketch Bill's indifference curve below with tickets on the horizontal axis and cases of tape on the vertical axis. Does this curve show the declining marginal rate of substitution? Carefully explain why.

   b. Draw another indifference curve on the same set of axes you used above that shows Bill's preferences for the following pairs of points.

Tickets	Cases of Tapes
4	20
6	12
8	9
10	7

   Which set of combinations of tickets and tapes does Bill prefer and why?

c. Suppose that the tickets to shows and the cases of tape are both priced at $20 each. If Bill has $240 to spend, what is the maximum number of shows that he can see? What is the maximum number of cases of tape that he can purchase? Use these values to draw in Bill's budget line on the axes you drew for part a.

d. How many shows will Bill see and how many cases of tape will he buy? How do you know?

e. Suppose that the price of a case of tapes falls to $10. Draw Bill's new budget line. How many cases of tapes will he buy and how many shows will he see now?

f. What is the quantity demanded of cases of tapes when the price is $20 per case? $10 per case? Sketch Bill's demand curve for cases of tapes.

Answers to Questions for the Appendix

True-False Questions

1. True
2. False. Utility is constant along an indifference curve so it cannot increase as Ian moves down along the curve.
3. True
4. True
5. False. The marginal rate of substitution is the rate at which one good can be substituted for another holding the level of utility constant (as along an indifference curve). However, the marginal rate of substitution is not constant along an indifference curve. The marginal rate of substitution declines along an indifference curve because of the law of diminishing marginal utility. As equal amounts of one good are

INTRO TO MICROECONOMICS

sacrificed, larger amounts of the second good are required to keep utility constant.
6. True
7. True
8. True
9. False. In order to derive a demand curve for a good, only that good's price should be changed while holding income and the prices of other goods constant.
10. False. The indifference curve approach and the marginal-utility-to-price ratio approach to deriving demand curves arrive at the same result. That is, they show downward-sloping demand curves reflecting the law of demand.

Multiple-Choice Questions

1. b
2. b
3. e
4. d
5. b

6. a
7. b
8. b
9. c
10. b

Discussion Questions

1. Even though the idea of linking the law of demand to the law of diminishing marginal utility by comparing the choices consumers make as price changes alter marginal-utility-to-price ratios makes perfectly good sense, it depends on the notion of measuring utility. The measurement is done in hypothetical units called utils. Therefore, economists have developed an alternative method for deriving demand curves that gets the same result. This is the indifference curve approach. All that is required of consumers using the indifference curve approach is that they be able to rate the utilities of sets of goods as greater, less than, or equal to the utilities of other sets of good.

2. Indifference curves are drawn downward sloping and convex to the origin, thus exhibiting the declining marginal rate of substitution. The declining marginal rate of substitution arises from the fact that as the consumption of one good increases by equal amounts, a consumer will accept smaller and smaller sacrifices of the other good, holding utility constant. That is because the consumer experiences the law of diminishing marginal utility as consumption of the one good increases by equal amounts. The diminishing marginal utility is borne out in the smaller and smaller sacrifices of the second good the consumer is willing to accept.

3. It makes sense that utility levels are higher for indifference curves that lie farther from the origin because these curves correspond to the consumption of larger amounts of the two goods represented by an indifference map. As consumption increases, utility levels increase too.

4. The method for deriving a demand curve with indifference curves and budget lines is straightforward. Use the prices of the goods and the consumer's income to determine the endpoints of the budget line on the axes for the two goods. This is done by dividing the income by the price of each good to find out the maximum amount of each good the consumer could buy if only that good was purchased. Connect the two endpoints to form the budget line. Then find the tangent point of the budget line to the consumer's highest indifference curve. This is the utility-maximizing combination of the two goods given the prices and incomes. Now, let one of the good's prices decrease by some amount. Find the new endpoint for the line by dividing income by the new price. The new line will be tangent to an indifference curve that lies farther from the origin than did the first one. Record the prices and quantities consumed at each price. Plot these prices and quantities demanded to draw a demand curve. You've done it!

Problems

1. a. This curve does show the declining marginal rate of substitution. Moving from 16 cases of tapes to 8 cases of tapes, Bill receives 2 additional tickets for a marginal rate of substitution equal to -8/2 or -4. From 8 cases of tapes to 4 cases of tapes, Bill gets 2 more tickets for a marginal rate of substitution equal to -2. From 4 cases of tapes to 2 cases of tapes, Bill acquires two more tickets for a marginal rate of substitution equal to -1. He gives up fewer and fewer tapes to obtain 2 additional tickets. So, the marginal rate of substitution is declining.

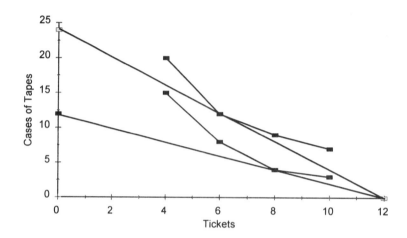

b. The second indifference curve is farther from the origin and shows a higher utility level so it is preferred to the first set of combinations of tickets and tapes. This makes sense because each level of ticket consumption is matched with a bigger level of tape consumption in the second set of combinations.

c. With $240, Bill can see a maximum of 12 shows at $20 per show. He could also purchase a maximum of 12 cases of tapes.

d. Bill will purchase 8 tickets, so he'll see 8 shows and buy 4 cases of tapes. These quantities correspond to the tangent point between the budget line and the indifference curve.

e. The new budget line cuts the cases of tapes axis at 24. Bill will now go to 6 shows and purchase 12 cases of tapes. These combinations of tickets and tapes correspond to the tangent point of the budget line to the higher indifference curve.

f. At $20 per case, Bill purchases 4 cases of tapes. At $10 per case, Bill buys 12 cases of tapes. These price and quantity demanded combinations yield a typical downward-sloping demand curve when they are graphed.

CHAPTER 6

PRICE CEILINGS AND PRICE FLOORS

Chapter in a Nutshell

So far, the prices we've discussed have all been market determined. The interaction of demand and supply guides prices to their equilibrium levels where the quantity demanded is equal to the quantity supplied. There can never be an excess demand or an excess supply in equilibrium when prices are market determined.

Market-determined prices reflect the market reality. When demand increases, the price increases. That's the market reality. Usually, we can accept the reality. However, in some circumstances, the market reality of a price skyrocketing overnight or, alternatively, decreasing dramatically in a short period of time, is unacceptable to society. In these situations, market-determined prices may have to be abandoned. If a price suddenly begins to rise too rapidly, the government can stop the increase by setting a **price ceiling** in the market. The price ceiling is a maximum price. Of course, the ceiling creates problems of its own — **chronic excess demand,** for one. But society may prefer coping with chronic excess demand, perhaps by using **ration coupons**, to watching prices go through the roof. This is exactly the political decision that was made during World War II.

In other cases, where prices are falling too low, **price floors**, or minimum prices, can be set by the government. There are problems associated with price floors — most obviously, what to do with the **chronic excess supply** that a price floor generates. Yet, living with chronic excess supply might be preferable to society to seeing a price keep tumbling over time. The United States made a decision to limit the decline of agricultural prices in the 1930s by introducing a set of **price floors** for farm products in order to maintain **parity** between agricultural and nonagricultural prices.

Government interference with market-determined prices has a long history. For example, **usury**, or the charging of interest on debts, was forbidden in biblical times. This ban on interest was a price ceiling set at zero. **Usury laws** persist to this day, setting maximum rates of interest that can be charged in many states and in countries around the world.

For the most part, markets do a great job setting equilibrium prices so that the quantity demanded and quantity supplied are equal. However, these equilibrium prices are, in rare cases, unacceptable, prompting government to establish price ceilings and/or price floors. This chapter focuses on these exceptions to the rule of market-determined prices.

After you study this chapter, you should be able to:

- Describe circumstances where **price ceilings** and **price floors** might be appropriate.
- Show how a price ceiling causes **chronic excess demand**.
- Discuss the use of price ceilings during World War II.
- Explain how **rationing** works.
- Show how a price floor causes **chronic excess supply**.
- Give reasons for setting price floors in agricultural markets during the 1930s.
- Compare **parity pricing** with **target pricing**.
- Evaluate **crop limitation** programs.

Concept Check — See how you do on these multiple-choice questions.

1. A **price ceiling** will have no impact on a market if it is set
   a. below the equilibrium price
   b. by knowledgeable government officials
   c. to maintain parity
   d. above the equilibrium price
   e. below last year's average price

Think about whether a price ceiling is introduced because the price in the market is too high or too low.

2. **Rent controls** are examples of
   a. price floors
   b. price ceilings
   c. parity prices
   d. target prices
   e. equilibrium prices

Were rent controls imposed because rents were too high or too low?

3. **Ration coupons** are used to
   a. cope with chronic excess supply
   b. cope with price floors
   c. establish parity between farmers' incomes and nonfarm incomes
   d. raise prices in a market
   e. cope with chronic excess demand

Rationing becomes necessary when there isn't enough to satisfy the quantity demanded.

4. The **parity price ratio** is the
   a. price ceiling divided by the price floor
   b. ratio of prices received by farmers to the prices paid by farmers
   c. formula used to calculate target prices
   d. ratio of farm prices to the value of their ration coupons
   e. price ceiling divided by the price floor in a market

Are farm prices increasing or decreasing relative to nonfarm prices?

5. **Target prices** are established to guarantee that farmers receive the
   a. equilibrium price
   b. difference between the target price and the equilibrium price
   c. target price
   d. parity price
   e. price floor

Be sure you understand the difference between parity pricing and target pricing.

INTRO TO MICROECONOMICS

Am I on the Right Track?

Your answers to the questions above should be **d, b, e, b,** and **c**. This chapter should improve your skills working with demand and supply diagrams at the same time that you learn some economic history. The story of price controls during World War II is an example of government intervention that worked effectively to shift resources from peacetime to wartime production. Price floors were introduced in agricultural markets because farmers were, in a very real sense, too successful. Technological advances in agriculture during this century have pushed agricultural supply curves to the right faster than the demand has increased, causing a long-run decline in the prices of agricultural products relative to those for manufactured goods. Farm incomes have declined relatively as a result. The questions that follow will develop your knowledge of the details of these stories.

Key Terms Quiz — Match the terms on the left with the definitions in the column on the right.

1. price ceiling   _____ a. payments made to farmers so they receive the target price on their output
2. ration coupon   _____ b. the ratio of prices received by farmers to the prices paid by farmers
3. rent control   _____ c. a maximum price set by government below the equilibrium price
4. price floor   _____ d. a coupon that one must have in order to purchase a good
5. parity price ratio   _____ e. a minimum price that is set by government above the equilibrium price
6. target price   _____ f. a price guaranteed to farmers by the government
7. deficiency payments   _____ g. a price ceiling for rent

Graphing Tutorial

Let's look at the effect of a rent control law, like those imposed during World War II, on a rental housing market that had been in equilibrium. Consider the graph below:

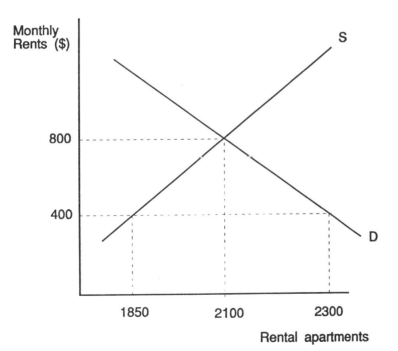

The demand for rental apartments is negatively sloped because as rents are lowered, more people are willing and able to rent apartments — as opposed to living with parents, sharing an apartment with others, or being homeless. The supply of rental apartments is positively sloped because fewer apartments are supplied in the short run as rents are lowered. People find it less worthwhile to rent out that extra room or basement apartment as rents decrease. The graph on the previous page shows that the market equilibrium monthly rent is $800, and at that price, quantity demanded and quantity supplied are equal to 2,100 apartments. Because the market is in equilibrium, there is no excess demand or excess supply.

Now suppose that government decides that $800 is too high a price for renters to pay. Out of concern for renters, the government imposes a rent control law that sets a maximum monthly rent of $400. This certainly reduces the cost of housing to renters, doesn't it? But look at the graph to see the effects on the rental housing market. The quantity demanded of apartments increases to 2,300, while the quantity supplied drops to 1,850. This means that there is now an excess demand (or shortage) of 450 rental apartments. Renters who are lucky enough to get a rent-controlled apartment are better off because they are paying $400 instead of $800, but others are worse off because they can't get an apartment at all. This shortage will persist as long as rent controls are in effect.

In fact, the shortage of rental apartments is likely to become worse in the long run. Landlords who are receiving lower rents have less incentive to maintain their properties, so many will eventually be abandoned or torn down. Low rents will also deter potential landlords from building new rental properties. Over time, the supply of housing will probably decrease.

Graphing Pitfalls

Consider the effects of a target pricing system on an agricultural market. Here, the government guarantees farmers a particular price for their output by promising to make up the difference between the target price and the equilibrium price. Consider the example shown in the graph below.

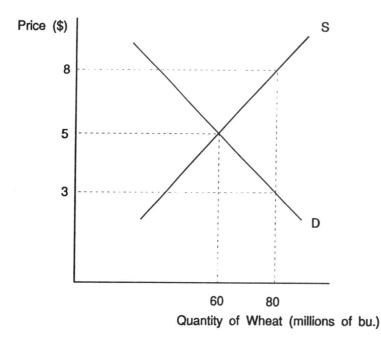

INTRO TO MICROECONOMICS

The free market equilibrium price is $5, and the equilibrium quantity demanded and supplied is 60. If the government sets a target price of $8, quantity supplied increases to 80. To induce consumers to buy 80 million bushels of wheat, the equilibrium price must fall to $3. The amount of the deficiency payment made to farmers is ($8 − $5) × 80 = $240.

Make sure you understand that the equilibrium price and quantity have both changed in response to the target pricing program. Even though you may be accustomed to thinking of equilibrium as the intersection of the demand and supply curves, in this case, you must interpret the outcome differently. Jumping to the market equilibrium solution of price equal to $5 and quantity supplied of 60 will give you the wrong answer for a target pricing problem.

True-False Questions — If a statement is false, explain why.

1. During a war, resources must be shifted from producing civilian goods to defense goods, and the prices of civilian goods rise to much higher levels as a result (T/F)

2. Because consumer sovereignty is so ingrained in American culture, government price controls are banned by law. (T/F)

3. A national security crisis might be a reason to impose price controls if the burden of the crisis is borne disproportionately by the poor. (T/F)

4. A price ceiling sets a minimum price for a good. (T/F)

5. Chronic excess demand cannot exist if price is set below the market equilibrium. (T/F)

6. One way to deal with the problem of chronic excess demand is to issue ration coupons. (T/F)

7. A price floor keeps a good's price from falling too low. (T/F)

8. Agriculture in the United States experienced such rapid improvement in technology during the first two decades of the twentieth century that prices began falling as supply curves shifted to the right. (T/F)

9. A target price policy results in lower prices for consumers than a parity price policy. (T/F)

10. Deficiency payments are made to farmers to cover the difference between the target price and the equilibrium price for the output a farmer produces. (T/F)

11. If a price floor is set below the equilibrium price, the price floor will have no effect on the market. (T/F)

12. Mechanization and the introduction of chemical fertilizers have had little long-run impact on farm output over time in the United States. (T/F)

13. Incomes of farmers in the United States have risen relative to nonfarm incomes during this century. (T/F)

14. The Commodity Credit Corporation (CCC) was created to make loans to farmers that could be repaid with crops farmers were unable to sell. (T/F)

15. By replacing parity pricing with target pricing, government subsidies to agriculture in the United States were eliminated. (T/F)

Multiple-Choice Questions

1. When a price ceiling is imposed in a market,
    a. a persistent surplus results
    b. a persistent shortage results
    c. sellers of the product are made better off
    d. no one is made better off
    e. quantity supplied is greater than the quantity demanded

2. All of the following are problems associated with price ceilings **except**
    a. chronic excess demand
    b. an eventual decline in the number of suppliers
    c. the need to use ration coupons to purchase the good
    d. chronic excess supply
    e. landlords failing to maintain rent-controlled properties adequately

3. When target pricing replaced parity pricing in 1973 as an attempt to reform agricultural policy in the United States,
    a. farmers were simply to receive the equilibrium price
    b. price floors were increased
    c. price ceilings were increased
    d. deficiency payments were made to achieve the target prices for crops
    e. the prices farmers received were deemed to be deficient

4. One way to cope with chronic excess demand is to
    a. simply give the goods away for free
    b. force parity between the quantity demanded and the quantity supplied
    c. issue ration coupons for the quantity supplied
    d. lower the price ceiling
    e. impose crop limitations

INTRO TO MICROECONOMICS

5. When a price floor is imposed, it has an impact on a market if it is set
   a. below the equilibrium price
   b. at the equilibrium price
   c. above the equilibrium price because quantity demanded exceeds quantity supplied
   d. above the equilibrium price because quantity supplied exceeds quantity demanded
   e. below the equilibrium price because quantity demanded exceeds quantity supplied

6. Some economists consider price controls to be socially beneficial in cases where
   a. the economy is currently stable, but erratic changes are forecast
   b. there are many producers and consumers
   c. prices are considerably out of line with their historical levels, causing great disruptions in their markets
   d. the price of a good in excess demand needs to be held lower
   e. the government checks excess demand by raising the equilibrium price

7. Price floors were established in agricultural markets for all of the following reasons **except to**
   a. keep farmers' incomes in parity with nonagricultural workers' incomes
   b. prevent surpluses of agricultural goods from occurring
   c. counteract falling agricultural prices caused, over the long run, by technological change
   d. counteract the low price elasticity of demand for farm goods
   e. counteract the low income elasticity of demand for farm goods

8. Technological progress in agriculture has been beneficial for _____ but harmful to _____ because the output of farm goods has grown so rapidly as a result.
   a. small farmers, large farmers
   b. consumers, farmers
   c. farmers, consumers
   d. the United States, other countries
   e. other countries, the United States

9. Unlike parity pricing, under target pricing farmers are
   a. paid target lump-sum cash grants
   b. paid the equilibrium price if they produce an output targeted by government
   c. paid the average of commodity prices from 1910 to 1914
   d. paid according to their targeted incomes
   e. guaranteed a target price

10. The Conservation Reserve Program was designed to
    a. encourage farmers to set aside funds to pay for future topsoil erosion
    b. encourage farmers to set aside highly erodible acres to restrict supplies of crops
    c. encourage farmers to clear additional acres so more crops can be exported
    d. develop new techniques of farming that minimize topsoil erosion
    e. regulate the rents that farmers can charge for their land

11. Living with chronic excess demand requires that
    a. the government shift resources from producing goods with excess supplies to those with excess demands
    b. an alternative to price, such as ration coupons, be used as a rationing mechanism
    c. the government shift resources from producing goods with excess demands to those with excess supplies
    d. consumers shift part of their income from spending to saving
    e. suppliers find additional resources to produce those goods in excess demand

12. The Commodity Credit Corporation was established in the 1930s to
    a. provide loans to farmers that commercial banks refused to grant
    b. stimulate farmers to expand acreage and increase production
    c. help farmers pay off mortgage debt left over from the Great Depression
    d. provide credit to farmers who invest in commodity speculation
    e. provide loans to farmers based on expected sales that could be paid for with surplus crops

13. Parity pricing was designed to
    a. create income equality among farmers
    b. maintain farmers' purchasing power relative to nonfarmers' purchasing power
    c. provide an incentive for farmers to leave farming for nonfarming economic activity
    d. encourage investment in agriculture by providing below-equilibrium prices for agricultural equipment
    e. restore market prices in agriculture to their equilibrium levels

14. One of the factors that contributed to the gradual decline in farm income in the United States during much of the twentieth century was
    a. World War I
    b. World War II
    c. unemployment among farmers
    d. the low price and income elasticities of demand for farm goods
    e. slow technological change in agriculture

15. The Agricultural and Consumer Protection Act in 1973 was revolutionary because it
    a. created a new division of meat inspectors employed by the United States Department of Agriculture
    b. ended the use of price floors, dramatically lowering food prices to consumers
    c. ended government subsidization of agriculture
    d. made fraud in the labeling of food packages a criminal offense
    e. established the minimum amount of aid to a farm family at $20,000 per year

16. One lesson to be drawn from our discussion of price ceilings and price floors is that
    a. government intervention in the economy should be routine and extensive
    b. the government can easily solve most economic problems
    c. price ceilings work better than price floors
    d. in most cases, prices should be set by the interaction of demand and supply
    e. price controls work best if left in place over long periods

17. One criticism of the role played by the Office of Price Administration during World War II is that
    a. the controls were largely ineffectual since most producers and consumers ignored them
    b. the burden of the war effort still fell disproportionately on poor people
    c. most price ceilings were set above their market equilibrium, so they had no real impact
    d. rent controls discouraged investment in new housing, intensifying the chronic housing shortage
    e. it created price speculation that ended up raising all prices above their equilibrium levels

18. Usury laws establish
    a. maximum rates of interest on loans; thus they are price floors
    b. minimum rates of interest on loans; thus they are price floors
    c. maximum rates of interest on loans; thus they are price ceilings
    d. minimum rates of interest on loans; thus they are price ceilings
    e. market rates of interest on loans

INTRO TO MICROECONOMICS

19. If the average of prices paid by farmers is 100 and the average of prices received by farmers is 120, then the parity price ratio, expressed as a percent, is equal to
   a. 100
   b. 10
   c. 12
   d. 120
   e. 220

20. Price floors in agricultural markets tended to
   a. slow down the rate of technological progress in agriculture
   b. reduce the number of family farms
   c. increase the incomes of farmers while increasing food prices for consumers
   d. help small farmers more than large farmers
   e. create a favorable climate for democracy

Fill in the Blanks

1. During World War II, the United States was forced to shift resources from the production of _____ to _____, causing dramatic _____ in the prices of _____ goods.

2. The _____ in agriculture has caused a dramatic decline in _____ prices relative to _____ prices during the twentieth century.

3. The intent of _____ pricing was to restore _____ between _____ and nonfarm prices.

4. The _____ of 1933 established both the price _____ system and the _____ Corporation to absorb the _____ created by parity pricing.

5. Laws against _____ fix the _____ price of borrowing money.

Discussion Questions

1. Why might a war create circumstances that necessitate price controls? Would the anticipated size and length of the war make a difference in the need for price controls?

2. Much of the literature produced by the Office of Price Administration explaining price controls during World War II was prefaced by disclaimers from the economists who constructed the price ceilings and floors. These economists wanted to make it clear that they didn't agree with the use of price controls as a general practice. Why would economists find price controls so abhorrent? Is there an alternative method for protecting the poor from dramatic price increases? Might it have its own drawbacks? Explain.

3. Why has technological progress created problems for farmers, but hasn't created problems in other industries subject to rapid technological change such as computers? Think about elasticities of demand.

4. What role did acreage restriction programs like the Conservation Reserve Program (Food Security Act of 1985) play in moderating the size of deficiency payments made to farmers under target pricing? Were these acreage restriction programs successful? Why or why not?

Problems

1. a. The table below shows figures for the prices received by farmers and the prices paid by farmers from 1936 through 1940. Calculate the parity price ratio as a percent and enter this value in the fourth column for each year.

Year	Prices Received by Farmers	Prices Paid by Farmers	Parity Price Ratio
1936	100	100	
1937	110	120	
1938	105	130	
1939	115	150	
1940	100	145	

INTRO TO MICROECONOMICS

b. Given the data presented in the table, what happened to the level of farm incomes relative to nonfarm incomes? Assume that output in each sector was constant over these years.

c. Sketch a graph that shows trend lines for prices received by farmers, prices paid by farmers, and the parity price ratio over these years. Axes are provided below.

2. The quantities demanded and supplied at different prices in the bagel market in Yellow Springs, Ohio, are shown in the table below.

Price ($/bagel)	Quantity Demanded	Quantity Supplied
0.20	200	50
0.30	170	70
0.40	140	90
0.50	110	110
0.60	80	130
0.70	50	150

a. On the axes provided below, sketch a graph to show the demand and supply for bagels in Yellow Springs. What is the equilibrium price, and what are the quantities demanded and supplied at the equilibrium price?

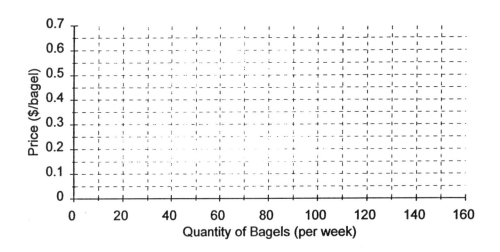

b. Suppose that the village mayor, David Foubert, decides that bagels are extremely healthy for villagers to eat and issues an edict that the price of a bagel in Yellow Springs is never to exceed $.40. Is Foubert establishing a price floor or a price ceiling? What are the quantity demanded and quantity supplied at this price? Is there a problem of excess demand or excess supply? How will consumers react to this policy? Bagel producers? Explain.

c. After a few months, Foubert decides that he has made a mistake. The price of bagels is too low at $.40. So, he issues another edict that the price of bagels is never to fall below $.60. Is this a price ceiling or floor? Discuss the ramifications of this price change.

3. Consider the graph below representing the market for soybeans.

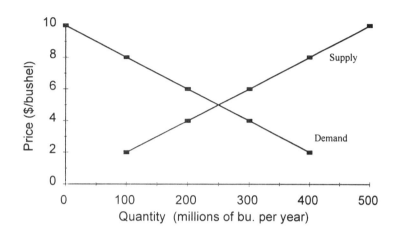

a. Suppose the government imposes a $6 price floor in this market. What is the quantity of soybeans demanded? The quantity supplied? What is the size of the subsidy that will be paid to farmers? Explain how you calculated the subsidy.

b. Now suppose the government changes its farm policy to target pricing with acreage restrictions. The target price is set at $6 per bushel, and, with acreage restrictions, farmers produce 250 million bushels per year. What is the quantity demanded, and how much do consumers pay? Do consumers prefer price floors or target pricing? Why?

c. How does the size of the subsidy change with target pricing? Explain how you arrived at your answer.

Everyday Applications

One area that is a prime candidate for price regulation now is the cable television industry. What has happened to cable rates in your area over the last several years? In many areas, cable rates have risen dramatically. Does this justify the imposition of a price ceiling? Suppose a price ceiling were placed on cable rates. Do you think the quantity supplied would decline as a result? Why or why not?

Economics Online

Congress recently eliminated target pricing for most crops grown by U.S. farmers. Prices for almost all farm products are set by the interaction of demand and supply. This has been a significant change for many farmers. To find out more about farm commodities, their production, and their prices, visit the site (*http://www.fsa.usda.gov/daco/co.htm*). Do you agree with Congress's action to remove target prices? Explain.

Answers to Questions

Key Terms Quiz

a. 7   f. 6
b. 5   g. 3
c. 1
d. 2
e. 4

True-False Questions

1. True
2. False. Although consumer sovereignty usually guides market behavior in the United States, in exceptional cases price controls have been introduced.
3. True
4. False. A price ceiling sets a maximum price.
5. False. Chronic excess demand does exist if price is set below the equilibrium because the quantity demanded will be greater than the quantity supplied.
6. True
7. True
8. True
9. True
10. True
11. True
12. False. These changes in agricultural technology have increased agricultural output enormously.
13. False. Farm incomes have fallen relative to nonfarm incomes in the United States during this century due to the decline in farm prices resulting from increases in supply and the low price and income elasticities of demand for farm products.
14. True
15. False. Government subsidies were reduced somewhat with target pricing, and a $20,000 cap was placed on the maximum subsidy that individual farmers could receive.

Multiple-Choice Questions

1. b	6. c	11. b	16. d
2. d	7. b	12. e	17. d
3. d	8. b	13. b	18. c
4. c	9. e	14. d	19. d
5. d	10. b	15. b	20. c

Fill in the Blanks

1. civilian goods; defense goods; increases; civilian
2. technological revolution; farm; nonfarm
3. parity; parity; farm
4. Agricultural Adjustment Act; floor; Commodity Credit; excess supply
5. usury; maximum

Discussion Questions

1. A war might require that large amounts of resources be shifted out of civilian goods production into defense goods production. Such a shift along a country's production possibilities curve would cause dramatic decreases in the supplies of civilian goods, causing their prices to skyrocket. These higher prices could pose a harsh burden for the poor in a country at war. Price controls may be necessary to minimize this burden. The longer the war and the bigger it is anticipated to be, the greater the need for price controls.

2. These economists prefaced the OPA literature with such disclaimers because they knew that price controls (in this case, price ceilings, for the most part) came with their own set of problems. They knew that chronic excess demand would result from price ceilings, that suppliers might leave markets with controlled prices if they could find more profitable lines of business, and that black markets for the short supplies of goods available were likely to emerge. The alternative to the imposition of price ceilings was to let markets adjust to new equilibrium prices at much higher levels, and then give poorer households income subsidies so that they could continue to subsist during the war. However, these income subsidies would have to be financed with new taxes that would result in distortions of their own. The question of who would receive the subsidies was also problematic.

3. The demands for farm products tend to be price and income inelastic. If demand is price inelastic, a decrease in price leads to a decrease in total revenue. Likewise, if demand is income inelastic, an increase in income leads to a less than proportionate increase in the quantity demanded. This is Engel's law in action. Computers, on the other hand, have demands that are relatively price and income elastic. Rapid technological change that causes the price of computers to fall could lead to increases in revenue for computer producers. Also, as income increases, the quantity demanded of computers will increase more than proportionately.

4. By restricting supply, acreage restriction programs were intended to reduce chronic excess supply in agricultural markets. With a smaller quantity supplied, the deficiency payments owed to farmers under target price policies would be reduced. However, the problem with acreage restriction programs is that farmers tend to remove their least fertile acres from production. Thus, the impact on agricultural supply may be minimal. Although target price policy with deficiency payments was an improvement over parity pricing with price floors, especially for consumers, the failure of acreage restrictions to limit supply very much resulted in deficiency payments that ran at high levels through the late 1980s into the 1990s.

Problems

1. a. The completed table is shown below.

Year	Prices Received by Farmers	Prices Paid by Farmers	Parity Price Ratio
1936	100	100	100
1937	110	120	92
1938	105	130	81
1939	115	150	77
1940	100	145	69

b. Farm incomes fell over the five-year period. The prices received by farmers in 1940 were only 69 percent of the prices they paid compared to the parity that existed in 1936.

c. The graph is shown below.

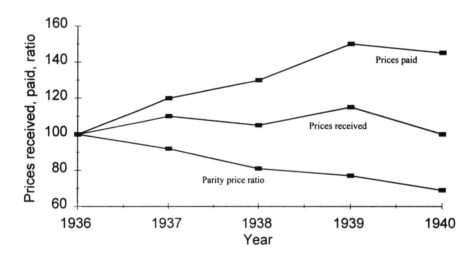

2. a. The demand and supply curves for the bagel market in Yellow Springs are shown in the graph on the next page. The equilibrium price is $.50 and the equilibrium quantity is 110.

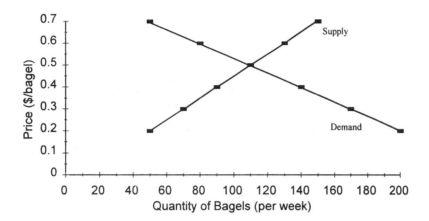

b. Foubert is setting a price ceiling since the $.40 per bagel price is a maximum price. Quantity demanded is equal to 140 bagels per week while quantity supplied is equal to 90 bagels per week at $.40 per bagel. There is an excess demand for bagels equal to 50 bagels per week. The consumers who are able to purchase the 90 bagels at $.40 per bagel are happy about the policy. They save $.10 per bagel. However, consumers previously purchased 110 bagels at $.50 per bagel, so fewer healthy bagels are being eaten as a result of the policy. Producers are also frustrated by the policy because they sell fewer bagels and earn less revenue.

c. The $.60 per bagel price is a price floor since it is a minimum price. At $.60 per bagel, the quantity demanded is 80 while the quantity supplied is 130 bagels per week. Under these circumstances, the village of Yellow Springs will have to purchase the 50 excess bagels supplied each week. Villagers will have to pay for these bagels with higher taxes. Moreover, bagels are more expensive for consumers in Yellow Springs. However, bakers who produce bagels love the policy. They earn more revenue as a result.

3. a. At the $6 price floor, the quantity demanded of soybeans is 200 million bushels, and the quantity supplied is 300 million bushels. The subsidy paid to farmers will be the cost of the excess supply of soybeans that must be purchased by the government, which is equal to $6 times 100 million bushels, or $600 million.

   b. If 250 million bushels are produced, consumers of soybeans will pay $5 to purchase 250 million bushels. Therefore, the deficiency payments to farmers will be $1 per bushel ($6 − $5) × 250 million bushels or $250 million. Consumers prefer this policy because the price of soybeans is $1 lower, and they get 250 million bushels instead of 200 million bushels.

   c. The subsidy is $350 million lower with the target price policy, or $600 million minus $250 million.

CHAPTER 7

BUSINESS OWNERSHIP AND ORGANIZATION: PROPRIETORSHIPS, PARTNERSHIPS, AND CORPORATIONS

Chapter in a Nutshell

A wide variety of different types of business firms operate in our economy. Not only do they differ according to the types of product they make, but they differ in how they are owned and organized. We can classify the vast array of business firms into three categories — **proprietorships, partnerships, and corporations**. Each category has distinct rules regarding the ownership and organization of firms. For example, **sole proprietorships** and **partnerships** are subject to **unlimited liability** — the owners of these businesses are personally liable for all of the debts they may incur. Corporations, on the other hand, have **limited liability**, meaning that shareholders can lose only what they have invested in the company. The financing of proprietorships, partnerships, and corporations differs significantly too. This chapter should make you keenly aware of the fact that no one type of business organization is ideal in all circumstances. Each has unique advantages and disadvantages.

After you study this chapter, you should be able to:

- Explain the implications of **unlimited liability** for **sole proprietorships**.
- Contrast **proprietorships** with **partnerships**.
- Describe the way **limited liability** works for **corporations**.
- Distinguish between **stocks** and **bonds** as methods of financing corporations.
- Present a scenario for a corporate takeover.
- Outline the organization of businesses in the United States.
- Profile stockholders of U.S. corporations.
- Compare and contrast **international** and **multinational corporations**.

Concept Check — See how you do on these multiple-choice questions.

1. The single most important advantage of a **sole proprietorship** is
   a. the ease of incorporation
   b. the ability to finance expansion through stock sales
   c. limited liability
   d. unlimited liability
   e. the independence it affords the owner

INTRO TO MICROECONOMICS

2. In a **partnership**, liability is _____ and _____ partner can be held liable for the business' entire debt.
   a. limited; neither
   b. limited; each
   c. high; all
   d. unlimited; each
   e. unlimited; neither

3. A corporate owner's — or **shareholder's** — liability is limited to the value of his or her shares because a corporation
   a. is less risky than a proprietorship or partnership
   b. exists as a legal entity independent of its owners
   c. provides liability insurance for shareholders
   d. can never go bankrupt
   e. can issue stocks

4. One disadvantage to the **corporate form of business organization** is that
   a. corporate dividends are taxed twice, once as corporate income and once as personal income
   b. decision making is complicated by the large number of shareholders
   c. the threat of a takeover looms large most of the time
   d. bondholders have first claim to a corporation's profits
   e. stockholders demand and get large dividends if any profits are made

5. The basic difference between **international corporations** and **multinationals** is that
   a. only international corporations have production facilities located overseas
   b. international corporations are larger
   c. only multinationals have production facilities located overseas
   d. multinationals export more than international corporations
   e. multinationals pay higher dividends to shareholders

Am I on the Right Track?

If you answered the questions above **e, d, b, a,** and **c**, then you're off to a great start. Most of the material in this chapter is descriptive. You may find it a nice break from the more analytical work we've been doing. Work through the questions below to make sure you understand the terms and concepts that are used to describe business ownership and organization.

Key Terms Quiz — Match the terms on the left with the definitions in the column on the right.

1. sole proprietorship
2. partnership
3. unlimited liability
4. corporation
5. stocks
6. stockholder/shareholder
7. corporate bond
8. dividend
9. multinational corporation

___ a. shares of a corporation that are claims on the firm's assets
___ b. an owner of part of a corporation
___ c. a firm owned by two or more people with unlimited liability
___ d. a corporation with production facilities overseas
___ e. a firm owned by one person
___ f. a part of a corporation's net income paid to stockholders
___ g. personal responsibility of the owners for all of the firm's debts
___ h. a corporate IOU
___ i. a firm with a legal identity separate from the people who own its stock

CHAPTER 7 BUSINESS OWNERSHIP AND ORGANIZATION

True-False Questions — If a statement is false, explain why.

1. Virtually all businesses in the United States are large corporations. (T/F)

2. The primary difference between a sole proprietorship and a partnership is that the partnership has more than one owner. (T/F)

3. The term *unlimited liability* means that a sole proprietor or a partner is personally responsible for all of the firm's debts. (T/F)

4. In a partnership, the partners and the firm are legally inseparable. (T/F)

5. Because a corporation is a separate legal entity, the shareholders' liability is limited to the value of their investments. (T/F)

6. One advantage of a partnership is the ability to acquire greater access to capital resources by taking on new partners. (T/F)

7. The law treats a corporation as a separate legal entity. (T/F)

8. Preferred stockholders are paid dividends before convertible stockholders. (T/F)

9. Common stock is defined as stock that allows its holder a vote in corporate decisions proportional to the stockholder's share of the outstanding common stock. (T/F)

10. Preferred stockholders, in addition to being allowed to vote on corporate decisions, are paid dividends before common stockholders. (T/F)

11. It might be better for a corporation to fund its activities by selling common stocks than by selling bonds because bondholders have first claim on any corporate profits, whereas a stock dividend need not be distributed. (T/F)

12. One difference between a bondholder and a stockholder in a corporation is that bondholders are lenders to the corporation while stockholders are actual owners of the corporation. (T/F)

13. A disadvantage of the corporate form of organization is that corporate profits are taxed twice, once as corporate profits and again as the personal income of dividend recipients, whereas profits for proprietorships and partnerships are only taxed once. (T/F)

INTRO TO MICROECONOMICS

14. A corporate takeover can occur when an individual or group is able to buy and control more than 50 percent of a corporation's outstanding common stock, thus controlling corporate decision making. (T/F)

15. A multinational corporation sells its products overseas but produces them domestically. (T/F)

Multiple-Choice Questions

1. Businesses in the United States exhibit different forms of business organization because
   a. diversification leads to lower risks
   b. each form has unique advantages that satisfy particular firms
   c. common stockholders vote to have different types of business organization in different firms
   d. establishing a corporation is complicated so few proprietorships and partnerships ever try
   e. proprietorships and partnerships are typically more profitable than corporations

2. A sole proprietorship is a business where all of the following are true **except** that
   a. the owner has complete control over decision making
   b. profits are only taxed once as the proprietor's income
   c. the proprietor is liable for losses to the extent of his or her personal assets
   d. the proprietorship is the most numerous type of business in the United States
   e. the proprietor can sell stock to increase its capital resources

3. Unlimited liability for sole proprietors means that
   a. they can lose everything they own if their businesses fail
   b. they should form corporations instead
   c. proprietors are liable for all the value of all the shares they own in a business
   d. a partnership appears relatively more attractive
   e. sole proprietorships are less risky to operate than corporations

4. In a partnership, the owners
   a. are sheltered somewhat from unlimited liability
   b. always split profits and losses 50 - 50
   c. may have access to more venture capital, but each loses some independence in decision making
   d. enjoy limited liability
   e. cannot be sued separately in the event of a business failure

5. The limited liability associated with the corporate form of ownership results from
   a. corporations existing as legal entities, separate and apart from their owners
   b. corporations being much less likely to experience losses
   c. banks that offer loans to corporations at low interest rates
   d. lower taxes on dividends
   e. the many stockholders who share liability

6. Common stock allows the holder to do all of the following **except**
   a. have a voice in day-to-day corporate decision making
   b. share in profits if a dividend is declared
   c. suffer a loss if the stock loses value
   d. sell out of the business quickly
   e. avoid double taxation

7. The order in which dividends are paid to different types of stockholders is
   a. common, preferred, convertible
   b. convertible, preferred, common
   c. convertible, common, preferred
   d. preferred, convertible, common
   e. common, convertible, preferred

8. Corporate bonds might be preferred to stocks by someone who wants to hold less risky assets because
   a. the government guarantees that bondholders will be reimbursed in the case of bankruptcy
   b. in the event of poor corporate performance, bondholders are paid before stockholders
   c. dividends are always lower than the interest paid on bonds
   d. corporations that issue bonds rarely incur losses
   e. bond prices always increase over the long run

9. Preferred stockholders receive their dividends _____ common stockholders and are _____ in corporate decisions.
   a. before; nonvoters
   b. before; voters
   c. after; nonvoters
   d. after; voters
   e. at the same time as; voters

10. Most stockholders are people who have
    a. only a small investment of a few thousand dollars in the stock market
    b. invested millions because only the very rich can afford to buy stocks
    c. lost and made thousands of dollars at a time because the market is so unpredictable
    d. large holdings in blue-chip stocks
    e. portfolios that total over $100,000

11. The primary difference between multinational corporations and international corporations is that
    a. multinationals sell in overseas markets whereas international corporations both sell and produce overseas
    b. international corporations sell in overseas markets whereas multinationals both sell and produce overseas
    c. multinationals are more profitable because they operate in more countries
    d. international corporations adopt technologies from all countries while multinationals use the technologies appropriate only to their home countries
    e. international corporations are more powerful financially

12. All of the following are characteristics of sole proprietorships **except** that
    a. there is a single owner
    b. profits are taxed twice
    c. liability is unlimited
    d. they are the most numerous type of business
    e. they may have a difficult time raising funds to expand the business

INTRO TO MICROECONOMICS

13. All of the following are characteristics of corporations **except** that
    a. the power of corporate managers is complete and cannot be challenged by stockholders
    b. liability is limited
    c. the corporation is a separate legal entity
    d. the corporation may gain access to funds by issuing more stock
    e. the management in a corporation may be threatened in the event of a takeover bid

14. When economists say that corporate profits paid to shareholders as dividends are taxed twice, they mean that
    a. the tax rate on corporate profits is twice as high as the tax rate on income
    b. corporations must pay sales taxes and taxes on profits before paying dividends
    c. people who own shares in corporations typically pay double the amount of non-shareholders in taxes
    d. dividends are taxed first as corporate profits, then as personal income for shareholders
    e. shares of stock are taxed when they are purchased and when they generate dividends

15. Two differences between common stock and preferred stock are that common stockholders receive dividends only after preferred stockholders receive theirs, and
    a. preferred stockholders can buy new shares at lower than market prices
    b. preferred stockholders have unlimited liability
    c. preferred stockholders are able to convert their shares to common stock
    d. preferred stockholders have voting privileges
    e. common stockholders have voting privileges

16. Between 1970 and 1993, the percentage of U.S. businesses that were proprietorships
    a. decreased so substantially that they became "an endangered species"
    b. stayed approximately the same, at roughly 25 percent
    c. decreased slightly, from 90 to 84 percent
    d. increased slightly, from 69 to 75 percent
    e. dwindled almost to zero as the family farm disappeared from the American landscape

17. In 1993, corporations were _____ in number compared to proprietorships and partnerships. However, their receipts account for approximately _____ of total business receipts in the U.S. economy.
    a. large; 75 percent
    b. small; 10 percent
    c. large; 90 percent
    d. small; 90 percent
    e. large; 10 percent

18. Stock ownership in the United States in 1992 was
    a. concentrated among a few wealthy, elderly people
    b. spread over 90 percent of the population
    c. declining as ownership became concentrated in the hands of corporate managers
    d. spread over about a quarter of the adult population
    e. limited essentially to stock brokers who understand how the stock market works

19. Indirect stock ownership is
    a. fairly rare because most people want to control their assets
    b. more widespread than direct ownership of stock through pension plans and life insurance policies
    c. very risky because of limited knowledge of portfolio composition
    d. centered in rural areas where access to financial markets is difficult
    e. on the wane in the United States due to low savings rates

20. A company whose export business overshadows its domestic business is referred to as
    a. a foreign firm
    b. an export specialist
    c. a multinational corporation
    d. an international corporation
    e. a foreign partnership

Fill in the Blanks

1. Both _____ and _____ are subject to unlimited liability.

2. One advantage for a corporation is _____ while a disadvantage is the _____ of dividends.

3. Nearly 75 percent of businesses in the United States are _____.

4. Many people own stock indirectly through _____ and _____.

5. A(n) _____ sells its products in overseas markets while a(n) _____ both produces and sells its products in overseas markets.

Discussion Questions

1. Why is there tremendous diversity in the types of businesses in most U.S. industries?

2. Discuss the advantages and disadvantages inherent in each of the following business types.

   a. Sole proprietorships

   b. Partnerships

INTRO TO MICROECONOMICS

    c. Corporations

3. Explain how corporate profits are taxed twice.

4. What are the rights and responsibilities of a common stockholder?

5. How do convertible, preferred, and common stocks differ from each other?

6. Is it riskier for a corporation to finance expansion through stocks or bonds? Why?

7. Which is a riskier asset for an individual to own, stocks or corporate bonds? Why?

8. Does the large number of proprietorships reflect the true extent of the role played by small businesses in the American economy?

9. How do the numbers of corporations in different size categories compare with their shares of total corporate receipts?

10. Who owns stocks? How much stock does the average shareholder own?

INTRO TO MICROECONOMICS

Everyday Applications

Interested in chartering your own corporation? It's relatively easy to do in Delaware. Each state has its own procedures for becoming a corporation, and Delaware's have long been regarded as simpler than other states. That is why so many corporations have Delaware charters. You can write to Delaware Registry Ltd., 3511 Silverside Rd., #105-EC, Wilmington, DE 19810 for a free kit that will get you started.

Economics Online

Every major corporation has a homepage now. Visit the Coca-Cola site (*http://www.coca-cola.com/*) and the McDonald's site (*http://www.mcdonalsds.com/main.html*) to get a feel for how these popular companies present themselves to the public on the Internet.

Answers to Questions

Key Terms Quiz

a. 5
b. 6
c. 2
d. 9
e. 1
f. 8
g. 3
h. 7
i. 4

True-False Questions

1. False. Corporations included 18.6 percent of American businesses in 1993. Proprietorships included some 75 percent of businesses and partnerships made-up the remaining 6.4 percent in 1993.
2. True
3. True
4. True
5. True
6. True
7. True
8. False. Convertible stockholders are paid dividends before preferred stockholders.
9. Truc
10. False. Preferred stockholders cannot vote on corporate decisions.
11. True
12. True
13. True
14. True
15. False. A multinational corporation sells and produces overseas.

Multiple-Choice Questions

1. b
2. e
3. a
4. c
5. a
6. a
7. b
8. b
9. a
10. a
11. b
12. b
13. a
14. d
15. e
16. d
17. d
18. d
19. b
20. d

CHAPTER 7   BUSINESS OWNERSHIP AND ORGANIZATION

Fill in the Blanks

1. sole proprietorships; partnerships
2. limited liability; double taxation
3. proprietorships
4. pension plans; life insurance policies
5. international corporation; multinational

Discussion Questions

1. Sole proprietorships, partnerships, and corporations coexist in most industries because some entrepreneurs prefer proprietorships and partnerships as ways to organize their firms. They may be operating on a different level of production than the corporations in their industries. Each type of business organization offers unique advantages and disadvantages.

2. a. Sole proprietorships have the advantages of independence of decision making and single taxation. The big disadvantage is unlimited liability. Also, it may be difficult to raise funds for business expansion.

    b. Partnerships have the advantages of somewhat greater access to funds for expansion and single taxation. However, they have all the disadvantages of proprietorships in addition to the fact that the partners may not always agree on appropriate policies.

    c. Corporations benefit from limited liability. However, their profits are taxed twice, and corporate managers may not always serve the interests of stockholders.

3. Corporate profits are taxed first as corporate net income. Then, because part of corporate profits is distributed as dividends, they are taxed a second time as personal income for shareholders.

4. Common stockholders have the right and responsibility to vote in corporate elections as well as the right to share in corporate profits if a dividend is declared. In theory, common stockholders exercise control over a corporation because they hire and fire management. Only rarely, however, do common stockholders succeed in drawing together the 50 percent plus one share votes necessary to oust management.

5. Preferred stockholders are paid dividends before common stockholders, but they cannot vote in corporate elections. Convertible stockholders are paid a dividend before preferred stockholders and can convert their shares to common stock if they so choose. Common stockholders have voting rights, and they may or may not get a dividend.

6. Bonds are riskier because the bondholders must be reimbursed out of corporate assets in the event of a poor business performance. On the other hand, firms have no obligation to pay dividends to stockholders.

7. Stocks are riskier because the entire investment can be lost, and no dividend is guaranteed. Bondholders have a prior claim over stockholders on the corporation's assets and are more likely to be reimbursed in the event of a poor business performance.

8. No, because proprietorships are large in number but their total receipts are small relative to corporations'. Proprietorships make up some 75 percent of businesses in the United States, but corporations account for almost 90 percent of business receipts.

9. Approximately three million corporations in the United States have receipts under $1 million

per year, and these account for 82.3 percent of all corporations. However, these smaller corporations comprise only 5.7 percent of corporate receipts. Corporations with receipts in excess of $50 million per year account for 67.5 percent of corporate receipts.

10. About one in four adult Americans owns stocks, but their holdings amount to, on average, only a few thousand dollars. Many more Americans are indirect owners of stock through pension plans and life insurance policies.

PART 2 — INTRODUCTION TO MICROECONOMICS

COMPREHENSIVE SAMPLE TEST

Give yourself 50 minutes to complete this exam and see how you do. The answers follow. Don't look until you are finished!

True-False Questions — If a statement is false, explain why. Each question is worth 2 points.

1. The price elasticity of demand measures the sensitivity of price to changes in quantity demanded. (T/F)

2. Goods that are complements have positive cross elasticities of demand. (T/F)

3. Total revenue increases when price decreases and demand is elastic. (T/F)

4. A consumer maximizes utility by consuming goods so that the ratios of marginal utility to price are equal to each other. (T/F)

5. Consumer surplus is the difference between the total utility of a good and its price. (T/F)

6. The law of diminishing marginal utility says that additional units of consumption add less to total utility. (T/F)

7. One result of price ceilings during World War II was the need to ration the available supply of many goods through ration coupons. (T/F)

8. Price floors for agricultural products lead to lower prices for consumers because surpluses are produced. (T/F)

9. A sole proprietorship has the benefit of limited liability. (T/F)

10. In the event of bankruptcy, stockholders can sue a corporation for the amount they invested. (T/F)

INTRO TO MICROECONOMICS

Multiple-Choice Questions — Each question is worth 2 points.

1. If corn prices increase by 20 percent and the quantity demanded of corn decreases by 10 percent, then the price elasticity of demand is
   a. .5
   b. 2
   c. 20
   d. 10
   e. 1

2. Ranked from the most to the least price elastic, we have
   a. market-day supply, short-run supply, long-run supply
   b. short-run supply, market-day supply, long-run supply
   c. long-run supply, market-day supply, short-run supply
   d. market-day supply, long-run supply, short-run supply
   e. long-run supply, short-run supply, market-day supply

3. Engel's law states that the demand for food is
   a. price inelastic
   b. price elastic because so many food alternatives exist
   c. income elastic because food choices depend on income level
   d. income inelastic because food consumption is insensitive to income changes
   e. completely insensitive to price changes

4. On Sundays, the Billy Goat Tavern in Chicago offers a Bears football cheeseburger special for $.95, which is $.50 less than the regular price. The tavern discovers that its total revenue from cheeseburgers increases. This suggests that
   a. the demand within the $.95 to $1.45 price range is inelastic
   b. the demand within the $.95 to $1.45 price range is elastic
   c. the price elasticity of demand within the $.95 to $1.45 price range is less than one
   d. the price elasticity of demand within the $.95 to $1.45 price range is one
   e. we need more data on specific prices and quantities to know the price elasticity of demand between these prices

5. All of the following pairs of goods **except** _____ could have a cross elasticity of demand equal to four.
   a. tea and coffee
   b. Miller Lite and Bud Lite
   c. chicken and fish
   d. hamburger and french fries
   e. rice and pasta

6. If the slope of a total utility function is positive and decreasing, then it exhibits
   a. the law of increasing costs
   b. the law of diminishing marginal utility
   c. negative marginal utility
   d. interpersonal comparisons of utility
   e. consumer sovereignty

140   PART 2   COMPREHENSIVE SAMPLE TEST

7. As the price of a good decreases, its marginal-utility-to-price ratio increases, causing consumers to purchase
   a. more, indicating a downward-sloping demand curve
   b. more of all substitute goods
   c. less of all complementary goods
   d. only goods that maximize utility
   e. more than their budgets will allow

8. If it is possible to make interpersonal comparisons of utility, a higher tax rate for upper-income individuals that transfers income to poorer individuals could
   a. contribute to an increase in society's utility level
   b. decrease the marginal utility of money for the rich
   c. create incentives for the rich to give more to charities
   d. increase the utility enjoyed by the rich
   e. decrease utility levels among the poor

9. Suppose the following chart represents the marginal utilities you derive from consuming hamburger, chicken, and bacon. The prices are as follows: hamburger = $2, chicken = $2, and bacon = $1. If you had a $10 budget, how much of each good would you buy?

Quantity	Hamburgers	Chicken	Bacon
1	32	38	20
2	30	35	17
3	28	31	15
4	25	26	12
5	21	22	10

   a. 1 hamburger, 2 chickens, 4 bacon
   b. 1 hamburger, 3 chickens, 2 bacon
   c. 2 hamburgers, 2 chickens, 2 bacon
   d. 2 hamburgers, 3 chickens, 0 bacon
   e. 3 hamburgers, 1 chicken, 2 bacon

10. Jennifer consumes both apples and bread. If Jennifer is consuming quantities of apples and bread such that the marginal-utility-to-price ratio for apples is higher than it is for bread, in order to maximize utility, she should
    a. spend more on apples and less on bread
    b. spend more on both goods
    c. check to make sure she has money left over and spend it on apples
    d. check to make sure she has money left over and spend it on bread
    e. spend more on bread and less on apples

11. If a price ceiling is imposed on gasoline, one can expect
    a. suppliers of gasoline to reduce their supplies so that the price rises to match the ceiling
    b. demanders to increase their demands so that the price rises to match the ceiling
    c. a chronic excess supply of gasoline to result
    d. a chronic excess demand for gasoline to result
    e. a temporary increase in the price of gasoline

INTRO TO MICROECONOMICS

12. The complete end to subsidization of agriculture in the United States would lead to
    a. a burst of new farmers entering the newly deregulated industry
    b. an increase in the rate at which farmers leave agriculture
    c. a rise in the demand for farm products
    d. an increase in deficiency payments
    e. the government having to buy the surpluses

13. When target pricing replaced parity pricing in 1973, farmers were to be paid subsidies if
    a. they had very low incomes
    b. the equilibrium price fell below the target price
    c. they were family farmers
    d. they exported most of their product
    e. their soil was prone to erosion

14. An effective price floor lies
    a. below the equilibrium price
    b. above the equilibrium price
    c. below the target price
    d. above the target price
    e. equal to the equilibrium price

15. One problem with acreage restriction programs intended to reduce agricultural surpluses is that
    a. farmers were unwilling to participate
    b. farmers tended to retire their worst acreage with little effect on supply
    c. consumers complained about the higher prices that resulted
    d. deficiency payments rose to even higher levels
    e. exports were reduced

16. Suppose that Tom's Hats, a corporation, sells the majority of its hats in other countries but produces them in only one factory located in Peoria, Illinois. This company is a(n)
    a. multinational corporation
    b. national corporation
    c. monopoly corporation
    d. regional corporation
    e. international corporation

17. The largest share of total receipts from business sales in the United States is generated by
    a. corporations
    b. small businesses
    c. proprietorships
    d. partnerships
    e. firms with unlimited liability

18. For investors, compared to stocks, bonds are
    a. more risky
    b. less risky
    c. similar in risk levels
    d. able to generate higher dividends
    e. a better way to gain influence over corporate decisions

19. A clear advantage of proprietorships over corporations is
    a. unlimited liability
    b. limited liability
    c. single taxation of profits
    d. easier access to funds for expansion of the business
    e. the absence of business partners

20. One reason for a corporation to prefer stocks to bonds as a means to raise funds for expansion is that
    a. new stockholders who vote in corporate decisions provide management with new insights
    b. the corporation does not have to make payments to stockholders
    c. bondholders aid management in their daily activities
    d. the government taxes bonds twice
    e. stocks are cheaper to sell than bonds

Discussion Questions/Problems — Each question is worth 10 points.

1. a. Suppose that the price of fresh artichokes increases from $1.00 each to $1.60 each and Mary's quantity demanded per week falls from 5 to 2. What is Mary's price elasticity of demand for artichokes between these prices? Show your work. Interpret the number you have calculated.

   b. If other consumers in the artichoke market have elasticities similar to Mary's, will total revenue for suppliers of artichokes rise or fall as a result of the increase in artichoke prices? Explain.

2. Julien is preparing for a trans-Atlantic flight and is purchasing prerecorded cassette tapes and magazines in an airport shop. The tapes cost $5 each and the magazines cost $3 each. The table below shows Julien's marginal utilities from consumption of different quantities of tapes and magazines.

Quantity	MU from Tapes	MU/P for Tapes	MU from Mags	MU/P for Mags
1	100		60	
2	85		55	
3	70		45	
4	50		30	
5	25		20	
6	10		10	

a. If Julien has $24 to spend on tapes and magazines, how many of each will he purchase? Complete the marginal-utility-to-price columns in the table and use the information to justify your answer.

b. Suppose the price of magazines falls to $2. How many tapes and how many magazines will Julien purchase now? How did you get your answer?

c. Sketch Julien's demand curve for magazines. Why does it slope downward?

3. The graph below shows the market for corn under parity pricing.

a. What is the price floor in this diagram? Is there an excess supply? If so, how large is it? Explain

b. What is the size of the subsidy to farmers in this case? Show your calculations.

c. Suppose this market is allowed to adjust to its equilibrium. Explain in detail what would happen as a result.

INTRO TO MICROECONOMICS

4. Describe each of the three forms of business organization and identify the main advantages and disadvantages associated with each type.

Answers to the Sample Test over Part 2

True-False Questions

1. False. The price elasticity of demand measures the sensitivity of quantity demanded to changes in price.
2. False. Goods that are complements have negative cross elasticities of demand.
3. True
4. True
5. False. Consumer surplus is the difference between what a consumer is willing to pay for a good and what he or she actually pays.
6. True
7. True
8. False. Price floors raise food prices above their equilibrium levels, making food more expensive for consumers.
9. False. A sole proprietorship is subject to unlimited liability.
10. False. Stockholders assume the risks and uncertainties of enterprise. If the firm goes bankrupt, shareholders lose their investment in the firm.

Multiple-Choice Questions

1. a	6. b	11. d	16. e
2. e	7. a	12. b	17. a
3. d	8. a	13. b	18. b
4. b	9. b	14. b	19. c
5. d	10. a	15. b	20. b

Discussion Questions/Problems

1. a. The price elasticity of demand for artichokes between these prices is equal to

$$e = \frac{\frac{5-2}{\frac{5+2}{2}}}{\frac{1-1.6}{\frac{1+1.6}{2}}} = 1.857$$

A 1 percent increase in price leads to a 1.857 percent decrease in the quantity demanded of artichokes.

b. Total revenue will fall because demand is elastic and price increases lead to a more than proportional decrease in the quantity demanded. Thus, total revenue, equal to price times quantity, must fall. Mary's demand for artichokes is elastic.

2. a. The completed table is shown below.

Quantity	MU from Tapes	MU/P for Tapes	MU from Mags	MU/P for Mags
1	100	20	60	20
2	85	17	55	18.33
3	70	14	45	15
4	50	10	30	10
5	25	5	20	6.67
6	10	2	10	3.33

Julien will purchase items in the following order — magazine, tape, magazine, tape, magazine, tape. These purchases will exhaust his budget of $24.

b. The MU/P column for magazines changes to 30, 27.5, 22.5, 15, 10, and 5. The order of purchases is now magazine, magazine, magazine, tape, tape, magazine, tape. Julien spends $23 of his $24 this way. Thus, he buys 4 magazines and 3 tapes.

c. Julien's demand curve for magazines is shown on the next page. It slopes downward because as the price decreases, Julien's satisfaction per dollar spent on magazines increases, so he purchases more of them.

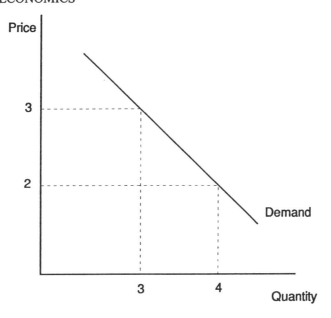

3. a. The price floor in the diagram is $7.50. The excess supply is 1,200 minus 400 equals 800 bushels. This is the difference between the quantity supplied and the quantity demanded at the price floor.

   b. The subsidy to farmers is equal to $7.50 times 800 bushels or $6,000.

   c. The market would adjust to the equilibrium price of $5.00 per bushel as suppliers competed with each other, lowering the price from the $7.50 level. As the price decreases, the quantity supplied decreases and the quantity demanded increases until the two are equal at 800 bushels. Consumers are better off and farmers are worse off as a result.

4. Sole proprietorships are just that — businesses owned by one person. Independent decision making is the primary advantage associated with this type of business. Many sole proprietorships are family businesses, including family farms.

   While proprietorships enjoy the advantages of operating independently, they are subject to unlimited liability should the business fail. This is because the proprietor and the business are legally one entity. A sole proprietor risks almost everything he or she owns if the business fails.

   Having a partner means spreading some of the risks and acquiring access to more capital that can be used in the business. However these advantages over a proprietorship have their own drawbacks. Decision making too, must be shared. And business partners don't always agree. Moreover, the risks assumed by partners are not always evenly spread. Suppose you are in partnership with someone who has zero wealth. If the business fails, you may be totally liable for all debts since your partner has nothing to contribute.

   Relief from unlimited liability comes in the form of the corporation, which exists as a separate legal entity. A part owner or shareholder in a corporation is liable for the corporation losses only to the extent of the value of the shares. If all you own is $100 worth of stocks, that's all you're liable to lose. Your personal assets are protected. A shareholder or group of shareholders needs to own only 50 percent plus one of the corporation's common stock or shares to control it. Each share gives its owners one vote out of the total votes that represent the total shares outstanding. A sole proprietor can change his or her business to a corporation and maintain complete control as long as the proprietor owns all the shares. Many proprietors have done that.

Corporations can issue new stock in order to raise more capital for business expansion. New shares are printed and sold to old or new stockholders. In this way, ownership becomes more diverse. The primary reason people own stock is to earn profit, which they receive in the form of dividends. Some shareholders are willing to forgo their right to vote for a better chance at dividends. They buy **preferred stock**, which gives them priority over common stock when dividends are issued. A third type of stock is **convertible stock**. Its owners have highest priority when dividends are paid, and although the owners have no voting rights, they have the option of converting these stocks to common stock.

Corporations can also raise capital by selling corporate bonds. These are the corporation's IOUs that people buy on the bond market. The corporation promises to pay a fixed rate of interest on the bonds. Bonds are less risky than stocks because bondholders are paid before any stockholder receives dividends.

You probably wonder why anyone would prefer to operate as a proprietorship or partnership when they can incorporate and avoid unlimited liability. The main disadvantage of the corporation is that profit is taxed twice — first it is taxed as corporate profit, then the after-tax profit is taxed again as personal income of the dividend recipients. Another disadvantage is that individual stockholders, although owners, really have no influence on corporate decision making.

CHAPTER 8

COSTS OF PRODUCTION

Chapter in a Nutshell

This chapter gives an in-depth look at the **costs of production** for firms, both in the **short run** and in the **long run**. Although production techniques may differ from one industry to another, and even among firms operating in the same industry, there are features of production costs that are common to all firms. When an **entrepreneur** makes a decision to start a business, this commitment usually involves **total fixed costs** for items such as mortgage payments and insurance. Total fixed costs do not vary with the level of output. Even if the firm produces nothing at all, total fixed costs exist. When output is produced, the firm incurs **total variable costs** that correspond to payments made for resources such as labor and materials. The sum of total fixed costs and total variable costs is equal to **total costs**. Total fixed costs, total variable costs, and total costs can be graphed to show the three total cost curves.

From these three total cost curves, we can derive four other cost curves. **Average total cost** is found by dividing total costs by output. Similarly, **average variable cost** is total variable costs divided by output, and **average fixed cost** is total fixed costs divided by output. **Marginal cost** is the change in total costs that occurs when one more unit of output is produced. We will examine the usual shapes of all of these curves, as well as the special relationships among them.

Labor is often the most important of the variable cost items, and its importance is reflected in the shape of the total variable cost curve. **Labor costs** tend to increase at a decreasing rate when output is low, but as output increases, labor costs eventually rise at an increasing rate. The character of the total variable cost curve reflects labor costs by rising at a decreasing rate at low levels of output and at an increasing rate as output increases. The portion of the total variable cost curve that rises at an increasing rate exhibits the **law of diminishing returns**. In the short run, some resources used in production are fixed, while it is possible to vary the amount of labor employed. Adding more labor to production when these resources are fixed will increase total product, but by smaller and smaller amounts.

The firm's **long-run average total cost curve** shows the envelope curve formed by drawing a line tangent to the firm's short-run average total cost curves. The long-run average total cost curve shows the firm in its long-run position when it is able to change the quantity of all the resources used in production. When the long-run average total cost curve is decreasing, there are **economies of scale**; when it is a horizontal line, there are **constant returns to scale**; and when it is increasing, there are **diseconomies of scale**.

The characteristic shapes of the cost curves that are presented in this chapter are supported by ample empirical evidence.

After studying this chapter, you should be able to:

- Describe how someone becomes an **entrepreneur**.
- Explain **short-run** commitments to **fixed costs**.
- Distinguish between **total fixed costs** and **total variable costs**.
- Construct an example to show the **law of diminishing returns**.
- List and explain the determinants of **labor costs**.
- Draw curves to show **total costs**, **average total costs**, **average variable costs**, and **marginal costs**.

- Contrast **economies of scale**, **constant returns to scale**, and **diseconomies of scale**.

Concept Check — See how you do on these multiple-choice questions.

1. One of the requirements for success as an **entrepreneur** is
   a. access to funds to start the business
   b. choosing a low-risk business to enter
   c. beginner's luck
   d. a college education
   e. an aversion to risk taking

Not everyone can become an entrepreneur. Why is that? Will you be able to start your own business with no outside help after you graduate?

2. Committing to **fixed costs** often means that an entrepreneur must
   a. produce services instead of goods
   b. study the history of costs
   c. borrow to finance the purchase of plant and machinery
   d. vary expenditures on fixed costs as output varies
   e. cut these costs when output is low

What sort of goods are purchased with fixed-cost expenditures?

3. As output increases, **average total cost** and **average variable cost** approach the same value because
   a. average fixed costs are always quite low
   b. total costs don't include fixed costs
   c. fixed costs are sunk costs
   d. marginal cost is less than average total cost
   e. average fixed costs decrease as output increases

Remember that average total costs equal the sum of average variable costs and average fixed costs.

4. **Diseconomies of scale** result from
   a. economies of scale
   b. constant returns to scale
   c. problems with technology
   d. problems managing a large firm
   e. higher fixed costs

This question is related to the reason for the upturn in long-run average costs at high levels of output.

5. **Average total cost** decreases as long as **marginal cost** is
   a. zero
   b. less than average total cost
   c. less than average fixed cost
   d. rising
   e. greater than average variable cost

If your next test score in economics is lower than the average of all your test scores, what happens to the average?

THE MICROECONOMICS OF PRODUCT MARKETS 151

Am I on the Right Track?

Your answers to the questions above should be **a, c, e, d,** and **b**. One critical aspect of this chapter is to relate the calculation of costs to the way they are graphed. After you work through the Key Terms Quiz, a graphing tutorial is presented that walks you through the calculation of average costs and marginal costs and carefully considers how the graphs for the average cost concepts are drawn.

Key Terms Quiz — Match the terms on the left with the definitions in the column on the right.

1. total fixed costs
2. total variable costs
3. law of diminishing returns
4. labor productivity
5. quality of labor
6. total costs
7. average total cost
8. average fixed cost
9. average variable cost
10. marginal cost
11. economies of scale
12. diseconomies of scale
13. constant returns to scale
14. short run
15. long run

_____ a. the addition to total cost from producing one more unit
_____ b. output per laborer per hour
_____ c. decreases in average cost that accompany increases in scale of output
_____ d. addition to output from each additional worker diminishes
_____ e. time enough to change only some of the resources for production
_____ f. total fixed cost divided by the quantity produced
_____ g. costs per unit of output that are constant as the scale of production increases
_____ h. time enough to change all of the resources for production
_____ i. costs that don't change with the level of production
_____ j. average fixed cost plus average variable cost
_____ k. total fixed costs plus total variable costs
_____ l. costs that vary with the level of production
_____ m. differences between workers in ability and experience
_____ n. total variable cost divided by the quantity produced
_____ o. increasing average total costs due to management problems as the scale of production increases

Graphing Tutorial

There are quite a few new graphs to learn in this chapter. In this section, we'll focus on the average total cost, average variable cost, average fixed cost, and marginal cost curves. These curves are frequently drawn together, and they are very important for work you will do in the next several chapters. A picture of a firm's average cost and marginal cost curves can be combined with price information to find out whether the firm will be profitable or not. Certainly, this is an important issue. We'll address the problem of maximizing profit in the next chapter. Right now, our goal is to understand the nature of a firm's costs of production and how to properly represent them in a graph.

Consider the following data for the Merkle Broom Company in Paris, Illinois. The table on the next page shows the monthly output of brooms, total fixed costs, total variable costs, and total costs for the broom company. The first column shows monthly broom output measured in thousands. The second column shows the total fixed costs of producing from 0 to 10,000 brooms per month. Notice that it is fixed at $15,000. This fixed expenditure corresponds to the fixed cost of the factory. If the owners of Merkle Broom Company took out a loan to build their factory and the monthly payment on the loan is $15,000, then these are its fixed costs. Look at the third column in the table. This column shows the total variable costs of producing different quantities of brooms. The variable costs vary with the quantity of brooms produced. Variable costs correspond to labor costs and the costs of the raw materials that go into the manufacture of brooms — broom corn, twine for binding, and wooden handles, in addition to paint, dyes, and packaging materials. To produce more brooms requires more of all of these inputs. Of these inputs, labor is the most important. Look at how total variable costs change as output increases. At first, total variable costs rise at a decreasing rate up to an output level of

4,000 brooms. Then, total variable costs rise at an increasing rate. Beyond 4,000 brooms, each additional 1,000 brooms produced costs more than the previous 1,000 brooms. This is due to the law of diminishing returns. As more workers are added to production, each one adds less to total product than did the one before. Therefore, proportionately more labor must be hired to get the same 1,000-broom increase; hence, total variable costs begin to increase at an increasing rate. The fourth column shows the total costs of producing these different quantities of brooms. If you were to graph total variable cost and total cost, the two curves would lie parallel to each other with the vertical distance between them equal to total fixed cost.

Quantity of Brooms (1,000s)	Total Fixed Costs ($1,000s)	Total Variable Costs ($1,000s)	Total Costs ($1,000s)
0	15	0	15
1	15	12	27
2	15	18	33
3	15	22	37
4	15	24	39
5	15	30	45
6	15	39	54
7	15	54	69
8	15	72	87
9	15	94	109
10	15	122	137

Suppose that Oscar Merkle, the owner of Merkle Brooms, wants to know the average costs of production. This is clearly an important piece of information. By comparing the average cost of a broom with its price, Oscar will know whether he is making or losing money on each broom produced. Average costs can be computed from the data presented in the table above. For example, average fixed cost is equal to total fixed cost divided by quantity. This quotient gives you the fixed cost per broom. Similarly, average variable cost is equal to total variable cost divided by quantity, and average total cost is equal to total cost divided by quantity. A table showing the average costs of production for the various output levels is shown on the following page. One other variable is included in the last column of the table — marginal cost. Marginal cost is the change in total cost divided by the change in output. You could also calculate the marginal cost from the total variable cost by dividing the change in total variable cost by the change in output. Do you see why these two computations give the same result? The only difference between total cost and total variable cost is total fixed cost. So, our calculations show that the marginal cost per broom of the first 1,000 brooms is $12,000/1,000 or $12. For the second 1,000 brooms we have $6,000/1,000 or $6. Make sure you understand where all these numbers came from.

THE MICROECONOMICS OF PRODUCT MARKETS

Quantity of Brooms (1,000s)	Average Fixed Cost ($/broom)	Average Variable Cost ($/broom)	Average Total Cost ($/broom)	Marginal Cost ($/broom)
0				
1	15.00	12.00	27.00	12
2	7.50	9.00	16.50	6
3	5.00	7.33	12.33	4
4	3.75	6.00	9.75	2
5	3.00	6.00	9.00	6
6	2.50	6.50	9.00	9
7	2.14	7.71	9.86	15
8	1.88	9.00	10.88	18
9	1.67	10.44	12.11	22
10	1.50	12.20	13.70	28

Now that we have our data organized, we can proceed with graphing the average cost and marginal cost curves. As usual, we plot the quantity on the horizontal axis and the cost values, measured in dollars per broom, vertically. A graph of these curves is shown below.

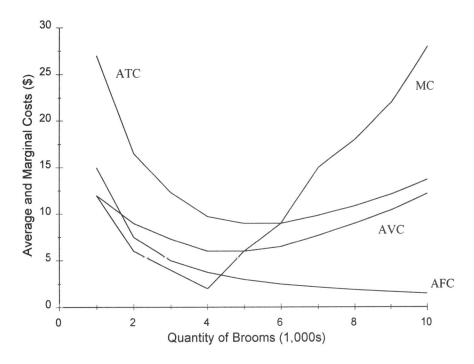

The marginal cost, average total cost, average variable cost, and average fixed cost curves are labeled MC, ATC, AVC, and AFC, respectively. Note that the ATC, AVC, and MC all have characteristic U-shapes. The ATC and AVC approach each other as output increases because the difference between them is the AFC, which gets smaller as output increases. The MC intersects the AVC and the ATC at their minimums. When MC is less than AVC or ATC, the average costs must fall because a marginal cost that is less than the average is added to the total cost. You see, don't you? The smaller marginal cost value pulls the average costs down. Similarly, when MC is greater than AVC or ATC, the average costs must rise because a marginal cost that is greater than the average is added to total cost. The larger marginal cost value pulls the average costs up.

You will encounter this kind of a picture of a firm's average and marginal costs often from this chapter onward. The exercises below give you a chance to practice interpreting and drawing average and marginal costs.

Graphing Pitfalls

Consider the average total cost and marginal cost curves shown below. What's wrong with them? These curves aren't drawn correctly. Marginal cost always intersects average total cost at its minimum.

This graph is incorrect because the marginal cost curve doesn't intersect the average total cost curve at its minimum point.

True-False Questions — If a statement is false, explain why.

1. More people would probably become entrepreneurs if start-up capital were more readily available. (T/F)

2. Entrepreneurs rarely, if ever, have much experience in the businesses they enter. (T/F)

3. The short run refers to a time period of one year or less. (T/F)

4. Fixed costs rise as the level of output rises. (T/F)

5. In general, a larger outlay for fixed cost assets provides a firm with greater productive capacity. (T/F)

6. Total variable cost is unaffected by the law of diminishing returns. (T/F)

7. Labor is typically the most significant component of total variable costs. (T/F)

8. Labor productivity increases continuously as the size of the labor force is increased. (T/F)

9. Beyond some point in production, total variable cost increases at an increasing rate. (T/F)

10. Average total cost is equal to total cost divided by quantity. (T/F)

11. For the law of diminishing returns to apply, at least one factor of production must be held constant. (T/F)

12. Whenever marginal cost is less than average total cost, average total cost must be decreasing. (T/F)

13. A firm can avoid encountering diseconomies of scale in production by continuously increasing the number of its manufacturing plants. (T/F)

14. If an increase in the scale of a firm's operations causes a decrease in the average total cost, then the firm is said to benefit from economies of scale. (T/F)

15. Diseconomies of scale exist because of overcrowded labor conditions. (T/F)

Multiple-Choice Questions

1. Entrepreneurship is attractive to those who practice it because
    a. it is a chance to make high profit without having financial or technical expertise
    b. it provides an alternative to working for someone else
    c. it is based mainly on luck or chance
    d. it means never having to face unemployment
    e. unlike others forms of activity, very few actually lose money

2. If a firm is operating in the short run, then
    a. some of the resources used in production are fixed
    b. all resources used in production are fixed
    c. increases in output can be achieved only by increasing the use of one resource
    d. there is ample time to alter both the amount of labor and the amount of capital employed
    e. all resources used in production can be changed

3. By purchasing a larger fixed-cost item, like the maxiboat discussed in the text, an entrepreneur incurs higher start-up costs but benefits from
   a. greater freedom from risk
   b. lower operating costs
   c. greater fixed-cost flexibility
   d. paying off larger debt at lower rates of interest
   e. greater production capacity

4. Labor productivity refers to the
   a. work ethic of the firm's laborers
   b. willingness of workers to work overtime until a job is done
   c. output per laborer per hour
   d. quality of work a laborer does
   e. human capital associated with a particular labor skill

5. Imagine a situation where the firm's total fixed cost is zero. In this case, the firm's
   a. MC curve is a straight line
   b. TC curve is a straight line
   c. TVC curve is a straight line
   d. ATC = AVC
   e. MC = ATC

6. Some cost items are referred to as variable cost items because
   a. they vary from firm to firm in an industry
   b. they vary from industry to industry
   c. they vary from country to country
   d. their costs vary depending on the level of production
   e. their costs vary over time

7. Labor is a variable cost item whose costs will usually rise with production levels at a(n) _____ rate at first but then rise at a(n) _____ rate because of changes in labor productivity, quality, and price.
   a. decreasing; increasing
   b. increasing; decreasing
   c. constant; decreasing
   d. constant; increasing
   e. increasing; constant

8. The graph shown on the next page depicts total variable costs such that beyond an output level of 10,000
   a. output increases at an increasing rate
   b. total variable cost rises at an increasing rate
   c. total variable cost rises at a constant rate
   d. total variable cost is constant
   e. the firm should cut back

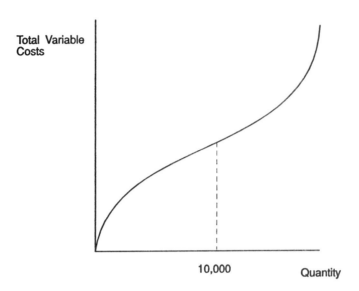

9. Because total cost is the sum of total fixed cost and total variable cost, the total cost curve has the same shape as the _____ curve but is shifted _____ by the amount of total fixed costs.
   a. average cost; up
   b. total fixed cost; up
   c. total fixed cost; down
   d. total variable cost; down
   e. total variable cost; up

10. The "envelope curve" refers to
    a. the long-run average total cost curve
    b. the economies of scale segment of a cost curve
    c. the curve business people believe explains their costs of production
    d. the short-run average total cost curve
    e. the socioeconomic environment that defines a cost curve

11. Marginal cost and total cost are related such that
    a. marginal cost is the change in total cost resulting from a change in the quantity produced
    b. marginal cost is total cost divided by the level of output
    c. marginal cost is greater than total cost at any level of output
    d. marginal cost is decreasing when the total cost curve's slope becomes very steep
    e. marginal cost is always greater than total cost

12. Marginal cost and average total cost are related such that
    a. when marginal cost is decreasing, average total cost is increasing
    b. when marginal cost is at a minimum, so is average total cost
    c. when average total cost is at a minimum, marginal cost and average total cost are equal
    d. when marginal cost is at a minimum, marginal cost and average total cost are equal
    e. marginal cost is always less than average total cost

13. Average total cost is defined as _____ while marginal cost is defined as _____.
    a. the change in total cost divided by the change in quantity; total cost divided by quantity
    b. total cost divided by quantity; the change in total cost divided by the change in quantity
    c. the change in quantity divided by the change in total cost; quantity divided by total cost
    d. quantity divided by total cost; the change in quantity divided by the change in total cost
    e. average variable cost minus average fixed cost; any small addition to costs

14. Diseconomies of scale result when
    a. diminishing returns become apparent
    b. a particular input becomes more expensive at high levels of output
    c. technology fails to improve
    d. average total costs increase at high levels of output due to inefficiencies in management
    e. further growth for the firm is impossible

15. The long run is a time period long enough so that all of the following are true **except** that
    a. the firm has no fixed commitments
    b. no costs are fixed
    c. firms can alter the size of their operations
    d. marginal cost is at a minimum
    e. all costs are, by definition, variable costs

16. Suppose that you are the manager of a factory producing compact discs. You observe that for the first ten workers hired, each one adds increasing amounts to total product, but starting with the eleventh worker, they each add smaller and smaller amounts to total product. You are observing
    a. the law of increasing cost
    b. diseconomies of scale
    c. the average total cost curve
    d. the law of diminishing returns
    e. the law of diminishing total product

17. Economies of scale exist when _____ and diseconomies of scale exist when _____.
    a. increasing firm size leads to lower average total costs; increasing firm size leads to higher average total costs
    b. firms that increase their size are successful; businesses fail
    c. firms can change all resources; firms can change only some resources
    d. firms are large; firms are small
    e. firms expand; firms contract

18. The text says "behind every cost curve is a socioeconomic structure." This means that
    a. social status often dictates which entrepreneurs succeed and which fail
    b. the ability to produce efficiently depends, to a large extent, on human relations
    c. firms count on government as well as social institutions and habits to control cost
    d. the availability of social institutions, such as schools and hospitals, is a prerequisite to modern production
    e. every material cost, whether fixed or variable, has an unintended effect on social relations

THE MICROECONOMICS OF PRODUCT MARKETS

19. When a firm engages in downsizing along its long-run ATC, it typically
    a. increases its productive capacity to reduce its short-run ATC
    b. reduces its productive capacity to reduce its short-run ATC
    c. increases its productive capacity to capture economies of scale
    d. decreases its productive capacity to capture diseconomies of scale
    e. lowers its long-run ATC curve to reduce its short-run ATC

20. Most business managers _____ with the economists' conception of the U-shaped average total cost curve because _____.
    a. agree; their own cost curves are U-shaped
    b. agree; they believe other firms have U-shaped cost curves, even if they don't
    c. disagree; they rarely produce in the range where average total costs are rising
    d. disagree; they rarely produce in the range where average total costs are falling
    e. disagree; they know no two firms are alike so that average total cost could be, or not be, U-shaped

Fill in the Blanks

1. An example of a _____ is a monthly payment that a business must make regardless of the level of production.

2. The cost of labor increases at a(n) _____ rate at a low level of output and at a(n) _____ rate at higher levels of output for three reasons.

3. The reasons for the behavior of the cost of labor just described are _____, _____, and _____.

4. As output increases, the average _____ cost approaches the average _____ cost because the average _____ cost decreases.

5. In the _____, at least one factor of production is fixed, but in the _____, all factors of production can be varied.

Discussion Questions

1. Why do some people decide to become entrepreneurs, and why do others choose to work for a wage or a salary?

2. What is the difference between fixed and variable costs? Explain the shape of the total variable cost curve and explain why the total cost and total variable cost curves are parallel.

3. How does a firm such as the Merkle Broom Company described in the graphing tutorial use its average total cost curve to find out if a given price will result in a profit or a loss? What is the lowest price that the Merkle Broom Company could sell brooms for and still avoid a loss? Explain.

4. What is the difference between marginal cost and average total cost?

5. Discuss the factors that give rise to economies of scale and diseconomies of scale.

Problems

1. Suppose that you are the owner of a new microbrewery in a midwestern college town. The table below shows your total costs of production per month.

Quantity of Beer (cases per month)	Total Fixed Cost ($)	Total Variable Cost ($)	Total Cost ($)
0	1,000	0	1,000
100	1,000	600	1,600
200	1,000	1,000	2,000
300	1,000	1,300	2,300
400	1,000	2,200	3,200
500	1,000	3,300	4,300
600	1,000	4,800	5,800

THE MICROECONOMICS OF PRODUCT MARKETS

a. On the axes provided below, sketch the total fixed cost, total variable cost, and total cost curves.

b. How are the total variable cost and total cost curves positioned relative to one another in your sketch? What accounts for this positioning?

c. Does the total variable cost curve have the shape that you would expect from the discussion presented in the text? What accounts for this shape?

2. a. Using the information presented in problem 1, fill in the following table.

Quantity of Beer (cases per month)	Average Fixed Cost ($/case)	Average Variable Cost ($/case)	Average Total Cost ($/case)	Marginal Cost ($/case)
0				
100				
200				
300				
400				
500				
600				

b. On the axes provided on the next page, graph the information you calculated in the table above.

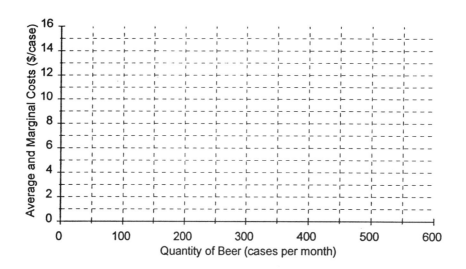

c. Suppose the price of a case of beer is $10. What is the minimum number of cases per month that you could produce and sell and still cover your costs of production? How do you know?

3. Suppose there's a firm that manufactures umbrellas called the Rain All You Want But I Don't Get Wet Company. The table below displays some of its cost structure.

Quantity of Umbrellas	TFC	TVC	TC	MC	ATC	AVC	AFC
0							
1							
2							
3							
4							
5		24	34				
6		38					
7			68				
8			98				

a. What is the total fixed cost of producing 2 umbrellas? How do you know?

b. What is the marginal cost of the sixth umbrella? How do you know?

c. Calculate the average fixed cost of the fifth unit. Show your work.

d. Calculate the total variable cost and the average variable cost of producing 8 units. Show your work.

Everyday Applications

Nearly everyone has had the opportunity to be part of a fund-raising effort for an organization. Fund raising is hard work, and costly too. Consider your own experience with the business of collecting cash donations. Did the process involve fixed and variable costs? Was there a marginal cost associated with generating additional dollar donations? How did the revenues generated compare to the costs?

Economics Online

Costs of production figure importantly in the work of engineers. Cost engineers are concerned with combining fixed and variable cost resources to produce output. Often, the goal is to achieve a certain level of output at minimum cost. The Association for the Advancement of Cost Engineering through Total Cost Management has a site (*http://www.aacei.org/*). Do you notice differences in the way economists and engineers view costs of production?

Answers to Questions

Key Terms Quiz

a. 10
b. 4
c. 11
d. 3
e. 14
f. 8
g. 13
h. 15
i. 1
j. 7
k. 6
l. 2
m. 5
n. 9
o. 12

True-False Questions

1. True
2. False. Entrepreneurs typically have some background in the businesses they enter.
3. False. The short run is the period of time in which a producer can vary some, but not all, of the resources used in production.
4. False. Fixed costs don't change with the level of output.
5. True
6. False. Total variable cost rises at an increasing rate because of diminishing returns.
7. True
8. False. Labor productivity might fall due to the law of diminishing returns and hiring workers with less experience and ability.
9. True
10. True
11. True

12. True
13. False. Diseconomies of scale mean that the firm's long-run average total cost increases. By cutting back on the size of the operation and streamlining complex managerial and bureaucratic hierarchies, the firm can decrease long-run average total cost.
14. True
15. False. Diseconomies of scale stem from problems associated with managing a very large firm.

Multiple-Choice Questions

1. b
2. a
3. e
4. c
5. d
6. d
7. a
8. b
9. e
10. a
11. a
12. c
13. b
14. d
15. d
16. d
17. a
18. d
19. b
20. c

Fill in the Blanks

1. fixed cost
2. decreasing; increasing
3. labor productivity; labor quality; labor cost
4. variable; total; fixed
5. short run; long run

Discussion Questions

1. Some people prefer not to be employed by others. They may have strong leadership qualities that are suited for running a business firm. Entrepreneurs usually have a good working knowledge of the business that they are entering. They may have been employed in the industry for a time and then decided to found a new business. A willingness to take risks is a common characteristic among entrepreneurs.

2. Fixed costs are constant as output increases. The firm must pay its fixed costs whether it produces or not. Fixed costs are associated with the firm's plant and capital. Frequently, money is borrowed to start a firm, and the regular payments that must be made for these debts represent fixed costs. Variable costs increase with the level of output. Variable costs include the cost of labor and raw materials that go into production. In lower ranges of output, total variable costs increase at a decreasing rate. The total variable cost curve becomes flatter. Each worker adds more to output than to variable costs in this range. However, at some point as output increases, the total variable cost curve begins to rise at an increasing rate. Each worker adds less to total output than the one before. The law of diminishing returns is apparent in this range.

3. A firm can compare the price of its output with the average total cost at that output to figure its profit or loss. If the price is above the average total cost, the firm makes a profit. If it is below, the firm suffers a loss. The lowest price that Merkle Broom could receive and not face a loss is $9.00 at an output level of 6,000 brooms.

4. Marginal cost is the addition to total cost from producing one more unit of a good. It can also be expressed as the change in total cost divided by the change in quantity. Average total cost is total cost divided by output. Average total cost is computed at a specific level of output. Marginal cost is computed between two levels of output.

5. Economies of scale are marked by decreasing average total costs of production that occur as a result of an

THE MICROECONOMICS OF PRODUCT MARKETS

increase in the scale of a firm's operation that happens over the long run. The firm is able to vary the levels of all resources used in production. As the scale of production increases, by adding new plant, capital, and technology in addition to more laborers, the firm can take advantage of new opportunities for specialization and division of labor. Labor productivity rises as a result. Diseconomies of scale arise from the problems associated with managing a very large firm. Bureaucracies become entrenched. Managerial responsibilities become confused. Communication is unclear within the firm. Inefficiencies are the result with rising average costs of production in the long run. The long-run average cost curve begins to turn up, and if the firm wants to lower its average costs, it must downsize.

Problems

1. a. The graph you sketch should look like the one shown here.

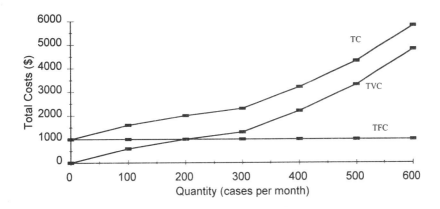

   b. Total cost and total variable cost are parallel to one another because the difference between them is total fixed cost, which is constant.

   c. The shapes of both the total variable cost curve and the total cost curve are similar to the shapes encountered in the text. It is primarily the nature of labor's contribution to costs that accounts for the shape of these curves. At lower levels of output, each additional worker adds more to total output than to costs. Therefore, total variable and total costs rise at a decreasing rate. However, as output increases, the contribution from each additional worker to output begins to diminish — diminishing returns set in — and output rise more slowly than costs, so the total variable and total costs begin to rise at an increasing rate.

2. a. The values in your table should correspond to those shown on the following page.

Quantity of Beer (cases per month)	Average Fixed Cost ($/case)	Average Variable Cost ($/case)	Average Total Cost ($/case)	Marginal Cost ($/case)
0				
100	10	6	16	6
200	5	5	10	4
300	3.33	4.33	7.67	3
400	2.5	5.5	8	9
500	2	6.6	8.6	11
600	1.67	8	9.67	15

b. Your graph should look like the one shown below.

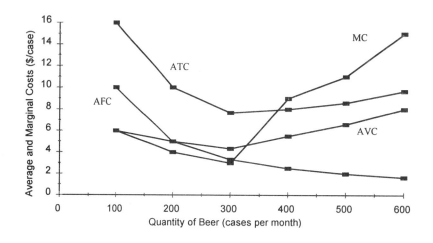

c. Your microbrewery would have to sell at least 200 cases of beer per month because the average total cost of producing 200 cases is $10 per case. The price would just cover the average total cost of a case of beer.

3. a. The total fixed cost is the difference between the total cost and the total variable cost at any level of output. Therefore, it is equal to 34 − 24 or 10.

b. The marginal cost of the sixth umbrella is the change in total cost divided by the change in quantity, or 38 − 24 divided by 1 or 14. Marginal cost can be computed from either the total variable cost series or the total cost series. Marginal costs have to be variable costs because they correspond to costs that vary with output.

c. The average fixed cost of the fifth unit is 10 divided by 5 or 2. Total fixed cost is 10. Average fixed cost is total fixed cost divided by the quantity, which was 5 in this case.

d. The total variable cost of producing 8 units is 98 − 10 or 88. The average variable cost of producing 8 units is 88 divided by 8 or 11.

CHAPTER 9

MAXIMIZING PROFIT

Chapter in a Nutshell

In Chapter 8, we hinted at how you might determine whether a firm is making a profit or a loss by comparing the price of a good with its average total cost of production. A profit is, of course, preferred to a loss, but entrepreneurs usually want to do more than just make a profit. They want to make the maximum profit possible. You'll learn precisely how they do it in this chapter. The rule they follow to achieve **profit maximization** is to produce at an output where **marginal cost equals marginal revenue**. In a step-by-step fashion, the entrepreneur can choose the best output level by comparing the extra revenue that can be obtained by selling one more unit of output with the extra cost of producing that unit. Once the profit-maximizing level of output has been selected, total profits can be found by multiplying the difference between price and average total cost by the output.

On occasion, when the firm's only prospect is incurring losses, the same MC = MR rule guides the entrepreneur to **loss minimization**. If the price at the loss-minimizing level of output is high enough to cover average variable costs, the firm should continue to produce in the short run. If the price at the loss-minimizing level of output is below average variable costs, the firm should **shut down**, producing nothing to minimize losses. Either way, the entrepreneur will face a loss because the firm's fixed costs cannot all be covered in the short run. If this situation persists into the long run, the entrepreneur will go out of business.

Some economists and other social scientists have questioned whether businesses actually follow the MC = MR approach to profit maximization and loss minimization. In general, economists believe that they do behave this way, even though not all entrepreneurs are aware of the MC = MR rule.

After you study this chapter, you should be able to:

- Discuss the decisions entrepreneurs make about production and prices.
- Define **profit**.
- Calculate **total revenue, marginal revenue,** and **average revenue**.
- Explain why the **marginal cost equals marginal revenue rule** achieves profit maximization.
- Identify the area of profit on a graph showing average total costs, marginal cost, and marginal revenue.
- Justify **producing at a loss** when total variable costs are covered by total revenue.
- Evaluate alternative theories to profit maximization.

Concept Check — See how you do on these multiple-choice questions.

1. Entrepreneurs must be expert in **two distinct worlds of enterprise**. These are
   a. hiring and firing workers
   b. employing capital and labor
   c. issuing stocks and bonds to raise capital
   d. overseeing production and marketing activities
   e. entering and leaving new markets

What sorts of activities must an entrepreneur oversee in the pursuit of the maximum possible profit?

2. **Profit maximization** identifies the output level that has
   a. the lowest average total cost of production
   b. marginal revenue equal to marginal cost
   c. a high price for its output
   d. the biggest difference between marginal revenue and marginal cost
   e. the biggest difference between average revenue and marginal cost

What is the rule for profit maximization?

3. **Loss minimization** occurs when a firm produces at an output level where
   a. price covers its fixed costs but not its variable costs
   b. it sets marginal revenue equal to marginal cost
   c. price covers its variable costs but not its fixed costs
   d. it sells for a price that is greater than marginal cost
   e. it sells for a price that is less than marginal cost

The rule for loss minimization is the same as the rule for profit maximization.

4. The **Lester-Machlup controversy** called into question the
   a. importance of marginal analysis to modern firms
   b. results of survey studies in economics
   c. ability of entrepreneurs to anticipate price changes
   d. ability of entrepreneurs to anticipate production costs
   e. mathematics behind the marginal cost equals marginal revenue rule

Not all social scientists agree that firms try to maximize profits following the MC = MR rule.

5. In John K. Galbraith's view, the **primary goal for a corporate manager** is
   a. profit maximization
   b. loss minimization
   c. corporate survival
   d. to maximize the price of stocks
   e. to merge with other corporations

According to Galbraith, the primary goal for a corporate manager may be different from the primary goal for the corporation's stockholders.

Am I on the Right Track?

Your answers to the questions above should be **d, b, c, a,** and **c**. One key to mastering this chapter is to understand the logic of the marginal cost equals marginal revenue rule and to be able to work with this rule using a graph of the firm's average costs, marginal costs, and marginal revenue. The graphing tutorial and questions that follow the matching quiz on key words will help to better acquaint you with **marginal analysis**.

THE MICROECONOMICS OF PRODUCT MARKETS

Key Terms Quiz — Match the terms on the left with definitions in the column on the right.

1. profit maximization
2. average revenue
3. marginal revenue
4. MC = MR rule
5. loss minimization
6. shut down

_____ a. total revenue divided by the quantity of goods sold
_____ b. output level at which profits will be maximized
_____ c. when total revenue is less than total variable cost
_____ d. strategy for the firm when TR < TC
_____ e. the addition to total revenue from selling one more unit
_____ f. the greatest difference between total revenue and total cost

Graphing Tutorial

In a graph featuring (1) the average total cost, (2) average variable cost, (3) marginal cost, and (4) marginal revenue curves, profit maximization, loss minimization, and shut down are all possible outcomes. The firm always produces at an output level where marginal revenue and marginal cost are equal. It is the firm's profit-maximizing or loss-minimizing level of output. The profit or loss can be computed by multiplying the difference between price and average total cost by the output level. However, if a firm incurs a loss, it will shut down if its price is less than its variable costs. This makes sense. After all, why would a firm continue to produce if it were unable to pay for labor and other variable cost items? Fixed costs are unavoidable. But if a firm can pay its variable costs, it will continue to produce at a loss. Business could turn around for the firm. In the real world, firms are not always profitable.

Consider the Merkle Broom Company from the last study guide chapter. Suppose the price of a broom is $18 and the company can sell as many brooms as it wants at this price. Each time another broom is sold, $18 are added to total revenue. This price generates a marginal revenue curve that is a horizontal line at $18. The marginal revenue function is shown in the graph below with the Merkle Broom Company's average total cost and marginal cost functions.

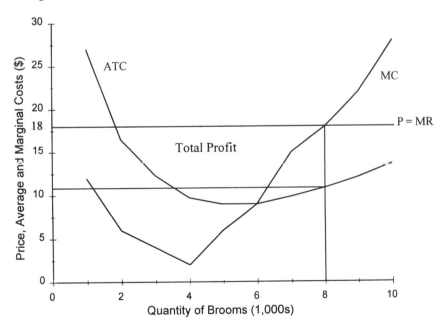

Merkle Broom maximizes profits by producing where MC = MR. When MR = 18, the profit-maximizing level of output is 8,000 brooms. The firm's profit is shown as the rectangle,
($18.00 − $10.88) × 8,000 = $56,960. The average total cost is equal to $10.88 at the 8,000-broom level of

output.

Suppose the price drops from $18.00 per broom to $7.50 per broom. The graph below shows the new marginal revenue curve at $7.50 per broom. MC = MR at 5,400 brooms, the loss-minimizing output level.

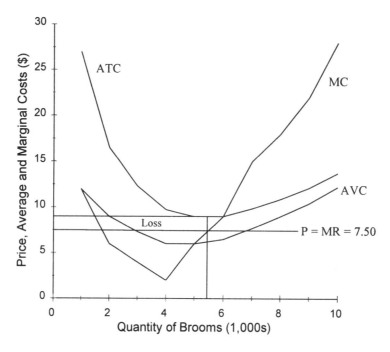

The average total cost at 5,400 brooms is $9.00. Therefore, the loss is ($9.00 − $7.50) x 5,400 = $8,100. Since the price is greater than average variable cost, the firm continues to operate at a loss. The loss is less than the $15,000 loss (the amount of total fixed costs) that would be incurred at zero output. The firm is covering all of its variable costs and $6,900 of its fixed costs.

Suppose that the price of brooms falls to $6.00. The P = MR curve is shown as a horizontal line at $6.00 and MC = MR at 5,000 brooms in the graph on the following page. The loss is the difference between average total cost ($9) and the price ($6) multiplied by the output level (5,000) or $15,000. This equals the firm's total fixed cost. At a price of $6.00, Merkle Broom Company is just able to cover its total variable costs. If the price drops below $6.00, the loss will exceed $15,000 so that it pays the firm to shut down.

THE MICROECONOMICS OF PRODUCT MARKETS

An easy way to tell whether a firm is making a profit or a loss is to see if the marginal revenue curve is above or below the average total cost curve. If it's above, then the firm earns a profit. If it's below, then the firm incurs a loss.

Graphing Pitfalls

One common graphing mistake is to identify the area of profit incorrectly as shown below. The mistake is to identify the minimum point on the average total cost curve (where marginal cost intersects average total cost) as the profit-maximizing level of output. Follow the MC = MR rule for profit maximization and you won't make this mistake.

The profit-maximizing level of output is where MC = MR, not where MC intersects ATC.

True-False Questions — If a statement is false, explain why.

1. To be successful, an entrepreneur needs to be able to monitor production and marketing decisions at the same time. (T/F)

2. The goal for an entrepreneur is to maximize total profit. (T/F)

3. Total profit is found by taking the difference between price and average total cost and then dividing by quantity. (T/F)

4. Marginal revenue is equal to total revenue divided by quantity. (T/F)

5. If price is constant, it is equal to marginal revenue, but greater than average revenue. (T/F)

6. Just as a firm maximizes its profit by producing where MR = MC, it minimizes its losses by producing where MR = MC. (T/F)

7. An entrepreneur can avoid all costs in the short run by simply not producing. (T/F)

8. In the short run, a firm should stop producing if its price cannot cover its average variable cost. (T/F)

9. Professor Richard Lester's survey research of entrepreneurs supports the MR = MC theory of profit maximization. (T/F)

10. Shut down refers to a decision to cease production and incur a loss equal to the firm's fixed cost. (T/F)

11. Berle and Means have argued that a firm may be driven by management's desire to enhance the firm's image, as opposed to pure profit maximization. (T/F)

12. To John K. Galbraith, the primary goal of a modern corporation is a good return for stockholders. (T/F)

13. A basic theme of critics of the MR = MC rule for profit maximization is that modern corporations may be owned by stockholders who desire high profits, but they are run by managers whose goals may be quite different. (T/F)

THE MICROECONOMICS OF PRODUCT MARKETS

14. Economists who support the MC = MR rule for profit maximization believe that this rule perfectly reflects firm behavior in the real world. (T/F)

15. As long as a unit of a good's marginal revenue is greater than its marginal cost, profit can be increased by producing and selling it. (T/F)

Multiple-Choice Questions

1. The key to success for most entrepreneurs is
   a. a commitment to hard work and having access to "deep pockets" for financial support
   b. an ability to judge when the stock market will make sharp changes
   c. being satisfied with moderate profit making
   d. a fair knowledge of production processes, coupled with luck
   e. personal drive, management skills, and an ability to correctly anticipate price changes

2. To maximize profits, a firm will produce where
   a. marginal revenue exceeds marginal cost by the largest amount
   b. average total cost is at a minimum
   c. sales are maximized
   d. marginal revenue is equal to marginal cost
   e. marginal cost is at its lowest

3. If the market price for fish is $4, regardless of how many units are sold, then the firm's
   a. average revenue will be greater than $4
   b. marginal revenue will be greater than $4
   c. average revenue will be less than $4
   d. marginal revenue will be less than $4
   e. marginal revenue will be equal to $4

4. Suppose the market price increases to $5. If the firm produces 200 fish and its average total cost is $2, then its profit is
   a. $1,000
   b. $600
   c. negative
   d. $3
   e. $500

5. If price remains at $5 and the firm increases its output to 300 fish, raising its average total cost to $3, then
   a. there is no change in the firm's profit or loss position
   b. profit increases
   c. profit decreases
   d. loss increases
   e. loss decreases

6. The firm should shut down in the long run if it total revenue cannot cover its
   a. marginal cost
   b. total cost
   c. fixed cost
   d. total variable cost
   e. average total cost

7. The firm's marginal revenue will be constant as long as
   a. the market price is constant
   b. the marginal cost is constant
   c. profit is constant.
   d. no new firms enter the industry
   e. entrepreneurs continue to accurately predict prices

8. Suppose prices don't change. If by producing and selling one more unit, the firm's total revenue increases more than its total cost increases, all of the following are true **except** that
   a. profit will increase
   b. marginal revenue is greater than marginal cost
   c. producing and selling the unit was a sound business decision
   d. average revenue increases
   e. the firm produces closer to the level of profit maximization

9. Shut down refers to
   a. a firm reaching the MC = MR level and remaining at that production level
   b. the first phase in a firm's decision to stop producing one good and start up another
   c. the maximum number of firms that can make a profit
   d. the disruption of production due to overuse of the firm's productive capacity
   e. the situation in which the firm's loss minimization occurs at zero output

10. How much profit a firm makes when the firm maximizes profit is determined by
    a. the MC = MR rule
    b. price times quantity, that is, PQ
    c. price minus total cost times quantity, that is, (P – TC)Q
    d. price minus average total cost times quantity, that is, (P – ATC)Q
    e. marginal revenue minus total cost times quantity, that is, (MR – TC)Q

11. To maximize profit, a firm should continue to produce additional units of output as long as marginal revenue is greater than marginal cost because
    a. profit continues to increase
    b. this is where total revenue will be at a maximum
    c. this is where total cost will be at a minimum
    d. this is where the difference between total revenue and total cost is the greatest
    e. average total cost will begin to decrease

12. The average revenue for a firm is
    a. higher than the price for the first unit sold and lower than the price for the last unit sold
    b. increased with increasing sales
    c. the same as the price
    d. equal to the quantity sold divided by total revenue
    e. equal to the change in total revenue divided by the change in output

THE MICROECONOMICS OF PRODUCT MARKETS 175

13. Marginal revenue is defined as
    a. total revenue divided by quantity
    b. total revenue divided by total cost
    c. the change in total revenue divided by the change in quantity
    d. the change in total cost divided by the change in total revenue
    e. the difference between total revenue and total cost

14. If a firm produces at a loss in the short run, its
    a. total revenue must be greater than or equal to average variable cost
    b. total revenue must be greater than or equal to total variable cost
    c. marginal revenue must be at least equal to the minimum of the average variable cost curve
    d. total revenue must be at least equal to total fixed cost
    e. total revenue must be greater than total cost

15. If a firm produces where marginal revenue is greater than marginal cost, then we know that
    a. profits are being maximized
    b. profits could be increased by increasing output
    c. profits could be increased by decreasing output
    d. the difference between total revenue and total cost is maximized
    e. the firm's costs are minimized

16. When economists refer to an entrepreneur "thinking on the margin," they mean that the entrepreneur
    a. is preoccupied with minor detail
    b. is concerned with how the next unit produced will affect profit or loss
    c. is concerned with past decisions
    d. wants to take every opportunity to improve the image of the firm
    e. wants to avoid the marginal loss

17. Professor Richard Lester suggests that entrepreneurs
    a. consciously equate MR and MC in deciding production levels
    b. do not follow the MR = MC rule in production decisions
    c. are more interested in empire building than profit maximization
    d. hire managers to maximize the value of the firm's stock
    e. are preoccupied with avoiding losses.

18. If marginal revenue is equal to marginal cost at the minimum point on a firm's average total cost curve, then
    a. the firm will incur a small loss
    b. profit for the firm is zero
    c. average revenue does not equal marginal revenue
    d. the firm should shut down
    e. the firm is not pursuing profit maximization

19. If a firm chooses an output level where MR = MC and P > ATC, then all of the following will be true **except** that
    a. the firm will have maximized profits
    b. total revenue will exceed total cost by the largest amount
    c. the firm should produce more output
    d. on a graph, profit is the rectangular area equal to per unit profit times output
    e. profit is equal to price minus average total cost multiplied by quantity

20. Empire building refers to the fact that
    a. most industries are intent on achieving supremacy in the market
    b. modern corporations are more intent on increasing their size than maximizing profit
    c. the typical firm converts profit into investment in order to grow
    d. profit leads to monopoly, which leads to industrial empires
    e. profit is to the entrepreneur what empires are to sovereigns

Fill in the Blanks

1. Entrepreneurs live in two very different worlds of economic life — the world of _____ and the world of _____.

2. A firm maximizes its profits by producing where _____.

3. If price is constant, then _____ revenue is equal to _____ revenue.

4. If, at the level of output where MC = MR, the price is less than average variable cost, the firm should _____.

5. Some economists argue that a possible problem with the MC = MR rule as it is applied to modern corporations may be that corporate managers are more concerned with _____ than with _____.

Discussion Questions

1. Why are firms often better able to predict their costs of production than the price of their product?

2. Discuss some alternative theories to profit maximization to describe the way firms behave. Why do most economists still subscribe to the notion that firms are profit maximizers?

THE MICROECONOMICS OF PRODUCT MARKETS

3. If profit is equal to total revenue minus total cost, then how do we derive the equation profit = (P − ATC)Q? Show your work.

4. Why should a firm increase its output when MR > MC and decrease its output when MR < MC? Explain.

Problems

1. Titleless produces golf balls and can sell them for $15 each. The output, price, average revenue, marginal revenue, marginal cost, average variable cost, and average total cost are shown in the table below.

Quantity (1000s)	Price ($/ball)	AR ($/ball)	MR ($/ball)	MC ($/ball)	AVC ($/ball)	ATC ($/ball)
0	15			6	6	30
1	15			3	5	16
2	15			2	4	10
3	15			1	3.5	8
4	15			3	3	7
5	15			6	3.5	6
6	15			10	4	7
7	15			15	6	8.5
8	15			21	9	11
9	15			28	13	14.5
10	15			36	18	19

a. Fill in the values for average revenue and marginal revenue in the table above.

b. On the axes provided below, plot the marginal revenue and the average total, average variable, and marginal costs. What is the profit-maximizing level output? How do you know? How much profit will the firm make? Shade the area of profit on the graph.

2. Using the same data presented in the table above, suppose the price of golf balls drops to $3. Show the profit-maximizing or loss-minimizing level of output. Should this firm continue to produce at this price? How do you know? Calculate the amount of profit or loss at this price. Shade this area on the graph.

3. Suppose the price of golf balls drops to $2. What should the firm do now? How do you know?

Everyday Applications

Are you a grade point maximizer? How do you approach studying for a set of exams that are scheduled together? Subconsciously, I'll bet you use marginal analysis to maximize the average of your grades on the exams. You weigh your current knowledge of the material against what you will gain from extra hours of studying. And, if you maximize correctly, you'll study until the marginal gain in your grade is equal to the marginal cost of another hour of studying. Through an economist's lenses, life is full of subtle calculations of marginal revenues (gains) and marginal costs.

Economics Online

Many small businesses are in the service sector. They are as concerned as the next firm with maximizing profits. It's no surprise, then, that there is a thriving market for business software to help service sector firms maximize profits. One addition to this market is Pacific Turn-Key Systems Profitmaster program. Check out their site (*http://www.carpetmaster.com/produc.../Maximizing_ProfitMaster/index.htm*) and look for the application of the MC = MR rule.

Answers to Questions

Key Terms Quiz

a. 2   d. 5
b. 4   e. 3
c. 6   f. 1

True-False Questions

1. True
2. True
3. False. Total profit is price minus average total cost times quantity.
4. False. Marginal revenue is equal to the addition to total revenue from selling one more unit of a good.
5. False. If the price is constant, then it is equal to both marginal revenue and average revenue.
6. True
7. False. Fixed costs must still be paid even when output is zero.
8. False. A firm should stop production when it cannot cover its variable costs.
9. False. Lester's research suggested that entrepreneurs have goals other than pure profit maximization.
10. True
11. True
12. False. To Galbraith, the primary goal for the corporation is survival.
13. True
14. False. Economists who support the MC = MR rule view it as a first approximation to reality that is logical and empirically verifiable.
15. True

Multiple-Choice Questions

1. e	6. b	11. a	16. b
2. d	7. a	12. c	17. b
3. e	8. d	13. c	18. b
4. b	9. e	14. b	19. c
5. a	10. d	15. b	20. b

Fill in the Blanks

1. production; markets
2. MC = MR
3. average; marginal
4. shut down
5. corporate survival; profit maximization

Discussion Questions

1. Costs of production are usually known in advance. They involve items, such as labor, that have been contracted for over a long period of time. On the other hand, the price of a firm's output may be subject to extreme fluctuations, depending on the market. Changes in either demand or supply conditions in the market may affect the price of the firm's output. Changes in the national economy may also have an effect on the price of the firm's output. For example, a general downturn in the economy may cause people to stop purchasing the good.

2. Richard Lester's survey work suggested that entrepreneurs don't think in terms of marginal units. Goals other than profit maximization may be more important. These could include empire building, improving the image of the firm, or simply corporate survival. Most of these theories suggest that there is a basic split in a modern corporation between stockholders who want to see profits maximized and management, whose goals may be quite different. Most economists think that the MR = MC thinking dominates for most firms, small and large in our economy. Even if the theory is at odds with some business behavior, it is a good first approximation of reality. Moreover, it can be shown empirically that most firms are profit maximizers.

3. Profit = TR − TC
    = P(Q) − ATC(Q)
   Factoring, Profit = (P − ATC)Q

4. If MR > MC, then producing and selling one more unit of output adds more to total revenue than it does to total cost. Therefore, profit increases. Similarly, if MR < MC, cutting output subtracts more from total cost than it does from total revenue. Therefore, profit increases.

Problems

1. a. The average revenue and marginal revenue are the same as price. They are all $15.

   b. The graph shown on the following page gives the profit-maximizing output and level of profit. The firm maximizes profit by producing 7,000 balls. Profit is ($15.00 − $8.5)7,000 = $45,500. The profit-maximizing level of output occurs where MR = MC.

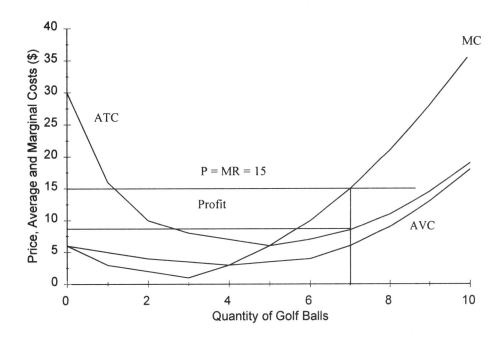

2. The firm's loss is shown below as the area defined by ($7 − $3) x 4,000 = $16,000. The average total cost is $7, and the marginal revenue equal to price is $3. The firm should continue to produce because price covers average variable cost.

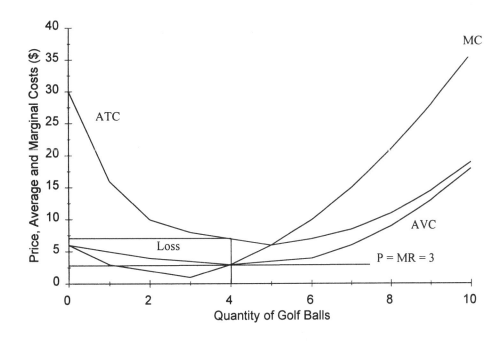

3. The firm should shut down. The lowest point on the AVC curve is at $3, and the $2 price is below that.

CHAPTER 10

IDENTIFYING MARKETS AND MARKET STRUCTURES

Chapter in a Nutshell

When should we consider goods to be part of the same market? Clearly, two identical goods belong to the same market. But what about a pair of goods that are similar — like a Hershey's bar and a Nestlé's bar? Are they part of the same market? We need to be able to define the **relevant market**. The first part of this chapter explores how it is possible to identify markets. You'll find that the cross elasticity of demand is a useful measure to help us determine whether or not two goods are part of the same market. The rest of the chapter is devoted to a descriptive analysis of different **market structures**. The range of market structures extends from markets with one firm — **monopoly** — markets with a few firms — **oligopoly** — to markets with many firms — **monopolistic competition** — to markets with considerable numbers of firms — **perfect competition**. You'll come to appreciate the variety in market structures.

After studying this chapter, you should be able to:

- Use the **cross elasticity of demand** to define the **relevant market**.
- Describe the four types of **market structures**.
- Discuss the conditions necessary for **monopoly** to exist.
- Contrast **oligopoly** and **monopolistic competition**.
- Account for the existence of advertising in many markets.
- Detail the characteristics of **perfectly competitive markets**.

Concept Check — See how you do on these multiple-choice questions.

1. If two goods are in the same **relevant market**, then the cross elasticities between these goods are
    a. less than one
    b. zero
    c. positive and relatively high
    d. difficult to measure
    e. negative

The cross elasticity coefficient allows us to categorize goods as substitutes or complements. If two goods are in the same market, are they substitutes or complements?

2. **Monopoly** and **perfect competition** represent
    a. the only two market structures that are identifiable
    b. the two extremes on the spectrum of market structures
    c. market structures that exist in theory only
    d. market structures where product differentiation is practiced
    e. the most profitable market structures

Think about the number of firms in each of these market structures.

THE MICROECONOMICS OF PRODUCT MARKETS 183

3. Exclusive access to resources, acquisition, and **patents** are ways that a natural monopoly
   a. maintains barriers to entry
   b. enters more competitive markets
   c. guarantees a profit
   d. maximizes the price of the firm's stock
   e. avoids losses

Being a monopolist is an attractive prospect for a firm. How does a monopolist stay a monopolist?

4. **Brand loyalty** permits a firm in monopolistic competition or oligopoly to
   a. maintain a monopoly
   b. prevent entry
   c. expand market share
   d. make the demand for its product more inelastic
   e. prevent product differentiation

Think about your favorite soft drink. Would you still drink it if the price went up a nickel a can? Why?

5. In **perfect competition**, the market share for the firm is
   a. insignificant
   b. growing through aggressive advertising
   c. dependent on the elasticity of demand for the firm's product
   d. dependent on brand loyalty
   e. usually very large

What is the relationship between the size of firms and the size of the market in perfect competition?

Am I on the Right Track?

Your answers to the questions above should be **c**, **b**, **a**, **d**, and **a**. Grasping the material in this chapter requires careful reading and the application of some logical reasoning. For example, the fact that a perfectly competitive firm is extremely small relative to the market has implications for the shape of its demand curve. The demand curve facing the firm is horizontal at a price that is determined in the market. That's why the firm is called a price-taker. The logic is clear. If the firm is so small that it cannot influence the market price, then it must be able to sell all it wants to at the market price. Hence the demand curve for the perfectly competitive firm is horizontal. On the other hand, a firm that has some control over its price, such as a monopoly or monopolistic competitive firm, faces a demand curve that is downward sloping. Thinking this way will allow you to move through the chapter smoothly.

Key Terms Quiz — Match the terms on the left with the definitions in the column on the right.

1. relevant market
2. market structure
3. mutual interdependence
4. monopoly
5. industry
6. natural monopoly
7. patent

_____ a. price changes by one firm in oligopoly affect pricing by other firms
_____ b. a few firms that produce goods that are close substitutes
_____ c. one firm producing a good with no close substitutes
_____ d. consumer willingness to buy a good at a price higher than the price of its substitutes
_____ e. a set of goods with high cross elasticities among them
_____ f. the percentage of total market sales produced by a particular firm
_____ g. large number of firms producing goods that are perfect substitutes

8. monopolistic competition   _____ h. a set of market characteristics common to a group of firms

9. oligopoly   _____ i. physical or perceived differences among substitute goods in a market

10. product differentiation   _____ j. only one firm able to produce profitably in a market given demand and costs

11. brand loyalty   _____ k. many firms that produce differentiated goods that are close substitutes

12. market share   _____ l. a monopoly right on a new technology or production of a new good

13. perfect competition   _____ m. a collection of firms producing the same good

Graphing Tutorial

Natural monopoly results when the combination of the market demand and the firm's costs is such that only one firm is able to produce profitably in a market. Typically, the fixed cost involved in setting up production for the goods supplied by a natural monopoly is so high that the firm must have access to a large market in order to bring its average total cost down sufficiently to allow for profitable operation. Examples of natural monopolies include major league sports franchises (the stadium with luxury box seats is a fixed cost), city bus companies, municipal water companies, the electric company, and the gas company.

The key to graphing a natural monopoly is to be careful to draw the average total cost curve so that it slopes downward in the range of output being considered. The demand curve is positioned so that only one firm can operate profitably within this range of output. The graph drawn below shows a natural monopoly — the municipal water company. The average total cost curve is pulled down over the range of output corresponding to the city's demand for water because of the high fixed cost of supplying water — wells, pipes, a water tower, purification system, etc.

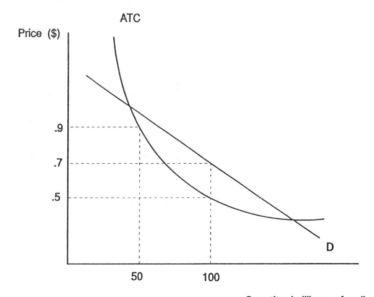

Suppose the water company maximizes profits by producing 100 million gallons of water at a price read from the demand curve equal to $.70 per gallon. The monopoly's profits are ($.70 − $.50) × 100 million gallons = $20 million. What would happen if a second water company entered the market? It would be split between the two firms, each supplying 50 million gallons at an average total cost equal to $.90 per gallon.

Each firm would charge $.70 per gallon; thus, the loss for each firm would be equal to ($.90 − $.70) x 50 million gallons = $10 million. Neither firm could survive.

Graphing Pitfalls

A problem you might encounter drawing the graph for a natural monopoly is to mistakenly place the demand curve too far above the average total cost curve so that the market could support more than one firm profitably. The graph below shows this situation.

With one water company supplying the community, the firm's profits are equal to ($.70 − $.20) x 150 million gallons = $75 million. Suppose we split the market between two firms. Each firm's profits are equal to ($.70 − $.50) x 75 million gallons = $15 million. Certainly, one firm is more profitable than two. But the market is big enough to support two firms profitably. Therefore, this graph does not represent natural monopoly.

True-False Questions — If a statement is false, explain why.

1. A relevant market contains a set of goods whose cross elasticities with others in the set are relatively high and whose cross elasticities with goods outside the set are relatively low. (T/F)

2. Since movie theaters and video arcades provide highly substitutable services, they may be considered part of the entertainment market. (T/F)

3. Because DuPont controlled 80 percent of cellophane production in the early 1950s, the courts ruled that it exercised monopoly power. (T/F)

4. The cross elasticity of demand is the percentage change in quantity demanded for one good generated by a percentage change in price for another good. (T/F)

5. Mutual interdependence is a term economists use to describe any price change made by one firm in an oligopoly that affects the pricing behavior of other firms in the oligopoly. (T/F)

6. Firms in a market that is perfectly competitive produce goods that are perfect substitutes for each other. (T/F)

7. The most important characteristic that distinguishes one market structure from another is the size of the firms in the market (T/F)

8. According to F. M. Scherer, a cross elasticity of 3.0 is high enough for a pair of goods to be considered part of the same market. (T/F)

9. A firm in perfect competition is free to set price at whatever level it pleases. (T/F)

10. In monopoly, the firm is the industry. (T/F)

11. A monopolist's demand curve will be horizontal at the market price. (T/F)

12. The intended effects of advertising are to increase the market share for a firm and to make the demand for the product more elastic. (T/F)

13. Entry into monopolistic competition or oligopoly is not free, but it is possible. (T/F)

14. Natural monopolies typically have high fixed costs, so only one firm is able to serve the market at a profit. (T/F)

15. Brand loyalty describes the willingness of consumers to buy a good at a higher price than the price of its close substitutes. (T/F)

THE MICROECONOMICS OF PRODUCT MARKETS

Multiple-Choice Questions

1. In the DuPont case discussed in the text, the government argued that DuPont had a near monopoly position in the market for cellophane; thus, DuPont
   a. was broken up into smaller competitive companies to produce cellophane
   b. had to show that the relevant market was the broader market for packaging materials
   c. had to lower its price for cellophane
   d. voluntarily reimbursed consumers for overcharging them
   e. stockholders fired their managers and replaced them with a more competitive group

2. In cases of antitrust violations, the key issue is often
   a. identification of the market
   b. the amount of advertising done
   c. whether a patent is valid
   d. environmental damage
   e. price elasticity of supply

3. All of the following are true about two goods with high cross elasticities of demand **except** that
   a. they cannot be in the same market because each has complete control of its own market
   b. they must be in the same market
   c. a small percentage increase in the price of one good will lead to a large percentage increase in quantity demanded for the other good
   d. they are close substitutes
   e. they must serve very similar needs for consumers

4. If the cross elasticity of demand between two goods is _____, then they are considered to be in different markets.
   a. 2
   b. 4
   c. 6
   d. 8
   e. 16

5. Courts have decided cases by considering cross elasticities of demand in order to
   a. measure monopoly profit
   b. help alert consumers to unfair business practices
   c. determine the degree of competition in industries where antitrust suits are involved
   d. distinguish between oligopoly and monopolistic competition
   e. distinguish between monopolistic competition and perfect competition

6. In oligopoly
   a. firms compete with each other only by raising and lowering quantity because prices are fixed
   b. the fewness of firms creates mutual interdependence in pricing among the firms
   c. the firm is the industry
   d. firms have no difficulty entering and leaving the market
   e. the firm having a natural monopoly sets price for the others

7. The difference between a market and an industry is that
   a. industries consist of markets producing the same good while markets consist of firms producing substitute goods
   b. industries consist of firms producing the same good while markets consist of industries producing substitute goods
   c. industries are collections of markets while markets are collections of firms
   d. firms make up a market while markets make up an industry
   e. industries are substitutes for markets, but markets are not substitutes for industry

8. Product differentiation refers to
   a. different prices for the same good
   b. different goods that have identical prices
   c. differences among goods in a market that make them close, but not perfect substitutes for each other
   d. markets that differ from industries because their goods are essentially different
   e. the firm's ability to create different goods while using the same technology and resources

9. Which of the following is **not** characteristic of natural monopoly?
   a. a declining average total cost over the firm's relevant range of production
   b. a prohibitively high average total cost for each firm if two or more firms are in the market
   c. production in an environment of high fixed costs
   d. a desire to earn the maximum economic profit
   e. a marginal cost curve that is above the average total cost curve

10. The monopolist's demand curve is _____ whereas the perfectly competitive firm's demand curve is _____.
    a. always downward sloping; always horizontal
    b. always horizontal; always downward sloping
    c. the market demand curve; the industry demand curve
    d. fixed because it represents just one firm; variable because it is only a fraction of the industry's demand
    e. inelastic along its entire range; unit elastic along its entire range

11. All of the following are characteristics of a monopoly **except** that
    a. its demand curve is the same as the industry demand curve
    b. the monopoly's size, that is, its scale of production, is always very large
    c. as long as it's a monopoly, there is absolutely no entry into its industry
    d. it is the only firm in the industry
    e. its demand curve is downward sloping

12. All of the following are true about advertising **except** that it
    a. plays a more effective role in monopolistically competitive markets than in perfectly competitive markets
    b. is used to reduce product differentiation
    c. is used to make a firm's demand curve more inelastic
    d. is used to increase a firm's market share
    e. is used to reduce consumer sensitivity to price changes

THE MICROECONOMICS OF PRODUCT MARKETS 189

13. As a firm loses its monopoly status, becoming more competitive as new firms enter the market, the ex-monopoly firm's demand curve
   a. remains the same but is now only part of market demand
   b. shifts to the left and becomes more elastic
   c. shifts to the left and becomes more inelastic
   d. shifts to the right and becomes more elastic
   e. shifts to the right and becomes more inelastic

14. As new firms continue to enter a market once dominated by a monopoly, the market structure changes from monopoly to
   a. oligopoly, to perfect competition, to monopolistic competition
   b. monopolistic competition, to oligopoly, to perfect competition
   c. perfect competition, to oligopoly, to monopolistic competition
   d. oligopoly, to monopolistic competition, to perfect competition
   e. monopolistic competition, to perfect competition, to monopolistic competition

15. Ordering market structures according to the ease of entry for new firms from easy entry to more difficult entry, we have
   a. monopoly, oligopoly, monopolistic competition, perfect competition
   b. perfect competition, oligopoly, monopolistic competition, monopoly
   c. perfect competition, oligopoly, monopolistic competition, natural monopoly
   d. perfect competition, oligopoly, monopoly, monopolistic competition
   e. perfect competition, monopolistic competition, oligopoly, monopoly

16. Brand loyalty refers to
   a. a firm's decision to stay with a particular good even though profit margins have fallen
   b. a firm's decision to develop a good with brand visibility so that sales will increase
   c. a consumer's decision to stay with a particular brand of a good no matter which firm produces it
   d. a consumer's choice of good depends on the firm's willingness to advertise a particular brand
   e. the willingness of consumers to buy a good at a price higher than the price of its close substitutes

17. A firm's influence over the price of the good produced in monopoly, oligopoly, monopolistic competition, and perfect competition is, respectively,
   a. complete, considerable, little, none
   b. none, little, considerable, complete
   c. considerable, none, little, complete
   d. little, none, complete, considerable
   e. complete, little, considerable, none

18. All the following are reasons why it is difficult for new firms to compete in an existing monopoly market **except** that the existing monopoly
   a. is a big firm
   b. is a natural monopoly
   c. has exclusive access to resources
   d. has a patent
   e. acquires potential new entrants

19. Which of the following is **not** a characteristic of perfect competition?
    a. product differentiation
    b. insignificant market share
    c. free entry
    d. inability to influence price
    e. large number of firms

20. A firm in perfect competition faces a horizontal demand curve for all of the following reasons **except** that
    a. the firm takes the price as given from the market
    b. the firm is unable to influence the market price because of its small size
    c. the product the firm sells is identical to the product sold by other firms in the market
    d. the firm's sales are limited so it is impossible for the firm to sell more and lower the price
    e. the firm can sell as much as it wants at the price established in the market

Fill in the Blanks

1. _____ is an important tool used to identify which goods belong to which markets.

2. _____ and _____ are marked by the potential entry of firms, although entry may be difficult.

3. Advertising can play a significant role in _____ and _____.

4. Monopoly is maintained through barriers to entry that may include _____, _____, _____, and _____.

5. Perfect competition consists of _____ producing goods that are _____.

Discussion Questions

1. How does one identify a market?

2. Why are court decisions involving identification of markets sometimes overturned on appeal as in the Alcoa case?

THE MICROECONOMICS OF PRODUCT MARKETS 191

3. Distinguish between an industry and a market.

4. Consider your two favorite soft drinks. Suppose the price of a two-liter bottle of your second choice falls. How much of a price decrease would it take to induce you to substitute the second for your first choice? Estimate the cross elasticity of demand for the drinks. Are they part of the same market?

5. Explain how the number of producers in a market varies from one market structure to another.

6. Suppose a market becomes more competitive over time. What happens to the elasticity of demand for a particular firm's good as its market becomes more competitive?

Everyday Applications

Think about your daily purchases. How are they distributed among the different industry structures that were presented in the chapter? For example, what sort of goods do you purchase from monopolists, oligopolists, monopolistically competitive firms, and perfectly competitive firms?

Economics Online

Farmers' markets, street markets, and flea markets are increasingly popular. Each is a collection of markets offering thousands of products — some are more competitive than others. Explore this side of the world of markets at this site (*http://www.openair.org/*). Try to pick out elements of monopoly power and evidence for perfect competition in these different settings.

Answers to Questions

Key Terms Quiz

a. 3
b. 9
c. 4
d. 11
e. 1
f. 12
g. 13
h. 2
i. 10
j. 6
k. 8
l. 7
m. 5

True-False Questions

1. True
2. True
3. False. The courts ruled that cellophane was a part of the broader market for packaging materials.
4. True
5. True
6. True
7. False. The most important characteristic that distinguishes one market structure from another is the number of firms in the market.
8. True
9. False. The firm does not choose the price — it is set in the market by market demand and market supply.
10. True
11. False. A monopolist's demand curve is the industry demand curve, so it is downward sloping.
12. False. The intended effects of advertising are to increase the market share for the firm and to make the demand for the product more inelastic. In this way, the firm can raise price without losing many sales.
13. True
14. True
15. True

Multiple-Choice Questions

1. b
2. a
3. a
4. a
5. c
6. b
7. b
8. c
9. e
10. a
11. b
12. b
13. b
14. d
15. e
16. e
17. a
18. a
19. a
20. d

THE MICROECONOMICS OF PRODUCT MARKETS

Fill in the Blanks

1. Cross elasticity
2. oligopoly; monopolistic competition
3. oligopoly; monopolistic competition
4. natural monopoly; patents; acquisition; exclusive access to resources
5. many, many firms; perfect substitutes (or identical)

Discussion Questions

1. The best way to identify a market is to compare the cross elasticities of goods. If they are relatively high they belong to the same market. A market consists of a set of goods whose cross elasticities are relatively high and whose cross elasticities with goods outside the set are low.

2. Identifying a market is primarily a judgment call. Reasonable people can look at the same evidence and arrive at different conclusions. What the courts attempt to do is to hand down impartial judgments about what constitutes a relevant market. There are no hard and fast rules by which to do this. However, measures of the cross elasticity of demand are a guide to determining the extent of the relevant market.

3. Industries consist of firms producing the same good. Markets consist of sets of industries producing close substitute goods. Using the example in the text, the construction market consists of the steel, concrete, and aluminum industries.

4. Clearly, the answer to this one depends on your tastes. Take me, for example. My two favorite soft drinks are 7 Up and Sprite. I have a slight preference for 7 Up, but it is so slight that if the the price of 7 Up were to increase by one penny, I would always buy Sprite. That creates a very high cross elasticity of demand. In my case, 7 Up and Sprite are almost perfect substitutes and belong to the same market.

5. A market with one producer is a monopolist; with a few, an oligopoly; with many, monopolistic competition; and with many, many firms, perfect competition.

6. Increased competition leads to increased elasticity. This makes sense because the essence of increased competition is a larger number of firms producing goods that are close substitutes for each other. One of the determinants of the price elasticity of demand is the number of close substitutes. As the number of close substitutes increases, the price elasticity of demand increases. Demand curves in markets where competition is increasing become flatter over time; that is, they become more elastic.

CHAPTER 11

PRICE AND OUTPUT IN MONOPOLY, MONOPOLISTIC COMPETITION, AND PERFECT COMPETITION

Chapter in a Nutshell

Now that we understand the characteristics of different market structures, we ask the question in this and the following chapter: How are prices and output levels determined for firms pursuing profit maximization in different market structures? This chapter analyzes price and output determination for firms in monopoly, monopolistic competition, and perfect competition. We leave the discussion of price and output in oligopoly for the next chapter.

A monopolist is a **price-maker**, since it makes its own pricing and output decisions. At the other extreme, a perfectly competitive firm must take the market-determined price as given and chooses only an output level, so it is a **price-taker**. Despite these differences, firms in all types of market structures maximize profits by selecting an output level where MR = MC. Monopolists and monopolistic competitive firms must then also find the price that corresponds to this output level on their demand curves. For any type of firm, if total revenue is greater than total cost (which consists of both explicit and implicit costs), there is an **economic profit**. If total revenue is equal to total cost, then there is a **normal profit** and the firm breaks even. **Maximum efficiency**, the production of goods at the lowest possible average total cost, can occur only with perfect competition. A monopoly could earn economic profits that persist even in the long run because of barriers to entry. However, perfectly competitive and monopolistic competitive firms can only earn normal profits in the long run, since there is free entry and exit of firms.

An important issue explored toward the end of this chapter is whether perfect competition or monopoly is more desirable. Economists in the Alfred Marshall tradition argue that small competitive firms tend to generate lower prices because with many firms pursuing innovations simultaneously, costs are driven down. However, Schumpeter, Galbraith, and others have argued that larger firms with greater monopoly power are able to realize economies of scale and spend part of their profits on research and development so that lower-cost production technology can be introduced.

After studying this chapter, you should be able to:

- Derive the monopolist's marginal revenue curve.
- Explain how profit is derived in monopoly and why it persists.
- Discuss short-run equilibrium in monopolistic competition.
- Use a graph to show long-run equilibrium in monopolistic competition.
- Distinguish between **economic profit** and **normal profit**.
- Graphically show short-run equilibrium and long-run equilibrium in perfect competition.
- Explain maximum efficiency in perfect competition.
- Present examples of **price-makers** and **price-takers**.
- Relate the perfectly competitive firm's supply curve to the market supply curve.
- Evaluate arguments offered to show the desirability of perfect competition versus monopoly.

THE MICROECONOMICS OF PRODUCT MARKETS

Concept Check — See how you do on these multiple choice questions.

1. The **primary goal of a monopolist** is to
   a. produce at the most efficient output level to maximize profit
   b. select the highest possible price
   c. earn the maximum profit
   d. ensure corporate survival in the face of intense competition
   e. maximize market share

Why would a monopolist's goal be any different from that of other firms?

2. The monopolist's decision to produce where **marginal revenue is equal to marginal cost** generates
   a. an efficient level of production
   b. production to the left of the minimum of the average total cost curve
   c. production to the right of the minimum of the average total cost curve
   d. chronic excess demand
   e. a price that is higher than consumers are willing to pay

What would an efficient level of production be?

3. What is the relationship between **economic profit** and **normal profit**?
   a. They are identical
   b. Only normal profit is earned in the long run by a price-taker
   c. Normal profit is greater than economic profit
   d. Economic profit is just enough to keep a firm in the market whereas normal profit is greater
   e. A firm will earn economic profit in the long run, but no normal profit

Which type of profit must an entrepreneur earn to stay in business in the long run?

4. A **price-maker** can _____ while a **price-taker** must _____ to maximize profits.
   a. raise price; lower price
   b. select price; accept the market price
   c. dictate prices to others; follows the price lead of the price-dictating firm
   d. advertise; rely on brand loyalty to control price
   e. enter new markets to control price; innovate to control price

Which type of firm has some control over the price it charges?

5. Firms that enjoy **economies of scale** can
   a. increase production but suffer increasing short-run average total cost
   b. increase production and at the same time have constant average total cost
   c. avoid diseconomies of scale by increasing the size of the firm
   d. enjoy higher stock prices as more shares are issued
   e. increase production and enjoy decreasing long-run average total cost

What is the shape of the long-run average total cost curve when a firm experiences economies of scale?

Am I on the Right Track?

Your answers to the questions above should be **c, b, b, b,** and **e**. One technical detail that you need to learn in order to reason correctly about price and output determination is the distinction between the marginal revenue curve that a perfectly competitive firm faces compared to the marginal revenue curve for other market structures. For these firms, marginal revenue lies below the demand curve. For a perfectly competitive firm, marginal revenue and demand are the same. The graphing tutorial will explore this difference.

Key Terms Quiz — Match the terms on the left with the definitions in the column on the right.

1. economic profit
2. normal profit
3. price-maker
4. price-taker
5. economies of scale

_____ a. a firm that accepts the market price as its own
_____ b. as output increases, long-run ATC decreases
_____ c. total revenue minus explicit and implicit costs
_____ d. the entrepreneur's opportunity cost
_____ e. a firm that can choose among combinations of price and output

Graphing Tutorial

Let's work through graphing the downward-sloping marginal revenue curve using a numerical example. Consider the local cable television service. This is a monopoly. Suppose the local cable company is the sole provider of a service with no close substitutes. The table below shows the price and quantity combinations of basic cable service that are demanded per month from the local company. The total revenue and marginal revenue are shown in the third and fourth columns of the table.

Price ($/month)	Quantity (# of cable subscribers)	Total Revenue ($)	Marginal Revenue ($)
35	500	17,500	
30	1,000	30,000	25
25	1,500	37,500	15
20	2,000	40,000	5
15	2,500	37,500	-5
10	3,000	30,000	-15
5	3,500	17,500	-25

How is the marginal revenue calculated? Between the prices $35 per month and $30 per month, the total revenue increases by $12,500, and the quantity of subscribers increases by 500. Marginal revenue is equal to $12,500/500 or $25. The demand curve and the marginal revenue curve are plotted on the graph on the next page. Note that the marginal revenue curve lies below the demand curve.

THE MICROECONOMICS OF PRODUCT MARKETS

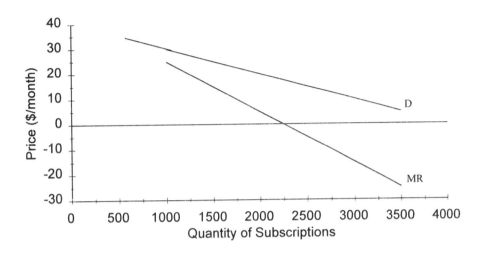

Given the demand curve and the marginal revenue curve, it is possible to superimpose on this graph the marginal cost and average total cost functions for the cable company to determine the profit-maximizing level of output and price. Then, profits can be shown on the graph.

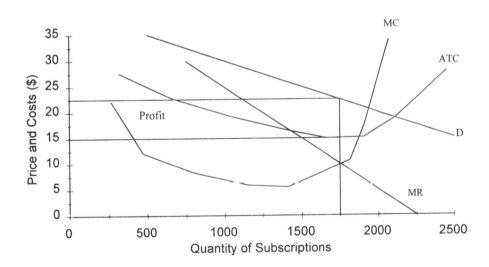

The cable company will maximize profit by setting output where MR = MC at an output level of 1,750 subscriptions. They will charge $22.50 per month, the price read from the demand curve. At 1,750 subscriptions, the average total cost is $15, read from the average total cost curve. Therefore, the economic profit this firm earns is defined by the rectangle labeled profit between $22.50 and $15 up to an output level of 1,750. The cable company's profit is equal to ($22.50 − $15) × 1,750 = $13,125.

Graphing Pitfalls

Suppose we have a monopolist with the demand, marginal revenue, average total cost, and marginal cost shown below. Pretend that you are an economics professor and ask one of your favorite students, Jeremy Lynch, to label the profit-maximizing price and output level with P* and Q*, respectively. Jeremy labels the points as shown below. Has he done this correctly?

Even though Jeremy is one of your prize students, he's made a mistake this time. He read price from the marginal revenue curve after locating the intersection of marginal revenue and marginal cost. So, he has labeled the correct profit-maximizing level of output with Q*, but no self-respecting monopolist would charge such a low price. **Price should always be read from the demand curve!** After all, that is what people are willing and able to pay.

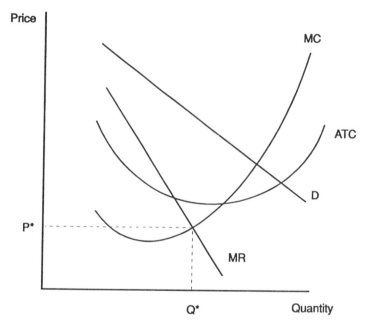

Price should be read from the demand curve, not from the point where MR = MC.

True-False Questions — If a statement is false, explain why.

1. What a monopolist most wants to do is to raise prices. (T/F)

2. A monopolist will never lower price. (T/F)

3. A monopolist's marginal revenue curve is constant at the market price. (T/F)

4. A monopolist can earn economic profit if the price is less than the average total cost at the profit-maximizing level of output. (T/F)

THE MICROECONOMICS OF PRODUCT MARKETS

5. A monopolist will maximize both profits and efficiency. (T/F)

6. If a monopolist's barriers to entry break down, then entering firms will cause the monpolist's profits to decline. (T/F)

7. Only normal profits are earned by a monopolist in long-run equilibrium. (T/F)

8. In monopolistic competition, all firms in an industry produce an identical product. (T/F)

9. In long-run equilibrium, a perfectly competitive firm produces where price is equal to marginal cost, both of which are equal to the minimum average total cost. (T/F)

10. Firms in monopolistic competition earn only normal profits in the long run. (T/F)

11. In short-run equilibrium, a firm in monopolistic competition can earn economic profit. (T/F)

12. An entrepreneur will leave an industry if there is zero economic profit to be earned. (T/F)

13. A firm earning an economic profit is also earning a normal profit. (T/F)

14. A monopolistically competitive firm produces at the minimum of its average total cost curve. (T/F)

15. Firms in perfect competition are described as price-makers. (T/F)

Multiple-Choice Questions

1. Explicit costs include all the monetary payments associated with an enterprise, while implicit costs equal
   a. explicit costs minus the opportunity costs of using resources owned by the entrepreneur
   b. explicit costs plus the cost of the entrepreneur's labor
   c. explicit costs minus the cost of the entrepreneur's labor
   d. the opportunity costs of using the resources owned by the entrepreneur
   e. explicit costs plus the opportunity costs of using resources owned by the entrepreneur

2. All of the following are true about a firm in a perfectly competitive industry **except** that the firm
   a. will always make a profit if it follows the rule of profit maximization
   b. will never advertise to increase its market share
   c. can enter and exit the market easily
   d. faces many buyers in the market
   e. produces a good that is a perfect substitute for goods produced by other firms in the industry

3. The demand curve for an individual firm in perfect competition is horizontal because
   a. it is inelastic throughout every price range
   b. it is elastic throughout every price range
   c. competitive markets always grow so any firm can sell as much as it wants at the market price
   d. the firm can sell as much as it wants at the market price since the firm's output is small relative to market demand
   e. sales are very flat in a competitive market

4. One difference between a perfectly competitive firm and a monopoly is that
   a. a monopoly sets price equal to marginal revenue, while a perfectly competitive firm sets price equal to marginal cost
   b. a monopoly faces a downward-sloping demand curve, while a perfectly competitive firm faces a horizontal demand curve
   c. perfectly competitive firms advertise while a monopoly does not
   d. while neither type of firm can control price, a monopolist can control output
   e. a monopoly is always very much larger than a competitive firm

5. A monopolistically competitive firm may realize
   a. economic profit in the short run, but only a normal profit in the long run
   b. a normal profit in the short run, but economic profit in the long run
   c. a level of production at the minimum of the average cost curve
   d. economies of scale in production if barriers to entry exist
   e. that product differentiation creates long-run economic profit

6. Monopoly profit tends to persist in the long run because
   a. monopolists are more innovative than other producers
   b. monopolists' costs decrease as their outputs increase
   c. monopolists can raise price any time costs increase
   d. monopolists are the shrewdest entrepreneurs
   e. of barriers to entry

7. The demand curve for a firm in monopolistic competition is downward sloping because
   a. the firm enjoys a degree of brand loyalty
   b. the good it produces is a perfect substitute for the goods other firms in the industry produce
   c. of product similarities
   d. consumers are unable to find close substitutes
   e. firms in monopolistic competition started out as monopolies

8. An entrepreneur will stay in an industry where zero economic profit is earned because
   a. it is costly to shift to a new industry
   b. profit may not be what is driving this entrepreneur
   c. the entrepreneur still earns his/her opportunity cost
   d. the entrepreneur prefers being the owner of a business to working for others
   e. there may be the potential to earn an economic profit in the future

THE MICROECONOMICS OF PRODUCT MARKETS

9. The supply curve for a competitive firm in the long run is given by that portion of the marginal cost curve that
    a. lies above the average variable cost curve
    b. lies above the average total cost curve
    c. lies above the average fixed cost curve
    d. is elastic
    e. is downward sloping

10. All of the following are conditions for long-run equilibrium in perfect competition **except** that
    a. all firms earn economic profits
    b. all firms earn normal profits
    c. no firms have incentive to leave the industry
    d. price is equal to marginal cost and minimum average total cost
    e. no firms have incentive to enter the industry

11. Which of the following is true of the relationship between price and marginal cost in monopolistic competition in long-run equilibrium?
    a. P = MC at all levels of output
    b. P = MC at the profit-maximizing level of output
    c. P > MC at the profit-maximizing level of output
    d. P < MC at the profit-maximizing level of output
    e. P = MC = minimum of the ATC at the profit-maximizing level of output

12. In monopolistic competition, the positioning of the demand curve facing an individual firm relative to market demand depends on the
    a. shape of the firm's marginal revenue curve
    b. shape of the firm's average total cost curve
    c. shape of the firm's marginal cost curve
    d. firm's supply curve
    e. number of firms in the market

13. A feature of monopoly that distinguishes it from competitive firms is that
    a. earning high long-run profit, it typically pays higher wages than do competitive firms
    b. it provides consumers with many differentiated products, rather than identical products
    c. being relatively large, it typically produces more than would be produced by competitive firms
    d. it produces unique goods that would not have been produced by competitive firms
    e. it uses resources more efficiently than a perfectly competitive market

14. Economies of scale mean that if a firm were to double its output
    a. long-run average total cost would decrease
    b. average total cost would remain unchanged
    c. average total cost would increase
    d. short-run average total cost would remain unchanged
    e. short-run average total cost would more than double

15. The following graph represents a
    a. monopolist earning economic profits
    b. firm in monopolistic competition earning normal profit
    c. very large and influential competitive firm
    d. monopolist suffering a loss
    e. competitive firm in disequilibrium

16. Since a firm in monopolistic competition earns zero economic profit in the long run
    a. the allocation of resources is as efficient as under perfect competition
    b. the entrepreneur earns only his/her opportunity cost
    c. price is equal to marginal cost
    d. the firm produces at its minimum average total cost curve
    e. the demand curve for its good is identical to the demand curve facing firms in perfect competition

17. An innovator firm in perfect competition will be able to
    a. raise the price of its product
    b. earn economic profit in the long run
    c. earn economic profit until other firms adopt the innovation
    d. achieve monopoly power in the market
    e. differentiate its product from those produced by other firms

18. All of the following are characteristics of the monopolist's marginal revenue curve **except** that it
    a. lies below the demand curve
    b. represents the addition to total revenue generated by producing and selling one more unit
    c. is greater than price at every output level
    d. is downward sloping
    e. eventually becomes negative

19. The graphs in panels A, B, and C best represent long-run equilibrium situations for _____, _____, and _____, respectively.
    a. monopolistic competition; perfect competition; monopoly
    b. perfect competition; monopolistic competition; monopoly
    c. perfect competition; monopoly; monopolistic competition
    d. monopolistic competition; monopoly; perfect competition
    e. monopoly; monopolistic competition; perfect competition

20. Firms in perfect competition are more efficient than firms in either monopolistic competition or monopoly in the long run because
    a. many small firms innovate more than one large firm or several medium-sized firms
    b. in the long run, perfectly competitive firms produce at close to zero marginal costs
    c. monopolists and monopolistically competitive firms make profit
    d. monopolists and monopolistically competitive firms have to advertise
    e. perfectly competitive firms operate at minimum average total cost

Fill in the Blanks

1. Rather than producing where _____ is at its minimum, the monopolist produces where _____ in order to _____.

2. The more unique and desirable a product supplied by a monopolistically competitive firm, the more _____ will be its demand curve.

3. The existence of profit in a perfectly competitive industry results in _____, which causes the market _____ to increase and _____ to fall.

4. Because the _____ curve represents the quantities supplied at varying prices and since a perfectly competitive firm in the long run always produces where P = MR = MC, the competitive firm's _____ curve is that portion of its _____ curve that lies above the _____ curve.

5. _____ believed that bigness could be an advantage for an innovating firm because of _____ and low average costs of production.

Discussion Questions

1. Why are the monopolist's and the monopolistically competitive firm's demand curves downward sloping while the competitive firm's demand curve is horizontal?

2. Outline the various ideas that economists have proposed to explain the relationship between the size of firms and the extent of innovation undertaken by firms. Which of these competing theories seems most reasonable to you? Why?

3. How is long-run equilibrium different for monopolistically competitive firms compared to perfectly competitive firms?

4. Why is a perfectly competitive firm's long-run supply curve the same as its marginal cost curve above the average total cost curve?

Problems

1. a. The following table shows price and quantity data for a jeans manufacturer's demand schedule. Complete the columns for total revenue and marginal revenue; then plot the demand and marginal revenue curves on the graph below that show the average total cost and marginal cost for the firm.

Price ($s/pair)	Quantity	Total Revenue	Marginal Revenue
30	1,000		
25	2,000		
20	3,000		
15	4,000		
10	5,000		
5	6,000		

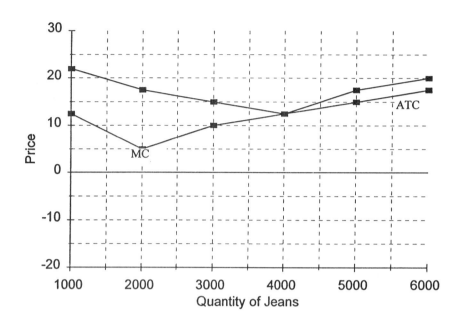

b. What is the firm's profit-maximizing level of output? Will this firm make a profit? If so, shade the area, label it profit, and calculate the size of the profit.

c. Assuming that the jeans industry is monopolistically competitive, has long-run equilibrium been achieved? Why or why not? State the condition necessary for long-run equilibrium.

2. The two graphs drawn below show a perfectly competitive firm in a short-run equilibrium and in long-run equilibrium. Which is which? How do you know? In each graph, label the profit-maximizing level of output with Q*, the profit maximizing price with P*, and shade the area of profit or loss. How will this market make the transition from short-run to long-run equilibrium?

THE MICROECONOMICS OF PRODUCT MARKETS

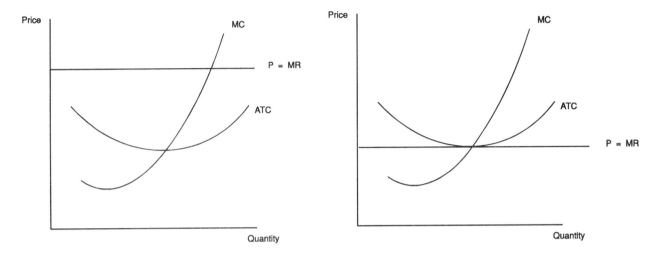

3. Consider the graph of the perfectly competitive firm shown below. Does this firm make a profit or a loss? Shade the area of profit or loss. If the firm is incurring a loss, should it continue to produce in the short run? The long run? Explain.

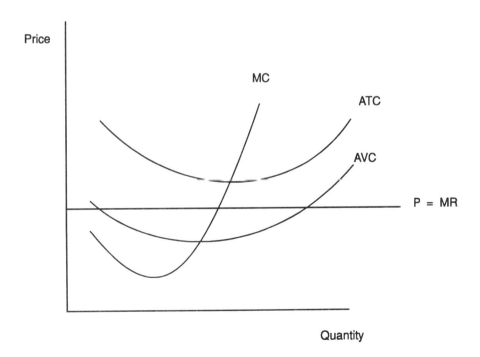

Everyday Applications

In the last decade, we have experienced remarkable changes in our telephone service. Instead of one choice for local and long-distance service, we now have a variety of choices for long-distance service. How does the experience of the last few years with firms entering the long-distance market compare to the story told about the increasingly competitive ice market? Aside from government intervention in the market, what technological factors played a role in making the long-distance market more competitive?

Economics Online

Check the Web sites for long-distance carriers to look for evidence of competition among them. AT&T's site is (*http://www.att.com/*); Sprint's site is (*http://www.sprint.com*); and MCI's site is (*http://www.mci.com/*).

Answers to Questions

Key Terms Quiz

a. 4
b. 5
c. 1
d. 2
e. 3

True-False Questions

1. False. Monopolists desire to maximize profits. Price is determined at the profit-maximizing level.
2. False. A monopolist will lower price if profits increase as a result.
3. False. Marginal revenue is a downward-sloping curve below the demand curve.
4. False. If price is less than average total cost, the monopolist incurs a loss.
5. False. A monopolist typically produces to the left of the minimum of the average total cost curve.
6. True
7. False. A monopolist's economic profit can persist in the long run due to barriers to entry.
8. False. There is product differentiation in monopolistic competition.
9. True
10. True
11. True
12. False. If economic profit is zero, an entrepreneur will stay in the market as long as he/she can earn normal profit.
13. True
14. False. The monopolistic competitive firm typically will produce to the left of the minimum of the average total cost curve.
15. False. Firms in perfect competition are price-takers.

THE MICROECONOMICS OF PRODUCT MARKETS

Multiple-Choice Questions

1. e	6. e	11. c	16. b
2. a	7. a	12. e	17. c
3. d	8. c	13. b	18. c
4. b	9. b	14. a	19. e
5. a	10. a	15. a	20. e

Fill in the Blanks

1. average total cost; MR = MC; maximize profit
2. inelastic
3. entry; supply; price
4. supply; supply; marginal cost; average total cost
5. Schumpeter; economies of scale

Discussion Questions

1. The monopolist's and the monopolistically competitive firm's demand curves are downward sloping because, in the case of the monopolist, there is no close substitute for the product sold, and, in the case of the monopolistic competitor, there are close but not perfect substitutes for the product sold. Hence, each firm can raise price and not lose all of its sales. Alternatively, in order to sell more, both types of firms must lower price. For the perfectly competitive firm, its good is a perfect substitute for all the other firms' goods. Furthermore, the firm is insignificant relative to the market, so its decision to sell more doesn't affect market price. Therefore, the perfectly competitive firm can sell all it wants at the market price. If it raised price, its sales would immediately drop to zero because consumers would go to a competing firm to buy the perfect substitute. That is why the perfectly competitive firm's demand curve is graphed horizontally.

2. Schumpeter holds that there may be advantages to monopoly and larger-sized firms in general. Specifically, these firms are able to employ modern technologies that give the firm economies of scale. Thus, even though the monopolist may earn economic profit, because of the lower average cost of production, the price it charges may be lower than what a competitive firm would charge. Moreover, the monopoly profits are a source of funds for further research and development of new technologies. The zero long-run economic profit situation faced by a competitive firm makes such innovation much more difficult. John Kenneth Galbraith shares this view. He argues that most innovation comes from large firms with the resources to support the necessary scientists and engineers.

    However, Alfred Marshall has argued that due to the sheer number of competitive firms, innovation will happen faster in perfect competition. More firms working generate more innovations. These firms have a strong incentive to innovate because it is the one sure way for them to earn economic profit in the short run.

    Which side is correct is a matter for debate. In some industries, experience indicates that larger firms do most of the innovating in our economy. However, many smaller, more competitive firms have shown innovative strength in recent years especially in the computer and pharmaceutical industries.

3. In both cases, in the long run the demand curve is tangent to the firm's average total cost curve, so the firm earns zero economic profit. However, in the case of the perfectly competitive firm, the demand curve is horizontal, so the point of tangency occurs at its minimum average total cost. Here, price is equal to

marginal revenue, marginal cost, and the minimum of average total cost. P = MR = MC = ATC gives consumers the lowest possible price. Competition results in maximum efficiency as well.

In monopolistic competition, because the demand curve is downward sloping, the point of tangency occurs to the left of the minimum average total cost, and price is greater than marginal cost at the profit-maximizing level of output. So, even though the firm earns only a normal profit, it doesn't achieve maximum efficiency because the output level is less than that associated with the minimum of the average total cost curve.

4. A perfectly competitive firm's long-run supply curve is that portion of its marginal cost curve that lies above the upward-sloping portion of the average total cost curve. If price falls below average total cost, the firm will shut down. In the long run, the firm will supply more if price increases, following the MR = MC rule, producing output levels that correspond to points on the marginal cost curve. Therefore, the marginal cost curve above the average cost curve traces out combinations of prices and quantities that the firm is willing to supply — the firm's long-run supply curve.

Problems

1. a. The completed table is shown below.

Price ($/pair)	Quantity	Total Revenue	Marginal Revenue
30	1000	30,000	
25	2000	50,000	20
20	3000	60,000	10
15	4000	60,000	0
10	5000	50,000	-10
5	6000	30,000	-20

The graph with the demand and marginal revenue curves plotted is shown below.

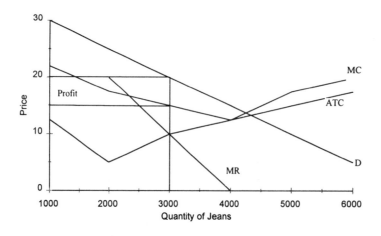

b. The firm's

b. The firm's profit-maximizing level of output can be read from the graph above as 3,000 pairs of jeans. This is the level of output that corresponds to MR = MC. The price at this level of output is read from the demand curve — $20 per pair. The firm makes a profit that is equal to the area of the rectangle labeled profit — ($20 - $15) x 3,000 = $15,000.

c. No, long-run equilibrium has not been achieved. As long as the firm is earning economic profit, there is incentive for new firms to enter the market. As new firms enter, the market demand is divided among a larger number of firms, and this firm's demand curve will shift to the left until profits are erased. This occurs when the demand curve is tangent to the average total cost curve. The firm earns only normal profit, so there is no incentive for firms to enter or leave the market. Long-run equilibrium has been reached because price is equal to minimum average total cost.

2. The graph to the left shows the firm in short-run equilibrium earning economic profit. This has to be a short-run situation because the profit won't persist in the long run. The profit will be a signal for new firms to enter the market. As entry occurs, the market supply curve will shift to the right causing the price to fall. Entry continues and price falls until economic profit is zero. This occurs when the marginal revenue curve is tangent to the average total cost curve at its minimum point, shown in the graph to the right.

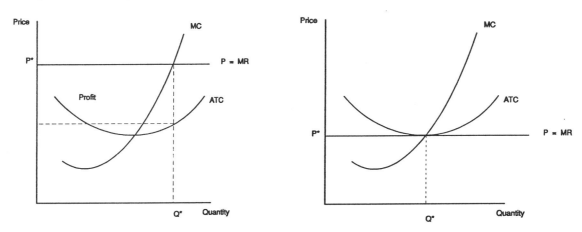

3. This firm incurs a loss. The area of the loss is shown in the graph below as the rectangle labeled "loss" that is bounded on top and to the right by the dashed line. This firm should continue to produce in the short run because it has enough total revenue to cover its total variable costs and a portion of its total fixed costs. We know this is the case because the price (marginal revenue) is greater than the minimum of the average variable cost curve.

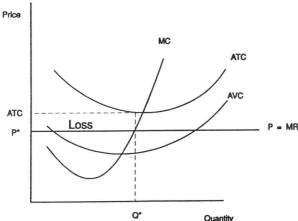

CHAPTER 12

PRICE AND OUTPUT DETERMINATION UNDER OLIGOPOLY

Chapter in a Nutshell

We reserved the discussion of price and output determination under oligopoly for a separate chapter because it's more complicated than the other market structures. First, this chapter considers the problem of describing the degree of oligopoly in a market. Oligopoly can occur in different forms — e.g., **balanced** and **unbalanced oligopoly**. The degree of market power, that is, the ability to control price and output, can be estimated with either a **concentration ratio**, which is the percentage of sales of the leading firms, or the **Herfindahl-Hirschman index**, which is the sum of the squares of all the firms' market shares. The concentrated market power that may exist in oligopoly markets can be increased by mergers. Mergers can be **horizontal**, **vertical**, or **conglomerate**. **Cartels** arrived at through **collusion** can give rise to greater concentrations of market power without mergers. Because oligopoly is such a varied market structure, it should come as no surprise that several theories exist to explain price and output determination in oligopoly. These include **game theory pricing**, the **godfather** or **price leadership theory**, the **kinked demand curve**, **brand multiplication**, **price discrimination**, and **cartel pricing**.

After studying this chapter, you should be able to:

- Use **concentration ratios** and the **Herfindahl-Hirschman index** to characterize different forms of oligopoly.
- Describe trends in concentration ratios.
- Distinguish between **balanced** and **unbalanced oligopoly**.
- Compare the extent of oligopoly markets in the United States and in other industrialized countries.
- Discuss the types of **mergers** and the impact of different types of mergers on industry concentration.
- Give examples of **cartels** and **collusion**.
- Present theories of price and output in oligopoly including **game theory**, **price leadership**, the **kinked demand curve**, **brand multiplication**, **price discrimination**, and **cartel pricing**.

Concept Check — See how you do on these multiple-choice questions.

1. In an **unbalanced oligopoly**, market power is
   a. controlled by collusion
   b. distributed evenly among firms in the industry
   c. distributed unevenly among firms in the industry
   d. constantly changing over time
   e. constantly changing according to the industry

Balanced and unbalanced oligopoly are two general forms of this market structure. How do they differ?

2. **Concentration ratios** tend to be overstated because
    a. they exclude industries producing goods that have high cross elasticities
    b. they exclude imports
    c. they exclude second-hand markets
    d. b and c are correct
    e. a, b, and c are correct

What happens to concentration ratios if we include the items suggested in a, b, and c in their calculation

3. **Game theory** is a useful tool for describing oligopoly price and output decisions among firms that are
    a. interdependent
    b. independent
    c. regulated
    d. international
    e. merging

In game theory models, the outcomes for different players depend on their strategies and those of the other players.

4. The **price leadership** model best explains
    a. cartel pricing
    b. pricing with brand multiplication
    c. pricing in horizontal mergers
    d. pricing in vertical mergers
    e. pricing in unbalanced oligopoly

Does a price leader take into account the price and output decisions of other firms in the market? Why or why not?

5. In the **kinked demand curve** model, the price tends
    a. to fall as firms cheat on cartel agreements
    b. toward stability
    c. to be sensitive to changes in marginal cost
    d. to rise as a result of cartel formation
    e. to be quite volatile

In the kinked demand curve model, what happens to the firm's total revenue if it either raises or lowers the price?

Am I on the Right Track?

Your answers to the questions above should be **c, e, a, e,** and **b**. By now, you should have acquired the tools of analysis necessary to construct a variety of models to describe the most prevalent and probably the most interesting of the market structures, oligopoly. So we'll run through the key words, then get on with questions about oligopoly so that you can master the complexity of this market structure.

Key Terms Quiz — Match the terms on the left with the definitions in the column on the right.

1. concentration ratio
2. market power
3. unbalanced oligopoly
4. balanced oligopoly
5. kinked demand curve
6. price discrimination
7. price leadership
8. horizontal merger
9. vertical merger
10. conglomerate merger
11. cartel
12. collusion
13. game theory
14. Herfindahl-Hirschman index
15. brand multiplication

_____ a. a merger between firms that have a supplier-purchaser relationship
_____ b. oligopoly where the sales of leading firms are distributed unevenly
_____ c. a merger between firms in unrelated industries
_____ d. a group of firms that collude to limit competition
_____ e. the practice of firms to negotiate price and market-share decisions
_____ f. ratio of total sales of the leading firms in an industry to total industry sales
_____ g. a merger between firms producing the same good in the same industry
_____ h. a theory of strategy in oligopoly where the firms' behavior is mutually interdependent
_____ i. a firm's ability to select and control market price and output
_____ j. sum of the squares of the market shares of all the firms in the industry
_____ k. variations on one good produced in order to increase market share
_____ l. oligopoly where the sales of the leading firms are distributed evenly
_____ m. sale of the same good or service at different prices to different people
_____ n. elastic demand for price increases, inelastic demand for price decreases
_____ o. price decisions of a firm are accepted and followed by other firms in the industry

Graphing Tutorial

The kinked demand curve model can be somewhat intimidating on first sight. However, if you keep in mind what the model is intended to explain, it makes good sense. The model explains why price rigidity in oligopoly is commonly observed. Consider General Motors' decision to raise or lower the price on its new model cars. GM may interpret its situation as follows. If GM raises the prices of its new cars, GM's competitors will not follow GM's lead and will leave their prices unchanged. Thus, GM will lose many sales along a relatively elastic demand curve. However, if GM lowers the prices of its new cars, other firms will follow GM's lead, and only a small number of new sales will be made along a steep inelastic demand curve because GM's competitors are cutting prices at the same time. In effect, GM faces two demand curves — one that is relatively elastic for prices above the current (or start) price and one that is relatively inelastic for prices below the current price. The demand curve has a kink at the current price.

If there are two distinct demand curves for GM, then there must also be two distinct marginal revenue curves, one for each of the demand curves. Thus, there is a relatively flat marginal revenue curve that corresponds to the elastic demand curve above the current price. And, there is a relatively steep marginal revenue curve that corresponds to the inelastic demand curve below the current price. A graph representing GM's kinked demand curve, the two marginal revenue curves, and the marginal cost curve is shown on the following page.

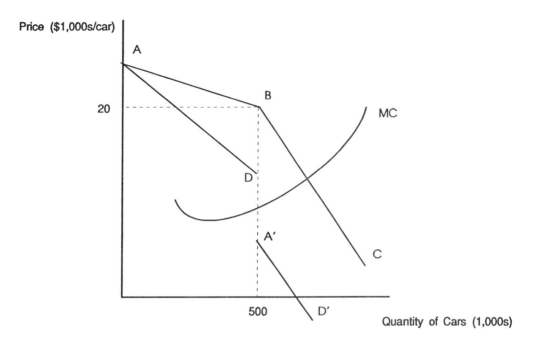

The elastic portion of the demand curve is the segment labeled AB, above a price equal to $20,000 per car, and the inelastic portion of the demand curve is the segment BC below the $20,000 price. Corresponding to demand segment AB is marginal revenue segment AD, and corresponding to demand segment BC is marginal revenue segment A'D'.

The marginal cost curve has been drawn so that it passes through a gap between the two segments of the marginal revenue curve. The gap between the marginal revenue curves, occurring above the output level of 500,000 cars, is significant because GM is able to equate MR and MC to maximize profits anywhere within this gap. GM has no incentive to raise or lower price — profits are maximized at the price $20,000 and an output level of 500,000 cars. Moreover, the marginal cost curve could shift within the gap between the marginal revenue segments, and GM would still not change either price or output. Thus, the kinked demand curve model demonstrates price rigidity in oligopoly.

Graphing Pitfalls

The kinked demand curve model is just that — a graph that shows a kink in the demand curve. However, the kink in the demand curve causes there to be a gap between the segments of the marginal revenue curve that correspond to the elastic and inelastic segments of the demand curve. The marginal revenue curve isn't kinked. So don't try to represent this model with both a kinked demand curve and a kinked marginal revenue curve, as shown on the following page!

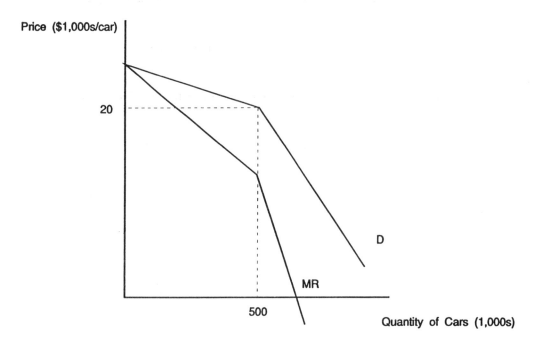

Only the demand curve has a kink, not the marginal revenue curve — there should only be a gap between the segments of the marginal revenue curve.

True-False Questions — If a statement is false, explain why.

1. Firm behavior under oligopoly is more varied than under perfect competition. (T/F)

2. Oligopoly has fewer firms and is more concentrated than monopolistic competition. (T/F)

3. Perfect competition is the most prevalent market structure in the United States. (T/F)

4. The concentration ratio describes the percentage of industry sales controlled by a specific number of firms. (T/F)

5. Brand multiplication is a means used by an oligopolist to increase market share. (T/F)

6. The Herfindahl-Hirschman index measures the industry sales of the four leading firms in an industry. (T/F)

7. In unbalanced oligopoly, one firm controls a much higher percentage of sales than the others. (T/F)

8. Concentration ratios are understated because imports are not included in their calculation. (T/F)

9. The oligopoly character of U.S. industry is unique in world markets. (T/F)

10. The kinked demand curve explains why prices in oligopoly are relatively stable. (T/F)

11. A horizontal merger occurs when two firms in the same industry combine. (T/F)

12. Because smaller firms are typically ignored in oligopoly, they can easily charge a different price than the price set by the godfather or price leader. (T/F)

13. Vertical mergers are the most common merger form observed in the United States. (T/F)

14. Cartel members determine a common price and output policy for their industry. (T/F)

15. The game theory view of oligopoly argues that prices are subject to fits of change as firms test each other's responses. (T/F)

Multiple-Choice Questions

1. The extent of oligopoly power in the United States can be measured by the
   a. low concentration ratios observed
   b. large number of firms in all industries
   c. number of very large firms in all industries
   d. high concentration ratios observed
   e. percentage of national sales accounted for by the four largest firms in various industries

2. The more inelastic segment of the kinked demand curve model describes a situation where rivals _____ price changes, while the more elastic segment describes a situation where rivals _____ price changes.
   a. follow; don't follow
   b. earn higher profits with; earn lower profits with
   c. don't follow; follow
   d. advertise; don't advertise
   e. consider; don't consider

3. Karl Marx made the incorrect prediction that
   a. oligopoly power would increase in capitalist countries
   b. concentration ratios would fall
   c. all oligopolies would become balanced
   d. all oligopolies would become unbalanced
   e. all monopolies would eventually become oligopolies because barriers to entry would be overcome

4. If an oligopoly industry is balanced, then
   a. the leading firms in the industry have approximately the same market shares
   b. one firm controls substantially more of the market than the others
   c. the industry is in equilibrium
   d. the concentration ratio is very low
   e. the concentration ratio is diminishing

5. Concentration ratios can be misleading because
   a. firms systematically withhold information
   b. they change so rapidly over time
   c. they can't be measured accurately
   d. they include foreign firms
   e. they don't include goods from industries with high cross elasticities, imports, and second-hand markets

6. Concentration ratios for industries in other industrialized countries are
   a. much higher than in the United States
   b. much lower than in the United States
   c. rising rapidly compared to the United States
   d. similar to those in the United States
   e. falling more rapidly than those in the United States

7. The most commonly observed type of merger is a
   a. vertical merger
   b. horizontal merger
   c. conglomerate merger
   d. hostile merger
   e. concentrated merger

8. If a horizontal merger occurs in the shoe industry, then the concentration ratio in that industry is likely to
   a. increase
   b. decrease
   c. stay about the same
   d. resemble those in similar industries
   e. follow a historical trend

9. A vertical merger with a dominating oligopolist in an industry allows the merged firms to
   a. become a monopoly
   b. control most levels of production in an industry
   c. survive indefinitely
   d. block entry by foreign competitors
   e. lower price while, at the same time, raising profit

10. A major reason why firms form a cartel is because the cartel can
    a. delay economic development
    b. lead to a situation resembling monopoly
    c. accelerate economic development
    d. lead to lower prices for consumers and higher profit for the cartel
    e. lead to higher total output for all cartel members

11. In an unbalanced oligopoly, when a firm's price decisions are tacitly accepted and followed by other firms, there is
    a. a cartel
    b. price leadership
    c. reduction in differentiated products
    d. mutual interdependence among the firms
    e. price and profit increases

12. If we consider the game theory explanation of pricing for two firms, then all of the following are likely scenarios **except** that
    a. the two firms will equate their own marginal revenue and marginal cost curves independently
    b. the two firms might maximize joint profits by both setting a high price
    c. the two firms could suffer from competitive price cutting
    d. the two firms' pricing decisions are interdependent
    e. one firm can undercut the other by setting a lower price

13. The godfather theory of oligopoly pricing argues that the
    a. smaller firms dictate the price to the godfather because the smaller firms typically collude
    b. smaller firms' price is higher than the godfather's because smaller firms cannot capture economies of scale
    c. godfather and smaller firms price independently, but the godfather ends up with the largest share of the market
    d. godfather sets price and output where its marginal revenue equals its marginal cost and the smaller firms accept that price
    e. demand curve is downward sloping for the godfather and horizontal for the others

14. The "gray area" of price discrimination refers to the idea that
    a. a firm is never certain that it has segmented the market correctly
    b. customers who purchase the good at a lower price resell at a higher price, causing profits to decrease
    c. to practice price discrimination, a firm must offer identical products or services at different prices
    d. oligopolists are uncertain as to the maximum price to charge segments of the market
    e. it is uncertain that price discrimination leads to higher profits

15. In the kinked demand curve model of oligopoly, if one firm cuts its price, then
    a. other firms will follow with price cuts of their own
    b. other firms will follow with price increases to increase short-run profit
    c. the demand curve facing the firm becomes very elastic, increasing profit
    d. its profit increases dramatically in the long run
    e. other firms won't respond at all because they are already maximizing profit

16. The existence of a marginal revenue gap in the kinked demand curve model of oligopoly is derived from
    a. price rigidity
    b. the gap in the demand curve
    c. the kink in the demand curve
    d. a shifting marginal cost curve
    e. uncertainty about the position of the demand curve

17. Brand multiplication in oligopoly occurs due to the desire of firms to
    a. satisfy consumers' changing tastes
    b. respond to changing cost structures
    c. increase market share without lowering prices
    d. lower price and increase output and profit
    e. keep demand highly elastic to maintain maximum profit

18. Price discrimination by firms results in all of the following **except** that
    a. firms are able to extract consumer surplus that would otherwise go to consumers
    b. identical goods or services have different prices, depending on who is buying them
    c. the total revenue of firms that practice price discrimination is higher
    d. some consumers are not allowed to purchase certain goods, based on their ethnic, racial, or cultural backgrounds
    e. firms find some way to distinguish one type of consumer from other types of consumers

19. One advantage to the Herfindahl-Hirschman index as a measure of market power compared to the four-firm concentration ratio is that
    a. the index allows for greater concentration than does the four-firm concentration ratio
    b. the index gives greater weight to the leading firms in the industry than does the four-firm concentration ratio
    c. the index is more complicated to calculate, so it is more accurate
    d. by squaring the percentages of market sales, greater weight is given to firms with smaller market shares
    e. the economy appears to be more competitive based on results of Herfindahl-Hirschman index calculations

20. A strong argument that can be made to show the inherent instability of cartels is
    a. cartel members are prone to be unprofitable in the long run
    b. cartels seldom set the price at the profit-maximizing level
    c. some cartel members may be able to increase their profits by exceeding their quotas
    d. quotas are established that inevitably create a surplus situation
    e. governments make every effort to break them up

Fill in the Blanks

1. A relatively even distribution of market power exists in _____, while an uneven distribution of market power exists in _____.

2. The three types of merger activity that are observed include _____, _____, and _____.

3. Price and output decisions by oligopolists tend to be _____, and _____ theory is often used to describe their behavior.

4. Oligopoly firms often attempt to increase market share through _____.

5. In the kinked demand curve model, if the firm raises its price, rivals will _____, while if it

lowers its price, rivals will _____.

Discussion Questions

1. How does the term *market power* relate to the concentration ratio in a particular industry?

2. Contrast the four-firm concentration ratio and the Herfindahl-Hirschman index as measures of the degree of concentration in an industry.

3. Which types of mergers are most likely to lead to higher concentration ratios? Why?

4. Explain why airlines price discriminate. For example, why would an airline lower price for special weekend getaways or for senior citizens? Does charging different prices to coach and first-class passengers represent price discrimination? Why or why not?

Problems

1. a. Suppose the 35 mm camera industry consists of two firms, Blinkon and Cannon, and that their pricing behavior can be represented by the kinked demand curve model. The following table shows price and quantity combinations for Blinkon under the assumptions that Cannon does and does not follow its pricing behavior. Complete the table to show Blinkon's total revenue and marginal revenue, and then graph the demand and marginal revenue functions for Blinkon.

Demand When Cannon Does Follow Blinkon				Demand When Cannon Does Not Follow Blinkon			
Price ($/camera)	Quantity Demanded	Total Revenue	Marginal Revenue	Price ($/camera)	Quantity Demanded	Total Revenue	Marginal Revenue
250	50			200	50		
200	100			175	100		
150	150			150	150		
100	200			125	200		
50	250			100	250		

THE MICROECONOMICS OF PRODUCT MARKETS

b. Identify the equilibrium price and output level. Explain your choice. That is, why aren't other price and output combinations profit maximizing for Blinkon?

c. By how much could the marginal cost shift without causing the profit-maximizing price to change? Explain.

2. The following table provides hypothetical sales data for 10 firms that comprise the television industry. Ignoring the fact that these companies are from different countries, calculate the four-firm concentration ratio and the Herfindahl-Hirschman index from these data. Show your work. Does this industry seem to be very concentrated at the international level? Explain.

Brand	Sales (millions of $s)
Zenith	25
Magnavox	15
Sony	38
Mitsubishi	22
Phillips	12
RCA	15
Panasonic	24
Samsung	28
Hitachi	10
Motorola	8

3. Suppose you are the chief executive officer for the major U.S. brewing company, Riceweiser. At the annual Brewers Association Meetings held in Milwaukee, you and your fellow CEOs from other brewing companies decide (secretly, of course) to collude on price and to allocate shares of the market between firms. Suppose that the price is set at $30 per barrel of beer and your share of the market is set at 2 million barrels per year. The demand, marginal revenue, average total cost, and marginal cost curves for Riceweiser are shown in the graph below.

a. Will Riceweiser make a profit under the cartel agreement? If so, how much profit? Identify the area of profit on the graph?

b. Does Riceweiser have an incentive to cheat on the agreement? Why or why not? Use the graph to justify your answer.

THE MICROECONOMICS OF PRODUCT MARKETS

4. Suppose that Riceweiser is the dominant firm in the brewing industry. What will Riceweiser's output level be as the godfather?

Everyday Applications

The first paragraphs of this chapter in your textbook describe the breakfast cereal aisle in any supermarket. There are many brands, but how many firms are actually producing all these brands? What phenomenon are you observing firsthand? Check the soft drink aisle. Observe the prices on two-liter bottles of various brands of soft drinks. Not much difference, is there? What model of price and output determination under oligopoly could you use to explain the observed stability in soft drink prices?

Economics Online

OPEC, the Organization of Petroleum Exporting Countries, has a Web page (*http://www.opec.org/*). How does the image OPEC presents in its home page compare to the behavior predicted by the theory of cartels presented in this chapter? Does cartel instability seem to be a problem for OPEC based on the information presented at this Web site?

Answers to Questions

Key Terms Quiz

a. 9
b. 3
c. 10
d. 11
e. 12
f. 1
g. 8
h. 13
i. 2
j. 14
k. 15
l. 4
m. 6
n. 5
o. 7

True-False Questions

1. True
2. True
3. False. Oligopoly is the most prevalent market structure in the United States.
4. True
5. True
6. False. The HHI is the sum of the squares of the percentage market shares of all firms in the industry.
7. True
8. True
9. False. The extent of oligopoly power in other industrialized countries is similar to that observed in the United States.
10. True
11. True
12. False. The godfather determines a price that other, smaller firms tacitly accept.
13. False. Conglomerate mergers are the most common form in the United States.
14. True
15. True

226   CHAPTER 12   OLIGOPOLY

Multiple-Choice Questions

1. e	6. d	11. b	16. c
2. a	7. c	12. a	17. c
3. a	8. a	13. d	18. d
4. a	9. b	14. c	19. b
5. e	10. b	15. a	20. c

Fill in the Blanks

1. balanced oligopoly; unbalanced oligopoly
2. vertical mergers; horizontal mergers; conglomerate mergers
3. interdependent; game
4. brand multiplication
5. not follow; follow

Discussion Questions

1. Market power is the ability of a firm to control the price and output in an industry. As the four-firm concentration ratio increases, the leading four firms in an industry control a larger percentage of total industry sales. For this reason, a strong correlation exists between greater market power and higher four-firm concentration ratios.

2. Both the four-firm concentration ratio and the HHI can be used to measure the degree of concentration in an industry. The four-firm concentration ratio gives the ratio of total sales of the four leading firms in an industry to total industry sales. The HHI is calculated by summing the squares of the percentage market shares for all the firms in the industry. By squaring the market shares, the HHI gives greater weight to firms with relatively higher market shares. The HHI has the advantage of highlighting the role that a dominant firm might play in an oligopoly industry. The dominant firm's position could be obscured by the four-firm concentration ratio. For example, if the dominant firm has 40 percent of the market, and there are many other small firms, the four-firm concentration ratio might only be 50 percent. Using the HHI, however, the dominant firm will contribute 1,600, a relatively large sum, to the index value.

3. Horizontal mergers lead to an immediate increase in an oligopoly's concentration ratio by decreasing the number of firms. Vertical mergers, too, can lead to an increase in concentration by giving the merged firm a cost or marketing advantage over its competition. A supplier-purchaser relationship is subsumed by a vertical merger that may allow the merged firm to gain access to resources at lower cost than can other firms. Conglomerate mergers have little effect on concentration ratios because the firms merging are from unrelated industries.

4. An airline will attempt to sell as many seats as possible at the upper end of the demand curve at higher prices. But the airline knows that every empty seat represents potential revenue that has been lost. The marginal cost of filling that empty seat is close to zero. After all, the plane flies whether it is full or not. If the airline can devise a way of selling tickets for these otherwise empty seats at lower prices without affecting the sales of other seats, it adds to revenue. That's why there are senior citizen discounts and special weekend getaway rates for Saturday night stayovers.

    Even though coach and first-class passengers are charged different prices for the same flight, the product isn't the same, so this practice does not represent price discrimination. Circumstances for travelers in first class are vastly superior to those most of us experience in coach. The seats are bigger, the food is

THE MICROECONOMICS OF PRODUCT MARKETS

better, and the lavatory is available without a long wait, to name just a few of the differences.

Problems

1. a. The completed table and graph, showing the kinked demand curve and the marginal revenue curves for Blinkon are presented below.

Price ($/camera)	Quantity Demanded	Total Revenue	Marginal Revenue	Price ($/camera)	Quantity Demanded	Total Revenue	Marginal Revenue
250	50	12,500		200	50	10,000	
200	100	20,000	150	175	100	17,500	150
150	150	22,500	50	150	150	22,500	100
100	200	20,000	-50	125	200	25,000	50
50	250	12,500	-150	100	250	25,000	0

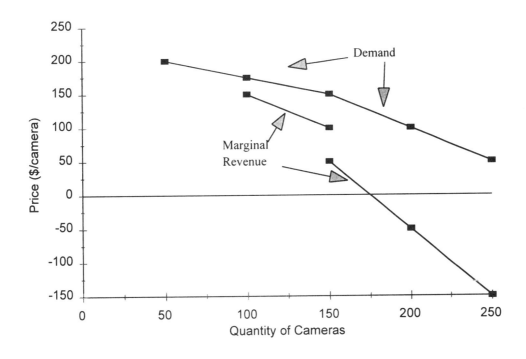

b. The demand curve is kinked at the price of $150 and sales of 150 cameras. The price will be rigid at $150 because an increase in price would not be followed by Cannon. Therefore, Blinkon would lose sales along the elastic portion of the demand curve above the $150 price level. A decrease in price from $150 puts Blinkon on the more inelastic demand curve, causing a decrease in total revenue from $22,500 to $20,000.

c. Marginal cost could shift anywhere in the gap between the marginal revenue curves at an output level of 150. The gap is $50 — so marginal cost could fluctuate by as much as $50 with no change in the profit-maximizing price.

2. Computing the four-firm concentration ratio — the top four firms are Sony, Samsung, Zenith, and Panasonic. The total of their sales is equal to $115 million. Total sales in the industry are $197 million. The four-firm ratio is 115/197 = .58, or 58 percent.

To compute the HHI, we need the market shares expressed as a percent, then squared and summed. The following table presents these calculations.

Brand	Sales (millions of $)	Market Share as % (S)	Market Share Squared (S^2)
Zenith	25	12.6	158.8
Magnavox	15	7.6	57.8
Sony	38	19.4	376.4
Mitsubishi	22	11.1	123.2
Phillips	12	6.2	38.4
RCA	15	7.6	57.7
Panasonic	24	12.2	148.8
Samsung	28	14.2	201.6
Hitachi	10	5.1	26.0
Motorola	8	4.0	16
Sum	197	100	1,204.7

On a national level this industry would be very concentrated. For example, suppose we consider Zenith, Magnavox, RCA, and Motorola to be U.S. companies. The four-firm concentration ratio for U.S. firms is 100 percent! The HHI for these four firms is 2,921. However, on an international level, the apparent market power wielded by U.S. firms is diffused by the existence of large firms from other countries.

3. a. Riceweiser will make a profit under the cartel agreement. The area of profit given the cartel is shown in the graph on the next page by the heavy-lined rectangle. The profit is ($30 − $10) × 2 million barrels = $40 million.

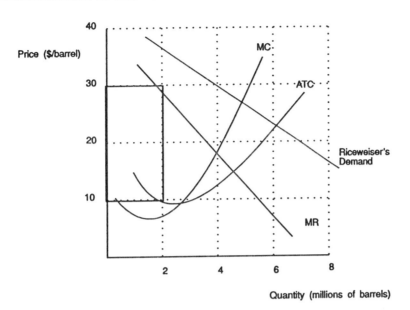

b. Riceweiser has incentive to cheat because the profit maximizing level of output is 4 million barrels — MR = MC at 4 million barrels. Riceweiser's profits could be ($30 − $12) x 4 million barrels = $72 million. The profit is shown below as the area inside the heavy-lined rectangle.

4. Riceweiser will act like a monopolist in this situation. The second graph from problem 3 illustrates the profit-maximizing output, price, and profit. Whatever share of the market is left can be soaked up by the other firms at the price that Riceweiser mandates.

CHAPTER 13

ANTITRUST AND REGULATION

Chapter in a Nutshell

Perfect competition is the exception rather than the rule in the real world. Because there are so few perfectly competitive markets in the economy, most firms do not produce efficiently — that is, at minimum average total cost. Should something be done about this? What about the relative prices that are formed in markets dominated by monopoly and oligopoly? These question are explored in this chapter. A variety of policy options are discussed. The easiest policy is to do nothing — the **laissez-faire** approach. A laissez-faire approach makes sense if the markets being considered for regulation are **contestable markets** where at least the threat of competition exists, or if there is **countervailing power**. In other cases, **regulation** is more appropriate, especially with natural monopoly. Price choices are left to the regulatory agency, where **"fair" price and marginal cost pricing** are alternatives. Other options for dealing with monopoly and oligopoly power include **deregulation, nationalization,** and **antitrust policy**. Deregulation of a previously regulated industry is carried out with the hope that competition will thrive and place limits on monopoly power. Nationalization occurs when the government takes over a firm or industry and then controls price and production decisions. Antitrust policy involves enacting and enforcing laws that affect the structure and behavior of firms. Some of these policies are more appropriate than others for particular situations, and each of these policies has its advantages and disadvantages.

After studying this chapter, you should be able to:

- List and explain the options available for coping with monopoly and oligopoly.
- Compare graphically the **"fair" price** and **marginal cost pricing** approaches to regulation.
- Explain how **deregulation** can lead to lower prices.
- Discuss the feasibility of **nationalizing** an industry.
- Distinguish between **contestable** and **noncontestable** markets.
- Present examples of **countervailing power** in industries.
- Define **creative destruction.**
- Provide an overview of **antitrust** legislation and its enforcement in the United States.

Concept Check — See how you do on these multiple-choice questions.

1. The **rule of reason criterion** states that
    a. market power should always be limited
    b. only public utilities should be allowed to be monopolies
    c. monopolies are acceptable if they don't abuse their market power
    d. the bigger the firm, the more monopolistic is its behavior
    e. a monopoly convicted of an antitrust violation usually wins on a reasonable appeal

Should monopoly ever be allowed to exist? Under what conditions?

2. If the government decides to pursue a policy of **laissez-faire** with respect to monopoly and oligopoly, it will
   a. regulate the firms
   b. nationalize the firms
   c. apply antitrust policy
   d. leave the firms alone
   e. encourage concentration of the industry

What does the French phrase mean?

3. One problem with applying **marginal cost pricing** to regulate a monopolist is that the
   a. monopolist will earn profits that are too high
   b. monopolist may incur a loss
   c. price may be above average total cost
   d. monopolist's shareholders begin selling their holdings
   e. price will also equal average total cost

In cases of natural monopoly, the average total cost curve is decreasing over a wide range of output. If average total cost is decreasing, then marginal cost must be less than average total cost.

4. The purpose of **deregulation** is to
   a. guarantee competitive pricing
   b. abide by court decisions regarding government regulation
   c. provide a way for monopolies to avoid having to abide by court decisions to regulate
   d. provide a way for monopolies to avoid having to abide by regulatory commission decisions
   e. dismantle the regulatory controls that have been imposed on a regulated industry

Regulation in the United States has typically imposed a set of controls on an industry that are enforced by a commission. Deregulation . . . .

5. The first piece of **antitrust legislation** in the United States was the _____ passed by Congress in _____.
   a. Sherman Act, 1914
   b. Clayton Act, 1914
   c. Sherman Act, 1890
   d. Celler-Kefauver Act, 1951
   e. Interstate Commerce Commission Act, 1881

Learn the different acts, their provisions, and the effectiveness of each in limiting monopoly practices.

Am I on the Right Track?

Your answers to the questions above should be **c, d, b, e,** and **c**. A virtual grab bag of options exists for dealing with monopoly and oligopoly markets. One of these options is to do nothing — the laissez-faire approach. The problem is to determine which policy is most appropriate given the economic circumstances. The theory of production along with the theories of firm behavior we have studied help guide the choice of policy regarding concentration of market power in monopoly and oligopoly markets.

CHAPTER 13 ANTITRUST AND REGULATION

Key Terms Quiz — Match the terms on the left with the definitions in the column on the right.

1. laissez-faire
2. countervailing power
3. contestable market
4. creative destruction
5. regulation
6. patent
7. rule of reason criterion
8. marginal cost pricing
9. per se criterion
10. deregulation
11. antitrust policy
12. nationalization

_____ a. pricing and output decisions are made by a regulatory agency
_____ b. price is regulated equal to marginal cost
_____ c. laws to foster competition that prohibit the exercise of excessive market power by monopolies
_____ d. market power of one economic bloc is checked by the power of a competing bloc
_____ e. government ownership of a firm or industry
_____ f. size alone is enough to indicate a violation of antitrust law
_____ g. market where the threat of entry exists
_____ h. government policy of nonintervention in the market
_____ i. firm's size alone is insufficient to indicate a violation of antitrust laws
_____ j. monopoly right granted for 20 years to market a product or process
_____ k. competition that exists between highly concentrated industries
_____ l. the process of converting a regulated industry into an unregulated industry

Graphing Tutorial

This chapter uses the graph depicting a natural monopoly to show how a natural monopoly can be regulated by either the "fair" price method or the marginal cost pricing policy. Each of these alternatives has its own advantages and drawbacks. Suppose the Bumpke Waste Removal Company has a natural monopoly on hauling garbage in Springfield. Recall from Chapters 10 and 11 what this means. Given the size of the market, only one company can be supported to haul trash at a low average total cost. The average total cost curve is downward sloping in the range of output being considered. The downward slope of the average total cost reflects the high fixed costs that are associated with a natural monopoly. As output increases, average total costs continue to fall because declining average fixed costs pull them down. Because average total cost is decreasing, marginal cost is less than average total cost in this range of output. A natural monopoly is shown below with demand and marginal revenue curves.

THE MICROECONOMICS OF PRODUCT MARKETS

Since Bumpke is a price-maker with no regulation, the firm will set output at 200 tons per week, where marginal revenue is equal to marginal cost, and charge $8 per ton from the demand curve. Suppose the Springfield community decides this is unacceptable and chooses to regulate the fee charged by Bumpke for waste haulage. One choice is to set a "fair" price where the demand curve crosses the average total cost curve. The price charged would be $4, and 275 tons per week would be hauled with this form of regulation. Bumpke receives a normal profit, just as it would under perfect competition. This solution is far from perfect, however. As discussed in the text, the problem becomes, "Who regulates the natural monopoly's average total cost?"

The other alternative is for Springfield to impose marginal cost pricing on Bumpke. The demand curve crosses the marginal cost curve at a price equal to $2 and an output of 325. Springfield residents benefit because more trash is hauled at a lower cost. And, society is willing the pay $2 for hauling the 325th ton, exactly the cost of the resources used to haul that last ton. The P = MC rule yields the socially optimum use of resources. However, there is clearly a problem for Bumpke because the $2 price is below the $3.90 average total cost of hauling the 325th ton. In order for this pricing rule to work, Bumpke must be subsidized an amount equal to $1.90 per ton on 325 tons, or $617.50. The subsidy must be paid from tax revenues.

Graphing Pitfalls

Finding the "fair" price and the marginal cost pricing prices and levels of output is easy in the graph of a natural monopoly if you simply follow the demand curve downward to the point where it crosses the average total cost, which gives the "fair" price and output, then further down to where the demand curve crosses the marginal cost curve, which gives the marginal cost pricing price and output. Don't make the mistake of stopping where the demand curve intersects the average total cost curve and reading the marginal cost pricing price and output from this same quantity level as illustrated below. The marginal cost pricing level of output will always be larger than the "fair" price level of output for a natural monopoly.

The marginal cost pricing price level should be $2 per ton, not the 2.10 per ton shown in the graph above. Moreover, the output level should be 325, not 275 as shown above! Marginal cost pricing yields a larger output level than does "fair" pricing.

True-False Questions — If a statement is false, explain why.

1. Economists prefer perfect competition to other market structures because competition creates the lowest prices. (T/F)

2. Perfect competition is the dominant market structure in the U.S. economy. (T/F)

3. A fair price for a natural monopolist would be P = ATC. (T/F)

4. Monitoring costs of production is a difficult task for regulatory commissions. (T/F)

5. The United States practices a laissez-faire approach to the problems of monopoly and oligopoly pricing. (T/F)

6. If the threat of entry to an oligopoly or monopoly market is enough to cause prices to be reasonably low, then the market is said to be contestable. (T/F)

7. Antitrust legislation prohibits the excessive exercise of market power by monopolies and oligopolies. (T/F)

8. Consumers pay a lower price to a natural monopolist under a price equals marginal cost pricing policy than under a price equals average total cost policy. (T/F)

9. A natural monopolist regulated to set price equal to marginal cost can operate without a subsidy. (T/F)

10. Regulatory commissioners typically oppose the interests of regulated firms. (T/F)

11. The Sherman Act failed to clearly define what constituted "an attempt to monopolize" and "restraint of trade," which made the act difficult to enforce. (T/F)

12. By implementing an extensive regulatory apparatus in 1978, Alfred Kahn, then head of the CAB, was able to create lower airfares. (T/F)

13. The Clayton Act closed loopholes in the Sherman Act by incorporating four specific anticompetitive activities. (T/F)

14. A nationalized monopoly should be expected to be managed very differently from a private monopoly. (T/F)

15. The rule of reason holds that if a firm is large relative to the total market, then it has excessive monopoly power. (T/F)

Multiple-Choice Questions

1. Some economists believe that, if perfect competition ever existed, it is no longer obtainable, because
   a. modern technology dictates that firms be very large in order to realize economies of scale
   b. concentration ratios are low
   c. of government interference with prices
   d. regulatory commissions find it easier to regulate a few big firms
   e. production is inefficient when P = MC

2. Some economists propose that monopolies and oligopolies be allowed to price without interference because
   a. the high prices they charge are good for industry profits
   b. these large firms are able to capture economies of scale and end up pricing at levels at least as low or lower than firms in perfect competition
   c. they are too complex to regulate
   d. these industries could never be contestable
   e. regulatory commissions are inevitably staffed by self-interested personnel

3. A regulatory agency that is charged with overseeing a monopoly will most likely be involved in
   a. regulating the monopoly's profit margins
   b. regulating what monopolies can advertise
   c. encouraging the monopolist to adopt new technologies
   d. disallowing the monopoly from placing a limit on output
   e. setting the price the monopolist is allowed to charge

4. The problem with "fair" price regulation is that the regulated firm
   a. won't benefit from economies of scale any longer
   b. will earn only normal profit
   c. will earn extraordinary economic profits
   d. has little incentive to control average total cost
   e. will not submit to such regulation

5. The reason that marginal cost pricing is difficult to implement in the regulation of natural monopolies like utility companies is that
   a. marginal cost is below average total cost for a natural monopoly
   b. consumers will not pay for the resources used to produce the last unit of output
   c. marginal cost pricing would allow the monopoly economic profits
   d. such regulation might promote entry into the industry
   e. no one can figure out exactly what the marginal cost is

6. The laissez-faire approach to dealing with monopoly and oligopoly pricing behavior might be appropriate in cases where
    a. nationalization has failed
    b. firms block attempts to regulate them via court injunctions
    c. markets are contestable
    d. the firm's costs are difficult to estimate
    e. antitrust violations are difficult to prove

7. The Interstate Commerce Commission's decision to regulate trucking, as well as the railroad industry, was made to
    a. serve the interest of the trucking industry
    b. serve the public interest
    c. keep trucking prices from increasing
    d. serve the interests of the railroad industry
    e. hasten the decline of the railroad industry

8. Deregulation tends to have the most beneficial results in industries where
    a. entry is relatively easy
    b. fixed costs are very high
    c. markets are not contestable
    d. potential profits are rather low
    e. barriers to entry are significant

9. A problem that nationalized firms have faced in the past is that
    a. they are inherently less efficient than private firms
    b. they have tended to be firms that have operated at a loss over a long period of time
    c. the previous private owners have not been adequately compensated
    d. government bureaucrats make poor managers
    e. they suffer from a lack of technical expertise

10. One problem with the theory of contestable markets is that
    a. even when markets are contestable, profits are excessive
    b. entry into an oligopoly market would dilute profits
    c. it depends on the existence of countervailing power
    d. laissez-faire permits economic profit to persist in all market structures
    e. it is difficult to determine what constitutes a credible threat of entry

11. The theory of countervailing power states that oligopoly power is restrained because
    a. competition among economic blocs forces prices down
    b. the threat of entry into the industry is sufficient to keep prices down
    c. firms can quickly divert resources from one line of production to another
    d. the government can use nationalized firms to check the power of oligopoly
    e. firms will self-regulate in order to prevent government regulation

12. A contestable market is a highly concentrated market in which
    a. a balanced oligopoly ensures that prices are maintained at competitive levels
    b. a monopoly is imminent due to the intense competition among oligopolists
    c. prices are moderated by the potential threat of firms entering the market
    d. firms contest each other in the same way that firms compete
    e. power blocs exist that check the exercise of market power

THE MICROECONOMICS OF PRODUCT MARKETS

13. The primary goal of antitrust policy in the United States has been to
    a. allow firms to stay large if they experience economies of scale
    b. regulate essential industries
    c. create subsidies for competitive firms
    d. reduce profit to normal profit
    e. limit the prices charged by monopolists

14. The Clayton Act improved upon the Sherman Act to combat anticompetitive behavior by
    a. making conspiracies to restrain trade illegal
    b. creating four specific categories of anticompetitive behavior
    c. permitting interlocking directorships
    d. allowing firms to buy voting stock in competing firms
    e. allowing for natural monopolies to exist

15. The Federal Trade Commission uses all of the following methods to combat unfair trade practices **except**
    a. investigating unfair trade practices
    b. nationalizing monopolies
    c. holding public hearings
    d. initiating complaints
    e. issuing cease and desist orders

16. The Robinson-Patman Act is aimed at preventing _____ while the Celler-Kefauver Act was intended to prevent _____.
    a. disguised merger through purchase of physical assets; selective discount deals
    b. selective discount deals; disguised merger through purchase of physical assets
    c. selective discount deals; disguised merger through stock purchases
    d. disguised merger through stock purchases; selective discount deals
    e. disguised merger through stock purchases; disguised merger through purchase of physical assets

17. The courts' rule of reason criterion, as it is applied to antitrust, maintains that
    a. because monopolists are reasonable people, profit margins are constrained
    b. all monopolies unreasonably restrain trade
    c. through a process of reason monopoly can be restrained
    d. monopoly is illegal only if the firm unreasonably restrains trade
    e. it is reasonable to presume that competition is preferred

18. In 1945, the Supreme Court established the per se doctrine, which declares that
    a. a monopoly is acceptable if no other firm has attempted entry into the industry
    b. a firm's size is insufficient for a court to rule against it in antitrust cases
    c. size alone is enough for a court to rule against a firm in an antitrust case
    d. a court must find evidence of wrongdoing to declare a monopoly illegal
    e. if the monopolist can prove that the market is contestable, per se, it is acceptable

19. Supreme Court decisions in antitrust cases since the 1970s have
    a. continued to use the per se criterion
    b. have evolved to embody both the rule of reason and the per se criterion
    c. have shifted from per se to the rule of reason
    d. have been aggressive in breaking up monopolies
    e. have succeeded in ending monopoly practice in the United States

20. Critics of conglomerate mergers argue that while they involve firms from different industries, they
    a. may influence the competitive nature of the economy as a whole
    b. have impeded the creation of economies of scale
    c. cause an increase in the Herfindahl-Hirschman index
    d. cause a decrease in the Herfindahl-Hirschman index
    e. violate antitrust laws

Fill in the Blanks

1. By setting P = MC, a regulatory agency achieves the socially _____ of resources.

2. A _____ is an exclusive grant by government to _____ a product or process for _____ years.

3. The Clayton Act of 1914 made it illegal for firms to _____, _____, _____, and _____.

4. The _____ holds that a firm's size alone is insufficient evidence for a court to rule against it in an antitrust suit.

5. The _____ holds that a firm's size is sufficient evidence for a court to rule against it in an antitrust suit.

Discussion Questions

1. Do you agree that monopoly and oligopoly are inevitable outcomes of modern technology? Why or why not?

2. Why do regulatory commissions set fair prices for public utilities?

3. Compare the P = ATC pricing with the P = MC pricing for a regulated natural monopoly.

4. Discuss the various arguments in favor of a laissez-faire approach to monopoly.

5. Did antitrust legislation have much effect on the exercise of monopoly power in the United States prior to 1914?

Everyday Applications

How would you feel if you had only one choice for long-distance telephone service? Until fairly recently, that's the way it was. AT&T (Ma Bell) was the only option. Ask your parents what has happened to their long-distance bills since the introduction of competition to the market for long-distance telephone service. Do they think deregulation has led to a better situation for consumers?

Economics Online

Do you feel that you've been the victim of unfair trade practices? Do you want to get even? The information you need to get started with the process of redress may be found in the Web page for the Federal Trade Commission. The FTC Web page states that the FTC is "working for consumer protection and a competitive marketplace." Let's hope so. Visit the site (*http://www.ftc.gov/*).

Answers to Questions

Key Terms Quiz

a. 5   f. 9   k. 4
b. 8   g. 3   l. 10
c. 11 h. 1
d. 2   i. 7
e. 12 j. 6

True-False Questions

1. True
2. False. Monopolistic competition and oligopoly are both more dominant market structures in the United States.
3. True
4. True
5. False. The United States has practiced many approaches to dealing with monopoly and oligopoly market power including laissez-faire, regulation, nationalization, and antitrust.
6. True
7. True
8. True
9. False. A subsidy will be needed to compensate the natural monopolist for the loss incurred. Marginal cost is less than average total cost at the output level that corresponds to the intersection of demand and marginal cost.
10. False. Frequently, those who regulate a firm are drawn from the industry itself and share its concerns.
11. True
12. False. Kahn spearheaded the drive to deregulate the air travel industry, leading to lower fares.
13. True
14. False. There seems to be little difference between the efficiency performance of nationalized and private firms.
15. False. Size alone is not enough for the courts to rule against a firm in antitrust suits under the rule of reason.

Multiple-Choice Questions

1. a   6. c   11. a   16. b
2. b   7. d   12. c   17. d
3. e   8. a   13. e   18. c
4. d   9. b   14. b   19. c
5. a   10. e   15. b   20. a

Fill in the Blanks

1. optimum use
2. patent; market; 20
3. price discriminate; use exclusive contracts; buy out competitors' voting stock; sit on the boards of directors of competing firms
4. rule of reason
5. per se criterion

Discussion Questions

1. To the extent that modern technology favors those firms that can achieve economies of scale, then monopoly and oligopoly are outcomes of modern technology. This is not to say that small firms cannot coexist alongside large firms in particular industries. Recall the godfather model of oligopoly.

2. Public utilities are engaged in supplying households with the basics — water, gas, and electricity. These firms are characterized by their high fixed costs of production and are natural monopolies. The markets for their services are too small to support more than one firm at output levels high enough to allow the firms to realize low average total costs of production. Therefore, it makes sense to have one firm supply the water, gas, or electricity and to make certain that a fair price is charged.

3. The diagram below shows a natural monopoly being regulated at the P = ATC level and the P = MC level. P = ATC regulation occurs where the demand curve intersects the average total cost curve. P = MC regulation occurs where the demand curve intersects the marginal cost curve. Output is larger under a P = MC policy than a P = ATC policy. But, in the P = MC regulation case, the price is less than average total cost so the monopolist must be subsidized for the loss.

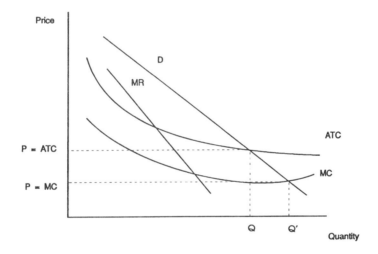

4. A strong argument could be made for a policy of laissez-faire when the markets under consideration are contestable. The threat of entry into the market by other firms will cause the monopolist or oligopolist to moderate prices. The existence of countervailing power can also justify a policy of laissez-faire. The ability of a firm to raise prices might be checked by some other economic power bloc. For example, an oligopolistic supplier of a supermarket chain, also an oligopolist, might be unable to raise prices on goods supplied to the supermarket chain because the chain purchases such a large volume of goods. Market power checks market power.

5. The Sherman Act was passed in 1890, but though it made contracts, combinations, and conspiracies in restraint of trade illegal, and the pursuit of a monopoly a felony, the act was quite vague and difficult to enforce. Therefore, in spite of victories by the Department of Justice against Standard Oil and American Tobacco, monopoly power in the United States was largely unchecked. In 1914, the Clayton Act was passed; it had more specific language to describe anticompetitive practices that were listed as illegal, including price discrimination among purchasers, exclusive contracts where purchasers would agree not to buy from competitors, the purchase of the voting stock in a competing firm, and board members sitting on the board of directors of competing firms.

CHAPTER 14

EXTERNALITIES, MARKET FAILURE, AND PUBLIC CHOICE

Chapter in a Nutshell

So far, this book has described consumption and production of goods where all of the costs and benefits are borne directly by those who do the consuming and producing. However, many types of consumption and production activities spill over to affect **third parties**. These unintended spillover effects are called economic **externalities** by economists. Externalities may be negative or positive for third parties. For example, a negative externality might be having Beavis and Butthead in the dorm room next to yours coming home late at night and playing AC/DC and Metallica when you have an economics exam at 8:00 a.m. the next day. An example of a positive externality is your dorm neighbors playing the same music (assuming you like AC/DC and Metallica) when you are in a mood to have fun, not sleep. If you like these bands and your rowdy neighbors play them regularly, then you can be a **free rider**, enjoying the benefits of hearing the music without paying for them.

Negative externalities impose costs on third parties for which they aren't compensated. Positive externalities are benefits that third parties enjoy without having to pay. In either case, the market has failed. Because no one pays for the costs resulting from negative externalities, too much of these types of activities occurs in a market. On the other hand, because people who create positive externalities aren't paid for the benefits they create for others, the market will generate too few of these activities.

Government can correct these **market failures**. A variety of approaches can be used to address the problem of negative externalities. For example, the government can impose a pollution compensation tax on an activity that creates negative externalities in order to bring the private cost in line with the social cost of the activity. **Creating new property forms** is another alternative. Here, instead of government directly regulating an activity to make sure that resources are allocated efficiently, resources may be privatized so that individuals will have an incentive to exercise **property rights** to the resources efficiently. Or, the government may impose obligatory controls regarding certain activities. For example, most municipalities don't allow leaves to be burned or dogs to roam freely.

In cases of positive externalities, the role for government is to encourage more of an activity to be undertaken. Government can do this by subsidizing the activity from tax revenues or by simply providing the activity itself, as in the case of **public goods** such as national defense, lighthouses, clean air, and clean water. However, **government failure** can occur if government fails to buy the quantity of public goods that generates maximum efficiency. Government failure can arise because, even with an honest effort, political representatives are unable to accurately measure our preferences regarding the purchase of public goods. Another potential problem is that government's choices of public goods may reflect the preferences of **special-interest lobbies** rather than the public's interest. Economists who hold this view of **public choice** believe that the production and allocation of public goods are dictated primarily by the need for government officials to keep their jobs.

After studying this chapter, you should be able to:

- Explain the difference between **negative and positive externalities**.
- Discuss why poorly defined **property rights** cause externalities.

THE MICROECONOMICS OF PRODUCT MARKETS

- Use graphs to show how **market failure** can be corrected for both types of externalities.
- Compare and contrast the different approaches for correcting negative externalities.
- Define and give examples of **public goods**.
- Distinguish between a **pure public good** and a **near-public good**.
- Describe the opposing views of **public choice**.

Concept Check — See how you do on these multiple-choice questions.

1. The reason that so many economic activities create **externalities** is that
   a. free riders exist
   b. third parties become involved in decision making
   c. special-interest groups lobby for them
   d. property rights are poorly defined
   e. government failure prevents them from being halted

Externalities exist as a result of market failure. What is the source of market failure in the case of externalities?

2. If the **social cost** of supplying a good or service is higher than the private cost, then
   a. the production of the good or service should be subsidized
   b. the price of the good or service is too low
   c. the price of the good or service is too high
   d. obligatory controls are the only way to correct the situation
   e. the good or service is a public good

Think about the position of the social cost curve relative to the private cost (supply) curve in this case.

3. The **public choice** view of the provision of public goods holds that
   a. government officials always try their utmost to act in the public's best interest
   b. government failure occurs only rarely
   c. the public chooses government officials in elections and is ultimately responsible for the provision of public goods
   d. special-interest lobbies play an important role in determining the level of provision of various public goods
   e. voting is the best way to determine the level of provision of public goods

The public choice view holds that self-interest guides a large part of political behavior. Would catering to the needs of special-interest lobbies be in the self-interest of government officials who aim to keep their jobs?

4. A **public good** is a good whose benefits are
   a. diminished as it is consumed and whose benefits cannot be withheld from anyone
   b. not diminished as it is consumed and whose benefits cannot be withheld from anyone
   c. not diminished as it is consumed and whose benefits can be withheld from anyone
   d. concentrated among a select few
   e. enjoyed by everyone in society

Be able to distinguish between a private good and a public good. There are also near-public goods.

244   CHAPTER 14   EXTERNALITIES, MARKET FAILURE, AND PUBLIC CHOICE

5. A **special-interest lobby** attempts to
   a. make certain that just the right amounts of public goods are provided
   b. persuade government to act on its behalf
   c. eliminate negative externalities
   d. eliminate positive externalities
   e. promote efficiency in government to avoid government failure

Could successful special-interest lobbying lead to government failure?

Am I on the Right Track?

Your answers to the questions above should be **d, b, d, b,** and **b**. There are some strong similarities between the material in the last chapter and this one. In both cases, the market outcome is shown to be undesirable because it fails to create an efficient allocation of society's resources. In both cases, appropriate government action can help to correct the problems with the market outcome. This chapter shows the role that government can play in correcting negative externalities and providing public goods. Economic principles help guide the development of policies to combat market failure.

Key Terms Quiz — Match the terms on the left with the definitions in the column on the right.

1. third parties   _____ a. unintended costs or benefits imposed on third parties
2. market failure   _____ b. the failure of government to buy the quantity of public goods that
                                       generates maximum efficiency
3. externalities   _____ c. view that the allocation of public goods is determined by the need
                                       for government officials to keep their jobs
4. public goods   _____ d. the cost to society of producing a good including both the private
                                       costs and the externalities costs
5. free rider   _____ e. people upon whom the externalities are imposed
6. public choice   _____ f. the right to own a good or service and to enjoy the benefits that
                                       the use of the good or service provides
7. property rights   _____ g. benefits from these goods aren't diminished by consumption and
                                       cannot be withheld from anyone
8. government failure   _____ h. a group organized to influence government concerning the
                                       costs and benefits of particular public goods
9. social cost   _____ i. the failure of the market to achieve an optimal allocation of the
                                       economy's resources
10. special-interest lobby   _____ j. someone who consumes a good or service without paying for it

Graphing Tutorial

A new graph that shows the effect of negative externalities on a market is presented in this chapter. Actually, this graph is a variant of the demand and supply diagram with which you are now familiar. To show the effect of a negative externality on a market in a graph, let's consider the market for steel. Suppose that the production of steel involves dumping waste water in a river upstream from a fishery specializing in trout. Clearly, the waste water is a negative externality for the fishery, which depends on clean water. The private cost of supplying a ton of steel is less than the social cost of supplying a ton of steel. Suppose that the pollution cost associated with producing steel is a constant $5 per ton. How would the private cost of producing steel be affected if the pollution cost were included? The private cost would be shifted upward vertically by $5. Adding the pollution cost of producing steel to the private cost generates the social cost curve of producing steel. This scenario is represented by the graph shown below.

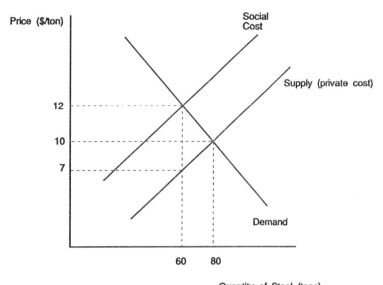

Before the cost of pollution is included in the supply of steel, the supply curve reflects the marginal cost of producing steel to the steel producers only. Thus, the supply reflects only the private costs of producing steel. However, the cost of pollution is a constant $5 per ton. Therefore, the social cost of producing steel is shifted up from the supply (private cost) curve by a vertical distance of $5.

How can we correct this problem? This can be done with a pollution compensation tax equal to $5 per ton of steel. Before the tax, 80 tons of steel would be produced and sold for $10 per ton. The tax forces producers and consumers of steel to consider the full social cost of their actions. The price per ton rises to $12 and the quantity consumed falls to 60 tons. With less steel being produced, less pollution is created. Furthermore, revenue is generated from the tax equal to $5/ton x 60 tons = $300, and this revenue can be used to fund more extensive clean-up efforts.

Graphing Pitfalls

Make certain that when you represent the effect of a negative externality on a market, you shift the supply curve (the private cost) upward and to the left to generate the social cost curve. Remember, the idea is that the private cost curve doesn't reflect all of the costs to society of a particular activity. The social cost curve must lie above the private cost curve because the cost to society for any level of production is higher than the private cost. You can't show the effect of a negative externality with a graph like the one drawn on the following page.

CHAPTER 14   EXTERNALITIES, MARKET FAILURE, AND PUBLIC CHOICE

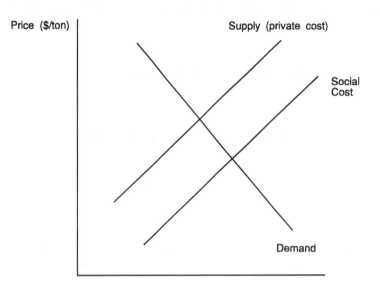

In a graph that shows the effect of a negative externality on a market, the social cost curve has to lie above the supply (private cost) curve!

True-False Questions — If a statement is false, explain why.

1. Third-party effects can be either harmful or beneficial to those who experience them. (T/F)

2. Without government intervention, negative externalities are borne directly by the producer of a good or service, so they diminish profit. (T/F)

3. Ideally, a pollution compensation tax will exactly match the cost of a negative externality. (T/F)

4. Third-parties who reap benefits without paying are called free riders. (T/F)

5. If property rights are poorly defined, then market failure results. (T/F)

6. The social cost is equal to the private cost plus the cost of the negative externality. (T/F)

7. A free market can still be efficient when negative or positive externalities are present. (T/F)

8. If steel production causes a negative externality, then the market generates a price for steel that is too low. (T/F)

9. A market price below the marginal cost is an indication that too many resources are devoted to an activity. (T/F)

10. The Coase theorem applies in cases where many parties are involved in a property rights dispute. (T/F)

11. By taxing polluters an amount per unit of the good produced equal to the cost of the negative externality, the quantity of pollution generated is reduced. (T/F)

12. Typically, if the government chooses to tax polluters, pollution levels fall to zero. (T/F)

13. A public good is not diminished by consumption and cannot be withheld from consumption. (T/F)

14. If people choose not to pay for a public good, they can be excluded from consuming it. (T/F)

15. A special-interest lobby will consider only the broader interests of society in its lobbying efforts. (T/F)

Multiple-Choice Questions

1. A third-party effect is one that involves
   a. a challenge to our two-party political system
   b. careful consultation by decision makers with those who are affected
   c. a harmful or beneficial consequence not considered by decision makers
   d. the EPA
   e. pollution taxes

2. Pollution is an example of market failure because
   a. the equilibrium price is higher than the efficient price
   b. the equilibrium price is less than the efficient price
   c. property rights are poorly distributed
   d. the market does not produce enough of the good
   e. those who suffer from pollution are compensated outside the market

3. In order for someone to be a free rider, an activity must be undertaken that
   a. arranges for ride-sharing at rush hour
   b. creates benefits for people who can't be forced to pay for them
   c. beautifies a neighborhood
   d. improves national defense
   e. identifies the beneficiaries and forces them to pay

4. All of the following are goods for which property rights are hard to identify **except**
   a. a river running along a field of corn
   b. the atmosphere over a field of corn
   c. crows that eat the corn on the field
   d. the ozone layer
   e. a field of corn

5. When there are negative externalities, the price should be adjusted so that it is equal to
   a. social cost
   b. private cost
   c. the amount of the externality
   d. zero
   e. the number of free riders

6. The Coase theorem suggests that private negotiation will lead to the correction of market failure when
   a. only a few people are involved
   b. property rights are clearly recognized
   c. negotiation costs are low
   d. people are willing to cooperate
   e. a, b, and c must hold true

7. The social cost curve lies above the supply (private cost) curve for the producer in cases of
   a. positive externalities
   b. negative externalities
   c. public goods
   d. near-public goods
   e. public choice

8. An example of the government creating a new property form in order to deal with the problem of a negative externality would be
   a. the establishment of the EPA
   b. taxing air and water pollution
   c. requiring catalytic convertors on automobiles
   d. administration of the national parks through the Department of the Interior
   e. auctioning rights to pollute to electric utility companies

9. A clear problem associated with the use of pollution compensation taxes is that
   a. it is not easy to arrive at the exact size of tax to be imposed
   b. taxing polluters is inherently unfair
   c. the tax is easy to avoid
   d. new technologies will be developed to cut down on pollution
   e. pollution levels will increase in spite of the tax

10. A clear advantage of using obligatory control directives to deal with negative externalities is that they
    a. reduce the need for bureaucrats
    b. reduce pollution to zero
    c. are relatively simple
    d. are costless to monitor and enforce
    e. are fair to polluters

11. If a per unit tax is imposed on a producer of a good with a negative externality, then the tax shifts the producer's
    a. marginal cost curve to the right
    b. marginal cost curve to the left
    c. total fixed cost to the left
    d. total fixed cost to the right
    e. price downward

12. In the case of a pure public good, one person's consumption of the good
    a. depletes the supply of the good for others
    b. increases the supply of the good
    c. denies the opportunity to consume the good to others
    d. excludes others from consuming the good somewhat
    e. neither depletes the good nor excludes others from consuming it

13. Near-public goods are distinguishable from pure public goods by the fact that
    a. consumption can result in some depletion and some exclusion
    b. they are not provided by government
    c. consumption can result in some exclusion but no depletion
    d. consumption can result in some depletion but no exclusion
    e. consumption of the good must be rationed by government

14. Government failure occurs when
    a. social cost lies to the left of private cost
    b. the good it purchases has a greater negative externality than a positive one
    c. the quantity of public goods it purchases is less than the socially optimal quantity
    d. it pays a higher price for a public good than it would pay on the private market
    e. obligatory controls are imposed

15. Public choice holds that
    a. public officials serve the community's interest
    b. government failure cannot occur
    c. society does not consume enough public goods
    d. we should presume self-interested behavior on the part of public officials
    e. given the number of parties running for public office, the people's choice is limited

16. Voting fails to generate the efficient quantity of a public good because
    a. lobbying groups use bribes to change people's votes
    b. public goods are not depleted by consumption
    c. public goods cannot be withheld from consumption
    d. voting doesn't accurately reflect the magnitude of benefits from public goods
    e. markets are always the best way to achieve efficiency

17. A public good differs from a private good because it
    a. serves a public need
    b. creates benefits that are not exclusive
    c. creates benefits that are consumed only by government
    d. creates restricted benefits
    e. is more costly because it is produced by government

250 CHAPTER 14 EXTERNALITIES, MARKET FAILURE, AND PUBLIC CHOICE

18. All of the following are examples of obligatory controls **except**
    a. the "No Smoking" signs posted in public buildings
    b. automobile emissions testing requirements
    c. restrictions on the transportation of hazardous wastes
    d. trading in pollution rights between electrical utility companies
    e. the requirement that cars all use unleaded fuel

19. The EPA's "living in an imaginary bubble" approach to pollution control
    a. is another example of obligatory controls
    b. allows plants to buy and sell pollution rights to one another
    c. reduces pollution to zero
    d. holds each plant under the bubble to the same level of pollution control
    e. involves setting different taxes for different plants under the bubble

20. Suppose that farmers decide individually whether or not to get their own cattle vaccinated against anthrax. Which of the following results?
    a. there is market failure because the equilibrium quantity of vaccine is too low
    b. there is market failure because the equilibrium price of vaccine is too low
    c. there is market failure because both the equilibrium price and quantity of vaccine are too high
    d. there is no market failure because the market will tend toward equilibrium
    e. there is no market failure, although both the equilibrium price and quantity of vaccine are too high

Fill in the Blanks

1. Costs and benefits that affect unsuspecting third parties are called _____ and

   _____ externalities, respectively.

2. If property rights were _____, externalities would not exist.

3. Correcting for negative externalities means forcing producers to face the _____ of their

   actions.

4. In the case of a pure public good, consumption does not _____, the good and consumption

   of the good cannot be _____.

5. Groups that are organized to persuade government to take actions that serve their interests are called

   _____.

Discussion Questions

1. Why do economists use the word *external* to describe third-party effects that are harmful or beneficial?

2. Increasingly, groundwater pollution is being recognized as a serious problem in many regions. How does the difficulty associated with assigning property rights to groundwater contribute to the problem of groundwater pollution?

3. Compare and contrast the advantages and disadvantages of the three approaches that government can take to cope with the problem of external costs.

4. What's the difference between a pure public good and a near-public good?

5. What are the competing views on public choice held by economists?

Problems

1. a. Suppose that a steel firm is a monopoly and has the demand, marginal revenue, and marginal cost functions shown in the graph below. What price and output combination will the monopoly select? Explain your choice.

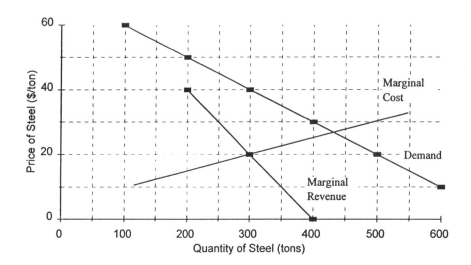

b. Suppose the production of steel generates water pollution in a nearby river that costs a constant $10 per ton of steel produced. What is the size of the negative externality? If the monopolist included the cost of the negative externality in its marginal costs, how would the marginal cost curve shift? Draw in the social cost curve that includes the cost of the negative externality in the monopoly's marginal costs.

c. If a tax equal to the negative externality is imposed on each unit of steel produced, what price will the monopolist charge and how much steel will be produced? Will this policy improve the quality of water in the river? How?

2. The town of Edisto Beach, South Carolina, has a horrible mosquito problem from May through October each year. The table below shows the community's demand and supply schedules for spraying for mosquitoes.

Price ($/spraying)	Quantity Demanded	Quantity Supplied
80	2	14
70	4	12
60	6	10
50	8	8
40	10	6
30	12	4
20	14	2

Suppose the town derives a positive externality of $20 for every spraying for mosquitoes. What is the extent of market failure in this situation? What price and quantity does the market generate? What price and quantity are consistent with an efficient level of spraying? How can the efficient level of spraying be realized? Illustrate your answer using the axes provided below.

Everyday Applications

Tomorrow, as you go through the day, make a list of all the negative and positive externalities that you experience. Externalities are everywhere in modern life. Consider the negative and positive externalities that you create on any given day. What if you were taxed for the negative externalities you create and compensated for the benefits you create generating positive externalities? Would you have a net gain or a net loss?

Economics Online

The Political Economy Research Center is an environmental organization unlike many others because it focuses on market approaches to solving environmental problems. Economic principles are the basic tools for analysis used by researchers at PERC. The Coase theorem that is discussed in your text figures prominently in much of PERC's analysis. For a closer look at the work done by PERC, visit their Web site (*http://www.perc.org/*).

Answers to Questions

Key Terms Quiz

a. 3
b. 8
c. 6
d. 9
e. 1
f. 7
g. 4
h. 10
i. 2
j. 5

True-False Questions

1. True
2. False. External costs are external to the producer of a good or service so they don't diminish profit.
3. True
4. True
5. True
6. True
7. False. If negative and positive externalities exist, then the market has failed to create a socially optimum allocation of resources.
8. True
9. True
10. False. The Coase theorem applies when the number of parties involved in a dispute is small.
11. True
12. False. If the tax is set equal to the marginal externality cost, then pollution is reduced to its socially optimum level.
13. True
14. False. In cases of public goods, the good cannot be withheld from consumption.
15. False. A special-interest lobby considers the particular interests of its members in its lobbying efforts.

Multiple-Choice Questions

1. c
2. b
3. b
4. e
5. a
6. e
7. b
8. e
9. a
10. c
11. b
12. e
13. a
14. c
15. d
16. d
17. b
18. d
19. b
20. a

Fill in the Blanks

1. negative; positive
2. clearly defined
3. social costs
4. diminish; withheld
5. special-interest lobbies

Discussion Questions

1. The word *external* suggests that the third-party effect was external to the decision maker's thinking about whether to undertake an activity. The costs or benefits are external to the person creating them, so they are

THE MICROECONOMICS OF PRODUCT MARKETS

not taken into consideration when the action that creates them is undertaken.

2. Assigning property rights to groundwater is difficult. Simply deciding how much water is in an aquifer is a problem. One also has to consider the rate at which an aquifer recharges through rainfall. To assign property rights, one would have to develop a system to measure withdrawals of water and to prevent pollution from occurring. Also, a system whereby exchanges of water rights to the groundwater could be accomplished would be necessary so that a market price for the groundwater be established. Once property rights to groundwater are clearly defined, the users will realize the true value of the water and will have greater incentive to protect the water from pollution.

3. Obligatory control directives are simple and direct. However, there is no guarantee that the socially optimal level of the externality will result. Creating a new property form is a good approach if property rights can be defined easily. But this may be problematic. Taxing the activity that generates the externality is a workable approach if the marginal externality cost can be measured accurately.

4. A pure public good is not diminished by consumption and cannot be withheld from consumption. The benefits from a pure public good are completely external. The benefits from a near-public good are not completely external. The benefits may be diminished somewhat with consumption, and/or it may be possible to withhold them from others to some extent.

5. Some economists hold that public officials make public choices with the public interest in mind. However, other economists view public choices as skewed by the lobbying efforts of special interests. If this second view of public choice is correct, then government will rarely purchase the socially optimum quantity of public goods. Therefore, government failure is almost always a problem.

Problems

1. a. The monopolist will produce 300 tons of steel and charge $40 per ton for it. The output level of 300 tons corresponds to the point where MR = MC, and the price of $40 per ton is the price read from the demand curve at that output level.

   b. The size of the negative externality is $10(300) = $3,000. Because of the negative externality, the social cost curve is shifted up by $10 vertically from the monopolist's marginal cost curve, as shown on the following page.

   c. The tax will make the marginal cost of steel equal to the marginal social cost. Now, the monopolist will choose an output level where MR = MSC, or an output level equal to approximately 260 tons of steel. The price read from the demand curve at this output level is approximately $43 per ton. Steel output is lower, so the external cost of pollution becomes $10(260) = $2,600. The tax generates enough revenue to cover the damage from the negative externality.

256   CHAPTER 14   EXTERNALITIES, MARKET FAILURE, AND PUBLIC CHOICE

2. The extent of the market failure in this case is that the town will not spray often enough for mosquitoes because the market does not take into account the $20 per spraying positive externality. Taking the positive externality into account shifts the demand curve upward by $20 at every quantity, as shown on the graph below. Instead of purchasing 8 sprayings at a cost of $50 per spraying, the community will purchase the efficient level of 10 sprayings at a cost of $60 per spraying. The sprayings will be purchased through subsidization. For example, the buyers will pay the price read from the demand curve labeled Demand', and then get a $20 rebate drawn from general revenues to support the spraying program.

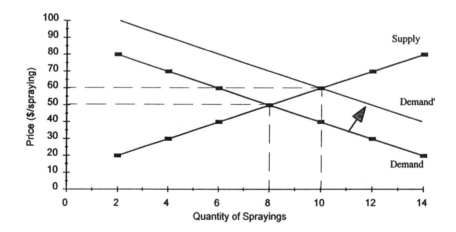

PART 3 — THE MICROECONOMICS OF PRODUCT MARKETS

COMPREHENSIVE SAMPLE TEST

Give yourself 50 minutes to complete this exam and see how you do. The answers follow. Don't look until you are finished!

True-False Questions — If a statement is false, explain why. Each question is worth 2 points.

1. Marginal cost intersects the average total cost curve at its minimum point. (T/F)

2. The long-run average total cost curve will be horizontal if diseconomies of scale are apparent. (T/F)

3. To maximize profit, a firm should set output where MR = demand. (T/F)

4. In oligopoly, there are many firms producing differentiated products, and entry into the industry is relatively easy. (T/F)

5. In monopolistic competition, long-run economic profit for the firm is zero. (T/F)

6. Schumpeter and Galbraith argue that firms in perfect competition will develop new technologies faster than firms in other market structures because the competition is so intense. (T/F)

7. Oligopoly is identified by the fewness of firms. (T/F)

8. The kinked demand curve model predicts that oligopolists will change price whenever the marginal cost changes. (T/F)

9. If a market is contestable, the laissez-faire approach is a reasonable one for dealing with monopoly power. (T/F)

10. If pollution exists, then the social cost is less than the producer's marginal cost. (T/F)

Multiple-Choice Questions — Each question is worth 2 points.

1. As output increases, the average variable cost and the average total cost converge because
   a. fixed costs decrease as output increases
   b. there are no fixed costs in the long run
   c. average fixed cost increases as output increases
   d. technological change blurs the distinction between fixed and variable costs
   e. average fixed cost decreases as output increases

2. The reason that the total variable cost curve eventually begins to increase at an increasing rate as output increases is
   a. the law of increasing costs
   b. new opportunities for specialization and division of labor
   c. the law of diminishing returns
   d. marginal cost is greater than average total cost
   e. diseconomies of scale

3. The difference between the short run and the long run is that
   a. the short run is less than one year while the long run is one year or more
   b. at least one resource used in production is fixed in the short run whereas no resources are fixed in the long run
   c. diminishing returns are a long-run problem and diseconomies of scale are a short-run problem
   d. economies of scale are evident in the short run while constant returns to scale are evident in the long run
   e. the firm must cover its fixed costs in the short run and its variable costs in the long run

4. When marginal revenue is greater than marginal cost, a profit-maximizing entrepreneur will
   a. increase output
   b. keep output the same if marginal revenue exceeds marginal cost by the maximum possible amount
   c. decrease output
   d. add to production capacity
   e. produce at the minimum of the average total cost curve

5. Average revenue is always the same as
   a. marginal revenue
   b. total revenue
   c. marginal cost when profit is maximized
   d. price
   e. average total cost when profit is maximized

6. A firm facing a price that is less than the average variable cost should
   a. increase output
   b. produce where MR = MC to minimize the loss
   c. decrease output
   d. shut down
   e. fire the less productive workers on the payroll

THE MICROECONOMICS OF PRODUCT MARKETS

7. All of the following are characteristics of perfect competition **except**
   a. easy entry into and easy exit from the market
   b. a low cross elasticity of demand between products of different firms in the market
   c. many, many firms
   d. identical products from all firms
   e. no influence over price

8. The demand curve facing a monopoly is likely to be _____ and _____ than the demand curve facing a monopolistically competitive firm.
   a. more inelastic; higher
   b. more elastic; higher
   c. more inelastic; lower
   d. unit elastic; higher
   e. less inelastic; higher

9. In the 1953 case against DuPont, the government charged that DuPont had illegally monopolized the cellophane market, but the Supreme Court ruled for DuPont because
   a. of the rule of reason
   b. of the per se criterion
   c. the relevant market was flexible packaging materials, not cellophane
   d. the antitrust division of the Justice Department is underfunded
   e. Roosevelt's court was pro-business

10. In order to sell another unit of output, a monopolist must lower price because
    a. the firm has little control over price
    b. the monopolist's demand curve is the downward-sloping industry demand
    c. marginal revenue is less than price
    d. the profit-maximizing level of production is to the left of the minimum of the average total cost
    e. marginal revenue is equal to marginal cost at a lower price

11. In long-run equilibrium, a firm in monopolistic competition will earn
    a. an economic profit
    b. a loss because these industries become overcrowded in the long run
    c. a loss because the firm does not produce at the minimum of the ATC
    d. a normal profit
    e. the maximum difference between marginal revenue and marginal cost

12. The main point of the Schumpeter hypothesis is that
    a. perfect competition is preferred because so many firms competing leads to a faster rate of technological progress
    b. perfect competition is preferred because it leads to the greatest output at the lowest price for consumers
    c. modern technology gives rise to economies of scale, which favor larger firms
    d. monopoly is preferred to perfect competition because profits persist in the long run
    e. monopoly is preferred to perfect competition because markets are contestable

13. The main reason to prefer the Herfindahl-Hirschman index to the four-firm concentration ratio as a measure of market concentration is that the
    a. four-firm concentration ratio considers only domestic firms
    b. four-firm concentration ratio doesn't consider substitute goods with high cross elasticities
    c. HHI considers all the firms in the industry when it is calculated
    d. HHI gives greater weight to firms with high market power than the four-firm concentration ratio
    e. HHI considers second-hand markets

14. When comparing concentration ratios in the United States to those in other industrialized countries, it is clear that
    a. there is little difference in the ratios observed across countries
    b. U.S. industries are less concentrated because of rigorous enforcement of antitrust laws
    c. the rule of reason has led to more concentration in U.S. industry
    d. U.S. firms are bigger and industries are more concentrated as a result
    e. firms in other industrialized countries are larger but there is lower concentration because of intense international competition

15. A cartel agreement is likely to be unstable if
    a. the profit-maximizing level of output for the cartel is not reached
    b. the cartel member's quota is less than the profit-maximizing output for the firm
    c. countervailing forces exist
    d. the market is split between only a few firms
    e. there is no godfather to enforce the agreement

16. The basic problem with using marginal cost pricing to regulate a natural monopolist is that
    a. the regulatory agency cannot distinguish between average cost and marginal cost
    b. the regulatory agency's members are drawn from the industry so they go along with the monopolist's inflated cost estimates when price is being set
    c. marginal cost may be less than average total cost for a natural monopolist
    d. the market can support only one firm at low average total costs in natural monopoly
    e. marginal cost pricing is inefficient

17. One strategy that Bill Gates and Microsoft might use to avoid prosecution under antitrust laws is to make the case that the market for computer operating systems and software is
    a. extremely concentrated
    b. marked by barriers to entry
    c. declining
    d. contestable
    e. perfectly competitive

18. A free rider problem exists when people find that it is possible to
    a. enjoy the benefits of an activity without paying for it
    b. save money by growing flowers and vegetables at home
    c. carpool for less money than commuting alone
    d. enjoy a summer sunset from the back porch
    e. maximize consumer surplus

THE MICROECONOMICS OF PRODUCT MARKETS 261

19. All of the following are examples of pure public goods **except**
    a. programs for universal vaccination against infectious diseases
    b. national defense
    c. fire protection
    d. an uncrowded toll road
    e. clean air

20. In cases of negative externalities, when the social costs are introduced to cost calculations, the effect is to
    a. shift the marginal cost curve upward to the left
    b. cause the price to decrease to the optimum level
    c. create a positive externality
    d. signal the market to divert more resources to this activity
    e. cause the equilibrium output to increase

Discussion Questions/Problems — Each question is worth 10 points.

1. Explain the difference between the short-run average total cost curve and the long-run average total cost curve. Use graphs to illustrate your answer.

2. Use a graph to show why a natural monopolist will have to be subsidized if the firm is regulated by marginal cost pricing. Would setting price equal to average total cost be preferred? Why or why not?

3. Using graphs and in words, show a firm in perfect competition earning profits in short-run equilibrium and in long-run equilibrium. Explain the transition between short-run equilibrium and long-run equilibrium. Does perfect competition have some desirable features? Discuss.

4. Suppose an oligopolist producing steel is dumping waste into a nearby river. The government imposes a tax on the oligopolist equal to the cost of the negative externality. If this oligopolist steel firm faces a kinked demand curve, will the price of steel increase as a result of the tax? Will steel output change? Explain. Is a pollution tax an effective policy to reduce pollution levels in this case?

THE MICROECONOMICS OF PRODUCT MARKETS

Answers to the Sample Test over Part 3

True-False Questions

1. True
2. False. If diseconomies of scale are apparent, the long-run average total cost curve will be upward sloping
3. False. To maximize profit, a firm should set output where MR = MC.
4. False. Oligopoly is characterized by few firms, a product that may or may not be differentiated, and difficult entry.
5. True
6. False. Monopoly and oligopoly firms will develop technology faster because they experience economies of scale with economic profit that can be used for research and development.
7. True
8. False. Marginal cost can shift in the marginal revenue gap without a change in price.
9. True
10. False. If pollution exists, the social cost is greater than the producer's marginal cost.

Multiple-Choice Questions

1. e	6. d	11. d	16. c
2. c	7. b	12. c	17. d
3. b	8. a	13. d	18. a
4. a	9. c	14. a	19. d
5. d	10. b	15. b	20. a

Discussion Questions/Problems

1. The difference between short-run average cost and long-run average cost is that in the short run, some costs are fixed, so the firm can change some but not all of the resources devoted to production. For example, a firm in the fishing industry could change the amounts of labor, bait, lines, nets, etc. — variable cost items — that are employed in the short run, but not the boat itself. The cost of the boat is a fixed cost that must be paid whether any fish are caught or not. However, in the long run, the firm could choose to add another boat or sell the existing boat. All resources used in production can be changed in the long run. Output levels are more limited in the short run than in the long run. The long-run average cost curve is also called the envelope curve and corresponds to the curve that encloses the firm's short-run average total cost curves.

   The graphs drawn below show the short-run average total cost with marginal cost intersecting it at its minimum point and the long-run average cost curve showing economies of scale, constant returns to scale, and diseconomies of scale.

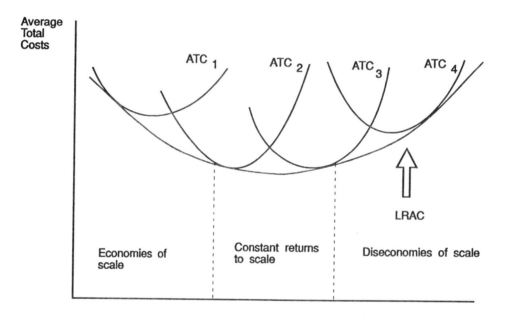

2. In a natural monopoly, marginal cost is below average total cost in many cases because the natural monopoly has high fixed costs that cause the average total cost curve to decline over a wide range of output. The firm's marginal costs are typically low. Marginal cost is less than average total cost if the average total cost is decreasing. Therefore, if price is set equal to marginal cost, at the point where demand intersects marginal cost, the monopolist will earn a loss and must be subsidized. This is illustrated in the graph on the following page.

THE MICROECONOMICS OF PRODUCT MARKETS

Setting price equal to average cost is simpler insofar as the monopolist will earn a normal profit and won't have to be subsidized. However, the price is higher to consumers and the quantity consumed is lower, shown as Q in the diagram above.

3. The graphs for a perfectly competitive firm in short-run equilibrium and long-run equilibrium are shown below. In the short run, the firm earns economic profit that signals new firms to enter the industry. As new firms enter, the market supply curve shifts to the right, and the price falls. Entry continues until economic profit is driven to zero. Hence, all firms in the industry earn only a normal profit and produce at the minimum of the average cost curves, so price is equal to marginal cost is equal to the minimum of the average cost. This is desirable because the market generates the largest output at the lowest price possible.

4. A graph of the kinked demand curve model showing the demand curve, the marginal revenue gap, and a representative marginal cost curve is shown below. The oligopolist maximizes profit by producing where MR = MC, which is in the gap between segments of the marginal revenue curve in the graph below. Marginal cost could shift up or down in the gap, and the oligopolist would still produce at Q* and charge the price, P*. A pollution tax would shift the marginal cost curve, and, if it shifted within the gap, the oligopolist won't change the output or the price. However, the tax may still reduce pollution. The tax will reduce the oligopolist's profits. If the cost of reducing pollution is less than the tax, the oligopolist will have an incentive to reduce pollution in order to avoid the tax. Thus, the tax causes incentives to be structured in a way that encourages the oligopolist to reduce pollution.

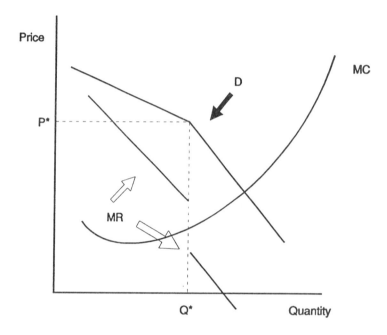

CHAPTER 15

WAGE RATES IN COMPETITIVE LABOR MARKETS

Chapter in a Nutshell

This chapter examines how wage rates are determined in competitive labor markets. Suppose that a firm hires workers in a labor market where all of the workers have roughly the same skills. As the firm begins hiring workers, the **marginal physical product of labor** (the change in output that results from adding one more unit of labor) may increase as more workers are able to take advantage of opportunities for division of labor and specialization. However, beyond some point, additional workers will add smaller and smaller increments to output, reflecting the **law of diminishing returns**. The marginal physical product of labor eventually decreases because of the law of diminishing returns. The marginal physical product of labor can be converted to revenue by multiplying each worker's marginal physical product by the price of the output. This gives the **marginal revenue product of labor** — the addition to total revenue from adding one more unit of labor.

How much labor will the firm hire? The firm continues to hire as long as the marginal revenue product of labor is greater than the **wage rate**. In a competitive labor market, the firm hiring labor cannot influence the market-determined wage rate. The **marginal labor cost** — the addition to **total labor cost** from hiring one more worker — is equal to the wage rate. The firm will stop hiring workers when the marginal revenue product of the last worker hired is equal to the wage rate. Thus, the marginal revenue product of labor is the firm's demand curve for labor. Each point on the marginal revenue product curve tells us how many workers the firm would hire given a specific wage rate. The firm's demand curve for labor increases (shifts to the right) when the price of the good being produced increases or when the workers hired have become more productive through, say, an improvement in technology. The industry demand for labor is the sum of the individual firms' demands for labor.

The labor supply curve is upward sloping. The higher the wage rate, the greater the quantities of labor workers are willing to supply. Shifts in the supply curve of labor occur as a result of changes in alternative employment opportunities, changes in population size, and changes in wealth. The intersection of the industry demand for labor and the supply of labor determines the market wage rate.

Why do wage rate differentials exist? Sometimes these differences in wage rates are geographic. For example, in the United States, wages in the North, until fairly recently, tended to be higher than wages for the same jobs in the South. The differential reflected, in part, the fact that northern workers had more capital to work with than did southern workers. However, this differential has all but disappeared as workers moved to the North and capital migrated to the South. Wage differentials will persist if labor and capital cannot move freely. Another reason for persistent wage differentials is **noncompeting labor markets**. Special talents are required in certain labor markets, so workers without these skills are excluded from competing.

The minimum wage is the source of much debate among economists and politicians. The purpose of the minimum wage is to provide workers who are stuck in low-wage labor markets with a wage rate that provides a decent living. However, the minimum wage acts as a price floor in labor markets and, as such, creates unemployment. Economists hold strong views on the minimum wage issue, but there is no real consensus about whether the gains to employed workers more than offset the losses to unemployed workers.

After studying this chapter, you should be able to:

- Define the **marginal physical product** of labor.
- Give examples of the **law of diminishing returns**.
- Derive the **marginal revenue product** of labor from the marginal physical product of labor.
- Explain why the marginal revenue product of labor is the demand curve for labor.
- Show why the **marginal labor cost** for a firm in a competitive labor market is equal to the wage rate.
- Graph the profit-maximizing level of employment for a firm in a competitive labor market.
- Discuss reasons for changes in the demand for labor.
- Draw a labor supply curve and explain its shape.
- Examine the logic behind the backward-bending supply curve of labor.
- Account for wage differentials.
- Evaluate the impact of minimum wage laws.
- Explain the logic behind **efficiency wages**.
- Understand the argument that competitive wages are ethical.

Concept Check — See how you do on these multiple-choice questions.

1. The **marginal physical product** of labor is defined as the
    a. total output of labor divided by the amount of labor employed
    b. the change in total output generated by a change in the amount of labor hired
    c. the change in total revenue generated by a change in the amount of labor hired
    d. the value of the last worker hired
    e. demand for labor

What units do we use to measure the marginal physical product of labor?

2. The **marginal revenue product** curve for labor slopes downward because
    a. of the law of diminishing returns
    b. as the price of a good decreases, quantity demanded increases
    c. of technological change
    d. the demand curve slopes upward
    e. of minimum wage laws

The demand for labor is the marginal physical product of labor multiplied by the price of the output.

3. In a competitive labor market, the **marginal labor cost** is equal to the
    a. market supply of labor
    b. firm's demand for labor
    c. firm's supply of labor
    d. minimum wage
    e. lowest wage unskilled workers will accept

Can a firm in a competitive labor market influence the wage rate?

THE MICROECONOMICS OF FACTOR MARKETS

4. The demand for and supply of labor model shows that a **minimum wage** set above the equilibrium wage will
   a. decrease employment in the labor market
   b. cause workers to offer less along the backward-bending supply curve of labor
   c. increase the equilibrium wage rate
   d. decrease efficiency wages
   e. increase employment in the labor market

A minimum wage acts like a price floor in a labor market.

5. The **ethic of wages equal to MRP** is
   a. hard to justify
   b. from each according to his or her contribution, to each according to his or her contribution
   c. from each according to his or her ability, to each according to his or her need
   d. easier to justify than the ethic underlying minimum wages
   e. based on the marginal physical product, not the marginal revenue product

People are paid at the rate the market values them in a competitive labor market.

Am I on the Right Track?

Your answers to the above questions should be **b**, **a**, **c**, **a**, and **b**. By now you should have thoroughly mastered the use of marginal analysis. Studying labor markets affords us with yet another chance to apply this useful technique. There are a few new terms to learn, and the graphing is a bit different, so we'll proceed with the key terms quiz and a short graphing tutorial, then it's time to get to work on some questions.

Key Terms Quiz — Match the terms on the left with the definitions in the column on the right.

1. marginal physical product   _____ a. quantity of labor employed multiplied by the wage rate
2. noncompeting labor markets   _____ b. the change in output from adding one more unit of labor
3. marginal revenue product   _____ c. the price of labor
4. total labor cost   _____ d. as more units of a resource are added to production with at least one input fixed, the addition to output eventually declines
5. wage rate   _____ e. markets whose requirement for specific skills excludes workers who do not have the required skills
6. marginal labor cost   _____ f. a wage rate higher than the market's equilibrium wage that a firm pays to decrease turnover and increase productivity
7. law of diminishing returns   _____ g. the change in total labor cost from adding one more unit of labor
8. efficiency wages   _____ h. the change in total revenue from adding one more unit of labor

Graphing Tutorial

The demand for labor shows how much labor an employer is willing to hire at different wage rates, just as the demand for a good shows us how much of the good people are willing to purchase at different prices. We begin our derivation of the demand for labor with the marginal physical product of labor. Let's work through a numerical example to see how the marginal physical product of labor is derived and how it is related to the marginal revenue product of labor — the firm's demand for labor.

Suppose we have a fishing operation where the number of people working on the fishing boat is related to the quantity of fish produced, as shown in the first two columns of the table below.

Workers	Fish Output (lb./run)	Marginal Physical Product (MPP)	Total Revenue (price = $3/lb.)	Marginal Revenue Product (MRP)
0	0			
1	1,000	1,000	$ 3,000	$3,000
2	3,000	2,000	9,000	6,000
3	6,000	3,000	18,000	9,000
4	8,500	2,500	25,500	7,500
5	10,500	2,000	31,500	6,000
6	11,500	1,500	34,500	3,000
7	12,000	500	36,000	1,500

Note how fish output changes as more workers are added, all other factors of production held constant. Fish output increases at an increasing rate for the first three workers — 1,000, 3,000, and 6,000 pounds of fish. From the fourth worker through the seventh worker, output increases at a decreasing rate — 8,500, 10,500, 11,500, and 12,500 pounds of fish.

The third column shows the marginal physical product of labor. The marginal physical product of labor is the change in output that results from adding one more unit of labor. The law of diminishing returns is reflected in the declining MPP of the fourth through the seventh worker.

Total revenue is computed by multiplying fish output by the price of fish. These revenues are shown in the fourth column, assuming the price of fish is $3 per pound.

The marginal revenue product is shown in column five. The marginal revenue product is the addition to total revenue generated by the addition of one more worker.

Marginal physical product is plotted in the graph below. Note the upward-sloping segment that reflects the effects of specialization and division of labor. This portion of the curve corresponds to the first three workers. The curve is downward sloping for the fourth through the seventh worker. This reflects the dominance of the law of diminishing returns.

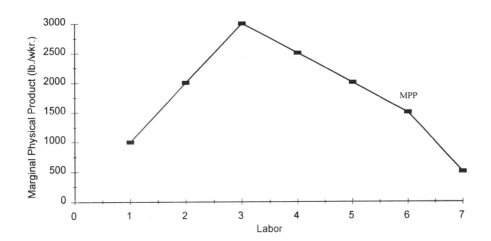

The following graph shows the marginal revenue product of labor. Note that the values for the first two workers have been left out of the graph. That is because the MRP is still increasing for these workers. The demand curve for labor is the downward-sloping portion of the marginal revenue product curve. A firm would never stop hiring workers while the marginal revenue product was still increasing.

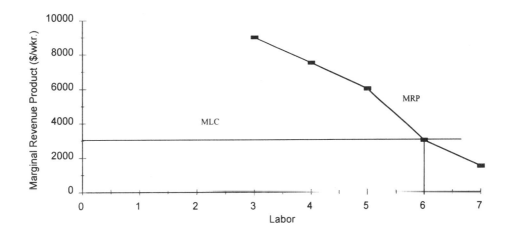

The marginal revenue product of labor curve is the firm's demand curve for labor. This makes sense because the MRP shows how much each worker contributes to total revenue. The firm will be willing to pay for a worker an amount equal to the worker's contribution to total revenue. How many workers will the firm hire? This depends on the wage rate, which is the same as the marginal labor cost in a competitive labor market. Each worker adds to total cost an amount equal to the wage rate. Suppose the wage rate in this case is $3,000 for a one-month fishing run. This firm will hire 6 workers. That is where the marginal revenue product curve intersects the marginal labor cost. For all the workers hired up to the sixth worker, the MRP is greater than or equal to the MLC. The firm keeps hiring because each of these workers adds more to total revenue than to total cost. What about the seventh worker? This worker adds $1,500 to total revenue and $3,000 to total cost. The firm won't hire this worker because its profit would decline if it did.

Finding the profit-maximizing number of workers to hire is very much like finding the profit-maximizing level of output of goods for a firm. Remember, we set output where MR = MC to find the profit-maximizing level of output. Now we are setting MRP = MLC; that is, the marginal revenue product is equal to the marginal labor cost. The marginal analysis is the same.

Graphing Pitfalls

A major difference between the marginal cost curves we used to show the change in total cost from producing one more unit of output for the firm and the marginal labor cost curve that we use to show the addition to total labor cost from hiring one more unit of labor is that the marginal cost curve is upward sloping while the marginal labor cost curve is a horizontal line at the market wage rate. A firm in a competitive labor market can hire as much labor as it wants without affecting the market wage rate. Therefore, the wage rate that it pays for labor will be constant, so the addition to total labor cost from adding one more unit of labor is constant too.

You are probably in the habit of drawing a marginal cost curve that is upward sloping by now. Beware! The marginal labor cost curve is horizontal. It shouldn't be drawn as shown below.

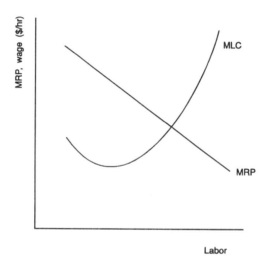

The marginal labor cost curve for the firm should be horizontal — it's the supply of labor for the firm — because the firm takes the wage rate set in the labor market and can hire as much labor as it wants to without influencing the market wage rate. Don't let yourself by force of habit draw an upward-sloping marginal labor cost curve!

True-False Questions — If a statement is false, explain why.

1. The wage rate, that is, the price of labor, is the same for all firms that hire labor in a competitive labor market. (T/F)

2. The marginal physical product of labor is the change in total output resulting from adding a unit of labor to production. (T/F)

3. The law of diminishing returns explains why adding workers to production doesn't increase output. (T/F)

4. The marginal revenue product is the addition to total revenue resulting from adding a unit of labor to production. (T/F)

5. The marginal revenue product is the marginal physical product multiplied by the wage rate. (T/F)

6. In a competitive labor market, a firm can hire workers at a wage lower than the equilibrium if it chooses, but cannot hire as many workers as it chooses. (T/F)

7. The marginal labor cost curve for a firm in a competitive labor market is upward sloping. (T/F)

8. A profit-maximizing firm will hire labor as long as the marginal revenue product is greater than or equal to the marginal labor cost. (T/F)

9. An increase in the price of a firm's product causes the marginal physical product curve to shift to the right. (T/F)

10. If the price of a firm's product increases, then its demand curve for labor shifts to the right. (T/F)

11. New technology that makes labor more productive will lower a firm's demand curve for labor. (T/F)

12. The industry demand for labor represents the sum of individual firms' demands for labor at different wage levels. (T/F)

13. The supply of labor reflects both people's preferences between work and leisure and the employment alternatives available in a community. (T/F)

14. Most workers are unwilling to supply larger quantities of labor because their wages are high enough to put them on the backward-bending portions of their labor supply curves. (T/F)

15. Workers tend to migrate from lower-wage areas to higher-wage areas, while industries tend to migrate from higher-wage areas to lower-wage areas. (T/F)

Multiple-Choice Questions

1. Output typically increases at an increasing rate as the first few workers are added to a production process because
   a. they are paid efficiency wages
   b. it is possible to take advantage of opportunities for specialization and division of labor
   c. management can carefully monitor job performance for just a few workers
   d. economies of scale are realized
   e. the first worker has done the most demanding activity by the time new workers arrive

2. When diminishing returns set in,
   a. the marginal physical product of labor increases
   b. the marginal physical product of labor decreases
   c. the marginal physical product of labor is greater than the cost of hiring labor
   d. total output decreases
   e. the marginal labor cost increases

3. The marginal physical product can by converted to the marginal revenue product by
   a. dividing it by the price of output
   b. adding in the price of output
   c. multiplying it by the price of output
   d. multiplying it by the wage rate
   e. dividing it by the wage rate

4. When the marginal physical product and the marginal revenue product are graphed, you can see that
   a. no similarities between the graphs exist because they represent different concepts
   b. they converge after the first few workers
   c. they diverge after the first few workers
   d. the MRP curve is equal to the MPP curve multiplied by the price of the output
   e. they are identical

5. The constant marginal labor cost that a firm in a competitive labor market faces means that
   a. it must raise the wage rate to hire more workers
   b. it can increase profit by increasing output
   c. the law of diminishing returns applies
   d. it can hire all the labor it wants without having to raise the wage rate
   e. labor-saving technology cannot influence how many workers the firm hires

6. In a perfectly competitive labor market, a firm is able to
   a. dictate the wage rate it offers workers
   b. hire the most efficient workers first at a higher wage rate than it offers other workers
   c. hire as many workers as it desires at the market wage rate
   d. influence wages if no union is present
   e. hire only a few workers since so many firms compete for them

7. A firm hiring workers in a perfectly competitive labor market will continue to hire more labor until
   a. the marginal revenue product is equal to the wage
   b. the marginal revenue product curve slopes downward
   c. the marginal revenue product is greater than the marginal labor cost
   d. no more workers are available at that wage
   e. demand for the firm's output is exhausted

8. The introduction of a new technology that makes labor more productive causes the demand curve for labor to
    a. shift inward since fewer workers are needed
    b. be greater than the supply curve
    c. be less than the supply curve
    d. shift outward since the marginal revenue product has increased
    e. approximate those found in other high-tech industries

9. If the demand curve for labor decreases while technology is unchanged, the decrease may be explained by
    a. a decrease in the workers' productivity
    b. a decrease in the price of the output
    c. a decrease in the wage rate
    d. an increase in the supply of labor
    e. an increase in industry output

10. The upward-sloping market supply curve for labor reflects the fact that
    a. firms must meet the higher opportunity costs of the new workers added to production
    b. workers prefer leisure
    c. not all wages are efficiency wages
    d. the most productive workers command the highest wages
    e. if wage rates are cut, workers must work longer hours

11. Expanding employment opportunities in a community are likely to
    a. decrease the prices of most goods
    b. decrease wage rates
    c. shift the demand curve for labor to the right
    d. shift the demand curve for labor to the left
    e. raise prices of most goods

12. If the supply curve for labor is backward bending at very high wage rates, it is an indication that
    a. beyond some point, higher wages made consumption of other goods more attractive than leisure
    b. some people just don't want to work regardless of the wage rate
    c. leisure is always preferred to work
    d. labor productivity is on the rise
    e. workers are willing to sacrifice higher income for more leisure

13. The effect of people's migrating from low-wage to higher-wage regions is to
    a. increase wage rates in both regions
    b. reduce wage differentials between regions
    c. increase wage differentials between regions
    d. shift the supply curve of labor to the right
    e. decrease wage rates in both regions

14. NBA basketball players earn high incomes for all these reasons **except** that
    a. professional basketball players work in a noncompeting market
    b. their MRPs are very high
    c. the revenues earned by basketball teams are very high
    d. they work hard and spend long hours practicing as well as playing scheduled games
    e. people are willing to pay high prices for tickets while others enjoy watching games on TV

276 CHAPTER 15 COMPETITIVE LABOR MARKETS

15. The impact of minimum wages on low-wage earning people is
    a. to raise their wages and employment
    b. to shift the demand curve for their labor to the left
    c. to shift the demand curve for their labor to the right
    d. to reduce the price ceiling on labor
    e. dependent on the elasticities of demand for and supply of labor

16. When the labor market for miners is in equilibrium, all the following are true **except** that
    a. the quantity of miners demanded equals the quantity of miners supplied
    b. for miners, w = MRP
    c. wage differentials between the market for miners and all other labor markets disappear
    d. all miners receive the same wage rate, which is equal to the MRP of the last miner hired
    e. all miners are paid the market wage equal to the marginal labor cost

17. People who earn high wage rates in noncompeting labor markets tend on average to
    a. be more intelligent than the average worker
    b. have more experience at their jobs than others
    c. possess unique skills that shelter them from competition
    d. benefit from government legislation that limits entry into their field
    e. be the most mobile workers, that is, most willing to leave a job for a higher wage rate

18. An increase in the minimum wage rate will definitely lead to
    a. improvement in the lot of low-wage workers
    b. significant unemployment
    c. increased employment since many new workers will enter the labor market
    d. less effort exerted by workers already employed
    e. an increase in income for workers employed at the new minimum wage

19. An example of a pair of noncompeting labor markets is
    a. cabbies and chauffeurs
    b. doctors and chiropractors
    c. police officers and security guards
    d. professional landscapers and private gardeners
    e. baseball players and tennis players

20. By paying efficiency wages, a firm hopes to
    a. encourage higher productivity in the firm
    b. increase turnover to keep the labor force fresh
    c. drive out its competition
    d. increase specialization and division of labor
    e. realize economies of scale in labor resources

Fill in the Blanks

1. Decreases in the _____ and the _____ cause decreases in the demand for labor.

2. The law of diminishing returns states that as more and more units of one _____ are

added to production, while _____ remain unchanged, output will increase by

_____ and _____ increments.

3. The market supply of labor reflects the _____ of each individual worker.

4. The wage rate is equal to the _____, which is the cost of adding a worker to

   production.

5. A difference in wage rates between two regions will result in movement of labor to the _____ wage

   region and movement of capital to the _____ wage region, causing wage differences to

   _____.

Discussion Questions

1. Why do improvements in technology lead to an increase in the demand for labor in a competitive labor market? Doesn't technological change cause unemployment?

2. Why is rapid population growth, coupled with the law of diminishing returns, particularly troublesome for workers in developing countries striving to raise living standards?

3. How do the elasticities of demand and supply of labor affect the impact of minimum wage laws?

4. Discuss the ethics of $w = MRP$.

5. How would a policy of open immigration, such as we had during the nineteenth century, affect wage differentials and living standards in the United States today?

Problems

1. Return to the graphing tutorial above. Suppose the price of fish rises to $6 per pound. How does this affect the demand curve for labor and the profit-maximizing number of workers the firm should hire? Fill in the columns for the total revenue and marginal revenue product in the table below and graph the marginal revenue product on the axes provided. If the marginal labor cost stays at $3,000, how many workers will the firm hire?

Workers	Fish Output (lb./run)	Marginal Physical Product (MPP)	Total Revenue (price = $6/lb.)	Marginal Revenue Product (MRP)
0	0			
1	1,000	1,000		
2	3,000	2,000		
3	6,000	3,000		
4	8,500	2,500		
5	10,500	2,000		
6	11,500	1,500		
7	12,000	500		

THE MICROECONOMICS OF FACTOR MARKETS

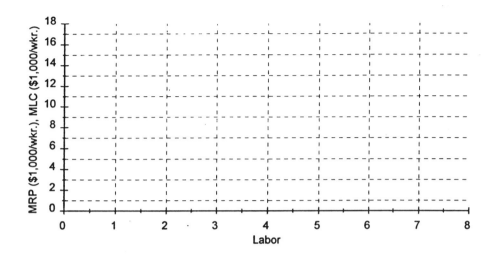

2. Suppose that a minimum wage law is passed for the fishing industry that sets the wage at $6,000 per run. How will the choice of a profit-maximizing level of employment for the firm shown above be affected by the law? What do you predict will happen to employment throughout the fishing industry as a result of the law? Will people employed in the fishing industry be supportive of the law? Discuss.

3. The following table shows the demand and supply schedules in the U.S. and Mexican labor markets for daily laborers.

United States			Mexico		
Wage	Q_D (millions)	Q_S (millions)	Wage	Q_D (millions)	Q_S (millions)
$70	30	70	$40	0	16
60	40	60	35	4	12
50	50	50	30	8	8
40	60	40	25	12	4
30	70	30	20	16	0

What is the wage differential between the United States and Mexico? What kinds of changes would you expect to occur in both the supply of and the demand for labor in both countries if labor and capital were allowed to move across the borders freely?

Everyday Applications

Have you ever worked for the minimum wage? If you have not, you probable know a friend who has. In your experience, does the minimum wage accomplish the goal for which it is intended? That is, does the minimum wage provide a decent living for low-wage earners? Have you or your friends experienced fewer employment opportunities as a result of recent increases in the minimum wage?

Economics Online

For more facts on the minimum wage and for other labor-related information, visit the Web site of the Bureau of Labor Statistics (*http://stats.bls.gov/blshome.html*).

Answers to Questions

Key Terms Quiz

a. 4
b. 1
c. 5
d. 7
e. 2
f. 8
g. 6
h. 3

True-False Questions

1. True
2. True
3. False. The law of diminishing returns explains why adding more workers will cause output to increase by smaller and smaller increments.
4. True
5. False. The MRP = MPP multiplied by the price of the output.
6. False. Firms in competitive labor markets must offer the equilibrium wage rate no matter how many workers they choose to hire.
7. False. The marginal labor cost curve is a horizontal line at the wage rate.
8. True
9. False. An increase in the price of a firm's product causes the MRP to shift to the right.
10. True
11. False. New technology causes the MPP to increase, which causes the MRP to increase. This is the same as an increase in the demand for labor.
12. True
13. True

THE MICROECONOMICS OF FACTOR MARKETS

14. False. Although the backward-bending supply curve of labor makes logical sense, most workers are on the upward-sloping portions of their labor supply curves.
15. True

Multiple-Choice Questions

1. b	6. c	11. c	16. c
2. b	7. a	12. e	17. c
3. c	8. d	13. b	18. e
4. d	9. b	14. d	19. e
5. d	10. a	15. e	20. a

Fill in the Blanks

1. marginal physical product of labor; price of output
2. factor of production; other factors; smaller; smaller
3. opportunity cost
4. marginal labor cost
5. high; low; diminish

Discussion Questions

1. Improvements in technology increase the marginal physical product of workers and, therefore, the marginal revenue product of workers, so firms in competitive labor markets will want to hire more. As long as the market for the goods produced is competitive, the firms will be able to sell their increased output. Therefore, an increase in employment, not a decrease, is associated with an improvement in technology.

2. As population increases, it shifts the supply of labor to the right. Because the demand for labor is downward sloping, the increase in the supply of labor will lower wage rates. The key to raising living standards in developing countries is to increase the demand for labor. This can happen by improving technology (raising the marginal physical product of labor), producing goods whose prices are increasing, and introducing new employment opportunities, that is, new industries.

3. If the supply and demand curves for labor are highly elastic, then a small increase in the wage rate caused by an increase in the minimum wage will create a large increase in unemployment. The more inelastic the supply and demand curves for labor are, the less is the unemployment.

4. The ethical appeal of the perfectly competitive labor market is that workers are paid the value of what they produce. In addition, a perfectly competitive labor market creates a link between effort and reward. The incentive exists for workers to acquire skills and become more productive so that they can earn higher wage rates. Inequality in the income distribution will exist. The phrase, "From each according to his or her contribution, to each according to his or her contribution," describes the ethic underlying the wage rates set in competitive labor markets.

5. Because wage rates are higher in the United States than in most countries of the world, wage rates in the United States could be expected to decrease as a result of increased immigration, while wage rates in the countries of emigration can be expected to rise. The impact on living standards is less clear. It may be that with a larger labor supply in the United States, increases in output in all industries would cause prices to fall and give consumers greater access to a wider array of goods. Larger markets might lead to the

282　　　CHAPTER 15　　COMPETITIVE LABOR MARKETS

achievement of economies of scale that didn't exist before. Living standards in sending countries should increase since these were low-wage countries to begin with. This is a complex question and this answer just scratches the surface.

Problems

1. The completed table and the graph are shown below. An increase in the price of fish increases the marginal revenue product, shifting the demand for labor to the right. Given a marginal labor cost equal to $3,000, the fishing operation will hire 7 workers.

Workers	Fish Output (lb./run)	Marginal Physical Product (MPP)	Total Revenue (price = $6/lb.)	Marginal Revenue Product (MRP)
0	0			
1	1,000	1,000	$ 6,000	$ 6,000
2	3,000	2,000	18,000	12,000
3	6,000	3,000	36,000	18,000
4	8,500	2,500	51,000	15,000
5	10,500	2,000	63,000	12,000
6	11,500	1,000	69,000	6,000
7	12,000	500	72,000	3,000

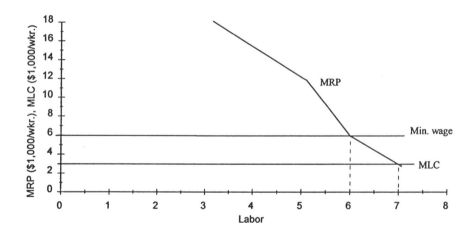

2. Looking at the graph above, a minimum wage law setting the wage rate at $6,000 per run will cause employment to fall from 7 to 6 workers. Employment throughout the fishing industry will be decreased. People in the fishing industry who get jobs at the minimum wage will be supportive of the law. Those who find themselves unemployed by the law may well be opposed to it. Owners of fishing businesses will oppose the law because it is likely to drive up total labor costs and drive down profits.

3. The equilibrium wage in the United States is $50, and the equilibrium wage in Mexico is $30. Therefore, labor will move from Mexico to the United States, causing the labor supply to shift to the right in the United States and to the left in Mexico. On the other hand, capital will flow from the United States to Mexico

causing the MRP of labor in the United States to shift to the left and the MRP of labor in Mexico to shift to the right. The impact of these changes is an increase in wage rates in Mexico and a decrease in wage rates in the United States — a reduction in the wage differential between the two countries.

Appendix

Who Earns What?

Appendix in a Nutshell

This appendix is devoted to an analysis of who earns what incomes, who is employed where, and what factors determine people's wages and employment. The "people characteristics" that lie behind specific MRP curves are examined. Characteristic patterns of employment in labor markets are also considered.

Clearly, an important determinant of people's incomes is productivity. Growth in productivity is strongly correlated with growth in real hourly compensation (which translates into the goods and services people take home). Since 1973, the slowdown in productivity growth has matched precisely the slowdown in the growth rate of real hourly compensation.

Another significant determinant of people's incomes is education. An overwhelmingly large percentage of managerial and professional people have college degrees. Educational attainment among people in lower-paying jobs, on the other hand, is generally lower.

Race and sex are also determinants of income levels. In 1997, for example, Hispanic males earned only about 68.3 percent of what white males earned in similar occupations. Black males earned only 77 percent of what white males earned in similar occupations. The disparity is, in large part, a reflection of discrimination both past and present. On average, women in similar occupations earned 75.5 percent of what men did in 1995. These disparities in earnings raise the issue of **comparable worth**, which is the concept that people with comparable skills should receive comparable wages.

At the low end of the income scale, earnings for many people are determined by minimum wages. The decades of the 1970s and 1980s were especially difficult for people earning minimum wages. The ratio of the minimum wage to the average wage fell steadily from 49 percent in 1970 to 35 percent in 1995.

True-False Questions — If a statement is false, explain why.

1. The data show convincingly that women are systematically paid less than men for similar jobs. (T/F)

2. There is little connection between productivity and earnings for workers. (T/F)

3. The ranks of blue-collar workers are populated by a large percentage of college-educated people who were unable to find white-collar jobs. (T/F)

4. The minimum wage expressed as a percentage of the average cash wage has fallen over the period from 1970 to 1995. (T/F)

5. Comparable worth means that people with comparable skills should be paid comparable wages. (T/F)

Multiple-Choice Questions

1. Steady growth in labor productivity in the United States has led to
    a. relatively less capital and more labor employed
    b. a rise in real hourly compensation
    c. a rise in wage rates, but at the expense of employment
    d. the elimination of the minimum wage
    e. the introduction of the minimum wage

2. The strong correlation between those employed in high-paying jobs and those who have finished at least high school suggests that
    a. as wage rates rise, people return for continuing education courses
    b. education is insignificant in determining someone's income-earning potential
    c. uneducated people lack the intelligence for these jobs
    d. education enhances people's income-earning potential
    e. people without high school diplomas are completely excluded from high-paying jobs

3. The fact that the earnings of black workers is 77 percent that of white workers suggests that
    a. current and past discrimination may play a role in the lower wages for blacks
    b. no blacks earn as much as whites
    c. affirmative action has not worked
    d. blacks don't work for minimum wages
    e. the outlook for higher incomes for blacks is bleak

4. Women's salaries most closely match men's in
    a. managerial occupations
    b. sales jobs
    c. service jobs
    d. precision production jobs
    e. agricultural jobs

5. Between 1970 and 1995, the ratio of minimum wages to average wages has
    a. risen steadily
    b. grown at the same pace as productivity
    c. fallen from 49 percent to 35 percent
    d. dropped because of new entrants to the labor force
    e. risen dramatically due to regular increases in the minimum wage

THE MICROECONOMICS OF FACTOR MARKETS

Discussion Questions

1. List and discuss the factors that most influence people's income-earning potential.

2. Does it follow from the theory presented in Chapter 15 that wages and productivity would change together over time in the United States? Explain.

Answers to Questions

True-False Questions

1. True
2. False. The correlation between productivity and earning is almost perfect over the years.
3. False. Most college-educated people work in higher-skill, higher-wage jobs.
4. True
5. True

Multiple-Choice Questions

1. b
2. d
3. a
4. e
5. c

Discussion Questions

1. Productivity influences people's income-earning potential. As productivity measured by real hourly output has increased, so has real hourly compensation. When they are graphed, the curves measuring productivity and real hourly compensation are almost indistinguishable.

   Education is an important determinant of people's income-earning potential. Some 66 percent of managerial and professional people, people who earn higher incomes, have college degrees. Most jobs in technical areas, sales, and administrative support are staffed by people with high school and college degrees. Almost 25 percent of operators, laborers, and fabricators are high school dropouts. Among these occupations, only 4.9 percent of workers have college degrees.

   Minority status and gender also make a difference in income-earning potential. Blacks, Hispanics, and women earn significantly less than white men in comparable jobs. These earnings disparities reflect a combination of current and past discrimination against minorities and women in the labor market.

2. It follows perfectly from the theory that wages and productivity would change together over time. The demand for labor is the marginal physical product of labor times the price of the output labor produces. The marginal physical product is a measure of labor productivity. As it rises, so does the demand for labor and the wage rate, given a constant labor supply.

CHAPTER 16

WAGES AND EMPLOYMENT: MONOPSONY AND LABOR UNIONS

Chapter in a Nutshell

We continue our discussion of labor markets in this chapter with **monopsony** labor markets. Instead of many buyers of labor, we assume there is only one buyer of labor — a monopsony exists. A monopsonist is able to reap a **return to monopsony power** by hiring workers up to the point where the MRP of labor is equal to the MLC and paying the workers a wage rate read from the labor supply curve, which lies below the MLC. However, monopsony labor markets are sometimes marked by the presence of **labor unions**, which bargain with the monopsonist for higher wages, shorter hours, and better working conditions. A labor union can confront the monopsonist with a horizontal MLC curve and, as a result, capture the return to monopsony power for the workers it represents.

An overview of labor history in the United States is presented in the chapter. The divergent goals of unions and their employers during **collective bargaining** are considered. Sometimes, the failure of collective bargaining results in a union declaring a **strike** in order to achieve its goals for wages, hours, and working conditions. The differences between **craft** and **industrial unions**, **closed** and **union shops** are discussed. Finally, important legislation regarding labor is reviewed.

After studying this chapter, you should be able to:

- Explain why the **monopsonist's** labor supply curve is the market supply of labor.
- Derive the marginal labor cost curve from the supply curve for labor.
- Describe how a **labor union** can alter the marginal labor cost curve to increase wages.
- Discuss the conflicts that arise between **unions** and **monopsonists** over wages and employment.
- Show how the elasticity of demand for labor can influence union strategies.
- Outline the historical development of unions in the United States.

Concept Check — See how you do on these multiple-choice questions.

1. A **monopsony** is
   a. the same as a monopoly only bigger
   b. a market with only one buyer
   c. a labor market with a union
   d. a closed shop
   e. a union shop

A monopoly is a single seller. A monopsony is a . . . .

2. The **marginal labor cost** for a monopsonist is
   a. the same as the market supply of labor
   b. above the market supply of labor
   c. below the market supply of labor
   d. lower with a union
   e. unchanged by the presence of a union

287

Remember that the market supply of labor is the monopsonist's supply of labor.

3. The **return to monopsony power** is
   a. the result of lower wages accepted by unions when their strikes are broken
   b. the difference between the marginal revenue product and the wage rate for the last worker hired
   c. larger as the power of a union increases
   d. smaller as the power of a union increases
   e. the difference between the marginal revenue product and the wage rate for the last worker hired multiplied by the number of workers hired

A monopsony won't pay the last worker hired his/her marginal revenue product.

4. When a **labor union** goes on strike, it is often the result of
   a. a failure to produce a contract acceptable to the union through collective bargaining
   b. unrealistic union demands
   c. unrealistic demands by the firm
   d. an unwillingness to negotiate
   e. carefully orchestrated union strategy to push the firm to bankruptcy

What is the process that usually precedes a decision to strike?

5. The most important piece of **labor legislation** in the United States has been the
   a. Norris-La Guardia Act of 1932
   b. Wagner Act of 1935
   c. Taft-Hartley Act of 1947
   d. Landrum-Griffin Act
   e. Civil Rights Act of 1964

This is one you need to know!

Am I on the Right Track?

Your answers to these questions should be **b, b, e, a,** and **b**. Analogies can be drawn between monopoly and monopsony. A monopoly is a single seller whereas a monopsony is a single buyer. The demand curve for a monopolist is the market demand curve, whereas the supply curve for a monopsony is the market supply curve. The marginal revenue curve for a monopoly is below the demand curve whereas the marginal labor cost for a monopsonist employer is above the labor supply curve. Wage and employment determination for a monopsonist is different from that of a firm hiring labor in a competitive labor market. We'll explore this difference in a graphing tutorial. Be sure to note the new key terms, many of which correspond to unions and their activities.

Key Terms Quiz — Match the terms on the left with the definitions in the column on the right.

1. monopsony   _____ a. a union representing workers of a single occupation regardless of the industry

2. labor union   _____ b. the withholding of labor by unions when collective bargaining fails

3. strike   _____ c. the firm may only hire union labor

THE MICROECONOMICS OF FACTOR MARKETS

4. collective bargaining   _____ d. the firm may hire nonunion labor, but once hired, they must join the union within a specified time period

5. return to monopsony power   _____ e. negotiation between a labor union and a firm employing labor

6. closed shop   _____ f. a labor market with only one buyer

7. union shop   _____ g. a union representing all workers in a single industry regardless of each worker's skill or craft

8. craft union   _____ h. the difference between the MRP and the wage rate of the last worker hired, multiplied by the number of workers hired

9. industrial union   _____ i. an association of workers that negotiates wages, hours, and working conditions

Graphing Tutorial

The key difference between competitive labor markets that we studied in the last chapter and monopsony that we consider in this chapter is that there are many buyers of labor in competitive labor markets and only one buyer of labor in monopsony. In a competitive labor market, the market demand for labor and the market supply of labor interact to set an equilibrium wage. Firms that hire labor cannot influence this equilibrium wage. They can hire as much labor as they want at the market wage rate. Therefore, the marginal labor cost curve is a horizontal line at the wage rate.

However, in a monopsony labor market, the market supply of labor is the firm's supply of labor because only one firm is hiring labor. Each time the firm wants to hire additional labor, it must increase the wage somewhat in order to match the opportunity cost of the additional workers hired. It must pay this increased wage to all workers hired previously at a lower wage rate. Therefore, the marginal labor cost is equal to the higher wage that must be paid to the additional labor hired, plus the increment to wages paid to workers hired previously at a lower wage rate. Thus, the marginal labor cost is above the supply of labor curve for the monopsonist.

Let's work through a numerical example and examine wage determination for a monopsony. Suppose that Janet Goulet has managed to acquire all the firms in the fishing industry described in the graphing tutorial for the previous chapter. She is a monopsonist — the sole buyer of labor in the fishing industry. Goulet Fishing, Unlimited faces the following labor supply function. The total labor cost and marginal labor cost are shown in the third and fourth columns of the table.

Workers	Wage ($/run)	TLC	MLC
10	500	5,000	500
20	1,000	20,000	1,500
30	1,500	45,000	2,500
40	2,000	80,000	3,500
50	2,500	125,000	4,500
60	3,000	180,000	5,500
70	3,500	245,000	6,500

Note that at every level of employment, the marginal labor cost is greater than the wage, so that when the labor supply curve and the marginal labor cost curve are graphed, the marginal labor cost curve will lie above the labor supply curve. These two curves are shown in the graph below with a marginal revenue product curve superimposed on them.

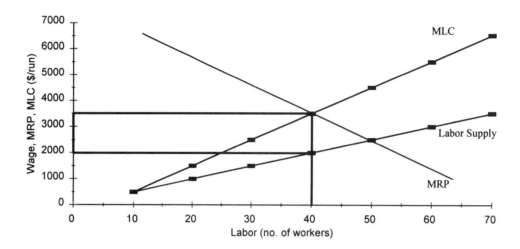

How many workers should Goulet Fishing, Unlimited hire? Janet will follow the same rule that the firm hiring in the competitive market did in the previous chapter. Namely, she will continue to hire workers until MRP = MLC. This intersection of the marginal revenue product and marginal labor cost occurs at 40 workers. What wage will they be paid? Wages are read from the labor supply curve. The 40 workers will each earn $2,000 per run. However, this is $1,500 below the $3,500 marginal revenue product of the 40th worker.

We can now use the graph to show the return to monopsony power. The monopsonist pays each worker $1,500 less than the marginal revenue product of the last worker hired. Therefore, the return to monopsony power is $1,500 multiplied by 40 workers or $60,000. This area is outlined by the heavy rectangle.

Graphing Pitfalls

Be sure that you don't confuse the labeling of the marginal labor cost curve and the labor supply curve in a graph that represents a monopsony. The marginal labor cost curve is always above the labor supply curve. The monopsonist pays workers wages that are read from the labor supply curve. However, in order to hire additional units of labor, the monopsonist must pay a higher wage rate, not just to the additional units of labor hired, but to all the labor hired previously at lower wage rates. Therefore, the marginal labor cost curve is above the labor supply curve.

Consider the way the two curves are labeled in the diagram below. Instead of reading down to the labor supply curve to find the wage rate, you would read up from the intersection of the MRP and MLC to find the wage rate. How would you calculate the return to monopsony power? It just doesn't compute.

THE MICROECONOMICS OF FACTOR MARKETS

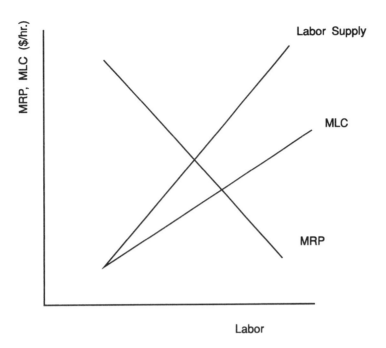

The MLC is always above the labor supply curve because a monopsonist that hires additional units of labor must pay a higher wage rate to those units, and that wage rate must also be paid to units of labor hired previously at lower wage rates.

True-False Questions — If a statement is false, explain why.

1. Monopsony exists when there is only buyer of labor in a labor market. (T/F)

2. A monopsonist can hire any quantity of labor at any wage rate it chooses. (T/F)

3. A monopsonist faces the market supply curve of labor. (T/F)

4. A monopsonist will hire workers until the marginal revenue product of labor intersects the labor supply curve. (T/F)

5. Under monopsony, marginal labor cost and the supply curve for labor are precisely the same. (T/F)

6. The marginal revenue product of the last worker hired under monopsony is less than the wage rate the worker receives. (T/F)

7. A union can increase both the wage rate and employment in a monopsony market by dictating a wage rate to the monopsonist that essentially changes the marginal labor cost curve. (T/F)

8. A union facing a monopsonist will always oppose the adoption of a new technology that results in increased labor productivity because jobs will be cut. (T/F)

9. The return to monopsony power is the difference between the marginal revenue product and the wage paid to the last worker hired. (T/F)

10. Firms that sell their output in highly competitive markets tend to have elastic demands for labor. (T/F)

11. A union attempting to raise the wage rate will cause fewer workers to be laid off if the demand for labor is highly inelastic. (T/F)

12. A union shop is one in which only union workers are hired. (T/F)

13. Early union activity in the United States was limited by court decisions holding that unions were criminal conspiracies. (T/F)

14. The Wagner Act forced businesses to accept unions as legitimate institutions in collective bargaining. (T/F)

15. The American Federation of Labor was interested in structural change in the economy, as well as obtaining higher wage rates for its members. (T/F)

Multiple-Choice Questions

1. A monopsony can always
    a. pick the wage rate it chooses to offer
    b. hire as many workers at a given wage as it wants
    c. compete successfully with other firms in the labor market
    d. outlast a union whenever a strike of long duration occurs
    e. find nonunion workers in cases of strikes

2. The supply curve of labor facing a monopsonist is always
    a. lower than the supply curve facing a competitive firm
    b. identical to the market supply curve of labor
    c. backward bending
    d. perfectly elastic
    e. horizontal at the market wage

3. The monopsony's labor demand curve is always
   a. the sum of the firms' marginal revenue product curves
   b. upward sloping because the labor market is competitive
   c. its marginal revenue product curve
   d. horizontal because the labor market is competitive
   e. downward sloping because the labor market is competitive

4. If a profit-maximizing monopsony is hiring workers at a point where its marginal revenue product is less than its marginal labor cost, it
   a. has hired too many workers
   b. has hired too few workers
   c. should shut down
   d. should shift the supply curve of labor to the left
   e. should shift the supply curve of labor to the right

5. Marginal labor cost is greater than the wage rate under monopsony because
   a. the monopsonist has trouble controlling costs with little competition
   b. hiring additional workers involves raising the wage rate of those workers already working
   c. marginal labor cost includes many new factors
   d. unions are unable to raise wage rates
   e. the revenue generated by the workers is less than the marginal labor cost

6. A profit-maximizing monopsonist will hire workers until MRP = MLC and
   a. workers are paid a wage equal to the MRP
   b. workers are paid a wage that is less than the MRP
   c. the labor supply is equal to the MLC
   d. workers are paid the difference between MRP and MLC
   e. the labor supply is greater than MLC

7. Monopsony induces workers to organize in a union because a union can
   a. raise MRP and therefore the wage rate
   b. fix the wage rate at which labor will be offered so the MLC is constant to the monopsonist
   c. increase the labor supply dramatically
   d. provide labor of higher quality to the firm
   e. prevent nonunion workers from taking their jobs

8. A successful union facing a monopsonist can
   a. increase the wage rate above the nonunion rate and still maintain the level of employment
   b. increase the wage rate above the nonunion rate, but only at the expense of employment
   c. decrease the MRP by striking frequently and in this way increase the wage rate
   d. reduce MLC, which creates a wider gap between MLC and MRP and serves to raise wage rates
   e. survive only by accepting wage rate cuts or by allowing layoffs

9. The return to monopsony power is measured by
   a. the difference between MRP and MLC multiplied by the number of workers employed
   b. the difference between union and nonunion wage rates multiplied by the number of workers employed
   c. the price that a monopsony charges for a good and the wage rate it pays to produce it
   d. the elasticity of MRP
   e. the difference between the MRP and the wage rate of the last worker hired, multiplied by the number of workers hired

10. One difference between a perfectly competitive labor market and a monopsony labor market is that in
    a. monopsony workers are paid their MRP
    b. competitive labor markets the labor supply curve determines how much workers receive
    c. perfect competition workers are paid less than their MRP
    d. monopsony workers are paid less than their MRP
    e. perfect competition workers are paid too much to allow the firm a normal profit

11. Workers resort to a strike
    a. in an effort to shift their MRP curve to the right, which allows for higher wage rates
    b. in an effort to shift their MLC curve to the right, which allows for higher wage rates
    c. to capture all or some of the return to monopsony power
    d. to reduce employment, which makes wage-rate increases easier to obtain
    e. to increase employment, enhancing union strength, which makes wage-rate increases easier to obtain

12. Given the choice, management prefers the union shop over the closed shop because
    a. union workers are more productive than nonunion workers
    b. a union shop permits a greater pool of labor from which to hire
    c. a closed shop shuts out union members, thereby risking labor strife
    d. closed shops demand higher wage rates
    e. union shops do not engage in strikes

13. Given a high elasticity of demand for labor in a monopsony market, a union will probably have greater success at
    a. raising employment rather than wage rates
    b. raising wage rates rather than employment
    c. raising neither wage rates nor employment, but improving benefits packages
    d. making the demand for labor even more elastic
    e. opposing any technology to increase labor productivity that may reduce employment

14. In the United States during the late eighteenth and early nineteenth centuries
    a. political and economic liberty favored union growth
    b. the courts denied unions legal status
    c. business regarded unions as conspiracies, but courts supported their right to organize
    d. union growth was rapid
    e. the CIO was the most successful union organization

15. The failure of collective bargaining will cause a union to
    a. begin a membership drive
    b. increase its wage demands
    c. go on strike
    d. increase the MRP curve
    e. form a closed shop

16. Samuel Gompers left the Knights of Labor in 1881 and formed the AFL in 1886 in order to
    a. better promote social equality and justice
    b. reap the benefits that accrue to union leaders
    c. promote strictly economic goals as a union leader
    d. form a union for industrial workers
    e. shield workers in America from foreign competition

THE MICROECONOMICS OF FACTOR MARKETS

17. The Congress of Industrial Organizations (CIO)
    a. represents specific crafts unions, such as welders, painters, and carpenters
    b. represents unions in specific regions, such as welders and painters in Oregon
    c. represents unions in specific industries, such as welders and painters in auto plants
    d. is the industries' (managements') response to union pressure to raise wage rates
    e. is designed to mediate disputes between management and unions to head off strikes that may be damaging to the nation's interest, e.g., railroad strikes or air traffic controller strikes

18. The Landrum-Griffin Act was passed in 1959 in order to
    a. protect union workers from rigged union elections and other abuses
    b. deal once and for all with the problem of closed shops
    c. close loopholes in the Norris-La Guardia Act
    d. encourage union formation in the agricultural sector
    e. pave the way for civil rights legislation in the 1960s

19. The Wagner Act of 1935 is called the Magna Carta of labor because
    a. American workers were all to be represented by unions
    b. unions were subsidized by federal grants
    c. unions were to be recognized by businesses as legitimate bargaining institutions
    d. unions were involved more heavily in the management of businesses
    e. the federal government guaranteed union workers better working conditions

20. The Taft-Hartley Act, the Landrum-Griffin Act, and the Civil Rights Act of 1964 all have in common that they
    a. outlawed certain types of unions
    b. limited the power of unions
    c. extended the power of unions
    d. placed union members on corporate boards of directors
    e. stopped businesses from discriminating against pro-union workers

Fill in the Blanks

1. In a monopsonist market, the marginal labor cost curve lies above the _____ because it includes the increase in the wages of workers already hired at _____ wages.

2. At the profit-maximizing level of employment, the difference between the MRP and the _____ multiplied by the level of _____ gives the return to _____.

3. The wage-maximizing supply curve of union labor presented to the monopsonist is _____ at the _____ level.

4. If new technology is adopted that shifts the demand curve for labor to the right, the union has the option of bargaining for higher _____ at the existing level of employment or _____ at the existing level of wages.

5. The American Federation of Labor was the organization of _____ while the Congress of

   Industrial Organizations was the organization of _____ .

Discussion Questions

1. Why does the marginal labor cost curve lie above the supply curve for labor in a monopsony?

2. In what sense is labor underpaid under conditions of monopsony?

3. Frequently, the comment is made that unions create unemployment by raising wage rates. Is this always the case? Explain.

4. Outline the major pieces of legislation that have affected union behavior over time.

Problems

1. Consider the labor market depicted in the graphing tutorial. What strategy would the labor union employ if it wanted to maximize wages? Show this on the graph presented below. How do union members benefit?

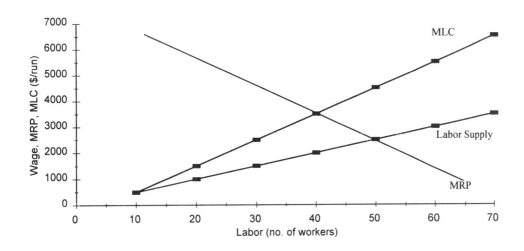

2. Continuing with the same example, what strategy would a union employ if it wanted to maximize employment? Show this on the graph. How do union members benefit?

3. Explain why a union will not demand wages that are higher than the MRP = MLC level.

Everyday Applications

Have you or any of your family or friends belonged to a labor union? What sort of activities did the union sponsor? Was the union representing workers employed by a monopsonist? Perhaps members of your family belong to professional organizations like the American Bar Association or the American Medical Association. How do unions and professional organizations differ? How are they the same?

Economics Online

To find out more about the sort of activities that unions pursue, visit the Web site for the United Auto Workers (*http://www.uaw.org/*).

Answers to Questions

Key Terms Quiz

a. 8
b. 3
c. 6
d. 7
e. 4
f. 1
g. 9
h. 5
i. 2

True-False Questions

1. True
2. False. The monopsonist must pay a wage read from the labor supply curve.
3. True
4. False. The monopsonist will hire workers until MRP = MLC.
5. False. The MLC is above the supply of labor.
6. False. The wage paid to the last worker hired is less than the MRP.
7. True
8. False. The new technology will increase the MRP, so the union must choose among increasing wages, increasing employment, or both.
9. False. The return to monopsony power is the difference between the marginal revenue product and the wage paid to the last worker hired, multiplied by the number of workers hired.
10. True
11. True
12. False. The workers hired may be nonunion, but they are required to join the union within a specified time period.
13. True
14. True
15. False. The AFL was most concerned about increasing wages and improving working conditions for its members.

Multiple-Choice Questions

1. a
2. b
3. c
4. a
5. b
6. b
7. b
8. a
9. e
10. d
11. c
12. b
13. a
14. b
15. c
16. c
17. c
18. a
19. c
20. b

THE MICROECONOMICS OF FACTOR MARKETS

Fill in the Blanks

1. labor supply curve; lower
2. wage; employment; monopsony power
3. horizontal; MRP = MLC
4. wages; higher employment
5. craft unions; industrial unions

Discussion Questions

1. The marginal labor cost curve lies above the labor supply curve because the monopsonist must raise the wage rate in order to attract more labor into the market and, in so doing, incurs the cost of that additional worker plus a wage rate increment that all previously hired workers receive to bring their wage rates up to that of the newly hired workers.

2. Workers are underpaid in the sense that the wage they receive is less than their marginal revenue product. The difference between the MRP and the wage rate for the last worker hired multiplied by the number of workers hired is called the return to monopsony power.

3. Unions in a monopsony market create unemployment only if they succeed in raising the wage rate above the workers' MRP. Otherwise, they can raise wages and capture the return to monopsony power without reducing the level of employment.

4. The first two pieces of labor legislation were pro-union. The Norris-La Guardia Act of 1932 outlawed "yellow-dog" contracts, which stated that a worker was automatically fired if he or she joined a union. The Wagner Act of 1935 is often called the Magna Carta of American labor because it forced businesses to accept labor unions as legitimate institutions in collective bargaining.

   After World War II, Congress passed a series of acts that limited the power of labor was passed. The first of these was the Taft-Hartley Act of 1947. This act outlawed the closed shop and prohibited unions' unfair labor practices including pressuring workers during union elections and striking to support other unions' strikes. Next came the Landrum-Griffin Act in 1959, also known as the Labor Management Reporting and Disclosure Act. This act forced unions to fully disclose their financial activities and sought to protect workers from rigged union elections. Union leaders were made liable for misusing union funds and were required to disclose the salaries of union officials. Finally, the Civil Rights Act of 1964 influenced union activity. The principal issue covered by this act was racial and sexual discrimination by unions; forcing unions to adopt affirmative action policies within their own ranks.

Problems

1. The union would make the marginal labor cost curve horizontal at the MRP = MLC level, which occurs at the $3,500 level. Union members benefit because the return to monopsony power that used to accrue to the monopsonist now goes to workers. The rectangle outlined by bold lines corresponds to the gain for the union. Note that even though wages are raised, employment is left unaffected.

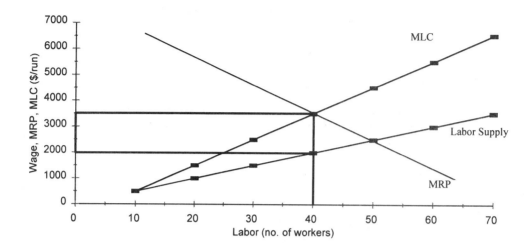

2. The union faces the monopsonist with a marginal labor cost curve at the wage rate $2,500 in order to maximize employment. The firm would hire 50 workers in this case. This is shown below with a bold line drawn for the MLC at the $2,500 wage and a bold line drawn down to the 50 worker level. Union members benefit from a $500 increase in their wages versus the non-union wage. Union membership also increases.

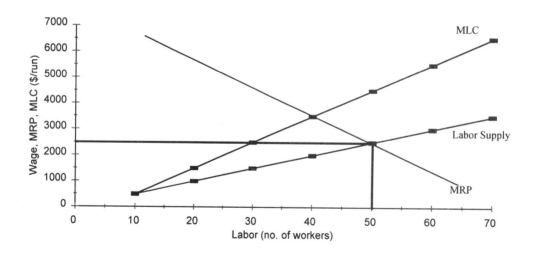

3. Two problems are encountered when a union attempts to increase wages beyond the MRP = MLC level. First, employment is reduced from the level achieved without a union. It would be bad for worker morale, to say the least, to join the union and achieve a wage increase, only to be laid off from work as a result. The other problem with raising the wage rate above the MRP = MLC level is that a larger quantity of labor will be supplied as a result. Many of these workers would be willing to work for less than the union wage. This could weaken the union's position significantly because of competition from nonunion labor.

CHAPTER 17

INTEREST, RENT, AND PROFIT

Chapter in a Nutshell

Our examination of resource markets in the previous two chapters has focused on labor. How are other resources like capital, land, and entrepreneurship priced? How much of each of these resources will a profit-maximizing firm hire? This chapter addresses these questions. Many of the same ideas that we used to study wage and employment determination are used to understand how **interest rates**, **rents**, and **profits** are determined. For example, it is possible to measure the **marginal revenue product of capital**, just as we did for labor. The marginal revenue product of capital is the marginal physical product of a dollar's worth of **capital equipment** multiplied by the price of the product the capital produces. The marginal revenue product of capital is the firm's demand for capital. A supply of capital in the form of loanable funds is provided by savers. The **interest rate** is determined by the intersection of the demand for loanable funds and the supply of **loanable funds** in the **loanable funds market**.

Land rents are set in land markets that reflect demand and supply for different types of land. **Differential land rent** arises from differences in the cost of providing land. Land that is close to the marketplace earns **location rent** because of lower transportation costs. The wages of people with specialized talents, like renowned artists, entertainers, and athletes, contain **wage-related rent**. These people would continue to perform for less than they actually earn each year.

Entrepreneurs earn **profit-related income**. Profit-related income paid to entrepreneurs arises from their willingness to assume the risks of enterprise. The dividend income received by people who own stocks is profit-related income.

After studying this chapter, you should be able to:

- Explain the terms **marginal physical product of capital** and **marginal revenue product of capital**.
- Distinguish between **loanable funds** and **capital equipment**.
- Verify that profits are maximized when a firm employs capital until the MRP = MFC.
- Graph the **loanable funds market** to explain the determination of the **rate of interest**.
- Discuss the ethics of income from interest.
- Use an equation to explain the relationship between interest rates and the **present values** of property.
- Give an economic definition for **rent**.
- Derive **differential rents on land** of different quality.
- Give examples of **wage-related rents**.
- Describe how entrepreneurs calculate their **profit-related income**.

Concept Check — See how you do on these multiple-choice questions.

1. The **marginal revenue product of capital** is calculated by
   a. adding the marginal physical product of capital and the price of the good the capital produces
   b. multiplying the marginal physical product of capital by the price of the good the capital produces
   c. subtracting the marginal physical product of labor from the marginal physical product of capital
   d. dividing the marginal physical product of capital by the price of the good the capital produces
   e. multiplying the marginal physical product of labor by the price of the capital good

Think about how we computed the marginal revenue product of labor.

2. The **supply curve of loanable funds** is upward sloping because
   a. as the price increases, the quantity supplied decreases
   b. of the law of diminishing returns
   c. of diseconomies of scale
   d. people are more willing to make the funds available at higher interest rates
   e. an increase in the interest rate leads to a decrease in the quantity of funds supplied

The interest rate is the price people are willing to pay to borrow money. How will people who lend money respond to changes in the interest rate?

3. The **present value** of a property is equal to the annual revenue generated by the property
   a. divided by its price
   b. multiplied by its marginal physical product
   c. divided by the interest rate
   d. multiplied by the interest rate
   e. multiplied by its marginal revenue product

The present value of a property is the amount someone is willing to pay today for the stream of expected future annual income a property generates.

4. **Land rent** is the difference between what an acre receives as payment for its use — the market price of the land — and the
   a. cost of bringing that acre into being — its supply price
   b. transportation costs of bringing an acre's production to market
   c. present value of the property
   d. annual revenue generated by the land
   e. cost of labor necessary to cultivate the land

When does land begin to earn rent?

5. **Profit** is what entrepreneurs earn for
   a. their expert managerial skills
   b. a salary
   c. making certain that stock prices increase
   d. implementing the latest technologies into production
   e. assuming the risks and uncertainties of enterprise

What do we mean by entrepreneurship?

Am I on the Right Track?

Your answers to the questions above should be **b, d, c, a,** and **e**. This chapter presents more examples of the application of marginal analysis. Keep following the basic rule — equating marginal revenue and marginal cost — and you'll have no trouble grasping the determination of interest, rent, and profit. This chapter has plenty of new terms, so pay close attention to them and their definitions.

THE MICROECONOMICS OF FACTOR MARKETS

Key Terms Quiz — Match the terms on the left with their definitions in the column on the right.

1. marginal revenue product of capital
2. rent
3. loanable funds
4. land rent
5. capital equipment
6. differential land rent
7. rate of interest
8. location rent
9. loanable funds market
10. wage-related rent
11. present value
12. profit

_____ a. a payment to landowners for the use of land
_____ b. the difference between what a resource receives in payment for its use in production and the cost of bringing it into production
_____ c. the value today of the stream of expected future annual income a property generates
_____ d. income earned by entrepreneurs
_____ e. the machinery that a firm uses in production
_____ f. money employed by a firm to purchase physical plant, equipment, and raw materials used in production
_____ g. the difference between the wage rate a person receives for working and the lowest wage necessary to keep that person employed
_____ h. the change in total revenue from adding one more dollar of loanable funds to production
_____ i. rent arising from differences in the cost of providing land
_____ j. rent arising from differences in land distances from the marketplace
_____ k. the price of loanable funds, expressed as an annual percentage return on a dollar of loanable funds
_____ l. the market in which the demand for and supply of loanable funds determines the rate of interest

Graphing Tutorial

The graph used to show differential land rent uses a different land supply curve than you have encountered thus far in the text. The supply curve has steps that correspond to the fact that there are differences in the cost of providing land. As population increases, it pays to bring more costly land into production. Once this more costly land is brought into production, land already in production earns rent per acre equal to the difference between the market price per acre and the supply price per acre.

    Consider the graph shown on the following page. With a limited population, the demand for land is represented by the demand curve labeled D that is closest to the origin. Under these circumstances, the least costly land is brought into production — 60 acres at a price equal to zero. Suppose that population increases so that the demand for land increases from D to D'. Now, more costly land is brought into production at a supply price equal to $100 per acre. The first 60 acres earns rent equal to the difference between the market price for land — $100 — and the supply price of the first 60 acres — zero. The per acre rent for the first 60 acres is $100. The total land rent earned is 60 acres x $100/acre = $6,000. This total land rent is represented by Area A. Suppose that the population continues to increase until the demand for land is given by D". The market price for land is now $200 per acre. This market price is high enough to cover the supply price of the third 60 acres of land. A total of 180 acres is now under cultivation. The first 60 acres in cultivation will earn a rent equal to $200 per acre and a total land rent equal to Area A + Area B = $12,000. The second 60 acres under cultivation will earn a rent equal to $100 per acre — the difference between the $200 market price and the $100 supply price. The total land rent for the second 60 acres is represented by Area C, equal to $6,000. What about the third 60 acres? It doesn't earn rent because the market price and the supply price are the same — $200. Thus, the total differential land rent earned (when the market price of land is $200) is Area A + Area B + Area C = $18,000.

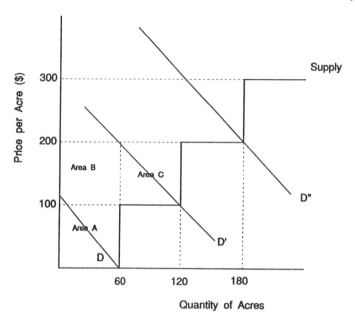

Graphing Pitfalls

The supply curve of land is drawn in steps rather than as a smooth, upward-sloping curve or upward-sloping straight line for the reason that land typically cannot be brought into production at a continuously increasing supply price. Fairly large plots of land with similar physical characteristics, such as grasslands, woodlands, hillsides, or floodplain, must be represented with a constant supply price; hence, the supply curve for land will be comprised of a series of steps. Each ascending step represents a more costly type of land to bring into production. The point here is not to make the mistake of trying to represent differential land rent with a smooth supply curve. Think of land as coming in big chunks that have similar characteristics and cost the same to bring into production. So, it doesn't make sense to try to represent differential land rent with the smooth, upward-sloping curve drawn below. A supply curve comprised of steps makes more sense from what we know of the physical world.

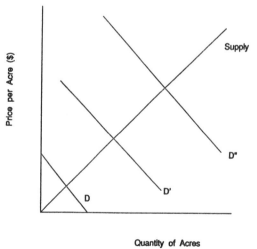

The supply curve representing differential land rent should be drawn as a series of ascending steps to represent differences in the cost of providing land that comes in large plots with similar physical characteristics and the same supply price.

THE MICROECONOMICS OF FACTOR MARKETS

True-False Questions — If a statement is false, explain why.

1. The marginal revenue product of capital is the change in total revenue that results from adding one more dollar of capital equipment to production. (T/F)

2. The marginal revenue product of capital curve is downward sloping because of the law of diminishing returns. (T/F)

3. The amount of capital equipment can be varied easily in the short run by simply adding more loanable funds. (T/F)

4. The marginal factor cost of loanable funds is equal to the interest rate. (T/F)

5. The quantity of loanable funds supplied in the market increases as the interest rate decreases. (T/F)

6. One justification for the income earned from interest payments on savings is that property holders with legitimate rights to property are entitled to receive the MRP the property generates. (T/F)

7. Marxists believe that interest income is justifiable because it represents abstinence from consumption. (T/F)

8. As interest rates decrease, the present value of property decreases. (T/F)

9. Profit-related income is the amount entrepreneurs earn over and above what they could be paid in the next best occupation plus the opportunity cost of the capital they have invested in a business. (T/F)

10. A celebrity's name can be a highly valued marketable asset. (T/F)

11. Economists define rent as the amount that a person pays to a landlord for the use of land or buildings. (T/F)

12. For acres of uniform quality, land rent is not paid unless the demand curve intersects the vertical supply curve somewhere above the horizontal axis. (T/F)

13. Differential rent arises from the fact that there are differences in the size of a country's population as time passes. (T/F)

14. Location rents for inner-city department stores tend to decline with the appearance of shopping malls on the outskirts of cities. (T/F)

15. The difference between the Rolling Stones' earnings on their "Bridges to Babylon" tour and the sum that would have been required for them to perform is called the wage-related rent. (T/F)

Multiple-Choice Questions

1. The marginal physical product of capital is the addition to
   a. total revenue generated by adding a unit of loanable funds to production
   b. total physical product generated by adding a unit of capital to production
   c. total revenue generated by adding a unit of capital to production
   d. total physical product divided by a unit of capital
   e. marginal revenue product

2. A unit of capital equipment, once employed,
   a. generates a rate of return equal to the marginal physical product of capital
   b. is unalterable in the short run
   c. can be altered only by borrowing more loanable funds
   d. completely substitutes for labor
   e. is always the most technologically advanced equipment available

3. A firm will employ loanable funds up to the point where the
   a. marginal revenue product is greater than the interest rate
   b. marginal revenue product is less than the interest rate
   c. marginal factor cost is equal to the interest rate
   d. marginal factor cost is equal to the rate of profit
   e. marginal revenue product is equal to the interest rate

4. The supply of loanable funds curve is upward sloping because as the interest rate increases,
   a. people are willing to save a larger portion of their incomes
   b. people are willing to borrow more from lending institutions
   c. people are willing to consume more big ticket items
   d. people are willing to save a smaller portion of their incomes
   e. the supply of savings decreases

5. If a nationwide campaign to increase saving is successful, it would shift
   a. the demand curve for loanable funds to the right, causing the interest rate to rise
   b. the supply curve of loanable funds to the right, causing the interest rate to fall
   c. both the demand curve for and the supply of loanable funds to the right, leaving the interest rate unchanged
   d. the demand curve for loanable funds to the left, causing the interest rate to fall
   e. the supply curve of loanable funds to the left, causing the interest rate to rise

6. The ethic that justifies someone receiving interest income earned on loanable funds supplied is that
   a. legitimate property holders are entitled to the MRP the property generates
   b. making money by any means is justified in a market-based economic system
   c. people should receive what they are able to earn on the market, even if they don't work
   d. income, from any source, always reflects what people contribute to production
   e. demanders of loanable funds make more income using the funds than do the suppliers

7. Interest rates are determined in the loanable funds market where
   a. the supply curve of loanable funds is upward sloping
   b. the marginal physical product of capital is downward sloping
   c. the marginal revenue product of capital is expressed as a percentage return on the dollar
   d. the interest rate is the marginal factor cost of capital
   e. all of the above

8. The present value of a property is equal to the
   a. price at which quantity demanded of the property equals quantity supplied
   b. minimum price set by an auctioneer at which bidding is to start
   c. annual income generated by the property divided by the interest rate
   d. annual income generated by the property multiplied by the interest rate
   e. sum of the interest earnings from the asset over a fixed number of years

9. If the price of cattle increases today, the likely effect on the present value of cattle ranches is
   a. a sell-off of cattle ranches resulting in big declines in their values
   b. an increase in the value of cattle ranches
   c. to cause cattle ranches' values to become more volatile in expectation of future price changes
   d. an increase in the demand for cattle so that ranch values increase
   e. to cause the value of cattle ranches to rise steadily over time

10. To economists, rent is the
    a. amount of money paid to occupy an apartment, house, or other fixed property
    b. difference between what a person pays for something and what it is worth
    c. difference between what a resource receives in payment and the cost of bringing the resource into production
    d. difference between what a resource is paid in the market and what the resource would be paid if it received the full value of its marginal revenue product
    e. value of any scarce resource

11. If one argues that land rent is strictly demand determined, then the underlying assumption must be that
    a. the supply of land is fixed and of the same quality
    b. the supply of land is variable and of unequal quality
    c. the demand for land is perfectly elastic and increasing
    d. the demand for land is perfectly inelastic and falling
    e. there is an excess demand for land

12. Because differential rent arises from the fact that all land is not of equal quality,
    a. farmers will cultivate the poorest land first, saving the best for last
    b. the cost of providing land of different qualities varies, creating different rents on different qualities of land
    c. the highest rent is paid for the worst land
    d. rent controls are necessary for the poorer land
    e. landlords can discriminate among tenants who cultivate the different qualities of land

13. Location rent arises because land that is located closer to the market has
    a. higher fertility than land farther away
    b. lower transportation costs than land farther away
    c. easier access to important breakthroughs in technology
    d. access to a better labor force
    e. been settled first so no clearing costs are incurred in the course of production

14. Suppose an author receives $1.4 million to write a new economics text. If the author would have been willing to write the text for only $100,000, then the
    a. $1.4 million represents wage-related rent received by the author
    b. $100,000 represents wage-related rent received by the author
    c. $1.4 million minus the $100,000 represents the publisher's actual economic profit
    d. $1.4 million minus the $100,000 represents wage-related rent received by the author
    e. $100,000 represents the publisher's potential economic profit

15. Implicit costs of an entrepreneur's labor time and capital refer to
    a. the entrepreneur's opportunity costs
    b. the total costs incurred by an entrepreneur in doing business
    c. the entrepreneurial risks associated with a business venture
    d. normal plus economic profit
    e. potential losses for the entrepreneur

16. Even though the stockholders may not be involved in day-to-day management of a corporation, they are regarded as "invisible entrepreneurs" because
    a. they earn differential rents from the corporation
    b. they choose, at annual corporate meetings, who will run the corporation
    c. they assume all the risks and uncertainties associated with the corporation
    d. they can also be employed in the corporation and in that combined capacity have the most input
    e. managers feel a strong allegiance to the stockholders

17. If land is situated so that it earns zero location rent, then the
    a. land must be of lower quality than other acres that earn location rent
    b. wages of workers farming the land must be higher than average
    c. supply price of the land is equal to the transportation costs
    d. cost of transporting goods to market is zero
    e. market price of the acre is less than its supply price

18. In the long run, total revenues must be sufficiently high for an entrepreneur to
    a. expand into new businesses
    b. cover his or her opportunity costs
    c. raise the price of the output
    d. exit the business
    e. buy all existing stock

19. The present value of an asset is defined as the
    a. sum of the stream of income the property generates
    b. interest rate multiplied by the annual income the property generates
    c. interest rate divided by the annual income the property generates
    d. value today of the stream of expected future annual income the property generates
    e. price set on the asset by an owner willing to sell it

THE MICROECONOMICS OF FACTOR MARKETS

20. As a country's population increases, we expect that
    a. the supply price of land will decrease
    b. land rent will increase, but differential land rent and location rent will decrease
    c. land rent and differential land rent will increase, but location rent will decrease
    d. land rent, differential land rent, and location rent will decrease
    e. land rent, differential land rent, and location rent will increase

Fill in the Blanks

1. Adding dollar increments of _____ to a production process increases total physical product, but by _____ and _____ amounts.

2. Laborers, loanable funds suppliers, landowners, and entrepreneurs receive _____, _____, _____, and _____, respectively, as payment for the resources they supply that are used in production.

3. Differential rent arises when the supply of land is not entirely _____.

4. Present value is calculated by dividing the _____ by the _____.

5. The equilibrium rate of interest is determined by the _____ and the _____ loanable funds.

Discussion Questions

1. Why can't the amount of capital equipment be altered simply by employing more loanable funds in the short run? How does your answer relate to the distinction we made earlier between fixed and variable costs of production?

2. How would a consumption tax influence the supply of loanable funds? (Hint: Think in terms of what you do with your income, that is, spend or save.) What would happen to the equilibrium interest rate and the level of employment of loanable funds if a consumption tax was introduced?

3. Explain why a decline in interest rates should lead to an increase in the average price of stocks on the stock market.

4. Suppose a friend approaches you with an idea to start a fast-food franchise in the middle of downtown Chicago. Does this sound like a paying proposition to you? Justify your answer using location rent theory.

Problems

1. Suppose you purchased a gourmet coffee shop/espresso bar in a shopping mall for $100,000. The interest rate is 10 percent, and the annual income from the investment is $20,000. Did you get a good deal on the place? Why or why not?

2. a. Suppose that the price of wheat is $4.00 per bushel, the costs of production are $2.00 per bushel, and the cost of transporting a bushel of wheat one mile to market is $.05. What is the furthest distance from the market that it would pay to transport the wheat? Will wheat be grown beyond this distance?

   b. What portion of the price of wheat would be location rent if the wheat were grown on a plot of land adjacent to the market?

3. a. Soundsgood CD manufacturers can employ different quantities of capital to produce blank compact discs priced at $.50 each. Calculate the marginal revenue product of capital for each of the following quantities of capital at the $.50 price.

Loanable Funds ($)	Total Product (CDs)	MPP of Capital	MRP of Capital ($)	Supply Price (per $)
200	400			0.03
600	600			0.10
1,000	750			0.16
1,400	850			0.25
1,800	900			0.30
2,200	925			0.40
2,600	935			0.50

b. Calculate the equilibrium rate of interest given the figures for the supply price of loanable funds.

Everyday Applications

Consider the ethics of income from interest and your own experience. Almost certainly you have saved money in the bank and earned interest income from the saving. Was this income ethically justified? Suppose you inherit a large sum from a wealthy relative. What is the ethical justification for your being entitled to this inheritance? Answering this question forces you to consider the broader question of what constitutes property and the limits of claims to property rights. If property rights to inheritance are ethically justified, what is the ethical justification for an inheritance tax? Suppose the inheritance tax were set at 100 percent. How would such a tax alter your and your family's economic behavior?

Economics Online

Perhaps the best place to look for examples of entrepreneurship in action in our economy is among the companies whose stocks are traded on the Nasdaq Stock Market. These tend to be smaller corporations that are newer and involved in technologically sophisticated and risky enterprises. Visit the Web site for Nasdaq (*http://www.nasdaq.com/homecontent.stm*).

Answers to Questions

Key Terms Quiz

a. 4
b. 2
c. 11
d. 12
e. 5
f. 3
g. 10
h. 1
i. 6
j. 8
k. 7
l. 9

True-False Questions

1. True
2. True
3. False. The amount of capital equipment is fixed in the short run.
4. True
5. False. The quantity of loanable funds supplied increases as the interest rate increases.
6. True
7. False. Marxists believe that interest income represents unearned income from property ownership; hence, it is unjustified.
8. False. The present value is equal to the annual income that an asset generates divided by the interest rate, so present values increase as interest rates decrease.
9. True
10. True
11. False. Rent is the difference between what a resource receives as payment and the cost of bringing the resource into production.
12. True
13. False. Differential rent arises from differences in the productivity of land.
14. True
15. True

Multiple-Choice Questions

1. b
2. b
3. e
4. a
5. b
6. a
7. e
8. c
9. b
10. c
11. a
12. b
13. b
14. d
15. a
16. c
17. c
18. b
19. d
20. e

Fill in the Blanks

1. capital; smaller; smaller
2. wages; interest; rent; profit
3. fixed
4. annual income; interest rate
5. demand for; supply of

Discussion Questions

1. Capital equipment is relatively fixed in the short run. It has a particular physical form that is difficult to

alter. When capital equipment is replaced, it is usually done all at once in big chunks, rather than in bits and pieces at a time. Capital equipment is a part of a firm's fixed costs since it cannot be changed in the short run.

2. A consumption tax would make saving seem more attractive to potential consumers because by saving a consumer can avoid the tax. If saving increases, then the supply of loanable funds will shift to the right, causing the equilibrium rate of interest to decrease. At a lower interest rate, firms will find it increasingly attractive to purchase more capital equipment by employing more loanable funds.

3. Stockholders expect to earn income in the form of dividends from their stock assets each year. The present value of a stock is the expected annual income from the stock divided by the interest rate. As the interest rate falls, the present value will increase, given a constant expected annual income.

4. Be very careful! This is a good idea only if you and your friend expect to earn an annual revenue greater than or equal to the interest rate times the purchase price of the asset. Property close to the center of a city earns very high location rents so the values of these properties are high as well. Typically, fast-food places don't generate enough revenue to justify the high location rents associated with city centers, unless you're McDonald's, Wendy's, or other fast-food franchises that have excellent name recognition.

Problems

1. The present value of the coffee shop is $20,000 divided by 10 percent or $200,000, so purchasing the coffee shop for $100,000 was a good deal indeed.

2. a. A farmer earns $2.00 per bushel in profit if located adjacent to the market where transportation costs are negligible. This $2.00 per bushel profit is location rent. If the farmer is 40 miles from the market, then transportation costs are 40 miles times $.05 per bushel per mile which is $2.00 per bushel. So a farmer located 40 miles from the market would earn zero location rent. Forty miles is the furthest the wheat can be transported without a loss to the farmer. Wheat may be grown beyond the 40-mile distance but only to satisfy household subsistence needs.

   b. Adjacent to the market, $2/$4 = 50 percent of the price is location rent.

3. a. The completed table is shown below.

Loanable Funds ($)	Total Product (CDs)	MPP of Capital	MRP of Capital ($)	Supply Price (per $)
200	400	2	1	0.06
600	600	0.5	0.25	0.08
1,000	750	0.375	0.1875	0.10
1,400	850	0.25	0.125	0.125
1,800	900	0.125	0.0625	0.15
2,200	925	0.0625	0.03125	0.20
2,600	935	0.025	0.0125	0.25

   b. The equilibrium interest rate is .125 or 12.5 percent. That is the rate where the marginal revenue product is equal to the supply price of capital.

CHAPTER 18

INCOME DISTRIBUTION AND POVERTY

Chapter in a Nutshell

One conclusion to be drawn from the preceding three chapters is that people who supply highly productive labor, capital, land, and entrepreneurial talent to the market earn higher incomes. Conversely, many people at the bottom of the income distribution are less productive and earn lower incomes as a result. The extent of inequality in the income distribution can be measured with the **Lorenz curve** and the **Gini coefficient**. The Lorenz curve measures the percentage of total income received by each quintile of the population. The Gini coefficient transforms the Lorenz curve into a single number. The diagonal of the Lorenz curve represents perfect equality in the income distribution. The right angle axes of the Lorenz curve show complete inequality in the income distribution. All income distributions lie somewhere between these extremes. The Gini coefficient is the ratio of the area between the diagonal and the Lorenz curve to the total area under the diagonal. These tools for measuring income inequality help us to trace out changes in a country's income distribution. Over time, the income distribution in the United States has remained fairly stable. The distribution of income in the United States is similar to that in other industrialized countries. Industrialized countries tend to have income distributions that are more equal than those in the most less-developed countries. The **distribution of wealth** can also be studied using the Lorenz curve and the Gini coefficient. In general, wealth is distributed more unequally than is income.

It is possible to make strong arguments for both **income equality** and **income inequality**. Income equality can be justified on the randomness of personal misfortune that leads to poverty, people's preference to avoid poverty over any other possible distribution of income, and the notion that income equality generates the maximum total utility for society. Arguments for income inequality relate high incomes to high levels of effort. Also, income inequality is more conducive to rapid economic growth that will improve circumstances for the poor over time.

Poverty can be described **relatively**, as a percentage of **median income**, or in **absolute terms**, as a minimally acceptable physical standard of living. The greatest progress against poverty in the United States occurred during the 1960s. Rates of poverty have remained fairly constant since then. There are a number of ways to fight poverty, including **cash and in-kind assistance** provided by the government and a **negative income tax**. In the final analysis, however, the one sure way to beat poverty is to enable people to become more productive.

After studying this chapter, you should be able to:

- Explain the reasons for **inequality** in the **distribution of income**.
- Measure a country's income distribution using a **Lorenz curve** or a **Gini coefficient**.
- Discuss differences in income distributions among industrialized and less-developed countries.
- Describe changes in income inequality over time in the United States.
- Contrast inequality in the distribution of income with inequality in the **distribution of wealth**.
- Discuss the advantages of inequality and equality in the distribution of income and wealth.
- Compare **relative and absolute definitions of poverty**.
- Describe methods for dealing with poverty.

THE MICROECONOMICS OF FACTOR MARKETS   315

Concept Check — See how you do on these multiple-choice questions.

1. The **Lorenz curve** is a representation of
    a. a Rawlsian "society in the making"
    b. a perfectly equal distribution of income
    c. a perfectly equal distribution of wealth
    d. the percentage of total income earned by each quintile of the population
    e. the percentage of poor people in a country

For a Lorenz curve, the percentage of households is measured horizontally, and the percentage of income is measured vertically.

2. The basic difference between income and **wealth** is that
    a. wealth is distributed more equally than income
    b. the rich have much wealth but little income, while the opposite is true for the poor
    c. wealth reflects the accumulated assets of a lifetime and income is what is earned in one year
    d. income grows faster than wealth
    e. wealth grows faster than income

Income is the amount a person earns in a year. How does one acquire wealth?

3. One way to define poverty is to arbitrarily select some percentage of the population's **median income** as
    a. the poverty threshold
    b. the fund for the poor
    c. necessary for in-kind assistance
    d. the minimal acceptable physical standard of living
    e. the definition of middle class

The median income is the income in the precise middle of the income distribution. Why would someone studying poverty find this a useful statistic to have?

4. Examples of **in-kind assistance** include all of the following **except**
    a. food stamps
    b. medical care
    c. Supplemental Security Income
    d. housing benefits
    e. Pell grants

What is the difference between **cash assistance** and **in-kind assistance**?

5. Although a **negative income tax** can bring a family up to a threshold level of income, it cannot immediately
    a. solve the problem of making the poor more productive
    b. eliminate other poverty programs
    c. provide the poor with the same cash assistance that Supplemental Security Income does
    d. replace in-kind assistance
    e. reduce the Gini coefficient

What is the basic reason for poverty?

Am I on the Right Track?

Your answers to the questions above should be **d, c, a, c,** and **a**. Measuring the extent of income inequality in a country is conceptually fairly simple. However, doing it in practice presents enormous challenges for economists. For example, accounting for the impact of government programs on the income distribution is a difficult problem to solve. The truly vexing question for economists and other social scientists who work on the problem of poverty is how to reduce levels of poverty in the long run. This requires raising the productivity levels of impoverished households.

Key Terms Quiz — Match the terms on the left with the definitions in the column on the right.

1. Lorenz curve
2. cash assistance
3. Gini coefficient
4. in-kind assistance
5. wealth
6. life-cycle wealth
7. median income
8. poverty threshold
9. negative income tax

_____ a. government assistance in the form of direct goods and services
_____ b. the midpoint of a society's income distribution
_____ c. cash payments to the poor that decrease as income increases — an income tax in reverse
_____ d. a curve depicting an economy's income distribution
_____ e. the accumulated assets of individuals
_____ f. numerical measure of the degree of income inequality in an economy
_____ g. the level of income below which families are considered poor
_____ h. government assistance in the form of cash
_____ i. wealth in the form of nonmonetary assets like a house, automobiles, and personal clothing

Graphing Tutorial

The Lorenz curve is a convenient way to portray the distribution of income in an economy. As with the other graphs we have studied, it is critical to know what variable is measured on which axis when constructing a Lorenz curve. The percentage of population is measured along the horizontal axis, and the percentage of total income the population receives is measured along the vertical axis. Typically, a Lorenz curve displays the cumulative population quintile shares of total income. Consider the following table that shows the population quintile shares of income received in the Yellow Springs economy.

Population Quintile	Percentage of Total Income Received
Poorest	12
Second	16
Third	20
Fourth	24
Richest	28

If income were distributed perfectly equally in Yellow Springs, each 20 percent of the population would receive 20 percent of the total income. Clearly, there is income inequality in Yellow Springs. The poorest 20 percent of the income distribution receives only 12 percent of the total income, while the richest 20 percent receives 28 percent of the total income. In order to construct the Lorenz curve for these data, we need to add up the quintile shares to arrive at the cumulative quintile shares. The cumulative quintile share for the poorest 20 percent of the population is 12 percent. For the bottom 40 percent of the population, the cumulative quintile share is 12 percent plus 16 percent, or 28 percent of total income. The bottom 60 percent of the population receives a cumulative percentage of total income equal to 48 percent, the bottom 80 percent receives

72 percent of total income, and the percentages all add up to 100 percent. These cumulative quintile shares are plotted in the graph shown below.

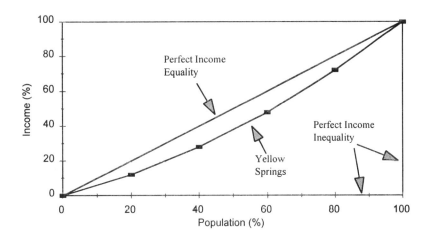

The Lorenz curve for Yellow Springs lies below the diagonal that represents perfect income equality. Along the diagonal, each 20 percent of the population receives 20 percent of the total income. Along the Yellow Springs curve, the poorest 20 percent receives only 12 percent of the total income while the richest 20 percent receives 28 percent of the total income. Perfect income inequality would be represented by the right angle axes marked by arrows. An income distribution with perfect income inequality would have one person receiving all the income in the economy.

Another measure that is used to describe an economy's income distribution is the Gini coefficient. The Gini coefficient is the ratio of the area between the diagonal and the Lorenz curve to the total area beneath the diagonal. The Yellow Springs Lorenz curve is shown below with areas produced by the Lorenz curve

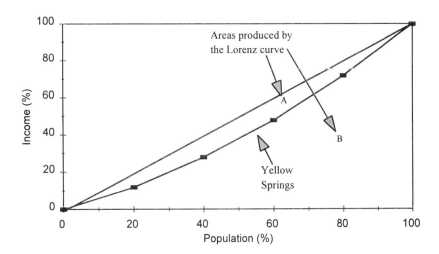

labeled A and B, respectively. The Gini coefficient, G, is calculated as G = A/(A + B).

An economy with a perfectly equal income distribution will have a Gini coefficient equal to zero since the area labeled A would be absent. What about the perfect income inequality distribution shown in the first graph? The Gini coefficient for perfect income inequality is 1 because the area labeled A would occupy the whole space under the diagonal.

The closer the Lorenz curve is to the diagonal, the more equal the income distribution and the lower the Gini coefficient. Drawn below is a Lorenz curve representing the income distribution for the Xenia economy, which displays greater inequality than the Lorenz curve for Yellow Springs.

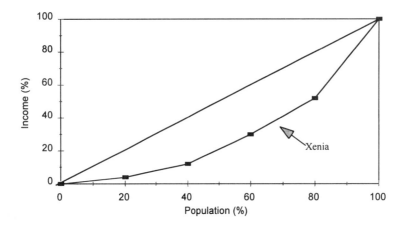

Clearly, the Lorenz curve for Xenia is farther from the diagonal than the one drawn for Yellow Springs. If we were to compute the Gini coefficient for Xenia, it would be larger than the Yellow Springs Gini because a larger area lies between the diagonal and the Lorenz curve in Xenia's case.

Graphing Pitfalls

The greatest potential pitfall you will encounter with Lorenz curves is graphing the data on the wrong axes. Suppose you make a mistake and plot the income data horizontally and the population data vertically. What sort of Lorenz curve would you get? Using data from the Xenia Lorenz curve drawn above, a Lorenz curve with income measured horizontally and population measured vertically is shown on the following page. This curve lies above the diagonal instead of below it. If you interpret this graph properly, it gives the same information as the graph shown above. However, it is more difficult to compare with other Lorenz curves that are drawn in the usual way. So, if you draw a Lorenz curve and it lies above the diagonal, you'll know you have your axes switched.

THE MICROECONOMICS OF FACTOR MARKETS   319

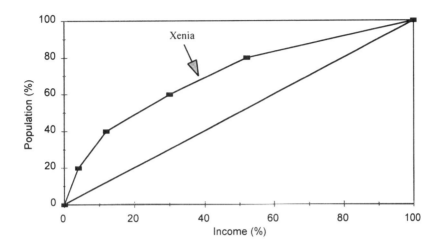

A Lorenz curve drawn with the axes switched will lie above the diagonal instead of below the diagonal. If this happens, simply redraw the curve with the axes labeled properly.

True-False Questions — If a statement is false, explain why.

1. Plato thought that, in order to minimize political discontent, the income of the richest citizen should be no greater than five times the income of the poorest. (T/F)

2. There is little connection between a person's productivity and his/her income level. (T/F)

3. People's occupations typically signal where they rank in the income scale. (T/F)

4. The Lorenz curve that consists of the right angle axes represents perfect income equality. (T/F)

5. The distribution of income is more equal in the United States than in Sweden and is reflected by a Lorenz curve that is closer from the diagonal than is Sweden's. (T/F)

6. The Gini coefficient is the ratio of the area between the diagonal and the Lorenz curve and the total area beneath the diagonal. (T/F)

7. A decrease in the Gini coefficient indicates a move toward greater income equality. (T/F)

8. The United States' income distribution fluctuates dramatically from year to year. (T/F)

9. Less-developed countries typically have income distributions that are more equal than do developed countries. (T/F)

10. Life-cycle wealth is common to nearly all income groups, while other wealth forms are more concentrated among the highest income groups. (T/F)

11. Wealth in the United States at the time of the American Revolution was distributed quite equally. (T/F)

12. People who believe that personal misfortune largely explains why people are poor are more likely to favor a more equal income distribution. (T/F)

13. Rawls's theory of justice suggests that people would prefer a more equal income distribution to the possibility of being at the bottom of an unequal income distribution. (T/F)

14. Assuming that everyone had the same utility functions for money, income equality would generate the highest level of total utility in society. (T/F)

15. The poverty threshold can be defined in relative terms as a certain percentage of the population's median income. (T/F)

Multiple-Choice Questions

1. Plato and Aristotle expressed the view that income inequality should be
   a. eliminated entirely
   b. encouraged because it is the source of prosperity
   c. limited to an acceptable degree
   d. what the labor market generates
   e. promoted because class differences are natural and should be reflected in income inequality

2. Wage earners
   a. are among the very poor in society
   b. usually have multiple sources of income
   c. move into upper-income brackets as their wage rates increase over time
   d. have little hope of ever seeing improvement in their lot
   e. are usually poorer than those with other primary income sources

3. A Lorenz curve that lies close to the diagonal suggests
   a. great inequality in the income distribution
   b. very limited redistribution of income and wealth in a society
   c. a relatively equal distribution of income
   d. that the wealth distribution is less equal than income distribution
   e. that the wealth distribution is more equal than income distribution

4. The Gini coefficient is
   a. the area between the diagonal and the Lorenz curve divided by the area under the diagonal
   b. the area under the diagonal divided by the area between the Lorenz curve and the diagonal
   c. a measure of people's wealth
   d. the difference between the highest 20 percent of income earners and the lowest 20 percent
   e. the ratio between the highest 20 percent of income earners and the lowest 20 percent

5. When the Gini coefficient increases,
   a. income inequality increases
   b. income equality increases
   c. the slope of the Lorenz curve decreases
   d. the slope of the Lorenz curve increases
   e. everyone is made better off

6. The income distribution in the United States has become _____ in the last 15 years.
   a. become more unequal
   b. become less unequal
   c. been higher than the poverty threshold
   d. remained constant from year-to-year
   e. become too difficult to measure

7. Comparing income distributions between countries is _____ because each includes different systems of taxes and cash payments by governments to individuals.
   a. complicated
   b. irrelevant
   c. impossible
   d. straightforward
   e. unfair

8. All of the following are reasons for the greater inequality in the income distribution in less-developed countries **except**
   a. low marginal revenue products of labor
   b. the agricultural character of production
   c. a definition of the poverty threshold that include 50 percent of the households
   d. a limited range of employment opportunities
   e. low levels of educational attainment among most of the population

9. People's net wealth reflects their accumulation of
   a. cars, houses, and other life-cycle wealth
   b. stocks and bonds
   c. knowledge
   d. cash assistance from the government
   e. assets over their lifetime and, perhaps, other lifetimes

10. According to John Rawls, if their own income status in society was uncertain, most people would choose _____.
    a. more income equality, being frightened by the possibility of being among the poor
    b. less income equality, being attracted by the possibility of "making it big"
    c. to let the market dictate who gets what because they view the market as unbiased
    d. to eliminate inheritance taxes because they create unnatural inequality
    e. to have government subsidize basic needs because they think that would be fair

11. Many socialists, especially Marxists, believe that income inequality arises principally from
    a. the unequal distribution of human skills
    b. unequal access to education
    c. differences in effort among individuals
    d. discrimination
    e. the unequal distribution of property

12. Lerner's argument that income equality tends to maximize utility in a society is based on the assumption that
    a. there are no interpersonal comparisons of utility
    b. everyone's utility function is unique
    c. everyone's utility function is the same
    d. there is increasing marginal utility of income
    e. there is decreasing marginal utility of income

13. An argument in favor of income inequality would be that
    a. personal misfortune leads to income inequality
    b. income inequality leads to greater total utility in society
    c. it provides incentives to work and invest, leading to faster economic growth
    d. income equality is impossible to achieve
    e. the poor will always be with us, no matter what is done

14. If government programs to assist the poor are successful at equalizing the income distribution, then the Lorenz curve should shift _____ and the Gini coefficient should _____.
    a. toward the diagonal; decrease
    b. away from the diagonal; increase
    c. toward the diagonal; increase
    d. away from the diagonal; decrease
    e. to a straight line; increase

15. In the period since 1960, the most progress in reducing the percentage of the population living in poverty has occurred between
    a. 1960 and 1970
    b. 1970 and 1980
    c. 1980 and 1990
    d. 1960 and 1980
    e. 1970 and 1990

16. Food stamps are a good example of a type of program that provides
    a. cash assistance
    b. in-kind assistance
    c. the possibility of improved skills and a better job
    d. enough aid to go above the poverty threshold
    e. food subsidies to everyone below the median income

17. One clear advantage to the negative income tax is that it gives the poor
    a. a guaranteed income that is higher than under current poverty programs
    b. incentive to work since the more income they earn, the more they can keep
    c. a variety of in-kind benefits
    d. the opportunity to pay in taxes for some of the benefits they receive
    e. a clear way out of poverty

THE MICROECONOMICS OF FACTOR MARKETS

18. One drawback of the negative income tax is that it
    a. does not bring the incomes of the poor up to the threshold poverty level
    b. does not address the problem of low productivity among the poor
    c. is ethically inappropriate to tax the incomes of the very poor
    d. creates a negative stigma for those who receive it
    e. is contrary to Rawls's theory of justice

19. Using Gini coefficients as the measure of income distribution, it appears that the income distribution in the United States is quite
    a. similar to that of Sweden
    b. different from that of the United Kingdom
    c. similar to that of Canada
    d. different from that of France
    e. similar to that of Japan

20. A winner-take-all market is one in which
    a. top performers are paid far more than others who are slightly less talented
    b. income equality is the goal
    c. a dominant firm, or godfather, sets price for other firms
    d. wages rates are carefully regulated instead of being set by market forces
    e. wage-related rents would rarely be apparent

Fill in the Blanks

1. People's incomes are derived from _____, _____, _____, and _____, or combinations of them.

2. The Gini coefficient is computed by dividing the area between the _____ and _____ by the total area under the _____.

3. Income inequality tends to be higher in _____ economies than in _____ economies.

4. Poverty can be described in _____, such as a percentage of median incomes, or in _____, such as a minimally acceptable physical standard of living.

5. A _____ transfers income to people whose pre-tax income is below a specific level, without creating _____ that are sometimes associated with government assistance.

Discussion Questions

1. Critique the following statement: "A sure way to eliminate poverty is simply to tax all incomes above $100,000 at a 100 percent rate and transfer the revenue to the poor."

2. Why is it important to determine whether a country's Lorenz curve is drawn before or after taxes are taken out of incomes and government-paid supplements are added back into incomes?

3. Why are income distributions so much more unequal in the less-developed world than in the industrialized world?

4. John Rawls describes a system whereby people who have no foreknowledge about their place in an income distribution will prefer a distribution of income that is more equal. Why do you think this is true? Consider Exhibit 6 in the text, which compares quintile shares of income between countries. Without foreknowledge of your place in the income distribution, in which of these countries would you choose to live? Is your choice consistent with Rawls' prediction?

5. How is poverty defined? How many people live in poverty now, and how has that figure changed since 1960? Why has progress in lowering the poverty rate been so slow since 1970?

THE MICROECONOMICS OF FACTOR MARKETS

6. Discuss the advantages and drawbacks of a negative income tax as a means to cope with poverty compared to in-kind assistance and cash assistance.

Problems

1. Complete the following table for a negative income tax, assuming that the tax rate is 20 percent and the minimum income level is $8,000.

Independent Income	Net Negative [-] or Positive [+] Tax	After-Tax Income
$ 0		
5,000		
10,000		
20,000		
25,000		
30,000		
35,000		
40,000		
45,000		

2. Suppose an economy consists of five people whose combined income is $200,000. Their individual incomes are as follows: Bob Rueppel, $85,000; Carol Young, $70,000; Fred Tiffany, $15,000; Larry Gwinn, $15,000, and Linda Lewis, $15,000. Draw a Lorenz curve that represents their economy's income distribution using the axes provided below.

3. Suppose the poverty threshold is defined as 50 percent of the economy's median income. Does anyone fall below the poverty threshold in Problem 2 above? Explain.

Everyday Applications

The trend of public policy toward the poor in recent years has been toward less automatic income redistribution and more emphasis on supporting efforts by the poor to gain skills through education and retraining that might help them to compete successfully in the job market. How do you feel about such a shift in policy? What if the policy results in greater income inequality over time even when taxes and income redistribution are considered? Would it still be an acceptable change in public policy to you? What would be the costs and benefits associated with greater income inequality compared to those associated with greater income equality?

Economics Online

For a lesson on how African Americans as a group have increased their productivity and experienced economic improvement, visit the Web site of the National Council on Economic Education (*http://www.economicsamerica.org*). Once you are there, choose *economics minute*, then *lesson archives*, then *Dr. Martin Luther King Jr.*

Answers to Questions

Key Terms Quiz

a. 4
b. 7
c. 9
d. 1
e. 5
f. 3
g. 8
h. 2
i. 6

True-False Questions

1. True
2. False. People who are highly productive typically earn higher wages.
3. True
4. False. The diagonal represents perfect equality in the income distribution.
5. False. Income is distributed more equally in Sweden than in the United States. The Lorenz curve for the United States is located further from the diagonal than is Sweden's.
6. True
7. True
8. False. The quintile shares in income have stayed fairly constant over time.
9. False. Less-developed countries have greater income inequality due to the predominance of agriculture and limited employment opportunities.

THE MICROECONOMICS OF FACTOR MARKETS

10. True
11. False. The data show significant inequality in the wealth distribution two centuries ago, similar to the distribution of wealth today.
12. True
13. True
14. True
15. True

Multiple-Choice Questions

1. c	6. a	11. e	16. b
2. e	7. a	12. c	17. b
3. c	8. c	13. c	18. b
4. a	9. e	14. a	19. c
5. a	10. a	15. a	20. a

Fill in the Blanks

1. wages; interest; rent; profit
2. diagonal; Lorenz curve; diagonal
3. less-developed; advanced industrial
4. relative terms; absolute terms
5. negative income tax; disincentives to work

Discussion Questions

1. This system is unlikely to work for the long run because it will create disincentives for people to earn incomes above $100,000. Why earn the additional income if it will all be taxed away? Moreover, the richest people in the income distribution do most of the saving. If there are fewer wealthy individuals, savings in the economy will be lower and so will investment in new capital equipment. The economy will grow more slowly as a result and may cause the poor to be in worse condition than if the income distribution had been somewhat unequal but with higher levels of investment and growth. This argument supports the existence of inequality in the income distribution.

2. Typically, if the Lorenz curve is drawn after taxes are taken out and government-paid supplements are added back into incomes, then it will likely shift closer to the diagonal. It will reflect greater income equality when compared to the Lorenz curve that is drawn to reflect only the distribution of payments to factors of production. Taxes and government-paid income supplements tend to equalize the income distribution somewhat.

3. People in less-developed countries have fewer job opportunities available to them, and those that are available are typically low-productivity, low-wage jobs. More limited access to education and training and to financial capital make it more difficult for people in less-developed countries to raise their marginal revenue products. Also, many less-developed countries are dependent on exports of agricultural goods and raw materials whose prices are quite volatile in world markets. Therefore, incomes in less-developed countries can fluctuate drastically at times.

4. It may be that people are simply averse to risk. The dread of being impoverished causes us to prefer a social structure that limits extremes in the distribution of income. Would you prefer the Netherlands as a place to live if you had no idea where you would stand in the income distribution scale? The Netherlands has the

most equal income distribution as measured by the Gini coefficient. Rawls would have predicted you would choose the Netherlands.

5. Poverty can be defined as the failure to achieve a threshold level of income, expressed perhaps as a percentage of the median income, or it can be defined as the failure to meet basic needs for people. The percentage of the population living in poverty in the United States fell from 22.6 percent of the population in 1960 to 12.6 percent of the population in 1970. The percentage of people living in poverty in 1995 was 13.8. Ultimately, the cause of poverty is low productivity. The persistence of the poverty rate since 1970 may be attributable to difficulty in raising productivity levels among the poorest members of society. Clearly, the antipoverty programs introduced in the 1960s have not been completely successful at eliminating poverty.

6. The advantage to a negative income tax is that people who are poor have an incentive to work under the scheme since the more money they earn, the more money they keep. Rather than being disqualified for benefits at a fixed level of income, the negative tax received by the poor is gradually phased out as independent income increases. The negative income tax should be simpler to administer than the many programs for the poor that currently exist. Whether it would be more effective than current programs is the topic of an intense and long-running debate about how best to cope with poverty.

Problems

1. To calculate the after-tax income, take the independent income and multiply by .2 to get the tax bill. Subtract the 20 percent tax from the income level, then add the $8,000 minimum income level to get the after-tax income. The net negative or positive tax is equal to -$8,000 (the negative income tax) plus the tax bill. The completed table is presented here.

Independent Income	Net Negative [-] or Positive [+] Tax	After-Tax Income
$ 0	-$8,000	$ 8,000
5,000	-7,000	12,000
10,000	-6,000	16,000
20,000	-4,000	24,000
25,000	-3,000	28,000
30,000	-2,000	32,000
35,000	-1,000	36,000
40,000	0	40,000
45,000	+1,000	44,000

2. The Lorenz curve is shown in the graph on the following page. The Lorenz curve is based on the data in the table below.

Cumulative Percentages

Percentage of Population	Percentage of Income
0	0
20	7.5
40	15.0
60	22.5
80	57.5
100	100.0

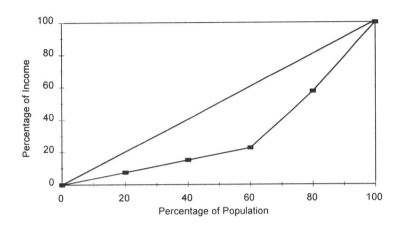

3. No one falls below the poverty line. In this example, the median income is $15,000. Fred, Larry, and Linda all make $15,000, so no one falls below $7,500, which is 50 percent of the median income.

PART 4 — THE MICROECONOMICS OF FACTOR MARKETS

COMPREHENSIVE SAMPLE TEST

Give yourself 50 minutes to complete this exam and see how you do. The answers follow. Don't look until you are finished!

True-False Questions — If a statement is false, explain why. Each question is worth two points.

1. In a competitive labor market, a firm can decide the wage it wants to pay workers. (T/F)

2. If labor and capital are free to move, then workers will migrate from low-wage regions to high-wage regions, while capital migrates from high-wage regions to low-wage regions, causing wage rates to equalize. (T/F)

3. If the demand for unskilled labor is very inelastic, a minimum wage law will cause more unemployment than if the demand for unskilled labor were elastic. (T/F)

4. In monopsony, the supply of labor for a firm is the same as the marginal labor cost curve. (T/F)

5. The return to monopsony power can be transferred from the monopsonist to a union if the union fixes the supply of labor at the marginal revenue product of the last worker hired. (T/F)

6. The American Federation of Labor advocated strictly economic goals such as higher wages, shorter hours, and better working conditions. (T/F)

7. The marginal revenue product of capital curve is downward sloping because of the law of diminishing returns. (T/F)

8. Differential land rent arises from differences in the cost of transporting goods from the location of the producing acres to markets. (T/F)

9. Poverty can be defined in relative terms as a minimal acceptable physical standard of living or in absolute terms as a percentage of the population's median income. (T/F)

10. Life-cycle wealth is wealth in the form of nonmonetary assets, such as a house, automobiles, and personal clothing. (T/F)

THE MICROECONOMICS OF FACTOR MARKETS

Multiple-Choice Questions — Each question is worth two points.

1. A firm in a competitive labor market will continue to hire labor as long as the marginal revenue product is
   a. greater than or equal to the marginal physical product
   b. decreasing
   c. less than the marginal labor cost
   d. greater than or equal to the marginal labor cost
   e. positive

2. In a competitive labor market, a firm can hire as many workers as it wants to at the market wage rate
   a. without affecting profits
   b. without affecting the wage rate
   c. in order to increase the wage rate for other firms
   d. in order to prevent unionization
   e. to increase the return to monopsony power

3. Labor supply curves can be backward bending at very high wages because
   a. the supply of labor decreases
   b. firms no longer demand as much labor at high wages
   c. at some point, wages get so high that workers want to enjoy more leisure
   d. jobs with such high wages are scarce
   e. workers skilled enough to earn high wages have alternative employment opportunities

4. If the labor demand and supply curves are very elastic, then the likely impact of a minimum wage set above the equilibrium wage is to
   a. increase wages and employment
   b. increase wages and reduce employment slightly
   c. decrease wages as firms substitute capital for labor in production
   d. create new opportunities for unskilled workers to enter the labor force
   e. increase wages and reduce employment significantly

5. The ethic underlying the "wages equal to the marginal revenue product of labor" rule is that
   a. most workers will be paid less than their marginal revenue products of labor
   b. low wages can always be compensated for with minimum wage legislation
   c. each worker receives the full measure of his/her marginal revenue product
   d. any resulting inequality in the income distribution creates incentives to work and invest
   e. from each according to their ability, to each according to their need

6. All of the following are determinants of a person's perceived MRP in the labor market **except**
   a. productivity
   b. education
   c. minority status
   d. stock ownership
   e. gender

7. As seen by a monopsonist, the supply curve of labor is
   a. upward sloping
   b. the market supply curve of labor
   c. below the marginal labor cost
   d. shifted to the right by increases in population
   e. all of the above

8. The difference between the marginal revenue product and the wage rate of the last worker hired, multiplied by the number of workers hired is called
   a. the return to monopsony power
   b. the return to monopoly power
   c. the return to union power
   d. wage-related rent
   e. monopsony profit

9. Suppose that a monopsony faced by a labor union introduces a new technology that increases the marginal physical product of labor. The union must decide whether it should
   a. demand higher wages or allow an increase in employment
   b. accept wage cuts to keep its members jobs or accept increases in unemployment
   c. use the new technology and lose members or risk layoffs by refusing to use the new technology
   d. pursue collective bargaining for better working conditions or for shorter hours
   e. raise union dues to limit membership or grow so that nonunion labor is unavailable to the monopsony

10. The Knights of Labor were a union in the United States in the late nineteenth century that
    a. failed to attract many members
    b. pushed for an end to private property
    c. pushed for structural changes in the economy as well as higher wages
    d. represented only skilled workers
    e. represented only unskilled workers in eastern industrial cities

11. The legislative act that forced businesses to accept unions as legitimate institutions in collective bargaining was the
    a. Civil Rights Act of 1964
    b. Landrum-Griffin Act of 1959
    c. Taft-Hartley Act of 1947
    d. Wagner Act of 1935
    e. Norris-LaGuardia Act of 1932

12. Money that a firm uses to purchase the physical plant, equipment, and raw materials used in production is called
    a. corporate profits
    b. variable costs
    c. fixed costs
    d. interest-based income
    e. loanable funds

13. The interest rate is determined in the loanable funds market by the intersection of the
    a. demand for loanable funds and supply of loanable funds
    b. marginal revenue product of labor and marginal revenue product of capital
    c. marginal revenue product of labor and marginal revenue product of land
    d. marginal revenue product of capital and marginal revenue product of land
    e. present value of an asset and the annual income it generates

THE MICROECONOMICS OF FACTOR MARKETS

14. If interest rates increase, then the present value of a property will always _____ when the annual income the property generates is _____.
   a. increase; constant
   b. increase; higher
   c. decrease; constant
   d. decrease; higher
   e. remain constant; constant

15. If the demand for a fixed quantity of land is such that it fails to intersect the supply curve at all, then land rent is
   a. extremely high
   b. impossible to measure
   c. the highest price demanders are willing to pay for an acre
   d. the difference between the prices paid by the first and second buyers of land
   e. zero

16. In the nineteenth century, frontier communities in the United Stated competed fiercely with one another to have rail lines run through them. These towns were competing with one another for control over
   a. land rents
   b. location rents
   c. differential rents
   d. wage-related rents
   e. transportation systems

17. Christal Morehouse has decided to quit her job as a waitress in a coffee shop and open her own expresso bar. She earned $20,000 as a waitress. Her stream of income from the expresso bar is $120,000. Christal's return to entrepreneurship is
   a. $120,000
   b. $20,000
   c. no more than $100,000
   d. $120,000 times the interest rate
   e. $120,000 divided by the interest rate

18. Given two Lorenz curves, the one that lies furthest from the diagonal represents an income distribution that is
   a. more unequal
   b. for a richer country
   c. for a poorer country
   d. more equal
   e. representative of the top 20 percent of the population

19. The argument advanced by A. P. Lerner for greater equality in the income distribution is based on the idea that
   a. equality in the income distribution maximizes the combined utility of money
   b. property is theft
   c. people prefer equality over the chance of extreme poverty
   d. inequality in the income distribution leads to less investment
   e. inequality in the income distribution leads to less incentive to work

20. The great advantage of the negative income tax is that it provides the poor with additional income while it preserves an incentive to work. However, the great disadvantage of the negative income tax is that it
   a. is extremely costly to administer
   b. requires the elimination of other programs that aid the poor
   c. does not ensure that the poor will produce more income
   d. sets an arbitrary minimum level of income
   e. cannot be based on a minimal acceptable physical standard of living

Discussion Questions/Problems — Each question is worth 10 points.

1. Consider the following perfectly competitive labor market for employees at fast food restaurants.

Workers	Marginal Revenue Product ($/worker per day)	Total Labor Cost ($)	Marginal Labor Cost
1	100	50	
2	80	100	
3	70	150	
4	60	200	
5	50	250	
6	40	300	
7	30	350	

a. Compute the marginal labor cost and fill in the values in the fourth column of the table.

b. How many workers will be hired? At what wage rate? Explain.

2. Havistar manufactures diesel trucks in Swingfield, Ohio. Havistar is the only employer of assembly line workers in Swingfield. The following table shows Havistar's MRP, wage rate, and total labor cost at different levels of employment.

Workers	MRP ($/worker per day)	Wage Rate ($/day)	Total Labor Cost ($/day)	MLC ($/worker per day)
10	200	30	300	
20	140	35	700	
30	100	40	1,200	
40	80	45	1,800	
50	70	50	2,500	
60	60	55	3,300	
70	54	60	4,200	

a. Calculate the number of workers Havistar will hire. What wage rate will the workers receive? Explain how you arrived at your answer.

b. Calculate the return to monopsony power for Havistar. Show your work.

c. Suppose that a union is organized at Havistar. What is the highest wage rate that the union can negotiate that is consistent with Havistar's current level of employment?

3. Present arguments for and against people receiving interest-derived income.

4. "There is no poverty problem that money can't solve." Discuss.

Answers to the Sample Test on Part 4

True-False Questions

1. False. The firm takes the wage set in the labor market as given because the firm is one of many and has no influence over the price of labor.
2. True
3. False. If the demand for labor is very elastic, a minimum wage causes more unemployment.
4. False. The marginal labor cost is above the supply curve of labor because in order to hire more workers, the monopsonist must pay a higher wage to the additional workers hired, as well as to the workers hired already at a lower wage rate.
5. True
6. True
7. True
8. False. Differential land rent arises due to differences in the cost of providing land.
9. False. Poverty can be defined in relative terms as some percentage of median income or in absolute terms as a minimal acceptable standard of living.
10. True

Multiple-Choice Questions

1. d	6. d	11. d	16. b
2. b	7. e	12. e	17. c
3. c	8. a	13. a	18. a
4. e	9. a	14. c	19. a
5. c	10. c	15. e	20. c

Discussion Questions/Problems

1. a. The marginal labor cost is constant at $50.

   b. The MRP = MLC at $50. Five workers will be hired at the $50 wage rate. For levels of employment below five workers, MRP > MLC so profits continue to rise as more workers are hired. For levels of employment above five workers, MRP < MLC, so profits would decrease if these workers were hired.

2. a. In order to calculate the number of workers that Havistar will hire, the MLC column in the table must be completed. The MLC is computed by dividing the change in TLC by the change in the number of workers. Be sure to note that the change in the number of workers is 10 between each employment level. The completed table is shown below.

THE MICROECONOMICS OF FACTOR MARKETS

Workers	MRP ($/worker per day)	Wage Rate ($/day)	Total Labor Cost ($/day)	MLC ($/worker per day)
10	200	30	300	30
20	140	35	700	40
30	100	40	1,200	50
40	80	45	1,800	60
50	70	50	2,500	70
60	60	55	3,300	80
70	54	60	4,200	90

Havistar will continue to hire workers until the MRP = MLC. This occurs at 50 workers. Havistar pays these workers a wage, read from the supply curve of labor, equal to $50.

b. The return to monopsony power is the difference between the MRP of the last worker hired — $70 in this case, and the wage paid to this worker — $50— multiplied by the number of workers hired 50. Therefore the return to monopsony power is $20 x 50 = $1,000.

c. The union should set the supply curve of labor at $70 — a horizontal line. The last worker hired will be paid $70 under these circumstances, so the return to monopsony power is completely acquired by the union.

3. Interest is earned on accumulated savings that are supplied to the loanable funds market. Savings may represent abstinence from consumption, or they may have been transferred from one generation to another as inherited wealth. People who live off interest-derived income have a property right to the loanable funds they possess that generate the interest. Viewed in this light, people who live off interest-derived income are no different from people who earn income from their intellectual and physical abilities. In each case, the income is derived from ownership of a property right.

However, some economists (primarily Marxists) reject the view that people have a right to income that, in their view, is unearned. They argue that the origins of property are in theft; hence there is no legitimate claim to private property, much less inherited private property.

4. This is a statement that might be made by someone who subscribes to the view that all poverty is relative. By giving people in poverty sufficient money, they can be brought above a poverty threshold that is stated as an arbitrarily selected percentage of the population's median income. A negative income tax might be able to accomplish this goal. Moreover, a proponent of this view would argue that the negative income tax preserves incentives to work by allowing poor households to earn income and still receive a portion of the cash payment associated with the negative income tax.

Still, just giving people in poverty more money may not guarantee that they begin to produce more income. The low productivity of people who live in poverty is the root of the problem. There may exist a "culture of poverty" that sets the poor apart from others. They may be unable to seize opportunities to increase their productivity. To change a "culture of poverty," large investments in the economic and social environments of the poor are required. This is a much more complex task than simply writing poor people checks.

CHAPTER 19

AGGREGATE DEMAND AND AGGREGATE SUPPLY

Chapter in a Nutshell

You learned in Chapter 1 that economics is divided into two main branches — microeconomics and macroeconomics. We begin our detailed analysis of macroeconomics with this chapter. Macroeconomics focuses on the economy as a whole, rather than on individual economic behavior. Macroeconomists typically address such questions as why there are periods of **recession** and **inflation**, what causes **prosperity**, and what causes economic growth. Some of the concepts used by macroeconomists to measure changes in the economy will be introduced. For example, the **gross domestic product (GDP)** measures the dollar value of all final goods and services produced in the economy in a year. The **consumer price index (CPI)** is a measure comparing the prices of goods and services that a household typically purchases to the prices of those goods and services purchased in a base year. The **GDP deflator** is a measure comparing the prices of all goods and services produced in the economy during a given year to the prices of those goods and services purchased in a base year. The concepts of **aggregate demand** and **aggregate supply** are used to show how the level of **real GDP** (GDP excluding price changes) and the **price level** are determined in the economy. These are a few of the new concepts presented in this chapter that will enable you to explore macroeconomic topics.

After you study this chapter, you should be able to:

- Describe the phases of the **business cycle**.
- Explain how **gross domestic product** is used to measure output in a country.
- Transform **nominal GDP** to **real GDP** using the **GDP deflator**.
- Graph **aggregate demand** and **aggregate supply**.
- Account for the shapes of the **aggregate demand** and **aggregate supply** curves.
- Explain how the economy moves toward **macroequilibrium**.
- Show how an economy can be in equilibrium with either **unemployment**, or **inflation**, or both.
- Distinguish among **demand-pull inflation, cost-push inflation,** and **stagflation**.

Concept Check — See how you do on these multiple choice questions.

1. The **business cycle** alternates between periods of _____, marked by **inflation**, and periods of _____, marked by relatively high unemployment.
    a. depression; recession
    b. recovery; recession
    c. prosperity; recession
    d. recession; depression
    e. unemployment; inflation

Which phase of the business cycle is characterized by inflation, which by high unemployment?

EMPLOYMENT, INFLATION, AND FISCAL POLICY

2. The difference between **nominal GDP** and **real GDP** is that real GDP
   a. is larger than nominal GDP
   b. measures the level of output including price changes, while nominal GDP holds prices constant
   c. measures the level of output and nominal GDP measures the price level
   d. measures the price level and nominal GDP measures the level of output
   e. measures the level of output in constant prices, while nominal GDP includes price changes

Which of these includes price changes and which doesn't?

3. If the **macroequilibrium** is at less than full employment, then
   a. the aggregate supply curve is relatively flat
   b. the aggregate supply curve is vertical
   c. the aggregate supply curve has a steep positive slope
   d. demand-pull inflation will be a problem
   e. cost-push inflation will be a problem

How does the shape of the aggregate supply curve change as GDP increases?

4. The **GDP deflator** is used to calculate real GDP by
   a. multiplying the GDP deflator by nominal GDP
   b. dividing nominal GDP by the GDP deflator and multiplying by 100
   c. dividing nominal GDP by the GDP deflator and dividing by 100
   d. dividing nominal GDP by the GDP deflator
   e. dividing the GDP deflator by nominal GDP

Learn this forumula.

5. **Demand-pull inflation** is caused by _____, and **cost-push inflation** is caused by _____.
   a. an increase in aggregate demand; a decrease in aggregate supply
   b. a decrease in aggregate supply; an increase in aggregate demand
   c. a decrease in aggregate demand; an increase in aggregate supply
   d. leveraged buyouts; government spending
   e. oil embargoes; leveraged buyouts

Inflation can have different causes.

Am I on the Right Track?

Your answers to the questions above should be **c, e, a, b,** and **a**. This chapter describes how the economy moves toward a macroequilibrium. Macroequilibrium occurs when the price level is such that the aggregate quantity demanded and aggregate quantity supplied are equal. This may occur when the economy's resources are fully employed or when there are unemployed resources in the economy. Critical to your understanding of macroequilibrium is the aggregate demand and aggregate supply model. The graphing tutorial below describes the shapes of the aggregate demand and aggregate supply curves and the determination of macroequilibrium. Before doing that, there are many new key terms to learn.

340 CHAPTER 19 AGGREGATE DEMAND AND AGGREGATE SUPPLY

Key Terms Quiz — Match the terms on the left with the definitions in the column on the right.

1. recession
2. real GDP
3. depression
4. consumer price index
5. prosperity
6. base year
7. inflation
8. price level
9. business cycle
10. GDP deflator
11. trough
12. aggregate supply
13. recovery
14. aggregate demand
15. peak
16. macroequilibrium
17. downturn
18. demand-pull inflation
19. gross domestic product
20. stagflation
21. cost-push inflation
22. nominal GDP
23. leveraged buyout

__3__ a. a severe recession
__6__ b. the reference year with which prices in other years are compared in a price index
__13__ c. a phase in the business cycle, following a recession, in which real GDP increases and unemployment declines
__1__ d. a phase in the business cycle in which the decline in real GDP lasts for at least six months with high unemployment
__14__ e. the total quantity of goods and services demanded by households, firms, foreigners, and government at varying price levels
__11__ f. the bottom of a business cycle
__9__ g. alternating periods of growth and decline in an economy's GDP
__20__ h. a period of stagnating real GDP, high inflation, and relatively high levels of unemployment
__17__ i. a phase in the business cycle in which real GDP declines, inflation moderates, and unemployment emerges
__12__ j. the total quantity of goods and services that firms in the economy are willing to supply at varying price levels
__5__ k. a phase in the business cycle marked by a relatively high level of real GDP, full employment, and inflation
__22__ l. GDP measured in terms of current market prices, unadjusted for inflation
__2__ m. GDP adjusted for changes in the price level
__18__ n. inflation caused primarily by an increase in aggregate demand
__19__ o. total value of all final goods and services, measured in current market prices, produced in the economy during a year
__10__ p. a measure comparing the prices of all goods and services produced in the economy during a given year to the prices of those goods and services purchased in a base year
__7__ q. an increase in the price level
__23__ r. a primarily debt-financed purchase of all the stock or assets of a company
__21__ s. inflation caused primarily by a decrease in aggregate supply
__15__ t. the top of the business cycle
__4__ u. a measure that compares the prices of consumer goods that a household purchases to the prices of those goods and services purchased in a base year
__16__ v. the level of real GDP and the price level that equate the aggregate quantity demanded and the aggregate quantity supplied
__8__ w. a measure of prices in one year expressed in relation to prices in a base year

Graphing Tutorial

This chapter introduces you to the aggregate demand and aggregate supply curves that we use to derive the macroequilibrium for an economy. Aggregate demand and aggregate supply curves must not be confused with demand and supply curves that we use to represent markets in microeconomics. Aggregate demand and aggregate supply measure the quantities of all goods and services demanded and supplied in the economy at varying price levels. Demand and supply measure the quantities of particular goods and services demanded and supplied in particular markets at different prices. The axes measure different variables for aggregate

EMPLOYMENT, INFLATION, AND FISCAL POLICY 341

demand and aggregate supply than we found for demand and supply graphs. For example, the horizontal axis in an aggregate demand and aggregate supply graph measures real GDP in dollars (trillions of dollars for the U.S. economy). The vertical axis in an aggregate demand and aggregate supply graph measures the price level. Recall that the axes for demand and supply graphs in microeconomics have quantity measured in physical units per unit of time on the horizontal axis and price measured in dollars per unit on the vertical axis. Presented below is a representative aggregate demand and aggregate supply graph.

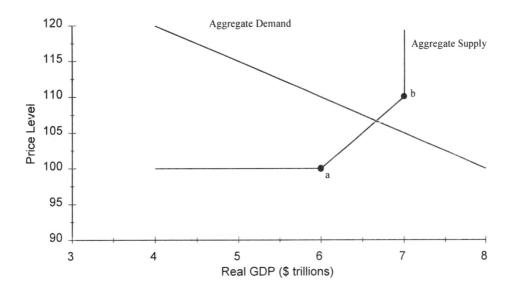

Note that the aggregate supply curve is drawn with three distinct segments. The horizontal segment shows that aggregate supply can increase up to point a without affecting the price level. In this range of GDP, there are readily available supplies of unemployed resources that can be used to increase aggregate supply with no increase in the price level. From point a to point b, the quantity of goods and services increases, but only with increases in the price level. Between points a and b, unused resources become less available, and firms may be willing to offer higher prices to employ them. The higher prices paid for these resources raises the prices of goods produced with them. Another way of explaining the upward-sloping segment is to suppose that the price level increases from 100 to 110. As the price level increases, so does the spread between prices and costs. Producers earn higher profits as a result. Higher profits stimulate greater production from existing firms and attract new firms into production. The vertical segment of the aggregate supply curve, above point b, shows the full-employment level of real GDP. Since all resources are fully employed, aggregate supply and real GDP cannot increase beyond the $7 trillion limit.

Aggregate demand represents the purchases of goods and services by households, firms, government, and foreigners. As the price level decreases, the total quantities demanded by these groups increase. Thus, the aggregate demand curve is downward sloping — as the price level decreases, the total quantities demanded of goods and services increases. This downward slope can be explained by three effects. First, the real wealth effect states that as the price level decreases, people's wealth (assets held such as cash, savings accounts, stocks, and government bonds) increases, so they can purchase more goods and services. Second, the interest rate effect states that a decrease in the price level means that people need to borrow less to make desired purchases. The decreased demand for borrowed money causes the interest rate (the cost of borrowed money) to fall. However, a decrease in the interest rate will make borrowing to purchase goods and services more attractive to households and firms. Thus, people will demand more goods and services as interest rates decrease due to a decrease in the price level. Finally, the international trade effect of a price level decrease will cause the total quantities demanded of goods and services to increase. If the price level in the United States decreases while price levels in the rest of the world stay the same, then U.S. goods are relatively less expensive to domestic consumers and foreigners. As a result, people will demand more goods and services as the U.S. price level declines.

Shifts in the aggregate demand and aggregate supply curves are fairly easy to explain. The aggregate demand curve shifts to the right (increases) as a result of increases in government spending or decreases in taxes; increases in spending by consumers, businesses and foreigners; and rising expectations about the future. As a result of decreases in government spending or increases in taxes, decreases in spending by consumers, businesses, and foreigners, and falling expectations about the future, the aggregate demand curve shifts to the left (decreases). Aggregate supply increases when it shifts to the right. Aggregate supply is shifted to the right by the increased availability of resources — more workers, more capital, more land, and more entrepreneurial energies. A decrease in resource prices also shifts the aggregate supply to the right. On the other hand, if resources become less available, or if their prices increase, the aggregate supply curve shifts to the left — a decrease in aggregate supply.

Macroequilibrium occurs at the price level and real GDP combination that equates aggregate demand and aggregate supply. In our diagram, this happens at the intersection of aggregate demand and aggregate supply — a price level of about 106 and a real GDP level of approximately $6.7 trillion. At price levels above 106, aggregate quantity demanded is less than the aggregate quantity supplied, so the price level begins to fall due to competition among suppliers. Conversely, for price levels below 106, aggregate quantity demanded is greater than aggregate quantity supplied, so the price level begins to rise due to competition among demanders. In each case, the macroequilibrium is restored.

Graphing Pitfalls

Graphs that represent demand and supply in particular markets in microeconomics are labeled with price, measured in dollars per unit on the vertical axis, and quantity, measured in physical units on the horizontal axis. The axes are different in the aggregate demand and aggregate supply diagrams that we use in macroeconomics. The price level, not price, is measured on the vertical axis. The price level is the average of all prices in the economy measured with an index number like the GDP deflator. The dollar value of real GDP is measured on the horizontal axis. All goods and service produced are included rather than the good or service produced in just one market. So the demand and supply diagram you learned in Chapter 3 and the aggregate demand aggregate supply diagram you are learning now are completely different. Don't mislabel the axes as shown in the graph on the following page.

EMPLOYMENT, INFLATION, AND FISCAL POLICY 343

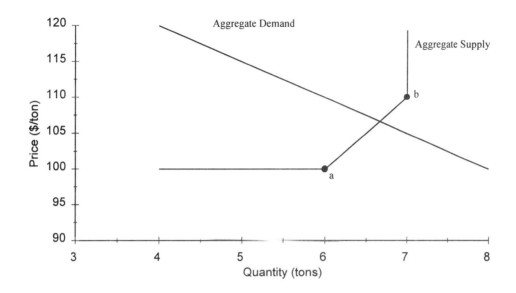

Don't make the mistake of mislabeling the axes on a graph of aggregate demand and aggregate supply in the same way you would for a demand and supply diagram in microeconomics. The price level is measured on the vertical axis, not price; and real GDP is measured on the horizontal axis, not quantity measured in some kind of physical units as shown above.

True-False Questions — If a statement is false, explain why.

1. Aggregate demand is basically the same concept as demand for a good or service, such as a banana or health services, that is the subject of analysis in microeconomics. (T/F)

2. One reason the aggregate demand curve is downward sloping is that as the price level decreases, real wealth increases so that people consume more. (T/F)

3. The horizontal segment of the aggregate supply curve suggests that ample resources are available to increase real GDP without causing inflation. (T/F)

4. The most inclusive measure of inflation is the consumer price index. (T/F)

5. Real GDP is equal to nominal GDP multiplied by 100, divided by the GDP deflator. (T/F)

6. If an increase in the price level creates higher profits and, as a result, causes real GDP to increase, then the aggregate supply curve must be vertical. (T/F)

7. The depression of the 1930s was a period in American economic history marked by significant cost-push inflation. (T/F)

8. Real GDP remains constant if increases in the price level alone cause nominal GDP to increase. (T/F)

9. In order for a recession to exist, a decline in the nation's real GDP must persist for at least half a year. (T/F)

10. Stagflation is a period of rapidly growing real GDP, inflation, and relatively high unemployment. (T/F)

11. During a recovery, real GDP increases and unemployment declines. (T/F)

12. The upward-sloping portion of the aggregate supply curve suggests that an increase in the price level will be associated with an increase in real GDP. (T/F)

13. A cut in government spending will cause the aggregate demand curve to shift to the right. (T/F)

14. Demand-pull inflation occurs when increases in aggregate demand shift the aggregate demand curve to the right while the aggregate supply curve remains unchanged at full-employment real GDP. (T/F)

15. The price level increase associated with increased aggregate demand during World War II was exacerbated by a decrease in aggregate supply caused by a labor force shift to the military. (T/F)

Multiple-Choice Questions

1. The upward slope of the trend line through a business cycle indicates that
   a. the economy is in a recovery phase
   b. the economy is in a period of stagflation
   c. there is a positive relationship between real GDP and the price level
   d. the economy's output increases in the long run
   e. the quantity supplied of a certain good increases as the price decreases

2. One characteristic of the recovery phase of the business cycle is that
   a. upward pressure on the economy's price level begins to build
   b. output reaches its maximum level
   c. a recession will soon follow
   d. inflation is moderating
   e. unemployment is increasing

EMPLOYMENT, INFLATION, AND FISCAL POLICY

3. One way that the government can increase aggregate demand is by
   a. reducing government spending
   b. reducing income taxes
   c. increasing taxes
   d. creating stagflation
   e. reducing the economy's supply of labor

4. The measure that compares the prices of all goods and services produced in the economy in any year to the prices of those goods and services produced in a base year is known as the
   a. GDP deflator
   b. real GDP
   c. nominal GDP
   d. CPI
   e. full employment GDP

5. All of the following conditions are consistent with general prosperity in the economy **except**
   a. unemployment is relatively low
   b. wage rates are relatively high
   c. real GDP is relatively high
   d. morale among workers and management is relatively high
   e. the price level decreases

6. It is important to control for price increases when comparing GDP between two years because
   a. nominal GDP can rise due to either an increase in output or an increase in the price level
   b. economists are only interested in price changes
   c. price increases are usually larger in relative terms than quantity increases
   d. price increases can reduce nominal GDP
   e. price increases can increase real GDP

7. If nominal GDP is $6 trillion in 1996 and the GDP deflator is 120, then real GDP is
   a. $5 trillion
   b. $50 trillion
   c. $7.2 trillion
   d. $72 trillion
   e. $12 trillion

8. The upward-sloping segment of the aggregate supply curve can be explained by
   a. tight resource markets, which, in turn, cause increases in the price of goods produced
   b. increases in the price level that raise profits, inducing firms to produce more
   c. the full employment of resources
   d. all of the above
   e. a and b

9. The aggregate supply curve shifts to the right when
   a. supplies of resources increase
   b. wage rates increase
   c. consumption decreases
   d. investment increases
   e. population decreases

10. Demand-pull inflation is the result of
    a. a leftward shift in the aggregate supply curve
    b. a rightward shift in the aggregate supply curve
    c. an increase in taxes
    d. a leftward shift in the aggregate demand curve
    e. a rightward shift in the aggregate demand curve

11. The difference between nominal and real GDP is that
    a. nominal GDP includes price changes while real GDP doesn't
    b. nominal GDP measures aggregate supply while real GDP measures aggregate demand
    c. real GDP is always equal to or higher than nominal GDP, depending on the phase of the business cycle
    d. real GDP includes price changes while nominal GDP doesn't
    e. real GDP is derived from the CPI while nominal GDP is derived from the GDP deflator

12. In the aggregate demand and aggregate supply model, the intersection of the AD and AS curves determines
    a. the price level and real GDP
    b. the equilibrium price and quantity combination
    c. the difference between real and nominal GDP
    d. the price level and the rate of inflation
    e. the rate of economic growth

13. The sequence of phases in a business cycle is
    a. recovery, recession, prosperity, downturn
    b. prosperity, recovery, downturn, recession
    c. prosperity, downturn, recovery, recession
    d. recession, recovery, prosperity, downturn
    e. recession, recovery, downturn, prosperity

14. The aggregate supply curve shifts to the right when
    a. consumers, with no change in nominal GDP, save less and consume more
    b. consumers, with no change in nominal GDP, save more and consume less
    c. people, with no change in the price level, decrease their supply of labor
    d. people, with no change in the price level, increase their supply of labor
    e. as a result of war, people shift from civilian to military production

15. If real GDP is $1,600 billion and the GDP deflator is 125, then nominal GDP is
    a. $2,000 billion
    b. $2,500 billion
    c. $1,800 billion
    d. $2,400 billion
    e. $1,000 billion

16. If the price level in the United States is constant while price levels in other countries increase, then
    a. aggregate supply in the United States shifts to the right
    b. aggregate demand in other economies shifts to the left
    c. real GDP in the United States increases more rapidly than in other economies
    d. U.S. exports increase, shifting U.S. aggregate demand to the right
    e. U.S. exports decrease, shifting U.S. aggregate demand to the left

EMPLOYMENT, INFLATION, AND FISCAL POLICY 347

17. The aggregate demand curve shifts to the left when
    a. consumers, with no change in the price level, save less and consume more
    b. consumers, with no change in the price level, save more and consume less
    c. people, with no change in the price level, decrease their supply of labor
    d. people, with no change in the price level, increase their supply of labor
    e. as a result of war, people shift from civilian to military production

18. If more capital is made available in an economy, one consequence will be
    a. a decrease in aggregate demand
    b. an increase in aggregate demand
    c. greater unemployment
    d. a shift to the right by the aggregate supply curve
    e. an increase in the slope of the upward-sloping portion of the aggregate supply curve

19. Cost-push inflation can be represented on a graph of aggregate demand and aggregate supply by
    a. a shift to the right of the aggregate demand curve
    b. a movement to the left along the aggregate supply curve
    c. a movement to the right along the aggregate supply curve
    d. a shift to the right of the aggregate supply curve
    e. a shift to the left of the aggregate supply curve

20. One of the main reasons for the recession and economic stagnation of the early 1990s was
    a. an OPEC-designed increase in oil prices that caused stagflation
    b. an increase in defense spending due to the war in the Persian Gulf
    c. a decrease in consumer spending in response to high levels of debt
    d. unsuccessful leveraged buyouts
    e. a commercial real estate boom

Fill in the Blanks

1. The business cycle consists of alternating periods of _growth_ and _decline_ in an economy's GDP.

2. The _base year_ is the reference year with which prices in other years are compared using a _price index_.

3. The aggregate demand curve is downward sloping due to the _real wealth_ effect, the _interest rate_ effect, and the _international trade_ effect.

4. If workers' _wages_ decrease while the price level remains constant, then the aggregate supply curve will shift to the _right_.

5. During World War II, aggregate demand shifted to the _right_ while the aggregate supply curve shifted to the _left_, causing the price level to _rise_.

Discussion Questions

1. Define gross domestic product. How can GDP increase over time?

2. How is the consumer price index constructed?

3. Why do we say that the GDP deflator is a more inclusive measure of inflation than the consumer price index?

4. What's the difference between nominal GDP and real GDP?

5. Why does the aggregate supply curve have three distinct segments?

6. Why is the aggregate demand curve downward sloping?

7. Distinguish between demand-pull inflation and cost-push inflation.

EMPLOYMENT, INFLATION, AND FISCAL POLICY 349

Problems

1. Suppose the GDP deflator is 140 for 1996. The base year is 1992. If nominal GDP in 1996 is $3.6 trillion, calculate real GDP in 1992 dollars. Show your work.

2. Suppose that the cost of the market basket of goods and services that represents the CPI is $3,000 in the base year, 1992. Suppose also that the cost of the same market basket of goods in 1994 was $3,300. What was the value of the CPI index for 1994? Explain what the 1994 CPI means.

3. Suppose the value of the market basket from question 3 was $4,000 in 1996. What was the average annual rate of inflation between 1994 and 1996? Show your work.

4. Use an aggregate demand/aggregate supply diagram to show what happened to the economy as a result of the OPEC-designed oil price increases of the 1970s. Explain your graph in words and make sure it is labeled carefully.

Everyday Applications

As you read the newspaper and watch the economic news on television, think about whether the U.S. economy is currently in macroequilibrium. What economic data would you use to answer this question? Is the aggregate demand/aggregate supply model relevant today?

Economics Online

Stat-USA is an Internet site that provides current and historical economic and financial data. The site is a service of the U.S. Department of Commerce. Find out changes in real GDP, the price level, and other key economic variables by visiting the site (*http://www.stat-usa.gov/*).

Answers to Questions

Key Terms Quiz

a. 3	f. 11	k. 5	p. 10	u. 4
b. 6	g. 9	l. 22	q. 7	v. 16
c. 13	h. 20	m. 2	r. 23	w. 8
d. 1	i. 17	n. 18	s. 21	
e. 14	j. 12	o. 19	t. 15	

True-False Questions

1. False. Aggregate demand refers to all goods and services purchased in the economy while demand refers to a particular good or service purchased in one market.
2. True
3. True
4. False. The most inclusive measure of inflation is the GDP deflator. The CPI measures the prices of goods and services typically bought by households, while the GDP deflator measures the prices of all goods and services produced in the economy.
5. True
6. False. Aggregate supply must be upward sloping for output to increase as the price level increases.

EMPLOYMENT, INFLATION, AND FISCAL POLICY

7. False. The depression of the 1930s was characterized by high unemployment and falling price levels caused by a dramatic decline in aggregate demand.
8. True
9. True
10. False. Stagflation is a period of stagnating or falling real GDP, inflation, and relatively high unemployment.
11. True
12. True
13. False. A cut in government spending will cause the aggregate demand curve to shift to the left.
14. True
15. True

Multiple-Choice Questions

1. d	6. a	11. a	16. d
2. a	7. a	12. a	17. b
3. b	8. e	13. d	18. d
4. a	9. a	14. d	19. e
5. e	10. e	15. a	20. c

Fill in the Blanks

1. growth; decline
2. base year; price index
3. real wealth; interest rate; international trade
4. wages; right
5. right; left; rise

Discussion Questions

1. Gross domestic product is the total value of all final goods and services produced in a country during a calendar year. GDP can increase if the quantity of goods and services produced increases or if the price of these goods and services increases.

2. The consumer price index is constructed by dividing the cost of a fixed market basket of goods and services purchased in a particular year by the cost of the same market basket of goods and services in a base year and multiplying by 100. The market basket represents purchases made by the typical American household.

3. The GDP deflator includes the prices of all final goods and services produced in a year, while the CPI includes only consumer goods and services that a household typically purchases. For instance, the GDP deflator includes airline ticket prices and the CPI does not.

4. Nominal GDP, measured in current market prices, includes the effect of price changes. Real GDP is adjusted for changes in the price level. Real GDP is equal to nominal GDP multiplied by 100 and divided by the GDP deflator.

5. Each segment of the aggregate supply curve reflects a different set of macroeconomic circumstances. For example, the horizontal segment reflects an economy operating well below full employment, so real GDP can be increased without any upward pressure on the price level. The upward-sloping segment shows that resources are becoming more scarce as the economy approaches full employment. Employers bid for

resources, driving up their prices, which causes costs of production and the price level to rise. Price level increases raise employers' profits so they increase output. In the vertical segment, full employment exists and resources are unavailable to increase real GDP. Only the price level can rise.

6. The aggregate demand curve is downward sloping because of the real wealth effect, the interest rate effect, and the international trade effect. As the price level decreases, the purchasing power of wealth increases, and consumption spending increases as a result. As the price level decreases, consumers and businesses don't have to borrow as much to finance their spending. Therefore, the demand for borrowed funds decreases and interest rates decrease. As a result of lower interest rates, spending by consumers and businesses increases. If the price level in the United States decreases while the price level in other countries stays the same, spending on U.S. exports by foreigners increases, and people in the United States buy fewer imports. As the price level decreases, foreign demand for exports increases and domestic demand for imports decreases.

7. Demand-pull inflation is caused by a shift to the right in the aggregate demand curve. Demand-pull inflation can result from an increase in aggregate demand beyond that necessary to achieve full employment. Spending by households, businesses, government, or foreigners or some combination of these can trigger demand-pull inflation. An example of demand-pull inflation is the inflation of the 1960s during the Vietnam War.

    Cost-push inflation is caused by a shift to the left in the aggregate supply curve. Cost-push inflation can result from decreasing availability of resources including labor, capital, land (natural resources), and entrepreneurial energies or from an increase in the prices of these resources. A good example of cost-push inflation is that caused by OPEC's increases in oil prices from 1973 through 1982. Because oil is an essential resource for many types of production and is used as a primary source of energy for heating and power generation, the prices of virtually all goods and services were affected by the increased price of oil.

Problems

1. Real GDP is equal to nominal GDP multiplied by 100 and divided by the GDP deflator. In this case, real GDP is equal to $3.6 trillion x 100/140 = $2.57 trillion.

2. The value of the CPI for 1994 is 3,300/3,000 multiplied by 100, which is 110. The 1994 CPI equal to 110 means that prices rose between 1992 and 1994 by 10 percent.

3. The value of the CPI for 1996 is 4,000/3,000 x 100 = 133. The average annual rate of inflation between 1994 and 1996 is (133 - 110)/110 multiplied by 100 then divided by 2, or 10.45 percent. You must divide by 2 because there are two years covered by the change in the CPI — 1994 -1996.

4. Your graph should look like the one shown on the following page. The OPEC-designed price increases caused the aggregate supply curve to shift to the left. These events are shown by a shift in the aggregate supply curve from AS to AS', a decrease in the equilibrium level of GDP to GDP', and an increase in the equilibrium price level to P'.

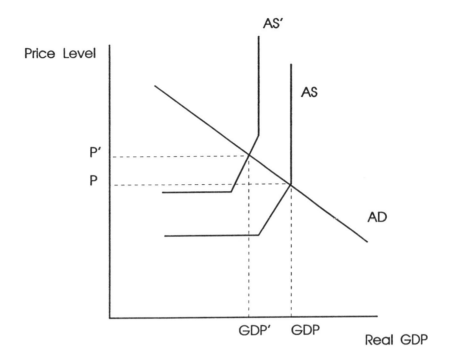

CHAPTER 20

GROSS DOMESTIC PRODUCT ACCOUNTING

Chapter in a Nutshell

Gross domestic product was introduced in the previous chapter as a basic measure of macroeconomic performance. This chapter identifies the component parts of GDP and describes their significance — personal consumption expenditures, gross private domestic investment, government purchases, and net exports. The **circular flow of goods, services, and resources** and the **circular flow of money** are used to show how gross domestic product can be viewed as either flows of expenditure on newly produced **final goods and services** or as equivalent flows of money income to people who provide the resources used to produce goods and services. These two views of GDP are represented by the **expenditure approach** and the **income approach to measuring GDP**.

The expenditure approach focuses on four categories of expenditures. **Personal consumption expenditures** are made up of spending by households for **durable goods, nondurable goods**, and services. **Gross private domestic investment** consists of spending for new plant and equipment, residential housing, and **inventory investment**. Government spending is comprised of federal, state, and local governmental purchases of goods and services. **Net exports** are the difference between a country's exports and imports. The 1996 GDP in the United States was over $7.6 trillion.

Although GDP is a comprehensive measure, certain types of goods and services are excluded from the calculations, including the value of housework, the value of leisure, and the **underground economy**. Also, changes in the quality of goods and services and the costs of environmental damage associated with production may not be accurately measured in the GDP accounts.

The income approach looks at the payments made to households that supply resources to the firms producing final goods and services. National income is the sum of all payments made to resource owners and includes the categories of employee's compensation, rental income, corporate profit, net interest, and proprietors' income. National income in 1996 was approximately $6.3 trillion, with about 70.8 percent representing payments to workers. When adjustments are made for **capital depreciation** and indirect business taxes, GDP and national income match, thus demonstrating the equivalence of the circular flows.

After studying this chapter, you should be able to:

- Explain the equivalence between the **circular flow of money** and the **circular flow of goods, services, and resources**.
- List the categories of spending on final goods and services used in the **expenditure approach** to measuring **GDP**.
- Distinguish between **durable and nondurable consumer goods**.
- Compare the relative magnitudes of the different components used in the **expenditure approach** to measuring GDP.
- Explain how economists bring GDP and **national income** into accord.
- Derive **personal income** and **disposable personal income** from **national income**.
- Explain why GDP is an imperfect measure of overall economic activity in a country.

EMPLOYMENT, INFLATION, AND FISCAL POLICY

Concept Check — See how you do on these multiple-choice questions.

1. The **circular flow of goods, services, and resources** shows how
   a. households and firms are independent from each other
   b. households supply their resources to firms in resource markets and demand goods and services in product markets
   c. the circular flow of money inaccurately measures real GDP
   d. households demand resources and firms demand goods and services
   e. too much spending on consumer goods can cause an economy to collapse

Between which two groups are the flows occurring in the circular flow model?

2. Changes in business inventories that are counted as **inventory investment** represent
   a. changes in the stocks of finished final goods, as well as stocks of resources used to produce those goods
   b. intended buildups of inventories
   c. the largest part of gross private domestic investment
   d. opportunities for firms to run inventory clearance sales
   e. accumulations of consumer durables

Why do businesses maintain inventories?

3. The difference between **GDP** and **GNP** is that
   a. GDP measures what is produced and earned by a nation's people and property and GNP measures what is produced and earned in the domestic economy
   b. GDP emphasizes ownership and GNP emphasizes location
   c. GDP measures what is produced and earned in the domestic economy and GNP measures what is produced and earned by a nation's people and property
   d. GDP includes depreciation and GNP does not
   e. GDP is always larger than GNP

Which of these measures emphasizes ownership and which emphasizes location?

4. All of the following are examples of **transfer payments** except
   a. government retirement benefits
   b. unemployment insurance benefits
   c. Social Security benefits
   d. rental income
   e. subsidies to farmers

Are transfer payments an addition to GDP?

5. Because most economic activity in the **underground economy** goes unreported, GDP is
   a. overstated
   b. unaffected
   c. understated
   d. understated, but this is offset by the inclusion of the value of housework
   e. overstated, but this is offset by the exclusion of the value of housework

How would GDP change if these activities were reported and included?

Am I on the Right Track?

Your answers to the questions above should be **b, a, c, d,** and **c**. There are two keys to your success in understanding the material in this chapter. First, make sure that you understand the circular flow of goods, services, and resources and the circular flow of money. These two circular flows are connected. Households supply flows of resources to firms in return for money payments — wages, interest, rent, and profit. Then the money payments to households for resources come back to firms as the expenditures on the final goods and services they have produced. The expenditure approach and the income approach to measuring GDP are embedded in these circular flow models. The second key to success with this chapter is to learn the key terms. As was true in the previous chapter, there are many new terms.

Key Terms Quiz — Match the terms on the left with the definitions in the column on the right.

1. circular flow of goods, services, and resources   _3_ a. the movement of income in the form of resource payments from firms to households, and of income in the form of revenue from households to firms

2. services   _6_ b. a method of calculating GDP by adding all the incomes earned in the production of final goods and services

3. circular flow of money   _20_ c. personal income minus personal taxes

4. inventory investment   _9_ d. the difference between the value of a good that a firm produces and the value of the goods the firm uses to produce it

5. final goods   _12_ e. the value of existing capital stock used up in the process of producing goods and services

6. income approach   _8_ f. the sum of all payments made to resource owners for the use of their resources

7. intermediate goods   _11_ g. all goods and services bought by households

8. national income   _1_ h. the movement of goods and services from firms to households, and of resources from households to firms

9. value added   _13_ i. the purchase by firms of plant, equipment, and inventory goods

10. gross national product (GNP)   _17_ j. all goods and services bought by government

11. personal consumption expenditures   _14_ k. GDP minus capital depreciation

12. capital depreciation   _19_ l. an economy's exports to other economies, minus its imports from other economies

13. gross private domestic investment   _4_ m. stocks of finished goods and raw materials that firms keep in reserve to facilitate production and sales

14. net domestic product (NDP)   _7_ n. goods used to produce other goods

15. expenditure approach   _23_ o. goods expected to last less than one year

16. personal income   _10_ p. the market value of all final goods and services in an economy produced by resources owned by people of that economy, regardless of where the resources are located

17. government purchases   _22_ q. the unreported or illegal production of goods and services in the economy that is not counted in GDP

18. transfer payments   _16_ r. national income, plus income received but not

EMPLOYMENT, INFLATION, AND FISCAL POLICY   357

19. net exports

20. disposable personal income
21. durable goods
22. underground economy

23. nondurable goods

earned, minus income earned but not received
___2___ s. productive activities that are instantaneously consumed
___21___ t. goods expected to last at least a year
___18___ u. income received but not earned
___15___ v. a method of calculating GDP that adds all expenditures made for final goods and services by households, firms, and government
___5___ w. goods purchased for final use, not for resale

True-False Questions — If a statement is false, explain why.

1. The circular flow of goods, services, and resources and the circular flow of money show equivalent streams measured in dollars. (T/F)   *True*

2. Personal consumption expenditures comprise about 20 percent of GDP. (T/F)

3. A final good or service is produced for resale. (T/F)

4. Sales of previously owned automobiles are included in GDP. (T/F)

5. Gross private domestic investment includes government spending on the National Guard but excludes other military spending. (T/F)

6. An increase in net exports causes GDP to decrease. (T/F)

7. An estimate of the value of production in the underground economy is included in official GDP statistics that are compiled by the government. (T/F)

8. Disposable personal income is equal to personal income minus personal taxes. (T/F)

9. Durable goods are expected to last for at least one year. (T/F)

10. Transportation facilities are among the goods and services that the government purchases. (T/F)

11. The sum of the values of intermediate goods will be equal to GDP. (T/F)

12. National income measures the sum of all payments made to resource owners for the use of their resources. (T/F) — **T**

13. People who provide firms with capital receive interest income. (T/F) — **T**

14. Stockholders in corporations receive proprietors' income. (T/F) — **F**

15. GDP and GNP are precisely equal to each other. (T/F)

Multiple-Choice Questions

1. The difference between GDP and GNP is that
    a. factor incomes to foreign-owned firms in the United States are included in GNP
    b. depreciation is excluded from GNP
    c. the corporate profits tax is excluded from GDP
    d. indirect business taxes are counted twice in GDP
    e. factor incomes to foreign-owned firms in the United States are included in GDP

2. The circular flow of goods, services, and resources shows the interdependence of
    a. the supplies of goods and the supplies of services
    b. firms and investment
    c. intermediate goods and final goods
    d. net imports and net exports
    e. households and firms

3. The smallest portion of personal consumption expenditures is accounted for by
    a. inventory investment
    b. productivity
    c. purchases of services
    d. purchases of nondurable goods
    e. purchases of durable goods

4. The expenditure approach to measuring GDP is the sum of expenditures in all of the following categories **except**
    a. gross private domestic investment
    b. personal consumption expenditures
    c. government spending on goods and services
    d. transfer payments by the government
    e. the difference between exports and imports

5. If C = $500, I = $200, G = $150, and X− M = −5, what is GDP?
    a. $850
    b. $855
    c. $845
    d. $755
    e. $745

EMPLOYMENT, INFLATION, AND FISCAL POLICY 359

6. If a large number of Egypt's citizens work overseas, then perhaps the best measure of the Egyptian people's economic health is
    a. the GDP deflator
    b. real GNP
    c. real GDP
    d. nominal GNP
    e. nominal GDP

7. The income approach calculates GDP with all of the following **except**
    a. interest
    b. wages
    c. rent
    d. investment
    e. profits

8. A decline in inventories shows up as
    a. a decrease in gross private domestic investment
    b. increases in production
    c. an increase in gross private domestic investment
    d. a decrease in production
    e. decreases in services

9. Disposable personal income is
    a. taxes and transfer payments
    b. households' consumption expenditures
    c. households' savings
    d. expenditures on luxury items by households
    e. the sum of personal consumption expenditures and saving

10. In the circular flow model of goods, services, and resources, _____ flow(s) from firms to households.
    a. labor
    b. capital
    c. land
    d. profits
    e. goods

11. GDP understates the total value of all final goods and services produced for all the following reasons **except**
    a. the costs of environmental problems are not included
    b. quality improvements in products are not included
    c. the value of leisure is not included
    d. the value of housework is not included
    e. the value of the underground economy is not included

12. All of the following are considered to be components of investment in calculating GDP **except**
    a. new residential construction
    b. net increases in inventory
    c. new factories
    d. purchases of new equipment by firms
    e. financial investment

13. If depreciation is zero,
    a. GDP is the same as NDP
    b. GDP will shrink over time
    c. gross investment exceeds depreciation
    d. inventory investment is positive
    e. the capital stock grows

14. It is necessary to subtract _____ from net domestic product in order to compute national income.
    a. indirect business taxes
    b. capital depreciation
    c. transfer payments
    d. net exports
    e. factor payments to the rest of the world

15. The largest share of national income is accounted for by
    a. corporate profit
    b. proprietors' income
    c. compensation of employees
    d. consumption of nondurable goods
    e. income taxes

16. Net domestic product (NDP) is GDP minus
    a. depreciation
    b. indirect business taxes
    c. GNP
    d. transfer payments
    e. personal taxes

17. All of the following are examples of transfer payments **except**
    a. Social Security benefits
    b. unemployment benefits
    c. the wages of government employees
    d. veterans' benefits
    e. Aid to Families with Dependent Children

18. The largest component of consumption expenditures is
    a. compensation to employees
    b. profits
    c. rents and royalties
    d. services
    e. proprietors' income

19. The value-added approach to GDP computation involves
    a. problems with double counting
    b. subtracting income from expenditures
    c. summing the addition to value at each stage in production
    d. summing the price times quantity for all intermediate goods
    e. improving technology so that value is added at each stage

EMPLOYMENT, INFLATION, AND FISCAL POLICY

20. One of the reasons for not including such items as leisure in the calculation of GDP is that
    a. including these items is conceptually difficult
    b. these are not government-sanctioned items
    c. it is difficult to accurately measure the value of these items on a consistent basis
    d. to include these items would cause GDP to decrease
    e. these are not productive items

Fill in the Blanks

1. The expenditure approach to measuring GDP consists of the sum of _____, _____, _____, and _____.

2. GDP has limitations as a measure of economic well-being because it excludes _____, _____, _____, _____, and _____.

3. National income is the sum of _____, _____, _____, _____, and _____.

4. One of the driving forces behind the underground economy is _____.

5. Gross national product is GDP _____ receipts of factor income from the rest of the world, _____ payments of factor income to the rest of the world.

Discussion Questions

1. How do the expenditure approach and the income approach to measuring GDP relate to the circular flow model?

2. Approximately what percentage of GDP is represented in each of the four categories of expenditure?

3. Why are inventories counted as part of investment?

4. Approximately what percentage of national income is represented in each of its categories?

5. Why would an economist, interested in a country's rate of growth, look at its NDP rather than GDP?

6. If you were studying living standards in a country, which measure would you find more informative, national income or personal income? Why?

Problems

1. Use the following data to calculate GDP, GNP, NDP, national income, personal income, and disposable personal income.

Personal Consumption Expenditures	1,000 GD
Interest	80
Corporate Profit	200
Government Purchases	400 GD
Depreciation	100 GN − 100 =
Rent	300
Gross Private Domestic Investment	400 GD
Compensation of Employees	750
Exports	100 GD
Imports	180 GD
Indirect Business Taxes	70
Proprietors' Income	220
Income Tax	200
Income Earned but not Received	110
Income Received but not Earned	200 (GD+GNP
Receipt of Factor Incomes from the Rest of the World	80 + GNP
Payment of Factor Incomes to the Rest of the World	70 − GNP =

1. GDP = 1,000.00 + 400 + 400 + 100 − 180 = 1,720
2. GNP = 1,720 + 80 − 70 = 1,730
   GDP + IGF − ICT =
3. NDP = GNP − D

2. Suppose that in the following year, economic activity for Problem 1 undergoes the changes that are listed in the table below. How does GDP change?

Corporate Profits	−100
Depreciation	50
Exports	+80
Income Earned but not Received	+10

364　　CHAPTER 20　　GROSS DOMESTIC PRODUCT ACCOUNTING

Everyday Applications

Think of some specific examples of the underground economy. Do you know anyone who has worked in the underground economy? How would a lowering of tax rates affect the underground economy and measured GDP? What would be the impact of legalizing marijuana?

Economics Online

One of the earliest groups that devoted itself to the collection of economic data like that included in the GDP accounts is the National Bureau of Economic Research (NBER). The NBER was founded in 1920 and continues to promote a better understanding of the economy through the research it supports. Visit the NBER Web site (*http://nber.harvard.edu/*).

Answers to Questions

Key Terms Quiz

a. 3　　f. 8　　k. 14　　p. 10　　u. 18
b. 6　　g. 11　　l. 19　　q. 22　　v. 15
c. 20　　h. 1　　m. 4　　r. 16　　w. 5
d. 9　　i. 13　　n. 7　　s. 2
e. 12　　j. 17　　o. 23　　t. 21

True-False Questions

1. True
2. False. In 1996, personal consumption expenditures accounted for approximately 68 percent of GDP.
3. False. A final good is produced for final use.
4. False. A used car has already been counted as part of a previous year's GDP.
5. False. Expenditures on the National Guard and other military expenditures are part of government purchases.
6. False. An increase in net exports causes GDP to increase.
7. False. The underground economy is left out of GDP calculations.
8. True
9. True
10. True
11. False. The sum of the value added for intermediate goods will equal GDP.
12. True
13. True
14. False. Stockholders receive corporate profit in the form of dividend income.
15. False. GNP is equal to GDP plus factor income to Americans producing overseas minus factor income to foreigners producing in the United States.

EMPLOYMENT, INFLATION, AND FISCAL POLICY

Multiple-Choice Questions

1. e	6. b	11. a	16. a
2. e	7. d	12. e	17. c
3. e	8. a	13. a	18. d
4. d	9. e	14. a	19. c
5. c	10. e	15. c	20. c

Fill in the Blanks

1. personal consumption expenditures; gross private domestic investment; government purchases; net exports
2. the value of housework; the underground economy; leisure; improvement in the quality of goods and services; the cost of environmental damage
3. compensation of employees; rental income; corporate profits; net interest; proprietors' income
4. tax avoidance
5. plus; minus

Discussion Questions

1. The expenditure approach corresponds to the money flow from households, businesses, government, and the international sector purchasing final goods and services. The income approach corresponds to the money flow from buyers of resources to the households that supply those resources for use in production. The two money flows are equivalent.

2. Consumption is by far the largest category of expenditure. Consumption accounted for some 68 percent of GDP in 1996. Government spending accounted for approximately 18 percent of 1996 GDP, investment accounted for another 15 percent, and net exports were negative. As a percentage of GDP, the difference between exports and imports was about 1 percent.

3. Inventories are unsold output. Firms keep stocks of finished final goods, as well as stocks of resources used to produce those goods, in reserve in order to promote efficiency in production and sales. A firm can't expect to sell or to produce if it doesn't have a stock of goods to sell or raw materials to use in production.

4. Compensation of employees dwarfs all the other categories with about 71 percent of the total in 1996. Rental income was only 2.3 percent of the total in 1996. Corporate profit, net interest, and proprietors' income were 12 percent, 6.8 percent, and 8.3 percent of national income, respectively, in 1996.

5. NDP is a better measure of a country's rate of growth because it excludes investment expenditures made to replace used-up capital. NDP focuses on investment over and above depreciation. An economy must have positive net investment in order to grow over time.

6. Personal income is probably more useful. This is because personal income shows the income that households actually receive, including transfer payments. Also, certain taxes that are withheld from income, like Social Security taxes, are accounted for by personal income. Personal income minus direct taxes gives disposable personal income.

Problems

1. GDP = Consumption + Investment + Government Purchases + Exports − Imports
   = 1,000 + 400 + 400 + 100 − 180 = $1,720

GNP = GDP + Factor Incomes from the Rest of the World − Factor Incomes to the Rest of the World
= 1,720 + 80 − 70 = $1,730

NDP = GDP − Depreciation = 1,720 − 100 = $1,620

National Income = NDP − Indirect Business Taxes = 1,620 − 70 = $1,550

Personal Income = National Income − Income Earned but not Received + Income Received but not Earned
= 1,550 − 110 + 200 = $1,640

Personal Income − Direct Taxes = 1,640 − 200 = $1,440

2. GDP will decrease by $20 to $1,700 because the $100 drop in corporate profits is partly offset by an $80 increase in exports. Changes in depreciation and income earned but not received have no effect on GDP.

CHAPTER 21

CONSUMPTION AND INVESTMENT

Chapter in a Nutshell

Producers and consumers make their production and consumption decisions simultaneously and independently of each other. This simple observation may help to explain why the economy can, at times, slide into recession and at other times bound into prosperity. For example, if production exceeds consumption, then inventories accumulate and firms will likely cut back production, causing an increase in unemployment. On the other hand, if consumption exceeds production, then firms will increase production, hire more workers, and cause unemployment to decrease. So it is critical to understand how households make consumption decisions.

Economists posit that a relationship exists between people's consumption and their disposable income. The **consumption function** is written as $C = f(Y)$, that is to say, consumption is a function of income. John Maynard Keynes developed the **absolute income hypothesis,** which states that as national income increases, consumption increases, but by diminishing amounts. Keynes believed that the **marginal propensity to consume (MPC)** decreased as the absolute level of income increased. However, Simon Kuznets's research showed that the MPC tends to remain fairly constant regardless of the absolute level of national income. New hypotheses about consumption were developed as a result of Kuznets's work. These included Duesenberry's **relative income hypothesis,** Friedman's **permanent income hypothesis,** and Modigliani's **life-cycle hypothesis.** As a result of the work done by these and other economists on the nature of consumption spending, we now represent consumption as a straight-line curve that increases as national income increases. Some consumption, called **autonomous consumption,** would occur at zero national income. The consumption curve shifts as a result of changes in real asset and money holdings, expectations of price changes, changes in credit and interest rates, and changes in taxation. Based on the fact that the part of national income not spent on consumption is **saving,** a saving curve can be derived from the consumption curve. The **marginal propensity to save (MPS),** which is the slope of the saving curve, is analogous to the MPC.

Another spending decision in the economy is that made by producers on investment. Economists use the concept **autonomous investment** to reflect the fact that investment is independent of the level of national income. Determinants of investment include the level of technology, the interest rate, expectations of future economic growth, and the rate of capacity utilization. Compared to consumption, investment is quite volatile, meaning that it can change quite dramatically over short periods of time. Together, consumption and investment form the two major building blocks of the Keynesian model.

After you study this chapter, you should be able to:

- Discuss Keynes's **absolute income hypothesis**.
- Define the **marginal propensity to consume**.
- Describe Duesenberry's **relative income hypothesis**.
- Explain Friedman's **permanent income hypothesis**.
- Present examples to illustrate the **life-cycle hypothesis** of consumption.
- List factors that cause shifts in the consumption curve.
- Derive the saving curve from the consumption curve.
- Write an equation for the consumption function.
- Discuss the determinants of **autonomous investment**.
- Explain the volatile nature of investment.

Concept Check — See how you do on these multiple choice questions.

1. Keynes's **absolute income hypothesis** states that as a person's
    a. income increases, his/her MPC decreases
    b. income increases, his/her MPC increases
    c. income increases, his/her MPC is constant
    d. income is more transitory, his/her MPC is lower
    e. age increases, his/her MPC decreases

Keynes believed that people's consumption behavior changed as their absolute level of income changed.

2. Duesenberry's **relative income hypothesis** states that the marginal propensity to consume is
    a. the same across different social classes
    b. lower for people with high incomes than for people with low incomes
    c. decreasing as income is increasing
    d. a function of disposable income
    e. a function of transitory income

How does a person's social class status influence consumption behavior in Duesenberry's theory?

3. **Autonomous consumption** is
    a. a function of disposable income
    b. a function of national income
    c. a function of GDP
    d. a function of saving
    e. independent of the level of income

What does autonomous mean?

4. When the consumption curve is linear, the **marginal propensity to save**
    a. is equal to one plus the MPC
    b. increases as income increases
    c. is the change in saving induced by a change in income
    d. decreases as income increases
    e. is that part of national income not spent on consumption

If the marginal propensity to consume is the change in consumption that results from a given change in income, then what would be the parallel definition of the marginal propensity to save?

5. **Autonomous investment** is determined by all of the following **except**
    a. income
    b. the level of technology
    c. the interest rate
    d. expectations of future economic growth
    e. the rate of capacity utilization

Again, what does autonomous mean?

EMPLOYMENT, INFLATION AND FISCAL POLICY

Am I on the Right Track?

Your answers to the questions above should be **a, b, e, c,** and **a**. You need to take four distinct steps to get on the right track in this chapter. First, you must understand the various hypotheses about consumption that have been advanced by different economists. Second, you need to be comfortable graphing the consumption curve and working with the consumption equation. That done, graphing the saving curve should be no problem because saving is the part of national income not spent on consumption. The last step is to understand the determinants of investment spending by firms and why economists use the concept of autonomous investment.

Key Terms Quiz — Match the terms on the left with the definitions in the column on the right.

1. consumption function — **4** a. consumption spending that is independent of the level of income
2. transitory income — **7** b. as national income increases, consumption spending increases at a constant rate
3. absolute income hypothesis — **12** c. investment spending that producers intend to undertake
4. autonomous consumption — **2** d. the unexpected gain or loss of income that a person experiences
5. marginal propensity to consume (MPC) — **10** e. a line drawn at a 45-degree angle showing all points at which the distance to the horizontal axis equals the distance to the vertical axis; same as income line
6. saving — **5** f. the ratio of the change in consumption spending to a given change income
7. relative income hypothesis — **8** g. the change in saving induced by a change in income
8. marginal propensity to save (MPS) — **1** h. the relationship between consumption and income
9. permanent income hypothesis — **14** i. investment that is independent of the level of income
10. 45-degree line — **13** j. the regular income a person expects to earn annually
11. life-cycle hypothesis — **6** k. that part of national income not spent on consumption
12. intended investment — **9** l. a person's consumption spending is related to his or her permanent income
13. permanent income — **3** m. as national income increases, consumption spending increases, but by diminishing amounts
14. autonomous investment — **11** n. typically, a person's MPC is high during young adulthood, decreases during the middle-age years, and increases when the person retires

Graphing Tutorial

It would be surprising to find any students who have not graphed linear equations in their high school algebra classes. Drawing these graphs wasn't terribly difficult then, and it isn't now. The consumption curve, saving curve and investment curve are all variants of graphs of equations for straight lines. Suppose that we have a consumption function in the form $C = a + bY$, where C is consumption spending, a is autonomous consumption, b is the MPC, and Y is the level of national income. Let $a = 100$ and $b = .75$. Now the equation reads $C = 100 + .75Y$. Graphing this equation is fairly easy because we know the value for autonomous consumption and the MPC. In algebraic terms, autonomous consumption is the vertical intercept for the graph of the consumption equation, and the MPC is the slope. We know that when $Y = 0$, $C = 100$ and that for every $100 increase in national income there is a $75 increase in consumption. That's all we need to know in order to graph the consumption curve. The consumption curve that corresponds to this consumption equation is shown on the following page along with the income line.

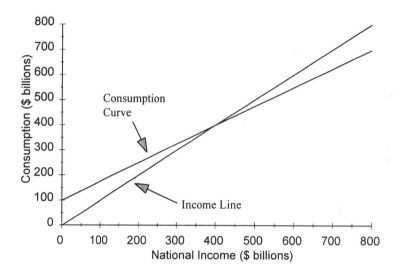

Note that the intercept on the consumption axis for the consumption curve is $100 billion. This is autonomous consumption — the value for a in the consumption equation. Also, for each $100 billion increase in national income, there is a $75 billion increase in consumption spending, which gives us a slope of .75 — the value for b in the consumption equation. The income line (also known as the 45-degree line) shows all of the points where the distance along the horizontal axis is equal to the distance along the vertical axis.

Now let's derive the saving function and graph the saving curve. We know that saving is the amount of national income that isn't spent on consumption. Therefore, national income minus consumption is equal to saving. Algebraically, we have $Y - C = S$, where S is saving. Substituting our expression $a - bY$ for C in the equation we have $S = Y - (a + bY)$. Factoring and rearranging terms, the saving equation can be written as $S = -a + (1 - b)Y$. In this equation, the vertical intercept is equal to $-a$ and the slope is equal to $1 - b$. Staying with the values for a and b used above for the consumption function, when income is equal to zero, saving is -$100 billion and the slope of the saving function (the marginal propensity to save) is equal to $1 - .75$, or .25. For every $100 increase in national income, there is a $25 increase in saving. The saving equation is $S = -100 + .25Y$. The saving curve that corresponds to this saving equation is shown below.

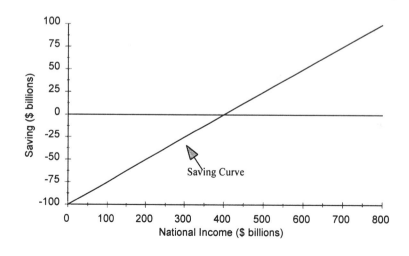

EMPLOYMENT, INFLATION AND FISCAL POLICY

Compare the consumption curve to the saving curve. Suppose that national income is $800 billion. In the graph of the consumption curve, when national income is $800 billion, consumption is $700 billion. Therefore, national income minus consumption *(Y - C)* is $100 billion. This is the value of saving at the $800 billion level of national income. The saving curve shows that saving is indeed $100 billion when national income is $800 billion.

Now find the point in the graph of the saving curve where saving is zero. This point corresponds to a national income of $400 billion. In the graph of the consumption curve, at an income level of $400 billion, the consumption curve intersects the income line. National income minus consumption, which is equal to saving, is zero at the $400 billion income level. You can see the correspondence between the points on the consumption curve and the points on the saving curve at different levels of national income.

Finally, we turn to graphing the investment curve. Investment is considered autonomous, that is, independent of the level of national income. Therefore, the investment curve can be graphed as a horizontal line at the level of autonomous investment. Suppose that the level of autonomous investment is $75 billion. A graph of this investment curve is shown below.

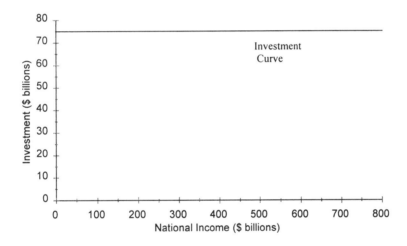

Graphing Pitfalls

The consumption curve, saving curve, and investment curve are all plotted on axes that measure national income on the horizontal axis and consumption, saving, and investment, respectively, on the vertical axis. Therefore, each of these curves will start from an intercept on the vertical axis. You will never find one of these curves starting from the national income axis. For example, the consumption curve drawn below, starting from the national income axis, makes no sense. What is autonomous consumption in this case? Why aren't there values for consumption when national income is below $100 billion? The consumption function always originates from an intercept on the vertical axis.

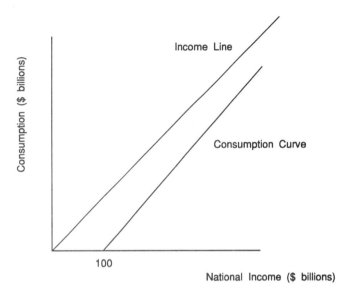

Never draw a consumption curve with the intercept on the national income axis. The intercept for the consumption curve is always on the consumption axis!

True-False Questions — If a statement is false, explain why.

1. Consumption spending decisions are carefully coordinated with production decisions in our economy. (T/F)

2. The most important factor determining people's consumption behavior is the level of their income. (T/F)

3. Keynes's absolute income hypothesis asserts that as national income increases, consumption increases, but at an increasing rate. (T/F)

4. Keynes believed that the marginal propensity to consume is constant. (T/F)

5. Simon Kuznets's data supported the idea that the marginal propensity to consume is constant. (T/F)

6. Duesenberry's relative income hypothesis suggests that the rich have relatively high MPCs and the poor have relatively low MPCs. (T/F)

7. If all people's incomes increase at the same rate, then their relative incomes increase as well. (T/F)

8. Modigliani's life-cycle hypothesis suggests that consumption fluctuates less than income over a person's lifetime. (T/F)

9. The expectation that the price level will increase induces consumers to save less and consume more now, which causes the consumption function to shift upward. (T/F)

10. If autonomous consumption increases, then the consumption curve shifts up and the saving function shifts down. (T/F)

11. An increase in interest rates shifts the consumption curve upward. (T/F)

12. We can determine consumption spending for any income level if we know the level of autonomous consumption and the marginal propensity to consume. (T/F)

13. The saving curve crosses the national income axis at the level of income where the consumption curve crosses the income line. (T/F)

14. Intended investment will increase when new technology is introduced. (T/F)

15. Because intended investment is related to the level of national income, it is called autonomous investment. (T/F)

Multiple-Choice Questions

1. All of the following are characteristics of intended investment **except** that
    a. its level is influenced by the rate of capacity utilization
    b. as the interest rate falls, the quantity of intended investment increases
    c. its size is dependent on the level of national income
    d. it is by nature volatile
    e. its level is influenced by the introduction of new technologies

2. Milton Friedman proposed the
    a. permanent income hypothesis
    b. life-cycle hypothesis
    c. absolute income hypothesis
    d. relative income hypothesis
    e. saving equals investment hypothesis

3. At a specific level of national income, saving can be measured by
    a. the MPS multiplied by the level of national income
    b. 1 + MPC multiplied by the level of national income
    c. the vertical distance between the income line and the consumption function
    d. the vertical distance between the consumption function and the saving function
    e. 1 − MPC multiplied by the level of national income

4. The life-cycle hypothesis on consumption behavior suggests that people at various stages of the life cycle,
   a. spend everything they earn so saving ends up at zero
   b. increase their marginal propensity to consume as income increases
   c. decrease their marginal propensity to consume as income increases
   d. have differing MPCs, which is still consistent with a constant MPC for the economy
   e. consume according to class status

5. All of the following are examples of Friedman's transitory income concept **except**
   a. a jockey winning the Triple Crown — the Kentucky Derby, the Preakness, and Belmont — in one year
   b. a $10 million winner of the Texas lottery
   c. a farmer whose crops are wiped out by a drought
   d. a physician experiencing a 20-fold increase in her patient load during a one-year epidemic
   e. David Letterman's $14 million salary at CBS

6. The marginal propensity to save (MPS)
   a. plus the MPC = national income
   b. plus the MPC = one
   c. plus intended investment = one
   d. minus national income = consumption
   e. represents the economy's level of savings

7. One conclusion to be drawn from the Modigliani life-cycle hypothesis is that consumption is
   a. a decreasing function of income for the entire economy
   b. a smaller fraction of income during a person's peak income years
   c. determined by one's class status
   d. very responsive to changes in transitory income
   e. virtually impossible to model because of its volatile nature

8. Because intended investment is independent of the level of national income, we graph the investment curve as
   a. downward sloping
   b. upward sloping
   c. horizontal
   d. vertical
   e. diagonal

9. The change in consumption divided by the change in income is
   a. Keynes's relative income hypothesis
   b. the marginal propensity to consume
   c. equal to a + bY
   d. equal to 1 + MPS
   e. equal to autonomous consumption

10. Keynes's absolute income hypothesis cannot be correct because studies have shown that
    a. as disposable income increases, consumption increases at a diminishing rate
    b. the marginal propensity to consume is constant
    c. rich households save a larger fraction of additional income than poor households
    d. income is never absolute and thus a hypothesis can't be formed
    e. autonomous consumption is zero

EMPLOYMENT, INFLATION AND FISCAL POLICY 375

11. Autonomous consumption refers to
    a. MPCs that are less than one
    b. MPCs that are greater than one
    c. consumption that is independent of the level of income
    d. permanent consumption associated with Friedman's permanent income hypothesis
    e. transitory consumption associated with Friedman's permanent income hypothesis

12. Shifts in the consumption curve are caused by all of the following **except** changes in
    a. asset holdings
    b. income
    c. price level expectations
    d. credit availability
    e. interest rates

13. If the consumption curve is drawn through the origin,
    a. consumption and income are the same
    b. the marginal propensity to consume is zero
    c. autonomous saving is very high
    d. autonomous consumption is zero
    e. the marginal propensity to consume will decrease as income increases

14. If the government increases income taxes, the
    a. intended investment curve shifts upward
    b. consumption curve shifts upward
    c. consumption curve shifts downward
    d. national income decreases because people's after-tax income has fallen
    e. actual investment curve shifts downward

15. When the MPS = 0.30 and autonomous consumption is $30 billion, then
    a. the MPC = 0.30
    b. consumption spending = $10 billion
    c. the MPC = 0.70
    d. consumption spending = $900 billion
    e. the MPC = 1.00

16. When the MPS = 0.30 and autonomous consumption is $30 billion, then the consumption equation is
    a. C = 90 + .3Y
    b. C = 10 + 30Y
    c. C = 0.3 + 30Y
    d. C = 30 + 0.3Y
    e. C = 30 + 0.7Y

17. The demand curve for investment is downward sloping. When it is graphed, it shows _____ on the horizontal axis and _____ on the vertical axis.
    a. income; investment
    b. investment; income
    c. investment; the interest rate
    d. the interest rate; investment
    e. income; the interest rate

18. All of the following are determinants of autonomous investment **except**
    a. interest rates
    b. credit availability
    c. the level of income
    d. changes in the level of income
    e. the pace of technological change

19. One difference between the short-run consumption function and the long-run consumption function is that the short-run consumption function
    a. has its intercept above the origin and the long-run consumption function runs through the origin
    b. runs through the origin and the long-run consumption function has its intercept above the origin
    c. runs through the origin and the long-run consumption is the income line
    d. has its intercept above the origin and the long-run consumption function has its intercept on the national income axis to the right of the origin
    e. has its intercept above the origin and the long-run consumption function has its intercept below the origin

20. If stock market prices increase dramatically so that those who own stock perceive that their wealth has increased, then, *ceteris paribus*
    a. the consumption function shifts downward because saving increases
    b. intended investment increases because it is now more profitable
    c. the saving curve shifts upward
    d. the saving curve is unchanged because only consumption is affected
    e. the consumption function shifts upward

Fill in the Blanks

1. The consumption function is a _____ relationship stating that a(n) _____ in income _____ consumption.

2. Friedman developed the permanent income hypothesis that distinguishes between _____ income and _____ income and states that consumption is dependent on _____ income.

3. Empirical research done by Simon Kuznets showed that contrary to Keynes's _____, the nation's _____ is constant.

4. The consumption function shifts due to changes in _____, _____, _____, and _____.

5. Because changes in investment tend to be unrelated to the level of _____, investment is regarded as _____.

Discussion Questions

1. Suppose that Keynes's absolute income hypothesis had been shown to be correct. What would happen to consumption spending as national income increased in a country? How would producers respond to this change in consumption spending and what would be the likely impact on GDP growth over time?

2. Suppose that your boss gives you a year-end bonus and you count it as transitory income. Suppose that this happens three years in a row. Would you continue to count this income as transitory? Why or why not?

3. Why does Duesenberry's relative income hypothesis predict that the MPC will be constant as national income increases?

4. What is the difference between a shift in the consumption curve and a movement along the consumption curve?

Problems

1. a. Suppose that autonomous consumption is $600 and the marginal propensity to consume is 0.60. Write an algebraic expression for the consumption equation.

   b. Sketch a graph of this consumption curve that corresponds to the consumption equation above. Include the income line in your drawing and label autonomous consumption.

c. Calculate the level of income at which income is equal to consumption, that is, where the consumption curve intersects the income line.

2. a. Using the consumption equation from problem 1, what is the MPS for the corresponding saving curve?

b. At what level of income will saving be zero? (Hint: What is the level of income where consumption is equal to income?) Use this point and the MPS to sketch the saving curve.

Everyday Applications

Duesenberry, Friedman, and Modigliani each presented very different hypotheses to explain consumption spending behavior. Apply each theory to your own family's experience. How well do these economists' ideas describe your family's consumption behavior? Does one theory seem to fit better than the others?

Economics Online

Most of you are entering young adulthood — the stage of the life cycle where people typically accumulate substantial debt. You may be incurring debt with your college education. Buying a home and a new car with borrowed funds are other ways that young adults add to their debt levels. You can generate considerable information about these key life-cycle consumption spending decisions from the Web. Intellichoice (*http://www.intellichoice.com*) is a site that provides dealer prices and ownership costs on many car makes and models. FinancCenter/Smartcalc (*http://www.financenter.com*) will calculate your car and mortgage payments and show you how much you need to save in order to retire. It's never too soon to start planning.

EMPLOYMENT, INFLATION AND FISCAL POLICY

Answers to Questions

Key Terms Quiz

a. 4   f. 5   k. 6
b. 7   g. 8   l. 9
c. 12 h. 1   m. 3
d. 2   i. 14   n. 11
e. 10 j. 13

True-False Questions

1. False. Consumption spending and consumption-production decisions are made independently of each other.
2. True
3. False. The absolute income hypothesis states that as national income increases, consumption increases at a decreasing rate.
4. False. Keynes believed that the marginal propensity to consume decreases as income increases.
5. True
6. False. Duesenberry's relative income hypothesis suggests that the poor have high MPCs and the rich have relatively low MPCs. The economy's MPC is constant, however.
7. False. If all incomes go up at the same rate, relative income is unchanged.
8. True
9. True
10. True
11. False. Consumer purchases of costly durable goods, which are typically financed, will fall, and the consumption curve shifts down.
12. True
13. True
14. True
15. False. Investment is called autonomous because it is unrelated to the level of income.

Multiple-Choice Questions

1. c   6. b   11. c   16. e
2. a   7. b   12. b   17. c
3. c   8. c   13. d   18. c
4. d   9. b   14. c   19. a
5. e   10. b   15. c   20. e

Fill in the Blanks

1. causal; increase; increases
2. permanent; transitory; permanent
3. absolute income hypothesis; MPC
4. real asset and money holdings; expectations of changes in the price level; credit and interest rates; taxes
5. national income; autonomous

Discussion Questions

1. Because Keynes's absolute income hypothesis for consumption spending states that the MPC decreases as national income increases, consumption spending would tend to rise at a rate slower than national income. Producers would probably note unsold goods piling up in their warehouses and would respond by slowing production. GDP growth would likely slow down over time as a result.

2. Probably not. Once income that is initially perceived to be transitory is received in consecutive years, it becomes part of permanent income. Is three years enough? Would you expect to earn a bonus every year? If so, this year-end bonus becomes a part of permanent income.

3. The relative income hypothesis states that the MPC differs between social classes with the poor and middle classes having a higher MPC than upper-class households. However, as national income increases, if everyone's income rises at roughly the same rate, the poor are still poor in relative terms. Therefore they will still have a higher MPC than those who earn higher incomes. On average, for the entire spectrum of social classes, the MPC remains unchanged.

4. A shift in the consumption curve is caused by a change in one or more of the determinants of consumption — real asset and money holdings, expectations of changes in the price level, credit and interest rates, and taxes. Movements along the consumption function are caused by changes in national income. If national income increases, then consumption increases at a rate determined by the marginal propensity to consume — the slope of the consumption function.

Problems

1. a. The consumption equation is $C = 600 + .6Y$.

   b. The graph of this equation is shown below.

EMPLOYMENT, INFLATION AND FISCAL POLICY

c. The consumption curve intersects the income curve at the $1,500 level of national income. This can be calculated by setting consumption equal to national income and solving for Y. We can write $C = 600 + .6Y = Y$. Then, $600 = .4Y$ and $Y = 1,500$.

2. a. Because we know that the MPC + MPS = 1, the MPS must be .4 if the MPC = .6.

   b. Saving will be zero at the $1,500 level of national income. This is because saving is that part of national income not spent on consumption. If consumption is equal to national income, then saving must be zero. The saving curve must run through the point $1,500 on the national income axis. In order to draw the saving curve, we need one more point. We can use the fact that the slope is .4 to find another point. Suppose there is a change in national income equal to $-1,500$. Then, $.4 =$ change in saving$/-1,500$. The change in saving is equal to $.4 \times -1,500 = -600$. When income is zero, saving is -600. A sketch of the saving curve is shown below.

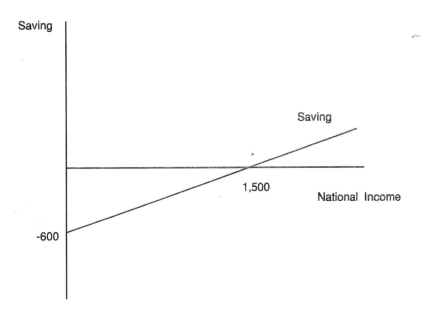

CHAPTER 22

EQUILIBRIUM NATIONAL INCOME

Chapter in a Nutshell

Two very different groups of people are always at work making decisions concerning spending, saving, and investment that affect each other. The income households earn is spent and saved: $Y = C + S$. Producers produce an equivalent value of goods and services in the form of consumption and investment: $Y = C + I$. By definition, $C + I = C + S$. But the I (investment) in this last equation is **actual investment**. It's what producers end up investing, not necessarily what they intended to invest, I_i. Sometimes they end up with more actual investment than they intended (creating **unwanted inventories**) and so cut output. At other times, their actual investment is less than what they intended to produce, and as a result, they increase output. How they respond to their actual investments and why they do it is what this chapter's about.

The total of what people spend on consumption, businesses spend on investment, government spends on its purchases, and foreigners spend on net exports is described as **aggregate expenditures**. Are these expenditures greater than, less than, or equal to the total income earned in the economy? The answer determines whether national income increases, decreases, or is in equilibrium. In any case, if the economy is not in equilibrium, it is always on its way there. Why is this so?

Suppose that consumers spend on consumption an amount less than what producers produced for consumption. Some consumer goods remain unsold as **unwanted inventories**. Actual investment is greater than intended investment. Producers lay off workers, employment declines, and national income declines until it reaches the **equilibrium level of national income** where aggregate expenditures equal national income at a lower level.

Now suppose that consumers spend on consumption an amount greater than what producers produced for consumption. Wanted inventories (investment goods) are converted into consumption goods. Actual investment is less than intended investment. Producers hire more workers to restore their inventories, causing both national income and employment increase. Aggregate expenditures and national income rise toward a higher equilibrium level of national income. Only when producers produce for consumption an amount equal to what consumers purchase for consumption will producers' intended investment be equal to saving by consumers. When producers' intended investment is equal to consumers' saving, the economy is in equilibrium.

Changes in intended investment cause the equilibrium level of national income to change. The relationship between these two changes is explained by the **income multiplier**. An increase in intended investment leads to an increase in income, a fraction of which is consumed (the marginal propensity to consume multiplied by the initial increase in investment) and becomes income for other people. Repeated rounds of income increases and consumption increases occur, with each round being smaller than the previous one. The multiplier, equal to $1/(1 - MPC)$, gives the factor by which the initial round of investment is multiplied into new income. Just as an increase in investment causes a multiple expansion in national income, a decrease in investment will cause a multiple decrease in national income.

The consumers' and producers' behavior that leads the economy to equilibrium also produces a rather surprising consequence known as the **paradox of thrift**. It says: The more people try to save, the more national income will fall, leaving them with no more, and perhaps less, saving in the end. Why? An increase

EMPLOYMENT, INFLATION, AND FISCAL POLICY

in saving is really the same as a decrease in consumption, which is a decrease in aggregate expenditures. It sets in motion a fall in national income to a new and lower level of equilibrium. There, saving is the same or less than it was at the original level of income.

After you study this chapter, you should be able to:

- Explain why consumption spending and **intended investment** spending decisions are independent.
- Define **aggregate expenditure** and graph the **aggregate expenditure curve**.
- Show how changes in inventories move the economy toward an **equilibrium level of national income**.
- Explain the relationship between **saving** and **investment**.
- Create an example to show the logic of the **income multiplier**.
- Illustrate the **paradox of thrift** with a numerical example.

Concept Check — See how you do on these multiple-choice questions.

1. **Aggregate expenditure** is equal to
   a. spending by consumers on consumption goods
   b. spending by businesses on investment goods
   c. spending by government
   d. spending by foreigners on net exports
   e. the sum of a, b, c, and d

Aggregate expenditure measures the total amount of spending in the economy.

2. The **income multiplier** is larger when
   a. the marginal propensity to consume is larger
   b. the marginal propensity to save is larger
   c. spending by government is larger
   d. the change in income is smaller
   e. the marginal propensity to consume is smaller

Under what circumstance does a change in intended investment cause a larger increase in the equilibrium level of national income?

3. An example of the **paradox of thrift** is
   a. consumers who attempt to save more but find they cannot go without basic consumption goods
   b. an increase in saving that leads to a lower equilibrium level of national income and the same or lower saving
   c. a high marginal propensity to save that is matched by a high marginal propensity to consume
   d. an increase in saving that leads to more investment, higher income, and higher consumption
   e. an increase in interest rates that leads to lower investment and lower saving

What is the impact of an increase in saving on the equilibrium level of national income?

4. If the level of national income is above the **equilibrium level of national income**, then
   a. autonomous consumption will fall and the economy will move toward equilibrium
   b. inventories will accumulate and production will fall, moving the economy toward equilibrium
   c. intended investment is equal to saving
   d. consumption spending is greater than the value of consumption goods produced
   e. the marginal propensity to save is too low to achieve equilibrium

The economy moves automatically toward equilibrium. Will national income rise or fall to move toward equilibrium in this case? How does it happen?

5. When **actual investment** is equal to intended investment,
   a. saving is zero
   b. unwanted inventories are increasing
   c. unwanted inventories are decreasing
   d. unwanted inventories are zero
   e. the economy is below the equilibrium level of national income

When do unwanted inventories become part of actual investment? When does the decrease in wanted inventories decrease actual investment?

Am I on the Right Track?

Your answers to the questions above should be **e, a, b, b,** and **d**. The consumption spending decisions by consumers and the production decisions by producers will match each other only by accident. Therefore, the level of national income that is produced is unlikely to be the equilibrium level of national income. If consumption spending is less than the production of consumption goods, unwanted inventories accumulate, production decreases, and national income declines toward its equilibrium level. If consumption spending is greater than the production of consumption goods, wanted inventories are converted to consumption goods, production increases, and national income rises toward its equilibrium level. The mechanics of these adjustments toward equilibrium will be explored in the graphing tutorial.

Key Terms Quiz — Match the terms on the left with the definitions in the column on the right.

1. aggregate expenditure _____ a. goods produced for consumption that remain unsold
2. aggregate expenditure (AE) curve _____ b. the more people try to save, the more income falls, leaving them with no more, and perhaps with even less, saving
3. equilibrium level of national income _____ c. the multiple by which income changes as a result of a change in aggregate expenditure
4. income multiplier _____ d. spending by consumers on consumption goods, by businesses on investment goods, by government, and by foreigners on net exports
5. unwanted inventories _____ e. a curve that shows the quantity of aggregate expenditures at different levels of national income or GDP
6. paradox of thrift _____ f. investment spending that producers actually make — that is, intended investment plus or minus unintended changes in inventories
7. actual investment _____ g. the level of national income where saving is equal to intended investment

EMPLOYMENT, INFLATION, AND FISCAL POLICY 385

Graphing Tutorial

This chapter presents a new graph that combines the consumption curve and the investment curve to show the equilibrium level of national income. Let's continue with the example presented in the graphing tutorial for Chapter 21 of the study guide to examine how the consumption curve and the investment curve are used to generate the aggregate expenditure curve in order to graph the equilibrium level of national income.

The consumption equation from the previous graphing tutorial is $C = 100 + .75Y$, and autonomous investment is $I_i = 75$. Autonomous investment is intended investment. These two equations are presented as curves along with the income line (45-degree line) in the graph below.

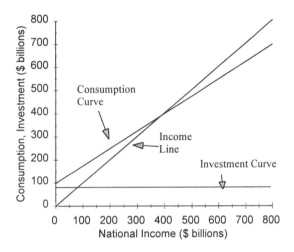

The aggregate expenditure curve can be drawn by adding the investment curve to the consumption curve. This will shift the consumption curve up by a constant $75 billion in the graph. The graph below shows the consumption curve and the aggregate expenditure curve that lies above and parallel to the consumption curve.

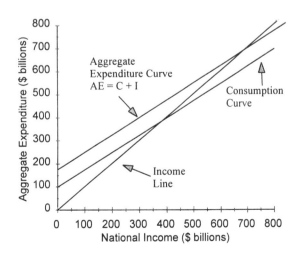

How do we locate the equilibrium level of national income in this diagram? We have defined the equilibrium level of national income as the level where $I_i = S$. In the graph, $C + I_i$ is the aggregate expenditure curve and $C + S$ is the income curve. Aggregate expenditure is equal to income where the two curves intersect at the $700 billion level of national income, so this is the equilibrium level of national income. At $700 billion, $I_i = S$.

Let's check our graph by calculating the equilibrium level of national income algebraically.

$$\begin{aligned} \text{In equilibrium} \quad & Y = C + I_i \\ \text{and} \quad & C = 100 + .75Y \\ \text{and} \quad & I_i = 75 \\ \text{then} \quad & Y = (100 + .75Y) + 75. \end{aligned}$$

Subtracting $.75Y$ from both sides of the equation and combining the constant terms gives us

$$.25Y = 175.$$

Finally, dividing both sides by .25 reduces the equation to

$$Y = 700.$$

This confirms our graph — the equilibrium level of national income is $700 billion.

What if we start at a level of national income other than the equilibrium level of national income? After all, it would be a chance event for the economy to automatically start out in equilibrium. How can we show the adjustment toward the equilibrium level of national income on the aggregate expenditure, national income graph? Consider the graph below, which shows just the aggregate expenditure curve and the income line.

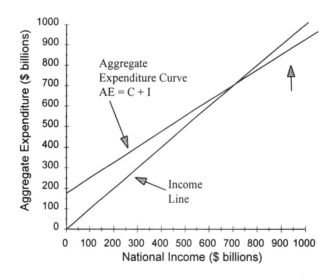

EMPLOYMENT, INFLATION, AND FISCAL POLICY

Suppose we start at a level of national income below the equilibrium, say, at $500 billion. The aggregate expenditure curve is above the income curve at $500 billion. Aggregate expenditure is greater than income so inventories decline. Wanted inventories are converted to consumer goods. Let's check our interpretation of the graph algebraically. Aggregate expenditure equals $C + I_i = 175 + .75Y = 175 + .75(500) = $550 billion. Aggregate expenditure exceeds national income by $50 billion. Therefore, producers increase output to restore their inventories, so employment and national income both increase as the economy moves toward the $700 billion level.

Suppose we start at a level of national income above the equilibrium, say, at $900 billion. The aggregate expenditure curve is below the income curve at $900 billion. Aggregate expenditure is less than national income so unwanted inventories accumulate. Checking our interpretation of the graph algebraically, we have $AE = 175 + .75Y = 175 + .75(900) = 850$. Now aggregate expenditure falls short of national income by $50 billion. Therefore, producers reduce output to rid themselves of unwanted inventories, so both employment and national income decrease as the economy moves toward the $700 billion level.

Graphing Pitfalls

When you add the investment curve to the consumption curve in order to draw the aggregate expenditure curve, make sure the aggregate expenditure curve is parallel to the consumption curve. Otherwise, you'll end up with the wrong equilibrium level of national income. It is tempting, perhaps, to draw the aggregate expenditure curve through the intersection of the consumption curve and the income curve, as depicted in the graph below. Don't make this mistake. Check to make sure that the consumption curve and the aggregate expenditure curve are parallel with the vertical distance between them equal to the amount of autonomous investment.

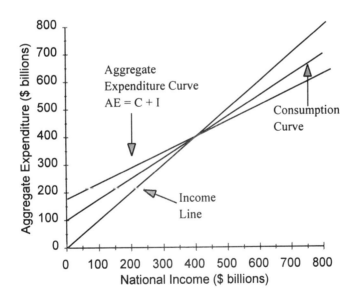

The aggregate expenditure curve should be parallel to and above the consumption curve by a vertical distance equal to autonomous investment.
The two curves should not intersect, as drawn above.

CHAPTER 22 EQUILIBRIUM NATIONAL INCOME

True-False Questions — If a statement is false, explain why.

1. The amount that people intend to save will automatically equal the amount that investors intend to invest. (T/F)

2. Actual investment exceeds intended investment when inventories accumulate. (T/F)

3. If inventories are less than intended (or wanted) inventories, then production, employment, and national income will increase. (T/F)

4. Assuming there is no government spending and no foreign trade, then aggregate expenditure is equal to consumption plus saving. (T/F)

5. Spending by consumers on consumption goods is equal to consumption goods production at the equilibrium level of national income. (T/F)

6. When autonomous investment increases by $100, national income will increase by $100. (T/F)

7. A decrease in autonomous investment will have a smaller effect on national income than an equal increase in autonomous investment. (T/F)

8. The paradox of thrift states that if everyone decided to save more, consumption spending would fall, which would decrease national income, and with less income, people would end up saving no more than they did before. (T/F)

9. If the marginal propensity to consume increases, the income multiplier decreases. (T/F)

10. A decrease in the price level along an aggregate demand curve is reflected by an upward shift in the aggregate expenditure curve. (T/F)

11. Intended investment equal to saving is a signal for firms to reduce their inventories. (T/F)

12. An upward shift in the aggregate expenditure curve, caused by an increase in autonomous investment, appears as a rightward shift in the aggregate demand curve. (T/F)

13. The multiplier effect of an increase in investment is a new round of spending equal to the new investment followed by successive rounds of increased income with each one larger than the preceding round. (T/F)

EMPLOYMENT, INFLATION, AND FISCAL POLICY   389

13. The multiplier effect of an increase in investment is a new round of spending equal to the new investment followed by successive rounds of increased income with each one larger than the preceding round. (T/F)

14. The multiplier is the reciprocal of the marginal propensity to consume. (T/F)

15. J. M. Keynes believed that aggregate supply was more important than aggregate demand in determining the equilibrium level of national income. (T/F)

Multiple-Choice Questions

1. If actual investment is greater than intended investment, then
   a. the economy is in equilibrium
   b. national income must rise
   c. inventory investment is negative
   d. consumers are purchasing fewer goods and services than are produced
   e. unemployment will decrease

2. In the aggregate expenditure model of equilibrium national income determination,
   a. aggregate supply is vertical
   b. aggregate demand increases as the price level decreases
   c. the price level is assumed to be constant
   d. investment is a function of income
   e. the economy may move away from the equilibrium level of national income

3. If you read in the paper that intended investment hasn't changed but inventories are accumulating, then it is likely that
   a. the economy is about to experience a period of rapid growth
   b. the price level will rise dramatically
   c. the economy will experience a drop in production, employment, and income
   d. the economy will experience a rise in productivity
   e. intended investment will change

4. The income multiplier means that changes in autonomous investment will lead to
   a. a quick end to recessions
   b. even larger changes in national income
   c. a larger marginal propensity to consume
   d. a larger marginal propensity to save
   e. lower autonomous consumption

5. Suppose that the consumption equation is C = $50 + 0.75Y and I = $200. The equilibrium level of national income is
   a. $10,000
   b. $1,000
   c. $100
   d. $750
   e. $333.33

6. Using the information given in question 5, if the level of national income is actually $1,200, then
   a. inventories will accumulate and production and income will fall
   b. inventories will accumulate and production and income will rise
   c. inventories will decline and production and income will rise
   d. inventories will decline and production and income will fall
   e. the economy will adjust to a new equilibrium

7. The graph below shows that if national income equals $800,
   a. inventories will decline and national income will increase
   b. inventories will decline and national income will decrease
   c. inventories will increase and national income will decrease
   d. inventories will increase and national income will increase
   e. intended investment and savings are equal

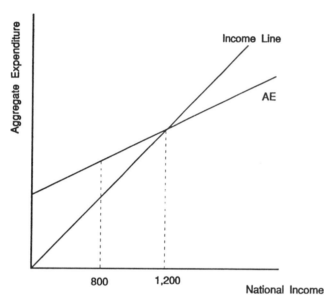

8. An increase in autonomous investment will
   a. lead to an equal increase in national income
   b. lead to an even larger increase in national income
   c. cause the marginal propensity to save to fall
   d. cause saving to decrease due to the increase in borrowing in the economy
   e. lead to an equivalent decrease in aggregate expenditures

9. Given a marginal propensity to consume of 0.90, an increase in investment spending equal to $100 will lead to a(n)
   a. decrease in national income of $1,000
   b. increase in national income of $1,000
   c. increase in national income of $100
   d. increase in national income of $900
   e. decrease in national income of $900

EMPLOYMENT, INFLATION, AND FISCAL POLICY

10. The basic idea behind the paradox of thrift is that
    a. by saving more people end up with higher incomes in the future
    b. it takes money to make money
    c. an increase in saving decreases national income so much that saving is, at best, unchanged
    d. it is impossible for savers to increase saving because somebody will always increase spending by an equivalent amount
    e. saving only benefits producers who invest, not the actual savers

11. If unwanted inventories cause a decrease in prices instead of in national income, then we can expect
    a. no increase in unemployment
    b. savings to rise faster than consumption
    c. a change in the equilibrium level of national income
    d. the income multiplier to work in reverse
    e. intended investment to increase

12. When consumption goods production is $2,400 billion and consumers purchase $2,000 billion of consumer goods, it is clear that
    a. not enough consumer goods are being produced
    b. to move toward equilibrium, national income must increae
    c. actual investment will be equal to intended investment
    d. the economy is in equilibrium
    e. actual investment will be higher than intended investment

13. The main reason why changes in the equilibrium level of national income should be expected is that
    a. consumption changes frequently
    b. saving changes frequently
    c. investment is fairly volatile
    d. the multiplier is quite large
    e. the rounds of spending in the multiplier keep increasing

14. If autonomous investment decreases by $200 billion and the marginal propensity to consume is 0.75, then national income will
    a. rise by $200 billion
    b. fall by $200 billion
    c. fall by $267 billion
    d. rise by $267 billion
    e. fall by $800 billion

15. An increase in the marginal propensity to save from 0.20 to 0.50 means that
    a. the marginal propensity to consume falls from 0.80 to 0.50
    b. less is saved at every level of national income
    c. more is consumed at every level of national income
    d. the marginal propensity to consume increases as well from 0.20 to 0.50
    e. intended investment increases by 30 percent

16. The "paradox" in the paradox of thrift is that as people try to save more
    a. aggregate expenditures increase
    b. national income increases
    c. investment increases
    d. income decreases and saving doesn't increase
    e. income increases and saving doesn't increase

17. The effect of an increase in the price level on the position of the aggregate expenditure curve is to
    a. shift the curve up parallel to the original curve
    b. shift the curve down parallel to the original curve
    c. increase the slope of the curve
    d. decrease the slope of the curve
    e. shift the curve down and decrease the slope of the curve

18. The equilibrium level of national income will not be reached automatically by pure chance because
    a. firms typically produce excessively so unwanted inventories accumulate
    b. firms typically produce less than is needed satisfy demand so wanted inventories are consumed
    c. the consumption goods production decisions by firms are unlikely to match the consumption spending decisions by households
    d. the price level cannot adjust to equate the quantity supplied and the quantity demanded
    e. autonomous investment is volatile

19. When the income multiplier works in reverse (is negative),
    a. the change in investment must have been negative
    b. the marginal propensity to consume must have fallen
    c. the marginal propensity to save must have fallen
    d. the consumption curve must have risen
    e. employment must increase

20. If the level of consumption equals the level of national income,
    a. the economy is in equilibrium
    b. autonomous consumption must be zero
    c. aggregate expenditure is equal to intended investment
    d. saving is zero
    e. saving equals consumption

Fill in the Blanks

1. If consumers purchase just as much as producers produce for consumption, then the _____ that producers intend to make will equal the _____ consumers make.

2. If wanted inventories are converted into consumption goods, then producers will increase _____ and _____ to replenish their inventory stock.

3. J. M. Keynes believed that _____ was primarily responsible for determining the equilibrium level of national income.

4. Actual investment is equal to intended investment plus or minus _____ in inventories.

EMPLOYMENT, INFLATION, AND FISCAL POLICY

Discussion Questions

1. What is the difference between actual and intended investment?

2. Why doesn't an increase in aggregate expenditures cause the price level to increase in the aggregate expenditure model of equilibrium national income determination?

3. Explain the logic of the multiplier.

4. Do Keynesian economists think that saving is a bad thing?

Problems

1. a. Suppose that the consumption function is $C = 80 + .8Y$ and the income level is $1,400 billion. Calculate what consumers intend to consume and save at this income level.

b. Continue with the information in part a. Now suppose that at an income level of $1,400 billion producers intend to produce $1,300 billion of consumption and intend to invest $100 billion. Is the economy in equilibrium? Explain, using a graph to aid discussion.

c. If this economy is not in equilibrium, what would the equilibrium level of national income be, assuming that intended investment remains at $100 billion? How does the economy adjust to the new equilibrium?

2. Suppose an economy is described by the following equations: $C = \$100 + 0.75Y$ and $I = \$300$.

   a. Calculate the equilibrium level of income.

   b. Graph the aggregate expenditures curve and the 45-degree line.

c. Suppose saving increases by $50 at every level of national income. How would the aggregate expenditures curve you drew be affected? Explain. Calculate the new equilibrium level of national income.

d. Calculate the level of saving at the original equilibrium and at the new equilibrium. Does this example demonstrate the paradox of thrift? Explain.

3. Illustrate the original equilibrium level of national income and the change in the equilibrium level of national income due to the increase in saving from problem 2 above using the saving and investment graph. Explain your graph carefully.

Everyday Applications

Have you worked in a business where inventory management was a key part of the job? Even if you have not, you can imagine the sequence of events once inventories build up to unwanted levels or fall to levels below those that are desired. When inventories begin to pile up, the inventory manager calls the producers telling them to stop sending so much. What else could happen but a cut in production? It's just the opposite when inventories are drawn down. The manager gets on the phone, says send us some more, and production, employment, and income all rise.

Economics Online

The Bureau of Economic Analysis, an agency of the U. S. Department of Commerce, is the nation's economic accountant. The agency prepares estimates of future levels of key economic variables. Visit its Web site (*http://www.bea.doc.gov/*) to learn more about how the agency makes estimates for key regional, national, and international economic variables.

Answers to Questions

Key Terms Quiz

a. 5
b. 6
c. 4
d. 1
e. 2
f. 7
g. 3

True-False Questions

1. False. Only by accident will intended investment be equal to saving because different groups make investment and saving decisions independent of each other.
2. True
3. True

EMPLOYMENT, INFLATION, AND FISCAL POLICY

3. True
4. False. Aggregate expenditure is equal to consumption plus intended investment.
5. True
6. False. An increase in autonomous investment causes national income to increase by a multiple of that amount.
7. False. Changes in autonomous investment that are equal in magnitude will have equal and opposite effects on the equilibrium level of national income.
8. True
9. False. As the marginal propensity to consume increases, so does the income multiplier.
10. True
11. False. If intended investment is equal to saving, then the economy is at the equilibrium level of national income, and there are no unwanted inventories.
12. True
13. False. The multiplier effect of an increase in investment is an initial increase in income equal to the increase in investment followed by successive increases in spending and income that diminish in each round.
14. False. The income multiplier is equal to 1/(1 − MPC).
15. False. Keynes believed that aggregate expenditure was more important than aggregate supply as a determinant of the equilibrium level of national income.

Multiple-Choice Questions

1. d	6. a	11. a	16. d
2. c	7. a	12. e	17. b
3. c	8. b	13. c	18. c
4. b	9. b	14. e	19. a
5. b	10. c	15. a	20. d

Fill in the Blanks

1. investment; saving
2. production; employment
3. aggregate expenditure
4. unintended changes

Discussion Questions

1. Intended investment includes the purchases of new plant and equipment and inventories that businesses plan to make. Intended investment is the same as autonomous investment. Actual investment includes unintended changes in inventories. For example, if consumers don't purchase all of the consumption goods that producers produce, there will be unintended inventory investment. On the other hand, if consumers purchase more consumption goods than producers produce, wanted inventories will be turned into consumption goods. Investment in inventories will be less than was intended.

2. The price level is assumed to be constant in the aggregate expenditure model for national income determination. An increase in aggregate expenditure causes output to increase via the income multiplier. The model assumes implicitly that output can increase without increases in the price level, meaning that ample supplies of resources are available to use for increased production.

3. The logic behind the multiplier is that an increase in autonomous expenditure becomes income for people,

who then spend a fraction of the increase as determined by the marginal propensity to consume. In turn, this increase in consumption becomes income for another group of consumers who spend a fraction of the increase. These rounds of spending go on and on, with each successive round becoming smaller. The multiplier process can also work in reverse, starting with a decrease in autonomous expenditure.

4. Keynesian economists don't believe that saving is a bad thing. Increased saving accompanied by increased investment is good and necessary because this is how society accumulates more capital to promote economic growth. The problems with saving arise when an increase in saving is not coupled with an increase in intended investment. Under such circumstances, the paradox of thrift is observed, national income declines, and at the new equilibrium, saving may be no more or even less than it was originally.

Problems

1. a. Consumers intend to consume $1,200 billion and save $200 billion.

   b. This economy is not in equilibrium because $100 billion of unwanted inventories will accumulate. As shown in the graph below, at an income level of $1,400 billion, aggregate expenditure falls short of national income. Consumer spending is $1,200 billion and investment spending is $100 billion. Unwanted inventories accumulate in the amount of $100 billion.

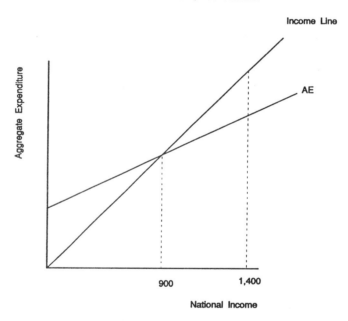

   c. The equilibrium is $900 billion. Aggregate expenditure is equal to $C + I_i = (80 + .8Y) + 100$. Solving for the equilibrium level of national income, we have $Y = 180 + .8Y$, which gives $Y = 900$. The economy adjusts to $Y = 900$ because inventories increase at the $1,400 level, causing firms to cut production and employment so that income falls to the $900 billion level.

2. a. The equilibrium level of income is calculated by setting $Y = (\$100 + 0.75Y) + \$300$ and solving for Y. The equation reduces to $Y = 400 + .75Y$. This becomes $.25Y = 400$, so $Y = \$1,600$.

b.

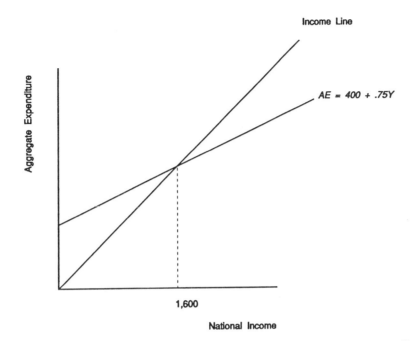

c. An increase in saving is represented by a downward shift in the aggregate expenditures curve by $50. The equilibrium level of income decreases to $1,400. These changes are shown in the graph. Aggregate expenditures falls from $AE = 400 + .75Y$ to $AE' = 350 + .75Y$, and the equilibrium level of income falls to $1,400 showing the multiplier effect. These changes appear in the graph below.

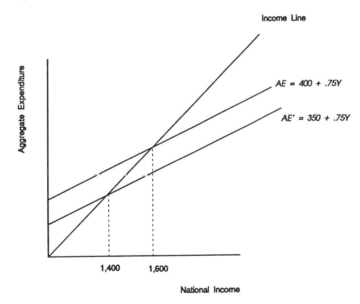

d. When $Y = 1,600$, $C = 100 + .75(1,600) = 1,300$. $S = Y - C = 1,600 - 1,300 = \$300$.
When $Y = 1,400$, $C = 50 + .75(1,400) = 1,100$. $S = Y - C = 1,400 - 1,100 = \$300$. Even though saving increased at the $1,600 level, the income multiplier caused national income to fall by $200 to $1,400, and the level of saving at this income level was the same as at the $1,600 level. This shows the paradox of thrift.

3. The saving and investment graph that corresponds to problem 2 is shown below. Because autonomous consumption is $100, we know that the vertical intercept for the saving curve is −$100. The saving curve, labeled S, intersects the investment curve at the $1,600 level of national income. Both saving and investment are equal to $300 in equilibrium. An increase in saving equal to $50 shifts the saving curve up by $50 parallel to the original curve. The new saving curve is labeled S'. At the $1,600 level of national income, saving is greater than investment on S'. Therefore, unwanted inventories accumulate, production decreases, employment decreases, and national income decreases along S' until the new equilibrium level of national income is achieved at $1,400. S = I = $300 at the new equilibrium, illustrating the paradox of thrift.

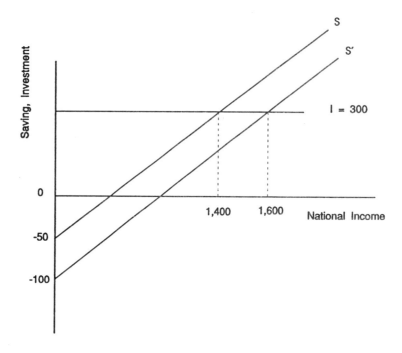

CHAPTER 23

FISCAL POLICY: COPING WITH INFLATION AND UNEMPLOYMENT

Chapter in a Nutshell

To say that an economy is in equilibrium tells us very little about the general state of the economy. The model showing the equilibrium level of national income presented in Chapter 22 allows for an economy to be in equilibrium at high levels of unemployment. Some of the unemployment is caused by insufficient aggregate expenditures. But unemployment can have other causes. Economists identify five types: **frictional unemployment**, **structural unemployment**, **cyclical unemployment**, **discouraged workers**, and the **underemployed**.

The Bureau of Labor Statistics (BLS), which establishes the official unemployment count and rate of unemployment for the economy, calculates the rate of unemployment by surveying households. Those who are either working or seeking employment are counted as being in the **labor force**. That excludes discouraged workers. The unemployment rate is the number of people who are not working but are seeking work, divided by the labor force. That excludes underemployed workers. The BLS defines this rate as the actual rate of unemployment.

Economists distinguish between the **actual rate of unemployment** and the **natural rate of unemployment**. The natural rate of unemployment consists of workers who are frictionally and structurally unemployed. It is "natural" and the result of positive dynamic forces in the economy — people looking for better jobs and technological change occurring — so the natural rate is not at all worrisome. What remains is cyclical unemployment. To economists, the economy is at **full employment** when the actual rate of unemployment is equal to the natural rate of unemployment. In other words, the economy is at full employment when cyclical unemployment is zero.

When inflation occurs, some groups of people are harmed while others benefit. Those who are hurt by inflation include people living on fixed incomes, such as landlords and savers. Those who gain from inflation include borrowers and, to some extent, the government. The government benefits from inflation when it borrows. Unions bargain for cost-of-living allowances in their wage contracts to protect themselves from the erosion of real wages.

What's the relationship between the full-employment level of national income and the equilibrium level? A **recessionary gap** exists when the equilibrium level of national income falls below the full-employment level. The amount by which spending must increase in order to achieve full employment defines the recessionary gap. An **inflationary gap** exists when the equilibrium level of national income is above the full-employment level. The inflationary gap defines the amount by which spending must decrease in order to achieve full employment without inflation.

Fiscal policy involves the government not only increasing or decreasing its spending, but also increasing or decreasing its tax take. Just as an increase in government spending creates a multiple increase in national income, an increase in taxes creates a multiple decrease in national income. The **tax multiplier** is $-MPC/(1 - MPC)$. When the government increases its spending and taxes by the same amount, both the income and tax multipliers are at work. The net effect is an increase in national income that equals the increase in spending and taxes. The **balanced budget multiplier** equals one. The government can create a **balanced budget** where $G = T$, a **surplus budget** where $T > G$, or a **deficit budget** where $G > T$.

CHAPTER 23   FISCAL POLICY

After you study this chapter, you should be able to:

- Describe the different types of unemployment.
- Calculate the **unemployment rate**, given the appropriate data.
- Explain the meaning of the **natural rate of unemployment**.
- Identify winners and losers from inflation.
- Understand **recessionary gaps** and **inflationary gaps** in the aggregate expenditure model.
- Show how **recessionary** and **inflationary gaps** can be closed using **fiscal policy**.
- Derive the **tax multiplier** and the **balanced budget multiplier**.

✓

Concept Check — See how you do on these multiple-choice questions.

1. **Cyclical unemployment** refers to workers who are unemployed because
    a. they have left one job to look for a better one
    b. of technological changes in production
    c. they are close to the retirement phase of the life cycle and no one will hire them
    d. new goods have been substituted for the goods they were trained to produce
    e. the economy is in a recession phase

When the rate of cyclical unemployment is zero, the economy is at full employment.

2. The **natural rate of unemployment** is equal to
    a. discouraged workers plus underemployed workers
    b. frictional plus structural unemployment
    c. cyclical plus structural unemployment
    d. cyclical plus frictional unemployment
    e. structural unemployment plus underemployed workers

Some unemployment is the natural result of dynamic forces in the economy.

3. A **recessionary gap** exists when
    a. structural unemployment is excessive
    b. frictional unemployment is excessive
    c. aggregate expenditure falls short of that needed to generate full employment
    d. aggregate supply falls short of that needed to generate full employment
    e. supply creates its own demand

A recession results when there is insufficient aggregate expenditure in the economy.

4. An appropriate **fiscal policy** to close a **recessionary gap** is to
    a. increase government spending
    b. decrease taxes
    c. decrease government spending
    d. increase taxes
    e. a and b are both appropriate policies

Aggregate expenditure must increase to close a recessionary gap.

EMPLOYMENT, INFLATION, AND FISCAL POLICY 403

5. Compared to the income multiplier, the **tax multiplier**
   a. causes a weaker income magnification
   b. is better for closing a recessionary gap
   c. is better for closing an inflationary gap
   d. causes a stronger income magnification
   e. causes an equal income magnification.

Suppose that taxes are decreased. Do households spend the full amount of the tax cut?

Am I on the Right Track?

Your answers to the questions above should be **e, b, c, e**, and **a**. Along with learning about the different types of unemployment and the impact of inflation on different groups in the economy, you need to be able to use a graph to distinguish between recessionary and inflationary gaps. A recessionary gap occurs when aggregate expenditure is insufficient to generate a full-employment level of GDP. An inflationary gap results when aggregate expenditure is more than is needed to generate a full-employment level of GDP. A variety of fiscal policy options exists to close both gaps.

Key Terms Quiz — Match the terms on the left with the definitions in the column on the right.

1. frictional unemployment
2. recessionary gap
3. structural unemployment
4. inflationary gap
5. cyclical unemployment
6. fiscal policy
7. discouraged workers
8. balanced budget
9. underemployed workers
10. tax multiplier
11. labor force
12. balanced budget multiplier
13. natural rate of unemployment

__9__ a. workers employed in jobs that do not utilize their productive talents or experience
__13__ b. an employment level at which the actual rate of unemployment is equal to the economy's natural rate of unemployment
__3__ c. unemployment that results from technological changes in production, or from the substitution of new goods for customary ones
__8__ d. government spending equals tax revenues
__11__ e. people who are gainfully employed or actively seeking employment
__1__ f. brief periods of unemployment caused by people who quit work to seek more attractive employment
__6__ g. government spending and taxation policy to achieve macroeconomic goals of full employment without inflation
__12__ h. the effect on the equilibrium level of national income of an equal change in government spending and taxes
__4__ i. the amount by which aggregate expenditure exceeds the aggregate expenditure level needed to generate equilibrium national income at full employment without inflation
__5__ j. unemployment associated with the downturn and recession phases of the business cycle
__10__ k. the multiple by which the equilibrium level of national income changes when a dollar change in taxes occurs
__13__ l. the rate of unemployment caused by frictional plus structural unemployment
__2__ m. the amount by which aggregate expenditure falls short of the level needed to generate equilibrium national income at full employment without inflation

14. budget deficit __16__ n. tax revenues exceed government spending
15. full employment __17__ o. unemployed people who give up looking for work after repeated failures trying to find work
16. budget surplus __14__ p. government spending exceeds tax revenues

Graphing Tutorial

This chapter uses the model of equilibrium national income presented in Chapter 22 to show recessionary gaps and inflationary gaps and the ways they can be closed with fiscal policy. Suppose we have an economy that is in equilibrium at a national income equal to $1,600 billion and the full-employment level of national income is $2,000 billion. The graph below represents the situation.

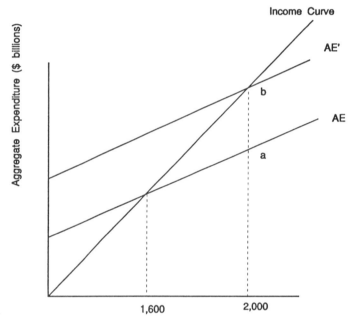

The vertical distance between the aggregate expenditure curves *AE* and *AE'* labeled *ab* defines the recessionary gap. It can be closed with a variety of fiscal policy options. Suppose that we choose to close the gap with an increase in government spending. Assuming the marginal propensity to consume is .75, the income multiplier is $1/(1 - MPC) = 1/(1 - .75) = 4$. We know that $\Delta Y = 4\Delta G$. National income must increase by $400 billion. So, $400 = 4\Delta G$, and $\Delta G = \$100$ billion. An increase in government spending equal to $100 billion will close the recessionary gap.

To illustrate an inflationary gap, suppose that the equilibrium level of national income is $2,400 billion and the full-employment level of national income is $2,000 billion. This situation is shown in the graph on the following page.

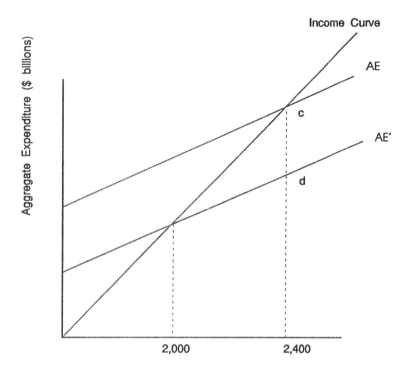

In this case, aggregate expenditure exceeds the amount necessary to achieve a full-employment level of national income. The vertical distance between *AE* and *AE'* labeled *cd* defines the inflationary gap — the amount by which aggregate expenditure must decrease to achieve the full employment level of national income. Suppose that we choose to close the inflationary gap with a tax increase and the *MPC* = .75. We know that the tax multiplier is $-MPC/(1 - MPC) = -.75/(1 - MPC) = -3$. Therefore, $\Delta Y = -3\Delta T$, and national income must decrease by $400 billion. So, $-\$400 = -3\Delta T$ and $\Delta T = \$133.33$ billion. A tax increase equal to $133.33 billion will shift the aggregate expenditure curve downward to achieve the full-employment level of national income.

Graphing Pitfalls

Closing a recessionary gap with an increase in government spending, a decrease in taxes, or some combination of the two results in an upward shift of the aggregate expenditure curve parallel to the original curve so that it intersects the income curve at the full-employment level of national income. Both the increase in government spending and the increase in consumption spending due to a tax cut compensate for a shortfall in autonomous investment that prevented the economy from reaching the full-employment level. You may think of the increase in government spending as public investment. In the context of our model, the impact of increased government spending is the same as an increase in autonomous investment — an upward shift of the aggregate expenditure curve parallel to the old curve. So don't make the mistake of rotating the aggregate expenditure curve upward so that its slope becomes steeper as shown in the graph on the following page. Remember, the marginal propensity to consume is the slope of the aggregate expenditure curve, and an increase in government spending (or a decrease in taxes of the kind discussed in your text) does not change the MPC.

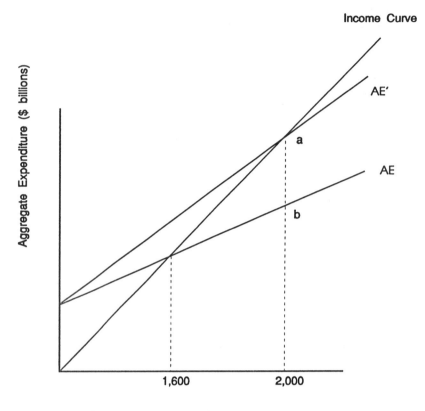

When a recessionary gap is closed with an increase in government spending, a cut in taxes, or some combination of the two, the aggregate expenditure curve shifts upward parallel to the original curve. It doesn't rotate upward as shown in this graph.

True-False Questions — If a statement is false, explain why.

1. Keynesians believe that the economy naturally moves toward equilibrium at full employment. (T/F)

2. The reason the economy may be at an equilibrium below full employment is that wages and prices are inflexible. (T/F)

3. The upward-sloping segment of the aggregate supply curve shows that increases in real GDP can only occur with increases in the price level. (T/F)

4. An inflationary gap can be closed by cutting taxes. (T/F)

5. The actual rate of unemployment is equal to the natural rate of unemployment when the rate cyclical unemployment is zero. (T/F)

6. According to Keynesians, reducing the budget deficit closes a recessionary gap, while increasing the budget deficit closes an inflationary gap. (T/F)

7. Structural unemployment is included in the natural rate of unemployment. (T/F)

8. Discouraged workers are not counted in the natural rate of unemployment but are included in the actual rate of unemployment. (T/F)

9. Banks that provide loans to businesses and individuals are losers during periods of high inflation. (T/F)

10. People living on a fixed income, such as retirees, are harmed by inflation. (T/F)

11. The tax multiplier is larger than the income multiplier. (T/F)

12. According to Keynesians, an increase in government spending generates an increase in national income equal to that created by an increase in private investment of the same magnitude. (T/F)

13. Closing a recessionary gap using deficit financing requires less government spending than financing the closing with a balanced budget. (T/F)

14. A deficit budget results when tax revenues are greater than the government's spending. (T/F)

15. One drawback to using budget deficits created by increased government spending to close recessionary gaps is that once government spending is introduced, it is hard to reduce. (T/F)

Multiple-Choice Questions

1. The economy is considered to be at full employment when the rate of _____ is zero.
   a. cyclical unemployment
   b. seasonal unemployment
   c. frictional unemployment
   d. structural unemployment
   e. discouraged workers

2. When a balanced budget increases by $120 billion, national income increases by
   a. $60 billion
   b. $120 billion ✓
   c. $240 billion
   d. $600 billion
   e. national income does not increase

3. Frictional unemployment can be the result of
   a. a change in the technology of production
   b. a recession
   c. people quitting one job to look for a better one ✓
   d. a decrease in government spending
   e. friction in the workplace between workers and their employers

4. The type of unemployment associated with technological displacement of labor is
   a. cyclical
   b. structural ✓
   c. frictional
   d. discouraged workers
   e. underemployed workers

5. When the economy is in equilibrium at a point on the vertical segment of the aggregate supply curve, an increase in government spending will
   a. cause a dramatic increase in national income
   b. cause the price level to increase with no change in national income ✓
   c. close a recessionary gap
   d. decrease the budget deficit
   e. be followed by an increase in taxes

6. All of the following groups tend to be harmed by inflation **except**
   a. retirees
   b. minimum wage workers
   c. landlords
   d. lenders
   e. renters ✓

7. The type of unemployment that fiscal policy is best suited to control is
   a. natural
   b. structural
   c. discouraged
   d. cyclical ✓
   e. frictional

8. According to the Bureau of Labor Statistics (BLS), all of the following make up the labor force **except**
   a. discouraged workers ✓
   b. underemployed workers
   c. frictionally unemployed workers
   d. cyclically unemployed workers
   e. structurally unemployed workers

EMPLOYMENT, INFLATION, AND FISCAL POLICY

9. People who are on fixed incomes are adversely affected by inflation because
   a. their incomes buy fewer goods and services
   b. while their income may increase with inflation, it increases at a lower rate than the rate of inflation
   c. they typically have large outstanding debts like a mortgage
   d. the minimum wage that they receive does not increase
   e. they are unable to pick cheaper goods and services to buy as they did before the inflation

10. Assuming that the government starts with a balanced budget, a subsequent $100 billion deficit results from a(n)
    a. increase in G by $140 billion and an increase in T by $40 billion
    b. increase in G by $140 billion and an increase in T by $140 billion
    c. decrease in G by $140 billion and an increase in T by $40 billion
    d. decrease in G by $140 billion and a decrease in T by $140 billion
    e. decrease in G by $40 billion and an increase in T by $100 billion

11. Suppose national income is $2,000 billion and the full-employment level is $2,400 billion. Given a marginal propensity to consume equal to 0.80, the amount by which taxes must change in order to reach full employment is
    a. $80 billion
    b. -$80 billion
    c. -$400 billion
    d. $100 billion
    e. -$100 billion

12. Given the same information as in question 11, full employment can be reached by which of the following changes in government spending and taxes?
    a. increase G by $240 billion and decrease T by $200 billion
    b. decrease G by $240 billion and increase T by $200 billion
    c. decrease G by $240 billion and decrease T by $200 billion
    d. increase G by $240 billion and increase T by $200 billion
    e. increase G by $200 billion and increase T by $160 billion

13. If government policy creates a deficit budget while the economy is already at full employment, then
    a. national income is falling
    b. fiscal policy is inflationary
    c. fiscal policy is recessionary
    d. the balanced budget multiplier must be less than 1
    e. the balanced budget multiplier must be greater than 1

14. The tax multiplier is
    a. 1/MPS
    b. -MPC/(1 - MPC)
    c. -1/(1 - MPC)
    d. MPS/(1 - MPS)
    e. T - G/(1+T)

15. Inflation can be the politician's friend when it causes tax revenues to
    a. increase without an increase in tax rates
    b. rise due to increases in people's real incomes
    c. fall due to tax cuts that are introduced to close inflationary gaps
    d. increase while people are distracted by increases in other prices
    e. increase at a time that tax increases are popular among voters

16. If the income multiplier is 4, government spending can increase by _____ and taxes by _____ to generate a $300 increase in national income.
    a. $250; $200
    b. $150; $100
    c. $200; $200
    d. $200; $250
    e. $300; $250

17. A frictionally unemployed person is one who
    a. lost a job due to a downturn or recession phase in the economy
    b. has retired from a job
    c. lost a job due to a technological change in the production process
    d. quit a job in order to find a better one
    e. takes a job that requires considerably less talent than that person has to offer

18. A budget surplus arises when
    a. the balanced budget multiplier generates a level of national income greater than the full-employment level
    b. the tax multiplier is greater than the income multiplier
    c. tax revenues exceed government spending
    d. the income multiplier is greater than the tax multiplier
    e. the tax increase necessary to balance the budget is more than the increase in government spending

19. If a $100 billion cut in government spending causes national income to fall by $500 billion, then the marginal propensity to consume is
    a. .75
    b. .8
    c. .9
    d. .25
    e. .2

20. Given a $10 billion recessionary gap and an MPC = 0.75, we know that the equilibrium level of national income is
    a. at the full-employment level of national income
    b. $30 billion below the full-employment level of national income
    c. $50 billion above the full-employment level of national income
    d. $30 billion above the full-employment level of national income
    e. $40 billion below the full-employment level of national income

Fill in the Blanks

1. The natural rate of unemployment consists of workers who are _____ and _____ unemployed.

EMPLOYMENT, INFLATION, AND FISCAL POLICY

2. A _____ exists when the equilibrium level of national income is below the full-employment level.

3. Some groups of people hurt by inflation include _____, _____, and _____.

4. Unions bargain for _____ in their wage contracts in order to protect themselves from the _____ of real wages due to inflation.

Discussion Questions

1. Suppose that the economy is below full employment. Is it necessary to use fiscal policy in order to eliminate the recessionary gap? Explain.

2. Define the unemployment rate. Does the definition include all the people of working age who don't have jobs? Explain.

3. Why do bankers lose because of inflation?

4. Which is the most difficult type of unemployment to eliminate and why?

5. Why is the balanced budget multiplier equal to 1?

Problems

1. Graph a recessionary gap and an inflationary gap using the aggregate expenditure model of equilibrium national income determination.

EMPLOYMENT, INFLATION, AND FISCAL POLICY

2. Suppose that the full-employment level of national income is $3,000 billion, the equilibrium level of national income is $2,500 billion, and the marginal propensity to consume is 0.8. By how much will government spending have to increase in order to reach full employment?

3. Suppose that the full-employment level of national income is $2,000 billion and the equilibrium level of national income is $2,500 billion. Given a marginal propensity to consume equal to 0.80, how much will taxes have to change in order to reach full employment?

4. Suppose that the government wants to close the inflationary gap in problem 3, but wants to limit the tax increase to $50 billion. By how much will government spending have to change to accomplish this goal? What is the size of the surplus or deficit budget that results?

Everyday Applications

During the winter and spring of 1998, a massive spending bill to finance highway repairs and new highway construction made its way through the U.S. Congress at a time when the economy was operating with the lowest levels of unemployment since 1970. Viewed from the perspective of fiscal policy, was this bill appropriate? Why or why not? Can large amounts of new spending on America's highways be justified on grounds other than fiscal policy? Explain.

Economics Online

The Joint Economic Committee of Congress was created when Congress passed the Employment Act of 1946 that committed the government to designing fiscal policy that would promote full employment with low inflation. You can visit the home page for the JEC to find out more about the formulation of fiscal policy (*http://www.house.gov/jec/welcome.htm*).

Answers to Questions

Key Terms Quiz

a. 9   f. 1   k. 10   p. 14
b. 15   g. 6   l. 13
c. 3   h. 12   m. 2
d. 8   i. 4   n. 16
e. 11   j. 5   o. 7

True-False Questions

1. False. Keynesians believe that the economy can be in equilibrium either below or above a full-employment
   level of national income.
2. True
3. True
4. False. A recessionary gap can be closed by cutting taxes; an inflationary gap can be closed by increasing taxes.
5. True
6. False. Closing a recessionary gap requires an increase in the budget deficit while closing an inflationary gap requires a budget surplus.
7. True
8. False. Discouraged workers are not counted as unemployed because they are not considered to be in the labor force.
9. True
10. True
11. False. The income multiplier is $1/(1 - MPC)$ which generates a larger income magnification than the tax multiplier, equal to $-MPC/(1 - MPC)$
12. True
13. True
14. False. A deficit budget results when government spending is greater than tax revenues..
15. True

Multiple-Choice Questions

1. a	6. e	11. e	16. b
2. b	7. d	12. d	17. d
3. c	8. a	13. b	18. c
4. b	9. a	14. b	19. b
5. b	10. a	15. a	20. e

Fill in the Blanks

1. frictionally; structurally
2. recessionary gap
3. savers; landlords; people on fixed incomes
4. cost-of-living allowances; erosion

Discussion Questions

1. Keynesians believe that it is usually necessary to use fiscal policy to eliminate a recessionary gap. They argue that the equilibrium level of national income is determined primarily by aggregate expenditure. The equilibrium level of national income can be at less than the full-employment level. Since this is an equilibrium level, there is no reason for income to change by itself. Therefore, fiscal policy will be necessary to eliminate the recessionary gap — either an increase in government spending, a decrease in taxes, or some combination.

   Other economists believe it may not be necessary to use fiscal policy because the economy will eventually adjust back to full employment automatically. For example, there may be a change in technology that prompts many entrepreneurs to invest in new capital equipment, causing an increase in aggregate expenditure. Or, old capital may just wear out and have to be replaced, causing an increase in investment. The drawback to such automatic adjustment is that it may take a very long time.

2. The unemployment rate is the percentage of the labor force that is looking for work. This definition does not include all people of working age who don't have jobs. Some people of working age are not in the labor force so they can't be unemployed. For example, discouraged workers are not included in the calculation of the unemployment rate.

3. Bankers lend money and are repaid the principal plus interest at a future date. If they lend $100 in 1995 and receive the full loan of $100 back in 2000 while but in the five intervening years, inflation totaled 50 percent, the quantity of goods and services that $100 buys for the bankers is only 50 percent of what they could have bought with the $100 in 1995. Bankers and other who lend money may try to anticipate the impact of inflation on the purchasing power of the money they lend. The interest rate that bankers charge typically includes a premium that is equal to their best estimate of the future rate of inflation. In this way, bankers can protect themselves to a degree from the impact of inflation on the purchasing power of the money they lend.

4. Structural unemployment is probably the most difficult type of unemployment to eliminate. Structural unemployment is the result of changes in tastes for goods that cause the demand for them to fall and/or changes in production technology that decrease the demand for certain skills. Either way, the workers affected may have difficulty finding other jobs because their skills are not immediately suited to the types of employment that are available. To ameliorate the problem of structural unemployment, retraining and education may be necessary to equip workers with skills that are in greater demand by employers. The

problem of structural unemployment is compounded by the extent to which the affected workers are late in their careers.

5. The balanced budget multiplier is the sum of the income multiplier, $1/(1 - MPC)$, and the tax multiplier, $-MPC/(1 - MPC)$. $1/(1 - MPC) + -MPC/(1 - MPC) = (1 - MPC)/(1 - MPC) = 1$.

Problems

1. Graphs of a recessionary gap and an inflationary gap are presented in the graphing tutorial.

2. The change in national income required in this case is $500 billion. The multiplier is equal to $1/(1 - MPC) = 1/(1 - .8) = 5$. Therefore, $500 = 5\Delta G$, so $\Delta G = \$100$ billion.

3. The change in national income required is -$500 billion. The tax multiplier is equal to $-MPC/(1 - MPC) = -.8/(1 - .8) = -4$. Therefore, $-500 = -4\Delta T$, so $\Delta T = \$125$ billion.

4. The change in national income required is -$500 and the tax increase is limited to $50 billion. The tax multiplier is -4, so national income will decrease by 4($50) = $200 billion due to the tax increase. The level of national income must be reduced by another $300 billion with cuts in government spending. The income multiplier is 5; therefore a cut in government spending equal to $60 billion will decrease national income by $300 billion. The increase in taxes equal to $50 billion plus the cut in government spending equal to $60 billion combine to generate a $110 billion budget surplus, assuming the original budget was balanced.

CHAPTER 24

ECONOMIC GROWTH, BUSINESS CYCLES,

AND COUNTERCYCLICAL FISCAL POLICY

Chapter in a Nutshell

Up to this point in our analysis of macroeconomics, our focus has been on understanding why the economy is either in or moving toward equilibrium. This chapter presents a very different approach to macroeconomic analysis. Instead of assuming that the economy moves incessantly toward equilibrium, it describes an economy that is always in motion, moving from one level of activity to another. The point of reference in this approach to macroeconomics is the **business cycle**.

The chapter opens with a discussion of **economic growth**. Being on a business cycle is not inconsistent with economic growth if, cycle after cycle, the economy's real GDP is increasing. What causes growth? Increases in the size of the labor force, with its specialization and division of labor, increases in the stock of capital, and improvements in technology are the principal factors we use to explain economic growth. Key variables that we track in studying the causes of economic growth include the **capital-labor ratio**, the **capital-output ratio**, and **labor productivity**.

Although economies grow over time, the growth path is by no means smooth and has many twists and turns. Economists have tried to figure out why the economy is subject to these twists and turns. Business cycle theorists offer a number of explanations, each of which can be viewed as belonging to either of two classes: **externally induced cycles** or **internally induced cycles**. Externally induced cycles are those triggered by causes that are external to the economy, such as wars, changes in climate, population booms, clustering of innovations, changes in consumer confidence, changes in government spending, or changes in the international scene. The internally induced cycle supposes that the economy is inherently cyclical. One theory that explains such an internally induced cycle shows how the multiplier and accelerator interact to create the cycle. The multiplier relates changes in investment to changes in income. The **accelerator** relates the level of investment to changes in income. A cycle can be triggered by a change in investment that changes income (the multiplier at work). That change in income changes the level of investment (the accelerator at work). That second round change in investment changes income (second round multiplier at work), and so on.

Not all economists accept the idea of the business cycle. **Real business cycle** theorists believe that there is no such thing as a business cycle marked by regular and distinct phases. Rather, the economy is highly dynamic, operating at full employment. What others diagnose as business cycles are, to them, really just sharp changes in the rate of economic growth that result from random changes in the rate of technological change.

Countercyclical fiscal policy can be used to moderate both the downturns and the prosperity phases of the cycle. The appropriate fiscal policy response to a downturn is to create a budget deficit by either raising government spending or lowering taxes, or both. To counteract inflationary pressures in the prosperity phase, the government should cut its spending, raise taxes, or both. Countercyclical fiscal policy is not always effective because it is not always clear where in the cycle the economy is positioned, or where it is heading. Anticipating the cycle's turning points is difficult. Moreover, even if it is clear what policy measure to use, there is still an **administrative lag** to overcome. The lag is the time interval between deciding on a policy and the execution of that policy. By the time a policy clears through the lag, it may no longer be appropriate.

CHAPTER 24   ECONOMIC GROWTH, BUSINESS CYCLES

After studying this chapter, you should be able to:

- Discuss the sources of long-run **economic growth**.
- Explain how the **capital-labor ratio, capital deepening,** and **labor productivity** are related to each other.
- Rank, according to their importance, the factors that have contributed to U.S. economic growth since World War II.
- Describe the **external theories of the business cycle.**
- Show how the multiplier and the **accelerator** can interact to generate an **internal cycle** in the economy.
- Contrast traditional theories of the business cycle with **real business cycle theory**.
- Discuss the design and implementation of **countercyclical fiscal policies**.

Concept Check — See how you do on these multiple-choice questions.

1. Adam Smith identified all of the following as principal causes of **long-run economic growth** except the
   a. wage rate
   b. size of the labor force
   c. degree of labor specialization
   d. size of the capital stock
   e. level of technology

Think back to the sources of economic growth that we identified in Chapter 2.

2. As the **capital-labor ratio** increases,
   a. labor productivity will decrease
   b. labor productivity will increase
   c. the capital-output ratio will increase
   d. saving will decrease
   e. consumption will decrease as resources are shifted to produce more capital goods

How do we define labor productivity? How would an increase in the capital-labor ratio affect labor productivity?

3. The idea of the **accelerator** is that
   a. once economic growth begins, it continues to accelerate
   b. an increase in investment triggers the income multiplier resulting in further increases in investment as expected sales rise
   c. countercyclical fiscal policy can accelerate rates of long-run economic growth
   d. to justify more capital stock, economic growth must accelerate
   e. technological advances accelerate economic growth

After an increase in investment, the multiplier effect is observed, then the accelerator.

4. The purpose of **countercyclical fiscal policy** is to
   a. eliminate large budget deficits
   b. experiment with changes in government spending
   c. learn precisely when turning points in the business cycle occur
   d. moderate the severity of the business cycle
   e. eliminate the real business cycle

EMPLOYMENT, INFLATION, AND FISCAL POLICY

Think about when specific types of fiscal policy are appropriate.

5. **Administrative lag** stems from
   a. the inability to design appropriate countercyclical policies
   b. the delay between deciding on an appropriate policy and its execution
   c. a belief in the real business cycle among most government economists that prevents them from taking countercyclical measures soon enough to prevent recessions
   d. a reluctance by a budget-conscious Congress to pursue new spending programs
   e. difficulty calculating the precise value for the income and tax multipliers and the accelerator

Countercyclical fiscal policies are designed and implemented by government. Does government in the United States typically move quickly?

Am I on the Right Track?

Your answers to the questions above should be **a, b, b, d,** and **b**. It may be useful for you to approach this chapter in three stages. First, you need to become comfortable with the terminology and methodology for examining economic growth. This is an extension of work we began in Chapter 2. Second, learn the various theories of the business cycle. Business cycle theory is a fascinating and colorful field. Finally, understand that countercyclical fiscal policy is intended to moderate the business cycle. To what extent is this possible given the difficulty of identifying business cycles and their phases and problems like administrative lag?

Key Terms Quiz — Match the terms on the left with the definitions in the column on the right.

1. economic growth   ___ a. the ratio of capital to labor, reflecting the quantity of capital used by each laborer in production
2. accelerator   ___ b. a rise in the ratio of capital to labor
3. labor productivity   ___ c. the time interval between deciding on an appropriate policy and the execution of that policy
4. countercyclical fiscal policy ___ d. an increase in real GDP, typically expressed as an annual rate of real GDP growth
5. capital-labor ratio   ___ e. the ratio of capital stock to GDP
6. administrative lag   ___ f. the quantity of GDP produced per worker, typically measured in quantity of GDP per hour of labor
7. capital deepening   ___ g. fiscal policy designed to moderate the severity of the business cycle
8. capital-output ratio   ___ h. the relationship between the level of investment and the change in the level of national income

Graphing Tutorial

One new graph describing the relationship between the capital-labor ratio and labor productivity is presented in this chapter. The labor productivity curve is fairly easy to draw and to interpret. Best of all, it conveys considerable information about an economy. Suppose we have an economy with 1,000 workers and $300,000 of capital. The capital-labor ratio is equal to $K/L = \$300,000/1,000 = \$300$. On average, each worker has $300 of capital to use in production. Suppose that with $300 of capital each worker contributes $70 to GDP. Labor productivity in this case is equal to $70, since GDP/L = output per laborer = $70. We can compute GDP from this information. GDP is equal to $70 per worker times 1,000 workers, or $70,000.

Now suppose that a $30,000 investment raises the economy's capital stock from $300,000 to $330,000. The capital-labor ratio has increased from $300 to $330,000/1,000 = $330. With more capital, each worker is more productive. Suppose that output per laborer rises to $77. GDP also rises from $70,000 to $77,000. Let's plot the capital-labor ratio on the horizontal axis and the output per laborer ratio on the vertical axis to explore the relationship between them further.

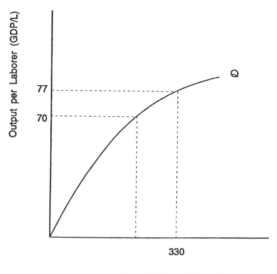

The graph shows that as the capital-labor ratio increases, output per laborer increases, but at a decreasing rate. The slope of the labor productivity curve becomes flatter as the capital-labor ratio increases, reflecting the law of diminishing returns. As each laborer has more capital to work with, labor productivity increases, but at a decreasing rate. Each additional unit of capital adds less and less to output per laborer. Economists refer to the rise in the capital-labor ratio along the horizontal axis as capital deepening.

The labor productivity curve can be used to show the effect of a change in technology. An improvement in technology can increase labor productivity without any change in the value of the capital stock. With better technology, the same dollar amount of capital per laborer results in a higher output per laborer. The impact of technological change is shown in the graph below. The labor productivity curve shifts from Q to Q' so that with $300 of capital, each laborer now generates $90 of output instead of $70.

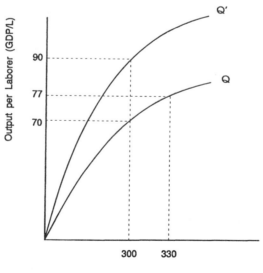

Graphing Pitfalls

Be certain that you draw the labor productivity curve with the correct slope. The slope should be positive and decreasing as *K/L* increases to reflect the law of diminishing returns — the fact that as capital is added for each laborer, output per laborer increases, but at a decreasing rate. It wouldn't make sense to have a labor productivity curve with a positive and increasing slope. Consider the example in the text where laborers are given double-bladed axes. Once each laborer has an axe, output per laborer will increase at a decreasing rate as the number of axes per laborer increases. So, the labor productivity curve won't look like the one drawn below.

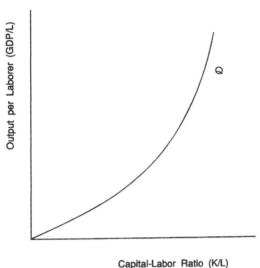

As the capital-labor ratio increases, output per laborer increases at a decreasing rate, not at an increasing rate as shown in this graph.

True-False Questions — If a statement is false, explain why.

1. External theories of economic cycles link cycles to external, random events. (T/F)

2. The U.S. economy grew faster from 1947 to 1973 than it did from 1973 to 1992. (T/F)

3. Our ideas about the causes of economic growth today are much different than those that were advanced by Adam Smith in 1776. (T/F)

4. The capital-output ratio tells us how many dollars' worth of capital are required to generate a dollar's worth of output. (T/F)

5. The model of economic growth based on the linkage between capital stock and GDP incorporates all the key factors associated with the growth process. (T/F)

6. Technological change contributed relatively less to economic growth in the period 1947-1973 than it did in the period 1973-1992. (T/F)

7. During the 20th century, the U.S. economic growth path traces out a steady, upward thrust in real GDP. (T/F)

8. There is a universal consensus among economists that business cycles exist. (T/F)

9. The sunspot theory associated movements through a business cycle with changes in solar activity. (T/F)

10. Marxists argue that governments use wars as a means to overcome economic recessions or depressions. (T/F)

11. New housing construction triggers the income multiplier that sparks the 15-to-20-year housing cycle. (T/F)

12. Simon Kuznets identified the innovation cycle which is linked to specific innovations that create major breakthroughs in technology that require massive investments. (T/F)

13. The multiplier-accelerator cycle is based on the premise that the economy is inherently cyclical. (T/F)

14. The accelerator principle states that an increase in the rate of innovation will induce a higher level of investment. (T/F)

15. Real business cycle theorists argue that what other economists believe to be the business cycle is really just variations in the rate of economic growth attributable to uneven variations in the rate of technological change. (T/F)

Multiple-Choice Questions

1. The effect of technological change on the labor productivity curve is to
   a. shift to a point further to the right on the curve
   b. shift to a point further to the left on the curve since less capital per laborer is required
   c. change the shape of the curve so that the slope is positive and increasing
   d. change the curve to a straight line as the law of diminishing returns is overcome
   e. cause the curve to shift upward

EMPLOYMENT, INFLATION, AND FISCAL POLICY

2. The sunspot theory of business cycles is most applicable to
    a. modern industrial economies
    b. an economy affected by global warming
    c. an agricultural economy
    d. an island economy like Great Britain
    e. an economy in a prolonged depression

3. The accelerator is the
    a. relationship between the level of investment and changes in the level of national income
    b. reciprocal of the multiplier
    c. rate of economic growth in the recovery phase of a business cycle
    d. relationship between changes in investment that cause changes in national income
    e. speed at which policy decisions are made in response to changes in the economy

4. The capital-output ratio
    a. describes how changes in investment affect the level of output in an economy
    b. describes how the level of investment affects changes in the economy's output
    c. describes the relationship between the economy's capital stock and its output
    d. is the key factor explaining why business cycles develop in an industrialized economy
    e. measures changes in output during one cycle, from peak to recession

5. William Stanley Jevons's sunspot theory relates
    a. economic performance to nuclear storms on the sun
    b. investment behavior of firms to seasons of the year
    c. changes in consumers' propensities to consume to seasons of the year
    d. changes in economic performance to government's fiscal policy
    e. changes in economic performance to changes in the interest rate

6. The real business cycle theory claims that
    a. business cycles occur because the economy is not competitive
    b. economic performance is linked to technological change that is totally random
    c. competition causes business cycles
    d. there are no adequate theories explaining why the economy experiences business cycles
    e. downturn phases of the cycle dominate the recovery phases

7. All of the following apply to the multiplier-accelerator model of the business cycle **except**
    a. the level of investment depends on changes in national income, which in turn depend on changes in investment
    b. the cycle is internally fueled, that is, it is inherent to the economic system
    c. the cycle dampens to a steady-state equilibrium in the long run
    d. the cycle, once triggered, will repeat
    e. it is not dependent on some external shock to the economic system, such as a war or population boom

8. In Schumpeter's innovation cycle,
    a. technological change dampens the cycle, forcing the economy to equilibrium
    b. government's randomly distributed investments in research and development trigger the cycle
    c. innovations cause uneven changes in labor productivity, which trigger the cycle
    d. clusters of innovations propel an economy into prosperity and, once exhausted, create a downturn
    e. innovations cause nominal GDP to depart from real GDP, which triggers the cycle

9. Most of the increase in GDP from 1947 to 1973 is explained by _____ while _____ explains most of the growth from 1973 to 1992.
   a. technological change; capital accumulation
   b. capital accumulation; increases in the labor force
   c. increases in the labor force; capital accumulation
   d. increases in the labor force; technological change
   e. technological change; increases in the labor force

10. War-induced cycles, sunspot-induced cycles, and the housing cycle have in common that they are
    a. triggered by misguided government policy
    b. triggered during the prosperity phase of the cycle
    c. internally induced; that is, each occurs because it is an integral part of the economic system
    d. caused by factors that are external to the economic system
    e. all by-products of the multiplier-accelerator cycle

11. An examination of the sources of U.S. economic growth from 1947 to 1973 and from 1973 to 1992 shows that
    a. technological change was a relatively more important source of economic growth in the later period
    b. capital inputs were a relatively more important source of economic growth in the earlier period
    c. total growth was faster in the later period
    d. technological change was a relatively more important source of economic growth in the earlier period
    e. labor inputs were the most important source of growth in both periods

12. The Kuznets cycle describes
    a. the relationship between cycles and housing construction
    b. volatile changes in GDP just prior to the Great Depression
    c. the relationship between changes in the real interest rate and changes in output
    d. how the economy's marginal propensity to consume can, by itself, generate cycles
    e. how immigration can trigger production booms in the economy that are soon followed by recession

13. Countercyclical fiscal policy is designed to
    a. moderate the severity of the business cycle
    b. create a balanced budget in each of the years of a cycle
    c. counter fiscal policies that create deficits, which trigger cycles
    d. curb the excessive powers of government's fiscal policy on cycles
    e. create a cycle whose phases are of equal length

14. An administrative lag
    a. reflects differences in the government's willingness to cope with inflation and unemployment
    b. is the time it takes fiscal policy to clear the bureaucratic channels of government
    c. is the time interval between making a fiscal policy decision and the actual execution of that policy
    d. the time interval between executing and later correcting inappropriate fiscal policy
    e. measures the number of government agencies required to approve any policy

15. A problem inherent in creating countercyclical fiscal policy when the economy is in a downturn is that
    a. the private sector may not go along with that policy, thus undermining the effort
    b. competition among firms in the economy creates a less-than-uniform response to any government policy
    c. government agencies fight among themselves — some want to curb unemployment, others inflation
    d. it is impossible to know where the economy is heading, on to recession or toward its recovery phase
    e. lack of consumer confidence undermines any government effort to initiate the recovery phase

EMPLOYMENT, INFLATION, AND FISCAL POLICY 425

16. All of the following are associated with capital deepening **except**
    a. a rise in the ratio of capital to labor
    b. an increase in investment that exceeds an increase in the number of laborers
    c. a movement along the labor productivity curve
    d. a shift upward in the labor productivity curve
    e. an increase in output per laborer

17. Investment-induced growth is dependent on
    a. consumption
    b. fiscal policy
    c. low unemployment
    d. innovation
    e. saving that is automatically converted to investment

18. A major difference between real business cycle theory and the innovation business cycle theory associated with Joseph Schumpeter is that real business cycle
    a. theory predicts that real GDP grows through innovation while Schumpeter's theory predicts that nominal GDP grows through innovation
    b. theorists regard innovations as clustered and connected while Schumpeter believed that innovations are random and unconnected
    c. theory predicts growth will be faster because it is less dependent on innovation than Schumpeter thought
    d. theorists regard innovations as random and unconnected while Schumpeter believed that innovations are clustered and related
    e. theorists support the use of countercyclical fiscal policy but Schumpeter's innovation business cycle theory argues against the use of countercyclical fiscal policy

19. Real business cycle theorists believe that the
    a. economy always operates close to full employment
    b. rate of economic growth is stable over time
    c. phases of the business cycle can be easily identified
    d. administrative lag is short
    e. economy's performance can be improved through government intervention

20. Data for the United States from 1950 to 1994 suggest that higher rates of economic growth are associated with
    a. lower saving rates
    b. lower rates of investment
    c. lower government spending
    d. higher saving rates
    e. paradoxically low rates of technological change

Fill in the Blanks

1. An economy's equilibrium may be more of a _____ than a specifically _____ GDP.

2. The four factors that Adam Smith identified as principal contributors to economic growth are

   _____, _____, _____, and

   _____.

3. Countercyclical fiscal policies are intended to moderate the _____ and the

   _____ phases of the business cycle.

4. Administrative lag is the time lapse between the government's _____ of a specific fiscal

   policy and the _____ of the policy.

Discussion Questions

1. How can economic cycles be related to the level of sunspot activity? Would you be comfortable predicting economic performance in the United States over the next five years based on sunspot activity? Why or why not?

2. Explain the innovation cycle.

3. How does real business cycle theory compare to the innovation business cycle theory?

4. Describe circumstances under which a countercyclical fiscal policy could be destabilizing even though it seemed to be the right thing to do when the policy was introduced.

EMPLOYMENT, INFLATION, AND FISCAL POLICY

Problems

1. Suppose the capital-output ratio is 4, and the initial level of income is $1,000, and the marginal propensity to consume is 0.80. Assume that there is no government and no foreign trade. Assume also that the dollar amount invested in one year increases the capital stock in the next year by the same amount. Compute values to fill the cells in the table below to show the level of income, the size of the capital stock, consumption, saving and investment for a four-year period. What is the rate of growth for this economy? What allows this economy to grow?

	Y	K	C	S	I
Year 1					
Year 2					
Year 3					
Year 4					

Everyday Applications

Since the brief recession in the early 1990s, economic growth in the United States has been quite robust. The signs of growth in all parts of the country are readily visible. What are some examples? Is there a particular business cycle theory that can explain this resurgence of growth? Consider the applicability of the various theories that we have examined.

Economics Online

Who doesn't like prosperity? There is a Prosperity Institute "dedicated to conducting and publishing research examining the causes of, and impediments to, high rates of economic growth and a higher standard of living for the American people." Be forewarned — this is a highly conservative group that opposes all but a limited degree of government intervention in the economy. Look for evidence of a belief in real business cycle theory on their home page (*http://prosperity-institute.org/*).

Answers to Questions

Key Terms Quiz

a. 5   **f.** 3
b. 7   **g.** 4
c. 6   **h.** 2
d. 1
e. 8

True-False Questions

1. True
2. True
3. False. Smith identified the same principal factors that we study today as the sources of economic growth.
4. True
5. False. Economic growth is a function of many other factors, such as labor inputs and technological change, that are left out of the growth model that links GDP to the size of the capital stock.
6. False. Technological change was relatively more important in the early period.
7. False. This period is marked by major fluctuations in real GDP.
8. False. Real business cycle theorists completely reject the idea of a business cycle.
9. True
10. True
11. True
12. False. Schumpeter is credited with the innovation business cycle theory.
13. True
14. False. The accelerator principle states that an increase in the rate of growth of GDP will induce a higher level of investment.
15. True

EMPLOYMENT, INFLATION, AND FISCAL POLICY

Multiple-Choice Questions

1. e
2. c
3. a
4. c
5. a
6. b
7. c
8. d
9. a
10. d
11. d
12. a
13. a
14. c
15. d
16. d
17. e
18. d
19. a
20. d

Fill in the Blanks

1. moving target; fixed
2. size of the labor force; degree of labor specialization; size of the capital stock; level of technology
3. recession; prosperity
4. choice; implementation

Discussion Questions

1. High levels of sunspot activity seem to be related to poor crop performance. This theory of the business cycle wouldn't be good for predicting cycles in the United States because agriculture accounts for such a small portion of our GDP. However, during the 19th century and earlier, when a larger percentage of the population farmed for a living, this theory was quite relevant.

2. The innovation cycle refers to technological changes that are clustered in particular industries and lead to high rates of investment in these industries. These innovations spur the economy into prosperity. When the innovations run their course, and the level of innovative activity falls, the economy slips into its downturn phase. A good example is the progress of transportation technology during the 19th century and into the 20th. New technologies and new industries replaced old ones as, for example, the automobile replaced the horse and buggy. These waves of investment can cause economic cycles.

3. Real business cycle theorists don't believe in a business cycle. Rather, they argue that the economy experiences periodic bursts of rapid growth associated with rapid technological changes that occur randomly in the economy. On the other hand, the innovation cycle focuses on technological changes that are significant enough to lead to major changes in investment, which starts the cycle process. The innovation business cycle theory maintains that innovations are clustered and related to one another, rather than random and unrelated.

4. Many answers are possible here. Suppose the economy was in recession and the president, hoping to moderate the economy's decline, decides on a massive spending program. By the time the program is approved by Congress and implemented, the economy has begun its recovery. But the program now takes effect, and instead of moderating the economy's fall, it contributes to the growing inflationary pressures. This is a classic example of administrative lag.

Problems

1. The completed table is shown below.

	Y	K	C	S	I
Year 1	1,000	4,000	800	200	200
Year 2	1,050	4,200	840	210	210
Year 3	1,102.5	4,410	882	220.5	220.5
Year 4	1,157.6	4,630.5	926.1	231.5	231.5

The cells are calculated as follows. In year 1, output is set at 1,000 and the capital-output ratio is 4. Therefore, the capital stock, K, is equal to 4,000. The MPC is given, equal to .8, so consumption is 800, saving is 200, and because saving is equal to investment, investment is equal to 200. In year 2, the I = 200 from year 1 is added to the capital stock, increasing K to 4,200. The capital-output ratio equal to 4 means that Y = 4,200/4 = 1,050 in year 2. Given the MPC = .8, consumption is .8(1,050) = 840, S = 210, and I = 210; add this to the capital stock, and follow the calculations for years 3 and 4.

This economy is growing at a constant 5 percent rate. Ultimately, it is saving that provides resources for investment that leads to capital accumulation, which allows this economy to grow.

PART 5 — EMPLOYMENT, INFLATION, AND FISCAL POLICY

COMPREHENSIVE SAMPLE TEST

Give yourself 50 minutes to complete this exam and see how you do. The answers follow. Don't look until you are finished!

True-False Questions — If a statement is false, explain why. Each question is worth two points.

1. The horizontal segment of the aggregate supply curve means that resources are fully employed. (T/F)

2. As the price level decreases, the quantity demanded of real goods and services increases because real wealth increases. (T/F)

3. The income and expenditure approaches to calculating GDP are equivalent. (T/F)

4. Modigliani's life-cycle hypothesis states that consumption varies exactly in proportion to income change over a person's lifetime. (T/F)

5. When the level of income is zero, consumption spending must be zero too. (T/F)

6. The accumulation of unwanted inventories is an indication that intended investment is greater than actual investment. (T/F)

7. In an economy with no government and no foreign trade the aggregate expenditure curve lies above and parallel to the consumption curve with the vertical distance between them equal to autonomous investment. (T/F)

8. An appropriate fiscal policy to close an inflationary gap is to cut taxes. (T/F)

9. A potential problem with increasing government spending to close a recessionary gap is that it is very difficult to cut government spending once it is introduced. (T/F)

10. The accelerator is an increase in investment causing income to increase, which is followed by the multiplier causing investment to increase further. (T/F)

Multiple-Choice Questions — Each question is worth two points.

1. Demand-pull inflation is the result of
   a. a leftward shift in the aggregate supply curve
   b. a rightward shift in the aggregate supply curve
   c. a leftward shift in the aggregate demand curve
   d. a rightward shift in the aggregate demand curve
   e. simultaneous shifts to the left in the aggregate demand and aggregate supply curves

2. A recession is defined as a period during which
   a. real GDP decreases for at least six months
   b. the GDP deflator decreases for at least six months
   c. nominal GDP decreases for at least six months
   d. real GDP decreases for at least a year
   e. the GDP deflator decreases for at least a year

3. If nominal GDP is $7 trillion in 1998 and the GDP deflator is 110, then real GDP is
   a. $7.7 trillion
   b. $6.89 trillion
   c. $7.11 trillion
   d. $6.36 trillion
   e. $7 trillion

4. If gross private domestic investment in the economy is less than depreciation, then
   a. GDP and NDP are equal
   b. the stock of capital is shrinking
   c. the stock of capital is growing
   d. unwanted inventories are accumulating
   e. the useful life for capital equipment is increasing

5. Of the following, the largest percentage component of national income is
   a. profits
   b. rents and royalties
   c. interest
   d. compensation to employees
   e. proprietors' income

6. For a country that has a large number of its citizens working abroad, the better measure of economic performance is
   a. the GDP deflator
   b. real GDP
   c. nominal GDP
   d. nominal GNP
   e. real GNP

7. Keynes's absolute income hypothesis for consumption behavior states that as income increases,
   a. consumption increases at a decreasing rate
   b. the consumption of leisure increases at an increasing rate
   c. consumption increases at an increasing rate
   d. the MPC increases
   e. the MPC is constant

EMPLOYMENT, INFLATION, AND FISCAL POLICY

8. All of the following are determinants of autonomous investment **except**
   a. the level of national income
   b. the level of technology
   c. the rate of capacity utilization
   d. the interest rate
   e. expectations of future economic growth

9. An increase in the marginal propensity to consume will cause
   a. the marginal propensity to save to increase
   b. autonomous consumption to increase
   c. autonomous consumption to decrease
   d. the marginal propensity to save to decrease
   e. the tax multiplier to increase

10. Keynes believed that saving would equal intended investment
    a. automatically, because saving and investment decisions are closely coordinated
    b. so that the economy can move toward equilibrium
    c. because unwanted inventories are equal to zero
    d. purely by chance because saving and investment decisions are made independently by different groups
    e. if the marginal propensity to save were sufficiently large

11. If saving is greater than intended investment, then
    a. aggregate expenditure is greater than national income
    b. national income will increase as the economy moves toward equilibrium
    c. national income is greater than aggregate expenditure
    d. wanted inventories are decreasing
    e. employment will increase

12. Suppose you read in the newspaper that the ratio of inventories to sales is increasing. It is likely that
    a. the economy is poised to experience a period of rapid growth
    b. employment, production, and national income will fall
    c. wanted inventories are decreasing
    d. the price level will rise significantly
    e. an inflationary gap will need to be closed

13. Suppose the consumption function is $C = 500 + .8Y$ and $I = 300$. The equilibrium level of national income is
    a. 4,000
    b. 400
    c. 40,000
    d. 40
    e. 1,600

14. Suppose there is a recessionary gap equal to $10 billion and the MPC is equal to .8. We know that the economy is in equilibrium at a level of income that is
    a. $80 billion below the full-employment level of income
    b. $80 billion above the full-employment level of income
    c. $40 billion below the full-employment level of income
    d. $50 billion above the full-employment level of income
    e. $50 billion below the full-employment level of income

15. One problem with using the balanced budget approach to close a recessionary gap is that
    a. full employment with a balanced budget happens purely by chance and cannot be achieved with conscious policy
    b. the increases in G and T necessary to achieve full employment may be quite large
    c. people will not tolerate the cuts in government spending necessary to balance the budget
    d. the tax increase necessary to balance the budget would cause a bigger recessionary gap
    e. the tax multiplier is very small

16. One conclusion to be drawn from our analysis of the income multiplier is that
    a. a recession due to a decrease in investment will be short-lived because of the income multiplier
    b. the decrease in national income due to a decrease in investment will be a multiple of the decrease in investment
    c. a decrease in investment will be matched by an increase in saving
    d. the income multiplier will guarantee a full-employment level of national income
    e. the value of the MPC and the multiplier are inversely related

17. Consider the following combinations of government spending and tax changes. The strongest policy to close an inflationary gap is a
    a. $100 billion increase in G; $100 billion decrease in T
    b. $100 billion increase in G; $100 billion increase in T
    c. $100 billion decrease in G; $100 billion increase in T
    d. $100 billion decrease in G; $100 billion decrease in T
    e. $100 billion decrease in G; no change in T

18. All of the following are examples of external theories of cycles **except**
    a. the sunspot theory
    b. war-induced cycles
    c. the housing cycle
    d. the innovation cycle
    e. the real business cycle

19. If we were to represent real business cycle theory using a production possibilities curve model, we would show
    a. shifts in the curve, some large, some small, that correspond to different rates of growth in the economy due to random and unrelated technological changes
    b. a continual shift in the curve to the right at a constant rate over time
    c. movements from points inside the curve to points on the curve that seem to happen randomly
    d. sequential shifts in the intercepts of the curve, first along the horizontal axis, then along the vertical axis
    e. an increase in the extent of the bowed-out shape of the curve as the economy becomes more specialized

20. The upward shift in the labor productivity curve over time is the result of
    a. capital deepening
    b. an increase in the capital-labor ratio
    c. technological change
    d. an increase in the capital-output ratio
    e. saving

Discussion Questions/Problems — Each question is worth 10 points.

1. a. What is aggregate demand? Draw an aggregate demand curve and explain its shape. What factors influence aggregate demand?

b. What is aggregate supply? Draw an aggregate supply curve and explain its shape. What factors influence aggregate supply?

c. What does macroequilibrium mean?

2. Describe Keynes's absolute income hypothesis to explain consumption spending behavior. Why is it incorrect? Present an alternative hypothesis to explain consumption behavior.

3. a. Suppose that consumption is $C = 600 + .75Y$ and $I = 400$ (all values are billions of dollars). Write an equation for aggregate expenditure, calculate the equilibrium level of national income, and sketch a graph of the aggregate expenditure curve to show the equilibrium level of national income.

b. Suppose the full-employment level of income is $6,000 billion. Is there a recessionary or an inflationary gap? How large is the gap? By how much would government spending have to change to close the gap? Show your work.

4. Discuss the problems inherent in designing a countercyclical fiscal policy.

Answers to Sample Test on Part 5

True-False Questions

1. False. The horizontal segment of the aggregate supply curve corresponds to ample unemployed resources in the economy that can be brought into production without an increase in the price level.
2. True
3. True
4. False. Modigliani's life-cycle hypothesis states that consumption spending will rise gradually during a person's life as income rises. The marginal propensity to consume changes significantly over a person's life. Typically, young adults have a very high marginal propensity to consume, middle-aged individuals have a lower MPC as they save for retirement, and retirees have a higher MPC.
5. False. Autonomous consumption, consumption when income is zero, is positive when people spend out of accumulated saving.
6. False. If unwanted inventories accumulate, then actual investment is greater than intended investment.
7. True
8. False. An appropriate fiscal policy to close an inflationary gap would be to increase taxes.
9. True.
10. False. The multiplier is an increase in investment causing income to increase. It is followed by the accelerator causing investment to increase further in order to create the productive capacity to support a higher level of expected sales that is associated with a higher level of national income.

Multiple-Choice Questions

1. d	6. e	11. c	16. b
2. a	7. a	12. b	17. c
3. d	8. a	13. a	18. e
4. b	9. e	14. e	19. a
5. d	10. d	15. b	20. c

Discussion Questions/Problems

1. a. Aggregate demand is the total quantity of goods and services demanded by households, firms, foreigners, and government at varying price levels. The aggregate demand curve is downward sloping as the price level decreases. The aggregate demand curve slopes downward because of the real wealth effect, the interest rate effect, and the international trade effect. The real wealth effect states that as the price level decreases, real wealth increases, so consumption spending will increase. The interest rate effect states that as the price level decreases, the demand for loanable funds decreases, so the interest rate decreases, causing consumption spending and investment to increase. The international trade effect states that as the price level decreases in the United States relative to other countries, the demand for U.S. exports increases. The position of the aggregate demand curve is influenced by changes in consumption spending, changes in investment spending, changes in government spending, and changes in spending on exports and imports. Increases in spending shift the curve to the right and decreases in spending shift the curve to the left. A graph of the aggregate demand curve is shown on the following page along with a graph of the aggregate supply curve.

   b. Aggregate supply is the total quantity of goods and services that firms in the economy are willing to supply at varying price levels. The aggregate supply curve is drawn in three distinct segments — a horizontal segment at low levels of real GDP, an upward-sloping segment as real GDP increases, and a vertical segment that corresponds to a full-employment level of real GDP. The horizontal segment describes low levels of real GDP where resources are unemployed and can be brought into production with no increase in the price level. The upward-sloping segment describes an economy approaching full employment. As unemployed resources become scarcer, employers must pay more to hire them, and these cost increases are passed on in the form of price increases. Alternatively, an increase in the price level will increase profit margins for firms, which then expand production or enter profitable industries causing real GDP to increase. The vertical segment corresponds to full employment — no more resources are available for production so real GDP cannot increase. The position of the aggregate supply curve is influenced by resource availability. As labor, land, capital, and entrepreneurial energies become more available, the aggregate supply curve shifts to the right. As resources become less available, the aggregate supply curve shifts to the left.

   c. Macroequilibrium occurs at the level of real GDP and the price level that equate the aggregate quantity demanded and the aggregate quantity supplied. This point is represented by the intersection of the aggregate demand and aggregate supply curves drawn below.

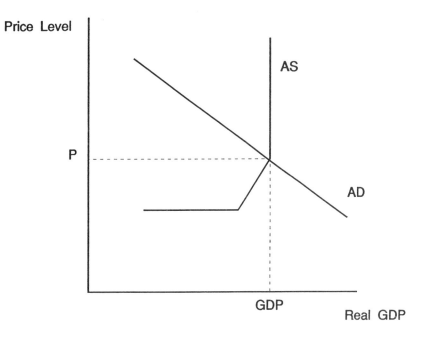

2. Keynes argued that consumption spending depended on the absolute level of national income. Consumption spending is a larger fraction on national income at low levels of national income than at high levels. Once income rises to a high enough level to meet the most pressing consumption needs, the desire to save a portion of income becomes more prominent. Therefore, the marginal propensity to consume decreases as income increases, according to Keynes. However, data examined by Simon Kuznets showed that consumption spending is a constant fraction of income. That is, the marginal propensity to consume is constant. The Duesenberry relative income hypothesis can explain this fact. People with low incomes spend nearly all of their income to meet immediate consumption needs. They have a marginal propensity to consume that is close to 1. Middle-income individuals also have a relatively high marginal propensity to consume. The rich are able to save a larger fraction of their income, so their marginal propensity to consume is lower. If each group's income level increases at approximately the same rate as national income over time, no group's relative position changes; therefore, the overall marginal propensity to consume is constant.

3. a. The aggregate expenditure equation is $AE = 1,000 + .75Y$. To solve for the equilibrium level of national income, set $AE = Y$. Thus, we have $1,000 + .75Y = Y$. Subtracting $.75Y$ from both sides gives $1,000 = .25Y$, so $Y = \$4,000$ billion. The graph on the following page illustrates this equilibrium level of national income.

   b. If the full-employment level of national income is $6,000 billion, then national income will have to rise by $2,000. A recessionary gap exists. The multiplier is equal to $1/(1 - MPC) = 1/(1 - .75) = 4$. $\Delta Y = 2,000 = 4\Delta G$. Therefore, $\Delta G = 2,000/4 = \$500$ billion. The recessionary gap is $500 billion, and government spending must increase by this amount to achieve the full-employment level of national income.

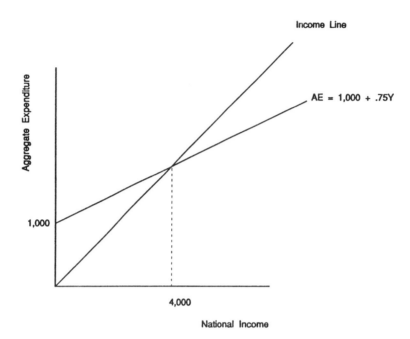

4. Countercyclical fiscal policy is designed to moderate the severity of the business cycle. Designing and implementing countercyclical fiscal policy is quite difficult. First, it takes time to recognize that a recession or inflation is beginning. Once a problem is recognized, a decision has to be made about whether policy action should be taken or not. This depends on the type of cycle the economy is entering. For example, if the economy dips into a recession, it could be very brief and largely self-correcting. If this is the case, no action is justified because a fiscal policy that increased spending might trigger inflation. However, perhaps the recession will deepen and be long-lasting. In this case, increased spending via a fiscal policy action is justified. How does one tell which way the cycle will go? No one can be certain. Suppose the decision is made to implement a fiscal policy to increase spending. The problem of administrative lag is then encountered — the time lapse between deciding on a policy and the implementation of the policy. A long administrative lag can result in a situation where the economy has already recovered before the policy takes effect, creating inflationary pressure. The problem of increased unemployment that is associated with a recession may be structural rather than cyclical unemployment. In that case, a job retraining program than fiscal policy would be more appropriate than fiscal policy. Finally, some believe there is no such thing as a business cycle — real business cycle theorists hold this view. If they are correct, then fiscal policy is never appropriate.

CHAPTER 25

MONEY

Chapter in a Nutshell

Although we know from experience that, under certain circumstances, **barter exchange** works, the complications associated with the requirements of a **double coincidence of wants** make the exchange of one good for another inefficient in the modern world. **Money** was invented to facilitate exchange. Money serves three functions. It is a **medium of exchange, a measure of value, and a store of value**. What properties must money have? It must be durable, portable, divisible, homoegeneous, and be relatively scarce. Gold has these characteristics and has long been used as money. Paper money — called fiat money — works as well, as long as it is universally accepted as the medium of exchange.

Let's look at our modern world of money. Money is described as a **liquid asset** because it exchanges easily for other assets. Our money supply is categorized according to its **liquidity**. **M1** is the most liquid. It includes currency and demand deposits (our checking accounts) and traveler's checks. **M2** is M1 money plus savings accounts, certificates of deposit, money market mutual funds, money market deposit accounts, repurchase agreements, and small-denomination time deposits. **M3** is M2 money plus other less liquid forms of money such as large denomination time deposits and large overnight repurchase agreements.

The relationship between an economy's prices and its money supply is expressed in the **quantity theory of money**, which derives from the **equation of exchange: MV = PQ**, where M is the money supply, V is the velocity of money, P is the price level, and Q the quantity of goods. The quantity theory of money restates the equation to read, assuming both V and Q are constant:

$$P = MV/Q.$$

We now see the direct relationship between money and prices (increase money, and the price level increases).

Economists hold different views concerning the velocity of money. **Classical economists** believe velocity is constant; **monetarists** believe it is not constant but stable and predictable; and **Keynesians** believe it is neither constant, stable, nor predictable. Economists' views on velocity affect their policy prescriptions. These show up in their theories of demand for money.

Classical economists believed that the demand for money is strictly a **transactions demand**, that is, a demand arising from the need to carry out transactions. They assume that since output is constant at full employment and velocity is constant, then the transactions demand for money depends on the price level. Monetarists accept the variability of velocity but believe that **MV = PQ** can still be a good tool for analysis because even though velocity is variable, it is predictable.

Keynesians believe that there are three motives for demanding (holding) money: **the transactions motive, the precautionary motive, and the speculative motive**. The speculative demand for money is inversely related to the interest rate. A fall in the interest rate increases the quantity demanded of money. Therefore, if the money supply increases, interest rates will fall and investment will increase, causing aggregate demand and real GDP to increase. To Keynesians, money matters. Classical economists and monetarists, on the other hand, believe that increases in the money supply only cause the price level to increase because the economy is continuously at full employment.

After you study this chapter, you should be able to:

- Explain why **money** has replaced **barter**.
- List the functions of money.
- Explain the **liquidity characteristics** of our money supply.
- Describe the **classical view of money demand** and the **quantity theory of money**.
- Explain **monetarism**.
- Contrast the **Keynesian** and the **monetarist** views of **money demand**.
- Account for the Keynesian belief that money matters.

Concept Check — See how you do on these multiple-choice questions.

1. A significant problem with **barter exchanges** in a modern economy is that
    a. only one party benefits from barter exchanges
    b. converted into money terms, barter prices typically are lower
    c. converted into money terms, barter prices typically are higher
    d. barter requires a double coincidence of wants, which is often difficult to achieve
    e. only agricultural comodities can be exchanged by barter

Barter is an exchange of one good for another.

2. **Liquidity** refers to
    a. money flows in the circular flow model
    b. flows of goods and services in the circular flow model
    c. the fact that gold is easy to melt and purify
    d. the fact that flows of debased coins drive out flows of good coins according to Gresham's law
    e. the degree to which an asset can be easily exchanged for money

What does it mean to say that an asset is liquid?

3. All of the following are included in the **M3 money supply** except
    a. currency
    b. corporate bonds
    c. savings accounts
    d. large-denomination time deposits
    e. large-denomination repurchase agreements

If a corporation is failing, how liquid would its bonds be?

4. The **quantity theory of money** states that
    a. the quantity of money in circulation depends on the velocity of money
    b. the price level is proportional to the quantity of money in circulation
    c. velocity and real GDP fluctuate significantly in the short run
    d. the quantity of money in circulation is proportional to the price level
    e. velocity is not constant, but it is highly predictable

The quantity theory of money focuses on the amount of money in circulation.

MONEY, BANKING, AND MONETARY POLICY 443

5. The **transactions demand for money**
   a. is the quantity of money demanded by households and businesses to transact their buying and selling of goods and services
   b. decreases as the interest rate increases
   c. increases as the interest rate increases
   d. is the only determinant of the demand for money, according to Keynesians
   e. is money held as insurance against unexpected needs

Why do people demand money?

Am I on the Right Track?

Your answers to the questions above should be **d**, **e**, **b**, **b**, and **a**. You can divide your study of this chapter into two parts. The first part focuses on the nature of money, its role in society, and the characteristics of the money supply. The material is largely descriptive. The second part of the chapter is more theoretical. Here, you need to learn the similarities and differences among the classical, monetarist, and Keynesian theories of money's role in the economy. The differences among these monetary theories are the source of enormous controversy and debate among economists.

Key Terms Quiz — Match the terms on the left with the definitions in the column on the right.

1. barter
2. M2 money supply
3. money
4. M3 money supply
5. fiat money
6. currency
7. equation of exchange
8. liquidity
9. quantity theory of money
10. transactions demand for money
11. M1 money supply
12. money supply
13. velocity of money

_____ a. coins and paper money
_____ b. the supply of the most immediate form of money that includes currency, demand deposits, and traveler's checks
_____ c. paper money that is not backed by or convertible into any good
_____ d. P = MV/Q — the equation specifying the direct relationship between the money supply and prices, assuming V and Q are constant
_____ e. the M1 money supply plus savings accounts, money market mutual fund accounts, money market deposit accounts, repurchase agreements, and small-denomination time deposits
_____ f. the exchange of one good for another, without the use of money
_____ g. typically, the M1 money supply — currency, demand deposits, and traveler's checks used in transactions
_____ h. the quantity of money demanded by households and businesses to transact their buying and selling of goods and services
_____ i. the M2 money supply plus large-denomination time deposits and large-denomination repurchase agreements
_____ j. any commonly accepted good that acts as a medium of exchange, a measure of value, and a store of value
_____ k. MV = PQ
_____ l. the degree to which an asset can easily be exchanged for money
_____ m. the average number of times per year each dollar is used to transact an exchange

Graphing Tutorial

Keynesians view the demand for money as comprised of three parts — the transactions motive (the source of demand for money according to the classical and monetarist views), the speculative motive, and the precautionary motive. The speculative demand for money arises from the fact that people have a choice about how they hold their assets. Assets can be held as money, which earns little or no interest, or as other financial assets that do earn interest such as interest-bearing notes, bills, and certificates of deposit. How people choose to split their assets between money and interest-bearing assets depends on the interest rate. As a result, we can graph the speculative demand for money as a downward-sloping function of the interest rate. As the interest rate decreases, people will choose to hold more money because the opportunity cost of holding money (what they give up in interest income from interest-bearing assets) has fallen. By holding a larger proportion of their assets in money, people place themselves in a better position to take advantage of buying opportunities that might arise. That is to say, they put themselves in a better position to speculate by holding more cash. The graph shown below shows the speculative demand for money.

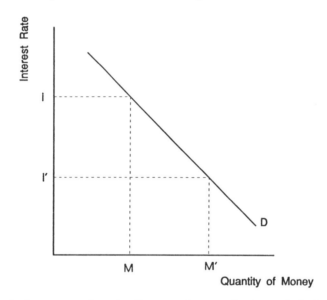

A decrease in the interest rate from i to i' causes the quantity demanded of money to increase from M to M'. Now we are in a position to understand how money matters to a Keynesian. Suppose the money supply curve, shown as a vertical line labeled S in Panel A on the following page, increases to S'. The increase in the money supply causes a decrease in the interest rate that results in an increase in the quantity of investment in Panel B. This increase in investment will cause the aggregate demand curve to shift to the right, raising the equilibrium level of real GDP if the economy is operating below the full-employment level.

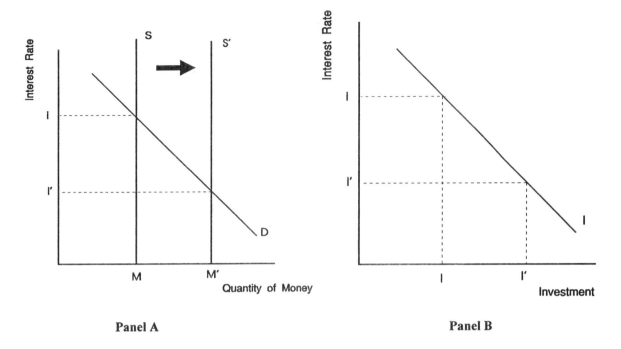

Panel A

Panel B

Graphing Pitfalls

As usual, labeling the axes incorrectly is a pitfall to avoid when graphing the speculative demand for money. The speculative demand for money is downward sloping — typical for a demand curve — and the quantity of money is measured on the horizontal axis — also typical — but the vertical axis doesn't measure price. The interest rate is the price of holding money in this case. The interest rate is what a person gives up in order to hold money rather than an interest-bearing asset. So label the vertical axis with the interest rate.

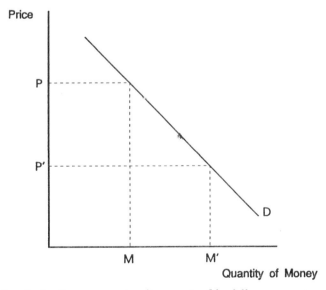

The interest rate is the opportunity cost of holding money, so the vertical axis is labeled with the interest rate, not price as shown above.

True-False Questions — If a statement is false, explain why.

1. Barter only works effectively when there is a double coincidence of wants. (T/F)

2. Gold has properties that make it a good form of money. (T/F)

3. Paper money that is backed by gold is called fiat money. (T/F)

4. According to Keynesians, when the economy is in a recession, an increase in the money supply would decrease the interest rate and, consequently, increase the level of investment and real GDP. (T/F)

5. An asset is considered to be liquid if it can be exchanged easily for money. (T/F)

6. As one compares the various forms of money supply in order — from M1, to M2, to M3 — increasingly liquid assets are included. (T/F)

7. Time deposits, such as people's savings accounts, are considered to be part of M1. (T/F)

8. The largest category of our M2 money supply is in the form of currency. (T/F)

9. The transactions demand for money refers to the amount of money necessary for people to transact the buying and selling of goods and services. (T/F)

10. If the velocity of money is equal to 1, then the transactions demand for money is equal to nominal GDP. (T/F)

11. The quantity of money demanded to satisfy people's speculative motive increases as the interest rate decreases. (T/F)

12. Assuming full employment and a constant velocity of money, an increase in the money supply will lead to a proportionate increase in the price level. (T/F)

13. Monetarists believe that the velocity of money is highly variable and impossible to predict. (T/F)

14. The three motives that Keynesians believe influence people's demand for money are transactions, precautionary, and speculative. (T/F)

MONEY, BANKING, AND MONETARY POLICY

15. Keynesians argue that money velocity is neither constant nor predictable, and is affected, in large measure, by changes in people's expectations of future prices. (T/F)

Multiple-Choice Questions

1. The most liquid form of money is
   a. M1
   b. M2
   c. M3
   d. gold
   e. barter

2. The creation of new financial innovations, such as NOW accounts and ATS accounts, has
   a. created distinct differentiations between M1 and M2 money
   b. created distinct differentiations between M2 and M3 money
   c. blurred the distinctions between M1 and M2 money
   d. blurred the distinctions between M2 and M3 money forms
   e. made credit cards, such as Visa and MasterCard, a new form of money

3. In 1997, M3 was approximately _____ the value of M1.
   a. 5 times
   b. equal to
   c. 50 times
   d. twice
   e. 4 times

4. In order to serve as a medium of exchange, money must fulfill all of the following requirements **except**
   a. divisibility
   b. homogeneity
   c. scarcity
   d. attractability
   e. durability

5. According to Keynes, the demand for money
   a. is an increasing function of the interest rate, that is, as the interest rate rises, the demand for money rises
   b. depends on the supply of money, which is determined by the government
   c. is based solely on the amount of money needed to transact aggregate supply
   d. is based on people's transactions, speculative, and precautionary motives for holding money
   e. exceeds the money supply when real GDP is greater than nominal GDP

6. All of the following statements about M1 are correct **except**
   a. M1, compared to M2 and M3, is the most readily available money form
   b. M1 includes checking accounts, which are generally more liquid than savings accounts
   c. M1 excludes currency, which is the least liquid form of mone
   d. travelers' checks are a form of M1 money
   e. the quantity of money ($ billions) that makes up M1 is less than the quantities that make up M2 and M3

7. The classical model of money demand holds that the demand for money is dependent on
   a. the money supply
   b. the interest rate
   c. nominal GDP and the velocity of money
   d. the precautionary and speculative motives for holding money
   e. changes in the velocity of money

8. According to the equation of exchange, MV = PQ, an increase in the money supply equal to 10 percent will cause the price level to increase by 10 percent if
   a. V is variable and Q is below full employment
   b. V is variable and Q is at full employment
   c. V is constant and Q is at full employment
   d. V is constant and Q is below full employment
   e. V is variable but predictable and Q is close to full employment

9. The main difference between the classical view of money's role in the economy and the monetarist view of money is that the classical school
   a. held that the economy was very competitive while monetarists saw the economy as dominated by monopoly power
   b. held that velocity was variable but predictable while monetarists argued that velocity was constant
   c. thought that the economy was always at full employment while the monetarists argued that persistent unemployment could arise
   d. saw money demand as solely a transactions demand while monetarists viewed money demand as stemming from precautionary and speculative motives
   e. held that the velocity was constant while monetarists argued that velocity could vary over time in ways that are predictable

10. The value of money diminishes as
    a. it becomes more divisible
    b. society abandons gold and silver for paper currency
    c. it becomes more plentiful relative to other goods
    d. an economy becomes more advanced
    e. credit cards come into widespread use

11. A Keynesian believes that velocity is
    a. constant
    b. variable but predictable
    c. constant but only in the short run
    d. decreasing over time
    e. highly variable and unpredictable

12. According to the classical view of the quantity theory of money,
    a. an increase in the money supply causes real output to increase
    b. velocity is highly variable in the short run
    c. an increase in the money supply causes nominal GDP to fall
    d. an increase in the money supply causes the price level to increase proportionately
    e. the impact of an increase in the money supply is impossible to predict

MONEY, BANKING, AND MONETARY POLICY

13. If nominal GDP is $5 trillion, and the money supply is $500 billion, then, according to the equation of exchange, the velocity of money is
    a. 5
    b. 0.5
    c. 10
    d. 100
    e. 2.5

14. The speculative motive for holding money is shown by John
    a. holding money, waiting for stock prices to rise
    b. holding money, "for a rainy day"
    c. not spending money in May because he plans to get married and honeymoon in June
    d. borrowing money from the local bank to finance his college education
    e. buying a large quantity of lottery tickets because he speculates "today's the day"

15. The precautionary motive for holding money is shown by John
    a. holding money "for a rainy day"
    b. borrowing money from the local bank to finance his college education
    c. sleeping with his cash under the mattress
    d. not spending money in May because he plans to get married and honeymoon in June
    e. holding money, waiting for stock prices to rise

16. According to Keynesians, changes in the money supply can affect real GDP in the following way:
    a. a money supply increase when the economy is at full employment
    b. a money supply decrease when the price level increases
    c. a money supply increase when the economy is below full employment
    d. a money supply decrease shifts the investment curve to the left, which increases real GDP
    e. a money supply decrease creates an excess demand for holding money, which raises real GDP

17. The money demand function is downward sloping because as interest rates
    a. decrease, the opportunity cost of investing increases
    b. increase, the opportunity cost of holding money decreases
    c. decrease, saving increases
    d. decrease, the opportunity cost of holding money decreases
    e. decrease, the opportunity cost of holding money increases

18. Barter exchange refers to
    a. exchange of one good for another
    b. the equilibrium price that arises after much bargaining and bartering occur in the market
    c. exchange of a good for a unit of currency other than gold
    d. exchange of a good for a unit of gold
    e. the sum of all values buyers and sellers place on the goods exchanged in an economy during a calendar year

19. Keynesians believe that money matters because an increase in the money supply causes the interest rate to _____ and the quantity of investment to _____ while monetarists believe that an increase in the money supply only causes the _____ to increase.
    a. increase; decrease; nominal GDP
    b. decrease; increase; real GDP
    c. decrease; increase; price level
    d. decrease; decrease; price level
    e. increase; increase; real GDP

20. According to classical economists, a 5 percent increase in the money supply coupled with a 5 percent increase in real GDP will create
    a. a 5 percent increase in the velocity of money
    b. a 5 percent increase in the price level
    c. no changes in the price level
    d. a 25 percent increase in the price level
    e. a 10 percent increase in the velocity of money

Fill in the Blanks

1. Barter requires a _____.

2. Money serves three functions. It is a _____, a _____, and a _____.

3. Monetarists view the demand for money as a _____ demand while Keynesians think that the demand for money consists of the _____ demand in addition to the _____ motive and the _____ motive.

4. The equation of exchange is written as $MV = PQ$ where M is _____, V is _____, P is _____, and Q is _____.

Discussion Questions

1. Discuss the advantages of money over barter.

2. Does a $100 nominal GDP imply a $100 money supply? Explain.

3. What's the difference between the equation of exchange and the quantity theory of money?

4. Suppose the economy is at full employment and that consumers increase their saving, causing aggregate expenditure to decrease. Explain what happens to real GDP and the transactions demand for money.

5. Using graphs, show how a decrease in the money supply could eliminate an inflationary gap. Label and explain your graphs carefully.

Everyday Applications

Consider the implications of eliminating currency from our economic life. Many people have already adopted purchasing habits that allow them to function without using currency. How would this affect your daily life? What would be the advantages and drawbacks of a world without currency?

Economics Online

The history of money is a fascinating topic. You can easily review the history of money from ancient times to the present on the Web at a site maintained by Roy and Glyn Davies titled, *A Comparative Chronology of Money from Ancient Times to the Present Day*. The address is (*http://www.ex.ac.uk/~RDavies/arian/amser/chrono.html*).

Answers to Questions

Key Terms Quiz

a. 6   f. 1   k. 7
b. 11   g. 12   l. 8
c. 5   h. 10   m. 13
d. 9   i. 4
e. 2   j. 3

True-False Questions

1. True
2. True
3. False. Fiat money is not backed by gold or any other good.
4. True
5. True
6. False. Less liquid assets are included as we move from M1 through M2 and M3.
7. False. Time deposits are part of M2.
8. False. The largest category of the M2 money supply is savings accounts.
9. True
10. True
11. True
12. True
13. False. Monetarists believe that velocity is fairly constant and predictable.
14. True
15. True

MONEY, BANKING, AND MONETARY POLICY

Multiple-Choice Questions

1. a
2. c
3. a
4. d
5. d
6. c
7. c
8. c
9. e
10. c
11. e
12. d
13. c
14. a
15. a
16. c
17. d
18. a
19. c
20. c

Fill in the Blanks

1. double coincidence of wants
2. medium of exchange; measure of value; store of value
3. transactions; transactions; speculative; precautionary
4. the money supply; velocity; the price level; the quantity of goods produced

Discussion Questions

1. The problem with barter is that it requires a double coincidence of wants in order to accomplish an exchange. In an economy with many people trading a wide variety of goods, finding double coincidences of wants to accomplish all the desired exchanges would be enormously difficult. That is why money is introduced as a universally accepted good for use in exchanges. Money becomes, as Adam Smith put it, a kind of universal pledge. Less time and energy are required to make exchanges with money instead of barter.

2. A $100 nominal GDP would imply a $100 money supply only when velocity is equal to 1. Typically, velocity is greater than 1. If the velocity were 2, a $100 nominal GDP could be supported with a $50 money supply.

3. The equation of exchange, $MV = PQ$, is an identity that shows that nominal GDP is equal to the money supply multiplied by the velocity of money. The quantity theory of money expresses a causal relationship: the price level is a function of the money supply, $P = MV/Q$ where V and Q are assumed to be constant.

4. Real GDP will decrease since the aggregate expenditure curve will shift down. This is an example of the paradox of thrift. At a lower level of real GDP, the transactions demand for money will be lower.

5. Panels A and B on the following page show the decrease in the money supply from S to S', an increase in the interest rate from i to i', and a decrease in the quantity of investment from I to I'. Panel C on the following page shows the aggregate demand curve shifting downward along the vertical portion of the aggregate supply curve to lower the price level to P', thus reducing inflation.

Panel A

Panel B

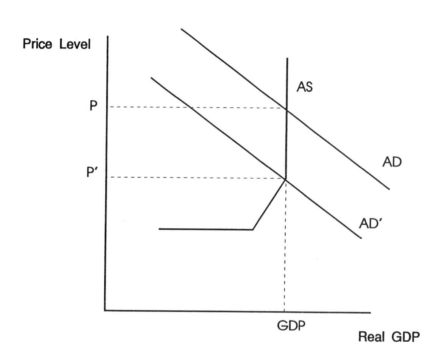

Panel C

CHAPTER 26

MONEY CREATION AND THE BANKING SYSTEM

Chapter in a Nutshell

The fundamental idea that explains how banks create money is the **fractional reserve system**. Fractional reserve simply means that banks have to keep in their vaults or at the Federal Reserve Bank only a fraction of what people deposit in their banks, even though these people have the right to withdraw their deposits on demand (which is why their deposits are called **demand deposits**). How can banks honor a promise to return deposits to people when their deposits aren't there? The answer is that customarily people don't ask for their deposits, certainly not all, and not all at one time. That's what banks count on and, most of the time, it works.

What do banks do with the deposits, if they're not there? That's the "creation" story. When a bank receives a new deposit, it can loan out a portion of the deposit, keeping a fraction of the deposit on hand as reserves. How large that fraction held in reserves must be is determined by the **Federal Reserve System (the Fed)**. That's why they are called **required reserves**. When the borrower who took out the loan spends it on, say, building a house, the housebuilder now has the money and deposits it in his own bank. This second bank is now able to loan a portion of this new deposit, keeping on hand a fraction as required reserves. Its own loan provides income for someone else who deposits it in a third bank, and so on. The process repeats and the money supply expands.

This money creation process doesn't go on forever because each round of deposits is smaller as more reserves must be set aside. Stretching it out, the new deposits eventually become close to zero. How much, then, does an initial deposit create in terms of total new deposits? The answer is found by using the **potential money multiplier** which is **1/LRR**, where **LRR is the legal reserve requirement** (in percentage terms).

The money supply is unlikely to expand to the extent indicated by the potential money multiplier for two reasons. First, banks may prefer to hold reserves in excess of those required. These are called **excess reserves**. Second, and more important, people may simply not borrow sufficiently to exhaust the full amount of the available reserves.

The money creation process can also run in reverse gear. When someone makes a withdrawal, it means the bank's loans are more than its new and lower deposits can support. It must reduce its loans. But that creates its own round-after-round sequence of loan and deposit reductions.

Banks sometimes fail when a large portion of the loans they made are not repaid. When people learn that someone else's bank is failing, they become nervous about their own deposits and may choose to withdraw them. If many people behave this way, they may cause a "run on the bank." If an exceptionally large number of withdrawals take place in a short period of time, loans must be called in, reducing the money supply and real GDP. **The Federal Deposit Insurance Corporation** was created to insure depositors' deposits up to $100,000 so they would be less anxious about the security of their deposits.

However, in spite of the FDIC and regular bank audits, banks do fail. During the 1980s and the early 1990s, bank failure rates rose significantly. A variety of causes account for these increased rates of bank failure. Savings and loans associations (S&Ls) also went through a difficult period during the 1980s as banks began to compete with them in the home mortgage market. Savings and loans failures were so extensive in the 1980s that a special government-sponsored corporation, the Resolution Trust Corporation, had to be established to handle the claims of depositors and creditors of the failed S&Ls.

In the absence of intervention by a central bank like the Fed, banking practice would tend to exacerbate the phases of the business cycle. During recession, a bank is less likely to lend for fear of not being repaid. The money supply shrinks as outstanding loans are called in, causing the interest rate to rise and the quantity of investment to fall, just when investment is needed the most. During prosperity, banks are more inclined to lend, which causes the money supply to grow more rapidly than otherwise, resulting in lower interest rates and more borrowing. With the economy near or at full employment, it creates an upward pressure on the price level. The Fed can counteract these outcomes by using some of its monetary tools.

After you study this chapter, you should be able to:

- Explain the concept of a **fractional reserve banking system**.
- Describe how **banks can create money** by making loans based on new deposits.
- Calculate the amount of money a banking system can create given a new deposit and the **legal reserve requirement**.
- Explain why banks may keep **excess reserves**.
- Show how the money supply shrinks when loans are repaid.
- Present reasons for **bank failures**.
- Justify the need for **deposit insurance** and bank audits.
- Recount events associated with the **savings and loan crisis** of the 1980s.
- Explain how a **central bank** can help to stabilize the banking system and manipulate the money supply to dampen the business cycle.

Concept Check — See how you do on these multiple-choice questions.

1. A **fractional reserve banking system** operates so that
   a. a fraction of depositors' money is available to them at any given time
   b. a fraction of depositors' money is held in reserve by banks
   c. banks lend the full amount of people's deposits
   d. all deposits are insured by FDIC
   e. the potential money multiplier is equal to 1

Are depositors likely to withdraw all of their deposits at any given moment?

2. The role of **financial intermediaries** in the economy is to
   a. provide loans to depositors and accept deposits from borrowers
   b. aid entrepreneurs by finding potentially profitable investment opportunities
   c. control the money supply so that inflation does not result
   d. conduct examinations of banks and savings and loans to make certain they will not fail
   e. provide loans to borrowers and accept deposits from depositors

Which two groups are linked through the activities of banks?

3. When a bank has **excess reserves**, it is
   a. operating with assets equal to liabilities
   b. able to make new loans if it chooses to do so
   c. required to call in loans to increase its required reserves
   d. contributing to the Federal Deposit Insurance Corporation
   e. causing the potential money multiplier to increase

MONEY, BANKING, AND MONETARY POLICY

What is the difference between required reserves and excess reserves?

4. The **potential money multiplier** is equal to
   a. 1/LRR
   b. 1/1 - LRR
   c. the legal reserve requirement
   d. 1/ID
   e. 1/1 - ID

Why is it called the **potential** money multiplier?

5. **Federal deposit insurance** is intended to assure depositors that
   a. they will earn the maximum possible interest on their savings accounts
   b. the bank holding their deposits has made sound loans
   c. their deposits are safe so they won't be easily inclined to withdraw their funds
   d. regular audits of banks will be conducted
   e. banks will continue to make loans during downturns in the business cycle

Why do bank deposits need to be insured?

Am I on the Right Track?

Your answers to the questions above should be **b, e, b, a,** and **c**. The money creation process is fairly clear if you follow the sequence of events — new deposits followed by new loans that are spent and become income, new deposits, and new loans. The logic behind the potential money multiplier is the same as the logic behind the income multiplier. Just as the income multiplier can run in reverse, so can the potential money multiplier, with money being destroyed rather than created. Make certain that you understand why a banking system without a central bank can exacerbate the recession and prosperity phases of the business cycle.

Key Terms Quiz — Match the terms on the left with the definitions in the column on the right.

1. fractional reserve system   _____ a. the percentage of demand deposits banks and other financial intermediaries are required to keep in cash reserves and deposits at the Fed
2. potential money multiplier   _____ b. the quantity of reserves held by a bank in excess of the legally required amount
3. balance sheet   _____ c. a banking system that provides people with immediate access to their deposits but allows banks to hold only a fraction of those deposits in reserve
4. excess reserves   _____ d. a government insurance agency that provides depositors in FDIC-participating banks 100 percent coverage on the first $100,000 of deposits
5. legal reserve requirement   _____ e. firms that accept deposits from savers and use those deposits to make loans to borrowers
6. Federal Deposit Insurance Corporation _____ f. the bank's statement of liabilities and assets
7. financial intermediaries   _____ g. the increase in the money supply that is potentially generated by a change in demand deposits

CHAPTER 26   MONEY CREATION AND THE BANKING SYSTEM

True-False Questions — If a question is false, explain why.

1. Banks keep all of their deposits on hand as reserves. (T/F)

2. The legal reserve requirement is the amount of capital that a bank must have in order to be chartered by the state. (T/F)

3. The legal reserve requirement is determined by the president. (T/F)

4. Banks may fail when an exceptionally large number of borrowers default on the loans they received from the bank, destroying, in this way, a large part of the bank's financial assets. (T/F)

5. One of the causes of the savings and loan crisis of the 1980s was the increased regulation of the banking industry. (T/F)

6. Increases in the legal reserve requirement increase the amount of money the banking system can create. (T/F)

7. Banks are eager to provide loans, thereby expanding the money supply, during a recession. (T/F)

8. The cave illustration in the text shows how a fractional reserve system came into being. (T/F)

9. A demand deposit is the bank's asset; the loan it makes possible is the bank's liability. (T/F)

10. If a bank is allowed to lend $900 on a new deposit of $1,000, then the legal reserve requirement is 0.10. (T/F)

11. The potential money creation associated with a new deposit may be larger than the actual money creation because not all of the money that is made available for loans is actually loaned out. (T/F)

12. If the legal reserve requirement is 0.50, then a $100 deposit in the Paris First National Bank will allow the bank to create loans of $50. (T/F)

13. An unregulated banking system without a central bank will tend to create too little money during a prosperity phase and too much money during a recession phase. (T/F)

14. Excess reserves accumulate in a bank when the bank, intentionally or unintentionally, does not loan out the full potential of its assets, subject to the legal reserve requirement. (T/F)

MONEY, BANKING, AND MONETARY POLICY

15. The principal role of financial intermediaries, such as banks, savings and loan associations, and credit unions is to accept deposits from savers and make loans to borrowers. (T/F)

Multiple-Choice Questions

1. A fractional reserve banking system is one in which banks within the system
   a. can lend out all of their reserves
   b. keep on hand all of their reserves to honor depositors' needs for cash
   c. can lend out only a fraction of their reserves
   d. try to maximize their excess reserves
   e. pay higher rates of interest to depositors than they charge borrowers to maximize deposits

2. The potential money multiplier is equal to
   a. the income multiplier
   b. the interest rate
   c. one divided by the legal reserve requirement
   d. the legal reserve requirement
   e. one

3. The amount of money created in the banking system by a new deposit may be less than the amount generated by multiplying the initial deposit by the potential money multiplier because
   a. many banks, intentionally or unintentionally, may end up holding excess reserves
   b. many banks may end up with more liabilities than assets
   c. many banks may end up with more assets than liabilities
   d. the legal reserve requirements may be less than the requirements associated with the potential money multiplier
   e. double counting of deposits may occur among banks in the system

4. Prior to the 1980s, S&Ls were fairly stable financial institutions because they
   a. invested heavily in a buoyant stock market that produced relatively stable rates of return
   b. invested in high-risk, high-yielding bonds that earned higher than average rates of return
   c. were successful competing against commercial banks and credit unions for mortgage loans
   d. were able to open branches in more than one state, thereby diversifying their risks
   e. did not face competition from commercial banks in the home mortgage lending business

5. Suppose you deposit $1,000 in a bank and the reserve requirement is 0.25. Suppose also that the banking system has zero excess reserves. The total amount of new money (not counting your deposit) that can be created by the banking system is
   a. $3,000
   b. $4,000
   c. $1,000
   d. $250
   e. $750

6. If the Federal Reserve raises the legal reserve requirement from 0.10 to 0.20, then
   a. banks will lower the interest rate to make up for the loss of their loan volumes
   b. the potential money multiplier increases
   c. banks will reduce the loans they make and the money supply in the economy will fall
   d. banks will increase the loans they make and the money supply in the economy will rise
   e. excess reserves will increase by 10 percent

7. If the Federal Reserve sets the legal reserve requirement at 1.00, then
   a. banks could loan out as much money as they want
   b. banks could loan out only the amount they hold in deposit
   c. all bank deposits would be held as required reserves
   d. the potential money multiplier would be infinite
   e. each bank's liabilities would equal its assets

8. When you deposit $100 in your local bank, even though you can withdraw that amount at any time
   a. the bank becomes the legal owner of that $100 deposit
   b. it automatically and instantaneously creates $100 in the bank's reserves
   c. the bank's assets become $100 more than its liabilities
   d. the bank's balance sheet remains unchanged because its new asset equals its new liability
   e. the potential money multiplier increases by $100 times the legal reserve requirement

9. If you withdraw $100 from the bank the following month
   a. the bank's assets become $100 less than its liabilities
   b. it automatically and instantaneously creates $100 in the bank's excess reserves
   c. the potential money multiplier decreases by $100 times the legal reserve requirement
   d. the money supply will eventually decrease
   e. the money supply will eventually increase

10. Assuming that every bank in the banking system holds substantial excess reserves, a decision by the Federal Reserve to increase the legal reserve requirement will
    a. cause the money supply to contract, but only slightly
    b. cause the money supply to increase, but only slightly
    c. force banks to decrease their excess reserves
    d. create a wave of bank failures
    e. cause the potential money multiplier to increase

11. Bank runs are most likely to occur when
    a. depositors discover that other depositors were not able to withdraw their deposits from their own banks
    b. borrowers who borrowed at high interest rates learn that interest rates are falling and will stay low for some time
    c. banks are forced by government to become part of the FDIC
    d. the Federal Reserve announces a series of upcoming bank audits
    e. borrowers outnumber savers

12. The Federal Deposit Insurance Corporation (FDIC) is designed to
    a. protect depositors from losing all their deposits in the event of bank failure
    b. protect banks from being sued by depositors in the event of bank failure
    c. protect banks against the possibility of bank failure
    d. insure the deposits in the Federal Reserve System
    e. safeguard the banking system against bank fraud

13. During the 1970s, banks provided farmers with significant amounts of new debt because
    a. banks had considerable excess reserves they wished to divest
    b. farmers were more willing than urban businesses to pay the high rates of interest banks demanded
    c. prices of grain and land were rising, providing farmers with higher valued collateral to back the loans
    d. the government encouraged banks to make these loans in order to stabilize a sluggish farm economy
    e. they knew that Willie Nelson would bail them out with Farm Aid

14. Loans that U.S. bankers made to Mexico and Venezuela during the 1970s
    a. became very high-risk loans when the price of oil fell in the early 1980s
    b. were quickly repaid in the 1980s, providing U.S. banks with considerable excess reserves
    c. were at interest rates substantially higher than the U.S. rate, which caused many Latin American projects to fail
    d. were transformed by the Federal Reserve to outright grants in the 1980s
    e. were made at low rates of interest because of their commitment to fight poverty in Latin America

15. Prior to the 1980s, savings and loan associations were able to pay depositors relatively low rates of interest on their deposits because
    a. these rates were dictated by commercial banks
    b. mortgage lending was relatively unprofitable for them
    c. Regulation Q set ceilings on these rates
    d. the S&Ls were monopolists
    e. interest rates were falling dramatically in the early 1980s

16. Contrary to what the economy really needs, the banking system tends to _____ during periods of recession and _____ during periods of prosperity
    a. increase the money supply; decrease the money supply
    b. lower interest rates; raise interest rates
    c. decrease its liabilities; increase its assets
    d. increase its liabilities; decrease its assets
    e. decrease the money supply; increase the money supply

17. One argument opposing the FDIC is that by insuring deposits, banks are encouraged to engage in moral hazard, meaning that they will tend to
    a. make too few loans during a recession
    b. charge borrowers interest rates that are too high
    c. engage in race and gender discrimination when they evaluate loan applications
    d. make loans that are riskier than they otherwise would
    e. increase the fees charged to small depositors for routine bank services

18. If I find $1 million in my backyard and deposit the money in my local bank that has a legal reserve requirement equal to .2, then the banking system can create a maximum amount of **new money** (excluding the original deposit) equal to
    a. $1 million
    b. $10 million
    c. $5 million
    d. $4 million
    e. $2 million

19. Suppose that total reserves = $1,000,000, demand deposits = $5,000,000, and the legal reserve requirement = 10 percent. How large are the bank's excess reserves?
    a. $4,000,000
    b. $6,000,000
    c. $500,000
    d. $1,000,000
    e. $4,900,000

20. Waves of bank failures like those that occurred during the Great Depression exacerbate downturns in economic activity because
    a. with no banks to borrow from, the government cannot pursue a fiscal policy of increased spending
    b. as deposits are withdrawn, the money supply shrinks, interest rates increase, and the investment associated with failed loans is halted
    c. the money supply increases as people withdraw cash from banks and this causes inflation
    d. the Federal Reserve typically increases the legal reserve requirement
    e. failed banks are prevented from re-opening by stringent audit requirements

Fill in the Blanks

1. Fractional reserve banking is based on the idea that a bank need not keep all of its _____ on hand as _____.

2. If banks hold loans up to their _____ and checks are written on their deposits, then the banks must _____.

3. During an economic expansion, banks are more inclined to _____, which causes the _____ to grow and _____ to fall.

4. An increase in the legal reserve requirement will cause the potential money multiplier to _____.

Discussion Questions

1. Why is the potential money multiplier probably larger than the actual money multiplier?

2. Suppose you hear someone remark that "If there were no legal reserve requirement, banks would keep sufficient reserves anyway." Evaluate.

MONEY, BANKING, AND MONETARY POLICY

3. Why is the money supply too important to be left to the banks?

4. Outline the problems faced by financial intermediaries in the United States during the 1980s and early 1990s.

Problems

1. Suppose that Springfield National Bank has reserves totaling $100,000 on $1,000,000 of deposits. The reserve requirement is 10 percent. Can this bank make any new loans? Explain.

2. Suppose that Jeff Ankrom, fearing an impending financial crisis, withdraws $20,000 from his account at Springfield National Bank in question 1 and buries the cash in his backyard. By how much will the bank have to reduce its loans? Calculate the maximum amount the money supply may contract as a result. Show your work.

Everyday Applications

Have you seen "*It's a Wonderful Life*" — the classic Jimmy Stewart film? If not, rent it so you can see a marvelous depiction of a run on a small-town savings and loan. If you've seen it, watch it again, this time from the perspective of someone who understands fractional reserve banking.

Economics Online

The FDIC has its own Web site providing information of interest to the banking industry, public information, laws and regulations, and consumer news, along with other topics. To learn more about the FDIC visit the site (*http://www.fdic.gov/*).

Answers to Questions

Key Terms Quiz

a. 5
b. 4
c. 1
d. 6
e. 7

f. 3
g. 2

True-False Questions

1. False. Banks keep a fraction of their deposits on hand and at the Federal Reserve Bank to satisfy the legal reserve requirement. They lend the remaining reserves, assuming excess reserves equal zero.
2. False. The legal reserve requirement is the fraction of deposits that must be kept as reserves.
3. False. The legal reserve requirement is determined by the Federal Reserve.
4. True
5. False. The savings and loan crisis followed the deregulation of the banking industry.
6. False. Increases in the legal reserve requirement decrease the amount of money the banking system can create.
7. False. Bankers will be reluctant to make loans during a recession because economic conditions are bad.
8. True
9. False. A demand deposit is a liability for a bank and a loan is an asset.
10. True
11. True
12. True
13. False. An unregulated banking system tends to create too much money during periods of prosperity and too little money during a recession.
14. True
15. True

MONEY, BANKING, AND MONETARY POLICY

Multiple-Choice Questions

1. c	6. c	11. a	16. e
2. c	7. c	12. a	17. d
3. a	8. b	13. c	18. d
4. e	9. d	14. a	19. c
5. a	10. a	15. c	20. b

Fill in the Blanks

1. deposits; reserves
2. legal reserve requirement; reduce their loans
3. lend; money supply; interest rates
4. decrease

Discussion Questions

1. The potential money multiplier equal to $1/LRR$, where LRR is the legal reserve requirement, is probably larger than the actual money multiplier for three reasons. First, banks may choose to hold excess reserves over and above their legal reserves in an effort to be cautious. Second, potential borrowers may choose not to borrow the excess reserves that banks have to lend. Finally, not all the money that is loaned by banks is redeposited in other banks, and this will limit the extent of the money creation process.

2. It is correct, in most cases, that even without a legal reserve requirement, banks would keep sufficient reserves to cover the day-to-day needs of depositors. After all, a bank does not want to be vulnerable to a possible run on its deposits. The bank is in business to make a profit, and its stability is critical to achieving profitability. However, in some cases, in an effort to make a profit more quickly or out of sheer recklessness, banks may not keep sufficient reserves, find themselves vulnerable to runs on their deposits, and fail if the runs materialize. Also, a legal reserve requirement enables the Fed to directly influence the money supply and, as a result, the state of the economy. It is for this reason that a legal reserve requirement is imposed on banks.

3. Just as war is too important to be left to the generals, the money supply is too important to be left to the bankers. An uncontrolled banking system without a central bank will tend to create too little money during the recessionary phase of the business cycle and too much money during the prosperity phase. This pattern stands to reason. Bankers are self-interested people who will be disinclined to risk loans in a period when economic conditions are bad. Their natural tendency will be to increase their excess reserves during a recesssion as unemployment rises, incomes fall, and businesses fail. As a result, the money supply will contract, interest rates will rise, and the recession will be made worse. Just the opposite is observed during the prosperity phase of the business cycle. Bankers observe healthy economic growth and feel confident that any new loans they can make will be repaid in a timely manner. Hence, lots of lending occurs, the money supply grows more rapidly than it would otherwise, interest rates fall, spending increases, and the economy may be subject to higher inflation.

4. The rate of bank failures in the United States grew markedly during the early 1980s as a result of severe shocks to specific sectors in the economy. One of these was agriculture. Higher prices for agricultural products during the 1970s led to rising values for farmland that provided farmers with collateral on which they could borrow. Many farmers purchased land and machinery at inflated prices on borrowed funds. When farm prices and land values collapsed in the early 1980s, these same farmers began to default on loans, putting pressure on the banks that owned the loans.

Some large urban banks were hit during the same period by a decrease in oil prices that led to the need to restructure loans made to oil-exporting countries such as Venezuela and Mexico. A large number of bank failures occurred in states with oil-based economies such as Texas, Oklahoma, and Louisiana.

Finally, there is the Savings and Loan crisis of the 1980s and 1990s. S&Ls faced new competition from commercial banks in the home mortgage lending business as a result of deregulation in the banking industry. Also, Regulation Q, which had set a ceiling on interest rates paid on deposits, was discarded. S&Ls had to increase the interest rates they paid to depositors in order to compete with banks and other financial institutions like investment houses, which meant that the lower rates at which they had loaned money to homebuyers were no longer profitable. Therefore, S&Ls moved into new loan markets that were riskier, and fraud became evident in many of the operations. As a result, many S&Ls failed. Even though depositors were protected by the Federal Savings and Loan Insurance Corporation, the FSLIC was unable to cover all of the failed S&Ls' deposits, forcing the government to create the Resolution Trust Corporation to handle the disposal of the failed S&Ls.

Problems

1. No, it cannot because with a 10 percent reserve requirement, the $100,000 in actual reserves is exactly equal to the $100,000 in required reserves it must hold on deposits of $1,000,000.

2. Springfield National's reserves decrease by $20,000 to $80,000 when Jeff withdraws the $20,000 in cash. Its deposits fall to $1,000,000 - $20,000 = $980,000. Springfield National should have $98,000 in reserves to cover deposits equal to $980,000. Therefore, Springfield National must reduce its loans by $18,000, causing the money supply to contract by as much as $180,000 — the money multiplier multiplied by the amount by which loans must be reduced. Note that deposits can contract by as much as $200,000, including the initial reduction in deposits equal to $20,000.

CHAPTER 27

THE FEDERAL RESERVE SYSTEM AND MONETARY POLICY

Chapter in a Nutshell

If necessity is the mother of invention, then the experiences of our early banking system cried out for the invention of central banking. Overindulging banks chronically overissued currency, kept too few reserves, and engaged in too many high-risk loans, all of which time and again undermined the fragile, fledgling money economy in the United States. The Federal Reserve System came into existence in 1913 only after a history of failed attempts at central banking.

The money supply in 18th-century colonial America consisted of a variety of foreign currencies and coins. A paper money — the Continental, American money for the first time — was introduced during the revolutionary period, only to be devalued quickly by massive overprinting. After independence, the number of **state-chartered banks** grew dramatically. Many people feared that these state banks would overissue **bank notes** (promissory notes that could be redeemed for gold or silver) and renew inflation. In order to counter this fear, the **First Bank of the United States was established in 1791**.

But it didn't last long. Opponents of the First Bank saw it as unconstitutional and feared a money monopoly. Congress refused to recharter it. Soon after, the number of state banks and the amount of currency in circulation rose dramatically. Again, the money system was in trouble and a second try at central banking — the **Second Bank of the United States** — followed. Although widely regarded as having done a credible job, it too was unceremoniously discarded at the behest of Andrew Jackson during his second administration in the mid-1830s. Apart from the **National Bank Act** during the Civil War, the history of banking in the United States from the 1830s to the eve of World War I is one of growing banking power over the economy but without control or direction.

The Panic of 1907 that followed the **Knickerbocker Trust disaster** prompted U.S. political leaders to reconsider, once again, the need for a central bank. What emerged in **1913 was the Federal Reserve System (the Fed)**. The Fed is composed of **twelve district Federal Reserve banks**, each owned by **member banks** that contribute 3 percent of their capital to the district bank. The main purpose of the Fed is to safeguard our money system. The Fed's **Board of Governors** consists of seven members appointed by the President for fourteen-year terms. The chairman of the board is a member who is appointed for a four-year term. District Federal Reserve banks are also headed by boards of directors. **The Federal Open Market Committee**, one of the Fed's most important operating bodies, consists of twelve members, including the seven-member Board of Governors, the president of the New York Fed, and four other district presidents who rotate. The Federal Open Market Committee controls the money supply via **open market operations**, the purchase and sale of government bonds.

Among the Fed's tasks is to decide how much money to have printed by the Bureau of Engraving and Printing. The Fed also serves as a **bankers' bank**, keeping much of the commercial banks' reserves on deposit in its vaults, providing them with currency and loans, and clearing many of the billions of checks that travel cross-country through the banking system.

However, the Fed's principal goal is to manage the money supply. It has three operating tools at its disposal to achieve that goal. They are changing the **legal reserve requirement**, changing the **discount rate**, and engaging in **open market operations**. Suppose the Fed, worried about inflationary pressures in the economy, decides to decrease the money supply. What does the Fed do? It can raise the legal reserve requirement, which would force banks to hold a greater proportion of their deposits on reserve. In this way, banks lend out less, and the money supply decreases. Or the Fed can raise the discount rate (the rate it charges member banks who borrow from the Fed), which makes banks' borrowing from it less attractive. If they borrow less, the money supply decreases. Or the Fed may resort to its most effective and most frequently used monetary tool, its open market operations. The Fed can sell government securities to the public, to member banks, and to corporations, which draws money out of the banking system, thereby decreasing the money supply.

These same instruments can be used to increase the money supply, although their effectiveness in this direction is somewhat weaker. The Fed can lower the legal reserve requirement, making more reserves available for loans. Note, though, that the Fed can make reserves available, but it can't make people borrow. Similarly, the Fed can lower the discount rate, but banks still have to want to borrow to make that policy work. The Fed's best move here is to buy government securities on the open market, which will put more money in the hands of the securities' sellers. They may deposit the money in their banks, but someone still has to want to borrow.

An alternative to controlling the money supply in order to manage the money economy is for the Fed to control the interest rate, allowing the money supply to take its course. It uses these same tools — the reserve requirement, discount rate, and open market operations — to increase or decrease the interest rate. A number of ancillary tools, including **stock market margin requirements** and moral suasion, are available to the Fed.

The Fed tends to be more effective at fighting inflation in high employment periods than it is at combating unemployment during recessions. Occasionally, the Fed and the government pursue conflicting policies, one encouraging economic expansion while the other discourages it. Remember, the Fed is charged with managing the money economy. If it senses inflationary pressures mounting, it may curb economic activity even if that means creating unemployment. That's where the government steps in if it wants to protect jobs. It can use its fiscal policy to lower rates of unemployment at the same time the Fed uses its monetary policy to contain inflation. In this situation, they work at cross purposes. They did so through the mid-1980s when the Fed tended to maintain high interest rates while the government ran large, expansionary budget deficits.

After you study this chapter, you should be able to:

- Provide an account of the **history of money and banking** in the United States.
- Describe the **organizational structure of the Federal Reserve System**.
- List the **functions of the Fed**.
- Discuss the **tools of monetary policy** at the Fed's disposal.
- Contrast a **money supply target** with an **interest rate target** as policy options for the Fed.
- Show how the Fed can use **countercyclical monetary policy** to influence the macroeconomy.
- Explain how the Fed and the government can have **conflicting economic policy goals**.

Concept Check — See how you do on these multiple-choice questions.

1. The principal function of the **Federal Open Market Committee** is to
    a. set the discount rate
    b. determine the reserve requirement
    c. purchase goods and services required by the Federal Reserve System on the open market
    d. buy and sell U.S. government bonds to influence the money supply
    e. set the federal funds rate

MONEY, BANKING, AND MONETARY POLICY

In which market does the Open Market Committee make trades?

2. If the Fed pursues a **countercyclical monetary policy** in the downturn phase of the business cycle, then the Federal Open Market Committee will
   a. lower the discount rate
   b. lower the reserve requirement
   c. purchase U.S. government bonds
   d. lower the federal funds rate
   e. sell U.S. government bonds

Should the money supply increase or decrease if we are in the downturn phase of the business cycle?

3. The **discount rate** is
   a. a lower interest rate that commercial banks charge their best customers
   b. the interest rate banks are charged when they borrow from the Fed
   c. the same as the federal funds rate
   d. the interest rate that district Federal Reserve banks charge each other for loans
   e. the interest rate that commercial banks charge each other for loans

Sometimes banks find it necessary to borrow. The Fed is the bankers' bank.

4. If the Fed lowers the **reserve requirement**, we can be certain that the intention is to
   a. increase the money supply and lower interest rates
   b. decrease the inflation rate
   c. increase the money supply and increase interest rates
   d. lower the price of government bonds
   e. decrease the excess reserves held by member banks

Lowering the reserve requirement makes excess reserves available for banks to lend.

5. All of the following are functions of the **Federal Reserve System except**
   a. printing money
   b. holding the reserves of member banks
   c. controlling the money supply
   d. setting stock market margin requirements
   e. printing state bank notes

What are the functions of the Fed?

Am I on the Right Track?

Your answers to the questions above should be **d, c, b,** **a, and e**. Approaching this chapter in a step-wise fashion, you should first learn the basics of U.S. monetary history and the reasons for the creation of the Federal Reserve System in 1913. It is important to understand the structure of the Fed. Then you should become well-versed in the tools of monetary policy that the Fed uses. Be certain that you are clear about how each tool should be used under different economic circumstances. Finally, it is important to understand how monetary policy and fiscal policy relate to each other. The economic goals of the Fed are sometimes in conflict with those pursued by Congress and the president.

Key Terms Quiz — Match the terms on the left with their definitions in the column on the right.

1. bank note
2. countercyclical monetary policy
3. state-chartered bank
4. reserve requirement
5. nationally chartered bank
6. federal funds market
7. Federal Reserve System (the Fed)
8. federal funds rate
9. Federal Open Market Committee
10. open market operations
11. discount rate
12. margin requirement

_____ a. policy directives used by the Fed to moderate swings in the business cycle
_____ b. the central bank of the United States
_____ c. the interest rate on loans made by banks in the federal funds market
_____ d. a commercial bank that receives its charter from the comptroller of the currency subject to federal law
_____ e. the buying and selling of government bonds by the Federal Open Market Committee
_____ f. the Fed's principal decision-making body, charged with executing the Fed's open market operations
_____ g. the minimum amount of reserves the Fed requires a bank to hold, based on a percentage of the bank's total deposit liabilities
_____ h. a promissory note, issued by a bank, pledging to redeem the note for a specific amount of gold or silver
_____ i. the market in which banks lend and borrow reserves from each other for very short periods of time, usually overnight
_____ j. the maximum percentage of the cost of a stock that can be borrowed from a bank or any other financial institution, with the stock offered as collateral
_____ k. a commercial bank that receives its charter or license from a state government subject to the laws of that state
_____ l. the interest rate the Fed charges banks that borrow reserves from it

True-False Questions — If a statement is false, explain why.

1. Continental notes, issued by the Continental Congress to finance the American Revolution, were paper money backed by gold. (T/F)

2. Alexander Hamilton was in favor of a central bank, while the idea of a central bank was opposed by Jefferson and Madison. (T/F)

3. The Fed's primary goal, as mandated by Congress, is to promote full employment in the economy. (T/F)

4. At the very top of the Federal Reserve System is the Open Market Committee. (T/F)

5. Open market operations refer to the Fed's intervention in the stock market when it perceives that a decrease in stock prices might endanger the stability of the economy. (T/F)

6. In the event that a bank, at the close of a banking day, discovers it is short of required reserves, it can borrow the needed reserves from its district Federal Reserve bank, paying the discount rate. (T/F)

7. The biggest money problem faced in the United States from the late 18th century through the 19th century was the reluctance of banks to issue enough paper money. (T/F)

8. The most effective and frequently used tool the Fed has at its disposal to change the money supply is its open market operations. (T/F)

9. When the Fed sells a $100 government security to your local bank, the only immediate change in your bank's balance sheet occurs only in the composition of its assets; its liabilities remain unchanged. (T/F)

10. The Fed is often called the bankers' bank because commercial banks can make deposits in it and borrow from it. (T/F)

11. District Federal Reserve banks play a vital role in clearing the millions of checks that are written daily by people and businesses. (T/F)

12. A newly elected president has the opportunity to appoint a new chairman of the Federal Reserve Board of Governors and to replace the board with new members. (T/F)

13. The Federal Open Market Committee can increase the money supply by buying government securities. (T/F)

14. Because the Fed gets its policy cues from government, its monetary policy is always coordinated with the government's own fiscal policy. (T/F)

15. Because the Fed does not know the exact position of the demand curve for money in the money market, it cannot target both the money supply and the interest rate at the same time. (T/F)

Multiple-Choice Questions

1. When the United States' first central bank, the First Bank of the United States, was established in 1791
   a. no other country had a central bank
   b. the U.S. monetary system was plagued by the hoarding of bank notes
   c. unanimous support for the bank was given by Congress
   d. there were many other nationally chartered banks that served the functions of a central bank
   e. there were already central banks functioning in England, Holland, and Sweden

472   CHAPTER 27   THE FEDERAL RESERVE SYSTEM AND MONETARY POLICY

2. The National Bank Act of 1864, passed during the Civil War, legislated
   a. the establishment of an early version of the Fed
   b. funds for the South to reconstruct
   c. the creation of the comptroller of the currency
   d. a significant increase in taxes to win the Civil War
   e. greater competition in the banking industry

3. Financial panics in the United States in the late 19th century were sometimes touched off by country banks that
   a. made risky loans to farmers who had purchased land and equipment at inflated prices
   b. failed because they kept inadequate reserves
   c. had abandoned their national charters for state charters
   d. overissued Greenbacks
   e. withdrew deposits at city banks in the spring to make loans to farmers

4. It is impossible for the Fed to target both the interest rate and the money supply simultaneously because
   a. the money supply is hard to calculate precisely
   b. the Fed can't control money demand
   c. the interest rate is determined on the money market, not by the Fed
   d. Congress has veto power over the Fed's decision-making process
   e. this would be unconstitutional

5. All of the following are characteristics of the Fed **except**
   a. it is owned by its member banks
   b. all nationally chartered banks must be members of the Fed
   c. there are 12 district Federal Reserve banks
   d. it is better at combating recessions than inflation
   e. the Fed chairman is appointed by the president

6. All of the following are mechanisms the Fed can use to increase the money supply **except**
   a. selling government bonds on the open market
   b. buying government bonds on the open market
   c. lowering the reserve requirement
   d. lowering the discount rate
   e. lowering the margin requirement on loans to purchase stocks

7. The Federal Reserve Act of 1913 created the Federal Reserve System, not the Federal Reserve Bank, because
   a. the United States already had experience with a central bank, and it didn't work
   b. the government wanted to keep the entire money system, not just the banks, under its control
   c. Congress wanted a decentralized central bank
   d. state-chartered and nationally chartered banks were already operating in the economy
   e. the government planned to link the central bank to the Department of the Treasury

8. The discount rate is determined by
   a. supply and demand in the money market
   b. supply and demand in the federal funds market
   c. nationally chartered banks, although it applies as well to state-chartered banks
   d. the Fed
   e. the Department of the Treasury

9. Monetary policy is more effective at curbing inflation than reducing unemployment because during periods of high unemployment
   a. banks are more reluctant to lend to businesses and businesses are more reluctant to borrow
   b. businesses may wish to borrow, but banks are reluctant to lend
   c. the Fed can rely on the self-correcting behavior of the labor market
   d. providing easier credit never stimulates borrowing
   e. the government will act, making the Fed's participation unnecessary and even interfering

10. When the government tries to finance a deficit by issuing new government securities while, at the same time, the Fed pursues policies to encourage more borrowing by businesses,
    a. the government and the Fed should raise the interest rate
    b. the Fed should buy the government's new securities issues
    c. the government's policy and the Fed's policy have opposite effects on the interest rate
    d. the new government securities issues will lower the interest rate, which is what the Fed wants anyway
    e. the Fed should lower the interest rate, which will allow the government to sell the new securities more easily.

11. During a period of inflation, an appropriate pair of policies for the Fed to implement would be to
    a. lower the discount rate and purchase government securities
    b. increase the discount rate and purchase government securities
    c. raise the legal reserve requirement and lower the discount rate
    d. sell government securities and raise the discount rate
    e. raise the discount rate and lower the legal reserve requirement

12. Moral suasion and controlling stock market margin requirements are two of the
    a. strongest tools used by the Fed to control the money supply
    b. ancillary tools used by the Fed to control the money supply
    c. tools that are quite effective at fine-tuning monetary policy
    d. tools used only to decrease the money supply
    e. tools used only to increase the money supply

13. When the Fed raises the legal reserve requirement, it
    a. may force banks to call in loans and convert them to reserves
    b. decreases the amount of reserves banks are obligated to hold
    c. creates the conditions for bank loan expansion
    d. makes government securities more attractive because interest rates fall
    e. lowers the discount rate that the Fed charges commercial banks

14. When the Fed buys government securities in the open market, the effect on the asset positions of commercial banks is
    a. negative, forcing banks to call in loans and converting them to reserves
    b. positive, decreasing the amount of reserves banks are obligated to hold
    c. to increase bank reserves, which allow banks to increase lending
    d. a substitution of stocks and corporate bonds for government securities
    e. to increase banks' assets, but, at the same time, their liabilities

15. The most likely place for a commercial bank to go to increase its reserves for short periods is
    a. its district Federal Reserve bank
    b. the federal open market committee
    c. the federal funds market
    d. the Department of the Treasury
    e. Knickerbocker Trust

16. All of the following are roles played by the Fed as a bankers' bank **except**
    a. clearing checks
    b. providing currency
    c. providing loans
    d. providing customers for commercial loans
    e. holding the reserves of member banks

17. The main role of the Federal Reserve System is to safeguard the country's money system by
    a. controlling the money supply, interest rates, and the price level
    b. doing thorough monthly audits of all nationally chartered banks
    c. encouraging district Feds to monitor all business transactions generated in their districts that exceed $1,000,000
    d. putting in place monetary policy that helps Congress cut the deficit
    e. keeping very conservative bankers on the Board of Governors

18. The U.S. Bureau of Printing and Engraving in Washington, D.C., prints our currency
    a. but the Department of the Treasury determines when and how much should be introduced into the economy
    b. and determines how much of it should be introduced into the economy
    c. but district Federal Reserve banks determine when and how much should be introduced into the economy
    d. but the Federal Open Market Committee determines when and how much should be introduced into the economy
    e. but the government, through fiscal policy, determines when and how much should be introduced into the economy.

19. A Fed policy to increase the money supply to eliminate a recessionary gap will be most effective when the money demand
    a. and investment demand curves are steep
    b. and investment demand curves are flat
    c. curve is flat and the investment demand curve is steep
    d. curve shifts to the right and the investment demand curve shifts to the left
    e. curve is steep and the investment demand curve is flat

20. The Fed's use of moral suasion to control inflation
    a. is very effective because people know the alternative to moral suasion is strong government fiscal policy
    b. is always tried before the Fed resorts to other tools of monetary policy
    c. is inherently weak because it relies on voluntary compliance
    d. is preferred by banks because it is more convenient than having to pay the higher discount rates at the Fed
    e. is only used in combination with the Fed's other tools of monetary policy

MONEY, BANKING, AND MONETARY POLICY

Fill in the Blanks

1. The failure to renew the charter for the First Bank of the United States was due primarily to opposition from _____ and _____ states.

2. The main goal of the Fed is to provide the economy with an appropriate _____ consistent with a stable _____.

3. The Fed tends to be more effective in controlling _____ during periods of _____ than in combating _____ during periods of _____.

4. If the Fed chooses to target the money supply, then it cannot simultaneously target the _____ because it cannot control _____.

Discussion Questions

1. How stable were financial institutions in the United States prior to the establishment of the Federal Reserve System? Provide examples.

2. Why is monetary policy a more effective tool for controlling inflation than for controlling unemployment?

3. Outline the institutional structure of the Federal Reserve System. Why are there 12 district banks in the Fed instead of one central bank?

4. Describe the tools used by the Fed to influence the money supply and interest rates.

5. When might the Fed use a money supply target? When is it more likely to employ an interest rate target? Why?

Everyday Applications

Suppose we were considering the establishment of a central bank in the United States now just as we did in the period from 1907 to 1913. Would there be as much political pressure to create 12 district banks today as there was in the early part of this century? Consider the ways that changes in banking technology have reduced the need for decentralization in a central banking system even for a large country like the United States.

Economics Online

The Federal Reserve Board of Governors has an extraordinarily extensive Web site (*http://www.bog.frb.fed.us/*). Among the items that you can browse at this site are the transcripts of Federal Open Market Committee meetings, speeches by Federal Reserve Board members, press releases, enforcement actions, consumer information, and reports to Congress. There is a lot to explore. Have fun.

Answers to Questions

Key Terms Quiz

a. 2
b. 7
c. 8
d. 5
e. 10
f. 9
g. 4
h. 1
i. 6
j. 12
k. 3
l. 11

MONEY, BANKING, AND MONETARY POLICY

True-False Questions

1. False. Continental notes were not backed by gold or silver so as the quantity of notes in circulation increased, their value depreciated. In 1777 they traded 2 for 1 against silver, but by 1781 they traded 1,000 to 1 against silver.
2. True
3. False. The primary goal for the Fed is to provide a money supply that is consistent with stable prices.
4. False. At the very top of the Fed is the Board of Governors.
5. False. Open market operations refer to the purchase and sale of bonds by the Federal Open Market Committee in order to influence the money supply and interest rates.
6. True
7. False. The greater problem for banks in the United States during the late 18th and 19th centuries was their tendency to overissue paper money.
8. True
9. True
10. True
11. True
12. False. The chairman of the Fed serves a 4-year term and can be reappointed for up to 14 years.
13. True
14. False. The Fed's policies and the policy favored by Congress and the president may be different. For example, the Fed's primary concern is maintaining low or zero inflation, while Congress and the president may want to keep unemployment at a low level. Monetary and fiscal policy would then work in opposite directions.
15. True

Multiple-Choice Questions

1. e	6. a	11. d	16. d
2. c	7. c	12. b	17. a
3. e	8. d	13. a	18. c
4. b	9. a	14. c	19. e
5. d	10. b	15. c	20. c

Fill in the Blanks

1. southern; western
2. money supply; price level
3. inflation; prosperity; unemployment; recession
4. interest rate; money demand

Discussion Questions

1. The banking system was chronically unstable prior to the establishment of the Federal Reserve System. Among the most notable examples of instability are the suspension of specie payments by most banks in 1814 prior to the establishment of the Second Bank of the United States and the Knickerbocker Trust crisis in 1907. The problem that a central bank could have helped to solve was the tendency of banks to issue more currency than their reserves could support. A central bank could have forced banks to effectively back their notes with specie — that is, to redeem bank notes with specie on presentation. A central bank could also have provided loans of specie to banks when depositors' demand for specie exceeded the banks' reserves. Without a central bank, bank failures tended to occur in waves with no mechanism for stopping

the withdrawal of deposits from the nation's banks. For example, as a result of withdrawals of deposits sparked by the Knickerbocker Trust disaster, investment projects had to be suspended and sound businesses were left without credit and forced into bankruptcy. A severe recession was the result.

2. In order to lower the unemployment rate, the Fed would have to increase the money supply and lower the interest rate so that investment increases. There are two possible stumbling blocks in this process. First, while the Fed can make reserves for lending available to banks, it cannot force banks to lend these reserves. As we learned in the previous chapter, it is by lending that the money supply increases. The second potential stumbling block is that the reserves may not be borrowed. Neither the Fed nor banks can make investors borrow funds to pursue productive projects.

   Controlling inflation is easier. In this case, the Fed simply reduces the money supply, causing interest rates to rise, investment and consumption spending to fall, and aggregate demand to fall as a result. If the aggregate demand curve intersected the aggregate supply curve along its vertical segment, a decrease in aggregate demand would lower the price level and inflation.

3. The Fed is controlled by a seven-member board with one member appointed as the chair. The board members have 14-year terms, and the chair serves for four years with the potential for reappointments for up to 14 years. The Fed Open Market Committee consists of the board and five of the district Fed Presidents, one of whom must be the New York Fed president. District Fed presidents rotate on and off the Open Market Committee. Open market operations are the purchase and sale of government securities by the Fed. There are 12 district Feds to better serve the regions of the United States and to diffuse power throughout the Federal Reserve System.

4. The Fed can change the legal reserve requirement. An increase in the legal reserve requirement reduces the reserves available to banks to make loans and so decreases the money supply. A decrease in the legal reserve requirement makes more reserves available to banks for lending. The Fed can change the discount rate, the rate at which banks borrow from the district banks. An increase in the discount rate makes it more expensive for banks to borrow, so it has the effect of decreasing the money supply and increasing interest rates throughout the economy. A decrease in the discount rate has the opposite effect. The Fed can use open market operations to change the money supply and interest rates. By selling government bonds, the Fed reduces reserves available to banks to make loans, so the money supply shrinks and interest rates increase. By purchasing government bonds, the Fed increases reserves available to banks to make loans, so the money supply can increase and interest rates will fall. The margin requirement is the maximum percentage of a stock's value that can be borrowed when the stock is being purchased. By increasing the margin requirement, the Fed reduces the amount of borrowing to buy stocks and limits the money supply somewhat. Moral suasion is a technique that relies on people's voluntary compliance to the Fed's wishes. The Fed chair may urge banks to restrict lending, or firms to hold the prices of their goods constant, to combat inflation.

5. The Fed is most inclined to use a money supply target when inflation is a serious problem. By restricting the money supply, the interest rate will rise, the quantity of investment and aggregate demand will fall, and the price level should fall. An interest rate target is preferred to fight unemployment since, by lowering interest rates, investment and aggregate demand can be stimulated. The Fed's countercyclical policy works in either case no matter which target it chooses. However, in that last few decades, the money supply target has been preferred for battling inflation, and the interest rate target has been preferred for reducing unemployment.

PART 6 — MONEY, BANKING, AND MONETARY POLICY

COMPREHENSIVE SAMPLE TEST

Give yourself 50 minutes to complete this exam and see how you do. The answers follow. Don't look until you are finished.

True-False Questions — If a statement is false, explain why. Each question is worth two points.

1. The quantity theory of money states that the price level is directly related to the money supply in the short run because velocity is constant and the quantity of goods produced is constant. (T/F)

2. Monetarists believe that velocity is constant. (T/F)

3. According to Keynesians, as the interest rate decreases, the opportunity cost of holding money decreases, so the speculative demand for money is downward sloping. (T/F)

4. The potential money multiplier is equal to $1/(1 - LRR)$. (T/F)

5. One factor contributing to the savings and loan crisis during the 1980s was the increasingly risky loans that S&Ls began to make in order to stay profitable. (T/F)

6. The banking system could create more money if the legal reserve requirement were reduced. (T/F)

7. The Fed can decrease the money supply by open market purchases of government bonds. (T/F)

8. All of the banks in the United States are required to be part of the Federal Reserve System. (T/F)

9. The primary goal for the Fed is to close recessionary gaps. (T/F)

10. In order for the Fed to be able to lower the unemployment rate, banks must be willing to lend reserves and borrowers must be willing to borrow and invest them. (T/F)

Multiple-Choice Questions — Each question is worth two points.

1. An asset is more liquid if it is
   a. more durable and portable
   b. more homogeneous
   c. closer to universally acceptable
   d. more easily exchanged for money
   e. fixed in supply and easily divisible

2. The largest measure of the U.S. money supply is
   a. M1
   b. currency
   c. demand deposits
   d. M2
   e. M3

3. If velocity increases while the money supply and real GDP remain constant, then the
   a. quantity theory of money predicts that interest rates will increase
   b. speculative demand for money will increase
   c. the equation of exchange predicts that the price level will increase
   d. the equation of exchange predicts that the price level will decrease
   e. the quantity theory of money predicts that interest rates will decrease

4. Keynesians reject the monetarist view that the equation of exchange is a useful predictive tool because they believe that
   a. aggregate expenditure determines the equilibrium level of national income
   b. the aggregate supply curve is vertical at full employment
   c. money only affects the price level
   d. velocity is neither constant nor predictable and real GDP can be in equilibrium at levels below full employment
   e. velocity is not constant but it is predictable and real GDP is always moving toward equilibrium at the full-employment level

5. Monetarists believe that the investment demand function is _____ to changes in the interest rate and that the economy always operates on the _____ segment of the aggregate supply curve.
   a. very sensitive; vertical
   b. insensitive; vertical
   c. very sensitive; upward-sloping
   d. insensitive; upward-sloping
   e. very sensitive; horizontal

6. According to Keynesians, the demand for money is comprised by
   a. the transactions motive
   b. the speculative motive
   c. the transactions and the speculative motives
   d. the transactions, speculative, and investment motives
   e. the transactions, speculative, and precautionary motives

MONEY, BANKING, AND MONETARY POLICY 481

7. Suppose a bank accepts a new deposit of currency equal to $1,000 and the legal reserve requirement is .2. The money supply has
   a. increased by $1,000
   b. increased by $800
   c. not changed
   d. decreased by $1,000
   e. decreased by $800

8. If the bank in the previous question loans $800 based on the original deposit of $1,000, then it has created _____ of new money and the banking system can create a maximum of _____ new money (excluding the original deposit).
   a. $800; $4,000
   b. $1,800; $5,000
   c. $1,000; $5,000
   d. $800; $5,000
   e. $1,000; $4,000

9. All of the following contributed to the increased number of bank and savings and loan failures during the 1980s and early 1990s **except** the
   a. fall in agricultural prices
   b. rise of the stock market
   c. repeal of Regulation Q
   d. fall in oil prices
   e. entry of banks into home mortgage lending

10. An important function served by financial intermediaries is linking savers with borrowers so that people's savings can
    a. generate interest income for bankers
    b. generate profits for borrowers
    c. earn the maximum amount of interest
    d. be available for withdrawal
    e. be used to produce the maximum amount of goods and services

11. Suppose that the Federal Reserve increases the reserve requirement from 10 percent to 20 percent. If a bank holds loans up to its legal reserve requirement at 10 percent, the increase in the reserve requirement will force the bank to
    a. extend more loans to generate interest income to increase reserves
    b. stop meeting the demands of depositors for currency
    c. raise interest rates on loans
    d. wait for loans to be paid back to increase reserves
    e. convert demand deposits into reserves

12. The impact of an increase in the legal reserve requirement from 10 percent to 20 percent will be to
    a. cause an increase in lending
    b. cause an increase in the money supply
    c. shrink the money supply
    d. force banks to purchase government bonds to hold as reserves
    e. cause depositors to withdraw their deposits

13. The potential money multiplier equal to $1/LRR$ is called potential because
    a. banks never exceed the legal reserve requirement
    b. the legal reserve requirement is merely a suggested value and banks typically hold fewer reserves
    c. the actual reserve requirement is given by $1/(1 - LRR)$
    d. the FDIC creates moral hazard
    e. banks may not lend all of their excess reserves, borrowers may not borrow them, and loans may not be redeposited

14. The First Bank of the United States was created in 1791 in response to a proposal by _____ for a central bank to _____.
    a. Thomas Jefferson; make certain the paper dollars issued were backed by gold and silver
    b. James Madison; make certain that debts from the Revolutionary War were paid
    c. Alexander Hamilton; control the money supply and provide credit to the government
    d. George Washington; collect taxes to pay for the Revolutionary War
    e. the British; make certain the new nation had a stable price level

15. The Federal Reserve System, comprised of 12 district banks owned by member banks in each district, was created in 1913 instead of just one Federal Reserve Bank because
    a. 12 banks were necessary to create enough money for such a large economy
    b. Congress wanted a decentralized central bank
    c. central banking was poorly understood in the United States
    d. large regional banks demanded that they be designated District Banks
    e. the large number of bank failures had created a need for many new banks across the country

16. If the Fed Open Market Committee purchases government bonds from banks, the intention is to
    a. raise interest rates
    b. avoid increasing the discount rate
    c. make reserves more available to banks so that loans can be made to increase the money supply
    d. combat inflation
    e. allow the Treasury to finance a deficit government budget

17. A decision by the Fed Open Market Committee to sell government bonds is an appropriate policy when the economy is in equilibrium
    a. on the vertical segment of the aggregate supply curve
    b. on the horizontal segment of the aggregate supply curve
    c. below a full-employment level of national income
    d. with unwanted inventories of government bonds
    e. and the investment demand curve is very steep, close to vertical

18. Among the alternative tools available to the Fed for controlling the money supply, the one that has the greatest potential to immediately alter the reserves available to banks for lending is
    a. changing the legal reserve requirement
    b. changing the discount rate
    c. changing the federal funds rate
    d. open market operations
    e. changing the margin requirement for stock purchases

MONEY, BANKING, AND MONETARY POLICY

19. If the Fed chooses to target the interest rate, it cannot at the same time control the money supply because
    a. it has difficulty reducing unemployment if it controls the money supply
    b. it has difficulty combating inflation if it targets the interest rate
    c. interest rates and the money supply are directly related to each other
    d. it cannot control money demand
    e. there are several interest rates to target, e.g., the discount rate and the federal funds rate

20. If the government and the Fed have policies that work in unison during a period of high unemployment and recession, then a possible combination is a fiscal policy with a
    a. surplus budget and a monetary policy to purchase government bonds
    b. deficit budget and a monetary policy to sell government bonds
    c. deficit budget and a monetary policy to purchase government bonds
    d. surplus budget and a monetary policy to lower the discount rate
    e. deficit budget and a monetary policy to raise the discount rate

Discussion Questions/Problems — Each question is worth 10 points.

1. a. Use graphs to show why a Keynesian believes that an increase in the money supply can increase employment and the equilibrium level of real GDP with little impact on the price level. Explain your graphs carefully.

   b. Would a monetarist or classical economist agree with the Keynesian? Why or why not?

2. Suppose that a bank starts with zero excess reserves and the Fed purchases $10,000 in government bonds from the bank. What is the maximum amount of money that can be created as a result of this bond purchase if the legal reserve requirement is 20 percent? Show your work.

3. Why is it easier for the Fed to limit growth in the money supply than to increase the money supply? How does this influence the Fed's relative effectiveness at combating inflation and unemployment?

4. Why is the speculative demand for money downward sloping as the interest rate decreases?

Answers to the Sample Test on Part 6

True-False Questions

1. True
2. False. Monetarists believe that velocity may vary, but in predictable ways.
3. True
4. False. The potential money multiplier is equal to $1/LRR$.
5. True
6. True
7. False. The Fed can reduce the money supply by open market sales of government bonds.
8. False. Banks with national charters are members of the Federal Reserve System while state-chartered banks may choose, but are not required, to be part of the Fed.
9. False. The primary goal for the Fed is to provide a money supply that is consistent with a stable price level.
10. True

Multiple-Choice Questions

1. d	6. e	11. d	16. c
2. e	7. c	12. c	17. a
3. c	8. a	13. e	18. a
4. d	9. b	14. c	19. d
5. a	10. e	15. b	20. c

Discussion Questions/Problems

1. a. The graph in Panel A shows a shift in the money supply curve that causes the interest rate to fall from i to i'. The decrease in the interest rate causes investment to increase from I to I', as shown in Panel B. In Panel C, on the following page, the increase in investment causes the aggregate demand curve to shift to the right along the horizontal segment of the aggregate supply curve. Therefore, the equilibrium level of real GDP increases from GDP_1 to GDP_2, but the price level stays fairly constant because the aggregate supply curve is flat. Keynesians believe that there are ample unemployed resources in the economy so that an increase in aggregate demand will increase real GDP rather than the price level.

Panel A

Panel B

Panel C

b. Monetarists and classical economists would disagree with the analysis in part a of this question because they believe the economy is always at a full-employment level of GDP along the vertical segment of the aggregate supply curve. An increase in the money supply would cause a shift in the aggregate demand curve upward along the vertical segment of the aggregate supply curve, causing the price level to increase with no increase in real GDP.

2. The reserves created by this purchase would all be excess reserves for the bank; thus, the full $10,000 can be loaned. The potential money multiplier is equal to $1/LRR = 1/.2 = 5$. The maximum amount by which the money supply can expand is $5 \times \$10,000 = \$50,000$.

3. The Fed can effectively limit the ability of banks to lend by limiting their access to reserves. The Fed can do this by raising the legal reserve requirement, raising the discount rate, and selling government bonds. If banks don't have new reserves, they can't make new loans, and new money cannot be created. Increasing the money supply is harder to accomplish because the Fed can only make reserves more available to banks. It cannot make banks lend these reserves, nor can it force people to borrow the reserves. Only by lending and borrowing the reserves will the money supply grow. Therefore, combating inflation is easier for the Fed than combating unemployment. By limiting growth in the money supply, the Fed pushes up interest rates and reduces aggregate demand, which will lower the price level and lower inflation. It is harder for the Fed to increase the money supply, lower interest rates, and increase aggregate demand to increase employment and real GDP.

4. The speculative demand for money is downward sloping as the interest rate decreases because at a lower interest rate, the opportunity cost of holding money (the interest sacrificed by holding money rather than an interest-bearing asset like a bond) is lower, so people will hold more money. They hold more money because that puts them in a better position to speculate. It is easier for them to purchase an asset at an attractive price if the chance arises.

CHAPTER 28

CAN GOVERNMENT REALLY STABILIZE THE ECONOMY?

Chapter in a Nutshell

There is little consensus among economists on macroeconomic policy, not only because they have imperfect information to work with, but because they approach economic issues from very different political perspectives. It is not altogether surprising, then, that liberal economists tend to be more inclined to advocate government intervention in the economy than do conservative economists. The fact that our presidents typically choose economic advisers who share their political ideologies is also hardly surprising.

Macroeconomic theorists, who represent a wide range of ideologies, have focused most of their attention on why unemployment and inflation occur and what can be done about them. Different schools of thought — **classical, Keynesian, neo-Keynesian, rational expectations, and supply-side economics** — reflecting differences in ideology, have developed around the issues of unemployment, inflation, and policies to prevent them. Even within schools of thought there are significant differences of opinion.

The **classical school** believes that unemployment is a temporary phenomenon. Classical economists believe that markets are competitive, so prices are flexible and always moving toward equilibrium where quantity demanded equals quantity supplied. Under these circumstances, labor markets will always generate full employment. The appropriate policy for dealing with unemployment, then, is to not intervene. To classical economists, inflation is purely the result of too much money in circulation. The rate of growth of the money supply should match the rate of growth of real GDP so that prices remain stable, consistent with the quantity theory of money.

Keynesian economists see the world very differently. They argue that prices are rigid and markets are not competitive. A decrease in demand leads to a decrease in output rather than a decrease in price. Under these circumstances, unemployment can persist indefinitely if nothing is done to prevent it. Increases in government spending, decreases in taxes, and increases in the money supply are all appropriate policies for combating unemployment according to Keynesians. As long as the economy is at or below full employment, inflation poses no problems for Keynesians.

To the Keynesians' dismay, the 1970s and 1980s generated both high rates of unemployment and high rates of inflation. The term *stagflation* was coined to describe this unpleasant event. If the policy to cure unemployment was exactly the opposite of the policy to cure inflation, how could both be cured at the same time? Many Keynesians conceded that it just couldn't be done. Then what? Enter the **Phillips curve**. It was used to explain how a higher rate of inflation could be traded for a lower rate of unemployment. **Neo-Keynesians** developed a new version of the aggregate supply curve with an upward-sloping segment that depicts price level increases as full employment is approached.

Neo-Keynesians developed a new stabilization policy based on the Phillips curve. Suppose the government wants to lower the rate of unemployment. It increases its spending (that's what Keynesians would do), which raises GDP and employment. Workers now feel more comfortable to press for higher wages, which creates cost-push inflation. When cost-push inflation occurs because of the initial government spending to lower unemployment, workers discover that their real wages are falling and react by demanding wage increases to make up for the loss. If successful, these wage increases cut into firms' profit, discouraging production so that GDP falls and unemployment increases. Neo-Keynesians now concede that while government can lower unemployment rates in the short run, it is much less successful in keeping them low in the long run.

GOVERNMENT AND THE MACROECONOMY

Rational expectations theorists deny even these temporary short-run gains. They argue that the trade-off between unemployment and inflation suggested by the Phillips curve does not exist. Why? The reason is that workers are rational and can translate past experience into expectations about the future. Let's go back to the first announcement by government that it will increase spending to lower the rate of unemployment. Workers expect such a policy to create inflation so, before suffering the expected real wage erosion, they demand wage increases to compensate for the expected inflation. Their success undermines the government's employment policy because firms, paying the higher wages, have no incentive to increase production. The unemployment rate doesn't fall. According to rational expectations theorists, the government can't lower unemployment rates even in the short run. Any attempt to do so will only cause inflation.

Supply-side economists argue that the best way to attack the problem of unemployment and inflation is by implementing policies that will move the aggregate supply curve to the right more rapidly over time. Such policies include lower tax rates, less government regulation, and less government spending. In their criticisms of demand-side Keynesian policy, supply-siders emphasize the **crowding-out effect of fiscal policy**. To finance its spending and deficits, government resorts to selling its own securities (savings bonds, for example) on the securities market, competing directly with private firms that try to sell their own securities to finance private investment. The interest rate increases and some private investment is crowded out as a result.

Stabilization policy is described as discretionary, meaning that policy is a matter of judgment. However, to some extent, the economy automatically stabilizes. Unemployment insurance is one type of **automatic stabilizer**. During a recession, when unemployment increases, unemployment insurance payments increase and prop up aggregate demand somewhat. At full employment, these payments are lower, thus relieving inflationary pressure. The income and corporate profits taxes work similarly, adding to aggregate demand when the economy is in recession and tax revenues decrease and subtracting from aggregate demand when the economy is inflationary and tax revenues increase. If these automatic stabilizers are effective, then the need for active government intervention to stabilize the economy diminishes.

After you study this chapter, you should be able to:

- State why the **classical school** believes **stabilization policy** is unnecessary.
- Present the **Keynesian** argument for the existence of unemployment.
- Draw a **Phillips curve** and explain its shape.
- Discuss **neo-Keynesian** policies to cope with unemployment and inflation.
- Justify the vertical shape of the **long-run Phillips curve**.
- Explain what is meant by **rational expectations**.
- Contrast **supply-side** and Keynesian policies for economic stabilization.
- Describe how **automatic stabilizers** work.

Concept Check — See how you do on these multiple-choice questions.

1. The **classical economics** view of the economy is that
   a. without government interference, the economy will move toward an equilibrium rate of growth with full employment and zero inflation
   b. a central bank like the Fed is necessary to introduce a countercyclical monetary policy
   c. the Phillips curve provides policymakers with a menu of combinations of inflation and unemployment rates
   d. prices in the economy are flexible upward, but not downward
   e. the money supply should grow faster than the annual rate of growth of full-employment real GDP

Classical economists believe that markets are competitive and prices are flexible.

2. The **Keynesian economics** view of the economy is that
   a. without government interference, the economy will move toward an equilibrium rate of growth with full employment and zero inflation
   b. tax cuts and increases in government spending do little to increase aggregate demand
   c. the money supply should never grow faster than the annual rate of growth of full-employment real GDP
   d. wages and prices are flexible upward and downward
   e. equilibrium at full employment without inflation can be achieved by managing aggregate demand

Keynesian economists believe that markets are not competitive and wages and prices are not flexible.

3. The **Phillips curve** is a graph showing
   a. combinations of government spending and taxation that generate a full-employment GDP without inflation
   b. the inverse relationship between the economy's rate of unemployment and rate of inflation
   c. the direct relationship between the economy's rate of unemployment and rate of inflation
   d. the inverse relationship between the economy's rate of employment and rate of inflation
   e. the direct relationship between the rate of growth of the money supply and the rate of inflation

What happens to inflation as unemployment decreases?

4. A fundamental idea behind the **rational expectations** school of thought is that
   a. the Phillips curve is downward sloping
   b. the Phillips curve is upward sloping
   c. by anticipating the consequences of announced government policy and incorporating these consequences into their decision making, people undermine the policy
   d. most people know too little about economic theory to be able to anticipate the consequences of announced government policy
   e. policies designed to close recessionary gaps work quickly with no inflation, but policies designed to close inflationary gaps reduce inflation at the expense of a recession

According to the rational expectations school, how do workers react immediately after hearing that the Fed will increase the money supply? Why?

5. **Crowding out** is
   a. the decrease in the number of state banks that happened when the Fed was established
   b. a fall in government spending caused by an increase in private investment spending
   c. a fall in private investment spending caused by an increase in government spending
   d. a fall in government spending caused by increased deficit spending during the 1980s
   e. a decrease in inflationary pressure that occurs when government spending is cut

If the government borrows large sums, what happens to the ease with which those in the private sector can borrow?

Am I on the Right Track?

Your answers to the questions above should be **a, e, b, c**, and **c**. The key to success with this chapter is to ask the questions "Why unemployment?" and "Why inflation?" for each school of thought presented. The answers to these questions will help you to distinguish among the various schools. As you answer these questions for each school, you will gain an appreciation for the role played by the Phillips curve in different theories and the varying views on the usefulness of the Phillips curve as a tool for designing economic policy. The meaning of automatic stabilization and crowding out should also become clear to you.

GOVERNMENT AND THE MACROECONOMY

Key Terms Quiz — Match the terms on the left with the definitions in the column on the right.

1. rational expectations
2. classical school
3. stabilization policy
4. supply-side economics
5. Keynesian economics
6. crowding out
7. Phillips curve
8. automatic stabilizers
9. neo-Keynesian economics

_____ a. the use of countercyclical monetary and fiscal policy by the government and the Fed to stabilize the economy

_____ b. the school of thought that argues that people anticipate the consequences of announced government policy and incorporate these anticipated consequences into their decision making, thus undermining the policy

_____ c. a graph showing the inverse relationship between the economy's rate of unemployment and rate of inflation

_____ d. a fall in private investment spending caused by an increase in government spending

_____ e. the school of though that argues that through tax reductions, spending cuts, and deregulation, government creates the proper incentives for the private sector to increase aggregate supply

_____ f. the school of thought that argues that government can achieve the most acceptable combination of unemployment and inflation by managing aggregate demand

_____ g. the school of thought that emphasizes the possibility that an economy can be in equilibrium at less than full employment with inflation

_____ h. the school of thought that emphasizes the natural tendency for an economy to move toward equilibrium at full employment without inflation

_____ i. structures in the economy that tend to add to aggregate demand when the economy is in recession, and subtract from aggregate demand when the economy is inflationary

Graphing Tutorial

The Phillips curve is used to show the inverse relationship between the percentage rate of unemployment and the percentage rate of inflation. The Phillips curve originated with the economist A. W. Phillips who first observed the inverse relationship between the two variables in a study of British inflation and unemployment between 1861 and 1957. Phillips's study showed clearly that for Great Britain over this long time period, as unemployment decreased, inflation increased. A hypothetical Phillips curve is shown below.

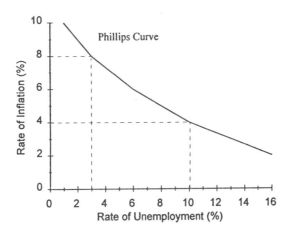

The Phillips curve relationship suggests that in order to decrease unemployment, it is necessary to accept a higher rate of inflation. For example, given the Phillips curve drawn on the previous page, to cut unemployment from 10 percent to 3 percent, one would have to be willing to tolerate an increase in inflation from 4 percent to 8 percent. This happens because a fiscal or monetary policy designed to increase aggregate demand and lower unemployment would do so with the cost of increased inflation. The Phillips curve suggests that inflation and unemployment can coexist and that there is a trade-off between the two — high inflation and low unemployment, or low inflation and high unemployment, or somewhere in between with moderate rates of inflation and unemployment.

The idea of a Phillips curve trade-off between unemployment and inflation was incorporated into the neo-Keynesian version of the aggregate supply curve with its upward-sloping segment as the economy approaches a full-employment level of GDP. The neo-Keynesian aggregate supply curve is drawn below.

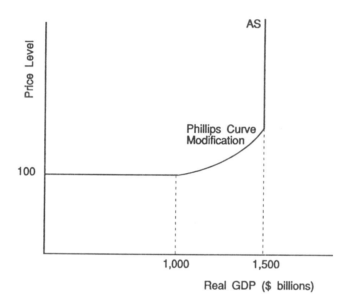

The Phillips curve modification shown in the neo-Keynesian aggregate supply curve suggests that as the economy approaches full employment, the price level will begin to rise. In the context of the Phillips curve, the upward-sloping aggregate supply curve corresponds to the rise in inflation that accompanies a fall in unemployment from, say, 10 percent to 3 percent.

Why does the economy behave this way? Neo-Keynesians argue that as the economy grows faster, approaching full employment, firms attempt to increase production by hiring more workers. Workers who are secure in their jobs begin to demand higher wages. Firms acquiesce to these demands for higher wages and pass the higher costs on as price increases. As a result, the price level rises as real GDP increases along the upward-sloping segment of the aggregate supply curve.

Graphing Pitfalls

Be sure that the Phillips curves you draw to represent the neo-Keynesian short-run view are caved in toward the origin, not bowed-out. Most of the data we have for the Phillips curve relationship suggest that as unemployment decreases, inflation increases at an increasing, not at a decreasing, rate. If the Phillips curve is drawn so that it is bowed-out from the origin, it would show an inflation rate that increases at a decreasing rate. An incorrectly drawn Phillips curve is shown on the following page.

GOVERNMENT AND THE MACROECONOMY

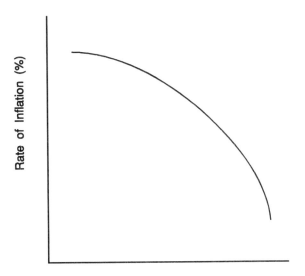

The Phillips curve relationship drawn above shows that the rate of inflation increases at a decreasing rate as unemployment decreases, not at an increasing rate as most data indicate.

True-False Questions — If a statement is false, explain why.

1. Political ideology may influence the way economists believe the economy works. (T/F)

2. A basic assumption underlying the classical school's view of the economy is that firms are highly competitive. (T/F)

3. The Keynesian idea of fine-tuning the economy rests on the belief that it is possible through fiscal and monetary policies to decrease rates of unemployment and inflation simultaneously. (T/F)

4. The Phillips curve shows the direct relationship between unemployment and inflation. (T/F)

5. If the long-run Phillips curve is vertical, then fiscal and monetary policy can permanently lower both inflation and unemployment. (T/F)

6. The Humphrey-Hawkins Act of 1978 defined 10 percent inflation and 10 percent unemployment as reasonable targets for fiscal and monetary policy. (T/F)

7. A beneficial effect of lowering the budget deficit is that government borrowing will decline, causing interest rates to decline as well. (T/F)

8. One advantage to automatic stabilizers is that no decision making is necessary for them to work. (T/F)

9. The classical school explains unemployment in the economy as the result, in part, of interference from unions and minimum wage laws in labor markets. (T/F)

10. A classical school economist would agree with a Keynesian that the cause of inflation is most likely a horizontal aggregate supply curve. (T/F)

11. A rational expectations theorist believes that only temporary victories over unemployment are possible through the use of fiscal and monetary policy. (T/F)

12. The main idea of rational expectations is that consumers and producers anticipate the effects of announced fiscal and monetary policy and react before it has time to influence aggregate demand, thus undermining the policy. (T/F)

13. If workers are successful in bargaining for wage increases to offset the increase in inflation associated with government policies to combat unemployment, then the long-run Phillips curve will be vertical. (T/F)

14. Raising tax rates to curb inflation is a cornerstone of supply-side economics. (T/F)

15. The upward-sloping segment of the aggregate supply curve suggests that as the economy approaches full employment, a higher price level must be tolerated, just as the Phillips curve suggests a trade-off between lower unemployment and higher inflation. (T/F)

Multiple-Choice Questions

1. An economist who states that the cause of inflation is excessive growth in the money supply is probably a
   a. Keynesian
   b. neo-Keynesian
   c. classical school economist
   d. supply-side economist
   e. rational expectations theorist

GOVERNMENT AND THE MACROECONOMY

2. In a world characterized by rational expectations, if the Fed announces that interest rates will be decreased, then workers will respond by
   a. withdrawing bank deposits
   b. bargaining with employers for a wage increase
   c. requesting that wages be cut to preserve employment
   d. increasing saving
   e. decreasing consumption

3. Supply-side economists argue that policies designed to make firms more profitable
   a. shift the aggregate supply curve to the right
   b. cause a decrease in tax revenue
   c. cause aggregate demand to shift to the right and aggregate supply to shift left
   d. lower unemployment but cause higher inflation
   e. cause the Phillips curve to shift up

4. All of the following are sources of inflation according to a neo-Keynesian economist **except**
   a. the influence of unions
   b. dramatic increases in prices of critical inputs like oil
   c. crop failures throughout much of the world
   d. the money supply growing at the same rate as real GDP
   e. excessive government spending

5. Classical economists believe that the economy will automatically adjust to full employment because
   a. aggregate demand will increase, causing real GDP and employment to increase
   b. aggregate supply will decrease, causing inflation to fall and employment to increase
   c. the economy is highly competitive and wages and prices are flexible
   d. successful unions will effectively promote higher levels of employment
   e. employers will raise wages to retain employees as real GDP and employment increase

6. The main difference between Keynesians and neo-Keynesians is that Keynesians believe it is possible to eliminate unemployment _____ and neo-Keynesians believe that in the battle over unemployment _____.
   a. permanently with zero inflation; only temporary victories with some inflation are possible
   b. only temporarily with some inflation; permanent victories with zero inflation are possible
   c. permanently with some inflation; only temporary victories are possible but with no inflation
   d. with great difficulty because of structural unemployment; structural unemployment is of little concern
   e. without government intervention; government intervention is necessary

7. An essential component of the rational expectations model is that
   a. wages are rigid, at least when aggregate demand falls
   b. unions' leaders can be made to see why stabilizing wages stabilizes prices
   c. unions are not very powerful
   d. wages are quite flexible
   e. monetary policy is quite effective when used to combat unemployment

8. All of the following would be consistent with supply-side policies **except**
   a. a cut in income taxes
   b. cuts in subsidies for research and development
   c. cuts in corporate profits taxes
   d. tax credits for firms that pursue research and development
   e. an increase in the capital gains tax

9. The Humphrey-Hawkins Act of 1978
    a. called on government to pursue zero unemployment and zero inflation policies
    b. acknowledged the impossibility of pursuing zero unemployment and zero inflation
    c. put rational expectations policies into effect
    d. forced unions to accept lower wage rate increases to keep unemployment rates low
    e. created wage and price controls to control both inflation and unemployment

10. All of the following are characteristics of the classical model of the economy **except**
    a. flexible wages
    b. monopoly power
    c. increases in the price level that are proportionate to increases in the money supply
    d. competitive markets
    e. flexible prices

11. Keynesians do not view inflation as a chronic problem because
    a. the aggregate supply curve shifts to the right at the same rate as aggregate demand
    b. central banks monitor the money supply
    c. the aggregate supply curve is horizontal until full employment is reached
    d. technology shifts the aggregate supply curve to the left, raising real GDP and lowering inflation
    e. the long-run Phillips curve is vertical

12. The neo-Keynesian view of the Phillips curve is that the curve
    a. is vertical in the short run, but becomes less steep in the long run
    b. is constant, although government policy may shift the economy's position on the curve
    c. shows no correlation between rates of unemployment and rates of inflation
    d. shifts upward over time because government keeps trying to lower the rate of unemployment
    e. is horizontal, so unemployment can be reduced to low levels without causing inflation

13. According to rational expectations theorists, the main effect of fiscal and monetary policy designed to increase aggregate demand is to
    a. lower the level of unemployment at the cost of somewhat higher inflation
    b. create a shift to the right in the aggregate supply curve
    c. cause workers to bargain for a wage increase in advance of an increase in the price level, causing inflation
    d. raise the rates of both autonomous and induced investment
    e. create a larger pool of savings from which investors can borrow

14. The most appropriate stabilization policy, according to the classical school, is to
    a. do nothing
    b. rely on monetary policy, not fiscal policy, in order to keep government interference minimal
    c. rely on aggressive fiscal policy immediately when problems arise to keep the problem from expanding
    d. make sure the Phillips curve does not shift in either direction
    e. apply wage and price controls to stabilize employment and inflation

15. An example of an automatic stabilizer is
    a. fiscal policy
    b. the Laffer curve
    c. the Phillips curve
    d. the Full Employment Act of 1946
    e. unemployment insurance

GOVERNMENT AND THE MACROECONOMY 497

16. In an attempt to prevent wage and price increases from undermining the cuts in unemployment resulting from government fiscal and monetary policy, neo-Keynesians advocated
    a. moral suasion
    b. wage-price controls
    c. raising interest rates
    d. cutting corporate profits taxes
    e. outlawing unions

17. The school of macroeconomic thought most closely associated with the idea that government can stabilize an economy that is in equilibrium below full employment without causing inflation is the
    a. Keynesian
    b. classical
    c. neo-Keynesian
    d. rational expectations
    e. supply-side

18. The Full Employment Act of 1946 made it government policy to ensure that
    a. real wages rise steadily over time
    b. there will be employment for all those willing and able to work
    c. deficit spending be used to increase aggregate demand
    d. unions represent workers who lose their jobs
    e. Keynesian economists be consulted before government makes economic policy decisions

19. One of the reasons why the coexistence of inflation and unemployment in the late 1960s and 1970s was a surprise to Keynesian economists was that
    a. Keynesians didn't think inflation would arise with high unemployment rates
    b. Keynesians didn't think inflation was possible in a modern economy
    c. fiscal policies to increase aggregate demand are naturally anti-inflationary
    d. inflation could be stopped successfully with wage-price controls
    e. inflation was viewed as only a temporary phenomenon with wages and prices adjusting back downward automatically once full employment was reached

20. The progressive income tax is an example of an automatic stabilizer because
    a. when GDP increases, tax revenues increase at a faster rate, reducing the upward pressure on prices
    b. the progressive income tax is a permanent structure in our economy
    c. taxes are withheld on paychecks so people automatically pay them
    d. people tend to forget their tax obligations when they consume, so aggregate demand is always high
    e. people pay taxes from saving, so consumption spending is unaffected

Fill in the Blanks

1. The five schools of macroeconomic thought related to the analysis of employment and inflation are the

    _____, _____, _____,

    _____, and _____.

2. Keynesian economists argue that markets are not _____ and that prices are downward

    _____.

3. The coexistence of _____ and _____ is referred to as stagflation.

4. Neo-Keynesians believe that a government policy that successfully reduces _____ will be followed by demands for _____ by unions, which, if successful, lead to _____ and an increase in unemployment.

Discussion Questions

1. Compare and contrast the Keynesian and classical school views on pricing in the economy. Use graphs in your analysis.

2. Sketch the Phillips curve diagram and explain the logic behind the relationship between inflation and unemployment that is represented.

3. Why is the long-run Phillips curve vertical?

4. How well do fiscal and monetary policies designed to lower unemployment rates work in a world of rational expectations? What about policies designed to reduce inflation? Explain.

5. Give some examples of supply-side policies. Critique the argument that supply-side economists make about the impact of their policies on the economy.

6. What is meant by the term "crowding out"? How could crowding out act as a drag on economic growth over time?

Everyday Applications

The late 1990s have been characterized by low and falling unemployment and virtually nonexistent inflation. Which of the schools of macroeconomic thought you have studied in this chapter is able to explain this remarkable bill of economic good health? Think creatively about this question. Several of the models we have worked with may be applicable.

Economics Online

The President's Council of Economic Advisers (CEA) is a group of distinguished economists who advise the president about what they think are appropriate stabilization policies given current and anticipated economic conditions. To find out the latest thoughts on stabilization policy at the White House, visit the CEA's Web site (*http://www.whitehouse.gov/WH/EOP/CEA/html/workingpapers.html*).

Answers to Questions

Key Terms Quiz

a. 3
b. 1
c. 7
d. 6
e. 4
f. 5
g. 9
h. 2
i. 8

True-False Questions

1. True
2. True
3. False. Fine-tuning involved developing policies to deal with either unemployment or inflation, not both at the same time.
4. False. Rates of unemployment and inflations are inversely related according to the Phillips curve.
5. False. Policies to increase aggregate demand will be ineffective at decreasing unemployment in the long run if the long-run Phillips curve is vertical.
6. False. The targets specified in the Humphrey-Hawkins Act were 3 percent inflation and 4 percent unemployment.
7. True
8. True
9. True
10. False. Classical economists associate inflation with excessive growth in the money supply. Keynesians, who believe the economy is operating on the horizontal segment of the aggregate supply curve do not see inflation as a problem.
11. False. Rational expectations theorists believe that even temporary victories over unemployment are impossible.
12. True
13. True
14. False. Supply-side economics favors tax cuts in order to shift the aggregate supply curve to the right.
15. True

Multiple-Choice Questions

1. c
2. b
3. a
4. d
5. c
6. a
7. d
8. e
9. b
10. b
11. c
12. d
13. c
14. a
15. e
16. b
17. a
18. b
19. a
20. a

Fill in the Blanks

1. classical; Keynesian; neo-Keynesian; rational expectations; supply-side
2. competitive; inflexible
3. inflation; unemployment
4. unemployment; wage increases; a decrease in GDP

Discussion Questions

1. The Keynesian and classical views can be compared using the following graphs. The left panel, depicting the classical view, shows a labor market in which wages are flexible. As the demand for labor falls from D to D', the wage rate falls from $10 to $8. Note that at the $8 wage rate, everyone willing to work has a job. That describes full employment. In the right panel, showing the Keynesian view, a fall in demand for automobiles from D to D' causes output and employment to decrease. Employment in the automobile industry will remain at lower levels as long as demand is lower. In the classical case, wages (and prices in goods markets are flexible), and in the Keynesian case, wages and prices are downward inflexible.

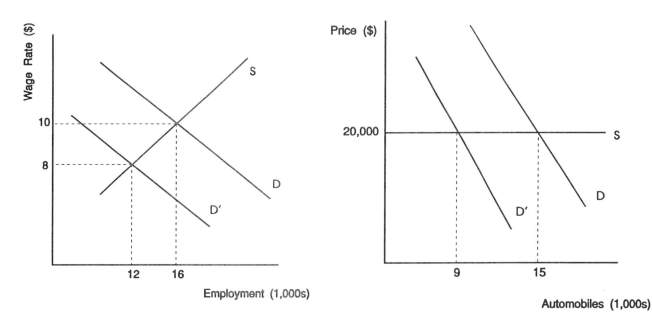

2. The Phillips curve shows the inverse relationship between rates of unemployment on the horizontal axis and rates of inflation on the vertical axis. As the economy approaches full employment, upward pressure on wages and prices causes inflation to rise, and vice-versa. A hypothetical Phillips curve is shown on the following page.

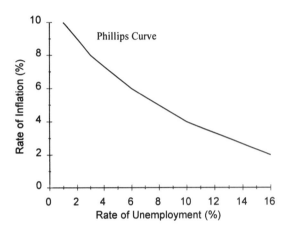

3. Suppose the government wants to lower the rate of unemployment. Government spending is increased, which raises GDP and employment. Unions now feel comfortable pressing for higher wages, which creates cost-push inflation. Workers and unions now discover their real wages eroding and react by demanding wage increases to make up for the loss. If successful, these wage increases cut into firms' profit, discouraging production so that GDP falls and unemployment increases. In other words, while government can lower unemployment rates in the short run, it is much less successful in keeping them low in the long run. If government keeps trying to lower unemployment rates, it can only succeed in raising the rate of inflation. On a graph, these attempts map out a vertical Phillips curve.

4. Fiscal and monetary policies designed to lower unemployment rates don't work at all because workers anticipate the increase in inflation the policies will cause and bargain for wage increases in advance, preventing the policy from having any effect other than to increase the price level. Policies designed to cut aggregate demand to fight inflation work well. Workers immediately accept wage cuts in anticipation of a lower price level, so the unemployment rate does not increase as aggregate demand falls.

5. Tax cuts are at the heart of supply-side policies. Supply-siders also advocate less government spending and less government regulation. In short, any policy that makes suppliers happy is a good supply-side policy. One impact of these policies is to increase their profits. The intended effect of the policies is to move the aggregate supply curve to the right more rapidly over time. If the aggregate supply curve shifts to the right, lower unemployment and lower inflation can be achieved simultaneously. One problem in the supply-side analysis is that tax cuts will also have the effect of shifting the aggregate demand curve to the right, negating to some extent the inflation reduction accomplished by the supply-side policy. Another problem with supply-side tax cuts is that they may increase the budget deficit if they aren't accompanied by sufficiently large cuts in government spending, as happened during the Reagan administrations during the 1980s.

6. Crowding out is the idea that government finance of deficit spending by borrowing pushes up interest rates. The government borrowing causes private investment to be crowded out of the economy in a manner that will slow down the accumulation of capital and create a lower rate of economic growth over time.

CHAPTER 29

GOVERNMENT SPENDING

Chapter in a Nutshell

The level and composition of government spending will always be topics for debate. Decisions about government spending are value judgments, as well as economic decisions. Government spending is more than an instrument of fiscal policy. Even if the economy was always at full employment without inflation, there would still be a role for government. After all, we do need city streets, interstate highways, schools, environmental protection, and national defense. These goods are not typically provided by markets, at least not in sufficient quantities. Economists call them **public goods** because they are basically nonexclusive and nonrival. Nonexclusive means that no one can be excluded from consuming the good, and nonrival means that any person's consumption of that good does not diminish the good for others. By contrast, milk is not a public good because the owner can exclude others from consuming it, and when one consumes it, it is not available for someone else to drink.

Aside from its stabilization and public-goods-provider roles, the government also legislates and administers **transfer payments**. Transfer payments are payments by government to particular groups in society. These are usually in the form of government services, price subsidies, or cash payments. In 1996, approximately 45 percent of federal spending was on transfer payments, and only 27 percent was for provision of public goods. By contrast, 78 percent of state and local government spending was for the purchase of public goods.

The chapter describes federal, state, and local spending item by item. Security is an important spending item. Most federal spending on security is for national defense. State and local spending is split among police, corrections, and fire protection. Federal spending on security has been falling as a percentage of total federal spending over the last quarter century.

There has always been strong support for public schools. Public education is one of Thomas Jefferson's cherished legacies. Over the period 1980 - 96, the annual rate of increase in real government spending on education at all levels was 2.8 percent, slightly above the 2.6 percent rate of increase in real GDP.

Transportation, natural resources, energy, and space are all areas receiving government support. These areas exhibit the characteristics of public goods, though to varying degrees. In each area, competing groups press for different levels of spending. Though the debate over the appropriate level of spending in these areas is fierce, each has its own history and reasons for existence.

Spending programs for agriculture and public assistance are more people-specific than spending on defense, education, or transportation. Agriculture receives public money because it is felt that farm incomes might suffer significantly otherwise, jeopardizing the health of regional economies. Public assistance shows up as spending on **Medicaid, Temporary Assistance for Needy Families, Supplemental Security Income**, and **food stamps**. Public assistance spending by the federal government totaled $95.5 billion in 1996, while state and local governments added another $74.6 billion.

Since the 1930s, government has taken on the job of providing social insurance. The best known of these insurance programs is **Social Security**. Social Security is a compulsory program that transfers income across income and age groups. Low-wage earners tend to receive more benefits relative to their contributions than do high-wage earners. Younger workers paying Social Security taxes subsidize people in retirement who receive benefits. **Unemployment insurance** is another type of government social insurance program. **Medicare** provides health insurance for the elderly. Between 1980 and 1996, social insurance payments rose as a percentage of GDP from 8.3 percent to 9.8 percent. Still, Social Security transfer payments in the United States are somewhat below average for the group of industrialized countries.

Interest payments on the government debt grew significantly during the 1980s. In 1996, the public debt reached $5.3 trillion, and $277.1 billion was spent on interest payments.

Government spending has increased from about 28.3 percent of GDP in 1970 to 34.5 percent of GDP in 1996. Among the major industrialized countries, the United States allocates a smaller share of GDP to government than any other country except Japan. As a share of GDP, federal, state, and local purchases of goods and services (excluding transfer payments) amounted to about 15.5 percent in 1996. To the extent that government spending moves resources away from the provision of private goods to the provision of public goods, resource allocation is affected. Over time, a rising share of our resources have been devoted to the provision of public goods.

After studying this chapter, you should be able to:

- Present a **public goods** argument to justify government spending.
- Give examples of **transfer payments**.
- Describe the relative size of different components of government spending.
- List the areas of **public assistance** provided by the government.
- Discuss how **Social Security** operates in the United States.
- Contrast the level of Social Security payments in the United States with levels in other countries.
- Rank levels of government spending as percentages of GDP for major industrialized countries.
- Explain the impact of government spending on the allocation of resources.

Concept Check — See how you do on these multiple-choice questions.

1. A **public good** is a good for which consumption is
   a. limited by scarcity
   b. expensive
   c. exclusive
   d. rival
   e. nonexclusive and nonrival

Does your consumption of national defense exclude someone else from enjoying the benefits? Are the benefits still there for someone else to enjoy after you consume national defense?

2. **Merit goods** are goods that the market
   a. produces in large amounts because of their high value
   b. does not produce enough of in some people's opinion
   c. produces even though they are public goods
   d. will not produce in sufficient quantities
   e. cannot create like art and music

"The world would be a much better place if more public money was used to support higher education," said Professor Wishart.

GOVERNMENT AND THE MACROECONOMY 505

3. Cash-payment **welfare** in the United States
   a. is an entitlement program for all who qualify
   b. is administered under the Aid to Families with Dependent Children program
   c. requires that those who are able participate in work activities within two years of receiving it
   d. is the food stamp program
   e. supports Medicaid

What changes were made in the welfare program recently?

4. **Social Security** is first and foremost a pension system where
   a. contributions are optional for all workers
   b. each worker contributes to his/her own retirement fund
   c. contributions are mandatory for wage earners
   d. the benefits are a larger percentage of contributions for the rich than for the poor
   e. the benefits are the primary source of income for most retirees

Who contributes to Social Security?

5. In the United States, **government spending as a percentage of GDP**
   a. is rising dramatically
   b. is less than in most other industrialized countries
   c. is quite volatile
   d. has declined since 1980
   e. rose from 1970 to 1980 but has declined since

How do Americans typically feel about "big" government?

Am I on the Right Track?

Your answers to the questions above should be **e, b, c, c,** and **b**. If you can organize your thinking about government spending so that you distinguish between spending on public goods, spending on merit goods, and transfer payments, you'll be on the right track. Then it is a matter of learning the different programs that fit in each category.

Key Terms Quiz — Match the terms of the left with the definitions in the column on the right.

1. Medicaid _____ a. a good whose benefits are not diminished even when additional people consume it and whose benefits cannot be withheld from anyone

2. Social Security _____ b. government-provided assistance — cash payments and goods and services — to the poor, the elderly, and the disabled

3. unemployment insurance _____ c. an aid program that provides low-income people with stamps that can be redeemed for food and related items

4. Medicare _____ d. a health care program administered through Social Security that is applicable to low-income and disabled people

5. food stamp program _____ e. a social insurance program that provides benefits subject to eligibility to the elderly, the disabled, and their dependents

6. welfare _____ f. a program of income support for eligible workers who are temporarily unemployed

7. merit good _____ g. a health care program administered through Social Security that is applicable to everyone over 65 years old

8. public good _____ h. a good that market demand and supply do not produce enough of, in some people's opinion

True-False Questions — If a statement is false, explain why.

1. Government spending on goods and services is strictly an economic decision. (T/F)

2. Your consumption of a public good does not exclude others from consuming it as well. (T/F)

3. The nonrival characteristic of a public good means your consuming it does not lessen the enjoyment others can get from it. (T/F)

4. If there was no government, no public goods would be available because the market would not produce them. (T/F)

5. Social Security doesn't really help those in retirement because they had to pay for what they receive earlier in their careers. (T/F)

6. Interest payments on the government debt declined after 1980. (T/F)

7. The largest share of federal government spending is on transfer payments. (T/F)

8. Determining the optimal amount to spend on national defense is extremely complex. (T/F)

9. The space program represents the most recent addition to the federal government's transfer payments program. (T/F)

10. The federal government's farm program represents transfer payments (from nonfarmers) to farmers. (T/F)

11. Food stamps can be legally converted to cash at most grocery stores. (T/F)

12. Medicare is available to those over 65 years old while Medicaid is a health care program for the poor. (T/F)

13. Social Security benefits go only to those who are over 65 years old. (T/F)

14. A legitimate argument for cutting government spending is that the private market will provide sufficient amounts of the sorts of goods and services that government provides and do it more efficiently. (T/F)

GOVERNMENT AND THE MACROECONOMY 507

15. As a percentage of GDP, government spending in the United States is less than government spending in West European economies. (T/F)

Multiple-Choice Questions

1. Government spending includes all of the following categories **except**
   a. public goods
   b. transfer payments
   c. merit goods
   d. interest payments on the national debt
   e. Social Security contributions

2. To say that a good is nonexclusive means that
   a. everyone will consume it
   b. no one can be denied its use
   c. it is easily privatized
   d. it is of low quality
   e. only the poor purchase it

3. A nonrival good is one such that
   a. my consumption of the good doesn't deplete it for others to consume
   b. it is the best of its kind on the market
   c. the good has no close substitutes
   d. its price is very low
   e. private firms will be likely to offer it in abundant quantities

4. One of the problems associated with a public good is that
   a. people who work in the private sector have low demands for it
   b. the market will provide too much of it
   c. chronic excess demand for it exists
   d. people feel that because others want it, they personally won't have to pay for it
   e. the market will provide too little of it

5. A case can be made that the U. S. international aid program serves all of the following roles **except**
   a. national security
   b. Social Security
   c. an expression of our humanitarian concern
   d. jobs creation
   e. transfer payment

6. The largest percentage of federal government spending is on
   a. purchases of goods and services
   b. grants-in-aid to state and local governments
   c. transfer payments
   d. foreign aid
   e. defense

7. As a percentage of total federal spending, from 1970 to 1996 spending on national defense in the United States
   a. rose
   b. fluctuated wildly between presidential administrations
   c. stayed the same
   d. fell
   e. failed to keep up with inflation

8. Spending on education in the United States
   a. is greater at the federal level than at the state and local level
   b. fell from 1980 to 1996
   c. was constant from 1980 to 1996
   d. rose in nominal terms but fell in real terms from 1980 to 1996
   e. is greater at the state and local level than at the national level

9. The largest share of spending on transportation is handled at the
   a. municipal level
   b. state and local level
   c. federal level
   d. regional level
   e. international level

10. Government spending on agriculture has been justified on the grounds that
    a. without aid, the farm economy and the national economy would be destabilized
    b. farm prices are rising so research and development need to be financed
    c. food prices can be kept low this way
    d. no one would farm otherwise
    e. farming is harder work than other occupations

11. One difference between Medicaid and Temporary Assistance for Needy Families (TANF) is that
    a. Medicaid serves the elderly and TANF serves the poor
    b. Medicaid provides in-kind benefits while TANF provides cash grants
    c. TANF guarantees that the poor will get jobs while Medicaid provides limited medical education
    d. TANF is an entitlement and Medicaid is not
    e. Medicaid is an entitlement and TANF is not

12. Government insurance protects individuals from all of the following **except** income losses due to
    a. retirement
    b. unemployment
    c. disability
    d. unexpected deaths of breadwinners
    e. fires

13. When Social Security transfers in the United States are compared to those in other developed countries as a percentage of GDP, the United States is spending
    a. somewhat less
    b. about the same
    c. an adequate amount
    d. an inadequate amount
    e. far more

GOVERNMENT AND THE MACROECONOMY

14. When government spending in the United States is compared to spending in other industrialized countries as a percentage of GDP, it is clear that spending levels in the United States
    a. are well above those in other countries
    b. are near the bottom of the range that is observed
    c. have risen much faster than in other countries
    d. need to be cut
    e. need to be increased

15. Throughout the 1970-96 period, government spending in the United States was
    a. within a few percentage points of half of GDP
    b. a much higher share of GDP than government spending in Canada
    c. slowly falling
    d. within a few percentage points of a third of GDP
    e. rising much faster than GDP

16. Government spending on public goods shifts resource allocation
    a. toward private goods
    b. away from private goods
    c. to less productive uses
    d. to more productive uses
    e. to transfer payments

17. All of the following are examples of merit goods **except**
    a. National Public Radio
    b. the Public Broadcasting System
    c. state universities
    d. private universities
    e. the National Endowment for the Arts

18. During the 1980s, interest payments on the national debt
    a. rose
    b. fell
    c. were constant
    d. were offset by increased tax revenue due to supply-side policies
    e. were halted for a time when the government defaulted

19. One reason that Aid to Families with Dependent Children was eliminated is
    a. the feeling that the program had served its function
    b. that it was bankrupting the nation
    c. the feeling that it undermined the recipients' motivation to work
    d. the rising cost of Social Security
    e. that food stamps served the same function

20. One reason for concern about the future of the Social Security and Medicare systems is
    a. that people no longer contribute to them
    b. the falling ratio of retirees to working people
    c. that people retire later in life now
    d. the rising ratio of retirees to working people
    e. that the trust fund is virtually depleted

Fill in the Blanks

1. Public goods are _____ and _____.

2. Transfer payments represent a _____ of income from taxpayers to _____.

3. Approximately 65 percent of all government spending is done by the _____ and the remaining 35 percent is done by _____.

4. Government decides what goods and services will be produced for approximately _____ percent of GDP.

Discussion Questions

1. What distinguishes government spending on public goods from transfer payments?

2. Explain why the government spends on agriculture. Is this spending a public good, a transfer payment, or part of the government's countercyclical fiscal policy?

3. How is Social Security financed in the United States? How is this system different from a private pension fund?

4. Discuss the recent changes in the welfare program in the United States.

Everyday Applications

How would your life change if government spending went to zero?

Economics Online

The Social Security Administration has a Web site (*http://www.ssa.gov/*). The page provides considerable information about the issue of social security's solvency in the coming decades as the baby boomers retire. This is an important matter for you — you'll be paying the taxes to support Social Security benefits for my generation.

Answers to Questions

Key Terms Quiz

a. 8
b. 6
c. 5
d. 1
e. 2
f. 3
g. 4
h. 7

True-False Questions

1. False. There is a political element to the choice of which public goods to purchase and how transfer payments should be allocated among various recipients and at what level.
2. True
3. True
4. False. The market would not supply enough of public goods.
5. False. People in retirement receive Social Security benefits that are paid for by those who are currently employed. Retirees' contributions to Social Security supported an earlier generation of retirees.
6. False. Interest payments on the national debt grew significantly during the 1980s.
7. True
8. True
9. False. The space program has characteristics of a public good and a merit good. It is not a transfer program.
10. True
11. False. Food stamps can only be legally exchanged for food.
12. True
13. False. Eligibility for benefits extends to the disabled and dependents of beneficiaries.
14. False. The market would not provide adequate quantities of public goods, and transfer payments would rarely occur without government.
15. True

Multiple-Choice Questions

1. e	6. c	11. b	16. b
2. b	7. d	12. e	17. d
3. a	8. e	13. a	18. a
4. e	9. b	14. b	19. c
5. b	10. a	15. d	20. d

Fill in the Blanks

1. nonexclusive; nonrival
2. redistribution; particular groups
3. federal government; state and local governments
4. 15.5

GOVERNMENT AND THE MACROECONOMY

Discussion Questions

1. Purchases of public goods by government correspond to the use of public money to buy specific amounts of goods and services that the market would not provide in sufficient quantities. These goods are nonexclusive and nonrival to some degree. Merit goods are also purchased by government. These are goods that the market would not provide enough of, according to some people. Determining the quantity of public goods to be purchased is a matter of controversy and debate in many cases. The decision to purchase public goods shifts the allocation of resources from one that is determined by consumer sovereignty in the private market toward an allocation that is partially determined by government. In the case of transfer payments, consumer sovereignty determines the allocation of resources because income is shifted from taxpayers to particular groups in society. Private individuals then decide what to purchase with the income that is redistributed.

2. Government spending on the farm community is essentially a transfer payment. Government farm programs end up taxing nonfarming populations and giving the income to the farming population. The agricultural sector has substantial political clout, which helps to maintain the transfer payment. The primary justification for government aid to farmers is that instability in the agricultural economy could contribute to instability in the national economy.

3. Social Security is financed by taxes paid jointly by employers and employees. Current employees pay for the benefits received by the current generation of retirees. Social Security differs from a private pension fund in three ways. First, Social Security is mandatory. Second, Social Security transfers income across income and age groups. A pension fund keeps funds that an individual deposits for that individual. Third, Social Security is a pay-as-you-go system financed by a payroll tax, half of which is paid by the employee with the remainder paid by the employer.

4. The major recent change in the welfare system in the United States has been the elimination of Aid to Families with Dependent Children. On August 22, 1996, the Personal Responsibility and Work Opportunity Reconciliation Act was enacted by Congress. This act created the Temporary Assistance for Needy Families program, which was to abolish entitlement in the welfare program. The federal government now provides states with capped block grants to administer their own welfare programs. Welfare recipients must participate in work activities within two years of receiving aid or risk losing it. Eligibility for a family on welfare runs out after five years of benefits. The idea behind the new program is to create incentives for people on welfare to gain skills and enter the labor force. However, many of these individuals have few skills, and the question remains whether enough low-skill jobs will be available to employ those going off the welfare rolls.

CHAPTER 30

FINANCING GOVERNMENT: TAXES AND DEBT

Chapter in a Nutshell

Public goods are not free goods. Resources are needed to produce city streets, just as they are needed to produce automobiles that drive up and down those streets. The opportunity cost of producing public goods — measured by how much we must give up of private goods — is always a matter of public debate. But even if we know how many public goods we want and are willing to make the sacrifice to acquire them, the question still remains: How does the government get the money it needs to provide those public goods?

In pre-modern societies, a government would often simply **commandeer** the resources it needed. If it needed labor to construct roads, it simply rounded up people to make the roads. The roads were built, but not necessarily in the most efficient way. In modern societies, government has shifted from commandeering resources to commandeering money. That's the essence of a tax system.

There are a number of ways to tax. Perhaps the simplest is a **poll (or head) tax**, say, $100, that is levied on every adult in a population. If there are 1,000 people, then the government's tax revenue is $100,000. An alternative way of taxing the population is by levying the tax on the person's income, rather than on the person. This is the income tax. An income tax structure can be **regressive** (the rich are taxed a lower percentage of their income than are the poor), **proportional** (the rich and poor are taxed the same percentage) or **progressive** (the rich are taxed a higher percentage). The government can also levy **taxes on corporate profits**, or on wealth (such as a **property tax** or estate and gift taxes). Perhaps the most widely used tax is levied not on a person's income or wealth, but on the person's consumption (**sales and excise taxes**). Contributions to the Social Security system are another form of taxation, but these are earmarked to finance the benefits the Social Security system is obligated to pay.

What does the U.S. tax structure look like? At the federal level, the income tax is the most important source of revenue. Its structure is progressive, with five tax brackets. The richer you are, the higher the tax rate on your higher income. If you are married and you and your spouse together earned $300,000, you paid 15 percent on your first $41,200; 28 percent on the income over $41,200 up to $99,600; 31 percent on income over $99,600 up to $151,750; 36 percent on income over $151,750 up to $271,050; and 39.6 percent on the income over $271,050 up to $300,000. Most states have their own state income taxes, but these are not as important a contributor to state revenue as their sales taxes. The property tax is the primary source of revenue for local governments.

For all but a few years since World War II, federal government spending has exceeded the tax revenues collected. How does government make up for the **deficit** (one year's contribution to the **public debt**)? The chapter focuses on the federal government's use of debt financing. The government sells securities through its Department of the Treasury. These securities are its IOUs. People loan money to the government in return for interest payments. The securities are regarded as very safe investments because the government has never defaulted on either interest or principal. The securities come in three forms: **Treasury bills**, which mature in one year or less; **Treasury notes**, which mature in 2 to 10 years; and **Treasury bonds**, which mature in 30 years.

The **public debt** has risen enormously since 1929, particularly since the 1980s, but so has GDP. The debt/GDP ratio was lower in 1996, by about one-third, than at the end of World War II. Big spurts in the

GOVERNMENT AND THE MACROECONOMY

debt/GDP ratio occurred in the decades of the 1930s, the 1940s, and the 1980s. The debt/GDP ratio for the United States is similar to those in other industrialized countries.

Government debt, like government deficits, is a contentious political issue. How much longer can the government finance its deficits by selling IOUs before it goes bankrupt? Are we placing a terrible financial burden on future generations?

Economists distinguish between an **internally financed debt** (its securities are purchased by its own population) and an **externally financed debt** (its securities are purchased by foreigners). An internal debt neither adds to nor subtracts from the nation's income. If 100 percent of the U.S. government debt is held internally (by U.S. citizens), then all the interest that the government pays goes to Americans. Where does the government get the money to pay for the interest? By taxing its citizens. In a sense then, Americans tax themselves to pay themselves. What about future generations? If future generations are forced to pay for the debt, they pay it only to themselves.

An external debt is different. The people who are taxed to pay the interest on the debt are not the same people who receive the interest payments. An external debt can burden future generations.

Internally financed debt can still cause problems. If the debt is held by few people, then everybody is taxed to pay the interest that goes to the few. In this way, the debt contributes to greater income inequality. It can also create over consumption because people view their securities holdings as real wealth and save less than they perhaps should. It can also contribute to inflation and crowding out of private investment.

Deficits and debt are not inevitable. A **balanced budget** exists if tax revenues match government spending. The extraordinary rise in the deficits and debt in the 1980s resulted from the tax reform acts of 1981 and 1986 that overhauled our tax rates and brackets, and with them, tax revenues. The Gramm-Rudman-Hollings Act of 1985 was intended to introduce discipline to the budgetary process by setting targets for deficit reduction. This act failed to achieve its goals. A constitutional amendment that would mandate a year-by-year balanced budget was seriously considered by Congress but failed. However, during the late 1990s, what many thought was impossible actually happened. The deficit shrank to zero. As a result of rising tax revenues due to increasing national income, coupled with cuts in government spending, the budget has become balanced.

After studying this chapter, you should be able to:

- Describe the various ways that governments have financed their activities over time.
- Discuss different systems of **income taxation**.
- Explain why an **excise tax** is a tax on consumption.
- Compare the magnitudes of **federal, state, and local tax revenues**.
- Describe how government spending can be financed through the sale of **government securities**.
- Evaluate the danger of a large **public debt** to our economic health.
- Recount the debate over the **federal budget deficit** during the 1980s and 1990s.

Concept Check — See how you do on these multiple-choice questions.

1. A **regressive income tax** is one where the poor
   a. have a lower percentage of their income taxed than the rich
   b. pay a larger dollar amount in taxes than the rich
   c. pay a tax that varies directly with their income
   d. have a higher percentage of their income taxed than the rich
   e. are able to use tax revenue to purchase basic goods

How do we distinguish among regressive, proportional, and progressive taxes?

2. The **public debt** is the total amount of
   a. debt held by the public
   b. government securities held by individuals, businesses, government agencies, and the Federal Reserve
   c. demand deposits held by banks
   d. outstanding commercial loans
   e. outstanding mortgages

How does the government issue debt?

3. The level of **external debt** rises when the U.S. Treasury
   a. prints more money
   b. sells securities to Americans
   c. increases the deficit
   d. decreases the deficit
   e. sells securities to foreigners

What is the difference between internal and external debt?

4. A **poll tax** is a tax levied
   a. on voters
   b. on those who respond to pollsters' questions
   c. per person
   d. on the value of property
   e. per village

The original meaning of the word "poll" is head.

5. **Property taxes** are
   a. an important source of state and local governments' revenue
   b. an important source of federal revenue
   c. proportional to income
   d. progressive
   e. consumption taxes

Which levels of government levy property taxes?

Am I on the Right Track?

Your answers to the questions above should be **d, b, e, c,** and **a**. This chapter is split into two distinct sections.

GOVERNMENT AND THE MACROECONOMY

The first deals with using various taxes to finance government. The array of available tax options is a tribute to the creativity of governments in need of funding. The second part of the chapter presents issues associated with the government's decision to borrow in order to fund spending. The decision to borrow has different implications for an economy depending on the circumstances.

Key Terms Quiz — Match the terms on the left with the definitions in the column on the right.

1. poll tax
2. unit tax
3. regressive income tax
4. sales tax
5. proportional income tax
6. customs duty
7. progressive income tax
8. excise tax
9. corporate income tax
10. public debt
11. property tax
12. savings bond
13. external debt

_____ a. a tax whose impact varies inversely with the income of the person taxed so that poor people have a higher percentage of their income taxed than do rich people

_____ b. a tax levied on the value of physical assets such as land or financial assets such as stocks and bonds

_____ c. a tax of a specific absolute sum levied on every person or every household

_____ d. a tax levied on a corporation's income before dividends are distributed to stockholders

_____ e. a sales tax applied to a foreign good or service

_____ f. a nonmarketable Treasury bond that is the most commonly held form of public debt

_____ g. public debt held by foreigners

_____ h. a fixed tax in the form of cents or dollars per unit levied on a good or service

_____ i. a tax that is a fixed percentage of income, regardless of the level of income

_____ j. any tax levied on a good or service, such as a unit tax, a sales tax, or a customs duty

_____ k. a tax levied in the form of a specific percentage of the value of the good or service

_____ l. the total value of government securities held by individuals, businesses, other government agencies, and the Federal Reserve

_____ m. a tax whose rate varies directly with the income of the person taxed so that rich people have a higher percentage of their income taxed than do poor people

True-False Questions — If a question is false, explain why.

1. Because people don't pay directly for public goods, these goods are described by economists as free goods. (T/F)

2. A poll tax is fair because every adult in a population must pay it. (T/F)

3. The difference between a deficit and the debt is that a deficit represents the accumulation of debts over many years, while a debt represents the amount by which government spending exceeds tax revenue in a single year. (T/F)

4. If the government raises interest rates on the bonds that it offers for sale, government debt may crowd out private investment. (T/F)

5. External debt is private debt and internal debt is public debt. (T/F)

6. The Gramm-Rudman-Hollings Act of 1985 called for across-the-board cuts in government spending if deficit reduction targets were not met. (T/F)

7. The largest holders of the U.S. public debt are foreigners, mainly Japanese and Saudi Arabians. (T/F)

8. The U.S. public debt in the mid-1990s was over 100 percent of GDP. (T/F)

9. When your salary bonus moves you up a bracket in a progressive income tax structure, all your income is now taxed at the new higher rate, which is why most people complain about tax increases. (T/F)

10. Compared to other industrialized countries, the tax/GDP ratio in the United States is relatively high. (T/F)

11. A principal difference between the income tax you pay and the contributions you make to Social Security is that your Social Security contributions are earmarked. (T/F)

12. The public debt consists of only one year's government securities, which must be paid back at the end of the fiscal year. (T/F)

13. If our public debt is held internally, Americans make payments on the debt to themselves. (T/F)

14. By borrowing in order to finance its spending, the government can alter the mix of goods purchased by its population to include more public goods and fewer private goods. (T/F)

15. Federal Reserve purchases of government securities issued to finance a deficit can create inflation because they cause the money supply to grow. (T/F)

Multiple-Choice Questions

1. All of the following are examples of regressive taxes **except**
   a. the poll tax
   b. excise taxes
   c. sales taxes
   d. customs duties
   e. the proportional income tax

GOVERNMENT AND THE MACROECONOMY

2. The revenue from Social Security taxes is
    a. invested in a pension fund for each individual to draw on at retirement
    b. earmarked for a trust fund out of which Social Security benefits are paid
    c. never sufficient to pay all the benefits for retirees and other beneficiaries
    d. handled in the same way that other tax revenues are handled
    e. about equal to the revenue generated by gift and estate taxes

3. Crowding out is the idea that as the government finances deficit spending by borrowing, it must
    a. lower interest rates, thus diverting funds away from private investment
    b. raise interest rates, thus diverting funds away from private investment
    c. keep private borrowers completely out of the market for investment funds
    d. accept the lower growth rate in the economy that inevitably results
    e. ask for higher and higher prices on the bonds it sells

4. The national debt is a burden to future generations to the extent that a portion of the debt is held by
    a. foreigners
    b. government institutions like the Social Security trust fund
    c. insurance companies
    d. national banks
    e. pension funds

5. The primary source of revenue for general spending by the federal government is
    a. property taxes
    b. income taxes
    c. tariff revenues
    d. inheritance taxes
    e. corporate income taxes

6. The main problem with the accumulation of a public debt that results from running deficit budgets each year is that
    a. financing the deficit becomes more difficult each year because the nation's credit is deteriorating
    b. interest rates have to be kept low so that the government can afford to borrow
    c. the deficit is climbing to very high levels as a percentage of GDP
    d. the government must pay a high interest rate to borrow and this tends to crowd out private investment
    e. private investment is nearly always more efficient than public investment, so most government activities should be turned over to the private sector

7. Until the 1980s, most of the federal debt accumulated as a result of
    a. natural disasters
    b. government spending that was grossly out of line with spending in other countries
    c. wars and recessions
    d. tax cuts
    e. the absence of a balanced budget amendment to the Constitution

8. The argument that the U.S. public debt is not a burden to future generations of Americans is correct insofar as the debt is held by
   a. the very rich
   b. Americans, with ownership of the debt spread evenly over the population
   c. foreigners who are paid in dollars
   d. international financial institutions like the World Bank
   e. the Social Security trust fund

9. One reason that the federal budget is so difficult to balance is that
   a. the Treasury is always issuing new securities
   b. people enjoy the benefits associated with government spending programs, so that cuts are unpopular
   c. there is very little wasteful spending that could be cut
   d. even minor spending cuts and tax increases would be disastrous for the economy
   e. the budget is far too complicated to expect balance to be achieved

10. The largest owners of the U.S. public debt are
    a. individual U.S. citizens
    b. commercial banks
    c. state and local governments
    d. foreigners
    e. federal agencies and trust funds

11. As a percentage of GDP, tax revenues in the United States
    a. are about 50 percent
    b. have ballooned since 1980
    c. tend to decrease after a national emergency has been addressed
    d. are somewhat lower than in other industrialized countries
    e. have stayed constant over our history

12. A progressive income tax is one in which
    a. everyone pays the same rate
    b. everyone must pay a fixed amount
    c. the poor pay a larger percentage of their income than do the rich
    d. the rich pay a larger percentage of their income than do the poor
    e. consumption is discouraged

13. The primary source of tax revenue for state and local governments is
    a. state income taxes
    b. estate and gift taxes
    c. sales and excise taxes and customs duties
    d. property taxes
    e. lottery revenues

14. The burden of the U.S. public debt consists primarily of that portion of the debt that is owned by
    a. all U.S. citizens
    b. U.S. commercial banks
    c. foreigners
    d. U.S. citizens who default on their share of the payments on the debt
    e. U.S. future generations who inherit the debt

GOVERNMENT AND THE MACROECONOMY

15. Deficit finance can be inflationary if it is done by
    a. purchases of government securities by foreigners
    b. purchases of government securities by Americans
    c. purchases of government securities by commercial banks
    d. purchases of government securities by the Federal Reserve
    e. tax increases

16. When the government's countercyclical fiscal policy to combat a recession creates a deficit that is financed by sales of government securities to the Federal Reserve, it can cause the all of the following to happen **except**
    a. an increase in the money supply
    b. lower interest rates
    c. higher rates of unemployment
    d. higher inflation
    e. higher consumption spending

17. Arranged from shortest to the longest time to maturity, the government securities are
    a. Treasury bills, Treasury notes, Treasury bonds
    b. Treasury notes, Treasury bills, Treasury bonds
    c. Treasury bonds, Treasury notes, Treasury bills
    d. Treasury bonds, Treasury bills, Treasury notes
    e. Treasury bills, Treasury bonds, Treasury notes

18. The tax reforms of 1981 and 1986
    a. raised tax rates, but ended up reducing tax revenues
    b. lowered tax rates that ended up reducing tax revenues
    c. created additional tax brackets to capture revenue from the very rich
    d. converted the income tax structure from progressive to proportional
    e. eliminated the federal sales tax, but increased federal tax rates on inheritances

19. A property tax is described as a flat-rate tax on wealth, so it is an example of
    a. a poll tax
    b. an income tax
    c. a proportional tax
    d. a progressive tax
    e. a regressive tax

20. One way that the United States' external debt could be reduced is for
    a. taxes to be decreased
    b. investment to increase
    c. the government to buy up bonds that are held by foreigners
    d. government spending to increase
    e. the government to sell bonds in foreign markets

Fill in the Blanks

1. The federal income tax structure is _____ with _____ tax brackets that range from _____ percent to _____ percent.

2. The federal debt represents the _____ of federal _____.

3. The 1997 federal budget deficit is zero due to a combination of _____ cuts and rising _____.

4. The government creates and sells _____ to finance its _____.

Discussion Questions

1. How does a progressive income tax differ from a proportional tax and a regressive tax? Which type of tax is the fairest? Why?

2. a. Suppose you are a debater and the topic is "The United States was correct in using public debt financing, rather than higher taxes, to finance its World War II effort." You take the affirmative. Make your case.

   b. Suppose you are given the negative. Make the case.

3. Why is the U.S. public debt not a burden when it is held by Americans? How does your answer depend on the distribution of the debt in the United States?

4. What did the Gramm-Rudman-Hollings Act of 1985 call for? Did it work? Why or why not?

5. Why was the commandeering of resources replaced by taxation as a way for governments to acquire the means to provide public goods?

Everyday Applications

There has been considerable discussion recently about what should be done with a federal budget surplus that is anticipated for 1998. Many Republicans favor using the surplus to finance a tax cut. Some prefer to pay back part of the government debt. Clinton and many Democrats want to use the surplus to safeguard Social Security. What would you do with the surplus? Why?

Economics Online

The U.S. Treasury is responsible for financing the deficit through the creation and sale of government securities. The Treasury has a Web page (*http://www.ustreas.gov/*). Visit the page to learn more about what happens in the Treasury Department.

Answers to Questions

Key Terms Quiz

a. 3
b. 11
c. 1
d. 9
e. 6
f. 12
g. 13
h. 2
i. 5
j. 8
k. 4
l. 10
m. 7

True-False Questions

1. False. Public goods are not free because an opportunity cost is associated with their provision by

government. The resources used to purchase public goods could have been used to purchase private goods.
2. False. A poll tax can be considered unfair because it is regressive.
3. False. The deficit is the amount by which government spending exceeds tax revenue in one year while the debt is accumulated deficits over the years minus surpluses.
4. True
5. False. External debt is owned by foreigners and internal debt is owned by Americans.
6. True
7. False. Federal agencies and trust funds hold most of the debt.
8. False. The U.S. public debt was approximately 69 percent of GDP in 1996.
9. False. Only the amount earned over the bracket is taxed at the higher rate.
10. False. The U.S. tax/GDP ratio is relatively low compared to other countries.
11. True
12. False. Different types of government securities have different lengths to maturity.
13. True
14. True
15. True

Multiple-Choice Questions

1. e	6. d	11. d	16. c
2. b	7. c	12. d	17. a
3. b	8. b	13. c	18. b
4. a	9. b	14. c	19. c
5. b	10. e	15. d	20. c

Fill in the Blanks

1. progressive; 5; 15; 39.6
2. accumulation; deficits minus any surpluses
3. spending; tax revenues
4. securities; deficits

Discussion Questions

1. A progressive income tax is one such that the rich are taxed a higher percentage of their income than are the poor. A proportional tax is one where rich and poor are taxed the same percentage of their income. A regressive tax is one where the poor are taxed a higher percentage of their income than are the rich. The progressive tax may be considered the fairest because the enjoyment loss from paying taxes will be approximately the same among the rich and the poor if the rich are taxed at a higher percentage rate than are the poor. If the rich and the poor were taxed at the same percentage rate, the rich would have to derive the same enjoyment from their last dollars of income taxed away as did the poor for the system to be considered fair. This seems implausible. After all, with their last dollars of income taxed away, the poor probably would have purchased goods considered to be more necessary for subsistence and would have received more enjoyment than would the rich. If taxes are to create an equal burden across income classes, then the progressive structure is the fairest.

2. a. Affirmative: The means used to finance the war is not a real issue. Getting it financed in a quick and responsive way is. If people believe that holding bonds gives them something in the future, fine! We need their money now to buy the military equipment to win the war. All we want to do is shift the economy's position along the production possibilities curve from civilian to military production. The sale

of government securities accomplishes this with less opposition than, say, a tax.

    b. Negative: While the sale of securities does the job, it is more dishonest than financing the war through taxation. People ought to know what they are fighting for and what it means in terms of sacrificing civilian goods. A tax tells them that in no uncertain terms. The public debt deceptive because people think the securities they buy add to their total wealth; they fail to realize that they eventually must pay themselves.

3. The debt is not a burden when one group of Americans is paying the interest and principal on the debt to another group of Americans. However, if the debt is held by the rich and the middle class and the poor pay taxes to finance the interest payments, then the debt can make the income distribution more unequal.

4. This act called for across-the-board cuts in federal government spending if certain specific deficit-reduction targets were not met according to a timetable. However, it didn't work largely because cuts in government spending are hard to achieve when many people benefit from the spending and fight the proposed cuts. For example, some in Congress attempted to exclude defense spending from the cuts and other attempted to exclude social welfare items. The Gramm-Rudman-Hollings deficit-reduction targets were revised in 1987 and 1991 and, in the end, simply didn't work.

5. Commandeering resources is very complicated, and you may not get the resources you need by commandeering them. Therefore, commandeering resources is unlikely to be an efficient way to provide public goods. As government became more complicated over human history, it is natural that money, with its high liquidity, would be the preferred form for payment of taxes to the government. By commandeering money, a government can gain more flexibility in the kind of goods and services it can acquire.

PART 7 — GOVERNMENT AND THE MACROECONOMY

COMPREHENSIVE SAMPLE TEST

Give yourself 50 minutes to complete this exam and see how you do. The answers follow. Don't look until you are finished.

True-False Questions — If a statement is false, explain why. Each question is worth two points.

1. Classical school economists believe that the economy adjusts to a full-employment GDP automatically. (T/F)

2. The Keynesian aggregate supply curve is upward sloping as GDP rises toward full employment. (T/F)

3. The long-run Phillips curve was downward sloping during the 1970s. (T/F)

4. Rational expectations theorists believe that a fiscal policy that attempts to close a recessionary gap will have no effect on unemployment and will cause higher inflation. (T/F)

5. The benefits from public goods are not diminished when additional people consume these goods, but the benefits can be withheld from people. (T/F)

6. Social Security contributions and benefits are examples of merit goods. (T/F)

7. Temporary Assistance for Needy Families is an example of an entitlement program. (T/F)

8. The public debt fell as a percentage of GDP from the end of World War II to the 1980s. (T/F)

9. Crowding out results in a shifting of resources from private goods production to public goods production. (T/F)

10. Tax revenues measured as a percentage of GDP are higher in the United States than in most other industrialized countries. (T/F)

GOVERNMENT AND THE MACROECONOMY

Multiple-Choice Questions — Each question is worth two points.

1. One area of agreement between neo-Keynesians and rational expectations theorists is that
   a. temporary victories over unemployment through the use of fiscal and monetary policy are possible
   b. the aggregate supply curve is horizontal up to a full-employment level of GDP
   c. the Phillips curve is downward sloping and stable
   d. fiscal policy is generally more effective than monetary policy
   e. the long-run Phillips curve is vertical

2. The stabilization policy that would be promoted by a classical economist is
   a. wage and price controls to halt inflation
   b. fiscal policy for recessionary gaps and monetary policy for inflationary gaps
   c. growth in the money supply that matches real GDP growth and no intervention in the economy
   d. tax cuts for recessionary gaps and slower growth in the money supply for inflationary gaps
   e. spending increases for recessionary gaps and higher interest rates for inflationary gaps

3. The Keynesian answer to the question "Why inflation?" is
   a. excessive monetary growth
   b. too much government intervention
   c. the influence of unions and minimum wage laws
   d. excessive aggregate demand
   e. high tax rates that stifle inflation

4. According to the Keynesian school of macroeconomic thought, there would never have to be a choice between
   a. fiscal policy and monetary policy
   b. a tax cut and a government spending increase
   c. growth in the money supply and lower interest rates
   d. a cut in government spending and slower growth in the money supply
   e. combating unemployment and combating inflation

5. The main idea expressed by supply-siders using the Laffer curve is that if
   a. tax rates are lowered, GDP will grow, and tax revenue will increase
   b. tax rates are lowered, GDP will grow, but the deficit will increase
   c. government spending is cut, GDP will fall, but the deficit will decrease
   d. business is deregulated, the aggregate supply curve will shift to the right
   e. government spending is reduced, crowding out will diminish

6. Keynesians and supply-siders agree that it is possible to reduce both the rate of inflation and the rate of unemployment, but Keynesians focus on changing _____ while supply-siders focus on changing _____ to accomplish these goals.
   a. fiscal policy; monetary policy
   b. government spending; taxes
   c. aggregate demand; aggregate supply
   d. the money supply; the tax rate
   e. aggregate supply; aggregate demand

7. To be effective, an automatic stabilizer should
   a. increase aggregate demand in the downturn phase and decrease aggregate demand in an inflationary phase
   b. increase aggregate demand at full-employment GDP and increase aggregate supply during a recession
   c. reduce wages during a recession and increase wage during an inflation
   d. increase the money supply during a recession and decrease the money supply during an inflation
   e. be studied carefully before it is allowed to operate

8. If the market demand for a product falls, a classical school economist predicts that _____ and a Keynesian economist predicts that _____.
   a. price and output will fall; price will fall and output will remain unchanged
   b. price will fall and output will remain unchanged; output will fall and price will remain unchanged
   c. output will fall and price will remain unchanged; price will fall and output will remain unchanged
   d. price and output will fall; price and output will remain unchanged
   e. price and output will fall; price will remain unchanged and output will fall

9. The government provides public goods because the private market would
   a. not provide any of them
   b. not provide enough of them
   c. provide too many of them
   d. charge prices that are too low
   e. only sell exclusive and rival public goods

10. A transfer payment does not affect the mix of public and private goods produced because
    a. only the poor receive transfer payments and they cannot afford public goods
    b. transfer payments do not affect consumer sovereignty
    c. the government determines what recipients can purchase with transfer payments
    d. the transfer payments are too small to affect the mix in a significant way
    e. transfer payments are supported with tax revenues and public goods are purchased with government debt

11. Which of the following is the largest item in the federal budget?
    a. government purchases
    b. transfer payments
    c. net interest
    d. defense spending
    e. public assistance

12. The program Temporary Assistance for Needy Families replaced
    a. the Personal Responsibility and Work Opportunity Reconciliation Act
    b. Social Security
    c. Medicaid
    d. Aid to Families with Dependent Children
    e. state-run welfare programs

13. One reason to expect that Social Security taxes may increase in the near future is that
    a. more people will be working to support a larger retired population
    b. the elderly population is less healthy than it used to be
    c. fewer people will be working to support a larger retired population as baby boomers retire
    d. Congress intends for Social Security to replace private pension plans
    e. more people are opting for early retirement so they can collect benefits at an earlier age

GOVERNMENT AND THE MACROECONOMY 529

14. Between 1970 and 1996, real government spending _____, and as a share of GDP, government spending _____.
    a. more than doubled; more than doubled
    b. increased slightly; more than doubled
    c. more than doubled; increased slightly
    d. remained constant; decreased
    e. fell; dropped dramatically

15. In a society where all incomes are equal, a poll tax is
    a. a regressive tax
    b. a proportional tax
    c. a progressive tax
    d. an excise tax
    e. a property tax

16. Measured as a percentage of GDP, tax revenues in the United States
    a. have been rising rapidly since the 1980s
    b. have been falling rapidly since the 1980s
    c. are among the lowest of the industrialized countries
    d. are among the highest of the industrialized countries
    e. are about average for industrialized countries

17. A customs duty is a tax placed on
    a. a customary activity like a wedding or funeral
    b. an imported good or service
    c. an exported good or service
    d. a luxury good like alcoholic beverages
    e. a basic good like milk or medicine

18. Which of the following is the largest source of federal tax revenues?
    a. Social Security contributions
    b. income taxes
    c. sales, excise, and customs taxes
    d. estate and gift taxes
    e. property taxes

19. One problem with the public debt is that not everyone holds the debt, so
    a. the poor may pay more in taxes than they receive in interest on the debt
    b. some are crowded out of receiving interest income
    c. those who do are adversely affected by inflation
    d. underconsumption and recession are likely results
    e. payments to the handful of foreigners who hold the debt are particularly burdensome

20. The successful balancing of the federal budget during the Clinton era is due to
    a. a growing feeling in America that government can solve social problems and a willingness to pay for the solutions
    b. a balanced budget amendment to the Constitution
    c. the Gramm-Rudman-Hollings Act
    d. tax reforms during the 1980s
    e. growth in GDP, rising tax revenues, and government spending cuts

Discussion Questions/Problems — Each question is worth 10 points.

1. Why do neo-Keynesians believe that temporary victories over unemployment are possible, while rational expectations theorists believe it is impossible to lower the unemployment rate even temporarily with fiscal or monetary policy?

2. Describe the events of the 1960s and 1970s that eroded the Keynesian belief in the possibility of fine-tuning the economy.

3. Suppose that a balanced budget amendment to the Constitution is passed. How would this affect the operation of automatic stabilizers during a recession?

4. Distinguish between the impact on future generations of an internally financed government debt and an externally financed government debt.

Answers to Sample Test on Part 7

True-False Questions

1. True
2. False. The neo-Keynesian aggregate supply curve is upward sloping as GDP rises toward full employment.
3. False. The Phillips curve shifted upward during the 1970s, creating a vertical long-run Phillips curve.
4. True
5. False. Consumption of public goods cannot be withheld from people.
6. False. Social Security contributions and benefits are examples of transfer payments.
7. False. Temporary Assistance for Needy Families requires that people engage in a work activity within two years of receiving benefits and benefits are limited to five years. The program effectively ends entitlement.

8. True
9. True
10. False. Tax revenues measured as a percentage of GDP are lower in the United States than in most other countries.

Multiple-Choice Questions

1. e	6. c	11. b	16. c
2. c	7. a	12. d	17. b
3. d	8. e	13. c	18. b
4. e	9. b	14. c	19. a
5. a	10. b	15. b	20. e

Discussion Questions/Problems

1. To a neo-Keynesian, a fiscal or monetary policy designed to lower unemployment will increase aggregate demand, causing employment and real GDP to rise. However, the price level increases as well. Workers observe that their real wages are eroded by the rising price level and bargain for wage increases. In an environment of rising GDP, businesses grant these wage increases. The higher wages increase production costs and lower profits. Therefore, both production and employment are cut. The policy served to decrease unemployment only temporarily.

    To a rational expectations theorist, even this temporary decrease in the unemployment rate is impossible to achieve. Once the fiscal or monetary policy aimed at decreasing the unemployment rate is announced, workers will immediately bargain for a wage increase because they correctly anticipate that the policy will cause higher inflation and erode their real wages. Therefore, output and employment fail to increase even temporarily. The only effect of the policy is to increase inflation.

2. During the early 1960s, Keynesian economists such as Arthur Okun, Paul Samuelson, James Tobin, Robert Solow, and Lawrence Klein believed that it was possible to fine-tune the economy to operate at full employment with zero inflation. It was simply a matter of creating policies to increase aggregate demand when the economy was in recession and reduce aggregate demand during periods of inflation. These economists thought that the problem would be either unemployment or inflation, not both at once. However, the Phillips curve showed that a decrease in unemployment would be associated with an increase in inflation. Neo-Keynesians argued that this relationship between inflation and unemployment could be explained by the market power wielded by unions, monopolies, and particular resource suppliers. For example, at high levels of employment, as were experienced in the United States during the mid-1960s, unions could ask for and receive higher wages. These higher labor costs would be passed on in the form of higher prices and higher inflation. During the early 1970s, it became apparent that high rates of unemployment and high rates of inflation could coexist. At that time, the OPEC-orchestrated oil supply shock led to higher costs of production and an increase in the price level. High inflation combined with unemployment — stagflation — marked the rest of the 1970s into the 1980s.

3. An amendment to the Constitution calling for a strict, year-by-year balancing of the federal budget would interfere with the operation of automatic stabilizers. For example, consider a year when the economy slips into a recession. As real GDP and employment decline, government spending increases automatically in the form of increased unemployment insurance payments and welfare benefits, so aggregate demand is propped up somewhat. At the same time, people slide into lower tax brackets as their incomes decline, so the government's tax revenues are automatically lower. Both of these phenomena boost aggregate demand, but cause the budget deficit to increase. With a balanced budget amendment, government would

be required to increase taxes, reduce spending, or some combination of the two in order to balance the budget. The effect of a tax increase and spending cut would be to decrease aggregate demand, making the recession worse.

4. An internally financed government debt is one that is held by Americans. Therefore, interest payments are made to Americans with tax dollars paid by other Americans. For a period of time, government spending rises, corresponding to the initial increase in the debt. A good example is the decision to use debt in order to finance a war effort, such as World War II. However, once the crisis passes, government spending returns to normal levels, and the interest on the debt is paid to one group of Americans by taxing another. As long as the debt is owned by a wide range of citizens, overconsumption is not promoted, inflation is not created, and the problem of crowding out is avoided, an internally financed debt is not a burden for future generations.

However, if the debt is externally financed — held by foreigners instead of Americans — then the debt will be a burden for future generations because the interest payments will be made by our children to people in other countries, causing a drain on American resources. Consumption levels in this country will decline as a result. One solution to this problem is for the government to buy back the debt that it issues.

CHAPTER 31

INTERNATIONAL TRADE

Chapter in a Nutshell

In the second chapter of the text, you were introduced to the concepts **absolute advantage** and **comparative advantage** that are the principles on which international trade is based. You may recall from Chapter 2 that by specializing in production activities that offer absolute and comparative advantages, a country can realize gains from trade. The benefits from **international specialization** and **free trade** are explored in more detail in this chapter. You will learn that free trade benefits some groups in the economy and hurts others. Competition from **imports** can drive down prices and profits, hurting some domestic producers and their employees. Entire industries in a country may be destroyed due to international competition. However, consumers benefit from the lower prices of the imported products. In addition, exporting firms and their employees can benefit from free trade and the resulting higher prices and profits. A persuasive case for free trade can be made because the gains from specializing and trading outweigh the costs.

Still, international trade is frequently limited by government policy. The principal barriers used to limit free trade are **tariffs** and **quotas**. However, the trend over the last few decades has been toward reducing these barriers. We'll examine some of the institutions and agreements involved in international trade, such as the **General Agreement on Tariffs and Trade**, the **European Economic Community**, and the **North American Free Trade Agreement**.

After you study this chapter, you should be able to:

- Explain the difference between **absolute and comparative advantage**.
- Make the case for **free trade**.
- Calculate the **terms of trade** for different countries.
- List the United States' major trading partners.
- Evaluate arguments against free trade.
- Describe how **tariffs** and **quotas** can be used to limit free trade.
- Distinguish between **customs unions** and **free trade areas**.

Concept Check — See how you do on these multiple-choice questions.

1. The advantages associated with **international specialization** in production result from
   a. cheaper labor in some countries than in others
   b. differences in the competitive strengths of countries
   c. reduced transportation costs
   d. differences in the opportunity costs of production among countries
   e. differences in demand among countries

Why not avoid trade altogether in order to be self-sufficient?

THE WORLD ECONOMY

2. If Sweden has an **absolute advantage** over Ireland in the production of automobiles, then this results from
   a. its ability to sell automobiles in Ireland for less than the cost of production in Ireland
   b. its ability to produce automobiles using fewer resources than Ireland
   c. the size of the Swedish market relative to the Irish market
   d. competitive free trade in automobiles
   e. its effective use of tariffs over many decades

Think back to the definition of absolute advantage that you learned in Chapter 2.

3. Changes in the **terms of trade** typically put less-developed countries at a disadvantage because
   a. they specialize and trade in agricultural goods rather than manufactured goods
   b. they have higher labor costs
   c. industrialized countries practice unfair trade with less-developed countries
   d. they specialize and trade in services like tourism
   e. tariffs and quotas are used more often in less-developed countries

The terms of trade are the ratio of export prices to import prices. What kinds of goods do less-developed countries export? What kinds of goods do they import?

4. The main reason for imposing a **quota** on imports of a good is to
   a. lower the price of domestic goods
   b. lower the costs of production of domestic goods
   c. encourage lower costs of production for foreign goods
   d. create a larger market share for domestic goods
   e. avoid the use of a tariff

Who would advocate the imposition of a quota?

5. If a **customs union** were established in South America, then these countries would
   a. raise tariffs on imports from non-South American countries
   b. practice complete free trade
   c. practice free trade within South America and have a common trade policy for other countries
   d. have a common trade policy within South America and free trade for other countries
   e. practice free trade within South America and let each South American country pursue an independent trade policy with other countries

How does a customs union differ from a free trade area?

Am I on the Right Track?

Your answers to the questions above should be **d, b, a, d,** and **c**. Understanding the economic principles of international trade requires that you apply what you have learned about opportunity costs and demand and supply analysis. If you find yourself confused or stuck on a question or problem, it might be a good idea to review what you learned in Chapters 2 and 3 of the text. The concepts of opportunity cost and demand and supply don't change when we use them to examine international trade, but the context is quite different.

Key Terms Quiz — Match the terms on the left with the definition in the column on the right.

1. free trade
2. tariff
3. international specialization
4. quota
5. absolute advantage
6. reciprocity
7. comparative advantage
8. General Agreement on Tariffs and Trade (GATT)
9. imports
10. customs union
11. exports
12. European Economic Community (EEC)
13. terms of trade
14. free trade area
15. dumping
16. North American Free Trade Agreement (NAFTA)

_____ a. goods and services bought by people in one country that are produced in other countries

_____ b. international trade that is not limited by protectionist government policies such as tariffs and quotas

_____ c. a country's ability to produce a good using fewer resources than are used by the country it trades with

_____ d. a country's ability to produce a good at a lower opportunity cost than the country with which it trades

_____ e. exporting a good or service at a price below its cost of production

_____ f. a trade agreement to negotiate reductions in tariffs and other trade barriers

_____ g. the use of a country's resources to produce specific goods and services

_____ h. a tax on an imported good

_____ i. a limit on the quantity of a specific good that can be imported

_____ j. goods and services produced by people in one country that are sold in other countries

_____ k. a set of countries that agree to free trade among themselves but are free to pursue independent trade policies with other countries

_____ l. an agreement between countries in which trading privileges granted by one to the others are the same as those granted to it by the others

_____ m. a free trade area consisting of Canada, the United States, and Mexico

_____ n. a group of countries that agree to free trade among themselves and a common policy for all other countries

_____ o. a customs union comprised of 16 European countries

_____ p. the amount of a good or service (export) that must be given up to buy a unit of another good or service (import)

Graphing Tutorial

The impacts of free trade and tariff policies on a domestic market can be represented in a demand and supply graph. The graph on the following page shows the demand and supply for wine in the United States assuming free trade. The intersection of the demand curve and the United States' supply curve gives the equilibrium quantity and price for the domestic market. The price of a case of wine would be $50, and U.S. consumers would purchase 300 million cases if no wine were imported. However, the world price for wine, shown in the graph at $30 per case, is lower than the domestic price, so the United States will import wine. Assuming free trade, domestic producers of wine supply 200 million cases to the U.S. market. At a $30 world price for wine, the United States will import 200 million cases since the total quantity demanded is 400 million cases. The world supply curve for wine is represented on the graph as a horizontal line at the $30 world price.

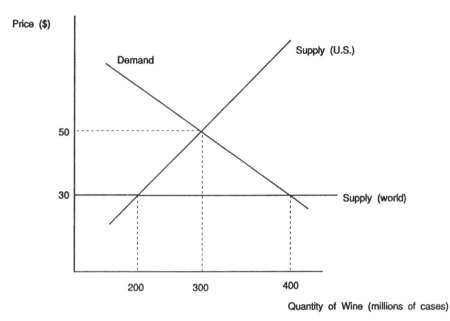

Suppose that U.S. wine producers demand protection from international competition and the government obliges them with a $10 per case tariff. The demand and supply graph shown below illustrates the effects of the tariff policy.

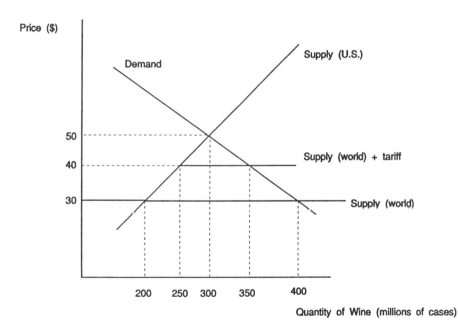

The tariff increases the price of imported wine by $10 per case to $40. The horizontal line at $40 per case starting at 250 million cases shows the effect of the tariff on the world supply curve. U.S. wine producers benefit because they are able to produce 250 million cases of wine at the $40 price. Imports are cut from 200 million cases to 100 million cases. The amount of wine consumed in the United States falls from 400 million cases to 350 million cases. The tariff will generate revenue equal to 100 million cases multiplied by the $10 per case tariff, or $1 billion.

When you draw a graph to show the effect of a tariff, first locate the position of the world supply curve, then shift it up by the dollar amount of the tariff to find the new quantity supplied and quantity demanded. The revenue generated by the tariff is equal to the tariff multiplied by the quantity of imports.

Graphing Pitfalls

A tariff is a tax on an imported good, and a tax on a good raises its price. However, it raises the price of the good from the world price, which is below the domestic equilibrium price, and not from the domestic price itself. So don't make the mistake of trying to show the effect of a tariff by increasing the domestic price by the amount of the tariff as shown in the graph below.

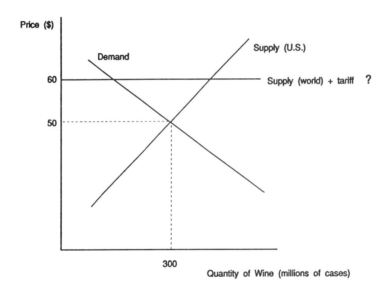

A tariff shifts the world supply up from a point below the domestic equilibrium price and quantity, not from the domestic equilibrium.

True-False Questions — If a statement is false, explain why.

1. If the opportunity costs of producing two goods differ between two countries, then specialization and free trade will benefit both countries. (T/F)

2. If all countries were endowed with the same natural resources, there would be fewer opportunities for specialization and trade. (T/F)

3. When two countries engaged in free trade benefit, this means that everyone in both countries benefits. (T/F)

4. If Italy uses fewer resources to produce wine than California, then Italy has a comparative advantage over California in wine production. (T/F)

5. The cheap foreign labor argument is a legitimate argument against free trade because the cheap labor leads to low costs of production. (T/F)

6. Political power was a more prevalent force influencing international prices and the distribution of gains from trade during the era of European colonialism in the 17th through the 19th centuries than today. (T/F)

7. The terms of trade equation for Mexico is the index of Mexican export prices divided by the index for Mexican import prices multiplied by 100. (T/F)

8. The world's industrialized countries buy most of their imports from less-developed countries because labor costs there are so much lower. (T/F)

9. The terms of trade have improved radically for most less-developed countries in recent years. (T/F)

10. Japan has a larger volume of imports and exports than any other country. (T/F)

11. NAFTA created a customs union between Canada, the United States, and Mexico while the European Economic Community is a free trade zone. (T/F)

12. The national security argument against free trade is that goods vital to the nation's security should be produced domestically. (T/F)

13. The infant-industry argument holds that protection should be withdrawn once an industry has had sufficient time to acquire expertise and experience. (T/F)

14. Dumping refers to a firm selling its goods in foreign markets below its domestic cost in order to drive competitors out of those markets. (T/F)

15. If a country is a most-favored nation under GATT, then tariff rates for that country are zero. (T/F)

Multiple-Choice Questions

1. If it takes Mexico 40 labor-hours to produce a barrel of wine and 30 labor-hours to produce a bushel of corn, then
   a. Mexico could not benefit from international trade
   b. Mexico has an absolute advantage in wine production
   c. Mexico has a comparative advantage in wine production
   d. the opportunity cost of 1 barrel of wine is 4/3 bushel of corn
   e. the opportunity cost of 1 bushel of corn is 4/3 barrel of wine

2. Suppose that a tariff and a quota both limit imports to the same quantity. On difference between them is that the
   a. quota gives more encouragement to domestic producers to become more competitive than the tariff
   b. quota raises the price by less than the tariff
   c. quota generates more revenue for the government than the tariff
   d. tariff generates tax revenue and the quota does not
   e. tariff raises the price by less than the quota

3. A country's terms of trade is the ratio of
   a. the quantity of its exports to the quantity of its imports
   b. the value of its exports to the value of its imports
   c. the index of its export prices to the index of its import prices, multiplied by 100
   d. domestic prices to international prices, multiplied by 100
   e. prices protected by tariffs to those prices subject to free trade

4. An arrangement that permits free trade among member countries and sets a common tariff policy for the rest of the world is called
   a. reciprocity
   b. a free trade area
   c. a trading bloc
   d. NAFTA
   e. a customs union

5. The infant-industries argument is used to
   a. promote indiscriminate free trade
   b. protect a new industry that employs unskilled labor
   c. protect textiles, especially children's wear, in most countries
   d. promote lower tariff rates on imports
   e. support the protection of newly established industries from foreign competition

Questions 6 and 7 refer to the table presented below. The table shows the number of labor hours required to produce cloth and wine in England and Portugal.

	Cloth (100 yards)	Wine (1 barrel)
England	100	120
Portugal	90	80

6. From the table it is clear that
   a. England has a comparative advantage in cloth production and Portugal has a comparative advantage in wine production
   b. the opportunity cost of 100 yards of cloth in England is 9/10 what it is in Portugal
   c. England has an absolute advantage in both activities
   d. England has a comparative advantage in wine production and Portugal has a comparative advantage in cloth production
   e. neither country can gain from specialization and trade

7. The opportunity cost of 100 yards of cloth in England is _____ barrel of wine, and the opportunity cost of 100 yards of cloth in Portugal is _____ barrel of wine.
   a. 6/5; 8/9
   b. 10/9; 3/2
   c. 9/10; 2/3
   d. 5/6; 9/8
   e. 1; 1

8. Because the less-developed countries were never really happy with GATT, they are allowed to
   a. impose stringent quotas on imports from industrialized countries
   b. practice dumping manufactured goods in industrial economies' markets
   c. enjoy the industrial economies' tariff concessions without having to reciprocate
   d. improve their terms of trade with additional tariffs
   e. improve their terms of trade with additional quotas

9. The argument for trade protection that supports the existence of a wide array of different industries is known as
   a. cheap labor industries
   b. infant industries
   c. specialization and division of labor
   d. economic development
   e. the diversity of industry argument

10. A country's ability to produce a good at a lower opportunity cost than the country it trades with gives a(n)
    a. superiority
    b. absolute advantage
    c. international specialization
    d. comparative advantage
    e. profit equal to the difference between the prices in the two markets

11. All of the following are arguments for trade restrictions **except**
    a. retaliation
    b. specialization
    c. cheap labor
    d. diversity of industry
    e. national security

12. Suppose that Brazil's terms of trade change from .9 to 1.2. Which of the following must be true?
    a. Brazil gets fewer real goods for a unit of its exports
    b. the index of import prices has increased
    c. Brazil gets more real goods for a unit of its exports
    d. the index of export prices has decreased
    e. Brazil's economy is primarily agricultural

13. If Chile increases its average tariff rate by 50 percent,
    a. Chilean customs duties will fall
    b. Chile's terms of trade equation will increase
    c. imports will be more expensive in Chile
    d. employment in Chile will increase due to increased exports
    e. Chilean imports will rise because import prices will fall

14. If the opportunity cost of producing onions is lower in Montana than in Ohio, then
    a. Montana has a comparative advantage in onions over Ohio
    b. Montana has an absolute advantage in onions over Ohio
    c. Ohio has an absolute advantage in onions over Montana
    d. Montana has more highly skilled onion farmers than Ohio
    e. Ohio has an absolute advantage in onion production over Montana

15. Free trade between Canada and the United States
    a. helps every Canadian and American
    b. generally hurts one country and helps the other
    c. allows for production specialization in Canada and the United States
    d. is more beneficial to the larger country, United States
    e. is more beneficial to the smaller country, Canada

16. The North American Free Trade Agreement (NAFTA)
    a. protects the United States from cheap labor production in Mexico
    b. created free trade between Canada and the United States, but protected both from Mexican cheap labor production
    c. created a customs union, similar to the European Economic Community, in Canada, the United States, and Mexico
    d. created a customs union, similar to the European Economic Community, in Canada and the United States
    e. created a free trade area that includes Canada, the United States, and Mexico

17. Most international trade takes place
    a. among the industrially developed countries, which trade primarily with each other
    b. between the industrially developed countries, which export, and the less-developed countries (LDCs), which import
    c. between the LDCs who export raw materials and the industrialized countries which import raw materials
    d. among the LDCs because they are mostly young, dynamic economies, such as Korea and Hong Kong
    e. among the LDCs because they have the largest populations, such as India, China, and Brazil

18. If the U.S. government places a quota on wheat, it is to
    a. restrict the quantity of wheat U.S. wheat producers can sell abroad
    b. raise government revenues from imports of wheat to the United States
    c. restrict the quantity of wheat that can be imported
    d. shift the domestic supply curve to the right in order to lower domestic wheat prices
    e. shift the domestic supply curve to the left in order to raise domestic wheat prices

19. With the exception of the 1920s and early 1930s, the trend in U.S. tariff rates since 1860 has been
    a. increasing
    b. decreasing
    c. constant
    d. increasing until the 1920s and decreasing after the early 1930s
    e. decreasing until the 1920s and increasing after the early 1930s

20. The main difference between a free trade area and a customs union is that
    a. the former includes all countries in the western hemisphere and the latter includes only France, Germany, Italy, Holland, Belgium, and Luxembourg
    b. the former requires tariffs for all members and the latter does not
    c. the former does not require tariffs for all members while the latter does
    d. the former allows free trade among members and individual tariff policies to be applied to nonmembers, while the latter allows free trade among members and a common tariff policy for nonmembers
    e. the former uses quotas for members and tariffs for nonmembers, and the latter uses tariffs for members and quotas for nonmembers

Fill in the Blanks

1. Differences in the _____ a specific good between two countries present opportunities for _____ which, when taken, result in _____.

2. In a two-country, two-goods world, each country will have a _____ advantage in a different good, and this will form the basis for _____.

3. The terms of trade for less-developed economies tend to deteriorate because changes in relative prices favor _____ over _____.

4. The practice followed under GATT whereby a tariff _____ offered to one member must be offered to all is known as _____.

Discussion Questions

1. List and critique the arguments opposed to free trade.

2. Why are less-developed countries at a disadvantage in the terms of their trade with industrialized countries?

3. What's the difference between a customs union and a free trade area?

4. Describe the pattern of U.S. tariffs from 1870 to the present.

Problems

1. The table presented below shows the number of labor-hours needed to produce an automobile or a computer in the United States and France.

	United States	France
Automobile	120	100
Computer	60	55

a. Which country has an absolute advantage in computer production? Comparative advantage? Explain.

b. If these countries specialize and trade, which country will specialize in automobiles? Computers? Explain.

c. If free trade exists between the United States and France, then what are the highest and lowest levels for the price of an automobile (expressed in terms of computers)? Which level favors the United States? France? Why?

2. Suppose that in one hour the United States can produce 180 computer microprocessors or 220 bushels of rice and that Japan in one hour can produce 160 microprocessors or 120 bushels of rice. (Note that in this problem the numbers refer to physical units, that is, microprocessors and bushels of rice, rather than labor-hours.)

   a. What is the opportunity cost of a microprocessor in the United States? In Japan? Who should specialize in microprocessor production? In rice production? Show your work.

   b. Suppose that these two countries begin to trade and that the price of one computer microprocessor is equal to one bushel of rice after trade. If the United States and Japan specialize according to their comparative advantages and trade, what are the potential gains from trade for each country?

   c. Identify which groups win and which groups lose as a result of trade in each country.

3. The following questions refer to the demand and supply diagram on the following page showing the market for bananas in the United States.

a. What are the equilibrium price of bananas and the equilibrium quantity before trade?

b. Let's now introduce free trade. Suppose banana producers from Honduras are willing to supply any quantity of bananas at a price of $.20 per pound. Draw the Honduran supply curve on the U.S. banana market in the diagram above. How many bananas will the U.S. producers supply? How many will the Honduran producers supply to U.S. consumers? How many bananas will U.S. consumers purchase?

c. Now suppose the United States imposes a $.20 per pound tariff on Honduran bananas. What is the new price for bananas in the United States? How many bananas will U.S. producers supply? How many will Honduran producers supply? How many bananas will U.S. consumers purchase? How much revenue will the tariff generate? Illustrate your answers in the graph.

THE WORLD ECONOMY

Everyday Applications

Consider how the reduction of barriers to free trade in recent years has affected your economic well-being. Are you a net beneficiary, or have you and your family suffered as a result? Do you have close relatives who work in industries that feel the pressure of increasing international competition? How would you go about calculating the benefits to yourself from freer international trade?

Economics Online

For a look into the latest developments in international trade and trade policy, visit the World Trade Organization's home page (*http://www.wto.org/*).

Answers to Questions

Key Terms Quiz

a. 9	f. 8	k. 14	p. 13
b. 1	g. 3	l. 6	
c. 5	h. 2	m. 16	
d. 7	i. 4	n. 10	
e. 15	j. 11	o. 12	

True-False Questions

1. True
2. True
3. False. Those in nonspecialized lines of production will be hurt by competition from international trade as the prices of goods they produce fall.
4. False. Italy has an absolute advantage because it uses fewer resources to produce wine than California. Comparative advantage refers to lower opportunity cost.
5. False. Cheap labor may be cheap, but it may also be less productive, so the per unit cost of producing a good may be relatively expensive.
6. True
7. True
8. False. Industrialized countries trade mostly with each other. Their labor forces are typically more productive.
9. False. The terms of trade have deteriorated for many less-developed countries in recent years.
10. False. The volume of trade is highest for the United States followed by Germany and Japan.
11. False. NAFTA created a free trade area and the EEC is a customs union.
12. True
13. True
14. True
15. False. Most-favored nation status means that a tariff concession offered to one member of GATT is offered to all members of GATT.

Multiple-Choice Questions

1. d	6. a	11. b	16. e
2. d	7. d	12. c	17. a
3. c	8. c	13. c	18. c
4. e	9. e	14. a	19. b
5. e	10. d	15. c	20. d

Fill in the Blanks

1. costs of producing; geographic specialization; more total goods produced
2. comparative; specialization
3. manufactured goods; agricultural goods
4. concession; reciprocity

Discussion Questions

1. The **national security argument** holds that goods essential to the national security should be produced domestically. The problem with this argument is that the list of goods deemed essential to national security tends to grow over time as industry lobbyists draw connections between their industries and national security.

    The **diversity of industry argument** holds that a wide range of industries should exist in a country to increase economic stability. The problem with this argument is that although it may apply to some highly specialized less-developed countries, it hardly applies to the diversified industrial economies, such as the United States, Canada, and France.

    The **antidumping argument** states that foreign competitors sell their goods in markets below their domestic cost of production in order to drive competitors out of the industry. Although dumping is illegal in many countries, including the United States, it is difficult to prove, which makes the legislation difficult to enforce.

    The **infant industry argument** support trade protection for industries that are just beginning in a country to afford them time to learn the industry and gain expertise. The problem is how to determine when the period of infancy is over.

    The **cheap labor argument** holds that industries cannot compete with other countries producing the same goods with much lower labor costs. However, the higher cost of labor in a country often stems from its labor being more productive. This means the higher-cost labor may actually result in lower production costs.

    The **retaliation argument** holds that the restriction of access to a country's markets is justified if it is in retaliation for trade restrictions on the other side. If the threat of retaliation or actual retaliation opens up foreign markets, then it is beneficial. But if retaliation doesn't work, it can make a country worse off by restricting the purchases of goods that were beneficial.

2. Less-developed countries are at a disadvantage because their exports are typically agricultural goods and natural resources. The prices of manufactured goods, produced primarily by industrialized countries, have risen relative to the prices of agricultural goods and natural resources. Therefore, the terms of trade, defined as the ratio of an index of export prices to an index of import prices, have declined for

THE WORLD ECONOMY 549

less-developed countries.

3. A customs union, like the European Economic Community, has a policy of free trade for members and a common tariff policy with respect to nonmembers. A free trade area, like NAFTA, requires free trade among members and allows each member to establish its own trade policy with respect to nonmembers.

4. From 1860 to 1870, tariff rates rose from less than 20 percent to over 45 percent. From 1870 to 1920, the average tariff rate fell gradually to a low point in 1920 of about 5 percent. Tariff rates climbed during the 1920s to about 20 percent in the early 1930s, but have fallen steadily since to an average rate of 5.9 percent in the early 1990s.

Problems

1. a. France has an absolute advantage in both computer and automobile production. It takes only 55 hours to produce a computer in France versus 60 hours in the United States and only 100 hours to produce an automobile in France versus 120 hours in the United States. However, the United States has a comparative advantage in computer production because the opportunity cost of producing 1 computer is .5 automobile whereas the opportunity cost of 1 computer in France is .55 automobile.

   b. In this case, the United States will specialize in computer production, and France will specialize in automobiles because the opportunity cost of producing computers is lower in the United States than in France, while the opportunity cost of producing automobiles is lower in France than in the United States. France gives up 1.82 computers to produce an automobile, and the United States gives up 2 computers to produce an automobile.

   c. The price for an automobile would range from the U.S. price of 2 computers to the French price of 1.82 computers. The U.S. consumer prefers the French price. The French producers prefer the U.S. price. Each country can sell its specialty for more in the other country.

2. a. The opportunity cost of a microprocessor in the United States is 11/9 bushels of rice. The opportunity cost of a microprocessor in Japan is 3/4 bushel of rice. The United States should specialize in rice production, and Japan should specialize in microprocessor production.

   b. Before trade, in one hour, the United States could have produced either 180 microprocessors or 220 bushels of rice. If the United States specializes in rice production, it can trade at the 1-to-1 rate for 220 microprocessors, 40 more than it could before trade. Similarly, before trade, in one hour, Japan could produce either 160 microprocessors or 120 bushels of rice. By specializing in microprocessor production, Japan can trade at the 1-to-1 rate for 160 bushels of rice, 40 more than it could before trade.

   c. In the United States, rice farmers gain an immediate advantage as a result of trade, while microprocessor producers are hurt. In Japan, rice farmers lose and microprocessor producers gain.

3. a. The equilibrium price of bananas prior to trade is $.50 per pound, and 50 pounds are sold.

   b. The Honduran supply curve of bananas shows as a horizontal line at $.20 per pound. U.S. producers will supply 20 pounds of bananas in competition with Honduran suppliers, who export 60 pounds of bananas to satisfy the 80 pounds of bananas that are demanded at $.20 per pound by U.S. consumers. The graph on the following page shows the Honduran supply at $.20 per pound.

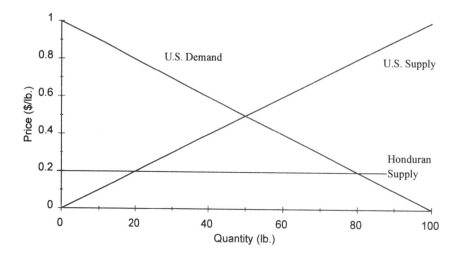

c. The new price for bananas in the United States will be $.40 — the price of Honduran imports plus the $.20 per pound tariff. Now U.S. suppliers will supply 40 pounds of bananas to U.S. consumers, and Honduran suppliers will export 20 pounds of bananas to satisfy the 60 pounds of bananas that U.S. consumers demand at a price of $.40 per pound. The graph below shows the situation with the tariff. The Honduran supply is raised by the amount of the tariff to the horizontal line at $.40 per pound. Tariff revenue is the area corresponding to the 20 pounds of bananas that are imported with a $.20 per pound tax. Tariff revenue is 20 x $.20 or $4.00.

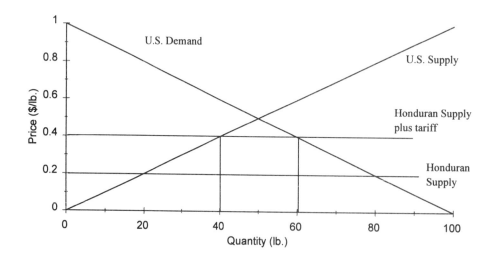

CHAPTER 32

EXCHANGE RATES, BALANCE OF PAYMENTS, AND INTERNATIONAL DEBT

Chapter in a Nutshell

Along with the flows of goods and services being traded between countries, there are corresponding flows of money. For example, in order to buy goods from Japan, we must acquire yen, the Japanese currency. In order for the Japanese to buy American goods, they must acquire dollars. Americans who want yen, Japanese who want dollars, and other traders buy and sell national currencies in **foreign exchange markets**. The price of one currency in terms of another country's currency is called the **exchange rate,** which is determined by the interaction of demand and supply for the currency in a floating exchange rate system. Fluctuations in a nation's exchange rate can have a significant impact on the nation's ability to import or export goods. A rise in the price of a nation's currency, called appreciation, can cause its exports to fall and imports to rise. Similarly, a decline in the price of a nation's currency, called depreciation, can cause its exports to rise and imports to fall.

The financing of a nation's international trade and its other financial transactions with the rest of the world are recorded in its **balance of payments**. The **balance on current account** itemizes the nation's imports and exports, its income receipts and payments on investment, and its unilateral transfers of funds. The **balance on capital account** itemizes changes in foreign asset holdings in the nation and the nation's asset holdings abroad. A deficit in the current account balance is matched by a surplus in the capital account balance. What defines a balance of payments problem? A current account deficit can be a problem for a country if it is forced to pay for the deficit by running down its stocks of foreign currencies, selling its assets to acquire other currencies, or borrowing other currencies excessively. Borrowing creates **international debt.** Moreover, interest must be paid on international debt. When the interest payments on the debt become too high a percentage of a nation's exports, the debt can become burdensome, resulting in a significant depreciation of the country's currency and a decline in living standards.

After studying this chapter, you should be able to:

- Explain how currencies are bought and sold on **foreign exchange markets**.
- Describe the factors that affect the demands for currencies and their supplies.
- Show how floating exchange rates allow currencies to **appreciate** and **depreciate**.
- Give an example of **arbitrage** in foreign exchange markets.
- Explain how **fixed exchange rates** work.
- Relate the **balance on current account** to the **balance on capital account** in the **balance of payments**.
- Present a set of options that a country might employ to service its **international debt**.

Concept Check — See how you do on these multiple-choice questions.

1. The purpose of **foreign exchange markets** is to allow people to
   a. practice arbitrage
   b. increase their country's current account balances
   c. increase their country's capital account balances
   d. finance international debt
   e. buy and sell different currencies

What is being traded in a foreign exchange market?

2. **Arbitrage** creates mutually consistent exchange rates because
   a. it causes a currency to appreciate to balance imports with exports
   b. it causes a currency to depreciate to balance exports with imports
   c. floating exchange rates are always in a state of flux
   d. when a currency is purchased at a low price in one market and sold at a high price in another, the prices converge
   e. when a currency is sold at a low price in one market and purchased at a high price in another, the prices converge

It makes sense to purchase a good (or a currency) where its price is _____ and sell it where its price is _____.

3. One potential problem for a country with **fixed exchange rates** is that
   a. a decrease in the demand for its currency can create a drain on foreign exchange reserves used to maintain the exchange rate
   b. the currency is probably prone to depreciation
   c. exchange rates are fixed as a result of the devaluation of the currency
   d. a current account deficit will result
   e. merchandise imports will exceed merchandise exports

If people become less willing to hold a nation's currency, how will it maintain a fixed exchange rate?

4. The **International Monetary Fund** was created to aid countries that have foreign exchange reserves problems by
   a. devaluing the country's currency
   b. lending the country foreign exchange reserves through purchase-and-resale agreements
   c. helping to re-establish the country's exchange rate at a higher level
   d. purchasing the country's assets abroad and converting them to foreign currencies
   e. helping the country find new markets for exports

How does one cope with a temporary cash flow problem?

5. A negative **balance of trade** for a country will not be a long-run problem if
   a. the country's foreign exchange reserves are depleted in order to finance it
   b. the country imports new capital equipment to improve its competitiveness in world markets
   c. the IMF stops lending the country foreign exchange reserves
   d. the country can sell important national assets to finance it
   e. the country also imports large quantities of services from the rest of the world

Ultimately, the solution to a balance of trade problem is for a country to become more productive.

THE WORLD ECONOMY

Am I on the Right Track?

Your answers to the questions above should be **e, d, a, b,** and **b**. Foreign exchange rates are determined by the interaction of demand and supply in foreign exchange markets, just as prices of other goods are determined in markets. The impact of erratic fluctuations in exchange rates can undermine the advantages of international trade because they contribute to uncertainty about the prices of imports and exports. Fixed exchange rates may appear to be a solution to floating exchange rates. However, fixed exchange rates create problems of their own, not the least of which is the possibility of accumulating excessive international debt in order to maintain the exchange rate. There are many key terms for this chapter. A key to your success in the chapter is understanding the new key terms and how they are used to explain the determination of exchange rates, the balance of payments, and international debt.

Key Terms Quiz — Match the terms on the left with the definitions in the column on the right.

1. foreign exchange market
2. balance of payments
3. exchange rate
4. balance on current account
5. floating exchange rate
6. balance of trade
7. appreciation
8. unilateral transfers
9. depreciation
10. balance on capital account
11. arbitrage
12. international debt
13. fixed exchange rate
14. debt service
15. foreign exchange reserves

_____ a. a rise in the price of a nation's currency relative to foreign currencies

_____ b. a rate determined and maintained by government by buying and selling its own currency on the foreign exchange market

_____ c. an itemized account of a nation's foreign economic transactions

_____ d. transfers of currency made by individuals, businesses, or the government of one nation to individuals, businesses, or governments in other nations without anything being given in exchange

_____ e. tariffs and quotas used by government to limit a nation's imports

_____ f. a market in which currencies of different nations are bought and sold

_____ g. an exchange rate determined strictly by the demands and supplies for a nation's currency

_____ h. a category that itemizes changes in foreign asset holdings in a nation and that nation's asset holdings abroad

_____ i. interest payments on international debt as a percentage of a nation's merchandise exports

_____ j. a system in which the government, as the sole depository of foreign currencies, exercises complete control over how these currencies can be used

_____ k. the stock of foreign currencies held by a government

_____ l. a category that itemizes a nation's imports and exports of merchandise and services, income receipts and payments on investment, and unilateral transfers

_____ m. the practice of buying a foreign currency in one market at a low price and selling it in another at a higher price

_____ n. the number of units of foreign currency that can be purchased with one unit of domestic currency

_____ o. government policy that lowers the nation's exchange rate, i.e., fewer units of foreign currency for a unit of its own currency

16. import controls   _____ p. the difference between the value of a nation's
                                    merchandise exports and its merchandise imports
17. devaluation   _____ q. an international organization formed to make loans of
                                    foreign currencies to countries facing balance of
                                    payments problems
18. exchange controls   _____ r. the total amount of borrowing a nation is
                                    obligated to repay other nations and international
                                    organizations
19. International Monetary Fund (IMF) _____ s. a fall in the price of a nation's currency relative to
                                    foreign currencies

Graphing Tutorial

Foreign exchange markets can be represented using demand and supply graphs. Buyers and sellers of different nations' currencies make exchanges in these markets, just as buyers and sellers of other goods make exchanges in markets. The equilibrium price in a foreign exchange market is called the exchange rate. The demand and supply graph presented below shows the foreign exchange market for zaps, the currency for the imaginary nation Zapland, priced in dollars. On the vertical axis we show the price of zaps in dollars — dollars per zap. On the horizontal axis we measure the quantity of zaps. The demand and supply curves are drawn to show the exchange rate — the equilibrium price of zaps measured in dollars — equal to $5 per zap.

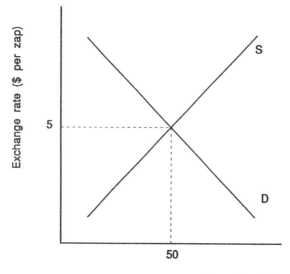

Quantity of Zaps (1,000s)

Why is the demand for zaps downward sloping? As the price of zaps measured in dollars decreases, goods from Zapland become more attractive to American consumers, and the quantity demanded of zaps increases. Why is the supply of zaps upward sloping? People in Zapland supply zaps in order to buy goods produced in the United States. As the price of zaps measured in dollars increases, U.S. goods are relatively cheaper for Zaplanders, so they supply larger quantities of zaps for dollars.

What causes the demand curve for zaps to shift? Suppose incomes in the United States increase. With higher incomes, Americans will buy more goods from Zapland; hence they will demand more zaps at all exchange rates. The demand for zaps shifts to the right, and the exchange rate for zaps increases from the $5 per zap level. A change in tastes would also shift the demand curve for zaps. If goods from Zapland become more fashionable, the demand for zaps will increase, causing the demand curve to shift to the right and the exchange rate to rise. Changes in interest rates in the United States and Zapland will influence the demand for zaps. If the interest rate in Zapland rises relative to the interest rate in the United States, then the demand for zaps increases as U.S. savers take advantage of the higher return in Zapland.

The supply curve of zaps is shifted by changes in the same factors in Zapland. If incomes in Zapland increase, they will demand more goods from the United States, and the supply of zaps shifts to the right. If Zaplanders' tastes change so that U.S. goods are more appealing, the supply of zaps shifts to the right. If interest rates in the United States rise relative to interest rates in Zapland, the supply curve shifts to the right as Zaplanders take advantage of saving opportunities in the United States.

A floating exchange rate is one determined strictly by the demand for and supply of a nation's currency. The factors that determine the demand for zaps and the supply of zaps would naturally change over time, causing the exchange rate of dollars per zaps to fluctuate. If the exchange rate increases from $5 per zap to $7 per zap, we say the dollar has depreciated (or weakened) relative to the zap because more dollars are required to purchase a zap. If the exchange rate decreases from $5 per zap to $3 per zap, the dollar has appreciated (or strengthened) relative to the zap because fewer dollars are required to purchase a zap. Erratic fluctuations in free-floating exchange rates can cause problems for businesses that import and export because unexpected changes in exchange rates result in unexpected changes in the price of goods being traded internationally.

Suppose that to avoid the problems of uncertainties associated with floating exchange rates, the U.S. government fixes the exchange rate at $5 per zap. Suppose further that the demand for zaps increases from D to D' as shown in the graph below.

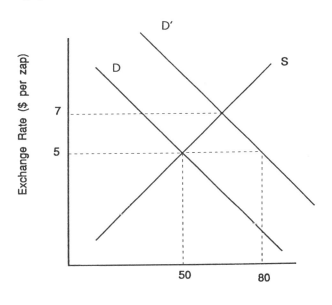

If the exchange rate were floating, it would rise from $5 per zap to $7 per zap — the new equilibrium exchange rate. However, the fixed exchange rate policy mandates that all exchanges of dollars for zaps occur at the $5 per zap rate. The graph shows an excess demand for zaps equal to 30,000 zaps at $5 per zap. The U.S. government must come up with its own supply of zaps — 30,000 in this case — to satisfy the excess demand. Problems with the fixed exchange rate policy could arise if the U.S. government runs out of zaps. These are described in detail in your text.

Graphing Pitfalls

Problems with labeling the axes sometimes arise when graphing foreign exchange markets. Remember that if the exchange rate measured along the vertical axis is dollars per zap, then zaps are being measured on the horizontal axis. Recall the fish market we examined in Chapter 3. The price of fish is measured in dollars per fish. Therefore, fish are measured on the horizontal axis. Don't make the mistake shown in the graph below of putting the exchange rate of dollars per zap on the vertical axis and dollars on the horizontal axis.

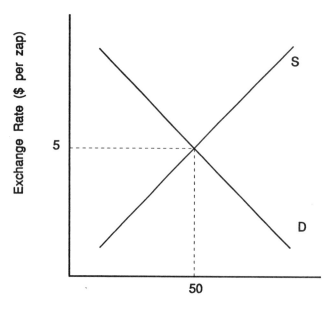

If the exchange rate on the vertical axis is dollars per zap, then the horizontal axis measures zaps, not dollars as shown above

True-False Questions — If a statement is false, explain why.

1. The foreign exchange market is where the international trade of goods and services takes place. (T/F)

2. An exchange rate is the number of units of one currency required to purchase one unit of another currency. (T/F)

3. As a nation's income increases, its demand for imports increases, creating an increase in its demand for foreign currencies. (T/F)

4. A currency depreciates if less of that currency is required to buy one unit of another currency. (T/F)

5. The supply curve of a currency will shift to the right when interest rates in that country fall relative to interest rates in other countries. (T/F)

6. If exports of merchandise are greater than imports of merchandise, then a favorable balance of trade exists. (T/F)

7. Arbitrage is the process whereby currencies are purchased in markets with low prices and sold in markets with high prices, creating mutually consistent exchange rates. (T/F)

8. One problem with a fixed exchange rate is that if the demand for imports continually increases, an excess demand for foreign currency will be generated at the fixed exchange rate that may deplete foreign currency reserves. (T/F)

9. An exchange control system requires exporters to convert any foreign exchange earned by trade into the domestic currency in order to replenish the government's supply of foreign exchange. (T/F)

10. The balance of payments account is an itemized account of a country's exports and imports of merchandise. (T/F)

11. Exports of goods and services and income receipts on investments from the rest of the world represent dollar inflows in the balance on current account. (T/F)

12. Low productivity contributes to a favorable balance of trade by making the domestic producers' goods relatively cheaper than goods from other countries. (T/F)

13. An American taking a vacation in Cancun has the same effect on Mexico's balance on current account as a Mexican businessperson exporting goods and services to the United States. (T/F)

14. The balance on capital account shows changes in the capital stock of all industries within a country. (T/F)

15. Foreign investment in the United States represents a capital inflow to the United States. (T/F)

Multiple-Choice Questions

1. One effect of an appreciation of the U.S. dollar is that
   a. it increases the demand for U.S. labor
   b. Americans can buy imports more cheaply
   c. American incomes decrease
   d. foreigners will demand more U.S. exports
   e. U.S. labor will become less productive

2. The supply curve of U.S. dollars on the foreign exchange market reflects the
   a. willingness of people in the United States to supply goods and services on the international market
   b. willingness of foreigners to demand U.S. goods and services on the international market
   c. willingness of people in the United States to demand foreign goods and services on the international market
   d. willingness of foreigners to demand U.S. dollars on the foreign exchange market
   e. the net exports (exports minus imports) that U.S. producers sell on the international market

3. All of the following are useful options for the government to pursue to bolster foreign exchange reserves **except** to
   a. impose exchange controls
   b. impose export controls
   c. adjust the exchange rate
   d. borrow foreign currencies
   e. permit a free floating exchange rate

4. An example of dollar inflows on the balance on current account is
   a. the export of services
   b. unilateral transfers of dollars to U.S. students in Europe
   c. changes in U.S. assets abroad
   d. the payments on foreign investments in the United States
   e. the import of services

5. The difference between the value of a nation's merchandise exports and its merchandise imports is its
   a. external debt
   b. balance on capital account
   c. balance of trade
   d. foreign exchange reserves
   e. foreign exchange rate

6. If the U.S. dollar appreciates relative to the Japanese yen, then
   a. more yen will be required to purchase one dollar
   b. fewer yen will be required to purchase one dollar
   c. the dollar has weakened relative to the yen
   d. Japan's demand for U.S. goods will increase
   e. the Japanese supply of yen will increase

7. Given an unfavorable balance of trade, the current account can still be favorable if
   a. there is a larger value for merchandise imports
   b. exports of services are less than imports of services
   c. unilateral transfers of dollars out of the United States exceed unilateral transfers of dollars into the United States
   d. sales of U.S. assets to foreigners increase
   e. exports of services are greater than imports of services

8. A persistent unfavorable balance on current account would represent a balance of payments problem if
   a. it were the result of declining productivity in the economy and an inability to compete in international markets
   b. it were the result of large imports of basic goods such as oil
   c. a strengthening of the nation's currency increased the price of its exports to foreign buyers
   d. reserves of foreign currencies increased
   e. the government pursued a surplus budget

9. People who practice arbitrage will create mutually consistent exchange rates if
   a. they operate in a country that practices exchange controls
   b. exchange rates are set properly by government
   c. productivity increases in the economy of the country whose currency is being traded
   d. they buy a currency in one market at a low price and then sell at a high price in another market
   e. the currency being traded appreciates

10. The impact of an Indonesian businessman purchasing a U.S. bond is to
    a. increase the current account deficit in the United States
    b. increase the balance on capital account in the United States
    c. increase the U.S. government budget deficit
    d. cause U.S. interest rates to rise
    e. contribute to a balance of payments problem in the United States

11. One consequence of a depreciation in a country's exchange rate is that
    a. its demand for foreign currencies increases
    b. its exports decrease
    c. its imports decrease
    d. other countries, in response, must depreciate theirs
    e. its government cannot borrow from the IMF

12. The demand for U.S. dollars on the foreign exchange market will increase when
    a. U.S. incomes increase
    b. foreign incomes decrease
    c. interest rates in the rest of the world rise dramatically while U.S. rates remain unchanged
    d. U.S. interest rates rise dramatically while those in the rest of the world remain unchanged
    e. U.S. exports increase

13. In an economy's balance of payments account,
    a. the capital and current accounts must add to one
    b. the current account is always greater than the capital account
    c. both the balance on current account and the balance on capital account are zero
    d. the capital plus current account balances must equal zero
    e. capital outflows must equal capital inflows

14. Floating exchange rates refer to
    a. the ability of exchange rates to even out when displaced by shocks to the foreign exchange market
    b. new issues of foreign exchange offered on the market
    c. an exchange rate determined by the demand for and supply of a nation's currency
    d. an excess demand for a nation's currency that causes its devaluation
    e. an excess supply of a nation's currency that causes its appreciation

15. Fixed exchange rates were designed to
    a. increase a nation's exports, if the fixed rate is low enough
    b. reduce a nation's imports, if the fixed rate is high enough
    c. reduce the uncertainties of international trade associated with floating exchange rates
    d. strengthen the nation's currency by curtailing the import of other currencies
    e. provide government with revenues

16. If Elrod is a student at the University of Toronto in Ontario, Canada, and his parents in Fresno, California, send him $75, the money is a
    a. private unilateral transfer, shown as a U.S. dollar outflow in the U.S. balance of payments account
    b. private unilateral transfer, shown as a Canadian dollar outflow in the Canadian balance of payments account
    c. current account transfer, shown as a U.S. dollar inflow in the U.S. balance of payments account
    d. capital account payment, shown as a U.S. dollar inflow in the U.S. balance of payments account
    e. capital account payment, shown as a Canadian dollar outflow in the U.S. balance of payments account

17. If the International Monetary Fund provides a loan of yen to the United States to help finance its unfavorable balance of trade, the
    a. IMF's supply of foreign reserves will increase
    b. United States balance on capital account will increase
    c. IMF will expect the U.S. to repurchase the dollars used to acquire the yen at a later date
    d. U.S. balance on current account will increase
    e. Japanese balance on current account will decrease

18. Debt service refers to
    a. interest payments on international debt as a percentage of a nation's merchandise exports
    b. the outflows from a nation's capital account to pay for its imports of foreign services
    c. the outflows from a nation's current account to pay for its imports of foreign services
    d. debt owed to a nation for the export of its services
    e. international debt representing all the services transacted on all nations' balance of payments accounts

19. A potential problem with free floating exchange rates is that
    a. people who practice arbitrage may gain from the losses of others
    b. uncertainty in exchange rate fluctuations may hinder international trade
    c. exchange rates may never reach equilibrium
    d. the currency markets may become monopolized
    e. less-developed countries may issue too much currency

20. Some countries may not worry about an unfavorable balance on current account because
    a. they know they can always borrow to cover the deficit
    b. they import capital goods to build up export industries that will eventually eliminate the deficit
    c. deficits are always a stimulant to economic growth, which is a higher priority
    d. they can, if necessary, fix the exchange rate to wipe out the deficit
    e. their capital account will be favorable since the balance of payments always ends up at zero

Fill in the Blanks

1. If the dollar-for-Mexican peso exchange rate falls, then Mexican goods are _____ for Americans, and the quantity demanded of pesos will _____.

THE WORLD ECONOMY

2. The _____ for Mexican pesos reflects the U.S. demand for Mexican goods and services, and the _____ of Mexican pesos reflects the Mexican demand for U.S. goods and services.

3. If a government finds it difficult to maintain a fixed exchange rate, the government can resort to policies such as _____, _____, _____, or _____.

4. If foreigners find attractive investment opportunities in the United States, the effect will be to cause the dollar to _____ relative to foreign currencies; hence foreign goods will become relatively _____ for Americans, and foreigners will find American goods relatively _____.

5. The debt service that is associated with a country's international debt is defined as the percentage of _____ that is accounted for by _____ payments on the debt.

Discussion Questions

1. a. Why is the demand curve for Mexican pesos downward sloping?

   b. Why is the supply curve of dollars priced in pesos upward sloping?

2. Describe the circumstances that led to the rise of the U.S. current account deficit during the 1980s.

3. Why is borrowing to finance an unfavorable balance on current account so dangerous for a less-developed country? Explain the nature of the long-run adjustment that will correct a current account deficit. Is this adjustment process painless for the less-developed country? Explain.

4. Under what circumstances would a country face a shortfall in its foreign exchange reserves? Discuss the role the International Monetary Fund plays in stabilizing a country's currency in times of crisis.

Problems

1. Graph the supply and demand for the foreign exchange market, expressed in terms of pesos per dollar. Show the equilibrium price at 5 pesos per dollar. Suppose the demand for dollars increases so that the new exchange rate is 7 pesos per dollar. Has the peso appreciated or depreciated? Which currency has strengthened? Is this good or bad for the United States? For Mexico?

2. Suppose the following data represent Mexico's international transactions measured in pesos.

THE WORLD ECONOMY

Merchandise exports	15		Merchandise imports	10
Change in foreign assets in Mexico	12		Change in assets abroad	8
Exports of services	7		Imports of services	5
Income receipts on investment	5		Income payments on investment	10
			Unilateral transfers	6

a. What is Mexico's balance of trade?

b. What is its balance on current account?

c. What is its balance on capital account?

Everyday Applications

An appreciation or depreciation in a country's currency can dramatically affect the finances of the country's citizens who are studying at universities and colleges in other countries. For instance, a decline in the value of the yen relative to the dollar can make it much more costly for Japanese students to study and live in the United States. Do you know any foreign students (perhaps you are one!) who have been affected by recent exchange rate changes? If their (or your) parents are assisting by sending money from home, do they have to spend more or less of their domestic currency to maintain the same level of assistance?

Economics Online

The IMF has a Web site (*http://www.imf.org/*). Visit the site to find out more about the structure of the IMF and its activities.

Answers to Questions

Key Terms Quiz

a. 7
b. 13
c. 2
d. 8
e. 16

f. 1
g. 5
h. 10
i. 14
j. 18

k. 15
l. 4
m. 11
n. 3
o. 17

p. 6
q. 19
r. 12
s. 9

True-False Questions

1. False. The foreign exchange market is a market for foreign currencies, not goods and services.
2. True
3. True
4. False. The currency depreciates if more of it is required to purchase one unit of another currency.
5. True
6. True
7. True
8. True
9. True
10. False. The balance of payments is an account of a country's entire international transactions.
11. True
12. False. Low productivity contributes to an unfavorable balance of trade because domestic goods are relatively more expensive than goods from other countries.
13. True
14. False. The capital account itemizes changes in foreign asset holdings in a nation and a nation's asset holdings abroad.
15. True

Multiple-Choice Questions

1. b	6. a	11. c	16. a
2. c	7. e	12. d	17. c
3. e	8. a	13. d	18. a
4. a	9. d	14. c	19. b
5. c	10. b	15. c	20. b

Fill in the Blanks

1. cheaper; increase
2. demand; supply
3. devaluation; import controls; exchange controls; borrowing foreign currencies
4. appreciate; expensive; cheaper
5. merchandise exports; interest

Discussion Questions

1. a. Suppose a Mexican hat sells in Mexico for 1 peso and the exchange rate is $5 per peso. If you buy that hat, you think of it as a $5 hat. If the exchange rate falls to $2 per peso, that same hat becomes a $2 hat. At that price, you may choose to buy more hats. As the exchange rate falls — U.S. dollars per peso — the Mexican good becomes cheaper, and therefore, the quantity demanded of pesos increases.

   b. Think of Mexicans buying U.S. goods. At $5 per peso, Javier Herrera can buy a VCR tape priced in the United States at $5 for only a peso. Suppose Javier buys 4 tapes. If the exchange rate falls to $2 per peso, then the $5 tape now costs him 2½ pesos. That's more expensive so he buys fewer tapes. As a result, the quantity supplied of pesos decreases as the exchange rate falls.

2. The strength and stability of the U.S. economy compared to other economies were an important factor contributing to the current account deficit. Foreigners perceived that the United States was a good place to

THE WORLD ECONOMY   565

invest, given the investment security and reasonable rates of return. Demand for U.S. dollars increased. Another factor was the relatively high interest rates in the United States. That, too, shifted the demand curve for U.S. dollars to the right, driving up the exchange rate for the dollar. A stronger dollar made foreign goods and services relatively cheaper for U.S. consumers.

3. Borrowing to finance an unfavorable balance on current account becomes problematic when the debt service rises to levels that are difficult to sustain. Exports must earn enough foreign exchange to pay the interest on the debt. A country cannot continually borrow if the debt service keeps rising because it simply won't be able to meet the interest obligations. Potential lenders will be unwilling to lend or will do so only at very high interest rates. However, there is an automatic correction mechanism that will reduce the unfavorable balance on current account. As a country imports more than it exports, its exchange rate will fall (currency depreciates) relative to others, making imports more expensive. At the same time, the country's exports become more attractive, so the trade gap will tend to shrink. This adjustment process may be very painful for a less-developed country, particularly if it depends on imports of food. As the exchange rate falls, food imports become more expensive, and living standards decline.

4. Suppose the U.S. government fixes the exchange rate at 5 French francs per dollar, and following this, the demand for French goods and, therefore, francs increases to create an excess demand of 20 million francs at the fixed 5 francs per dollar rate. The government is forced to use 20 million of the francs it held in reserve to buy $4 million on the foreign exchange market to maintain the fixed rate at 5 francs per dollar. But how deep are the government's pockets? How many francs does it need to have in reserve to continue to use its francs to buy U.S. dollars to support the fixed rate of exchange? What if it runs out of francs? Wouldn't the excess demand for francs undermine the fixed rate? If the government runs out of francs and still wants to maintain the fixed rate, it can appeal to the IMF for a loan of reserves, buying francs for dollars with the promise of later repurchasing its dollars with francs.

Problems

1.

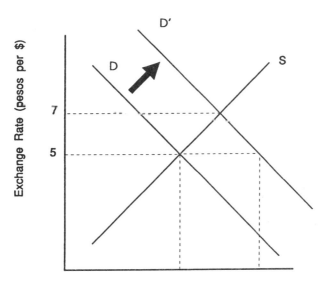

The peso has depreciated because it requires more pesos to buy one dollar. A depreciation of the peso means that the dollar has strengthened relative to the peso. One dollar buys more pesos —

7 rather than 5. Whether this is good or bad depends entirely on who you are. If you are a Mexican exporter to the United States, this is good because the price of your exports has fallen in dollars. If you are a consumer in the United States, this is good because Mexican goods are cheaper. However, it is bad for Mexican importers of U.S. goods who must pay more in pesos for a given amount of American goods.

2. a. Mexico's balance of trade is equal to merchandise exports minus merchandise imports = 15 − 10 = 5. Mexico has a positive or favorable balance of trade.

   b. Mexico's balance on current account is equal to merchandise exports + exports of services + income from investments − (merchandise imports + imports of services + income payments on investments + unilateral transfers) = 15 + 7 + 5 − (10 + 5 + 10 + 6) = 27 − 31 = −4. Mexico has a negative or unfavorable balance on current account.

   c. Mexico's balance on capital account is the difference between changes in foreign assets in Mexico and changes in Mexican assets in foreign countries = 12 − 8 = 4. This positive or favorable balance on capital account offsets the negative balance on current account.

CHAPTER 33

THE ECONOMIC PROBLEMS OF LESS-DEVELOPED ECONOMIES

Chapter in a Nutshell

Why do many people in the countries of Asia, Africa, and Latin America endure standards of living that barely support physical subsistence? Obviously, these people don't choose to remain poor. But the world they inhabit seems to afford them little choice. What can be done to improve their circumstances? Since the early 1950s, economists have focused some attention on the problem of persistent national poverty. Poor countries face challenges that are fundamentally different from those faced by the world's industrialized economies. For example, most poor countries are qualitatively different from industrialized countries. They lack a basic **infrastructure** — institutions and public facilities to support modern ways of producing goods and services. People in industrialized countries often take their economies' infrastructures for granted. Over the last 25 years, some **less-developed countries (LDCs)** have made considerable progress in modernizing their economies with accompanying increases in their per capita incomes, but many others haven't.

This chapter explores the characteristics of less-developed countries and the different approaches that they might take toward successful development. The pattern of low per capita incomes among LDCs is outlined. Rapid population growth in LDCs can contribute to slow growth in per capita incomes. **Economic dualism** — the coexistence of two separate and distinct economies within an LDC, one modern and the other traditional — is observable in many LDCs. Frequently, the basic prerequisites for economic development, such as political stability and infrastructure, are missing in LDCs. Two strategies for development, the **big push** and unbalanced development with **forward and backward linkages**, are compared. Finally, the roles played by foreign direct investment and foreign economic aid in economic development are considered.

After studying this chapter, you should be able to:

- Explain how the term **less-developed countries** came to be used by economists.
- Describe the variety of circumstances that exist in LDCs.
- Show how rapid population growth can slow down per capita income growth in LDCs.
- Discuss **economic dualism**.
- Contrast the **big-push** and the **unbalanced** strategies for economic development.
- Present arguments for and against **foreign direct investment** in LDCs.
- Contrast **foreign direct investment** and **foreign economic aid**.

Concept Check — See how you do on these multiple-choice questions.

1. The term **less-developed countries** is used instead of "underdeveloped countries" to describe the situations faced by economies in Asia, Africa, and Latin America because
   a. progress toward development has been significant in all of these countries
   b. per capita income in these countries is approaching per capita income in industrialized countries
   c. the term underdeveloped is too prejudicial and LDCs are the equals of industrialized countries on grounds other than economic
   d. the United Nations passed a resolution to use the term less-developed countries rather than underdeveloped countries
   e. the term underdeveloped countries masked differences between them more than the term less-developed countries does

Could "underdeveloped" be construed as pejorative language?

2. All of the following are examples of investments in **human capital except**
   a. productivity gains due to better education
   b. improved bridges and highways
   c. free vaccinations against polio for all children
   d. on-the-job training for newly hired factory workers
   e. a retraining program for unemployed workers

How do we define human capital?

3. **Economic dualism** means that
   a. the world consists of industrialized countries and less-developed countries
   b. an LDC has distinct modern and traditional economies
   c. some LDCs are politically stable and some are unstable
   d. infrastructure development is prevalent is some LDCs and absent in others
   e. two approaches to economic development exist — the big push and unbalanced development

In some LDCs, two distinct economies seem to exist alongside one another.

4. The **big-push** development strategy depends on
   a. backward and forward linkages
   b. first undertaking an unbalanced growth strategy
   c. foreign direct investment
   d. an integrated network of government-sponsored and financed investments
   e. generous foreign economic aid

Capital formation on a massive scale is necessary for development to begin in some LDCs.

5. **Forward linkages** refer to
   a. investments in one industry that create opportunities for profitable investments in other industries
   b. investments in one industry that create demands for inputs, thereby inducing investment in other industries
   c. connections between LDCs and industrialized countries created by foreign direct investment
   d. connections between LDCs and industrialized countries created by foreign economic aid
   e. connections between LDCs and industrialized countries that result from the colonial past

Learn the distinction between forward and backward linkages.

Am I on the Right Track?

Your answers to the questions above should be **c, a, b, d**, and **a**. Addressing the problems of less-developed economies requires that we first identify the most pressing of these problems and then arrive at strategies to remedy these problems. While there are many similarities among the problems facing LDCs, significant differences exist as well. The strategies appropriate for one LDC may or may not be appropriate for another. The problems associated with economic develoment are complex, making generalizations difficult. The questions that follow will help you begin to appreciate how difficult it can be for LDCs to realize successful development strategies.

THE WORLD ECONOMY

Key Terms Quiz — Match the terms on the left with the definitions in the column on the right.

1. less-developed countries
2. big push
3. human capital
4. forward linkage
5. economic dualism
6. backward linkage
7. infrastructure

_____ a. the investment in workers' knowledge, acquired through education and/or experience that enhances their productivity

_____ b. the basic institutions and public facilities upon which an economy's development depends

_____ c. the development strategy that relies on an integrated network of government-sponsored and financed investments introduced into the economy all at once

_____ d. investments in one industry that create demands for inputs, inducing investment in other industries to produce those inputs

_____ e. economies of Asia, Africa, and Latin America

_____ f. investments in one industry that create opportunities for profitable investments in other industries, using the goods produced in the first as inputs

_____ g. the coexistence of two separate and distinct economies within an LDC, one modern and the other traditional

Graphing Tutorial

Demand and supply diagrams can be used to represent the labor markets in the traditional and modern sectors of an LDC characterized by economic dualism. The demand and supply graphs in Panel A and Panel B below show the labor markets in the traditional and modern sectors, respectively.

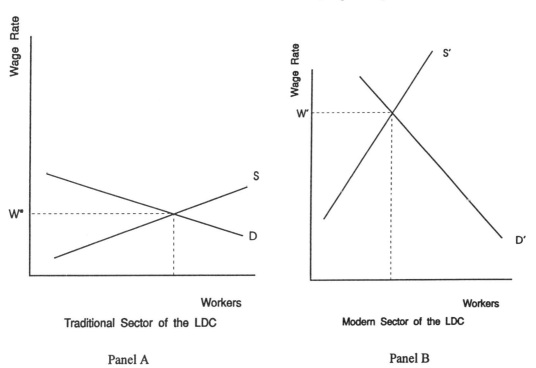

Panel A — Traditional Sector of the LDC

Panel B — Modern Sector of the LDC

In the traditional sector, the supply of labor is plentiful, as shown by the supply curve drawn far to the right, and the demand for labor is relatively low, reflecting traditional technology and weak prices. This combination yields a low wage level at W*. In comparison, in the modern sector, the demand for labor is higher, reflecting industrial technology applied to the export market where productivity and prices are higher.

570   CHAPTER 33   THE ECONOMIC PROBLEMS OF LESS-DEVELOPED ECONOMIES

However, the supply of labor is limited, and the curve is relatively steep, reflecting the scarcity of technical skills in the LDC. This combination of demand and supply yields a much higher wage rate at W'.

The problem with economic dualism is its tendency to persist. The skills of those in the traditional sector are inadequate for the modern sector. A large percentage of the population may be virtually trapped in poverty conditions.

Graphing Pitfalls

It is critical to position the supply curve for labor properly in graphs showing the labor market under conditions of economic dualism. Suppose we switch the supply curves for labor between the two sectors. The graphs this switch yields are shown below.

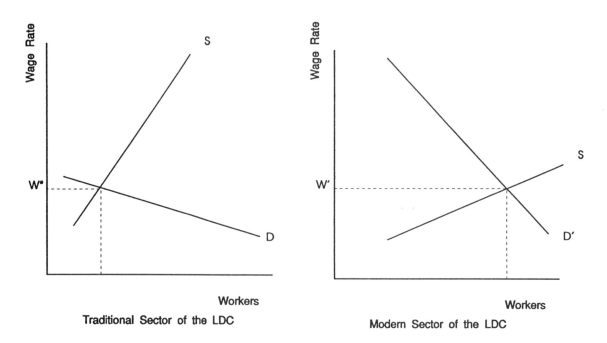

It should be apparent immediately that these graphs are drawn incorrectly because the wage rates in the two labor markets are approximately equal. That is because the supply curves have been switched. The supply curve for labor in the traditional sector should lie to the right, while the supply of labor in the modern sector is pushed up to the left, reflecting the scarcity of technical skills in the population. Be certain that your graphs make economic sense once you draw them.

True-False Questions — If a statement is false, explain why.

1. Economists have determined specific levels of per capita income and specific rates of output growth that identify countries as LDCs. (T/F)

2. Prior to the 1960s, LDCs were prejudicially described as economically backward and underdeveloped. (T/F)

3. Per capita income levels among many of the LDCs are at or near subsistence. (T/F)

4. The success of an economy in raising its per capita income depends not only on how well it generates economic growth, but also on how well it contains population growth. (T/F)

5. LDCs are characterized by an age distribution profile that loads the population in the under-15-years-old group. (T/F)

6. Investments in human capital have low payoffs, but they are realized very quickly. (T/F)

7. LDCs would be able to make larger investments in capital goods if production levels were further above subsistence. (T/F)

8. A characteristic of all LDCs is the complete absence of a modern, urban, export-driven sector. (T/F)

9. Economic dualism refers to the coexistence of both a modern and a traditional sector in an LDC. (T/F)

10. The labor demand and supply curves in the traditional sector of an LDC both tend to be relatively flat. (T/F)

11. Political instability in LDCs leads to uncertainty about property rights, which interferes with economic decision making. (T/F)

12. The power of traditionalism in an LDC is reflected in the way people in LDCs quickly adopt new technologies for producing goods. (T/F)

13. A country's infrastructure consists of its basic institutions and the public facilities, like transportation and communication systems, upon which development depends. (T/F)

14. A big-push development strategy relies on coordinated increases in investment in several industries at once in order to create interlocking markets for output. (T/F)

15. The unbalanced development strategy relies on private entrepreneurs to undertake investment projects that become profitable as a result of government-sponsored investment in infrastructure. (T/F)

Multiple-Choice Questions

1. People in LDCs are poor because
   a. they choose to be
   b. of their colonial legacies
   c. of slow population growth
   d. the world they inhabit affords them little choice
   e. of economic dualism

2. Levels of income have jumped dramatically in recent years in all of the following countries **except**
   a. Brazil
   b. Korea
   c. Hong Kong
   d. Ethiopia
   e. Taiwan

3. LDCs face a "double-whammy problem" when
   a. population growth rates are low and income growth is high
   b. population growth rates are low and income growth is low
   c. the modern sector and the traditional sector both fail to expand
   d. population growth rates are high and income growth is high
   e. population growth rates are high and income growth is low

4. The vicious circle of poverty in LDCs means that
   a. people are poor because they can't invest in capital goods and they can't invest in capital goods because they are poor
   b. their production possibilities curves are bowed-out from the origin
   c. investments in human capital have long payoff periods, so they aren't undertaken even though they are essential for economic growth
   d. investments in infrastructure have long payoff periods, so they aren't undertaken even though they are essential for economic growth
   e. the large fraction of an LDC's population that is poor and below the age of 15 ensures that the population will remain poor for years to come

5. Economic dualism in LDCs is reflected in the fact that most people live in the traditional sector where
   a. their skills allow them dual careers in both the traditional and the modern sectors
   b. most employment is in low-productivity agriculture or marginal service-related jobs
   c. some jobs pay high wages and some jobs pay low wages
   d. demand curves for labor are flat and supply curves of labor are steep
   e. the rich and the poor live side by side

6. It is possible to add significantly to a country's stock of human capital by
   a. investing in physical capital
   b. ending political instability
   c. improving the infrastructure
   d. ensuring that children receive primary education
   e. adopting the big-push strategy instead of the unbalanced strategy for economic development

7. Economic dualism would be best demonstrated in a country where
    a. some 20 percent of the population works for high wages in the modern sector and the rest work in the traditional sector
    b. the population is 80 percent urban and 20 percent rural
    c. production is virtually all agricultural compared to the industrialized countries nearby
    d. production is carried out with high-tech and low-tech methods in industry
    e. many people have jobs in both agriculture and industry

8. Political instability in an LDC interferes with economic development by causing
    a. uncertainty in economic decision making
    b. economic dualism
    c. the rise of single-party regimes
    d. the big-push strategy to be more difficult to adopt
    e. the unbalanced strategy to be more difficult to adopt

9. If a peasant in an LDC follows traditional methods of agriculture instead of adopting modern technology, it is likely that
    a. production will fluctuate more from year to year
    b. growth rates in output will be slower
    c. growth rates in output will be more rapid
    d. investment in agriculture will be high
    e. foreign direct investment will be higher

10. Even though the payoffs to investments in human capital are relatively high, these investments may not be made in an LDC because
    a. the LDC will not be able to compete internationally
    b. it is impossible for people in the traditional sector to take advantage of them
    c. the gains in productivity are realized gradually over a long period of time
    d. population growth will then increase
    e. only those in the modern sector can benefit from them

11. Although it is possible to transplant a modern Detroit automobile plant to an LDC such as Chad, the plant is unlikely to contribute much to Chad's economic development because
    a. Chad lacks the skilled personnel necessary to run the plant
    b. an adequate energy system to power the plant is lacking
    c. a system of good roads does not exist
    d. the Chadian banking system is still embryonic
    e. all of the above

12. A big-push development strategy emphasizes investment in
    a. one key industry
    b. the production of consumer goods for immediate marketing
    c. several industries at once that have interlocking markets
    d. the oil industry
    e. industries that require the most investment (big push) to get going

13. Government investment is emphasized by advocates of the big-push strategy because
    a. only government has the resources to finance the large investments required
    b. private investment is already fully utilized
    c. the government is likely to have a longer time horizon than private investors, making it possible for government to wait for the results of investment that come in the long run
    d. private investors are incompetent
    e. only the government has the personnel to implement and manage the big push in highly technical industries

14. The unbalanced development strategy is unbalanced because
    a. governments that undertake this approach are unstable
    b. forward linkages are stronger than backward linkages
    c. backward linkages are stronger than forward linkages
    d. an imbalance results between supply capacity and the creation of new demands
    e. government's role is completely eliminated so the process is completely private

15. Backward linkages in the unbalanced development strategy relate to increases in
    a. demands for inputs produced in other industries
    b. demands for the products of the backward traditional sector
    c. traditional practices that emerge in opposition to modernization
    d. links between businesses in the traditional sector
    e. links with government agencies that used to sponsor fledgling private-sector businesses

16. Foreign direct investment has the advantage that _____, which has to be weighed against the disadvantage that _____.
    a. growth is much faster; the environment is destroyed
    b. investment is financed by foreigners; images of the colonial past may be rekindled
    c. investment in foreign countries is profitable; domestic investment may languish
    d. domestic firms get funding; foreign firms lose employment
    e. LDCs profit enormously; industrialized nations suffer

17. U.S. foreign economic aid since 1970 has consisted mostly of
    a. arms exports
    b. direct food relief
    c. grants for development
    d. low-interest loans
    e. high-interest short-term loans

18. The idea behind the big-push development strategy is that by investing in many projects all at once,
    a. a few are likely to succeed
    b. the impact will spill over into the traditional economy
    c. foreign direct investment can be attracted to an LDC
    d. the country appears to be a better candidate for foreign economic aid
    e. ready markets for the investment projects will be created at the same time

THE WORLD ECONOMY   575

19. The main reason for the existence of forward linkages in the unbalanced development strategy is that investments in one industry will result in
    a. lower interest rates for other investors in other industries
    b. savings that can be transmitted to other industries
    c. opportunities for investment in new industries that use the output of the first as inputs
    d. the gradual replacement of the traditional economy by forward-looking entrepreneurs
    e. the expansion of infrastructure investment in the traditional sector

20. All of the following are explanations for the low level of development in the traditional sector of an LDC **except**
    a. low levels of literacy
    b. low levels of capital per person
    c. poor infrastructure
    d. attitudes opposed to modernization
    e. the absence of low-wage labor

Fill in the Blanks

1. Economic dualism is the _____ of two separate and distinct economies within an LDC, one _____, primarily urban, and export driven, the other _____, agricultural, and self-sustaining.

2. Foreign direct investment allows an LDC to create _____ goods production without having to sacrifice _____ goods production.

3. Many LDCs are caught in the vicious _____ — they are poor because they are unable to invest in _____, and the reason they don't is because they are _____.

4. The big-push strategy emphasizes investment in many projects _____ to create both _____ capacity and markets for the production.

5. The unbalanced strategy emphasizes private-sector development in key areas of the economy to create _____ and _____ linkages to new projects.

Discussion Questions

1. Why is rapid population growth considered to be a problem for many LDCs?

2. Contrast the role of government in the big-push development strategy and the unbalanced strategy.

3. List and discuss some basic prerequisites for economic development that may be absent in an LDC.

4. Why would an LDC welcome foreign direct investment? Why might an LDC be reluctant to allow foreign direct investment?

Everyday Applications

Often, a state government provides financial support for economic development within its borders. For example, it may offer tax incentives to new businesses thinking of relocating to the state or to established businesses thinking of leaving the state. Does your state engage in these types of efforts? In what ways is this process similar to the efforts of LDCs that wish to engage in economic development? In what ways is it different?

Economics Online

The World Bank supports development projects in many LDCs. Find out more about the World Bank's activities at its Web site (*http://www.worldbank.org/html/edi/home.html*).

Answers to Questions

Key Terms Quiz

a. 3
b. 7
c. 2
d. 6
e. 1
f. 4
g. 5

True-False Questions

1. False. Although specific levels for income and growth that can be used to label countries as less developed have not been identified, some levels are so low that economists have no trouble agreeing that these countries are LDCs.
2. True
3. True
4. True
5. True
6. False. The payoffs from investments in human capital are relatively high, but they are realized in the long run.
7. True
8. False. Economic dualism, the coexistence of a modern economy and a traditional economy in an LDC, frequently occurs.
9. True
10. True
11. True
12. False. Traditionalism is reflected in the slow pace at which new techniques are adopted.
13. True
14. True
15. True

CHAPTER 33 THE ECONOMIC PROBLEMS OF LESS-DEVELOPED ECONOMIES

Multiple-Choice Questions

1. d
2. d
3. e
4. a
5. b
6. d
7. a
8. a
9. b
10. c
11. e
12. c
13. c
14. d
15. a
16. b
17. c
18. e
19. c
20. e

Fill in the Blanks

1. coexistence; modern; traditional
2. capital; consumer
3. circle of poverty; capital goods; poor
4. all at once; productive
5. backward; forward

Discussion Questions

1. The main problem associated with rapid population growth in many LDCs is that it makes the achievement of per capita income growth more difficult. Per capita income growth is defined as income growth divided by population growth. If population grows faster than income, per capita income falls. In many LDCs, population growth is rapid and income growth is slow. Such LDCs face a double-whammy problem. Population growth rates in excess of 2.5 percent per year are not uncommon among LDCs, meaning that economic growth must exceed 2.5 percent per year in order for per capita income to grow at all.

   Another problem associated with rapid rates of population growth in LDCs is that the country's age distribution profile is weighted heavily in the under-15-years-old group. Even though children living in poverty in an LDC consume meagerly, they still consume more than they produce. The consumption requirements of the large numbers of children in LDCs make it more difficult for these countries to shift resources from consumption goods production to capital goods production in order to accelerate growth rates. So, high rates of population growth contribute to the vicious circle of poverty — people are poor because they can't invest in capital goods and they can't invest in capital goods because they are poor.

2. The role of government in the big-push development strategy is extensive. The idea behind the big-push strategy is that by pursuing a large all-at-once investment commitment in many different industries, ready markets for the interlocking projects will be created. Furthermore, the growing markets in the economy make many other investment projects attractive. Economists who advocate the big-push strategy believe that government is best suited to initiate, finance, and manage the set of infrastructure and development investments that comprise the big push. The main reason for relying on government to undertake the big push is that government has a sufficiently long time horizon to make the kinds of investments where payoffs may lie some time in the future. Once the big push is underway, the private sector is expected to participate because the big push creates a set of new, profitable investment opportunities.

   The unbalanced strategy relies less heavily on government investment in the economy. The unbalanced strategy is based on the idea that every investment will have its own set of backward and forward linkages. A backward linkage results when investment in one industry creates demands for inputs in another industry, inducing investment in it to produce those inputs. An example would be the construction of a railroad that creates a demand for steel rails, causing the steel industry to expand. A forward linkage is investment in one industry that creates opportunities in other industries that use the goods produced in the first as inputs.

THE WORLD ECONOMY

Continuing with the railroad example, a forward linkage from railroad construction might be the expansion of agricultural production for export to distant markets. The railroad provides transportation, an input critical to the expansion of agricultural exports. The unbalanced strategy emphasizes reinforcing imbalances caused by the continuous creation of new supplies and new demands in the economy. The emphasis on government investment is minimal. However, government funding and putting in place some of the economy's key infrastructure investments are still important for the unbalanced strategy to be successful.

3. Political stability is a basic prerequisite for development that is absent from many LDCs. If governments are routinely overthrown and replaced by new regimes in a country, people become very uncertain about their legal systems and their property rights. Economic decision making becomes difficult in such an uncertain environment.

Another basic prerequisite for development is a modern view of the world. Traditionalism may prevail in much of an LDC's population. People in LDCs may rely on custom in their economic relationships. They may be reluctant to part with traditional ways of producing goods for new and more productive ways. Economic modernization is very difficult if a country is tradition-bound in its economic relationships.

Finally, infrastructure is a necessary prerequisite for development that is absent in many LDCs. A country's infrastructure consists of the basic institutions and public facilities upon which production and development depend. Examples of infrastructure include an education system, a legal system, a financial system, as well as transportation, communication, and energy networks. It is virtually impossible to start using modern technologies in production without an infrastructure in place.

4. Foreign direct investment can be a boon to an LDC because it allows the country to expand economic development at zero opportunity cost. Instead of sacrificing consumption goods production in order to invest more in capital goods production, foreign capital is infused into the LDC. Thus, no consumption goods are sacrificed, and production increases due to the infusion of foreign capital. Typically, foreign direct investment brings new expertise to an LDC along with the new capital goods.

However, most LDCs hold some reservations about a development program based heavily around foreign direct investment. Some of these reservations are the result of lingering images from the LDCs' colonial pasts. Such LDCs may have been raw material supply bases for countries in the West. Their entrepreneurs may have had little freedom to operate except in restricted traditional production and retail activities. The best industries were reserved for the colonial power. The prospect of inviting back in the very colonial powers that the LDC threw off with independence is ironic indeed.

To avoid problems associated with their colonial legacies and foreign direct investment, LDC governments typically impose stringent regulations on foreign investors. For example, foreign investors may be excluded from certain fields of activity. They may be required to hire nationals in managerial positions and/or meet employment quotas. Finally, ceilings may be imposed on the amount of profit a foreign investor can take out of the LDC.

PART 8 — THE WORLD ECONOMY

COMPREHENSIVE SAMPLE TEST

Give yourself 50 minutes to complete this exam. The answers follow. Don't look until you are finished!

True-False Questions — If a statement is false, explain why. Each question is worth two points.

1. If two countries trade according to comparative advantage, then more goods will be available in both countries for consumption. (T/F)

2. A quota will restrict imports at the same time that it generates tax revenues for the government. (T/F)

3. A country's terms of trade will improve when the ratio between an index of export prices and an index of import prices increases. (T/F)

4. The most valid argument for trade restrictions is the cheap foreign labor argument. (T/F)

5. The exchange rate is the number of units of foreign currency that can be purchased with one unit of domestic currency. (T/F)

6. A depreciation of the yen relative to the dollar means that more yen are required to purchase a dollar. (T/F)

7. A negative balance on current account will be matched by a negative balance on the capital account. (T/F)

8. A massive, interlocking strategy of investments in infrastructure, manufacturing industries, and services is consistent with the big push. (T/F)

9. Economic dualism is the coexistence of two separate and distinct economies within an LDC, one modern and the other traditional. (T/F)

10. Foreign direct investment consists primarily of money for development that is granted to LDCs by the governments of industrialized countries. (T/F)

THE WORLD ECONOMY

Multiple-Choice Questions — Each question is worth two points.

1. The table below shows the number of hours required to produce either one ton of steel or one bushel of grapes in the United States and Chile.

	Labor-Hours to Produce:	
	1 ton of steel	1 bushel of grapes
United States	100	160
Chile	200	180

   The United States has an absolute advantage in _____ and a comparative advantage in _____.
   a. both activities; grape production
   b. both activities; steel production
   c. steel production only; grape production
   d. grape production only; both activities
   e. steel production; both activities

2. Using the data presented in the table for question 1, the opportunity cost of one bushel of grapes is _____ in the United States and _____ in Chile.
   a. one-half ton of steel; 9/10 tons of steel
   b. 10/9 ton of steel; 9/10 ton of steel
   c. 8/5 tons of steel; 9/10 ton of steel
   d. 5/8 ton of steel; 9/10 ton of steel
   e. 5/8 ton of steel; 10/9 tons of steel

3. A country could benefit from protection against free trade based on the infant-industries argument if
   a. its labor is cheaper than in foreign countries
   b. the protected industry successfully learns the trade
   c. the protected industry pays for the protection through higher taxes in the future
   d. the protected industry gains the expertise necessary to compete and accepts removal of protection
   e. the industry employs large numbers of workers

4. Suppose that a tariff equal to $2 per pound is imposed on imported sugar. The revenue from this tariff will be
   a. 0
   b. $100 million
   c. $200 million
   d. $400 million
   e. $600 million

5. The graph below shows the market for sugar in the United States, including imports.

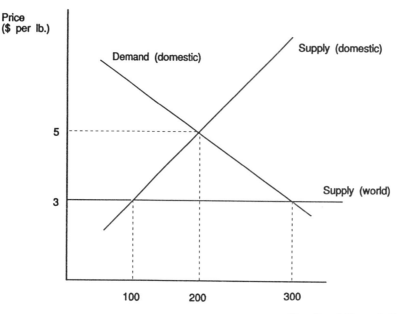

The graph shows that the world price for sugar is _____ and, with free trade, the United States will consume _____ million pounds of sugar per week.
a. $5 per pound; 200
b. $3 per pound; 200
c. $5 per pound; 100
d. $3 per pound; 100
e. $3 per pound; 300

6. Suppose that the terms of trade for a country specializing in gold exports have deteriorated due to a decline in gold prices. The best advice for this country would be to
a. impose a tariff on gold imports in order to raise the price
b. hold gold off the world market to raise its price
c. continue to export gold as long as it has a comparative advantage in gold production
d. stop trading in international markets because specialization is no longer beneficial
e. begin dumping gold in the world market

7. The most-favored nation clause in GATT requires that
a. new members be admitted to GATT only if they are favored by most of the existing members
b. a tariff reduction offered to one member be offered to all members
c. a tariff reduction be offered only to most-favored nations of GATT
d. tariff reductions be favored by most of the members of GATT
e. GATT nations be most favored compared to European Economic Community countries

8. If incomes increase in the United States, the demand for foreign currencies in the United States will be expected to
   a. decrease
   b. increase
   c. remain unchanged
   d. depend on tastes for foreign goods
   e. depend on the exchange rates

9. Suppose a decision is made by the U.S. government to fix the exchange rate between the dollar and German mark at $3/mark. An increase in the demand for German goods will force the United States to
   a. purchase marks in foreign exchange markets to make up the excess demand for marks
   b. purchase marks in foreign exchange markets to make up the excess supply of marks
   c. borrow marks from the IMF to make up the excess supply of marks
   d. supply marks at the $3/mark rate in order to satisfy the excess demand for marks
   e. supply marks at the $3/mark rate in order to satisfy the excess demand for dollars

10. Suppose the exchange rate between the dollar and German mark is fixed by the U.S. government at $3/mark. The equilibrium exchange rate in foreign exchange markets is $5/mark. Under these circumstances, there is a
    a. chronic excess demand for marks that could be eliminated by devaluing the dollar to $5/mark
    b. chronic excess supply of marks that could be eliminated by devaluing the dollar to $5/mark
    c. chronic excess demand for dollars that could be eliminated by devaluing the dollar to $5/mark
    d. reason to think the dollar will appreciate
    e. reason to think the mark will depreciate

11. The International Monetary Fund was created in 1944 to provide
    a. funds for development projects in newly independent LDCs
    b. advice on fixing currency exchange rates between members of GATT
    c. a forum for discussions on lowering tariffs around the world
    d. low-interest loans for entrepreneurs in LDCs
    e. temporary loans of foreign currencies to countries to help stabilize their currencies

12. When a country imposes import controls through tariff and quota adjustments, the purpose is to
    a. expand imports so that new capital equipment essential for development can be obtained
    b. eliminate the negative balance on current account
    c. eliminate the positive balance on capital account
    d. decrease the volume of imports so that the demand for foreign currencies is reduced
    e. increase the volume of imports so that the demand for foreign currencies is increased

13. The balance of trade is
    a. positive if the capital account balance is positive
    b. the difference between merchandise exports and merchandise imports
    c. the difference between service exports and service imports
    d. negative if the capital account balance is negative
    e. the same as the balance of payments

14. A balance of payments problem exists for the United States when
    a. currency reserves are run down to low levels to obtain the balance
    b. too many U.S. assets are sold to obtain the balance
    c. the United States borrows excessively in foreign exchange markets to obtain the balance
    d. the United States is unable to increase exports over time to eventually obtain the balance
    e. all of the above

15. Successful economic development could be represented on a production possibilities curve by
    a. a shift along the curve toward production of more consumption goods followed by an outward shift of the curve
    b. a shift along the curve toward production of more capital goods followed by an outward shift of the curve
    c. a change in the shape of the curve so that it is less bowed-out from the origin
    d. an inward shift of the curve as a result of foreign direct investment
    e. a move along the curve to a point where enough consumption goods are produced to meet subsistence needs

16. All of the following are possible results from rapid population growth in an LDC **except**
    a. slower per capita income growth
    b. an age profile that loads the population in the under-15-years-old group
    c. the need for the LDC to invest more in education
    d. an increase in wages over time as labor becomes scarcer
    e. greater investments in housing

17. In order for economic dualism to exist in an LDC,
    a. rates of per capita income growth must be negative
    b. a modern sector and a traditional sector must operate as two distinct economies in the country
    c. population growth rates must exceed 2.5 percent per year
    d. the terms of trade must deteriorate
    e. about half the population must be illiterate

18. The main reason for the emphasis on massive investments in the big-push development strategy is to
    a. establish a role for government in the economy
    b. demonstrate to private entrepreneurs that development is possible
    c. create ready markets for the new projects thereby inducing investment in other projects
    d. appear more receptive to foreign direct investment
    e. attract aid from foreign governments

19. A good example of backward linkages in an LDC would be
    a. an expansion of the country's fertilizer industry in response to expanded agricultural production
    b. an increase in the demand for teachers due to population growth
    c. the creation of a market for computer software due to growth in the computer manufacturing industry
    d. trade relationships that are established with poorer LDCs
    e. foreign direct investment coming from countries that were once colonial powers in the LDC

20. All of the following are basic prerequisites for successful economic development in an LDC **except**
    a. a colonial past
    b. political stability
    c. infrastructure
    d. a modern view of the world
    e. enough human capital to undertake modern investment projects

THE WORLD ECONOMY

Discussion Questions/Problems — Each question is worth 10 points.

1. The table from question 1 in the multiple-choice section is reproduced below.

	Labor-Hours to Produce:	
	1 ton of steel	1 bushel of grapes
United States	100	160
Chile	200	180

   a. Suppose that the United States and Chile each have 1,000 hours to devote to either steel production or grape production. Before trade, how much steel and how many bushels of grapes could each country produce if it devoted all its resources to producing one or the other?

   b. Now suppose that the United States and Chile each have 1,000 hours of labor available and they specialize and trade freely according to comparative advantage. Suppose that the international price is established at one ton of steel per one bushel of grapes. Show how both the United States and Chile can be better off as a result of specializing and trading according to comparative advantage at this price.

2. The graph from question 5 in the multiple-choice section is reproduced below.

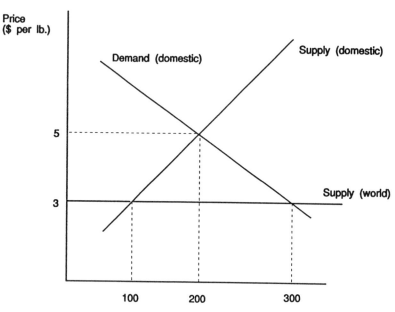

a. Suppose that a $1 per pound tariff is imposed on sugar imports. Sketch in the effect of this tariff on the graph above. Carefully label the new quantity supplied by domestic producers and the new quantity demanded. About how much sugar is imported now?

b. Approximately how much revenue does the tariff generate? Explain how you arrived at your answer.

3. Discuss the advantages and disadvantages of fixed exchange rates.

4. What is meant by the term human capital? What kinds of investments can an LDC make that will increase human capital? Why might an LDC be reluctant to make these investments?

Answers to the Sample Test on Part 8

True-False Questions

1. True
2. False. A quota will restrict imports, but it will not generate tax revenues because it is not a tax. A tariff both restricts imports and generates tax revenue.
3. True
4. False. If foreign labor is cheaper, it is because the labor is less productive. It makes more sense to buy goods where they are priced the lowest because that way the maximum amount of real goods can be purchased.
5. True
6. True
7. False. A negative balance on current account will be matched by a positive balance on the capital account.
8. True
9. True
10. False. Foreign direct investment is carried on by private businesses, not government.

Multiple-Choice Questions

1. b	6. c	11. e	16. d
2. c	7. b	12. d	17. b
3. d	8. b	13. b	18. c
4. a	9. d	14. e	19. a
5. e	10. a	15. b	20. a

Discussion Questions/Problems

1. a. If the United States devoted all 1,000 hours to producing steel, it could produce 1,000 hr./100 hr./ton = 10 tons of steel. If the United States devoted all 1,000 hours to producing grapes, it could produce 1,000 hr./160hr./bushel = 6.25 bushels.

    If Chile devoted all 1,000 hours to producing steel, it could produce 1,000/200 = 5 tons of steel. If Chile used all of its labor to produce grapes, it could produce 1,000/180 = 5.55 bushels of grapes.

    b. The United States has a comparative advantage in steel production. A ton of steel costs 5/8 bushel of grapes in the United States. In Chile, a ton of steel costs 10/9 bushels of grapes. The United States will specialize in steel and Chile in grapes.

    Suppose the United States uses the 1,000 hours to produce 10 tons of steel. At the 1:1 price ratio, the United States can trade those 10 tons of steel for up to 10 bushels of grapes. It can obtain 10 bushels instead of only 6.25 bushels. By the same logic, if Chile uses all of its labor to produce 5.55 bushels of grapes, it can trade for up to 5.55 tons of steel. This is greater than its no-trade amount.

2. A graph with the tariff and the new quantities supplied and demanded is shown on the following page.

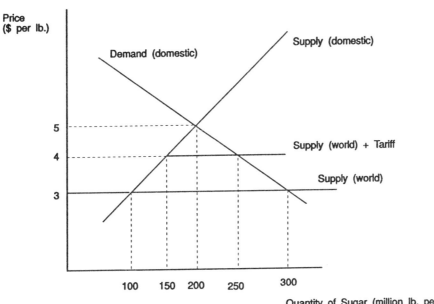

a. The tariff raises the price of imported sugar to $4. Domestic suppliers will increase their output by 50 million pounds per week to 150 million pounds per week. Consumption of sugar will fall from 300 million pounds per week to 250 pounds per week. The amount of sugar imported will drop to 100 million pounds per week.

b. Tariff revenue is equal to $1 per pound multiplied by the 100 million pounds imported, or $100 million.

3. The main advantage to fixed exchange rates is that they eliminate the uncertainty associated with flexible exchange rates. For example, suppose that a U.S. importer has contracted to purchase goods from Germany, and between the contract agreement and delivery, the German mark appreciates relative to the dollar (the dollar depreciates). The German goods become more expensive for the American importer as a result.

The disadvantage to fixed exchange rates is that if the exchange rate is set incorrectly, a chronic excess demand for or excess supply of foreign currencies will result. For example, suppose the United States sets the exchange rate between the mark and the dollar at $3/mark. Suppose the exchange rate for marks and dollars in foreign exchange markets is $5/mark. Under these circumstances, there will be an excess demand for marks in the United States, so the United States will be forced to cope with the excess demand. This can be done by supplying marks from U.S. foreign exchange reserves. Another alternative is for the United States to adjust the exchange rate to $5/mark (a depreciation of the dollar relative to the mark). The United States could impose import controls and adjust tariffs and quotas in order to limit imports and decrease the demand for marks. Exchange controls could also be imposed whereby exporters are required to turn over their earnings of foreign currencies at the fixed rate. Finally, the United States could go to the IMF to borrow marks to cover the excess demand for them.

However, problems are associated with each of these solutions to the problem of chronic excess demand for foreign currencies. For example, reserves of currencies might be drawn down to dangerously low levels. Currency depreciation makes imports more expensive for U.S. consumers. Import controls risk retaliation from other countries. Exchange controls limit the freedom of exporters in the United States. Borrowing from the IMF must be done with the expectation that the loan will be paid off after the currency crisis is over.

4. Human capital is the investment in workers' knowledge acquired through education, training, and/or experience, along with investments in the health of workers that enhance their productivity. An LDC can make investments in human capital by building new schools, training teachers, introducing job training, increasing the number of physicians, and expanding health delivery systems such as clinics and hospitals. Even though these investments may have high payoffs, the payoffs may not be realized until far in the future. An LDC that is anxious for quick, visible payoffs will be less inclined to invest in human capital than in other forms of capital, like a big manufacturing plant, where the payoff is relatively quick and highly visible.